NEIGHBORS, NOT FRIENDS

On the tenth anniversary of the 1991 Desert Storm campaign, Middle East expert Dilip Hiro provides the first full survey of events in Iraq and Iran since that war ended. Delving into the mutual hostility and deception that have marked America's continuing conflict with Iraq, *Neighbors, Not Friends* blows the cover on how Iraq cheated the UN inspectors on disarmament, and how Washington conversely manipulated and infiltrated the UN inspection teams to gather intelligence on Iraq and overthrow Saddam Hussein. Hiro describes graphically how Saddam maintains his brutal dictatorship and the suffering that UN sanctions have inflicted upon ordinary Iraqis. In the Iranian section of the book he tracks the upheavals in the domestic politics of the Islamic Republic, where a moderate presidency is engaged in a tug-of-war with the conservative religious establishment.

Combining first-hand journalistic accounts with political and analytical expertise, Hiro assesses the checkered history of the relationship between Iraq and Iran – neighbors in the oil-rich Gulf occupying a pivotal position in the world economy. Hailed as "perceptive," "balanced," and "definitive," Hiro's *The Longest War* and *Desert Shield to Desert Storm* won rave reviews for taking us from the trenches of the 1980–88 Iran–Iraq war to its inevitable climax in the armed conflict between Iraq and the US-led coalition. Completing the trilogy, *Neighbors, Not Friends* is a comprehensive account of Iraq and Iran since the two Gulf Wars, illuminated throughout by the author's lucid, incisive analysis.

Born in the Indian subcontinent, **Dilip Hiro** was educated in India, Britain and the United States, and has been living in London since the mid-1960s. He is a full-time writer and journalist, and a frequent commentator on Middle Eastern, Islamic and Central Asian affairs on radio and television in Britain and North America. His articles have appeared in the *Washington Post, Wall Street Journal, Los Angeles Times, International Herald Tribune, Sunday Times, Observer, Guardian* and *Toronto Star.* His books include *Inside the Middle East, Between Marx and Muhammad: The Changing Face of Central Asia,* and *Sharing the Promised Land: A Tale of Israelis and Palestinians.*

Reviews of previously published books by the same author

The Longest War: The Iran–Iraq Military Conflict
Routledge, New York

"Journalist Dilip Hiro, whose somber visage on the jacket cover photo suggests that he has seen his share of the conflict, takes us well beyond images of Khomeini dart boards and Saddam voodoo dolls to reveal calculating interest groups whom the West might have manipulated more skillfully."
Alex Raskin, *Los Angeles Times*

"The cold facts ... Hiro sets out, giving them their proper historic background and perspective."
Christopher Hitchens, *New York Newsday*

"A balanced analysis that fills a gap on most shelves."
Gil Taylor, *Booklist*

"Foresighted, this is one of the best books on the longest war of the 20th century."
Joseph Kechichian, *Library Journal*

"In a judicious narrative, the goals and actions of the two belligerent states, as well as various international actors involved in the conflict, are analyzed."
Mehrzad Boroujerdi, *Middle East Studies Association Bulletin*

The Longest War: The Iran–Iraq Military Conflict
Grafton Books/HarperCollins, London

"Hiro's work, clearly written and balanced, illustrated with photographs that portray the war in all its horror, is the best book on the subject so far."
Patrick Seale, *The Observer*

"Written with exemplary objectivity by journalist Dilip Hiro."
James Adams, *Sunday Times*

"*The Longest War* is beautifully impersonal, and its laying bare of the diplomatic wheels-within-wheels is outstandingly objective ... Exactingly chronicled ... Dilip Hiro provides, in his refusal to show excitement, an object lesson in how an accomplished journalist can and should reconstruct recent events of world-wide importance."
Justin Wintle, *The Independent*

"Balanced and thorough account ... Hiro's exacting, analytical approach is especially appropriate for a war which has never been quite what it seems."
Amanda Mitchison, *New Statesman*

"Hiro's book … is the first complete overview of the conflict – including its antecedents and aftermath. The author provides a competent account of events, and of the various international actors' responses. In the process he also reviews the economic consequences of the war for Iran and Iraq, and the main domestic political developments in the two countries."

Gerd Nonneman, *Middle East*

"Hiro, an international journalist, is, on the whole, even-handed in his narration of the ruthless strategies adopted by the two regimes."

Robert Irwin, *The Listener*

"Journalist Dilip Hiro tells the story of the Iran–Iraq war clearly and without taking sides."

Gerald Kaufman, *Manchester Evening News*

"*The Longest War* will remain the most authoritative account of one of the Middle East's most idiotic wars."

Middle East

Desert Shield To Desert Storm: The Second Gulf War
Routledge, New York

"Detailed … Hiro suggests that without the first Gulf War [between Iran and Iraq] … the second Gulf War might not even have occurred."

David Twersky, *New York Newsday*

"Mr Hiro is to be lauded for how much his book succeeds in being a definitive account of what happened politically, diplomatically and militarily before and during the Desert Storm."

Michael Hedges, *Washington Times*

"Dilip Hiro goes a long way toward offering a comprehensive, balanced and well-documented account of the historic, political, diplomatic, and to a lesser extent, military events leading to this strange encounter between a Third World country and a US-led international coalition numbering among its members not only Britain and France, but also Syria, Saudi Arabia and Egypt."

Edmund Ghareeb, *Middle East Insight*

"Despite this work's proximity in time to the Second Gulf War, *Desert Shield to Desert Storm* may well turn out to be the definitive work on this event."

David Snider, *Library Journal*

"A major contribution to the literature dealing with the history of the 1991 Persian Gulf War … It is impossible to read this book and not come away considerably more aware about an area of the world that many people tend to know, or care, far too little about."

Robert Nideffer, *Center for Iranian Research & Analysis Newsletter*

"Perceptive, detailed, and balanced account which should become the standard source on the second Gulf War (the first was, of course, the Iran–Iraq War)."
Research & Reference Book News

"Hiro is at his best in exploring historical continuities and interconnections. The narrative flows smoothly … Read this one for diplomacy."
Barton Gellman, *Washington Post*

Desert Shield To Desert Storm: The Second Gulf War
HarperCollins, London

"*Desert Shield to Desert Storm* tells the story like it should be told, from all sides without prejudice. Hiro writes dispassionately, methodically, painstakingly, accumulatively."
Justin Wintle, *Financial Times*

"The best book yet on the Gulf War … Quite without heroics Hiro, distancing himself from the scene, has produced a clear, thorough, exhaustive, carefully balanced survey that will not be easily or quickly superseded."
Godfrey Jansen, *Middle East International*

"*Desert Shield to Desert Storm* … is an excellent guide to the political economy of oil and indebtedness."
Christopher Hitchens, *Independent on Sunday*

"Hiro's analysis, based on long years of writing about the Middle East, is commendable."
Marie Colvin, *Sunday Times*

"The strength of Mr Hiro's new book – like that of his earlier volume on the Iran–Iraq conflict, *The Longest War* – is that the reader is provided with an encyclopedia of facts on war, untrammelled by the hysterical television journalism."
Robert Fisk, *Irish Times*

"The most meticulous and detailed study of the Second Gulf War produced to date and it is unlikely to be bettered in the near future."
George Joffe, *Sunday Tribune*

"The most comprehensive history of the Gulf War over Kuwait … The book is a clear and concise compendium of the causes and course of the conflict. An invaluable handbook for years to come."
Robert Fox, *Daily Telegraph*

Sharing The Promised Land: An Interwoven Tale of Israelis and Palestinians
Hodder & Stoughton, London

"Hiro is the perfect chronicler … As an Indian he is implicated neither by religion nor ethnicity … His success, as far as I am concerned, can be measured by my emotions as I read."
Gerald Kaufman, *Daily Telegraph*

"The book is fair and painstakingly accurate and it examines in detail … the different elements which make up Israeli society … Hiro does the same for the Palestinians … He produces some very useful documentation of elements in the story which are seldom put clearly before a world audience."
Michael Adams, *The Tablet*

"Encyclopedic in scope … sometimes a social and political study with a wide range of interviews conducted by the author; at other times a fascinating travel guide … It is in the portraits of contemporary life in a range of different Jewish and Arab communities that the book comes alive. Hiro has an eye for the detail that illuminates the broader picture."
Gerald Butt, *Church Times*

"[A] clear, non-judgmental and unbiased account of Israeli–Palestinian relations … a sober chronicle exuding neither idealism nor disaffection. Non-Jewish, non-Muslim and non-nationalist, Hiro owes nothing to either party, an advantage which allows him to present the facts in a lucid, often understated manner … . [A] good source of reference for anyone wishing to gain a distanced perspective on the world's most famous conflict."
Ori Golan, *Jerusalem Post*

"The author has captured the interwoven beliefs and conflicts in Jerusalem just as he has captured the differences between the daily lives of Palestinians and Israelis in that holy city … . Using his skills as a reporter and a historian, Dilip Hiro has written a book which is as lucid as it is objective."
Ranieh Muhammad, *Al Quds Al Arabi*

"An extensive chronological survey … In his many other books on the Middle East Dilip Hiro is not 'neutral' but fair-minded and his approach has been 'let the chips fall where they may' … This book's most useful collection of photographs and maps greatly increase the value of a publication that is still most interesting and informative."
G. H. Jansen, *Middle East International*

"[A] book which sets out to provide information and insights, and on the whole does it very well … . [T]he numerous biographies of personalities are useful, the comments intelligent, and the interviews often absorbing."
M. E. Yapp, *Times Literary Supplement*

NEIGHBORS, NOT FRIENDS

Iraq and Iran after the Gulf Wars

Dilip Hiro

London and New York

First published 2001
by Routledge
11 New Fetter Lane, London EC4P 4EE

Simultaneously published in the USA and Canada
by Routledge
29 West 35th Street, New York, NY 10001

Routledge is an imprint of the Taylor & Francis Group

Typeset in Baskerville by Bookcraft Ltd, Stroud, Gloucestershire

Printed and bound in Great Britain by Biddles Ltd, Guildford and
King's Lynn

British Library Cataloguing in Publication Data
A catalogue record for this book is available from the British Library

Library of Congress Cataloging in Publication Data
Hiro, Dilip.
Neighbors, not friends: Iraq and Iran after the Gulf Wars / Dilip Hiro.
p. cm.
Includes bibliographical references and index.
1. Iraq–Politics and government – 1991– 2. Iran – Politics and
government – 1979–1997. 3. Iraq – Relations – Iran.
4. Iran – Relations –Iraq. I. Title
DS79.75 .H57 2001
956.7044'3–dc21   2001020487

ISBN 0–415–25411–6 (hbk)
ISBN 0–415–25412–4 (pbk)

CONTENTS

PLATES

The plates appear between between Chapters 8 and 9.
Unless otherwise stated, all photographs are by Dilip Hiro.

President Saddam Hussein chairing a cabinet meeting in Baghdad, July 2000. On his immediate left is Tariq Aziz. The inset shows another cabinet meeting where, to Saddam Hussein's extreme left, sitting in a corner, is his personal secretary, Abid Hamid Mahmoud (al Khatib). *INA*

Saddam Hussein decorating his elder son, Uday, in Baghdad, January 2000. *AP/INA*

Taha Yassin Ramadan, vice-president of the Republic of Iraq. *INA*

Saddam Hussein with his younger son, Qusay, in Baghdad, December 1996. *Popperfoto/Reuters*

Izzat Ibrahim, vice-president of the Revolutionary Command Council of Iraq. *INA*

A painting at the Liberation Square, Baghdad.

Saddam Hussein's family tree at Imam Ali's shrine in Najaf, July 2000.

A portrait of Saddam Hussein at prayer at Imam Ali's shrine in Najaf, July 2000.

Iraqi Dinar 250 bank note, the highest Iraqi denomination, worth US$800 before August 1990 and US 12 cents in August 2000.

The United Nations headquarters in Baghdad, housing the offices of various UN agencies – from the humanitarian UNOHCI to the weapons monitoring BMVC. *UNOHCI*

The dilapidated state of a water treatment plant in Baghdad, August 2000.

Repairing sundry equipment, from hurricane lanterns to transistor radios, is a major activity at Shorja Souq, Baghdad, August 2000.

Open sewage is a common sight in Baghdad, July 2000.

A wall mural in Baghdad shows an Iraqi prisoner of war being tortured, with his arms being torn apart by two Iranian jeeps during the 1980–88 Iran–Iraq War.

Iraqi prisoners of war at an Iranian military camp near Tehran, demonstrating against Saddam Hussein and for Ayatollah Ali Khamanei, the then President of Iran, September 1986.

An Iranian military outpost along the Shatt al Arab/Arvand Rud near Khorramshahr, January 1989.

A spokesman for the UN Iran–Iraq Military Observer Group briefing journalists near Khorramshahr, January 1989.

A senior cleric addressing a Friday prayer congregation in Tehran, January 2000.

The Iranian Majlis, Tehran.

Hojatalislam Muhammad Khatami, Hojatalislam Ali Akbar Hashemi-Rafsanjani, Ayatollah Ali Khamanei, Ayatollah Muhammad Hashemi Shahroudi and Hojatalislam Mehdi Karrubi, Tehran, November 2000. *IRNA*

Office of the cleric attached to the Saadi Tile Factory at Islamshahr, with the picture of Ayatollah Ruhollah Khomeini on the wall, September 1986.

Shrine of Hadrat-e Maasuma, sister of Imam Ali Reza, Qom.

Mural of the Dome of the Rock, Jerusalem, near a mosque in Tehran. The inset shows a slogan reading 'Death to America 1378 (Iranian calendar)/1999' outside the Friday prayer site in Tehran.

ABBREVIATIONS

ABC	American Broadcasting Company
ABSP	Arab Baath Socialist Party
AIOC	Anglo-Iranian Oil Company
AIOC	Azerbaijan International Operating Company
AMOSSI	Agreement for Modalities of Sensitive Site Inspections
APOC	Anglo-Persian Oil Company
AWACS	Airborne Warning and Control Systems
BBC	British Broadcasting Corporation
BMVC	Baghdad Monitoring and Verification Center
bpd	barrels per day
CBS	Columbia Broadcasting Service
CESR	Center for Economic and Social Rights
CIA	Central Intelligence Agency
CIU	Concealment Investigation Unit
CNN	Cable News Network
CNPC	China National Petroleum Corporation
COC	Concealment Operations Committee
ECCS	Expediency Consultation Council System
EST	Eastern Standard Time (East Coast, US)
EU	European Union
FAO	Food and Agriculture Organization
FBI	Federal Bureau of Investigation
FIC	Free Iraq Council
GCC	Gulf Cooperation Council
GDP	Gross Domestic Product
GID	General Intelligence Department
GMT	Greenwich Mean Time
GS	General Security
IAEA	International Atomic Energy Agency
IAEC	Iraq Atomic Energy Commission
ICO	Islamic Conference Organization
ID	Iraqi Dinar

IFDEL	Iraqi Food and Drug Examination Laboratory
IIPF	Islamic Iran Participation Front
IKF	Iraqi Kurdistan Front
ILA	Iraq Liberation Act
ILSA	Iran–Libya Sanctions Act
IMF	International Monetary Fund
INA	Iraqi National Accord
INA	Iraqi News Agency
INC	Iraqi National Congress
INS	Immigration and Naturalization Service
IRGC	Islamic Revolutionary Guard Corps
IRNA	Islamic Republic News Agency
IRP	Islamic Republican Party
JACIO	Joint Action Committee of Iraqi Opposition
KAR	Kurdistan Autonomous Region
KDP	Kurdistan Democratic Party
KDPI	Kurdistan Democratic Party of Iran
KGB	Komitet Gosudarstvennoy Bezopasnosti (Committee for State Security)
LEF	Law Enforcement Forces
MCM	Movement for Constitutional Monarchy
MENA	Middle East and North Africa
Meto	Middle East Treaty Organization
MI	Military Intelligence
MIA	Missing in Action
MiG	Mikoyan i Gurevitz
MIE	Military Industrialization Establishment
MIMI	Ministry of Industry and Military Industrialization
MIR	Mujahedin of Islamic Revolution
MKO	Mujahedin-e Khalk Organization
MOU	Memorandum of Understanding
MP	Member of Parliament
MS	Military Security
NAM	Non-Aligned Movement
Nato	North Atlantic Treaty Organization
NGO	Non-Governmental Organization
NIOC	National Iranian Oil Company
NMD	National Monitoring Directorate
NPPF	National Progressive and Patriotic Front
NSA	National Security Agency
NSC	National Security Council
OPEC	Organization of Petroleum Exporting Countries
P5	Permanent Five (Members of the UN Security Council)
PKK	Partiye Karkeran Kurdistan (Kurdistan Workers Party)

POW	Prisoner of War
PUK	Patriotic Union of Kurdistan
RCC	Revolutionary Command Council
RFE/RL	Radio Free Europe/Radio Liberty
RG	Republican Guard
SA	Société Anonyme
SAS	Special Activities Staff
SAIRI	Supreme Assembly of Islamic Revolution in Iraq
SCC	Special Court for Clergy
SEC	Supreme Economic Council
SEINT	Signals and Electronic Intelligence
SICM	Special Information Collection Mission
SNSC	Supreme National Security Council
SOC	Servants of Construction
SOCAR	State Oil Company of Azerbaijan Republic
SOMO	State Oil and Marketing Organization
SRG	Special Republican Guard
SS	Special Security
SSD	State Security Department
UAE	United Arab Emirates
UK	United Kingdom (of Great Britain and Northern Ireland)
UN	United Nations
Unicef	United Nations International Children's Emergency Fund
Unikom	United Nations Iraq–Kuwait Observation Mission
Unmovic	United Nations Monitoring, Verification and Inspection Commission
UNOHCI	United Nations Office of Humanitarian Coordinator in Iraq
Unscom	United Nations Special Commission
US/USA	United States of America
VOA	Voice of America
WFP	World Food Program
WHO	World Health Organization
WMD	Weapons of Mass Destruction
WTO	World Trade Organization

GLOSSARY OF ARABIC, KURDISH AND PERSIAN WORDS

aam/ammaa	general or public
abu	father
adha	sacrifice
adil	just
akhbar	news
al/el/ol/ul	the
alaa	supreme
Alawi	follower or descendant of Imam Ali
amn	security
amr	command
ansar	helper
ashura	(*lit.*) tenth; (*fig.*) tenth of Muharram
askariya	military
asr	period or age
ayatollah	sign or token of Allah
baath	renaissance
baseej	mobilization
bin	son
bint	daughter
chador	(*lit.*) sheet; (*fig.*) veil
daawa	call
dairat	department
din	religion
-e	of
eid	festival
emir/amir	one who gives amr (command); commander
ershad	guidance
faqih (*pl.* fuquha)	one who practices fiqh; religious jurist
fath	victory
fatwa	religious ruling
fedayin (*sing.* fedai)	self-sacrificers

fi	of
fiqh	(*lit.*) knowledge; (*fig.*) Islamic jurisprudence
fursan	(*lit.*) horse riders; (*fig.*) knights
hadith	(*lit.*) narrative; (*fig.*) action or speech of Prophet Muhammad or a (Shia) Imam
hajj	(*lit.*) setting out; (*fig.*) pilgrimage (to Mecca)
haris	guard
hayat	life
hijab	cover or screen
himaya	emergency
hizb	party
hizbollah	Party of Allah
hojatalislam	proof of Islam
ibn	son
ijtihad	interpretative reasoning
imam	(*lit.*) one who leads prayers in a mosque; (*fig.*) religious leader
islam	state or act of submission (to the will of Allah)
istikhabarat	intelligence
jame	association
janbazan	self-sacrificers
jihad	(*lit.*) effort; (*fig.*) crusade or holy war
jihaz	corps
jumhouri/jumhuri	republican
jumhuriya	republic
kargozaran	servants
karkeran	workers
kayhan	world
khalq	people
khas	special
khums	one-fifth (of gains)
kiyan	existence
majlis	assembly
maktab	bureau
marja	source
medina/medinat	town or city
mobarez	combatant
mohareb	one who wages war
muderiye	directorate
mujahedin (*sing.* mujahid)	those who conduct jihad
mujtahid	one who practices ijtihad (interpretative reasoning)
mukhabarat	intelligence
mullah	cleric or preacher

munshiaa	establishment
murafaqin	companions
mustaqabal	future
mustazafin (*sing.* mustazaf)	the deprived or oppressed
nahda	awakening
nezam	system
nihayayt	end
peshmarga	(*lit.*) one who faces death; (*fig.*) soldier
qaid	leader
qasr	palace
qawami	national
quds	holy
quran/koran	recitation or discourse
quwat	forces
rahbar	leader
rais	president, chairman
resalat	mission
rud	river
ruhaniyat (*sing.* ruhani)	(*lit.*) spiritual beings; (*fig.*) clerics
ruhaniyun	clergy
sabil	path
sayyid	(*lit.*) lord or prince; (*fig.*) a hereditary title applied to male descendants of Prophet Muhammad
shah	king
shahab	youth
shaikh (*pl.* shuyukh)	(*lit.*) old man; (*fig.*) a title accorded to a senior man of power
Sharia	(*lit.*) path or road; (*fig.*) sacred law of Islam
sharif	noble
shatt	river, waterway
shia	partisan or follower
shoura	consultation
sunna	tradition or beaten path
sunni	derivative of 'ahl al sunna', people of the path (of Prophet Muhammad)
taqlid	emulation
tasnia	industrialization
tawaria	emergency
thawra	revolution
ulama (*sing.* alim)	possessors of (religious–legal) knowledge
umm	mother
umra	small pilgrimage (to Mecca)
va	and or by
vali	guardian

vilayat	rule
wa	and or by
waqf	(*lit.*) prevent; (*fig.*) religious endowment
wifaq	accord
-ye	of
yom	day
zakat	derivative of zakaa, to be pure; (*fig.*) alms or charity

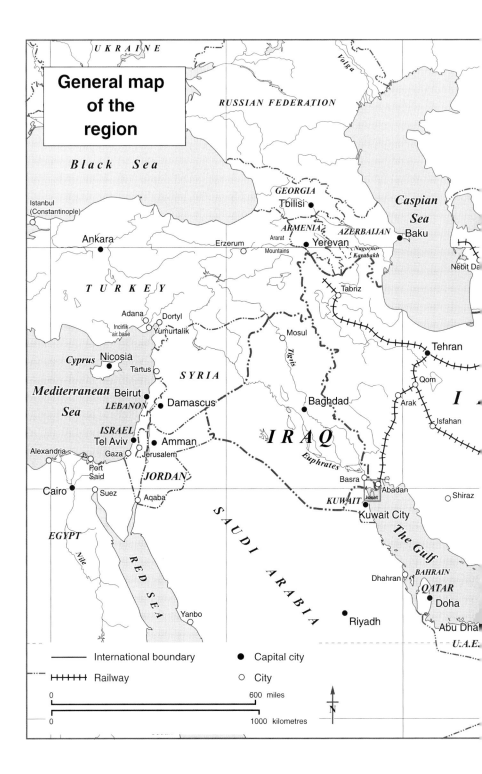

General map of the region

UKRAINE

RUSSIAN FEDERATION

Volga

Black Sea

GEORGIA
Tbilisi

Caspian Sea

Istanbul (Constantinople)

Ankara

Erzerum

ARMENIA
Ararat Mountains
Yerevan

AZERBAIJAN
Baku

Nagorno-Karabakh

Nebit Da

TURKEY

Tabriz

Adana   Dortyl
Incirlik air base   Yumurtalik

Mosul

Tehran

Cyprus Nicosia

Tartus

SYRIA

Tigris

Qom

Mediterranean Sea   Beirut
LEBANON   Damascus

Baghdad

Arak   I

ISRAEL
Tel Aviv

IRAQ

Isfahan

Alexandria
Gaza   Jerusalem   Amman

Euphrates

Port Said

JORDAN

Basra   Abadan   Shiraz

Cairo   Suez

Aqaba

KUWAIT
Kuwait City

EGYPT

Nile

SAUDI

The Gulf

RED SEA

ARABIA

Dhahran   *BAHRAIN*
QATAR
Doha

Yanbo

Riyadh

Abu Dha
U.A.E.

——— International boundary   ● Capital city

+H+H+ Railway   ○ City

0   600   miles

0   1000   kilometres

N

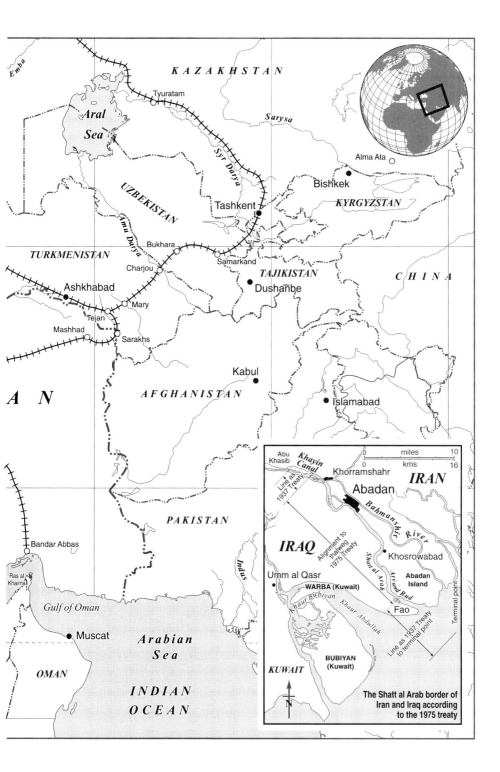

Emba

Tyuratam

Aral Sea

Sarysa

Syr Darya

Alma Ata

Bishkek

UZBEKISTAN

Tashkent

KYRGYZSTAN

Amu Darya

Bukhara

TURKMENISTAN

Charjou

Samarkand

CHINA

Ashkhabad

Mary

TAJIKISTAN

Dushanbe

Tejan

Mashhad

Sarakhs

Kabul

AFGHANISTAN

Islamabad

A N

PAKISTAN

Indus

Bandar Abbas

Ras al Khaima

Gulf of Oman

Muscat

Arabian Sea

OMAN

INDIAN OCEAN

Abu Khasib

Khayin Canal

Khorramshahr

Abadan

IRAN

miles 0 10

kms 0 16

Line as 1937 Treaty

Bahmanshir River

IRAQ

Alignment to thalweg 1975 Treaty

Khosrowabad

Umm al Qasr

Shatt al Arab

Arvand Rud

Abadan Island

WARBA (Kuwait)

Khaur Bubiyan

Fao

Terminal point

Khaur Abdullah

Line as 1937 Treaty to terminal point

BUBIYAN (Kuwait)

KUWAIT

N

The Shatt al Arab border of Iran and Iraq according to the 1975 treaty

Iran and the region

● Capital city
○ City
‑‑‑‑‑‑‑ International boundary

RUSSIAN
FEDERATION

Caspian Sea

GEORGIA
● Tbilisi

ARMENIA
AZERBAIJAN ● Baku
● Yerevan
Nakhichevan ○

TURKEY
Tabriz ○

TURKMENISTAN

Korpeje ○

Ashkhabad ●

UZBEKISTAN

Amu Darya

Mosul ○
Irbil ○
Kirkuk ○
Tikrit ○
Samarra ○
Baghdad ●
Zuhab ○
Qasr-e Shirin ○
Karbala ○
Kufa ○ Kut ○
Hilleh ○
Najaf ○
Amara ○
Shushtar ○
R. Karun
Basra ○ Khorramshahr
Abadan ○

IRAQ

Suleimaniya ○
Nahavand ○
Babol Sar ○ ○ Kord Kui
Neka ○
Qazvin ○
Abyek ○
Karaj ○ ● Tehran
Islamshahr ○
Hamadan ○
Qom ○
Arak ○
Khorramabad ○

Zagros Mountains

Isfahan ○
Masjad-e ○
Suleiman Husseinabad ○
Ahvaz ○
Bandar Khomeini ○

Mashhad ○

IRAN

Yazd ○

Behrman ○

AFGHANISTAN

PAKISTAN

KUWAIT
Jahra ○
Kuwait City ●

Kharg
Bushahr ○
Halile ○

Shiraz ○

SAUDI

ARABIA

Dhahran ○

BAHRAIN
QATAR
● Doha

● Riyadh

The Gulf

Lavan ○

Kish ○
Sirri ○

Bandar Abbas ○
Hormuz ○
Qeshm ○ Larak ○
Tunbs
Abu Musa

Bandar-e
Beheshti ○

Strait of Hormuz

Gulf of Oman

Abu Dhabi ●

U.A.E.

OMAN

● Muscat

Arabian
Sea

Tigris
Euphrates

| 0 | 300 miles |
| 0 | 500 kilometres |

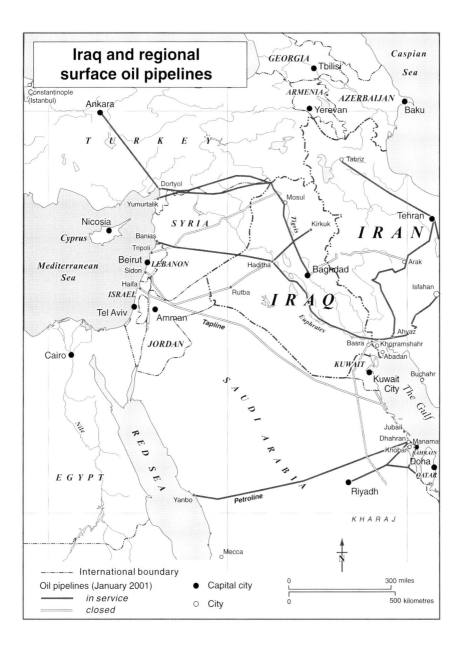

Iraq and regional surface oil pipelines

Constantinople (Istanbul)

Ankara

GEORGIA Tbilisi

Caspian Sea

ARMENIA Yerevan

AZERBAIJAN Baku

T U R K E Y

Tabriz

Dortyol

Yumurtalik

Mosul

Tehran

Nicosia

Cyprus

SYRIA

Banias

Tripoli

Beirut

Sidon **LEBANON**

Haifa

ISRAEL

Tel Aviv

Tigris

Kirkuk

I R A N

Baghdad

Arak

Isfahan

Haditha

Mediterranean Sea

Rutba

I R A Q

Euphrates

Ahvaz

Amman *Tapline*

Basra Khorramshahr

Abadan

JORDAN

Cairo

KUWAIT

Buchahr

Kuwait City

The Gulf

S A U D I

Jubail

Dhahran Manama

Khobar **BAHRAIN**

Doha

A R A B I A

QATAR

Nile

R E D

Riyadh

S E A

E G Y P T

Yanbo *Petroline*

K H A R A J

Mecca

N

--·-- International boundary

Oil pipelines (January 2001)

   in service

   closed

● Capital city

○ City

0 — 300 miles

0 — 500 kilometres

Iraq: no-fly zones

TURKEY

Habour
Zakho
Dohak

36° parallel
(June 1991–)

Hajj Umran
Shaqlawa   Hrian
Salahuddin   Ranya
Sinjar   Mosul   Irbil   Hiro
                    Qala Diza
Koy Sanjak

SYRIA

Tigris

Kirkuk
                    Suleimaniya

                    Halabja

Jabal
Maqbul   Alam   Kifri
Tikrit   Qasr-e Shirin
Tharthar   Dur   Kalar
Lake   Samarra   Khanaqin
Muthanna
                Dujayal

ANBAR
PROVINCE   Habbaniya   Taji **Baghdad**
              Ramadi   Rashidiya
                        Falluja

33° parallel
(Sept 1996–)   Hakam
              Trebil   Rafah   Musayib
                        Atheer   Kut
IRAQ   Karbala   Hilleh

32° parallel
(Aug 1992–   Kufa
Sept 1996)   Najaf
                        Amara

                    Ur   Qurna
                Nasiriyeh
SAUDI
                            Arvand
                            Rud
                Khorramshahr
ARABIA   Abadan
              Rumeila oilfield
              Umm al Qasr
                        Zubair   Shatt
                                  al arab
              KUWAIT

                        Kuwait City

IRAN

Euphrates

The
Gulf

···—··— International boundary

------- Iraqi front line

Area controlled by Kurdish
regional administration

Security zone
('Safe Haven' 1991)

N

0   200 miles

0   300 kilometres

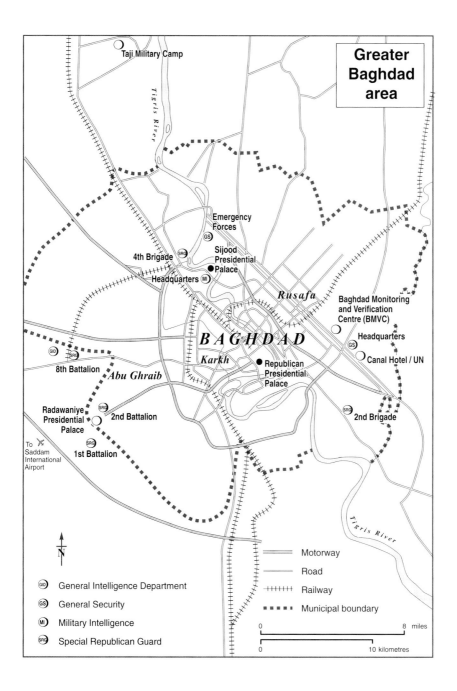

Taji Military Camp

Tigris River

Greater
Baghdad
area

Emergency
Forces

Sijood
Presidential
Palace

4th Brigade

Headquarters

Rusafa

Baghdad Monitoring
and Verification
Centre (BMVC)

BAGHDAD

Headquarters

Karkh

Canal Hotel / UN

8th Battalion

Abu Ghraib

Republican
Presidential
Palace

Radawaniye
Presidential
Palace

2nd Battalion

2nd Brigade

To
Saddam
International
Airport

1st Battalion

Tigris River

N

Motorway

Road

Railway

Municipal boundary

General Intelligence Department

General Security

Military Intelligence

Special Republican Guard

0   8   miles

0   10 kilometres

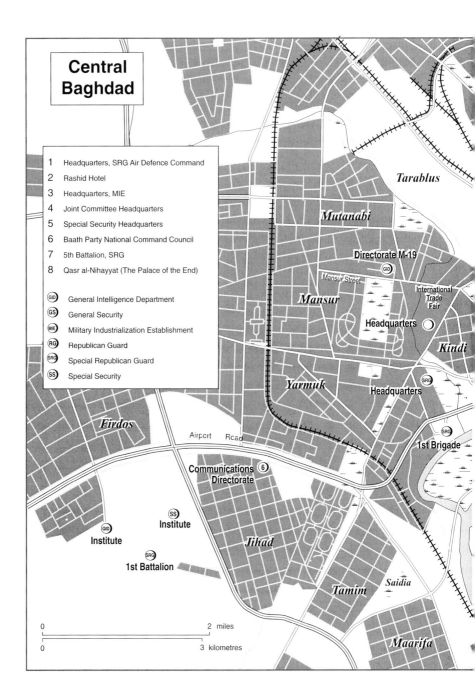

Central Baghdad

1 Headquarters, SRG Air Defence Command

2 Rashid Hotel

3 Headquarters, MIE

4 Joint Committee Headquarters

5 Special Security Headquarters

6 Baath Party National Command Council

7 5th Battalion, SRG

8 Qasr al-Nihayyat (The Palace of the End)

(GID) General Intelligence Department

(GS) General Security

(MIE) Military Industrialization Establishment

(RG) Republican Guard

(SRG) Special Republican Guard

(SS) Special Security

Tarablus

Mutanabi

Directorate M-19 (GID)

Mansur Street

Mansur

International Trade Fair

Headquarters

Kindi

Yarmuk

Headquarters (SRG)

(SRG) 1st Brigade

Firdos

Airport Road

Communications (6) Directorate

(SS) Institute

(GID) Institute

(SRG) 1st Battalion

Jihad

Tamim *Saidia*

Maarifa

| 0 | | 2 miles |
| 0 | | 3 kilometres |

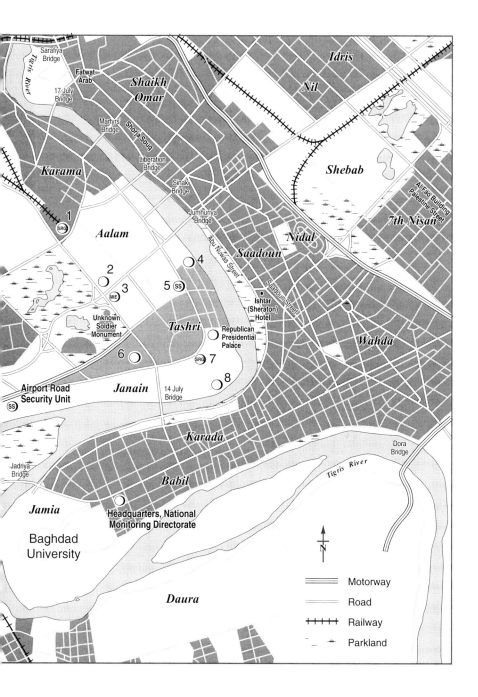

Tigris River

Sarafiya Bridge

Fatwat Arab

17 July Bridge

Shaikh Omar

Idris

Nil

Martyrs' Bridge

Shorja Souq

Liberation Bridge

Karama

Sinak Bridge

Shebab

Al Fao Building

Palestine Street

Jumhuriya Bridge

1

SRG

Aalam

Abu Nuwas Street

Saadoun

Nidal

7th Nisan

2

4

3 MIE

5 SS

Saadoun Street

Ishtar (Sheraton) Hotel

Unknown Soldier Monument

Tashri

Republican Presidential Palace

Wahda

6

SRG 7

Airport Road Security Unit

SS

Janain

14 July Bridge

8

Karada

Dora Bridge

Jadriya Bridge

Babil

Tigris River

Jamia

Headquarters, National Monitoring Directorate

Baghdad University

Daura

N

═══ Motorway

─── Road

+++++ Railway

- - ← Parkland

Saddam Hussein's family tree

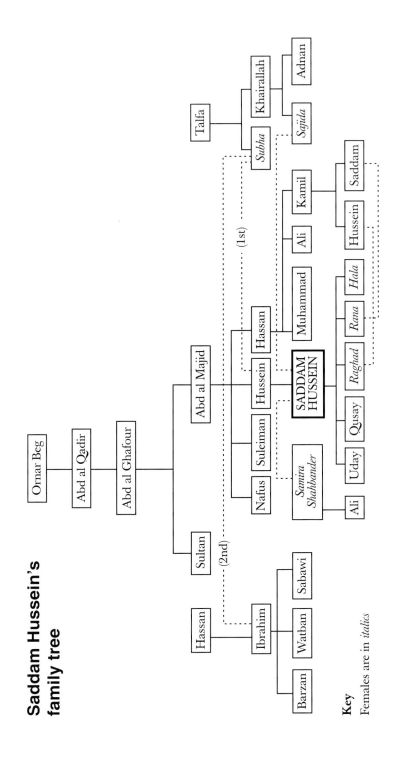

Key
Females are in *italics*

Iraqi chain of command

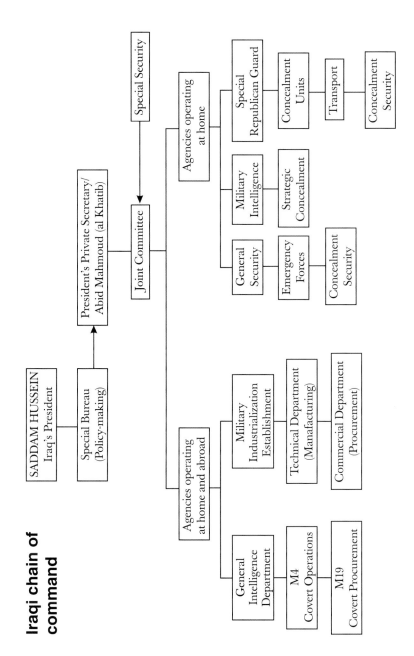

PREFACE

This is the last book in the trilogy which started with my book *The Longest War: The Iran-Iraq Military Conflict* – followed by *Desert Shield to Desert Storm: The Second Gulf War*. Its sub-title "*Iraq and Iran after the Gulf Wars*" is self-explanatory; and like its predecessors, it is meant for the general reader. The common thread that holds the trilogy together is Saddam Hussein, who became president of Iraq in 1979 and shows no sign of relinquishing office.

Iraq and Iran are heavyweights in the Gulf which possesses two-thirds of the global reserves of petroleum on which Western economies depend heavily. At the current rate of extraction these reserves will last eighty-three years. By contrast, at present production levels, the American oil deposits will be exhausted in ten years, the British in five, and the Norwegian in nine.[1] Between them, Iran and Iraq have a fifth of the world's petroleum reserves and its second largest natural gas deposits. They are the two most populous states in the region, and occupy strategic positions on the globe.

Each of them has the distinction of having impacted directly on recent US presidential elections. One of the main reasons why Democrat President Jimmy Carter (r. 1977–80) lost his campaign for re-election in 1980 was his failure to secure the release of the American hostages held by Iran. After his victory in the Second Gulf War between the US-led Coalition and Iraq in March 1991, President George Bush (r. 1989–92), a Republican, became so popular – with his ratings soaring to 91 percent – that his re-election in 1992 seemed assured. This perception discouraged leading Democrat politicians from entering the race for their party's nomination, and inadvertently paved the way for the election as president of a comparatively unknown governor of an obscure southern state of Arkansas, Bill Clinton (r. 1993–2000).

These, in short, are the compelling reasons why it matters a lot to the West what happens in Iraq and Iran.

The relationship between them has a long history. As part of the ancient Persian empire, the Mesopotamian plain to the west of the Zagros Mountains was called *Eraq* (Persian, lowland), the name that has survived to this day. And Baghdad is made up of the Persian words *Bag*, meaning God, and *dad*, meaning gift.

Since Persia (a derivative of Pars/Fars) was officially renamed Iran (a derivative of Arya) only in 1935, in the early parts of my text I have used the terms Persian and Iranian interchangeably, also the words Persian and Farsi for the local language.

In the Introduction I provide a historical perspective to the relationship between Iraq and Iran, and pick up the threads from my earlier two books. In Iran the death of Ayatollah Ruhollah Khomeini (r. 1979–89) about a year after the 1980–88 Iran–Iraq War was a watershed. And so was the 1990 invasion of Kuwait by Saddam Hussein in Iraq. Ten years on, Iraqis were still suffering its consequences.

Part I is a chronological account and analysis of what has happened in Iraq since the 1991 Gulf War between Baghdad and the United States-led Coalition. Most of the narrative deals with the troubled relationship between Iraq and the United Nations as defined by Security Council Resolutions 687 and 688 passed in April 1988. As the leader of the Coalition that expelled the Iraqis from Kuwait, the US – also the sole superpower in the world – was the pre-eminent player in the UN's dealings with Saddam Hussein. In any case, since Saddam Hussein is the only one who counts in Iraq,[2] there is no domestic politics in the conventional sense of the word – no public interplay between different ideas and personalities on how to run the country.

Contrary is the case in Iran, the subject of Part II. The Iranian political–religious system is evolving, helped by the fact that since the 1979 Islamic revolution there have been regular elections for the presidency, parliament and Assembly of Experts. Hence much of the narrative and analysis focus on internal politics.

The concluding chapter provides an analytical summary of the earlier text as well as informed speculation on the future.

The dates in bracket preceded by "r." after the first mention of a hereditary or elected ruler specify when he/she was in office. But a figure in brackets following a non-ruling personality indicates either his/her year of birth ("b.") or death ("d.").

A word about place names, and the spellings of Arabic and Persian words. While I have used the term "the Gulf" that divides Iran from the Arabian Peninsula, I have listed the two other names in common use – the Persian Gulf and the Arabian Gulf – in the index. There is no standard way of transliterating Arabic and Persian names. In each case I have chosen one of the most widely used spellings in the English-language print media – except when the spelling of the book author is different from mine. There I have merely reproduced the published spelling in quoted material. While using an index, a particular difficulty arises when different spellings of a proper noun, or an object, begin with a different letter – as in Koran/Quran; or Arbil/Erbil/Irbil. I have solved this problem by using one spelling in the text but including others as well in the index.

Iranians tend to use "e" where others prefer "i." Common examples are Esfahan rather than Isfahan, and Ezzat instead of Izzat. But I have followed the non-Iranian practice because, for instance, the name Izzat is common among both Iranians and Arabs.

Wherever appropriate, after the English translation of the name of an organization or concept I give the original title in Arabic or Persian in parentheses. I do this either because the Arabic or Persian term is better known – e.g., Special Security (*Amn al Khas*); or because the international newsagencies abbreviate the title to the point of distortion – e.g., University-Seminary Unity Consolidation Bureau (*Daftar-e Tahkim-e Vahdat-e Howza va Daneshgah*) shortened to Unity Consolidation Office.

Since many of the Arabic words used in the text are also part of the Persian vocabulary, I have prepared a combined glossary of Arabic, Persian and Kurdish words.

The custom about the family name of an Iraqi male deserves a brief explanation. After Iraq came under British Mandate in 1921, the Civil Register Law of 1927 required that the authorities must maintain a family register for all citizens. Hence arose the need for a "family name," which was to be added to the two identifying names in vogue, one given to the child at birth and the other being the father's. For the family name, the household head, always a male, chose the name either of the place or tribe or trade/profession – the respective examples being al Tikriti, al Ubaidi, and al Falaki. Thus all Iraqi males had at least three names, including the family name. This continued until 1972 when the four-year-old regime of the Arab Baath Socialist Party issued an order that men must stop using the family name and identify themselves by a maximum of three names – self, father and grandfather (the last one sometimes used with the prefix "al"). A typical example of the new law was Barzan Ibrahim al Hassan. This was done primarily to mask the fact that al Tikritis – originating in the native area of President Ahmad Hassan Bakr (r. 1968–79) and his relative, Saddam Hussein – occupied far too many positions at the top. However, since then the old family names have gradually re-surfaced even when the 1972 decree has not been formally revoked. So nowadays Barzan Ibrahim al Hassan is known as Barzan Ibrahim al Tikriti. And if the Iraqi president had to use three names he could call himself either Saddam Hussein al Tikriti or Saddam Hussein al Majid (being his grandfather).

At the first mention of an Iraqi male in the text, I provide his family name in parentheses even if he does not use it regularly. An example is Izzat Ibrahim (al Duri). In the index I give both names.

In Iran and Iraq women do not change their given and family names after marriage. So Jamila Kadivar, after marrying Ataollah Mohajerani, retains her maiden name.

The Iraqi Dinar is the currency unit in Iraq, and the Rial is the Iranian unit. Before the 1991 Gulf War the official exchange rates varied between ID 0.31 and ID 0.28 to US$1, and R 70 to R 85 to US$1. Since then these currencies have plummeted and, wherever appropriate, their wildly fluctuating rates appear in the text.

Between August 1999 and August 2000 I visited Iraq and Iran three times.

Dilip Hiro
London, April 2001

INTRODUCTION

On a clear day, from the embankment of the Shatt al Arab (*lit.*, The Arab River) – Arvand Rud (River), to the Iranians – near the Iranian city of Khorramshahr, you can see, beyond the mid-channel island covered with yellowing tall grass, Iraqi territory. Here the Shatt al Arab is only 75 yards (70 meters) wide, about a third of its girth at its mouth in the Gulf.

In January 1989 when I last visited the site it was strewn with marks of the Iran–Iraq War which had ended five months earlier: a sand-bagged bunker dug into the embankment with a helmeted soldier clutching his machine-gun, an armored personnel carrier covered by a dirty tarpaulin, and a rusty, sand-bagged fence near a quay. Not surprising. After all, the Shatt al Arab was at the core of the eight-year-long hostilities between Tehran and Baghdad.

For the last two-fifths of its 120 mile (190 km) length, the Shatt al Arab – beginning at the confluence of the Euphrates and Tigris rivers at Qurna, Iraq – forms a fluvial border between the neighboring countries. The demarcation of this placid, muddy waterway has been a most contentious issue between Iran and Iraq for many decades – with Baghdad claiming all of the Shatt al Arab, and Tehran demanding a division along its deepest mid-channel, called the thawleg line.

Competition and rivalry between Iran and Iraq date back to the era of the Ottoman Turkish empire (1517–1918) and the Persian/Iranian empire under the Safavids (1501–1722). Iraq was then the easternmost province of the Ottomans, and Iran the nucleus of the Safavid realm. Disputes between the competing empires revolved around boundaries and interference in each other's domestic affairs, conducted through ethnic and sectarian minorities across the ill-defined common frontier.

Until the first quarter of the nineteenth century the presence of migratory tribes in the border areas militated against fixed boundaries. Then tensions continued under the tutelage of European imperial powers, chiefly Britain and Tsarist Russia. Finally, from the 1920s onward the nominally independent states of Iraq and Iran maintained their historical animosity in changed circumstances, at first under the direct influence of Britain, and later – after 1958 – as truly independent countries pursing their respective national interests.

After the Safavid chief, Shah Ismail (r.1501–24), had consolidated his newly won territories he adopted Twelver Shiaism[1] as the official religion so as to appeal to the heterodox sentiments of his subjects and differentiate himself from the competing Sunni Ottoman Turks eager to incorporate Iran into their empire. Under his rule Shia theology and jurisprudence were systematized. The resulting religio-ideological unity helped him to lay a strong foundation for the Safavid empire. On the other side, the Ottomans feared that the Safavid might incite their own Shia subjects in Central Asia to rebel. As a result some 40,000 Shias in the Ottoman empire were massacred as spies for the Safavid.[2]

As the guardians of Shiaism, the Safavids wanted free access to the Shia holy shrines in Najaf and Karbala in southern Iraq. These cities, as well as Basra, Kufa and Samarra, figure prominently in the early history of Islam, when divisions among its adherents led to the creation of two major sects: Shias – derivative of Shiat Ali, "Followers of Ali," the cousin and son-in-law of Prophet Muhammad – and majority Sunni, people of Sunna, (*lit.*, custom) the tradition of Prophet Muhammad. Of the dozen Imams of Twelver Shias, six are buried in Iraq, and the last one is believed to have gone into occultation in Samarra.

The Safavids occupied Iraq from 1623 to 1638. Following its recapture by the Ottomans, the two sides signed the Treaty of Zuhab in 1639. It recognized Iraq as part of the Ottoman empire and dealt with frontier demarcation, as well as the problems of the Kurdish tribes settled in the northern Zagros Mountain region and the annual pilgrimage of Persian/Iranian Shias to the holy shrines in Iraq.

Although the treaty held for over a century the ethnic problem of the frontier areas persisted. In the north the Kurdish tribes continued to ignore the international boundaries while in the south Arabic-speaking tribes, keen to maintain their autonomy from the Ottomans, offered (nominal) allegiance to Persia.

The emergence of Muhammara in 1812 as an autonomous principality ruled by the chief of the Muhaisin tribe sharpened tensions between the two adjoining empires. War between them erupted in 1821. By then Britain and Tsarist Russia were the leading European imperial powers in the region. They came to regulate Ottoman-Persian relations. In 1821 London mediated between the belligerent neighbors, resulting in the First Treaty of Erzerum in 1823. Each of the signatories promised *inter alia* not to grant political asylum to dissident groups from the other empire.

Yet the two neighbors continued to interfere in each other's affairs. Persia encouraged the Kurds in Iraq to rebel. Tensions rose between 1834 and 1840, when the Ottomans attacked the port of Muhammara (later renamed Khorramshahr) and persecuted the Persian Shias living in Iraq. Britain and Russia intervened to resolve the conflict. A joint commission appointed in 1843 led to the signing of the Second Treaty of Erzerum four years later. Persia ceded Suleimaniya in Iraqi Kurdistan to the Ottomans, and received Muhammara/ Khorramshahr in return. And in exchange for some territory in the Zuhab-Qasr-e Shirin area, Persia got the Island of Khizr (later renamed Abadan) and the land between the Bahmanshir River and the Shatt al Arab. Thus the latest treaty shifted the fluvial borders between the two empires from the western bank of the

Bahmanshir river to the eastern bank of the Shatt al Arab for about the last two-fifths of the latter's length. However, the signatories still did not cease interfering in each other's domestic affairs.

A new factor was added to the complex equation when, in 1908, the British discovered oil in commercial quantities near Masjid-e Suleiman in Iranian Arabistan/ Khuzistan. The Shaikh of Muhammara persisted in his drive for independence while faction fighting among Kurds showed no sign of abating. This was the backdrop to the signing of the Protocol of Tehran in 1911. It outlined a basis for negotiations to settle all outstanding problems. In November 1913 the representatives of the Ottoman empire, Persia (renamed Iran in 1935), Britain and Russia met in Constantinople (later renamed Istanbul) to delineate the boundary from Mount Ararat to the Gulf, and redefine navigational rights in the Shatt al Arab. Keen to develop an oil industry in Persia, Britain needed extensive port facilities along the waterway. Unsurprisingly, the new protocol awarded to Iran one largish and five small islands in the Shatt al Arab between Muhammara/ Khorramshahr and the sea. After the confirmation of the Constantinople Protocol in 1914 came the appointment of the Delimitation Commission on which Britain and Russia had powers of arbitration. By the time World War I (1914–18) broke out later that year, a definitive map of the frontier had been produced and 227 boundary pillars erected.

World War I, the 1917 Bolshevik revolution in Russia and the dissolution of the Ottoman empire caused profound changes in the region. Iraq emerged as a quasi-independent state under British mandate in 1921. With this began the third phase of Iraq-Iran relations, where two (nominally) independent nation-states faced each other.

Iran refused to recognize the exclusive Iraqi control of the Shatt al Arab that Baghdad claimed, and used its own pilots to steer ships along it, arguing that the 1913 Constantinople Protocol had recognized the thawleg – the median line of the deepest channel – as the international boundary. It was only in 1929 that Tehran formally accorded diplomatic recognition to Iraq. Iran was then ruled by Reza Shah Pahlavi (r. 1926–41), who had seized the throne from the Qajar dynasty after proving his military prowess by crushing the semi-autonomous Shaikh Ahmad Khazal of Muhammara and renaming the province Khuzistan.

In 1931 the two countries exchanged envoys, and the next year Iraq, having acquired full independence, became a member of the League of Nations. The nature of the inter-state problems remained the same, centered on the minority Kurdish and Arabic-speaking tribes and the demarcation of the Shatt al Arab.

Iraq took the waterway issue to the League of Nations in 1934, but in the spring of 1936 it and Iran agreed to settle the matter through direct negotiations. While these were in progress, a military coup in October ushered in a government in Baghdad that was weak and confused. Under continued pressure from Iran, bolstered by the British oil interests and government, Iraq conceded the thawleg principle for 4 miles (6 km) opposite Abadan, which housed a vast oil refinery of the Anglo-Persian Oil Company (APOC, later Anglo-Iranian Oil

Company, AIOC). The result was the Iran-Iraq Frontier Treaty signed on July 4, 1937. It stated that the Shatt al Arab was open for navigation to all countries of the world. Confirming the land boundaries as set out in the 1913–14 accords, it amended only the fluvial frontiers.

Even though the 1937 Treaty was between two sovereign states the domineering presence of Britain was all too apparent. A British-led petroleum company had struck oil in northern Iraq in 1927, and the APOC was a giant in Iran's industrial and commercial life.

World War II destroyed whatever illusions the two states had of their sovereignty. In 1941 London intervened militarily to overthrow the nationalist government of Rashid Ali Gailani in Baghdad. During that year Britain and the Soviet Union deposed Reza Shah Pahlavi and occupied different parts of Iran. Both Iran and Iraq were used as staging areas by the Allies to supply weapons and goods to the beleaguered Soviet Union. This led to the building of a bridge over the Shatt al Arab and improved rail and road systems between the two neighbors.

After signing the Treaty of Good Neighborly Relations in 1949, the two states raised their diplomatic relations to the ambassadorial level. Relations improved further with the establishment of a military alliance between Turkey, Iraq, Iran, Pakistan and Britain in 1951, called the Middle East Treaty Organization (Meto) but popularly known as the Baghdad Pact. Among other things this alliance was a device for Britain – working in conjunction with the US – to maintain influence over Iran and Iraq. No wonder that in 1957 both endorsed the doctrine of US President Dwight Eisenhower (r. 1952–60) which promised support to any Middle Eastern government against "overt armed aggression from any nation controlled by international communism."

Two decades of fairly peaceful co-existence between Tehran and Baghdad ended in July 1958, when the pro-Western Iraqi monarchy was overthrown by nationalist, republican military officers. The event heralded the final expulsion of western imperialism from Iraq. With this Iraq and Iran entered a period when, as truly independent states, they were free to regulate their relations in the light of their sovereign rights, territorial integrity and national interests.

While republican Iraq adopted a non-aligned foreign policy by withdrawing from the Baghdad Pact in March 1959, monarchical Iran under Muhammad Reza Shah Pahlavi (r. 1941–78) signed a Military Cooperation Agreement with Washington in that month. This provided for American defense of Iran in case of external aggression. Thus fortified, the Shah revived the old Iranian demand that the thalweg formula be applied to all of the Shatt al Arab frontier. Iraqi Premier Abdul Karim Qasim (r. 1958–63) rejected the demand, arguing that Iraq had made the concession on the thalweg in 1937 for the anchorage area around Abadan due to unsettled conditions at home. Tension mounted as Iran threatened to use its own river pilots and stop paying tolls to Baghdad.

Iraq continued to be the weak party, partly because it lacked the military muscle of Iran and partly because of its unstable internal situation. Between 1958 and 1968, it experienced three coups and five governments. Only in July 1968, with the success of a coup dominated by the Arab Baath Socialist Party (ABSP), did the situation stabilize.

During their direct talks in February 1969, the Iranians declared that Iraq had failed to meet its obligations under the 1937 Treaty, and demanded once more that the fluvial frontier be drawn along the Shatt al Arab's thawleg. Iraq refused. The outbreak of the Iraqi Kurdish insurgency in March diverted Baghdad's attention, and emboldened the Shah. In April he unilaterally abrogated the 1937 Treaty. Iran went on to pilot its own ships in the Shatt al Arab, with its gunboats steaming up the waterway along the middle channel. Iraq complained to the United Nations, but to no avail. It expelled resident Iranians in large numbers. It revived the issue of Khuzistan/Arabistan which, it claimed, was Iraqi territory that had been surrendered to Iran during "the foreign mandate [of the Ottomans]."[3] A war of words ensued between the two capitals. But the Shah went beyond words. In January 1970 the Iraqi government accused him of sponsoring a military coup against it which it succeeded in foiling.

Earlier, in 1966, the Shah had agreed to act as a conduit for arms' supplies from Israel and the US to the Kurdish insurgents in northern Iraq. The Kurdish problem was of long standing. As descendants of the Indo-European tribes who settled in contemporary south-eastern Turkey, north-eastern Iraq and north-western Persia, Kurds trace their distinct history as mountain people to the seventh century B.C., appearing as Medes in the Bible. Racially, they are different from Turks and Semite Arabs, and their language, belonging to the Indo-European family, is akin to Persian/Farsi. After the dissolution of the Ottoman empire, the Kurdish-dominated Mosul province was added to Baghdad and Basra provinces to create contemporary Iraq. The importance of the Kurdish region rose sharply in 1927 when a British-dominated company struck oil near Kirkuk, the largest find in the world so far. A Kurdish insurgency for independence led by Shaikh Ahmad Barzani in 1931–32 was crushed in 1935 by a joint Iraqi-Turkish campaign. During World War II, Mustafa Barzani (1904–79), a brother of Ahmad, led another rebellion which failed. He escaped to Iran where, under the banner of the Kurdish Democratic Party, he co-founded the Kurdistan Republic in December 1945. When the Republic was overthrown by the Shah a year later, Barzani fled to the adjoining Azerbaijan Socialist Republic of the Soviet Union.

Following the 1958 coup in Iraq, Barzani returned home, and backed the new regime under Abdul Karim Qasim. In exchange Qasim legalized the Kurdish Democratic Party, which changed its name to the Kurdistan Democratic Party (KDP). Qasim promulgated a constitution which stated, "Arabs and Kurds are associates in this nation." This was a formal recognition of Kurds, forming about 17 percent of the national population, as a distinct ethnic minority. However, when Barzani advanced an autonomy plan, Qasim rejected it. He mounted an all-out campaign against Kurdish insurgents in September 1961. Though he was overthrown in February 1963 the Kurdish rebellion continued. It was not until June 1966 that a 12-point agreement was signed between the KDP and the central government, which had had to commit three of its five army divisions to fighting Kurdish guerrillas.[4] The pact included the official recognition of the Kurdish language and proportional representation for Kurds in the civil service. But in the absence of mutual trust the agreement failed to resolve the problem.

After seizing power in 1968, the Baathists began implementing part of the 12-point pact. But, considering the move inadequate, the KDP started an armed rebellion in March 1969. The fighting continued for a year, costing Baghdad about 30 percent of its annual budget.[5] This and the discovery of a Tehran-inspired military plot against it in January 1970 led the Baathist regime to conclude a 15-point pact with the KDP in March, to be implemented fully in four years. It promised a fair degree of autonomy to the region where Kurds were in majority (according to a census to be conducted) and the appointment of a Kurd as the Republic's vice-president. An interim constitution, promulgated in July 1970, recognized Kurds as one of the two nationalities of Iraq, the other being Arabs, and the Kurdish language as one of the two official languages in the Kurdish region. But the ruling Baathist Revolutionary Command Council (RCC), the highest authority in the country, rejected the KDP's nominee for vice-president.

Once again the accord failed to hold. As the central government earned three-fifths of its oil revenue from the Kurdistan region, it was unwilling to loosen its control over it. Baghdad failed to hold the promised census in the Kurdish areas and continued the previous regime's policy of Arabizing the oil-rich Kirkuk area through such means as deporting some 40,000 Fali (Shia) Kurds to Iran. On the other side, violating his promises, Barzani enlarged his guerrilla force and maintained contacts with Iran, Israel and America.

As Britain, the dominant Western power in the Gulf, prepared to withdraw from the region by December 1971, it and the US chose Iran to be the new guarantor of the security of the oil-rich Gulf, and a bulwark against revolutionary changes in the region. With London's active help, Iran added three strategically placed islands – the Lesser and Greater Tunbs (belonging to the Ras al Khaima principality) and Abu Musa (belonging to the Sharjah principality) – to a group it already possessed: Qeshm, Larak and Hormuz. Together these six islands form a crescent which covers the entrance to the Hormuz Straits through which a large part of the Gulf oil is shipped to the West and Japan.

As fervent Arab nationalists, Iraqi Baathists condemned the usurpation of Arab territory by the Shah. Severing its ties with Tehran and London, Iraq tilted more towards the Soviet Union. Its fifteen-year Treaty of Friendship and Cooperation with Moscow signed in April 1972 required the signatories to contact each other in case of "danger to the peace of either party or … danger to peace," and to refrain from joining an alliance aimed against the other. They also resolved to "continue to develop cooperation in the strengthening of their defense capacity."[6]

In response US President Richard Nixon (r. 1969–74) announced in May that the Shah could buy any non-nuclear American weapons he wanted.

Overall, the Iran–Iraq competition was unequal. Militarily and strategically, Iraq was much weaker than Iran. Since its coastline of a mere 40 miles (64 km) was short and shallow, its seaports could not maintain extensive and reliable communications with other regional ports. So an Iraqi claim to be a Gulf power was hard to substantiate. By contrast, Iran's coastline not only ran the full 570 mile (950 km) length of the Gulf but also extended into the Arabian sea. Politically, Iraq was isolated in the region. Because of the support it provided to republican forces against what it called "Arab reaction," it was much feared and hated by the Gulf's Arab monarchs.

The outbreak of the Arab–Israeli War in October 1973 demolished the Iraqi thesis that the Shah was a greater enemy than Israel and the West. During the hostilities Iraq dispatched troops to the Syrian–Israeli front, and re-established diplomatic links with Iran. However, there was no improvement in Baghdad–Tehran relations. Flushed with funds in hard currencies, thanks to the quadrupling of oil prices, the Shah embarked on ambitious plans to boost his military power. He tried to destabilize the Iraqi regime by bolstering the KDP whose agreement with Baghdad had collapsed.

In March 1974 the Iraqi government implemented the Kurdish autonomy law, stemming from its accord with the KDP four years earlier, as planned. Protesting against the exclusion of such oil-bearing areas as Kirkuk, Sinjar and Khanaqin from the Kurdish region, the KDP demanded postponement of the implementation until a fresh census revealed the exact distribution of Kurds in the region. When Baghdad ignored the demand, fighting resumed.

At its peak the conflict involved 45,000 Kurdish guerrillas who pinned down four-fifths of Iraq's 100,000-plus troops and nearly half its 1,390 tanks.[7] Barzani claimed to have liberated 25,000 sq miles (64,800 sq km) with a population of 1.5 million Kurds adjacent to the Iranian border. He achieved this with the assistance of the Shah who, besides supplying US and Israeli arms to the KDP, used his troops to cover the insurgents with artillery fire and anti-aircraft missiles. Periodic skirmishes erupted between the armies of Iraq and Iran all along their 750 mile (1,200 km) border. By early 1975 both sides realized the danger of a full-scale war, aware that it would lead *inter alia* to immediate destruction of their vital oil installations, which neither could afford. They therefore encouraged mediation, first by Turkey and then Algeria.

This was the background to the conclusion of an accord on March 6, 1975, in Algiers by the Shah of Iran and Saddam Hussein, then vice-president of Iraq, during a summit conference of the Organization of Petroleum Exporting Countries (OPEC). The parties agreed to delimit their river boundaries "according to the thalweg line" and "to end all infiltration of a subversive nature."[8] The Iran–Iraq Treaty of International Boundaries and Good Neighborliness, incorporating the Algiers Accord, was signed in Baghdad on June 17 and ratified by both parties on September 17, 1975. A joint commission was appointed to demarcate the new border in the light of Iran conceding territory around the villages of Zain al Qaus and Said Saad in the Qasr-e Shirin area to compensate Iraq for its concession on the Shatt al Arab.

A landmark in regional history, the Algiers Accord dominated Baghdad-Tehran relations for the next fifteen years. It incorporated the Iranian demand, first made over sixty years earlier, that the thalweg principle be applied to the frontier along the Shatt al Arab. And, just as the weakness of its government in 1937 had led Iraq to yield to the Iranian pressure to accept this formula for Abadan port, so too now. Harassed and exhausted by the Tehran-backed Kurdish insurgency, Baghdad agreed to extend the thalweg principle to the rest of the fluvial border. It was a bitter pill for Iraq to swallow which, as was to be revealed later, left its leaders acutely divided, with the military officers among them opposing the accord.

Domestically, however, Iraq benefited far more than Iran. Released from the debilitating task of countering Kurdish rebellion, the Iraqi government inaugurated an accelerated program of socio-economic development. It tried to tackle the long-simmering problem of Shias – denied power and status commensurate to their numerical majority – partly by increasing expenditure on economic projects in the south where Shias were concentrated. The funds for these ambitious plans came from exporting oil, the price of which had risen fourfold during 1973–74. By then Baghdad had nationalized all foreign holdings of the petroleum companies operating in Iraq, and was in total control of its most precious resource. Also the Baathists had consolidated their hold over state and society, and provided firm pan-Arabic ideological underpinning to the regime.

By contrast, the Shah's strong, highly centralized government in Iran lacked an ideological foundation. According to the 1906–7 Constitution, Twelver Shiasm was the state religion, and only a Twelver Shia could become king. Another article enjoined the monarch to promote the sect. In practice, though, Iran under the Shah was a secular state run by a highly Westernized ruling elite, uninterested in religion, politics or ideology. The Shah lacked a well-oiled party machine, inspired by a comprehensive social philosophy to underwrite the legitimacy of his regime.

The situation was parallel to the one that had existed in monarchical Iraq, from 1922 to 1958, when all political activity was banned. In 1950 the ABSP in Iraq was in its infancy and clandestine. It came into being as the Arab Baath Party in Damascus, Syria, in 1947 at a pan-Arab congress. Its founders were three teachers: Michel Aflaq (1910–89), a Greek Orthodox Christian; Zaki Arsuzi, an Alawi (i.e., follower of Imam Ali) Muslim;[9] and Salah al Din Bitar, a Sunni Muslim. The party's basic principles were unity and freedom of the Arab nation within its homeland, and a belief in the special mission of the Arab nation, that mission being to end colonialism. To achieve these ends, the party had to be nationalist, populist, socialist and revolutionary. While the party rejected the concept of class conflict, it favored land reform; public ownership of natural resources, transport, large-scale industry and financial institutions; trade unions of workers and peasants; and acceptance of non-exploitative private ownership and inheritance. It stood for a representative and constitutional form of government, and freedom of speech and association within the bounds of Arab nationalism. In 1952 the Arab Baath Party's union with Akram Hourani's Arab Socialist Party in Syria led to the composite name Arab Baath Socialist Party.

In Iraq the party (with a membership of about 200) held its first clandestine regional congress in 1955 when it decided to cooperate with other Arab nationalist groups. It played only a marginal role in the military coup that overthrew the monarchy in 1958. Despite suppression by the new ruler, Abdul Karim Qasim, the party grew. By the time the Baathists, joined by the non-Baathist sympathizers, overthrew Qasim in early 1963, the ABSP had 850 active members and 15,000 sympathizers.

Once in power, the Baathists fell out among themselves, allowing the non-Baathist Abdul Salam Arif (r. 1963–66) to usurp power in late 1963. He died in 1966. The failure of his brother, President Abdul Rahman Arif (r. 1966–68), to participate fully in the June 1967 Arab–Israeli War was used by the Baathists to bolster their popular support. In mid-July 1968 Baathist leaders and non-Baathist military officers overthrew Arif; and a fortnight later the Baathists elbowed out the non-Baathist conspirators and seized total power. The ABSP then had 5,000 active members.

The governing Revolutionary Command Council, headed by President Ahmad Hassan Bakr, institutionalized the interweaving of the party with state machinery and with secular society at large. The interim constitution of 1970 formalized party supremacy by stating that the RCC, the highest state body, had the right to select its new members from the regional (i.e., national) leadership of the ABSP. The party tightened its grip over the armed forces, police and intelligence. Once Saddam Hussein, who had earlier built up the party's militia, had acquired a seat on the 15-member RCC in November 1969, he busied himself with restructuring and strengthening the party. It set up cells in government departments, professional syndicates, educational institutions, publicly and privately-owned businesses, trade unions, agricultural cooperatives and women's associations – as well as the military. These cells were all the more effective because the Baathist cadres were required to keep their party affiliation secret. A well-planned internal security system held Baathist members responsible for safeguarding their street or neighborhood.

To broaden the popular base of the regime, the RCC sponsored the formation of the National Progressive and Patriotic Front (NPPF) of the Baath Party and other small like-minded groups in 1973, with the Baath firmly in the lead. With Iraq's oil income rocketing to $8,000 million in 1975 from $75 million three years earlier,[10] the Baathist government awarded hefty salary increments to its employees, expanded educational, health and public welfare services, and implemented ambitious economic projects.

But, whereas the Kurdish crisis receded with the signing of the 1975 Algiers Accord, disaffection among Shias came to the fore. As subjects of the Sunni Ottoman rulers, Shias had suffered discrimination. They were barred from public office. While the Ottomans allowed Sunni ulama (religious-legal scholars) to control waqfs (religious endowments) and derive income from them, they denied these rights to Shia ulama. They did not permit Shia ulama to exercise jurisprudence except in internal matters in their own centers. Shia clerics remained dependent on the contributions of their flock, mainly in the form of *zakat* (tithe for the poor; derivative of *zaka*, to be pure) and *khums* (*lit.*, one-fifth), one-fifth of annual profits as due to the descendant Imams of Prophet Muhammad.

Shias were mostly nomadic tribal people who had later settled as peasants and shepherds in the predominantly rural south. By the late 1940s Shia peasant tribesmen began migrating in large numbers to Basra and Baghdad, where they congregated in a shanty town later named Medinat al Thawra (Town of the Revolution), and then renamed Medinat al Saddam.

Since one of Abdul Karim Qasim's parents was Shia, he was neutral between Sunnis and Shias, in contrast to his successor Abdul Salam Arif, a rabid Sunni. With the secular Baathists seizing power in 1968, the government imposed strict censorship of religious publications, shut down various Islamic institutions, including a theological college in Najaf, began harassing Shia ulama and, for the first time in Iraqi history, allowed the sale of alcohol in Shia holy places.

It was against this backdrop that in 1969 al Daawa al Islamiya (*lit.*, The Islamic Call) was formed, clandestinely, with the blessing of the Najaf-based Ayatollah Muhsin al Hakim, the seniormost Shia clergy. As the Baathist regime, dominated by Sunni leaders, tried to interfere with some Shia public rituals and weaken the authority of the religious hierarchy, al Daawa gained ground. In December 1974 Shia religious processions turned into anti-government demonstrations. This was the first time in independent Iraq's history that Shias had, as a religious group, violently confronted the state. The government tried twenty-five Shia leaders clandestinely, and executed five.[11] At the same time it tried to placate Shias by increasing development funds to the south.

But Shia grievances went beyond redistribution of national wealth. They pointed out that they were grossly under-represented in the upper echelons of the police, military, intelligence, civil service and the Baath Party. None of the RCC members was Shia. Al Daawa attacked the rule of a party whose National (meaning pan-Arab) Command was headed by Michel Aflaq, a Christian, based in Baghdad. It also deplored the Baathists' neglect of Islam and Islamic institutions. Thus the simmering tension between Shia masses and the regime escalated steadily over the next few years.

It erupted violently at the height of a Shia ceremony in February 1977 when the government sealed off Karbala, the site of the shrine of Imam Hussein ibn Ali, who was killed there in 681 A.D. The police intercepted a procession of pilgrims on its way from Najaf, the site of the shrine of Imam Ali ibn Abu Talib (Caliph, 656–61 A.D.), to Karbala, at Haidariya. This triggered off rioting which spread to Najaf. It persisted for several days and the authorities called troops to quell it. Several dozen people were killed, and some 2,000 Shias were arrested.

They were tried by a special tribunal which ordered the execution of eight of them.

These events caused anxiety and fractious debate within the Baathist leadership which had just recovered from the divisive effect of the 1975 Algiers Accord. Some leaders, headed by President Bakr, advocated conciliating Shia protesters and accommodating party ideology to the rising wave of Islamic revival, while others, led by Vice-President Saddam Hussein, proposed repressing Shia dissent and reiterating Baathist commitment to secularism and separation of religion and politics. Saddam won.

He had fully grasped the gravity of the situation, aware that Shias formed three-quarters of the Arab population, forming about 80 percent of the total, the rest being ethnic Kurds, and that whereas the Kurdish activists were confined to the northern mountainous region, Shia activists, based in the plains, were part of the mainstream both socially and geographically.

Saddam combined merciless repression of the Al Daawa with determined moves to placate Shia masses through economic and political concessions. He allocated further sums to the development of the Shia-dominated south. And attempts were made to attract Shias to the membership rolls of the Baath Party where Saddam, though nominally number two in the hierarchy, enjoyed supreme authority.

His moves to tackle the Shia problem had not come a day too soon. For in Iran a revolutionary movement led by Ayatollah Ruhollah Khomeini, a towering Shia cleric, against the autocratic, secular regime of the Shah was about to gather steam. As it happened, Khomeini had been living as an exile in Najaf, only a few blocks away from Imam Ali's shrine, since October 1965, having clashed with the Shah in 1963–64. It was common among Shia clergy the world over to seek refuge in the shrine city of Najaf, the leading center of Shia learning. Given the animosity then existing between Baghdad and Tehran, there had been no objection from Iraqi President Abdul Salam Arif to granting political asylum to Khomeini. Later President Bakr solicited the ayatollah's backing in Iraq's quarrel with the Shah. But Khomeini refused to oblige. Indeed, being unhappy at the way the Baathist regime had been treating Shia clerics in Najaf and Karbala, he had expressed a wish to leave for Lebanon in 1972, only to have it rejected by the authorities. At the same time he kept scrupulously away from the Iraqi Shia underground. His sole interest lay in overthrowing the Shah in Iran.

Ruhollah Khomeini was born in 1903 to Sayyid Mustafa Musavi, the chief cleric of Khomein, a town 220 miles (350 km) south-west of Tehran. His father was murdered when Ruhollah was a year old. At 19, after he had finished his Persian schooling and religious instruction, he joined a seminary run by Ayatollah Abdul Karim Hairi-Yazdi in Arak. When the latter moved to Qom, a leading Shia center of learning, Khomeini went with him. In 1925 he completed his study in the Sharia (*lit.*, way or road) – consisting of the Quran and the Sunna, tradition of Prophet Muhammad as codified by Hadith (*lit.*, report; the sayings and doings of Prophet Muhammad) – ethics and spiritual philosophy. He married Khadija

Saqai at 25. Two years later he published his thesis on ethics and spiritual philosophy in Arabic, a language he had learnt as a child. Over time he established himself as a teacher who interrelated ethical-spiritual problems with contemporary social issues. After Hairi-Yazdi's death in 1936 Khomeini followed the leadership of Ayatollah Muhammad Borujerdi. In 1941 he published a book which attacked secularism and Reza Shah Pahlavi's dictatorial rule. Four years later he graduated to the rank of hojatalislam (proof of Islam), one below that of ayatollah (sign of Allah). This meant he could now collect his own circle of disciples who would accept his interpretation of the Sharia. Following Borujerdi's death in 1961 Khomeini's admirers urged him to publish his interpretations of the Sharia under the title *Clarifications of the Points of the Sharia*. It immediately secured him the rank of an ayatollah. In a series of sermons delivered at Qom's most prestigious seminary in early June 1963, Khomeini attacked the Shah's "white revolution" as phony. In early June, on the eve of the death anniversary of Imam Hussein, he vehemently attacked the Shah and his secular, pro-Western dictatorial policies. This speech transformed him into a national hero among the religious masses who despised the royal autocracy but dared not express their feelings. He was in and out of jail until November 1964 when he was deported to Turkey. After living in the Turkish city of Bursa for a year, he arrived in Najaf. From there he kept up his anti-Shah campaign. In 1971 his book, *Islamic Government: Rule of the Jurisprudent*, based on a series of lectures, was published. In it he argued that instead of prescribing dos and don'ts for believers, and waiting passively for the return of the Hidden Imam, the (Shia) clergy must attempt to oust corrupt officials and repressive regimes and replace them with the ones led by just *faqihs,* Islamic jurisprudents.

His anti-Shah campaign received a boost when, following the 1975 Algiers Accord, Baghdad allowed 130,000 Iranian pilgrims to visit the Shia holy places in Iraq annually.[12] It became comparatively easy for Khomeini to maintain regular contact with his acolytes in Iran, and guide them in their anti-Shah struggle through smuggled tape recordings. These audio-tapes became all the more important as the revolutionary process – consisting of massive and repeated demonstrations and strikes – gathered momentum from February 1977 to October 1978, when, with widespread strikes crippling the economy, the Shah became anxious. He urged Iraq to honor the Algiers Accord regarding suppressing subversive activities directed against the fellow-signatory. Baghdad complied swiftly by expelling Khomeini.

His expulsion was resented by Iraqi Shias, especially when it was soon followed by Saddam's escorting the Shah's wife, Farah Diba, around the Shia holy places. Khomeini flew to France where he discovered that he had greater freedom of action than in Najaf. He returned to Iran in triumph a fortnight after the Shah had left the country in mid-January 1979.

The victory of the revolutionary forces, led by Khomeini, over an apparently invincible Shah gave a fillip to Iraqi Shias. An indication of this came when Ayatollah Muhammad Baqir al Sadr of Najaf said in his congratulatory message to

Khomeini that "Other tyrants have yet to see their day of reckoning."[13] Obviously, by "Other tyrants" al Sadr meant the Baathist rulers, especially Saddam Hussein.

So, while Saddam had taken some steps to conciliate disaffected Shias, their expectations and aspirations underwent a qualitative change as a result of Iran's Islamic revolution. Now neither the Baathist regime nor Iraqi Shias could define their relationship without reference to the Iranian revolution.

After the Iranian revolution

For Iraqi Baathists, the Iranian upheaval could not have come at a worse time. The signing of the Egyptian–Israeli peace accord in September 1978 at the US presidential mountain retreat of Camp David in Maryland made Baghdad revise the ultra-radical, isolationist stance on the Arab–Israeli dispute it had taken since the October 1973 War. Alarmed at the loss of Egypt as Israel's enemy on the western front, the Iraqi government invited Syria's President Hafiz Assad (r. 1970–2000) to Baghdad, and offered to unite Iraq with Syria to create a strong eastern front against Israel. By so doing, and hosting the Arab League summit in Baghdad against the Camp David Accords in November, the Iraqi government ended its isolation in the Arab world. But the Iranian drama had a deleterious impact on the Iraqi–Syrian unity plans. While Assad enthusiastically praised the Iranian revolution in February 1979, Baghdad maintained a studied silence.

The overthrow against all odds of the powerful Shah in the midst of a booming economy made Iranian revolutionaries feel that their example would inspire the oppressed masses everywhere to rise up against their unjust, repressive rulers. They were particularly keen to aid the oppressed Muslim masses in the Gulf region to depose their rulers whom they considered either "corrupt" (as in the Arab Gulf monarchies) or "atheistic" or "non-Muslim" (as in Iraq). They considered the Iraqi Al Daawa, engaged in an anti-Baathist struggle, worthy of their support. That such a policy violated Iran's 1975 Treaty with Iraq, which specified non-interference in each other's domestic affairs, did not seem to enter their revolutionary thinking.

Overall, for Tehran three factors made Iraq the prime target for engineering an Islamic revolution: the secular nature of the Baathist regime; the oppression of the Shia majority; and the existence of six Shia holy shrines in Iraq. The Baathists, having consolidated their hold on state and society over the past decade, were determined to meet the challenge from Iran head on.

It was ironic that a hitherto pro-Western, conservative, secular regime in Tehran had been transformed into a revolutionary proselytizer, threatening the status quo which the erstwhile radical, pro-Soviet Iraq was keen to preserve in the region.

Soon it became evident that unless one or the other state changed tack they would clash on a large scale. The escalation, which culminated in the outbreak of war in September 1980, came in three stages: (a) the formal assumption of the supreme authority by Saddam Hussein in July 1979; (b) the failed attempt to assassinate Iraq's deputy premier, Tariq Aziz (a Christian, born Mikhail Yahunna, b.1936), followed by the execution of Ayatollah al Sadr in April 1980; and (c) the foiling of an attempted military coup in Iran on July 9–10, 1980.

Following his congratulatory telegram to Khomeini, al Sadr found himself under house arrest in Najaf, and then transferred to Baghdad. The news triggered demonstrations in the south and Baghdad's Shia district of Medinat al Thawra. The quelling of the rioting by the army led to scores of deaths and some 3,000 arrests. On June 10, Saddam submitted a list of men to be executed to President Bakr for his signature. Besides the leaders of the Shia demonstrations, the list included a number of senior military officers who had allegedly been secretly in touch with them. When Bakr objected to the inclusion of officers, he found himself under house arrest.[14] Some weeks later he resigned on "health grounds." On July 16, 1979, on the eve of the eleventh anniversary of the Baathist coup, Saddam Hussein became chairman of the RCC, president of the Republic and general secretary of the Regional (meaning Iraqi) Command of the Baath Party.

This was quite an achievement for a man born forty-two years earlier, on April 28, 1937, in a landless family of the Sunni al Bu Nasir tribe's Begat clan (originating with Omar Beg) in Auja, a village near Tikrit, a town 100 miles (160 km) north of Baghdad. Saddam's father, Hussein Abd al Majid, had died before his birth, and his mother, Subha Talfa (al Masallat), went on to marry Ibrahim Hassan, by whom she had three sons: Barzan, Watban and Sabawi. Saddam was raised by his maternal uncle, Khairallah Talfa (al Masallat), who had lost his military post for backing the nationalist Rashid Ali Gailani during World War II. In 1955, at 18, Saddam went to Baghdad for further schooling, and became involved in opposition activities. Two years later he joined the Baath Party as a candidate-member. After the 1958 coup he engaged in fights between the Baathists and the followers of Premier Qasim. He was part of the team that tried, unsuccessfully, to assassinate Qasim in October 1959, and was injured in the leg. He escaped to Syria, and then to Egypt, where he studied law at Cairo University.

Soon after the Baathists' seizure of power in early 1963, Saddam returned to Iraq and married Sajida Talfa, the school teacher daughter of his maternal uncle. During the rule of Abdul Salam Arif he was imprisoned, following a failed attempt to mount a Baathist coup. He escaped in July 1966. He was elected assistant general secretary of the Iraqi Baath Party. For the next two years he worked hard to reorganize and rejuvenate the party and its militia. He was only 31 when the Baath captured power in 1968. Though not a member of the ruling RCC, he was quite influential, thanks to his close relationship with RCC chairman, Ahmad Bakr, a cousin of Khairallah Talfa.

Once he had acquired the RCC membership in late 1969, the Bakr–Hussein duo came to dominate the party as a result mainly of their cunning decimation of their RCC colleagues. Saddam had many opportunities to use his considerable conspiratorial abilities, developed during his formative years as an underground Baathist activist, often on the run. As a youthful, energetic figure, he appealed to those Baathists who believed in strong ideology and commitment to socio-economic progress. By the mid-1970s he had outstripped Bakr in leadership, cunning, ruthlessness, organizational ability and charisma. It was he who signed the Algiers Accord with the Shah of Iran in 1975. However, he still needed Bakr, a former military officer with an avuncular personality whose moderation and piety went down well with the older, conservative segments of society. But as the Shia problem escalated into a series of crises, it strained the long-sustained alliance, since Bakr advocated compromise and Saddam confrontation.

Within a fortnight of assuming supreme power, Saddam discovered a major "anti-state conspiracy" involving sixty-eight top Baathist civilian and military leaders. All were tried summarily and twenty-one were executed. Saddam then purged the militia, trade unions and local and provincial governments of the elements he considered half-hearted in their support of him.

Stung by Iran's charges of his regime being "atheist" and "non-Muslim," Saddam resorted to praying at numerous holy shrines, Sunni and Shia. He undertook an extensive tour of the Shia region and announced programs for its socio-economic betterment. He declared Imam Ali's birthday a national holiday. During a speech in Najaf near Imam Ali's shrine, he pledged to "fight injustice with the swords of the Imams" and called for "a revival of heavenly values."[15]

But there was no let-up in his suppression of the al Daawa whose membership was now a capital offense. In March 1980 came the execution of ninety-seven civilians and military personnel, half of them al Daawa members. Repression of Shia militants had already led Ayatollah al Sadr to issue a fatwa (religious decree) that the Baathist regime was unIslamic.

To avenge the execution of their cadres, Al Daawa militants tried on April 1, 1980 – the first anniversary of the founding of the Islamic Republic of Iran – to assassinate Tariq Aziz. They failed. But this made Saddam more ruthless in his drive against the Shia underground. He also turned staunchly anti-Tehran. He ordered the bombing of Qasr-e Shirin, an Iranian border town, and expelled thousands of Iranian residents and Iraqi nationals of Iranian descent. He decreed the execution of Ayatollah Sadr and his sister Bint al Huda. They were executed in utmost secrecy on April 8. It was about a week before the news leaked. Khomeini, a long-time friend of Sadr, was livid. "The war that the Iraqi Baath wants to ignite is a war against Islam," he declared. "The people and army of Iraq must turn their backs on the Baathist regime and overthrow it … because this regime is attacking Iran, attacking Islam and the Quran."[16]

Iran started giving guerrilla training to Iraqi Shias and then sending them back to Iraq. It had already begun assisting Iraq's KDP, now led by Mustafa Barzani's sons, Idris and Masud, who had crossed into Iran in July 1979. Baghdad increased its aid to the secessionist elements among Iranian Kurds and Khuzistani Arabs.

In a way it was a re-run of past events during heightened tension between the two neighbors. Yet this time there was a major difference. Baghdad played host to major political and military figures of the Pahlavi era. Most prominent among them were Shahpour Bakhtiar (1914–91), the last premier under the Shah, and General Gholam Ali Oveissi, joint chief of staff under the monarch. Supplied with a radio station each by Baghdad, they broadcast specific advice to their partisans among the Iranian military and tribals. They tried to mount a military coup on May 24–25, but it was thwarted by Khomeini loyalists. On July 9–10 a further attempt by pro-Shah military officers in Iran, orchestrated and funded by Bakhtiar, to topple the Tehran regime failed.[17] On July 27, 1980, the Shah, who inspired monarchist generals and politicians, died of cancer in Cairo.

So far Saddam had counted on the success of the endeavors of the US and/or anti-Khomeini Iranian forces to overthrow the clerical rule in Tehran, or at least destabilize it. Now, with the Shah dead, there was no alternative to his performing the task himself.

He had several internal and external reasons for invading Iran. Above all, he feared that any recurrence of widespread Shia riots would encourage Kurdish secessionists to revive their armed struggle and plunge Iraq into a debilitating civil war. In his view the only certain way to abort such a possibility lay in destroying the source, moral and material, of Shia inspiration: the Khomeini regime.

Saddam was buoyed up by the accounts of rapid military, political and economic decline in Iran. There were persistent reports of conflict between Iranian President Abol Hassan Bani-Sadr (r. 1980–81) and religious leaders, low morale among military officers who had seen thousands of their colleagues purged, and rapid deterioration in the effectiveness of the US-made weapons in Iran's arsenals. Diplomatically, Iran was isolated. It had broken ties with America, which until then had been its most important arms' supplier. By refusing to release the American hostages, taken at the US embassy in Tehran in November 1979, it had invited an economic embargo by Western nations. Its relations with Moscow had soured in the wake of the Soviet military intervention in Afghanistan, a Muslim country, in December 1979. Its virulent attacks on the Gulf monarchs as unjust, corrupt rulers had left it friendless in the region.

In July 1980 the decision that Saddam had to take was not whether or not to attack Iran, but when. At the outset he decided to act before the US presidential poll in early November on the grounds that a newly elected American president would probably settle the hostage crisis and normalize relations with Tehran.

The personalities of Saddam Hussein and Ruhollah Khomeini impinged strongly on the course of events. Both were strong-willed, intransigent men who could not be intimidated. They believed absolutely in themselves and their doctrines. But their experiences were poles apart, and they ran different types of regimes. Khomeini had every reason to be confident of his inspirational charisma, but the social system he led had no parallel and was in its formative stage. By contrast, Saddam was in charge of well-oiled state and party machines which were awash with money and confidence. Additionally, he had

16

the active cooperation of the recently deposed Iranian military and political leaders, who possessed vital information and commanded the loyalties of hundreds of Iranians in key positions in the Islamic Republic. For once Baghdad felt that, in its long tussle with Tehran, the military and diplomatic balance was in its favor. So, Saddam concluded, the time was opportune to strike Iran.

After all, the Baathist regime had never really accepted the thalweg principle for the Shatt al Arab, enshrined in the 1975 Algiers Accord, as final. Here was a golden opportunity for it to retrieve its honor.

Once Saddam had finalized his plans and secured the Saudi and Kuwaiti rulers' active backing in August, events moved fast. There was a series of border clashes especially in the Qasr-e Shirin and the Zain al Qaus areas in the first half of September 1980.

In a televised speech to the recently elected National Assembly on September 17, after accusing Iran of violating the Algiers Accord by "intervening in Iraq's domestic affairs by backing and financing … the leaders of the mutiny [by Kurdish guerrillas] … and by refusing to return the Iraqi territory," Saddam said, "We consider the Accord as abrogated from our side, also." He then tore up Iraq's copies of the Algiers Accord and the subsequent Iran–Iraq Treaty of International Boundaries and Good Neighborliness (signed five years ago to the day). With this, according to Saddam, Iraq regained full sovereignty over the Shatt al Arab, and demanded that henceforth the Iranian ships using the waterway must engage Iraqi pilots and fly the Iraqi flag. Tehran refused. Heavy fighting erupted along the Shatt al Arab. On September 20, Iran called up its reserves.

Two days later, on September 22, 1980, Iraq invaded Iran at eight points on their common border with a third of its 240,000 troops, and bombed its military installations and economic targets.

The complex motivation of Baghdad was summarized by Shahram Chubin, a Gulf security specialist, thus: "Motivated by fear, opportunism and overconfidence, a mixture of defensive and offensive calculations, Iraq's decision to resort to force was a compound of a preventive war, ambition and punishment for a regional rival."[18]

The two Gulf Wars

In their war plans, Saddam Hussein and his Iranian collaborators visualized the attacking Iraqi forces, greeted as liberators by the ethnic Arabs of Khuzistan, capturing the oil-rich province in a week, then linking up with the Iranian Kurdish insurgents already battling Tehran's forces to the north. These liberated areas were then to be declared the "Free Republic of Iran" under Bakhtiar, operating from the temporary capital of Ahvaz. This was to be achieved within three weeks, with the establishment of the Free Republic acting as a catalyst to set off a widespread uprising against the Khomeini regime by discontented civilians as well as soldiers.[19]

In reality the fighting that Saddam initiated turned into the longest conventional war of the twentieth century. It went through eight distinct phases before ending on August 20, 1988, with a UN-mediated truce. According to the Stockholm International Peace Research Institute, it cost Iran $74–91 billion (the US meaning of "billion" is used throughout, i.e., a thousand million), plus military imports of $11 billion; and Iraq $94–112 billion, plus military imports of $25 billion. Iran's officially acknowledged human fatalities were 213,000, with the estimated figure for Iraq being 160,000 to 240,000.[20]

In the end, neither combatant lost much territory either on land or the Shatt al Arab bed; nor was there a change of regime in either country. But the war enabled Khomeini to mobilize all patriotic Iranians irrespective of their politics, and consolidate the Islamic revolution. Had Saddam not invaded Iran it is very likely that the Islamic Republic would have slipped into a civil war. He can therefore be perceived, rightly, as an inadvertent contributor to the consolidation of the Islamic revolution in Iran. However, it can also be argued that by getting the Khomeini regime entangled in a long, expensive war, Saddam succeeded in containing Islamic fundamentalism – a task which the Gulf monarchs and the West, particularly the US, also wanted him to perform. The downside of this for the West and the Gulf rulers was that, having expanded its military from less than a quarter of a million men to over a million during the war, Iraq under Saddam emerged as the most powerful nation in the Middle East, outstripping Turkey and Egypt.

Equally importantly, through relentless war propaganda Saddam succeeded in creating his own reality and having it accepted by Iraqis. According to him, the First Gulf War started not on September 22, 1980 – as recorded by journalists and historians the world over, and by the United Nations – but on September 4, when minor border clashes broke out between Iraq and Iran. And it ended not on September 20, 1988, as recorded by the UN which brokered the truce, but on August 8, 1988 (the easy-to-remember four 8s: 8/8/88). More seriously, he had his fellow-citizens believe that Iraq won the war. "On 8 August 88, we started dancing and singing in the streets, and this went on for three days," recalled "Hamza" (a pseudonym), a retired professor, in Baghdad, his eyes lighting up with the memory a decade after the event. "We were the victors."[21] The much-proclaimed defeat of Iran added to the stature of Saddam at home and enabled him to consolidate his one-man rule. It also fueled his ambition and made him over-confident. In short, it sowed the seeds for his invasion of Kuwait which came two years after the end of the Iran–Iraq War.

The long conflict in the 1980s militarized Iraqi society. Under the pressures of warfare, Saddam, a politician initially determined to keep the armed forces under strict civilian control, let military service and soldierly values dominate society and the Baath Party. Significantly, most of the deputies elected to the Second National Assembly in October 1984 had been active in the war effort. With the size of the regular military approaching a million and the Popular Army militia well past the half-million mark in the mid–1980s, Saddam realized that the armed forces were a far more effective tool to integrate society and state than the Baath. He instructed party cadres to imbibe military values and uphold discipline, patriotism and martyrdom.

Among military officers, Saddam put higher value on professional expertise than on ideological purity. As it was, the governing party's ideology changed. In the name of increasing production, the significance of Baathist socialism was downgraded and the private sector was encouraged to grow at the expense of the public sector. Pan-Arabism came to play second fiddle to Iraqi nationalism, which was promoted actively to motivate citizens to join the war effort.

It was during this war that Saddam Hussein's government resorted to manufacturing and using chemical weapons on a large scale. Indeed, deploying chemical arms was a crucial element in a series of successful offensives that Baghdad launched in spring 1988 to recover lost territory. By the time hostilities with Iran ended in August, it was seriously considering weaponizing biological warfare agents. The armed conflict with Tehran had resulted in Iraq accelerating its nuclear arms program as well as its plan to produce medium- and long-range missiles to deliver conventional and non-conventional weapons. When, in the course of disarming Iraq of non-conventional arms under UN supervision in the aftermath of the 1991 Gulf War, the full details of its weapons projects were winkled out of reluctant Iraqi officials over several years, the extent of Baghdad's progress in this field came as a shock to the regional countries and Western powers.

To counter the religious propaganda by Iran, Baghdad resorted to emphasizing Islam while extending its control of religious sites. The minister of waqfs (religious trusts) and religious affairs told the First Popular Islamic Conference held in Baghdad in April 1983 that three-fifths of the 3,183 Muslim religious sites were under total government supervision, and the rest partial, and that all 2,294 religious caretakers had become civil servants.[22] Saddam projected himself as a pious Muslim, offering much-publicized prayers at Shia holy shrines after the successful repulse of Iran's March 1985 offensive. During the holy month of Ramadan (in May–June) he decreed that government officials should hold public fast-breaking banquets, thus creating a symbiosis between the Baathist regime and Islam. He then published his family tree which showed him to be a descendant of Imam Ali, which entitled him to the honorific of *sayyid* (*lit.*, lord or prince) accorded to the male descendants of Prophet Muhammad. This was expected to endear him to Shias, who were originally known as Shiat Ali, Partisans of Ali.[23] The government distributed millions of copies of Saddam's family tree to emphasize his religious credentials. The offices of the caretakers of all Muslim religious sites were decorated with large, framed copies of the president's family tree. Rooted in Imam Ali, with its trunk carrying the names of the Twelver Shia Imams – followed by thirty descendants ending with Omar Beg (the progenitor of the Begat clan), the governor of Tikrit – it branched out, with Saddam son of Hussein son of Abd al Majid son of Abd al Ghafur son of Omar Beg appearing as an image on the outermost leaves.

By contrast, there was little change in the Islamic ideology of Iran, partly because no firm blueprint of the application of Islamic principles to administering a modern state and society had emerged by September 1980. Then the government used the war as a reason to postpone decisions on major socio-economic issues of land reform, ownership of foreign trade, personal taxation, labor relations and the role of the private sector. Meanwhile, Khomeini and his lieutenants reiterated the commitment of their regime to the relief of the needy, *mustazafin*, who provided the bulk of recruits for the Islamic Revolutionary Guard Corps (IRGC) and its auxiliary, the Baseej (*lit.*, mobilization) militia, both composed entirely of volunteers. But improvement in ordinary Iranians' living standards could not occur so long as the war had unquestioned priority over development projects.

Tehran's economic predicament was all the more acute because it decided to fund the war machine strictly out of its current resources, which dwindled dramatically when oil prices fell below $10 a barrel in the winter of 1985–86. Jealous of its newly-won independence, the revolutionary government refused to borrow money abroad. Indeed its loans to such countries as Syria and North Korea in unpaid supplies of Iranian oil rose to $5 billion.[24]

This was in stark contrast to Baghdad's policies. It borrowed $9–11 billion from the Soviet Union; $25–35 billion from the West and Japan; and $50–55 billion from the Gulf monarchies, chiefly Saudi Arabia and Kuwait – a total of $84–101 billion.[25] It also kept its economy running by employing 1.5 to 2 million foreign workers. That is how it managed to achieve an unrivalled force ratio – regular military personnel/1,000 inhabitants – of 63.3, nearly five times the figure for Iran.[26] By fighting the war on borrowed money and manpower, Saddam was able to continue building ambitious public works. It was during the war that four of the present twelve bridges over the Tigris in Baghdad were constructed, and the $7-billion Saddam International airport completed. Yet Iraq could not escape the economic consequences of the conflict completely. Its per capita income halved, and its infrastructure suffered an estimated damage of some $200 billion.

As a result Baghdad faced severe economic problems after the war ended. When it demobilized the first batch of 200,000 soldiers one year after the ceasefire there were no jobs for them. There were clashes between the returning Iraqi soldiers and Egyptian expatriates, the largest group of foreign workers, resulting in the death of several hundred Egyptians. Abroad, Kuwait pressured Iraq to repay the $12–14 billion it had borrowed from the emirate, a demand that was finally to lead to Baghdad's invasion of its small neighbor.

Thus, in retrospect, it can be seen that the 1980–88 Iran–Iraq War – also known as the First Gulf War – sowed the seeds of the Second Gulf War between Iraq and the US-led Coalition in 1991, which turned out to be the last major conventional war of the twentieth century.

While Saddam flamboyantly declared the outcome of the war with Iran as victory for Iraq, the mood in the Islamic republic was somber. In July 1988 Khomeini had described accepting unconditionally the UN Security Council

Resolution 598 of July 20, 1987 – specifying "an immediate ceasefire" and "withdrawal to internationally recognized boundaries" – as "taking hemlock."

The Iran–Iraq talks held under the UN auspices got bogged down when the Iraqis demanded the immediate clearance of the Shatt al Arab under the UN aegis while the Iranians insisted that, according to the 1975 Treaty, this was a joint responsibility of the two states. When Iraq argued that the 1975 Treaty no longer existed, Iran retorted that, being a border agreement, it was valid for ever and that it could not be abrogated unilaterally.

Iran, change of the leader

Reversing his previous policy of promoting Ayatollah Hussein Ali Montazeri (b. 1921) as his chosen successor, Ayatollah Khomeini made Montazeri resign his position of Deputy Leader on March 28, 1989. This went down well with Islamist radicals who disapproved of Montazeri's moderate policies. It also eliminated a potential threat to the rise of the alliance between President Hojatalislam Ali Husseini Khamanei (b. 1939) and Speaker Hojatalislam Ali Akbar Hashemi Rafsanjani (b. 1933) as the supreme authority in the post-Khomeini era. This was a boost for the centrist, pragmatic trend within the regime.

On April 24 Khomeini appointed a Constitution Review Panel of twenty-five members – twenty nominees of his and five of the Majlis (*lit.*, assembly), parliament – to reappraise the constitution within two months, with the main focus on the qualifications of his successor as the Leader; the powers of the president, the Majlis and the Expediency Consultation Council System (ECCS, Shoura-ye Tashkhis-e Maslehat-e Nezam); and the composition of the judiciary.

In mid-May Khomeini, afflicted with stomach cancer, fell seriously ill and expired on June 3. On his death bed, in the presence of two witnesses, he elevated Khamenei from hojatalislam to ayatollah – or mujtahid – the one who is qualified to practice *ijtihad*, interpretative reasoning, regarding the Sharia, Islamic Law, but lower than grand ayatollah (*ayatollah ozma*) or marja-e taqlid (*lit.*, source of emulation). (Every Shia is required to choose between the handful of living marja-e taqlids, to whom he is expected to hand over a fifth of his trading profits to be used for charitable purposes, and whose interpretations of the Sharia he is obliged to accept.) By so doing Khomeini, who had been pleased by Khamanei's speech on the tenth anniversary of the revolution in February, upholding the revolution's pristine values and decrying the slackness in morality and Islamic dress that had crept in, stressed political perspicacity as the pre-eminent qualification of the Leader.

Khomeini's demise marked the end of a remarkable era in Iranian history – eleven years of revolutionary turmoil and war, filled with dramatic events; the birth of a new socio-political system; and the upsetting of the regional balance of power that had prevailed since World War II. During those turbulent times, exercising his authority stemming from his popularity and charisma, he managed to hold together the vast country of 636,300 sq miles (1,648 million sq km) populated by ethnic Persians, Azeris, Kurds, Arabs, Baluchis and Armenians. He succeeded in maintaining amity among his squabbling followers who, holding different socio-economic views, kept on pulling in opposite directions, despite the pressures of war. To end the faction fighting, in mid-1987 he ordered the dissolution of the governing Islamic Republican Party (IRP) which had been established within a month of the February 1979 revolution. Above all, having led a revolution at 76, he went down in history as the oldest revolutionary ever.

In the midst of the overwhelming grief that seized the nation, the 83-member Assembly of Experts, made up of clerics, met and unanimously elected Khamanei the Leader. The chief executive's powers were then exercised by the Temporary Presidential Council, composed of Premier Mir Hussein Musavi, Speaker Rafsanjani and Chief Justice Ayatollah Abdul Karim Musavi-Ardebili. Contrary to the predictions of many Western specialists that, with the charismatic figure of Khomeini gone, personal squabbles and ideological differences among the leaders would tear the Islamic Republic apart, the Khamanei–Rafsanjani coalition held together well, and the transition of the supreme power to Khamanei, a comparatively junior cleric, albeit sanctified by the departed Leader, was smooth.

Born into a religious family in Mashhad, Ali Husseini Khamanei pursued his theological studies in Najaf and Qom, where he became a student of Khomeini. After Khomeini's deportation to Turkey in 1964, Khamanei returned to Mashhad and taught at the local theological college. During the next decade he was arrested six times for his anti-government activities. After his last spell in prison in 1975 he endured internal exile, which ended during the 1977–78 revolutionary upsurge. He returned to Mashhad and participated in the anti-Shah movement. He was one of Khomeini's first appointees to the Islamic Revolutionary Council, which assumed supreme power after the revolution. Later Khomeini appointed him the Friday prayer leader of Tehran, a highly revered position. In June 1981, during his sermon in a Tehran mosque, a bomb hidden in a tape recorder placed near him exploded, injuring his arm, lungs and vocal chords. Following the assassination of President Muhammad Ali Rajai in August, he was chosen the candidate of the governing Islamic Republican Party. He gained 95 percent of the votes cast. In the presidential poll in 1985 he won 89 percent of the votes. Yet when he tried to replace his radical prime minister Musavi (who had held the job since 1981), he found his hands tied. He and Musavi belonged to the opposing factions within the IRP, and could not reconcile their differences. This led to the dissolution of the IRP by Khomeini, the final arbiter, who was in the habit of praising the moderate faction (led by Khamanei) one week and the radical (led by Musavi) the next. In July 1988, instructed by Khomeini, Khamanei accepted the UN Security Council Resolution 598 for a truce in the First Gulf War. He chaired the Constitution Review Panel.

The forty-two amendments and additions to the constitution, including those pertaining to the qualifications of the Leader, which would later be ratified by a referendum, legitimized Khamanei's position. The important changes to the constitution, enlarged by two articles to 177, focused on the qualifications and powers of the Leader, and the powers of the president, Guardians Council, Majlis, and judiciary.

Article 109 in the old constitution described "the qualifications and attributes of the Leader" as:

a suitability with respect to learning and piety, as required for the functions of mufti (one who delivers religious rulings) and marja (source); and
b political and social perspicacity, courage, strength and the necessary administrative abilities for leadership.

These were amended to:

a scholarship, as required for the performing of the functions of mufti in different fields of fiqh (religious juriprudence);
b justice and piety, as required for the leadership of the Islamic ummah (community); and
c right political and social perspicacity, prudence, courage, administrative abilities, and adequate capability for leadership.

In other words, the Leader did not have to be a marja-e taqlid, a grand ayatollah. (At any given time there were no more than half a dozen grand ayatollahs in the Shia world.) This provision therefore caused a disjunction between the constitutional position of the Leader and the traditional Shia religious hierarchy.

The amended constitution increased the Leader's powers (Article 110), including "delineation of general policies after consultation with the Expediency Consultation Council System"; "supervision over the proper execution of the general policies of the system"; "resolving the problems, which cannot be solved by conventional methods, through the Expediency Consultation Council System," and the appointment of the head of the radio and television network. These were in addition to the original powers of the Leader – appointing the faqihs (jurisprudents) in the Guardians Councils, the chief of the joint staff and the chief commander of the IRGC. In the 1979 constitution there was no provision for the ECCS, established *ad hoc* by Khomeini in 1988. Also Article 122 of the old constitution was amended from "Within the limits of his functions and powers, the President is responsible to the people" to "Within the limits of his functions and powers, the President is responsible to the people, the Leader and the Islamic Consultative Council [Majlis]."

By dispensing with the prime minister's post – prescribed by Article 124 of the 1979 constitution – which had hindered efficient administration, and authorizing the president to appoint one or more vice-presidents, the new document ushered in executive presidency.

The first of the two new articles (176 and 177) established a 13-member Supreme National Security Council (SNSC) under the president. It consisted of heads of the three state organs: the chief of the supreme command council of the military, the highest official of the military and the IRGC, the head of the National Budget and Planning, the ministers of foreign affairs, interior and information (i.e., intelligence), a cabinet minister depending on the major subject under discussion, and two representatives of the Leader. It took over the functions of the now abolished Supreme National Defense Council. Its mandate was to:

1 determine the defense and national security policies within the framework of general policies determined by the Leader;
2 coordinate activities in the areas relating to political, intelligence, social, cultural and economic fields regarding general defense and security policies; and
3 exploit the country's material and intellectual resources to face internal and external threats.

In the administrative field, the Leader continued to maintain a multifarious network. In running his own secretariat, he had the assistance of four advisers, two of them military officers, with its main function being collecting and collating information domestically and internationally. He appointed personal representatives to twenty-three state and religious agencies, from the SNSC, military, IRGC and Baseej to the Islamic Propagation Organization, to Directorate of Mosque Affairs, the state-run media and various Foundations with enormous economic assets. In addition, he nominated the executive committee and secretariat of the Central Council of Friday Prayer Leaders. And his twenty-two provincial representatives reported to him direct.

The uniqueness of the social system which combined citizens' secular and spiritual spheres of life was aptly reflected in the existence of various centers of power: the Leader, elected by the Assembly of Experts; the popularly chosen president; the popularly elected Majlis; the 12-member Guardians Council, partly nominated by the Leader and partly elected by the Majlis, to vet legislation and supervise elections; the ECCS, appointed by the Leader to conciliate differences between the president, Majlis and the Guardians Council; the popularly elected Assembly of Experts; the chief of the judiciary, appointed by the Leader; the SNSC which *inter alia* formulates foreign policy; the military, the IRGC and the Baseej; religious and other foundations with independent financial resources, which gave much clout to their presidents; popularly elected local councils; voluntary Islamic Associations; and Friday Prayer Leaders. "Add to these religious rank and authority as another factor in the structure of power in modern Iran," writes Anoushirvan Ehteshami, a British academic of Iranian origin, "and you have a complex set of relationships which are in part based on personal contacts and authority, factional allegiances, kinship and marriage ties and a series of 'multi-directorships', and in part based on the authority derived from the office itself."[27]

On July 30, 1989, Iranians voted on the constitutional amendments as well as for presidential candidates. They endorsed the new constitution almost unanimously, and elected Rafsanjani as president by a plurality of 95 percent of the 14.2 million ballots cast.

Born into a religious family in Behraman, Kerman province, he studied theology in Qom where he became a student of Khomeini. After Khomeini's expulsion from Iran, he handled Islamic charities on his behalf. He was arrested and tortured in the mid-1970s. After the revolution, Khomeini appointed him to the Islamic Revolutionary Council. After his election as a Majlis deputy from Tehran in 1980, he was elected speaker, a post to which he was re-elected every year until the dissolution of the chamber in 1984. He held the same position in the Second Majlis (1984–88). Following Iran's military setbacks in the war with Iraq in spring 1988, Khomeini put him in overall charge of the war effort. Having realistically assessed the deteriorating situation, in July 1988 he persuaded the Assembly of Experts (of which he was deputy speaker) to recommend to Khomeini the truce called for earlier by the UN Security Council Resolution 598 of July 1987. Khomeini accepted the recommendation.

As president, Rafsanjani proved to be a pragmatic politician, committed to neo-liberal economics, reconstruction and adjustment at home, and mending of fences abroad. His cabinet of 22 ministers had only 4 clerics whereas there were 122 mullahs in the 270-member Majlis. Among the lay ministers, eight had degrees from American universities, including foreign minister Ali Akbar Velayati. Significantly, clerics held important politically-sensitive ministries: culture and Islamic guidance, Hojatalislam Muhammad Khatami (r. 1997–); intelligence, Ali Fallahian; interior, Abdullah Nouri; and justice, Muhammad Ismail Shushtari. Of these, Khatami would go on to succeed Rafsanjani as president, and Nouri would be tried and jailed for unIslamic behavior.

The immediate priority of the new government was to dissipate the economic crisis stemming from eight years of war. Between 1977–78 and 1989–90 per capita income had declined 45 percent. The 1986 census showed annual population growth of 3.9 percent, one of the highest in the world, with the marriage rate rising from 4.6 per 1000 in 1975 to 9.8 in 1983.[28] Khamanei's ruling that Islam did not enjoin believers to have large families, implying that birth control was not unIslamic, opened the door for the government to promote family planning. Which it did.

"Reconstruction" was the watchword of the Rafsanjani administration. This meant economic reform, correcting the changes in the economy that had happened due to the revolution and a long war, which had led to an unprecedented state intervention in the economy. Rafsanjani was quick to scrap the 1988 Five Year Development Plan and present a new version to the Majlis. Passed in January 1990, it became operational two months later once the Guardians Council had cleared it.

It envisioned an impressive 8 percent annual growth rate, with the share of the private sector expanding rapidly from its 25–30 percent share of the national economy in 1988. The ambitious economic reform package had two components – domestic and external. The domestic section included privatizing some

800 public sector enterprises, deregulating banking and financial services, liberalizing trade and commerce, modernizing Tehran's stock exchange, reducing subsidies in stages and allowing prices to be determined by market forces. The external component of economic liberalization included devaluing the Iranian Rial, borrowing from abroad, setting up free trade zones, encouraging foreign investment, and encouraging the return of the exiled capital and expertise.

With an Iranian diaspora of three million, two-fifths of it in America, the potential for tapping the expatriate source for specialized skills and capital was high. So the Iranian embassies were instructed to welcome all Iranians irrespective of their politics. Being a bureaucratic fiat, it was easy to issue and implement.

All other measures had to be legislated, however. Since the expansion of the state sector had occurred not due to any ideological commitment, but due to political pressures engendered by revolution and war, a political lobby had emerged to advance the process. In the Third Majlis (1988–92) it operated as "Followers of Imam Khomeini's line." Enjoying the support of the majority of the MPs as well as the Speaker, Hojatalislam Mehdi Karrubi, it was led by such social and political radicals as Hojatalislam Ali Akbar Mohtashami and Muhammad Musavi Khoeiniha. They got along well with Prime Minister Mir Hussein Musavi, a fellow-radical, but once he was gone and they had to deal with Rafsanjani as executive president from mid–1989 onwards, their relations with the executive branch cooled.

They were the founders of the Society of Combatant Clerics (*Majma-e Ruhaniyat-e*[29] *Mobraz-e Tehran*), popularly known as Majma. Formed on March 21, 1988, the Iranian New Year, with the tacit backing of Khomeini after the dissolution of the ruling Islamic Republican Party, it was composed of socio-economic radicals and headed by Karrubi. They broke away from the older Association of Combatant Clergy (*Jame-e Ruhaniyat-e Mobarez-e Tehran*), popularly called Jame. The nucleus of the Jame was formed in 1976 when the clerical followers of Khomeini began to meet clandestinely in Tehran to exchange and discuss socio-political information. The Jame arranged the smuggling of Khomeini's speeches on cassettes from Najaf, Iraq, into Iran. Its founders included Ayatollahs Murtaza Motahhari (assassinated in 1979), Muhammad Beheshti (assassinated in 1981) and Muhammad Reza Mahdavi-Kani, and Hojatalislams Javad Bahonar (assassinated in 1981), Rafsanjani and Khamanei. It played a vital role in engineering the Islamic revolution and has been highly influential since then.[30] Its general secretary since 1982 has been Mahdavi-Kani. As a clerical member of the Guardians Council in the 1980s, he declared land reform and foreign trade nationalization bills unIslamic. With the defection of leftist clerics from its ranks in 1988, the Jame, maintaining close ties with senior seminary theologians especially in Qom, affluent merchants and top civil servants, became an association of clerics who were socially conservative, wary of Western values which they regarded as incompatible with Islamization of Iran to which they were committed, but liberal in the running of the economy, advocating privatization and encouraging investment by local merchant-capitalists.

As such the MPs influenced by the Jame backed the economic liberalization plan unfolded by Rafsanjani. But they were a minority in the Third Majlis. Their rivals, influenced by the Majma, were in the majority, and they did not take kindly to Rafsanjani's program. Being a pragmatic politician, Rafsanjani avoided head-to-head confrontation with them, and sought compromise. Instead of insisting on wholesale privatization, he chose to proceed on a sector by sector basis, ready to switch policies to placate his leftist opponents while ensuring that the general thrust of his plan was not abandoned.

Iraq between the wars

Compared to the complexities of the composition and conduct of the Iranian Majlis, the elections and the subsequent proceedings in Iraq's National Assembly were boringly predictable. All that happened in the April 1989 poll to the 250-member Assembly was that the number of Baathist deputies fell from 184 to 150, and that elections to the Legislative Council of Kurdistan followed in September. Saddam tried to combine political reform with economic liberalization, with privatization plans, launched earlier, resulting in $2.2 billion worth of public sector companies being sold to private citizens.[31]

But Iraq's reconstruction plans were hamstrung by the demands of foreign debt servicing and high defense expenditure which consumed seven-eighths of the oil export revenue.[32] Its income was limited by the OPEC quota of 2.64 million bpd of oil. With Kuwait exceeding its OPEC quota after the Iran–Iraq War ceasefire, petroleum prices had been declining. Aware that Baghdad was economically vulnerable, Kuwait had chosen oil as the lever to pressure Baghdad to settle their long-standing border dispute.

That this was a deliberate Kuwaiti policy became evident with the later discovery of a memorandum from Brigadier Saad al Fahd al Sabah, director-general of Kuwait's State Security Department (SSD), to the interior minister, Salim al Salim al Sabah, on November 20, 1989, summarizing the agreements the brigadier had reached with William Webster, director of the US Central Intelligence Agency (CIA) during their meeting at the CIA headquarters in Langley, Virginia, on November 14. "We agreed … that information would be exchanged [between the SSD and the CIA] about the armaments and political structures of Iran and Iraq," read paragraph 2 of the document. "We agreed with the American side that it was important to take advantage of the deteriorating economic situation in Iraq to put pressure on that country's government to delineate our common border," stated paragraph 5.[33]

The situation in the emirate too was far from normal, with many of its enfranchised minority agitating for the restoration of parliament that Emir Jabar III al Ahmad al Sabah (r. 1977–) had dissolved in 1986. The police violently broke up a protest meeting in Kuwait City in January 1990. When in late April the ruler announced a 75-member National Council, including twenty-five nominees of his, as an advisory body, the agitators, calling themselves Constitutionalists, rejected the decree (and later boycotted the poll).

At the same time the Kuwaiti ruler also had to cope with the consequences of his flouting the OPEC quota. This and a similar action by the United Arab Emirates in the spring of 1990 depressed the oil price well below OPEC's reference level of $18 a barrel, fixed in November. During a closed session of the extraordinary Arab summit in Baghdad on May 30, Saddam Hussein alluded to "the failure by some of our Arab brothers to abide by the OPEC decision when they flooded the world market with more oil than it needed, thereby enabling clients to buy below the fixed [OPEC] price." For every US dollar drop in the price of an oil barrel, the Iraqi loss amounted to $1 billion annually, he said.

> War is fought with soldiers, and harm is done by explosions, killing and coup attempts, but it is also done by economic means sometimes … I say to those who do not mean to wage war on Iraq that this is in fact a kind of war against Iraq … [W]e have reached a point where we can no longer withstand pressure.[34]

Saddam's plea fell on deaf ears. Overproduction continued, with Kuwait exceeding its OPEC quota of 1.5 million bpd by 600,000 bpd, and the UAE by 450,000 bpd. In June the oil price fell to $11 a barrel, a level at which Iraq's oil income was barely enough to meet current expenses, leaving nothing to service foreign debts or fund minimum reconstruction that was urgently needed.

At Baghdad's behest the oil ministers of the Arab Gulf members of OPEC – Iraq, Kuwait, Qatar and Saudi Arabia – met in the Saudi city of Jiddah on July 11, and urged OPEC to cut overall output to raise the price from $14 to the $18 a barrel target. Two days later Kuwait dissociated itself from the statement.

Incensed, Tariq Aziz addressed a letter to Chadli Kilbi, the Arab League secretary-general on July 15.

> The war which Iraq was obliged to wage was not only intended to defend Iraq's sovereignty but also to defend the eastern flank of the Arab homeland, especially the Arabian Gulf region. This was confirmed by the Gulf leaders themselves … The value of the military hardware for which Iraq paid hard currency … amounted to $102 billion.

He put Iraq's loss due to the oil exports lost during the war at $106 billion.

> How can these amounts [i.e., interest-free loans from Kuwait and the UAE to Iraq] be regarded as Iraqi debts to its Arab brothers when Iraq made sacrifices that were many times more than these debts in terms of Iraqi resources during the grinding war and offered rivers of blood of its youth in defense of the [Arab] nation's soil, dignity, honor and wealth?[35]

Four days later Kuwait's foreign minister called on the Arab League to settle the Kuwaiti–Iraqi border dispute. On 25 July the US ambassador to Iraq, April Glaspie, had a meeting with Saddam Hussein in the presence of Tariq Aziz. Glaspie told Saddam:

> We have no opinion on the Arab–Arab conflicts, like your border disagreement with Kuwait. I was in the American embassy in Kuwait in the late 1960s. The instruction we had during this period was that we should express no opinion on this issue [of borders], and the issue is not associated with America. [US state secretary] James Baker has directed our official spokesmen to emphasize this instruction.[36]

Glaspie also referred to "a direct instruction from President [George] Bush to seek better relations with Iraq." Washington's positive attitude toward Baghdad had developed during the Iran–Iraq War, when Bush's predecessor, Ronald Reagan (r. 1981–88), a fellow-Republican, was the president. Saddam was seen as a strong, secular leader, well-motivated and capable of containing the revolutionary Islamic tide rising from Tehran, threatening to drown the ruling families of the Gulf monarchies, possessing nearly half of the world's petroleum reserves. America's ostensible neutrality in that conflict did not inhibit it from aiding Iraq materially and providing it with military intelligence on Iran, or from destroying or disabling half of Iran's navy in 1987–88. Over the years Saddam's government came to be perceived in Washington as secular and tolerable, a stabilizing influence in a region prone to volatility. Iraq's regime came off rather well when compared to those in such countries as Syria (penniless, tied to Moscow), Lebanon (wracked by a long and bloody civil war), Libya (headed by a megalomaniac maverick), or Egypt (debt-ridden and cripplingly bureaucratic). The continuing estrangement between Iran and the US even after Khomeini's death, a vehemently anti-American leader, encouraged Washington to cultivate Baghdad as a counterweight to its regional rival, Tehran. Also the Iraq connection had proved quite lucrative to the farming community in the US, with Baghdad emerging as the leading buyer of American agricultural produce. The US oil companies and other businesses too found Iraq attractive. It had the second largest petroleum reserves in the Gulf after Saudi Arabia, a population as large as all of the Arabian Peninsula countries combined, and a strong and varied economy. Moreover, Iraq quickly filled the gap left in US oil imports when President Reagan banned all Iranian imports in early 1987.

During her meeting with Saddam, Glaspie told him that Washington hoped he would be able to solve the border problem with Kuwait through the Arab League's secretary-general or "your Arab brothers." But the talks between Iraqi Vice-President Izzat Ibrahim (al Duri) (b. 1942) and Kuwaiti Crown Prince Shaikh Saad al Sabah in Jiddah on July 31 went badly. At one point Shaikh Saad told Ibrahim, "Don't threaten us. Kuwait has very powerful friends. You will be forced to pay back all the money you owe us."[37]

Among Shaikh's "powerful friends," America was the most important. "We remain strongly committed to supporting the individual and collective self-defense of our friends in the Gulf," stated the US defense department on July 31. It leaked information to the *Washington Post* that satellite pictures showed that six Iraqi divisions were deployed near the Iraq–Kuwait frontier. Expecting the worst, it put its naval force in the Gulf on high alert.

The behavior of the Pentagon and Shaikh Saad convinced Saddam that further negotiations with the Kuwaitis were futile. On the night of July 31–August 1 the Iraqi high command decided to attack Kuwait.

On August 2, 1990, Iraq invaded and occupied Kuwait within eight hours. Assisted by the US embassy, the Kuwaiti ruler and his entourage escaped to Saudi Arabia. The UN Security Council condemned Iraq, urging a ceasefire and withdrawal of its troops from Kuwait. On August 6 it passed Resolution 661 by 13 votes to none, imposing mandatory sanctions and embargo on Iraq and occupied Kuwait. That day King Fahd of Saudi Arabia invited US forces to his realm to bolster its defenses. President Bush dispatched 40,000 American troops to the Saudi kingdom. And, responding to the merger call by the "Provisional Free Government of Kuwait," Baghdad annexed Kuwait on August 8, calling it "the nineteenth province of Iraq."

In Cairo, the summit of the 21-member Arab League (boycotted by Tunisia) decided by 12 votes to 3 – with 5 members expressing reservations or abstaining – to condemn Iraq for its invasion and annexation of Kuwait, and to accept the request of Saudi Arabia and other Gulf monarchies to dispatch troops to assist their armed forces.

Saddam permitted the 100,000 Iranians in Kuwait to leave with all their belongings. President Rafsanjani condemned Iraq's invasion of Kuwait. While declaring that Iran would abide by the UN resolutions on Iraq, he demanded that all the foreign powers now in the region "to punish the aggressor" must leave once the crisis was over.

On August 14, to secure his eastern front, Saddam Hussein wrote a letter to Rafsanjani in which he agreed to abide by the 1975 Algiers Accord, withdraw troops from the occupied Iranian territory, and undertake an immediate exchange of prisoners of war. (During the conflict, Iran took some 70,000 Iraqi prisoners of war, and Iraq 40,000-plus.)[38] Rafsanjani accepted the offer, thus putting a final seal (hopefully) on the demarcation of the fluvial boundary of the two countries that had dogged their relations for several decades. While welcoming the new development, Rafsanjani repeated Iran's call that Iraq must vacate Kuwait. On August 21, exactly two years after the UN-supervised ceasefire, Iraq vacated all of the 920 sq miles (2,380 sq km) of the Iranian territory it had been occupying.

During his clandestine visit to Tehran on September 10, Tariq Aziz proposed a resumption of full diplomatic relations broken off towards the end of the First Gulf War, and Iran agreed. (They exchanged ambassadors on October 20.) Aziz reportedly offered $25 billion as Iraq's war reparations to Iran in exchange for establishing an Iran–Iraq Economic Cooperation Council which would coordinate supplies to Iraq while selling Iraqi oil abroad through the pipelines of Iran. Rafsanjani did not accept or reject the proposal. And Iran continued to observe strictly the UN embargo against Iraq.[39] However, both Rafsanjani and Khamanei condemned the US military build-up in the Gulf. Indeed, on September 12, Khamanei declared that those who confronted "America's aggression, greed, plan and policies aimed at committing aggression in the Persian Gulf region will have participated in a holy war in the path of Allah (*jihad fi sabilallah*), and anybody who is killed on that path is regarded as a martyr."[40]

During the Majlis debate on the subject, all factions condemned the presence of Western navies in the Gulf. But the call by Mohtashami, backed by the Majlis' foreign affairs committee chairman, Hojatalislam Sadiq Khalkhali, to create a broad military pact between Iraq and Iran against America and Israel did not go far, partly because public memories of Baghdad's aggression against Iran and the subsequent devastating war were fresh, and partly because the Iranian people, intent on reconstructing their country, did not want their government to defy the UN economic sanctions and suffer the consequences.

So the Tehran regime devised a two-track policy of demanding unconditional Iraqi evacuation of Kuwait and condemning Washington's military build-up in the Gulf which, in its view, was a disincentive to the regional Arab countries to find a diplomatic solution to the crisis. As for Iraq's remaining neighbors, Kuwait had been annexed by Baghdad; Saudi Arabia was in the forefront of the anti-Iraq campaign in the region; Syria had joined the US-led Coalition against Iraq; Turkey, a member of North Atlantic Treaty Organization (Nato), was firmly in the Coalition, ready to let the latter's warplanes use its Incirlik airbase in the south; and Jordan had adopted a pro-Iraqi neutrality. It was only Tehran which combined its condemnation of both Baghdad and Washington, albeit for different reasons, with a genuine interest in a peaceful resolution of the crisis.

Any hopes of such an outcome evaporated when, on November 29, the UN Security Council passed Resolution 687 by 12 votes to 2 (Cuba and Yemen), with one abstention (China), authorizing "all necessary means" by UN member-states cooperating with Kuwait to implement the earlier 11 related resolutions in order "to restore international peace and security in the area," unless Iraq fully implemented all these resolutions before January 15, 1991.

By then the US-led Coalition included 28 other UN members, including 11 Nato countries and 13 Arab and Muslim states. By the time the Coalition launched its Operation Desert Storm air campaign, on January 17 (0230 Iraqi time/January 16, 2300 GMT), its 850,000-strong forces faced 545,000 Iraqi troops in Kuwait and Iraq. For its campaign it deployed 2,900 warplanes and several warships to launch cruise missiles.

While firmly backing the UN demand for Iraq's evacuation of Kuwait, Rafsanjani declared that Iran would not allow the US-led Coalition to use its airspace or territory to launch attacks against Iraq or Kuwait. He called for an emergency meeting of the 45-member Islamic Conference Organization (ICO) to resolve the conflict speedily, but only ten members supported his initiative. With the Coalition's air sorties running at 2,000 a day, with half of these being bombing missions, on January 21 Tehran accused the Coalition of overstepping the UN mandate by hitting economic and other non-military targets in Iraq which had nothing to do with liberating Kuwait.

Five days later Tehran announced that, following requests from seven Iraqi military pilots to make emergency landings in Iran, they had been allowed to do so, and that their planes had been confiscated. However, the Coalition forces' commander-in-chief, US General Norman Schwarzkopf, put the number of such Iraqi planes at thirty-nine, and added that Tehran had given assurances that the aircraft would remain grounded until the war was over. Soon the number of Iraqi planes taking refuge in Iran rose to 148.[41] The fleeing Iraqi warplanes could not be intercepted by the Coalition forces because they made only short trips across the border from small airfields in northern Iraq.

As the total of the Coalition's air missions rose to 41,000 by early February, political temperature in the region and the Muslim world rose sharply. Responding to the pro-Baghdad calls by Pakistan's Islamist leaders, tens of thousands of Pakistanis signed up to fight for Iraq. The only way they could reach it was overland via Iran. But Iran's ambassador in Pakistan said that his government would not allow the Pakistani volunteers to cross its territory en route to Iraq.

When in early February, Mohtashami again urged the government to join the jihad with Iraq against the infidel forces of America and Israel, Ayatollah Ali Meshkini, chairman of the Assembly of Experts, retorted: "Do not connect this war with Islam... it is a war between dictators [Saddam and the Kuwaiti emir]."[42]

At the same time Tehran remained diplomatically active. On February 7, the *Sout al Kuwait* (Voice of Kuwait), a London-based newspaper, published an Iranian peace plan, to be launched with an appeal by Khamenei for a ceasefire. Iraq would then start withdrawing from Kuwait while he tried to "persuade" the Coalition forces to pull out of the region simultaneously. An Islamic peacekeeping force would be sent to Kuwait to act as a buffer between Iraq and the Coalition, and an Islamic committee would study all Kuwaiti–Iraqi disputes. The crowning point would be the conclusion of a regional non-aggression pact, covering economic, political and security questions. [43] Iraq took the plan seriously enough to dispatch Saadoun Hamadi (b. 1930), its deputy premier, to Tehran. But Iraq's final response was equivocal.

By then the Coalition had exhausted its list of military and economic targets in Iraq and Kuwait – having, for instance, reduced Iraq's electricity output of 9,000 mW by 75 percent, to its 1920 level.[44] The Coalition now turned its attention to destroying Iraq's infrastructure of roads and bridges to eliminate logistical facilities for its frontline troops, and softening up the elite Republican Guard (RG) posted in Kuwait and southern Iraq.

Iran protested at the punishment the Coalition was meting out to Iraq and its people. "Iran cannot be indifferent to the massacre of Iraqi Muslims and the destruction being inflicted upon Iraq," said Tehran Radio on February 9. Having failed to get the ICO to act, Iran cooperated with India at the Non-Aligned Movement (NAM) meeting in Belgrade on February 11–12 to sponsor a peace plan. However, the NAM plan, calling for a ceasefire once Iraq had declared its intention to quit Kuwait, failed to take off.

Direct high-level contacts between Iran and Iraq continued, with Hamadi visiting Tehran on February 18. Aware of the sympathy Iran's government and people felt for the Iraqis under continuous bombardment, Hamadi revealed to an Iranian newspaper, on February 19, that during the first twenty-six days the enemy bombing had killed 20,000 Iraqis and injured 60,000. This was to be the first and the last time that Iraq released such figures.[45]

On February 23, the Coalition mounted its Operation "Desert Saber" ground campaign from Saudi Arabia, where all foreign Muslim and non-Muslim troops were based. It lasted four days.

By noon on February 26, the Iraqi troops had withdrawn from Kuwait City and suburbs, and a long convoy of Iraqi tanks, armored personnel carriers, trucks, buses and hijacked vans and cars was on its way to Basra along the six-lane Highway 80. As it approached Mitla ridge, a sandy hill north of Jahra, 20 miles (32 km) west of Kuwait City, its head and tail were hit by US ground attack aircraft. The immobilized convoy was turned into a sitting duck. The slaughtering of the retreating Iraqis continued for the next forty hours until the truce at 0800 local time on February 28, turning the road into a "Highway to Hell." In the words of Colin Smith, the chief roving correspondent of the *Observer*, the aerial assault was "one of the most terrible harassments of a retreating army from the air in the history of warfare." When the weather turned unsuitable for aerial bombing in the afternoon, the task of "taking out" the retreating Iraqis fell to the US army and marines. Tony Clifton of the *Newsweek* reported:

> We got there [Highway 80] just before dusk, and essentially shot up the front of this column. The group of vehicles we hit included petrol tankers and tanks, so the tanks exploded in these great fountains of white flame from the ammunition ... You could see the little figures of soldiers coming out with their hands up. It really looked like a medieval hell – the hell you see in [the paintings of Hieronymus] Bosch, because of the great red flames and then these weird little contorted figures ... It was all conducted at a distance of say, half a mile, and in darkness.[46]

No wonder that the numbers of Iraqi casualties mounted sharply. With an estimated 25–30,000 fatalities caused by the Coalition's attacks on the twelve retreating Iraqi divisions (180,000 soldiers), added to an estimate of 32,600 deaths resulting from the Coalition's air campaign, the total came to 57,600–62,600. By contrast, the number of fatalities in the US military, providing two-thirds of the total Coalition troops, was 97 in the six-week combat and another 279 in accidents during the seven months. In its 110,00 air sorties the Coalition dropped on the Iraqi targets a total of 140,000 tonnes of explosives – the equivalent of seven nuclear bombs dropped on the Japanese city of Hiroshima during World War II.[47]

Of the $82 billion direct cost of the Second Gulf War, $51 billion were incurred by Kuwait and Saudi Arabia, which calculated the war's indirect cost, borne exclusively by it, at $22 billion. Washington's share was $18 billion. Once again there were no official figures of the war expenses by Baghdad. But Hamadi put the damage to Iraq's infrastructure during the first twenty-six days of the conflict at $200 billion. Later the Arab Monetary Fund estimated total Iraqi losses at $190 billion.[48] "Nothing we had seen or read [about Iraq] had quite prepared us for the particular form of devastation which had now befallen the country," said Martti Ahtissari, a (Finnish) UN undersecretary-general, in his report on the state of post-war Iraq. "The recent conflict has wrought near-apocalyptic results on the economic infrastructure of what was until recently a highly urban and mechanized society."[49]

Leading the victors, President Bush, in his victory speech to Americans on February 27, said, "Seven months ago, America and the world drew a line in the sand. We declared that the aggression against Kuwait would not stand. And tonight America and the world have kept their word."[50] He then laid out the terms for a permanent ceasefire, which included Iraq's acceptance of all Security Council resolutions. Once Baghdad had done so, a truce went into effect on the morning of February 28.

In Baghdad, contrary to Western and other reports, the newspapers asserted that Iraq had inflicted heavy losses on the Coalition, one headline declaring, "By God's will and the might of our leader Saddam Hussein, we foiled the aggressor's plot." They called on their readers to rejoice because their army had been able to keep its power intact.[51]

To make such claims when the Coalition bombing, preceded by the most comprehensive economic sanctions imposed by the UN, had plunged the country into a pre-industrial age and reduced its oil output by two-thirds, and when the Coalition's Western armies occupied over 2,000 sq miles (5,200 sq km) of Iraq south of the Euphrates between Samawa and the Kuwait border, was to defy reality.

But then it was not the first time that Saddam had gone into deep denial and offered the obverse of facts as reality; nor was it to be the last.

In Tehran, on March 1, Khamanei attacked both America and regional Arab leaders – describing them as "cowards" and "sheepish" – for inviting Washington to crush a Muslim nation. He vowed that the US would be kicked out by the region's Muslims if it did not leave of its own accord.[52] There is little doubt that Iranian leaders and masses were privately pleased to see Saddam's Iraq defeated and his military crushed, but they did give vent to these feelings in public.

Overall the Second Gulf War helped Iran to project a high profile, and to benefit from the high oil prices, which had almost trebled since the onset of the Kuwait Crisis.

Aftermath of the Second Gulf War

At the meeting of their military leaders at Safwan airstrip on March 3, Iraq and the Coalition formalized the terms of a truce, including the demarcation of the ceasefire line. While the Coalition aircraft were allowed to continue their reconnaissance flights all over Iraq, Baghdad's fixed wing aircraft were required to stay 4 miles (6 km) away from the ceasefire line.

The ink had hardly dried on this document when Saddam Hussein's regime faced a rebellion by Shia insurgents in the south. It began in Nasiriyeh, the headquarters of the army's south-western command, on March 2, when a group of armed men arrived from the nearby Suq al Shuyukh, a town under American control, and organized hundreds of Iraqi army deserters. Together they battled the government forces, stormed the garrison, severely injuring the commander, General Nizar Khazraji, and won.

Aware of the danger that thousands of army deserters might join the Shia rebels in the south, the government announced a general pardon for all deserters on March 4, and appealed to them to rejoin their units. But this had little effect on the uprising. It spread rapidly to other Shia-majority towns and cities: Amara, Kut, Hilleh, Basra, Karbala, Najaf and Samawa. By March 7, all these places had fallen into the hands of the Shia insurgents.

Popular protest, often triggered by the tearing-up of Saddam's posters by army deserters, and excited by the slogans like "There is no god but God, and Saddam is His enemy" (*La illah il Allah, Saddam adou Allah*), and "Saddam, lift your hand, the Iraqi people don't want you," escalated into an orgy of looting and destruction of public property and summary executions of local Baath leaders and intelligence and military officers.

Karbala, a city of a quarter of a million housing two holy Shia shrines – the tombs of Imams Hussein and Abbas – fell to the rebels on March 5, after an uprising in which tens of thousands participated. The insurgents attacked the army headquarters and seized weapons. Once in control, they destroyed the General Security (*Amn al Aam*) headquarters and municipal offices, and emptied the warehouses of food and medicine. They decapitated or hanged seventy-five military officers and Baathist officials, some of them Shia, and tortured many more, often using rooms and halls inside the precincts of the shrines.

Saddam was alarmed. He deployed his well-tried strategy of stick and carrot. His government immediately demobilized all soldiers aged 35 to 38 and all retired officers who had been called up during the Kuwait Crisis. It awarded bonuses to conscripts and Republican Guard personnel. It increased food rations, instituted in January 1991, by a quarter.[53] At the same time Saddam appointed the much-feared General Ali Hassan al Majid as interior minister.

During the early days of the insurgency, the participants and their sympathizers considered it to be a purely Iraqi phenomenon.

But this changed when, on March 7, Iranian President Rafsanjani intervened. "You know well that you are undesirable in your country as well as in the region," he said, addressing Saddam Hussein. "So, don't further stain your bloodied hands by killing more innocent Iraqis. Yield to the people's will, and step down." He appealed to the Iraqi opposition to close ranks.[54]

Rafsanjani's intervention coincided with persistent reports that thousands of armed men had crossed into Iraq from Iran. They reportedly included not only ranks of Iran's Islamic Revolutionary Guard Corps but also the forces of the Tehran-based Supreme Assembly of Islamic Revolution in Iraq (SAIRI). Formed in 1982 with the primary assistance of al Daawa al Islamiya and the Islamic Action Organization, SAIRI was led by Ayatollah Muhammad Baqir al Hakim, a Shia cleric with a long history of resistance to the Iraqi regime. During the Iran–Iraq War it built up an armed force of some 20,000 soldiers, most of them volunteers from among Iraqi refugees and prisoners of war, including its elite Badr and Tawabin brigades.[55] Along with these reports went statements by SAIRI leaders which stressed the Islamic nature of the uprising. This was contrary to the undertaking that SAIRI and other Shia leaders had earlier given to the Joint Action Committee of Iraqi Opposition (JACIO), a coalition of thirty-two opposition groups formed in Damascus in December 1990, that their struggle was aimed at overthrowing Saddam's regime to establish a secular, democratic state. Anthony H. Cordesman and Ahmed S. Hashim, American specialists on the Gulf, noted that

> [T]he initial uprisings were an explosion of pent-up rage and revenge, characterized by an orgy of looting and destruction without any sustaining organization or ideological vision. [W]hen the uprisings began to take on more organized form, they were led by Shia religious leaders and infiltrators from Iran. Many rebel leaders raised the green banner of Islam and portraits of Khomeini and Muhammad Baqir al Hakim … The atrocities committed against government officials were seen as the portent of the bloodshed to come if the rebels prevailed.[56]

Many Shias in southern Iraq, who joined the popular uprising to gain democratic freedoms, were angered and alienated when they realized that the aim of the leaders of the insurgency was to create an Islamic state on the Iranian model. After all, most of them had fought Iran for eight years to prevent such an outcome.

Iran's open intervention and SAIRI's dominance of the Shia uprising also alarmed Saudi Arabia, Kuwait and America. Earlier, President Bush had called on the Iraqi people to rebel against Saddam's regime. But once spontaneous uprising erupted in southern Iraq without any coherence or direction, except to wreak vengeance on government and party officials – followed by the assumption of its leadership by the Tehran-based SAIRI – Washington had second thoughts. Indeed, as Brent Scowcroft, the then US National Security Adviser, later told ABC Television, "I frankly wished [the uprising] hadn't happened. I envisioned a post-war government being a military government … It's the colonel with the brigade patrolling his palace that's going to get him [Saddam] if someone gets him."[57] This tied in neatly with the statement of Richard Haas, director for Near East affairs on the US National Security Council (NSC), on the day after the ceasefire, that "Our policy is to get rid of Saddam, not his regime."[58]

Clearly, the prospect of a fragmented Iraq, with the Shia south adjoining Saudi Arabia and Kuwait, siding with Iran, worried the Saudi and Kuwaiti rulers – not to mention the US administration. As one Saudi commentator was to put it later,

> Riyadh's worst scenario is a destabilized Iraq, a situation where Saddam Hussein can no longer hold the country together and it is split into three: a Kurdish north, a Sunni middle, and a Shia south, allied to Iran, right next to Saudi Arabia's eastern region where its Shias are concentrated.[59]

Inimical though they were to Saddam, they did not wish to see his regime replaced by one modeled on Iran, thus enabling Tehran to extend its influence to the Kuwaiti and Saudi borders, and emerge as the uncontested leader of the Gulf.

It was against this backdrop that the Baghdad government reassembled its forces in the south, particularly the Republican Guard, which was almost wholly Sunni, and its military hardware, including 700 tanks and 1,400 armored personnel carriers it had managed to withdraw from the Kuwaiti theater of operations before the ceasefire. It launched a counterattack against the Shia rebels on March 9. Unsurprisingly, the US forces did not intervene.

The ensuing fight was particularly bloody in Basra, Najaf and Karbala. On March 14, Iraqi soldiers and Republican Guard units, led by Colonel Hussein Kamil Hassan (al Majid), a son-in-law of Saddam, attacked Karbala, using mortars and occasionally ground-to-ground missiles. They faced stiff resistance, with the insurgents fighting the troops in the streets and houses. Finally, a hard core of 2–3,000 rebels retreated to Imam Abbas's shrine. It took 1,500 Iraqi soldiers and Guardsmen two days to overrun the rebel stronghold. The toll of human life and property was heavy. "All along Al Abbas Street, which leads to the Shia shrine of Imam Abbas, buildings were burnt out or smashed by gunfire," reported Patrick Cockburn of the *Independent*. "At the end of the street a tank stands in front of the porch of the shrine whose top has been hit." This shrine as well as Imam Hussein's suffered damage, including marks and holes caused by bullets and artillery shells. The military forced 70,000 Shias, including many clerics and most of the 8,000 theological students of Najaf, to flee across the border into Iran.[60] Having retaken Karbala, Saddam focused on Najaf, then a city of 600,000. Emulating their counterparts in Karbala, the insurgents in Najaf had set up their headquarters in the shrine of Imam Ali, father of Imam Hussein. It became the site of the final battle between them and Baghdad's forces led by Vice-President

Taha Yassin Ramadan (b. 1938). By the time Najaf reverted to government control, some 1,400 civilians were dead.

Once Basra, the second largest city of Iraq, was recaptured by the interior minister, General Ali Hassan al Majid, Saddam could claim, rightly, that he had regained all of southern Iraq. In an hour-long radio and television address, he accused Tehran of supporting "the saboteurs of the south and the stooges and agents of foreign enemies in the north." He said so on March 16, a day after Bush had issued a verbal warning to him to stop combat operations against the insurgents, and three days after Khamanei had appealed, in vain, to the Iraqi army not to fire at believers as this was forbidden in Islam.[61] Saddam Hussein marked the end of the rebellion in the south by visiting Najaf and praying at the shrine of Imam Ali. He allocated 44 lbs (20 kg) of gold, 110 lb (50 kg) of silver, and cash to rebuild the damaged shrine, and appealed to all Iraqis to donate money to the holy places of Iraq.[62]

Iran announced a day of mourning on March 18, for those Iraqis who fell in Baghdad's military onslaught in the south, and the desecration of the Shia holy shrines in Najaf and Karbala. Tehran Radio stepped up news of the rebellion, claiming that Saddam's forces had killed 12–16,000 civilians in recapturing Najaf and Karbala alone. The total death toll in the southern region was later put at 30,000.[63] Most of the deaths resulted from the artillery bombardment of residential areas by government forces.

While Saddam's attention was focused on the south, the Kurdish nationalists struck, building on the success that Masud Barzani's Kurdistan Democratic Party had in freeing the town of Ranya on March 4 – in the process depriving the Baghdad government of the control of 14 of its 18 provinces, the exceptions being Baghdad, Anbar (capital Ramadi), Salahuddin (capital, Tikrit) and Neineva (capital Mosul). Kurdish leaders were simultaneously participating in the JACIO conference in Beirut between March 11 and 13 to forge a common strategy to overthrow Saddam's regime and formulate the main features of the post-Saddam state.

On the morning of March 14, most of the troops of Fursan (*lit.* horse-riders), the 100,000-strong Iraqi army auxiliary force consisting of Kurds, changed sides. The regular Iraqi forces found themselves facing ultimatums from their Kurdish auxiliary units. Some fought, others surrendered. By the evening, in twelve major towns in a 100 mile (160 km) long arc, administrative and other authority passed to the Kurdish insurgents, known as *peshmargas* (i.e., those who face death). Since Saddam's invasion of Kuwait, Kurdish nationalist leaders had been cultivating the auxiliaries, most of them young recruits who had joined the Fursan either at the behest of their tribal chiefs, who received money and favors from Baghdad, or because they had lost their land and jobs in the forced resettlement of Kurds into protected villages in the government's drive to quell earlier Kurdish nationalist insurgencies.

Within a week the insurgents controlled not only the three provinces of Suleimaniya, Irbil and Dohak – forming the official Kurdistan Autonomous

Region (KAR) – but also large parts of the Tamim province, with the oil city of Kirkuk as its capital.

However, this did not last long. The loyalties of the Kurdish tribal chiefs, who had underpinned the success of the rebels, were fickle. But the more serious problem was the absence of geographical proximity and organizational linkage between the insurgencies in the north and the south. By the time the Shia and Kurdish opposition leaders confabulating in Beirut left the Lebanese capital on March 22 to take charge of their respective movements inside Iraq, it was too late. That day Saddam dispatched General al Majid to Mosul to re-organize the government troops in the north.

The next day Saddam carried out the promised reshuffle of the government, ceding his premiership to Sadoun Hamadi, a US-trained Shia, with a mandate to undertake post-war reconstruction, and divesting Tariq Aziz, a deputy premier, of foreign ministry. Bush dismissed the cabinet changes as cosmetic.

But his remark was peripheral to the dilemma he faced. Should America intervene militarily in an incipient civil war in Iraq by severing Baghdad's supply lines to the elite Republican Guard, compelling Saddam to keep his aircraft grounded, and arming the insurgents with anti-tank and anti-aircraft missiles? There was intense debate in Washington, with inputs from Riyadh, Ankara and Cairo.

All regional capitals advised the US against intervention. The prospect of southern Iraq under Shia control alarmed Riyadh. And the prospect of an independent Kurdistan worried Turkey, with a large Kurdish population concentrated in its south-eastern sector. During his meeting with Bush at Camp David on March 24, Turkish President Turgut Ozal explained how an independent Iraqi Kurdistan would become the nucleus for a Greater Kurdistan for the Kurdish populations of Turkey, Iran and Syria, thus destabilizing the whole region. "We're playing no part in that [Iraqi uprising], but it shows great unrest with the rule of Saddam Hussein," said Bush after this meeting. Urging outside powers "not to intervene in Iraq," Ozal remarked that "Iraqis will find the best way for themselves."[64] Two days later in his meeting with Scowcroft, who visited Saudi Arabia secretly, King Fahd too urged a similar course of action.

Following the US National Security Council meeting on March 27, the White House spokesman announced that President Bush had no intention of placing his administration in the midst of a civil war in Iraq, pointing out that "it had made no promises to the [Iraqi] Shias or Kurds." Reflecting the public mood, he added, "The American people have no stomach for a military operation to dictate the outcome of a political struggle in Iraq."[65]

Confident that the Shia revolt in the south no longer threatened his regime, Saddam turned his full attention to the Kurdish insurgency after having reiterated his acceptance of Kurdish autonomy on March 24. Four days later, using heavy artillery, multiple rocket launchers and helicopter gunships, the Iraqi armored and infantry divisions mounted an all-out assault on Kirkuk, and drove out the lightly armed rebels by nightfall.

Baghdad's swift success led to a massive Kurdish exodus to the mountainous Iranian and Turkish borders. As the Iraqi army recaptured town after town, the size of the Kurdish exodus increased, finally involving 1.5 million people, or about half of the region's population. The Kurds feared brutal and extensive reprisals by Baghdad, a repeat of its behavior in the mid-1970s and late 1980s.

Masud Barzani's desperate appeal on April 1, to America, Britain and France to act through the UN to save Kurds from "genocide and torture" fell on deaf ears. This happened primarily because the events did not fit the scenario that the Western powers had hastily conceived for post-war Iraq: a military coup against Saddam in the aftermath of the disastrous defeat his regime had suffered which would put the army in control of a united Iraq. It has emerged since then that in early March, Washington was informed by Minaf Hassan al Tikriti, a senior Iraqi diplomat in Moscow who had defected to the Saudi embassy there, that his brother, Gen. Hakim Hassan al Tikriti, commander of the helicopter forces in the army, was planning a military coup.[66]

If this was indeed the case, it was most likely that Hakim al Tikriti was put under intense surveillance by the Iraqi government or arrested after his brother's defection.

During the first week of April, Baghdad's forces retook Irbil, Dohak, Zakho and Suleimaniya, enabling the government to offer a general amnesty to rebellious Kurds. On 6 April the Revolutionary Command Council declared, "Iraq has totally crushed all acts of sedition and sabotage in all cities of Iraq."[67] It emerged later that "sedition and sabotage" had spread to all but four of the eighteen provinces of Iraq.

The RCC's statement came a day after the UN Security Council had passed Resolution 688 by 10 votes to 3 (Cuba, Yemen and Zimbabwe), with 2 abstentions (China and India). Aware of the dissident minorities within their own boundaries – on whose behalf the UN could interfere in their internal affairs in violation of Article 2.7 of the UN Charter in the future – China and India opposed the mention of "authority to use force" in the draft resolution which, like all previous resolutions on Iraq, referred to Chapter VII of the UN Charter. Entitled "Action with respect to Threats to the Peace, Breaches of the Peace, and Acts of Aggression," this Chapter authorized military action by member-states. China threatened to veto the document if put to the vote in its present form. The Western powers agreed to drop this provision, and the mention of Chapter VII, if China and India abstained. So they did. The final version condemned the repression of Iraqi civilians, including most recently in the Kurdish-populated area, and demanded that Baghdad should immediately end this repression, and allow access to international humanitarian organizations to help those in need of assistance in all parts of Iraq.

As it was, all Iraqis were in dire need of foreign economic help. The report by Martti Ahtissari, a senior UN official, published on March 22, said that the all-encompassing international sanctions on Iraq in August "seriously affected" its ability to feed its people. This was noted by the drafters of the Security Council's

Resolution 687, a long, comprehensive document of thirty-four paragraphs –
later nicknamed the "Mother of all Resolutions" after Saddam's description of
the Second Gulf War as the "Mother of all Battles." Adopted on April 3, 1991 by
12 votes to 1 (Cuba), with 2 abstentions (Ecuador and Yemen), it removed the
embargo on food, eased restrictions on essential civilian needs and unfroze Iraq's
foreign assets. However, the lifting of the remaining restrictions was tied to the
elimination of Iraq's non-conventional weapons, and the establishment of a
mechanism for Iraq to compensate those who had suffered from its actions.

Resolution 687 could be summarized as follows:

1 A formal ceasefire would come into effect only after Iraq officially accepted
   the document.
2 Iraq and Kuwait must respect the 1963 border until the UN demarcated it.
3 UN military observers would monitor a demilitarized zone extending 6 miles
   (10 km) into Iraq and 3 miles (5 km) into Kuwait, and their deployment
   would allow the Coalition to remove its troops from (southern) Iraq.
4 Baghdad must agree unconditionally to destroy or remove under international supervision all chemical and biological weapons, and all ballistic missiles with ranges greater than 94 miles (150 km), and related production
   facilities. A similar procedure would be instituted to remove all material
   usable for nuclear weapons. Iraq must provide lists of locations, amounts and
   types of these arms and materials as well as chemical and biological weapons
   by April 17. The UN secretary-general would set up a commission charged
   with making on-site inspections by May 17. These actions represented steps
   towards achieving the goal of establishing in the Middle East a zone free from
   weapons of mass destruction (WMD).
5 Iraq was liable for damages, without prejudice to its foreign debts, arising from its
   invasion of Kuwait. A fund would be created to meet the claims, and a commission established by May 2 to administer it. The amount to be paid into the fund
   would be based on a percentage of Iraq's oil revenues. Payment levels would take
   into account the needs of Iraq's people, its economy and foreign debts.
6 Iraq must pledge not to support international terrorism.

After protesting that the terms of Resolution 687, passed under the UN Charter's Chapter VII, impinged on Iraq's sovereignty, Baghdad accepted it on April
6. But it rejected Resolution 688 and stuck to this position.

These two Security Council resolutions would come to dominate society and
state within Iraq as well as Baghdad's external relations over the next decade.

Meanwhile, the feelings of ordinary Iraqis about the great tragedy that had
visited them was summed up succinctly in a diary that Nuha al Radi, an Iraqi
artist living in Baghdad, kept. Her entry on April 15, 1991, read,

> After the War ended, the Allies spent all day and all night flying over our
> heads and breaking the sound barrier. Our torture went on for months –

20 or 30 times, day and night, jets broke the sound barrier over our heads, horrific deafening noise, swooping down, rubbing our noses in the dirt … Bush says he has nothing against the Iraqi people … [But] It's us, and only us, who've been without electricity and water – a life of hardship.[68]

Part I

IRAQ

1

SADDAM CENTER-STAGE,
EXIT BUSH

The three Western permanent Security Council members – America, Britain and France – wasted little time in bending Resolution 688 to serve their own policies. On April 16, 1991, they argued that it entitled them to send troops to northern Iraq and establish secure encampments to provide supplies to Kurdish refugees. Iraq denounced this as interference in its internal affairs.

Following an undeclared ceasefire between the Kurdish insurgents and the Iraqi army on April 17, talks between the central government and the delegates of the seven-member Iraqi Kurdistan Front (IKF), led by Masud Barzani of the KDP and Jalal Talabani of the Patriotic Union of Kurdistan (PUK), began in Baghdad. The Kurdish leaders saw Saddam's current weakness as an opportune moment to strike a deal. A week later both sides announced an interim agreement which, based on the 1970 pact, reiterated Kurdish autonomy, and gave Kurds the additional right to return and revive the 3,800 villages and towns that had been razed during the past seventeen years.

Keen to receive international aid, Iraq signed a memorandum of understanding (MOU) with the UN secretary-general's Executive Delegate, Prince Sadruddin Agha Khan, on April 18. It permitted the UN to offer humanitarian aid – providing food, medical care, agricultural rehabilitation and shelter – to Iraqis, including those in the north, but only in cooperation with the central government. In its preamble the MOU mentioned Iraq's rejection of Resolution 688. Baghdad welcomed UN efforts to promote the voluntary return home of Iraqi refugees, chiefly Kurds. Yielding to Western pressures, Saddam Hussein deputed two Iraqi generals to meet the US commander in charge of Operation "Provide Comfort", launched to set up safe havens for the Kurdish refugees inside Iraq. To facilitate the process they agreed to withdraw Iraqi security forces from the border Zakho area. Little did they know that by so doing they had unwittingly started a process that would rob Baghdad of full control of the north for many years to come.

The UN began establishing its humanitarian presence in the 3,600 sq miles (9,320 sq km) of the safe haven area – later renamed "security zone" – that the Coalition had created in the Iraqi-Turkish border region with 16,000 troops. By late May more than half of the 500,000 Kurdish refugees in the region had left for home. (With the withdrawal of the Coalition's Western forces from the occupied southern territory on May 6, southern Iraq became totally free of foreign troops.) On June 7, the Coalition forces handed over all humanitarian tasks to the UN High Commissioner for Refugees. They started a 24-hour air surveillance of the region above the 36th Parallel to protect the "safe haven" for Kurdish refugees, declaring it to be a "no-fly" or "air exclusion zone" for Iraqi aircraft.

Domestically, the Iraqi government's decisions, taken in the latter half of May, to abolish the much dreaded revolutionary courts (established after the 1968 Baathist coup) and demobilize the Popular Army militia, were warmly received by the public. So too were the long prison sentences meted out to profiteers to control runaway inflation.

By now Saddam had consolidated his power, and formed the Special Bureau, composed of his innermost circle of senior advisers, with himself as the chairman. It included Izzat Ibrahim (al Duri), his loyal deputy; Abid Hamid Mahmoud (al Khatib), his private secretary; Gen. Ali Hassan al Majid, interior minister; Tariq Aziz, deputy premier; Gen. Hussein Kamil Hassan, the recently appointed defense minister; and Sabawi Ibrahim al Tikriti in charge of General Security (GS).

By foiling a coup plot led by General Bareq Abdullah, the commander of the Republican Guard, and a hero of the war with Iran, in early May, Sabawi Ibrahim al Tikriti had proved his worth to Saddam. And by so doing he had frustrated the plans of the Bush administration which had collaborated with Abdullah.[1] It was the second time in three months that Washington's attempt to overthrow Saddam by a coup had failed.

But success on the internal security had no impact on Iraq's economic condition. It was dire, despite the Security Council 661 Sanctions Committee's decision in mid-June to let thirty-one countries release over $3.75 billion in frozen Iraqi assets to enable Baghdad to buy food and other essential consumer goods. The Committee was named after Resolution 661 of August 6, 1990, which called on all states (members of the UN as well as non-members like Switzerland) to prohibit importing into their territories "all commodities and products originating in Iraq or [occupied] Kuwait." It also called on all states not to make available to the government of Iraq or any commercial, industrial or public undertaking in Iraq or [occupied] Kuwait, or any person living in Iraq or [occupied] Kuwait, any funds or any other financial or economic resources, or allow any resident in their territories to do so – except "payments exclusively for strictly medical or humanitarian purposes, and in humanitarian circumstances, foodstuffs". The sum of $3.75 billion had to be viewed in the context that Iraq needed about $10 billion annually just to service its foreign loans of $88–110 billion. It also faced a repair bill for its damaged infrastructure of $30 billion, with half of it to be paid in hard currency to be earned from resumed oil shipments.[2] With its electric output down to 22 percent of the pre-war level, there was insufficient power to ensure water purification and sewage treatment. According to a study by a team of Harvard University doctors, the Iraqi ration, supplying 1,300 calories a day, was nearly half the size needed to maintain normal health; and child mortality had doubled since the UN sanctions were imposed.[3]

It is worth noting that before August 1990, UN mandatory sanctions, authorized by Article 41 of Chapter VII of the UN Charter, had been imposed only twice: in 1966 against white-ruled Rhodesia (now Zimbabwe) and in 1977 against the neighboring white-ruled South Africa. (Since 1990 UN sanctions have been imposed in seven other cases.)

The easing or lifting of UN sanctions was linked to the disarmament of Iraq to be implemented by the Vienna-based International Atomic Energy Agency (IAEA), headed by Hans Blix, a Swede, that had been inspecting Iraq for possible military use of its nuclear facilities since the late 1970s, and the newly established United Nations Special Commission (Unscom) under the executive chairmanship of Rolf Ekeus, a Swedish diplomat, for Baghdad's chemical and biological weapons programs and its medium- and long-range missile projects. In an exchange of letters with the UN secretary-general, Javier Perez de Cuellar (1987–1991), in May 1991, the Iraqi foreign ministry agreed to grant unimpeded access to all sites and facilities that Unscom thought it necessary to inspect.

On May 15, the first post-war IAEA team paid a week-long visit to Iraq to list its nuclear facilities. During the visit of the second IAEA team, led by David Kay, an American, from June 23 to 28, the Iraqis obstructed their access to two sites on the basis that these had not been listed by Baghdad as nuclear facilities. On June 28, tipped off by US intelligence, Kay arrived with his team at the Military Transport Center at Falluja, 30 miles (50 km) west of Baghdad. When the team was refused entrance, Kay asked his inspectors, armed with cameras, to cover the exits. They took pictures of tractor-trailers loaded with massive electromagnetic isotope separators, called Calutrons, leaving the premises. Since Calutrons are used for producing weapons-grade uranium, it showed that Iraq had been engaged in nuclear weapons' development, an admission it had not made so far. The Security Council dispatched a high-level delegation to Baghdad to seek Iraq's assurance of full cooperation with the IAEA and Unscom. Washington threatened to bomb Iraq's remaining nuclear facilities if it did not disclose fully its nuclear program.

On its first day in Iraq during its July 7–18 visit, the third IAEA team discovered several kilograms of highly enriched uranium and large stocks of natural uranium. The next day the Iraqi foreign minister, Ahmad Hussein Khodayir, submitted details of Baghdad's nuclear program to the UN secretary-general, explaining that Iraq had withheld full information about its nuclear equipment because it feared that the US would launch an attack to destroy it. Baghdad now admitted enriching uranium by the old-fashioned method of electromagnetic isotopic separation (used by America for its Hiroshima bomb in 1945), and added that it had also tried the centrifuge process and chemical means. It conceded producing only half a kilogram of enriched uranium (whereas 25 kgs were needed for one atom bomb). On July 18, the IAEA formally condemned Iraq for violating its agreement with it by not being honest before.[4] The fourth IAEA team, led again by Kay, concluded at the end of its tour, from July 27 to August 10, that Baghdad had a nuclear military program contrary to its assertions that its program was for peaceful purposes.

As for Unscom, Iraq declared in its submission to the Special Commission that it possessed 1,005 tons of liquid nerve gas stored in vats, and 11,382 chemical warheads – with 30 fitted for Scud ground-to-ground missiles, and the rest for bombs or artillery shells, and that at least 2,700 chemical warheads were buried under debris caused by the Coalition bombing.

The task of the first two Unscom teams, arriving on June 30 and July 18, was to destroy ballistic missiles with ranges of over 94 miles (150 km), and launchers. During the visit of Unscom's third ballistic team from August 8–15, Baghdad admitted to the existence of a supergun, a 350 mm artillery piece. This weapon – as well as components of an even larger gun, Iskandariya, with a 1,000 mile (1,625 km) range – would be destroyed in early October by Unscom at Jabal Hamran north of Baghdad.

Baghdad's admissions led to a hardening of the Security Council stance. On August 15, it adopted Resolution 707 which demanded "full, final and complete" disclosure of its past weapons of mass destruction programs, and "an immediate, unconditional and unrestricted access" to the Unscom-designated sites to IAEA and Unscom inspectors. In addition, the Resolution entitled IAEA and Unscom teams to conduct "both fixed wing and helicopter flights throughout Iraq for all relevant purposes … and to make full use of their own aircraft and such airfields in Iraq as they may determine." Baghdad objected strenuously to such over-flights, aware that the US, acting on behalf of Unscom, had four days earlier flown its U–2 spy planes for high-altitude reconnaissance of Iraq.

During the visit of Unscom's fourth ballistic team from September 6–13, Baghdad refused to let it fly its own helicopters, and offered the use of Iraqi helicopters.

This team had hardly left Iraq when the IAEA's fifth team arrived for a week-long tour during which it found 2.2 tons of heavy water used in nuclear reactors. Hard on its heels came the IAEA's sixth team of forty-four inspectors led by David Kay. His second-in-command was Robert Galluci, the deputy executive chairman of Unscom, a former official of the Politico-Military section of the US state department.

As before, the team stayed at the 200-room Al Rashid Hotel in the Aalam district of central Baghdad. (Before the UN sanctions of August 1990, Al Rashid Hotel was part of the India-based Oberoi chain; afterwards it was run by Iraq's ministry of tourism.) On September 22, 1991, armed with hard intelligence, the IAEA team, accompanied by its Iraqi minders, entered the multi-story Nuclear Design Center near Al Rashid Hotel. It picked up several trunks of documents stored in a basement, including a report from the Atheer site detailing progress made on an implosion-type nuclear bomb. A quick perusal of these papers later in the day at the hotel picked up the codename PC–3. This (PetroChemical–3) turned out to be codename for Iraq's clandestine nuclear weapons program under Dr Jaafar Dhia Jaafar, deputy head of the Iraqi Atomic Energy Commission (IAEC).

The following day, after making an elaborate preparation and equipping themselves with a satellite telephone, the IAEA team set off for the headquarters of PC–3, which happened to be quite near al Rashid Hotel. The Iraqis accompanying the team were led by Dr Hatem Sami, a US-trained nuclear physicist. At the PC–3 premises the IAEA team began removing documents and videotapes from the building and putting them into their vehicles. Sami protested, and had all the inspectors expelled from the offices. He demanded that all the 60,000 documents be returned. Kay refused. Later, Sami's boss, Jaafar Dhia Jaafar, arrived. Kay dared him to remove the documents from the UN vehicles. This led to a stand-off, with the IAEA team sitting tight in the UN vehicles in the parking lot, and Jaafar barring their departure. As days passed, demonstrators gathered around the IAEA group, Kay began giving interviews to the Western media over his satellite phone, and Unscom support staff supplied food and water to the inspectors. Tariq Aziz accused Kay of being a CIA agent, and complained about the high percentage of Americans in his team. (As it was, using the satellite link, Galluci sent sensitive information, not to Unscom or the IAEA, but to this former employer, the US state department – a fact which leaked soon after. The UN admitted later that the team had been wrong in passing some information directly to the US government. But the UN secretariat did not condemn this publicly.)

Despite intense diplomatic activity at the UN headquarters in New York it took four days for a compromise to be devised. The IAEA team, accompanied by the Iraqis, would leave the parking lot with the documents. Then at the Unscom office at the Ishtar (Sheraton) Hotel[5] on Abu Nuwas Street along the Tigris, both sides would review them. The irrelevant documents would be returned to the Iraqis, and a list of the relevant ones and their photocopies would be given to them. After a day-long review, the IAEA team kept 5,000 pages, several thousand pictures and nineteen hours of videotape. According to Kay, the seized material showed how Iraq acquired materials for its nuclear program and gave details of the actual weapons development program.[6]

This episode had the two major elements that kept surfacing time and again over the next many years: systematic and determined attempts by Baghdad to conceal the true extent of its WMD projects, and Washington's misuse of the UN as a cover for spying on Iraq.

Later, based on the information provided by Gen. Hussein Kamil Hassan after his defection in the summer of 1995, it emerged that in May 1991 Saddam Hussein's Special Bureau had formed a Concealment Operations Committee (COC) under the chairmanship of his younger son Qusay (b. 1966), then head of Special Security, to oversee and safeguard information and material concerning the military programs prohibited by the Security Council Resolution 687.[7]

Kurdish refugees and UN embargo

There were two other facets to the UN involvement in Iraq: the welfare of the Kurdish refugees in the north, and its economic embargo on the country.

In his July 1991 report, Prince Sadruddin Agha Khan estimated the total cost of restoring Iraq's oil, electricity, water, sanitation, agriculture and public health sectors to pre-war levels at $22 billion.[8] Settling for a partial rehabilitation he came up with an estimate of $7 billion in the first year. Citing Paragraph 23 of Security Council Resolution 687, providing for exceptional sales to finance imports of food and medicine, he recommended allowing Baghdad to sell oil worth $7 billion in a year to meet its emergency requirements. He proposed allowing Iraq the use of its State Oil and Marketing Organization's (SOMO) frozen accounts in America to process the oil revenue under UN supervision.

When Security Council's members began discussing the Agha Khan's report, the three Western Permanent Members introduced the idea of earmarking part of the oil income for the UN Compensation Fund set up to pay reparations to those who had suffered due to the Iraqi invasion of Kuwait, and to cover all UN expenses, especially Unscom's. They also insisted that Iraq's oil revenue should be deposited in an escrow account controlled by the UN. China and Yemen objected, unsuccessfully, to the interweaving of humanitarian aid with disarmament and the degree of intrusion on Iraqi sovereignty – themes which would crop up repeatedly as time passed.

In the end, Resolution 706 that the Security Council passed on August 15, 1991, by 13 votes to 1 (Cuba), with 1 abstention (Yemen), authorized Iraq to sell up to only $1.6 billion worth of oil in a six-month period under UN auspices, and deposit 30 percent of the sum into the UN Compensation Fund and meet the UN expenses. Iraq rejected the resolution as an insult to its sovereignty, objecting particularly to the UN monitoring of every stage of oil sales as well as importation of food and medicine. The subsequent Resolution 712, adopted in September by 13 votes to 1 (Cuba), with Yemen abstaining, outlined the mechanism for implementing Resolution 706. After the deductions prescribed by these resolution, Baghdad would have been left with a net sum of $1.86 billion over a year, about a quarter of the figure Agha Khan had recommended.

Iraq was in desperate need of foreign exchange to finance its imports of food and medicine. The government also faced the twin problem of high inflation and rapid pauperization of the population. Within a year of Baghdad's occupation of Kuwait, the price of food had risen 15–20-fold. Annual inflation was running at 2,000 percent, and, at $18 a month, average earnings were one-tenth the pre-war level.[9]

The implications of the deteriorating economy impacted on politics. Saddam Hussein postponed indefinitely the parliamentary elections due in 1993. At the Baath Party Congress on September 13, Prime Minister Hamadi argued that reconstruction was possible only with liberalization of all aspects of life, and with strict adherence to the UN resolutions to allow Iraq to end its international isolation. Saddam did not like this. So the Congress expressed no-confidence in Hamadi, and he resigned. He also lost his place on the RCC. His successor, Muhammad Hamza Zubaidi, was another Shia, but he was a light-weight politician who lasted until 1993 when his failure to stop the slide of the Iraqi Dinar led to his dismissal.[10]

After visiting Iraq in August and September 1991, an 87-member international team of health experts, engineers and economists, sponsored by the UN International Children's Emergency Fund (Unicef), Oxfam, a British charity and twenty other non-governmental organizations (NGOs) published a report in October. Its conclusions were: four times as many children were dying now than before the Second Gulf War; one million were malnourished, and another million faced risk of starvation; and water-borne diseases were rampant among them. The report pointed out that the equipment to drive power stations and water purification plants was subject to vetting by the UN 661 Sanctions Committee. Responding to the report, the US state department said, "Saddam is now using children as human shields to ward off sanctions."[11] It pointed to the existence of Resolutions 706 and 712, allowing oil sales for purchase of food and medicine, which Iraq had spurned. This was all the more ironic because, according to a UN aid agency staff member involved in the oil-for-food discussions in Baghdad, "[T]he US intention was to present Saddam Hussein with so unattractive a package that Iraq would reject it and thus take on the blame, at least in Western eyes, for continued civilian suffering."[12]

During the first half of 1992 there was a series of meetings between UN and Iraqi officials in Vienna to hammer out a *modus vivendi* regarding Resolutions 706 and 712. It failed. Iraq informed the UN secretary-general, Boutrous Boutrous-Ghali (1992–96), that since these resolutions questioned its sovereignty, it could not accept them. Overall, in the words of Sarah Graham-Brown, a British specialist on the region, "The mixing of humanitarian exemptions with matters such as compensation and enforcement activities of Unscom muddied the waters, allowing the Iraqi government to object on other political or technical grounds. This made Western condemnation of its callousness less credible."[13]

Among other things Resolution 712 specified that Iraqi oil had to be exported by the Kirkuk–Yumurtalik pipeline passing through Turkey. This was meant not only to benefit Ankara but also to give a lever to the anti-Saddam leaders in Iraqi Kurdistan which had been placed under the Western air umbrella since June 1991. At the same time the Western powers – America, Britain and France – had, in an unpublished memorandum, warned the Baghdad government to keep away from the "safe haven/security zone," adding that they would monitor its behavior in all of Iraqi Kurdistan; and that its Military Coordination Center would remain in Zakho to do so.

Earlier, following two rounds of talks in May 1991, the chances of an agreement between the IKF and Baghdad had dimmed in June, partly because of growing dissension between Barzani and Talabani, and partly because of Saddam's insistence that IKF members cut all foreign links and close their radio stations. Also he refused to discuss the future of Kirkuk, insisting it was an Iraqi city. Little wonder that in late June the IKF rejected the draft agreement by a majority, and the Western powers' *démarche* to Baghdad followed soon after.

In mid-July, the Western troops withdrew from northern Iraq, leaving behind 270 unarmed UN guards. Ankara allowed the Western powers to station a force of 3,000 in south-eastern Turkey as part of their Operation "Poised Hammer," but only for three months. The other part of Operation "Poised Hammer" was the stationing of the US, British and French aircraft at Turkey's Incirlik air base to maintain air surveillance of Iraq above the 36th Parallel. An agreement to let the Western powers use this base for six months at a time needed to be approved by the Turkish parliament.

With the departure of the Coalition's Western forces, the Kurdish *peshmargas* and the Iraqi troops clashed in Irbil and Suleimaniya. Consequently the Iraqis vacated the centers of these cities and took up positions on the outskirts.

As the sowing season approached in September–October, most of the Kurdish refugees returned home to plant seeds. With this the need for the Western powers to maintain a "safe haven" for Kurdish refugees vanished.

On October 10, the Western forces withdrew from south-east Turkey. This emboldened the Iraqi forces. There were clashes between them and the Kurdish *peshmaragas* in south-eastern Kurdistan, especially Suleimaniya and the border towns of Kifri and Kalar. Then, in a sudden reversal of policy, Saddam Hussein withdrew his forces from the three Kurdish provinces. He coupled this with the imposition of an economic embargo on Kurdistan, which remained in force for almost five years. By the mid–1990s, protected by the Western air umbrella, the CIA had built up Iraqi Kurdistan as a spring-board for overthrowing Saddam's regime.

In October 1991, President Bush informed US Congress that he was escalating covert operations against Saddam through his Deputy National Security Adviser, Robert Gates, and wanted it to raise funding for them from $15 million to $40 million. Gates had made public his strong views on Iraq's president five months earlier. "Saddam's leadership will never be accepted by the world community," he said. "Therefore Iraqis will pay the price while he remains in power. All possible sanctions will be maintained until he is gone ... Any easing of sanctions will be considered only when there is a new government."[14] The consternation that Gates's statement caused at the UN was summed up by the headline in the *Los Angeles Times* of May 9, 1991: "US Sanctions Threat Takes UN By Surprise." Later that month Bush forwarded a White House "finding" on Iraq to the CIA director, William Webster, authorizing a covert operation "to create the conditions for the removal of Saddam Hussein from power." The task fell on Frank Anderson, the head of the CIA's Directorate of Operations' Near East Division. Following Congressional approval, his initial annual budget of $15 million was raised by another $25 million.

The conventional wisdom in the Bush administration was that as Iraqi people begin to suffer the devastating effect of the UN sanctions they will increasingly blame Saddam for their woes, and that will create an environment in which an irate but courageous member of his immediate family or bodyguard will assassinate him – The Silver Bullet Solution. Alternatively his overthrow will come about through a coup at the top by a few disaffected generals of the Republican Guard. In effect this meant implementing the Bush White House's policy encapsulated in the directive: "Get rid of Saddam, not his regime."

There were solid reasons for the Bush administration to opt for covert action leading to a military coup rather than overt backing for insurgency. The main flaw of the popular uprising scenario was that it was hard to forecast how, once unleashed, it would develop. History shows that when such a movement takes off, thanks to the coalescing of disparate forces with the common aim of toppling the status quo, the most organized group in the coalition invariably emerges as the leader after it success. This is what happened with the insurgency in southern Iraq after the Second Gulf War. (Also, the same thing happened in the case of the massive anti-Shah uprising in Iran. In the end Islamist forces led by clerics elbowed out all other anti-Shah groups – some of them secular, others Marxist – that had participated in the revolutionary process, and monopolized power.) Had Shia Islamists consolidated their position in the south, they would have encountered resistance from the Sunnis in central Iraq. And with Iraqi Sunni and Shia partisans engaged in warfare in the Mesopotamian plain, the Kurds in the north would have declared independence, and this in turn would have invited an immediate invasion by Turkey, determined to decimate an independent Kurdish entity in the region to abort any chance of its becoming an inspiration and a safe haven for the Partiye Karkeran Kurdistan (PKK, Kurdistan Workers Party), engaged in an armed struggle against Ankara to establish an independent Kurdistan. A civil war in Iraq, a country with such vast petroleum reserves, would have played havoc with oil prices, causing inflation and a downturn in corporate-America's profit margins, an unacceptable scenario for any US administration, Democrat or Republican.

So, given the uneasy relationship between Arabs and Kurds, and Sunnis and Shias, in Iraq, the American policy-makers concluded, rightly, that only a strong central authority could keep the country together. Also, this meant that it would take a long time for these ethnic and sectarian groups to learn to play politics according to democratic rules, and so the prospect of multi-party democracy rising out of the ashes of Saddam's brutal dictatorship was minimal. Little wonder that top US officials preferred an authoritarian regime in Baghdad to a democratic one, without of course ever acknowledging this publicly. They therefore focused on encouraging defections from among the Sunni elements surrounding Saddam. Replacing Saddam with one or more secular, Sunni generals, willing and ready to cooperate with Washington, would also make the region secure, as the aggressions committed by Iraq between 1980 and 1990 had stemmed essentially from the belligerent nature of Saddam (*lit.*, fighter or clasher), they surmised.

Saddam was fully aware of the American efforts, and acted to thwart them.

Within a week of the Second Gulf War ceasefire he established a bipolar equilibrium in the armed forces, placing the defense ministry and the Republican Guard (RG, *Haris al Jumhuri*) in the hands of officers who were from outside the Tikriti area, his home base: Gen. Saadi Tuma al Abbas and Gen. Mukhalif Iyad al Rawi. They were balanced by leading officers who were Tikritis: Gen. Hussein Rashid Wendawi as the military chief of staff; Gen. Medhahim Saib (al Tikriti) as the air force commander; and Hussein Kamil Hassan as the minister of industry and military industrialization. The two arms of civilian intelligence apparatus remained as before under Saddam Hussein's half brothers: Sabawi Ibrahim al Tikriti (General Security) and Barzan Ibrahim al Tikriti (General Intelligence) – with Military Intelligence assigned to Gen. Wafiq Jassim al Samarrai, a non-Tikriti. The appointment of a cousin, Gen. Ali Hassan al Majid, as interior minister in early March 1991 completed the grip of Saddam over the formidable intelligence and security machine of Iraq.[15] Such an even division of power in the military, intelligence and security services made a successful attempt to overthrow Saddam dependent on a highly unlikely alliance between the two poles of Tikritis and non-Tikritis, or the neutralization of one by the other.

At the operational level, following the post-war uprisings, Saddam had strengthened the intelligence agencies. Long before he became president in 1979, Saddam, who had run the internal security organ of the Baath Party, the Jihaz Hunein (*lit.*, Corps of Hunein, a reference to the Battle of Hunein in the early years of Islam) under the refurbished title of the General Relations Office, had supervised the restructuring and expansion of the state intelligence apparatus.[16] His control of the security and intelligence agencies played a vital role in his rise to the supreme authority in the republic, and since then he has spared no expense or effort to maintain these agencies in top form.

In 1970, soon after he became a member of the RCC, the country's most powerful body, Saddam Hussein set up the National Security Bureau (*Maktab Amn al Qawami*) under Nazim Kazar to coordinate and supervise the three existing intelligence agencies: (1) General Security (GS, *Amn al Aam*) with its focus on general public and governmental property; (2) General Intelligence Department (GID, *Dairat al Mukhabarat al Ammaa*), focusing on political opposition at home and abroad; and (3) Military Intelligence (MI, *Istikhabarat al Askariya*). After the failed coup attempt by Kazar on June 30, 1973, Saadoun Shakir (al Tikriti), a cousin and a long-time confidant of Saddam Hussein, became head of the National Security Bureau. In 1992 this job went to Qusay, the younger son of Saddam, who continues to hold it. By then Iraq had acquired two more security services, one civilian – Special Security Directorate (*Muderiye al Amn al Khas*) – and the other military, called Military Security (MS, *Amn al Askariya*).

General Security, dating back to the British Mandate in Iraq in 1921, dealt with general security of the state and its property, with some of its employees monitoring the daily life of the populace, looking for any sign of dissent, and others, operating at major police stations, specializing in questioning and, if need be, torturing suspects. A part of the interior ministry until the 1968 Baathist coup, General Security was manned by police and army officers as in the pre-1968 era. But in 1980 President Saddam Hussein appointed another cousin, Ali Hassan al Majid, as the director of the agency with instructions to infuse Baathist ideology into its personnel.

The task of turning General Security into a political police force, accomplished against the background of the Iran–Iraq War, earned the service an odium for using torture, kidnapping, murder and rape as means of intimidating dissenters and malcontents, real or potential. Its agents were ever-vigilant to sniff out the barest sign of disaffection. In 1987, after Gen. al Majid was appointed the military commander of Kurdistan, Gen. Abdul Rahman al Duri became its head. During the post-1991 Gulf War insurrection, General Security agents were the prime target of the insurgents. Once Baghdad had re-established control in the disturbed provinces, Saddam provided the agency with its own paramilitary arm, the Emergency Forces (*Qawat al Tawaria*), and placed it under his half-brother, Sabawi Ibrahim al Tikriti. In 1996 he was replaced by Gen. Taha Abbas Ahbabi. The agency has a large network of informers. For instance, the translator-guides provided by the ministry of information to the visiting journalists (who are required to use no others) routinely submit reports on their charges to General Security. And the drivers of the taxis based at hotels such as al Rashid in Baghdad report the movements of foreigners to the agency.[17]

Following a serious assassination attempt on him by a group of soldiers belonging to al Daawa al Islamiya on July 11, 1982, in Dujayal, 40 miles (64 km) north of Baghdad, in which ten of his bodyguards died,[18] Saddam Hussein set up a special section within General Security and called it Special Security. Two years later he raised it to a separate directorate under Gen. Fanar Zibin Hassan al Tikriti, who later gave way to Gen. Hussein Kamil Hassan. Its primary job was security of Saddam as well as his presidential palaces and guest houses. It performed this task through the Emergency Forces (*Qawat al Himaya*), made up of 200 bodyguards. They formed the second circle around Saddam – the first circle immediately around him consisting of the forty-strong Murafaqin (*lit.*, Companions), all of whom shared their al Bu Nasir tribal affiliation with him. They are divided into the Special Location Group charged with Saddam's security in the palaces he used; the Mobile Group (called Salih) charged with securing the president and his immediate cordon of bodyguards; and the Kulyab, consisting of his cook, butcher and food-taster, and his swimming and fishing companions. The Special Security's other duties were to keep a watchful eye on all other intelligence and security agencies, and maintain a close watch on top military brass. It did so in close cooperation with the Special Republican Guard (SRG, *Haris Al Jumhuri al Khas*) whose three brigades guarded the southern, northern and western arteries of Baghdad. (In addition, a division of the Republican Guard was stationed in the capital.)[19]

By the time Qusay Saddam Hussein took over Special Security in 1992, it was

5,000 strong. Armed with the latest in surveillance and communications equipment, it occupied two multi-story blocks in Baghdad, and had its own arsenal, prison and community centre. It played a central role in the regime's concealment program concerning proscribed weapons. "Without offices and computers and motor pools, the Amn al Khas will lose much of its ability to keep shunting the key weapons' stocks around the country and guaranteeing the personal security of Saddam Hussein," said a Western diplomat.[20]

By far the largest organ of intelligence was the GID, operating from its vast headquarters in Baghdad's upmarket Mansur neighborhood. It evolved out of the General Relations Office, the name the Baathist regime gave to the Baath Party's internal security organ. It operated both internally and externally. At home, it was divided into provincial bureaus; and abroad, its agents were attached to the Iraqi embassies. Its functions included keeping tabs on the Baath and other political parties; curbing Shia and Kurdish opposition; monitoring subversive activities and engaging in counter-espionage; maintaining surveillance of all embassies and other foreign missions inside Iraq and monitoring Iraqi embassies abroad; collecting intelligence overseas; conducting sabotage and subversion against hostile countries and aiding the groups opposed to their regimes; and establishing contacts with anti-regime groups in the countries opposed to Iraq. In the region, its agents were most active in Amman, the Jordanian capital, a focal point for the activities of the foreign intelligence agencies not only of the Arab countries but also Israel and America. They sniffed the city for any signs of plots against the Saddam regime. Within the boundaries of Iraq, the GID maintained clandestine contacts with its counterpart of the KDP – a fact which surfaced when, following Baghdad's military assistance to the KDP to wrest control of the regional capital of Irbil from its rival Patriotic Union of Kurdistan, its operatives swiftly got to work to kill the CIA agents.[21] It maintained a network of informers, often members of such popular organizations as the Union of Iraqi Students at home and abroad, and the Iraqi Women's Federation.

In 1973, the GID was headed by Saddam's half-brother, Barzan Ibrahim al Tikriti, an office he held for many years. So he was well qualified to publish, in May 1983, a highly publicized book, *Assassination Attempts on the Life of President Saddam Hussein*, including nine such attempts but excluding the latest at Dujayal.[22] But five months later, yielding to pressure from America to distance his regime from international terrorism to pave the way for the resumption of US–Iraq diplomatic ties, Saddam dismissed Barzan because of his close association with Abu Nidal (real name, Sabri al Banna), a Palestinian leader alleged to be deeply involved in terrorist actions. He then appointed Barzan as Iraq's ambassador to the UN in Geneva. His successor as head of the GID was Gen. Fadil Barrak al Tikriti, who in 1986 became a reserve member of the Regional (meaning Iraqi) Command of the Baath Party.

The military counterpart of the GID was Military Intelligence, with a history dating back to Iraqi independence in 1932. Its functions included assessing chief military threats to Iraq, overseeing security and counter-intelligence in the military, ensuring officers' loyalty to the regime, maintaining a network of informers in the countries of the region, and cooperating with foreign intelligence agencies. Its prestige suffered when Israel's warplanes surreptitiously destroyed a nuclear facility under construction near Baghdad in June 1981. It then focused on protecting the country's emerging military-industrial complex. It and the GID sought and received professional training and guidelines from the Soviet Union on how to conceal and camouflage Iraq's strategic military-industrial projects. The Soviet Komitet Gosudarstvennoy Bezopasnosti (KGB, Committee for State Security) taught the Iraqi operatives not only how to locate their industrial facilities in a way that reduced their vulnerability to air raids, and how to mask their identifiable features – as seen from the air – through trickery and practical means like masking heat sources, but also the vital importance of an early warning system and swift evacuation of a facility likely to be attacked. Among other things it recommended that Iraq should so design and build a new military-industrial facility that it could absorb the explosive impact of bombs, installing blow-away walls that leave the skeleton intact, and which can be rebuilt quickly following bombardment. By implementing these instructions, the Iraqis managed to deceive IAEA inspectors about their nuclear arms program during their six-monthly inspections before the Second Gulf War.[23] During the 47-day non-stop bombing by the anti-Iraq Coalition during the war, the MI, then headed by Gen. Sabir al Duri, managed to save most of the warplanes by having them stored in underground bunkers that withstood the impact of the Coalition's deadly, hi-tech bombs. After the war Duri was replaced by Gen. Wafiq al Samarrai. In early 1992 al Samarrai was transferred to a less sensitive job at the Presidential Office, and was followed by Gen. Muhammad Nimah al Tikriti.

Later that year, sensing disaffection in the officer corps, Saddam decreed the formation of Military Security and appointed Gen. Muhammad al Tikriti as its commander, instructing him to report directly to the Presidential Office. The MS's function was to maintain internal security within the armed forces. It did so by posting at least one unquestionably loyal officer in every military unit. Both the MS and the MI had their headquarters in the Kadhimiya neighborhood of Baghdad between the U-bend in the Tigris River.

In addition, the Baath Party maintained a military bureau, headed by Saddam Hussein, with a mandate to impart political education to the officer corps, and monitor its political-ideological allegiance.

The Baath had its own Party Security (*Amn al Hizb*), which kept tabs on members' loyalty and maintained security cells within the organization.

Finally, having crushed the post-Gulf War insurrections with the active backing of Sunni tribal leaders, Saddam set up the Tribal Chiefs' Bureau (*Maktab al Shuyukh*) to formalize the relationship between them and the state. In return for cash subsidies and arms supplies, loyal tribal chieftains agreed to crush dissidents within their tribes. Saddam put his younger son-in-law, Col. Saddam Kamil Hassan (al Majid), in charge of this bureau.[24]

By 1992, the total strength of the security and intelligence agencies of the state and ruling party was probably about the same as the estimate of 60–80,000 in 1984 during the Iran–Iraq War.[25] There were most likely an equal number of informers.

Iraqi opposition

Certainly, the Bush administration was aware of the ubiquitousness of Iraq's security and intelligence apparatus, and knew of the heavy odds against a successful overthrow of the tightly-run Saddam regime. But then it was pursuing a coup not as its sole option, but rather as part of a bigger game plan with diverse but complementary roles assigned to the UN sanctions (to further damage Iraq's economy and engender popular discontent); the maintenance of a no-fly zone in Iraqi Kurdistan (to highlight Saddam's loss of control in part of Iraq); and the upkeep of an American armada in the Gulf (to underscore Washington's commitment to its regional allies).

Bearing all this in mind, Frank Anderson at the CIA headquarters set out to expand his program. By then the agency had acquired many Iraqi "assets." Prominent among them was Ahmad Chalabi (b.1945), a portly Shia Iraqi. A wealthy, Westernized businessman, he had been living in London since 1989.

Born into a rich banking family in Baghdad, he and his parents fled Beirut in the wake of King Faisal II's overthrow and murder in 1958. After university education in Beirut, Chalabi enrolled at the Massachusetts Institute of Technology, and then obtained a doctorate in mathematics at the University of Chicago. He became a mathematics professor at the American University in Beirut. He stayed there until 1977 when, due to the Lebanese civil war, he moved to Amman. Here he set up Petra Bank during a time when petro-dollars were aplenty. Within a decade, it became the third largest bank in Jordan, only to be seized by the Central Bank of Jordan in mid–1989 due to shady foreign exchange transactions. This in turn led to a spate of allegations of embezzlement and fraud against Chalabi. His hasty exit allegedly in the boot of a friend's car to Damascus left many wondering. The State Security Court in Amman later (in 1992) convicted him *in absentia* in two cases, involving the embezzlement of many millions of dollars, and sentenced him to three- and six-year jail terms. He denied all charges, describing them as politically motivated.[26] In 1989 he moved to London, where he was later to acquire British citizenship. Following Iraq's invasion of Kuwait in 1990, he became politically active, carving out a place for himself in the world of Iraqi opposition.

His value to the CIA was threefold: he was Westernized and sophisticated; as a rich businessman he was a credible conduit for funding by the agency; and since he had no constituency inside Iraq he was the least threatening to other opposition groups, each of which had some sort of following and contacts at home.

When Chalabi convened a gathering of 300 opposition delegates in Vienna in

June 1992, they all assumed that he was the paymaster. In reality it was the CIA, which had reportedly set aside $20 million to back Chalabi.[27] The result was the formation of the Iraqi National Congress (INC), an umbrella body that gained the affiliation of nearly twenty groups, to be led by Chalabi. These included not only the long-established KDP and the PUK, but also the comparatively new Iraqi National Accord (INA), popularly known as *al Wifaq* (The Accord), which since its inception in 1990 had focused on staging a coup in Iraq.

The timing of the conference had suited the Kurdish leaders. Protected by the Western air umbrella, they had held a poll to the Kurdistan Legislative Council on May 19. The official outcome showed the KDP winning 50.8 percent of the vote and the PUK 49.2 percent after the votes of the smaller groups, which failed to pass the threshold of 7 percent, had been reallocated. The KDP and the PUK accepted a 50:50 power-sharing formula. At the Vienna convention, both Barzani and Talabani concurred with the INC leadership's decision to base the INC in Iraqi Kurdistan and build a liberation army composed of exiled and defector Iraqis. The end purpose was to set up a democratic regime in post-Saddam Iraq, which chimed with Washington's professed commitment to democracy and human rights.

But democracy was the last thing that the INA, or its generously funded patron, Saudi Arabia's foreign intelligence chief, Prince Turki ibn Faisal, had in mind for Iraq. The INA was the brain-child of General Adnan Nouri, Dr Iyad Alawi, and Salih Omar Ali al Tikriti, all of them defectors from the Iraqi regime. As a senior military defector, Nouri, a former general in the RG, was valuable to the anti-Saddam plotters. Based in London, he was in close touch with the local CIA station chief. The INA also included Salah al Shaikhly, a high official at the Iraq Central Bank before his defection in early 1980, and Dr Tahseen Muaala who had attended to the wounds of Saddam Hussein after a failed attempt on Abdul Karim Qasim's life in 1959.

Alawi first went to London as a post-graduate medical student in the early 1970s. There he became president of the Iraqi Students Union in Europe – and a valuable asset to the Iraqi authorities. He defected in 1975, and turned to business with the help of his Saudi patrons. But when he cultivated British Secret Intelligence Service (MI6) agents, he upset Baghdad. An assassination attempt on him in 1978 in his suburban London house left him injured. He then set up an additional home in Amman, and established contacts with Jordanian intelligence. His business connections with Saudi Arabia and his continued interest in gathering information led him to assist Saudi intelligence in establishing an anti-Baghdad radio station, Voice of Free Iraq, after Iraq's invasion of Kuwait. At the radio station, he worked with Salih Omar Ali al Tikriti, who had risen steadily in the Baathist hierarchy to become Iraq's ambassador to the UN in the late 1970s. In mid–1982 when Iran acquired the upper hand in its war with Iraq, and the future of Saddam Hussein looked uncertain, al Tikriti resigned his post to make himself available as a successor to Saddam. But nothing came of it. He later made his peace with Saddam, and found himself running Iraqi

Freight Services Limited, a government-owned company, in London. Repeating the pattern of the past, he jumped ship when Iraq came under UN sanctions in August 1990. Once more he joined the Iraqi opposition, and moved to Saudi Arabia. As a kinsman of the reputed coup plotters – Minaf Hassan al Tikriti and his brother Gen. Hakim Hassan al Tikriti – soon after the Second Gulf War, he claimed high-level contacts.[28]

Among other things the Voice of Free Iraq gave much publicity to the meeting of the Joint Action Committee of Iraqi Opposition held in Saudi Arabia in February 1992 and presided over by King Fahd. Among the fifteen groups attending the conference was the Shia organization, SAIRI. Its delegates were led by Ayatollah Muhammad Baqir al Hakim, who had a separate meeting with Fahd, a Sunni, during which he reportedly assured the monarch that he was committed to Iraq's territorial integrity and Arab character, and that in the post-Saddam Iraq there would be no discrimination against any religious or ethnic group or individual.[29]

Partly as a riposte to SAIRI's flirtation with Saudi Arabia, in April the Iraqi government mounted an armed campaign in the southern marshes, especially in the Amara region, using artillery fire and aerial bombardment, to flush out the Shia insurgents and army deserters hiding there, and generally depopulate the area and drain the marshes as part of an ambitious scheme to reclaim land for cultivation and oil extraction.

This move was also a measure of the confidence Saddam Hussein felt especially after his security services had aborted a coup attempt by the London-based Free Iraq Council (FIC). Led by an affluent Shia Iraqi exile, Saad Jabr, son of a former prime minister, Salih Jabr (r. 1947–48), FIC used Tehran as its base for the operation. The plotters included General Bashir Talib, commander of the Republican Guard when it was first formed as the president's personal force in late 1963 and later Iraq's ambassador to Libya, and Jassim Mukhlus, a former Iraqi ambassador, both Sunnis and natives of the Tikrit region. Having established contacts with the commanders of several anti-Saddam army units inside Iraq, Jabr traveled to Washington in February 1992 (against the background of the UN Security Council declaring Iraq to be in material breach of Resolution 687), to persuade the Bush administration to bomb Baghdad for forty-eight hours and hit the army garrisons loyal to Saddam with a view to creating confusion and letting the military units commanded by the plotters seize control. But before the plan could be finalized and implemented, Saddam's regime discovered the plot in April. Up to 300 army officers and civilians were arrested, and many were executed. A few months later Jabr addressed an open letter to the US secretary of state, James Baker, alleging that the CIA had leaked the plan to Iraq.[30]

During the rest of the decade, whenever an anti-Saddam coup attempt got exposed, the plotting Iraqi leaders would routinely blame the CIA, which, in their view, was not serious about toppling him. Despite growing evidence to the contrary, they refused to accept the fact that the Iraqi intelligence apparatus was extraordinarily efficient. This was particularly true of its Military Security and the GID. It was common knowledge that all Iraqi opposition groups operating abroad and in Iraqi Kurdistan were infiltrated by these agencies.

UN inspections

Reflecting the growing confidence of Saddam Hussein, in June 1992 his government refused to renew the MOU regarding humanitarian aid with the UN. London and Paris urged Unscom to ease off its pressure on Baghdad while efforts were being made to encourage Iraq to sign a fresh MOU.

Relations between Baghdad and Unscom–IAEA since the stand-off in September 1991 had been choppy. Iraq could argue, citing facts and figures, that between September 1991 and June 1992 Unscom's various ballistic teams had destroyed all medium- and long-range missiles as well as missile production facilities and equipment. Unscom's Chemical Destruction Group had supervised the destruction of Iraq's bulk stocks of mustard and nerve agents, precursor chemicals, and loaded munitions at Muthanna, as well as chemical bomb-making equipment. This was in addition to the destruction of 463 rockets containing sarin nerve gas at Khamissiya. During that period IAEA teams had destroyed all uranium-enrichment and reprocessing equipment as well as the facilities and equipment at Iraq's nuclear weaponization research and development center at Atheer, and removed highly enriched uranium from Iraq.

Friction had arisen between Iraq and the UN on Resolutions 707 (August 15, 1991) and 715 (October 11, 1991) on long-term verification and monitoring to prevent a reconstitution of Iraq's WMD programs. Baghdad continued to object to the provision in 707 which gave blanket powers to Unscom to conduct overflight anywhere in Iraq and demanded full cooperation from the Iraqi government. The latter's national security fears were not misplaced when there were press reports that Israel, using information obtained by the American U-2 spy planes, already working for Unscom, had been planning to assassinate Saddam Hussein (in 1992), but canceled the operation when members of its would-be hit squad were killed in a training accident.[31]

Regarding Resolution 715, Baghdad objected to the provisions requiring it to furnish "a full inventory of plants and other sites with the potential for making weapons of mass destruction, and all machinery, chemicals and other materials that might be devoted to such activity," and spelling out that UN inspectors were "entitled to travel anywhere within Iraq and enter any site they choose."

Since the UN Security Council considered Resolutions 707 and 715 to be extensions of Paragraphs 12 and 13 of Resolution 687, it declared on February 19, 1992, that, due to its rejection of 707 and 715, Iraq was "in material breach" of Resolution 687.

Participating in the Council's debate on the subject on March 11–12, Tariq Aziz argued that Unscom was trying to de-industrialize Iraq by insisting on listing many machines as having dual (i.e., both civilian and military) purpose, and thus subject to ongoing monitoring. He failed to convince the Council whose president stated that Iraq was not yet in full compliance of Resolution 687. Despite the diplomatic stalemate, in late June Baghdad backed down and accepted Resolution 707, permitting Unscom to deploy its helicopters for aerial inspection of Iraq. But it was not until November 1993 that Iraq reversed its rejection of 715.

By then the structure of Unscom, housed on the top floors of the Ishtar (Sheraton) Hotel, had become established, and so also had its protocol with the Iraqi government. The missile disarmament unit was led by Nikita Smidovich, a Russian; the chemical weapons unit by Dr Horst Reeps, a German; the biological warfare agents unit by Dr Gabrielle Kraatz-Wadsack, a German. The standard procedure was that at 8 p.m. on the day before an inspection, Unscom would give the Iraqis a copy of the Notification of Inspection, specifying the location, the size of the inspection team and the number of vehicles, to depart from the Unscom office at 8 a.m. the next day. In the case of "no notice" inspection, the document would not state the location. So the Iraqi office had twelve hours to assemble its batch of minders who would meet the Unscom team the next morning and accompany it wherever it went. The Unscom team was identified by a single or joint serial number (89/93 meant 89th chemical mission and 93rd biological mission), and its mandate could cover one or more inspections to be carried out during a one- to two-week period. But there were exceptions. Unscom 63, involving 100 inspectors and focusing on missiles, for instance, had operated for nearly two months. An inspection team had specialists under the direction of a chief inspector, who was a permanent staff member of Unscom (e.g., Scott Ritter and Nikita Smidovich), with the rest being employees with short-term contracts. A typical chemical team, for instance, would have four to five chemical experts, two computer technicians to scan databases for relevant information, technicians to run satellite telephones and other equipment, and a paramedic.[32]

On July 5 came another stand-off at the ministry of agriculture and irrigation in Baghdad near the PC–3 building, the site of the confrontation in September. Tipped off by two West European intelligence agencies, a Unscom team arrived in the Iraqi capital to inspect the ministry of agriculture, suspecting it of containing the archives of Iraq's WMD programs. When the Iraqis refused entry to the team, its leader, Mark Silver, posted UN vehicles at the three exits to ensure that no documents were removed. The stand-off continued for a fortnight as the two sides tried to reach a compromise, with the inspectors daily facing a crowd of angry Iraqi demonstrators.

After the Unscom chief, Rolf Ekeus, had rejected Iraq's argument that a Security Council resolution passed under Chapter VII of the UN Charter could not impose on a member-state conditions that violated its sovereignty, Tariq Aziz, in his meeting with Ekeus on July 18, proposed that a team of experts drawn from the non-aligned members of the Security Council be formed to inspect the ministry of agriculture, and report directly to the Council without involving Unscom. Ekeus rejected the proposal, arguing that it contravened the inspection procedure outlined in the Status Agreement of May 1991 signed by the UN and Iraq. However, urged by Aziz, he forwarded his proposal to the Council.

As the stand-off continued, President Bush threatened military action against Baghdad. But, to his disappointment, except Kuwait and Saudi Arabia, no other Arab country backed this course. Also there were no worthwhile military targets in Iraq left to strike. The Iraqi government wanted to see the UN inspectors end their watch. Its tactic of letting anti-UN protesters grow increasingly aggressive worked when, on July 21, facing a large, rowdy crowd of angry demonstrators, with some of them wielding knives and skewers, Silver lifted the UN cordon of the ministry by instructing the inspectors to leave. Soon the team returned to its regional base in Bahrain. This hardened the stance of Ekeus, then negotiating with the Iraqis at the UN in New York. Finally, a compromise was reached on July 26. Iraq agreed to let a team selected by Ekeus inspect the ministry on a verbal understanding that it would not contain American inspectors. On July 28, Ekeus arrived in Baghdad with a new Unscom team composed entirely of non-Americans. It inspected the building but found nothing. Evidently the Iraqis had removed whatever incriminating documents were stored at the premises as soon as Unscom inspectors withdrew from the scene a week earlier.

Among those who kept watch over the agriculture ministry from a Nissan Patrol was the team's operations officer, Scott Ritter, a former intelligence officer in the US marines with the rank of colonel. Seven years later he published a book, *Endgame*, in which he summarized the information concerning the materials and documents about Iraq's WMD and missile programs provided by Gen. Hussein Kamil Hassan – Saddam Hussein's senior son-in-law, who had headed the ministry of industry and military industrialization (1988–91), ministry of defense (1991–92) and the Military Industrialization Establishment, (MIE, *Munshiaa al Tasnia al Askariya*) (1992–95) – to Unscom and the CIA after his defection in August 1995.

After Qusay Saddam Hussein had been put in charge of COC by the Special Bureau, he formed a Weapons Control and Maintenance Committee. Working in conjunction with Gen. Kamal Mustafa, commander of the SRG, he selected a team of SRG officers for the task. They received technical assistance from the MIE (which took over the functions of the earlier Military Industrialization Commission and also dealt with the post-1991 War reconstruction), with logistical backing from the RG, the army, and several ministries. By June 20, the COC had received all the relevant materials it needed.[33]

But when the IAEA team led by David Kay had wrongfooted the Iraqis on June 28, 1991, and filmed them removing Calutrons from a military base in Falluja, the COC decided to focus on the critical materials and components of the military programs – to be listed by four task forces – and destroy the rest unilaterally or hand them over to the Unscom–IAEA personnel. Accordingly, the material essentials of the nuclear program were dispatched to the Tikrit area for storage at the presidential farms and villas. The critical materials and components of the chemical and biological programs and the missile projects were sent to Alam near the Tikrit military garrison. It was thus that in early July more than 100 trucks converged on Alam. Once the final winnowing was done by Colonel Mudhahim Suleiman al Latif of the SRG operations, the materials to be saved were hidden at sites belonging to top SRG and Special Security officers or President Saddam Hussein. This task and the destruction of non-essential materials were believed to have been completed by the end of July.

But the seizure of the documents about nuclear projects by David Kay's team at the Nuclear Design Center and the PC–3 headquarters in September made the top level Special Bureau revise the COC's strategy of letting the MIE's security arm move documents around. It instructed the COC to remove the remaining WMD and missile documents to safe houses for evaluation. Once this was done, different task forces separated the essential documents – whether on paper or computer discs – from the non-essential, with the latter marked for microfilming. They also classified the papers by discipline to facilitate their future use by MIE scientists. The job of protecting these archives was assigned to the Special Security, which was also instructed to hold the microfilm in reserve. By the end of 1991, Special Security had worked out a safeguarding plan of constantly moving the archives around from one innocuous-sounding place (like the ministry of agriculture and irrigation) to another. This was an essential part of the concealment strategy to ensure that if the exact location of the archives was leaked to Western agents inside or outside Iraq it should prove transient.[34]

While the upper echelons of the Iraqi government were engaged in a diplomatic tug of war with the UN Security Council, ordinary citizens were struggling to make ends meet. The ban on oil sales meant the drying up of the only source of foreign exchange needed by the government to buy food, 70 percent of which was imported before the Iraqi invasion of Kuwait. With the UN sanctions barring imports of seeds, pesticide, fertilizer and spare parts for farm machinery, there was a limit to the growth of agricultural output at home.

Under these circumstances, profiteering increased, with the Iraqi import–export firms based in Jordan becoming active, and conducting both legal and illegal trade, providing not only basic necessities for the common people but also luxuries for the elite. However, even items like cigarettes and beer had become luxuries. "A gang robbed Umberto's house of 1,000 crates of beer which he was storing for his [foreign] company," noted Nuha al Radi in her diary. "Each crate sells for 80 [Iraqi] Dinars – that's 8,000 Dinars right there: a fortune. No one steals electrical goods any more except for chandeliers."[35]

To curb profiteering and black economy, in the summer of 1992 the government executed about forty businessmen and sequestered their assets. Some of them were leading merchants and one, Salim Hamra, was the former chairman of the Baghdad Chamber of Commerce.[36] A major motivation behind the government's summary justice was to enable the inner circle of Saddam's regime to carve out a share in the lucrative import–export market – an unedifying objective. Nonetheless, its action probably had the approval of most people who were suffering the consequences of the UN economic embargo.

However, whatever relief these executions provided in terms of easing of prices proved temporary. The fundamentals of the economy were highly inflationary. The foreign oil revenue earned by exporting more than 3 million bpd, which accounted for most of the public exchequer's income, had dried up since August 1990. After the War, the government earned an insignificant amount by selling the oil products derived from 305,000 bpd of crude oil to local consumers in 1991, with the figure rising to 425,000 bpd in the following year.[37] At the same time it had engaged in large-scale reconstruction to repair the extensive damage done to its economic infrastructure by the US-led Coalition bombing during the Second Gulf War. It could do so only by printing bank notes, thus fueling inflation. The rampaging inflation dramatically reduced savings, and lowered living standards.

As the largest single employer, the government could have provided relief by raising salaries of civil servants and soldiers to keep pace with inflation. But that would have fueled inflation even further. Instead, it virtually froze salaries. As a result the salaried middle class suffered most.

Adnan Abdul Razak (a pseudonym), then a journalist with the state-run Iraqi News Agency (INA) in Baghdad, recalled the early 1990s thus:

> The first two years of the sanctions were really terrible for us. We did not know how to cope as we saw our salaries turn into dust. The experience was so new and so depressing we did not know who to turn to for salvation. What underwrote our bare survival was the rationing of basic necessities which were given to us almost free by the government since early 1991.

He held out the rationing document for a family, ensuring supplies of wheat flour, rice, sugar, tea, vegetable oil, milk, salt, lentils, white beans, detergent and toilet soap. It was a large single sheet with twelve vertical rows of stamps – a stamp signifying an item – one row for each month, with a wide column to the right carrying the address and other details of the household topped by a message from President Saddam Hussein:

To the Iraqi Woman

1   When the economic life of Iraq is organized according to the program that Iraq will win the war and hope that the battle will be resolved and benefit Iraq and the [Arab] nation.
2   The rationing is the socialist solution in this difficult period.
3   Rationing is the backbone on which to build the solidarity of our social life in this difficult period.[38]

Meanwhile, repairing of the devastated infrastructure continued. Of the 134 bridges destroyed during the war the government had by now restored 120. It had boosted the oil refining capacity from 5 percent to an impressive 65 percent. However, while the Iraqis had repaired many of the 84 hospitals and 234 health centers destroyed or damaged by the bombing, they were functioning at only one-third of their capacity. This was a considerable fall for a state which during the pre-sanctions days was regarded by the World Health Organization (WHO) as a developed country for health care, with 96 percent of the urban and 78 percent of the rural population having access to free health service.[39] A ban on dual (civilian and military) use machinery meant that health authorities were unable to import spare parts or replacement materials for chemotherapy units for treating cancer.

In America, while such groups as the Harvard-based international study team for Iraq were in the forefront of publicizing their disturbing findings of the devastating impact of UN sanctions on ordinary Iraqis, top US officials were focused on overthrowing Saddam's regime, or at least destabilizing it.

Having established the Iraqi National Congress in Vienna in June 1992, with the CIA's monetary assistance, six INC leaders traveled to Washington. In their meeting with the US secretary of state, James Baker, on July 29 they drew his attention to Baghdad's campaign in the southern marshes to flush out Shia fugitives, and proposed a safe zone in the south. At the Security Council, America, Britain, France and Belgium called on Max van der Stoel, the UN Special Rapporteur on human rights in Iraq, to submit his findings on the condition in the southern marshes. China, India, Zimbabwe and Ecuador objected to the Western move, arguing that the Security Council was concerned with security and peace, and not with human rights. But their reasoning was ignored. On August 11, van der Stoel recommended dispatching monitors to the area to get proper information. Meanwhile, Edward Perkins, the US ambassador to the UN, proposed a response similar to the one that the Western powers had given earlier in northern Iraq – that is, intervention on the ground. Caught between the extremes of the stances taken by America and the group of Non-aligned Movement members, the Security Council took no decision on the subject.

On August 17, in his address to the National Republican Convention in Houston, Texas, to renominate him as its presidential candidate, George Bush warned Iraq, but refrained from specifying any particular action against it. He did so even though, following consultations with Britain and France, he had already opted for a no-fly zone in the south – a move which he could authorize immediately, which did not involve risking American lives on the ground, and which in reality was punishment for Baghdad for obstructing the missions of Unscom and the IAEA. To spike a charge by his critics of exploiting a major foreign policy decision for partisan ends, he let British Prime Minister John Major (r. 1990–97) announce the decision of the Coalition's Western powers to impose an air exclusion zone for Iraqi planes below the 32nd Parallel in order to safeguard the Shias in the marshes. The enforcement of the southern no-fly zone started on August 27. Saddam Hussein accused the Western powers of attempting to dismember Iraq and seize its oilfields, but refrained from ordering his military to attack the patrolling Western aircraft.[40] The reason was spelled out by Tariq Aziz much later: active Iraqi resistance to the new air exclusion zone would have given an opportunity for Bush to flex his military muscle and boost his electoral chances, something Iraq was loath to do.

As it was, Bush lost to Democrat Bill Clinton in the presidential poll on November 3, 1992. The defeat of his nemesis, Bush, certainly pleased Saddam who felt that now there was a chance of a fresh beginning with the new occupant of the White House who had no personal animus against him. At the same time he felt that the transitional period, from early November to January 21, 1993, provided him with an opportunity to roll back the no-fly zone in the south for which he found no rhyme or reason – an aim he tried to achieve whenever he thought the moment was right, either because the White House was in an indecisive mood or because Arab public opinion had turned pro-Iraq.

In late December Saddam began challenging the southern air exclusion zone. In response a US F–16 shot down an Iraqi MiG fighter in the zone on the 27th. The next day American aircraft chased away two intruding Iraqi MiGs. Bush's perception that Baghdad was trying to test Washington's resolve during the hand-over period to his successor three weeks later proved prescient. After deploying twenty anti-aircraft missile launchers inside the zone, on January 4–5, Baghdad transported missiles to the launchers. The next day the three Western permanent members of the Security Council demanded that Iraq remove the anti-aircraft missiles from the southern no-fly zone within two days. While making defiant statements in public, Baghdad complied on the ground.

In view of the rising tension, Iraq demanded that Unscom planes arriving from Bahrain did not use the Iraqi airspace below the 32nd Parallel and instead approach Baghdad from the west. Unscom refused to do so. On January 10 Iraq banned the arrival by air of seventy Unscom inspectors. That day about 500 Iraqis, some of them armed, entered the demilitarized zone between Iraq and Kuwait to collect military equipment which they claimed belonged to them. The UN Security Council condemned Baghdad's actions, and warned of "serious consequences."

On January 13, 114 American, British and French planes, including 30 support aircraft, hit sites near the air bases of Amara, Basra, Najaf, Samawa and Talil, in the southern no-fly zone, targeting ground-to-air sites, radar sites and telecommunications systems. They managed to hit only half of the targets, and in the process killed nineteen people.

On January 15, Iraq rescinded its ban on UN flights, but insisted that the UN airplanes enter its territory from the west and not through the southern no-fly zone. Rejecting this Iraqi condition, on January 17 the US navy fired forty-five Cruise missiles at Zafaraniya factory on the outskirts of Baghdad, claiming it to be a nuclear facility even though it had been decommissioned during the earlier four Unscom inspections. One missile hit Al Rashid Hotel in Baghdad, much favored by visiting foreign journalists, killing three civilians. Washington justified its actions on the ground that Iraq was in violation of Resolutions 687, 707 and 715. The final Western attack on Iraq came, on January 18, when seventy-five aircraft struck the targets in the southern no-fly zone that they had missed earlier, and killed twenty-one people.[41]

On the eve of the inauguration of President Clinton on January 21, Baghdad announced a unilateral ceasefire "to enable the new [US] administration to study the no-fly zones."[42] But the Clinton White House showed no sign of reciprocating, and the clashes in the air exclusion zones did not cease until four days later.

Though militarily and diplomatically the latest confrontation between Iraq and the Western powers changed nothing, Saddam gained politically at home. The Western attacks in the southern no-fly zone and outside distracted Iraqis from their daily hardship. Instead of blaming Saddam, they rallied around him in the face of renewed US bombing, and began blaming the Western powers' intransigence rather than their own government's behavior for their economic plight.

Also, the initial response of President-elect Clinton to the latest Baghdad-Washington spat indicated that the new American chief executive would not be so uncompromising toward Saddam as Bush. In a long interview with *New York Times* editors on January 12, after expressing his support for the US action "taken today [i.e., January 12, on the East Coast]," Clinton added that if he were talking directly to Saddam Hussein, he would say, "If you want a different relationship with me, you could begin by upholding the UN requirements, to change your behavior." Turning to the editors, he said, "You know I am not obsessed with the man," and added, "My job is not to pick their rulers for them [foreign countries]." Finally, he said, "I always tell everybody, 'I'm a Baptist. I believe in death-bed conversions.' If Saddam wants a different relationship with the US and the UN, all he has to do is to change his behavior."[43]

However, as his close aides immediately impressed upon him that being soft on Saddam was a liability in domestic politics, Clinton distanced himself from his statements about the Iraqi dictator. Indeed, within a few months he convincingly established his hardline policy towards him.

2

ENTER CLINTON, SADDAM'S NEW NEMESIS

The first sign of Clinton's uncompromising stance on Iraq came in March 1993 at the UN Security Council. Following the 60-day review of the UN embargo against Iraq, France, Russia and China proposed that the customary Security Council president's statement after the review should acknowledge the cooperation that Baghdad had offered so far on the UN resolutions. But Washington, backed by London, rejected this. Like Bush (his predecessor), Clinton decided against combining carrot with stick in the case of Saddam.

His administration's overall policy on Iraq – as well as Iran – was spelled out on May 18, 1993, by Martin Indyk, Special Assistant to President on Near East and South Asian Affairs, working within the NSC, in his speech to the Washington Institute for Near East Policy. In it he announced the adoption of the "Dual Containment" policy towards Iraq and Iran.

"The end of the Cold War and the elimination of the Soviet empire also eliminated a major strategic consideration from our calculus in the Gulf." he said. "We no longer have to worry that our actions would generate Soviet actions in support of our adversaries in the region." Furthermore, he continued,

> as a result of the Iran–Iraq War and the Gulf War, a regional balance of power between both countries has been established at a much lower level of military capability. This makes it easier [for us] to balance the power of both of them.

He added,

> "Dual Containment" derives from an assessment that the current Iraqi and Iranian regimes are both hostile to American interests in the region. Accordingly, we do not accept the argument that we should continue the old balance of power game, building up to balance the other ... We reject it because we do not need it ... The coalition that fought Saddam remains together. As long as we are able to maintain our military presence in the region; as long as we succeed in restricting the military ambitions of both Iraq and Iran; and as long as we can rely on our regional allies – Egypt,

Israel, Saudi Arabia and the GCC [Gulf Cooperation Council], and Turkey – to preserve the balance of power in our favor in the wider Middle East region, we will have the means to counter both the Iraqi and Iranian regimes.

Regarding Iraq in particular, Indyk said,

We seek Iraq's full compliance with all UN resolutions, including Resolution 688, which calls upon the regime to end its repression of the Iraqi people. Some have tried to portray our policy as a softening. But by now it should be clear that we seek full compliance from all current or future Iraqi regimes … Now we have decided to seek the establishment of a UN Commission to investigate the charges of war crimes and crimes against humanity in Iraq itself. Our purpose is deliberate: it is to establish clearly and unequivocally that the current regime in Iraq is a criminal regime, beyond the pale of international society and, in our judgment, irredeemable. We are also providing backing for the Iraqi National Congress as a democratic alternative to Saddam Hussein.[1]

During both his terms as president, Clinton stuck to the dual containment policy regarding Baghdad and Tehran, and took an uncompromising stance on Iraq, which included its public commitment to bring about the downfall of Saddam's regime.

His administration soon launched aerial strikes against Iraq on a basis that was less than convincing. In mid-April George Bush visited Kuwait City as a guest of the emir, Shaikh Jaber III al Sabah, who wanted to show his gratitude to the former US president for forming and leading the anti-Iraq Coalition to liberate Kuwait. Immediately after the trip, Kuwait announced the arrest of sixteen men (eleven Iraqis and five Kuwaits) – described as agents of Baghdad – for plotting to assassinate Bush during his trip to the emirate. They were produced before a judge, and their trial was set for June 5. The US state department refrained from making any statement on the grounds that the case was *sub judice*. But that changed abruptly on June 25, when the White House announced that it had received a report from Federal Bureau of Investigation (FBI) agents sent earlier to Kuwait which said that the assassination plot against Bush had been "serious," and that Iraq was behind it. Baghdad denied the charge.

The next day the US navy fired twenty-three Tomahawk missiles at the six-winged headquarters of the GID in the Mansur district of Baghdad. Three missiles went astray, resulting in the destruction of neighboring houses and the deaths of eight people, including Leila Attar, a leading Iraqi painter. At the Security Council, Madeleine Albright, the US ambassador to the UN, argued that Washington's "retaliation" was in line with Article 51 in Chapter VII of the UN Charter. That Article reads,

> Nothing in the present Charter shall impair the inherent right of individual or collective self-defense if an armed attack occurs against a Member of the United Nations, until the Security Council has taken measures necessary to maintain international peace and security.

In the absence of "an armed attack" against America by Iraq, this provision of the UN Charter simply did not apply. But none of this seemed to matter to the Clinton administration. Nor did the cooking of the evidence, to show how a car bomb had been smuggled from Iraq into Kuwait across a fortified border, presented to a Kuwait court, or the execution of four of the accused, seem to bother the US decision-makers. By the time Seymour Hersh, an eminent American investigative journalist, had debunked the Kuwaiti charges in a *New Yorker* article four months after the US bombing, it was too late. Among other things he disclosed that far from "having a unique signature linking the [car bomb detonator to be used to kill Bush] to Iraq," the pictures that the US displayed at the Security Council in June showed "mass produced items, commonly used for walkie-talkies and model airplanes ... most likely made in Taiwan or Japan or South Korea."[2]

At the same time Baghdad's relations with Unscom continued to be fraught. In June Unscom insisted on destroying all the precursor agents and chemical production equipment because Iraq had acquired these for its chemical weapons program, and the equipment was such that it could easily be converted from permitted (civilian) purposes to prohibited (military) ones. Baghdad wanted to retain the equipment for civilian purposes. It refused to let monitoring cameras be installed at the rocket test sites at Musayib (south of Falluja) and Rafah (5 km from Musayib), arguing that cameras did not fall within the purview of Resolution 687, and that it had not accepted Resolution 715 specifying long-term monitoring. However, following Ekeus's visit to Baghdad in mid-July, Iraq relented on both issues, but refused to have the cameras activated. It was not until late September that it finally gave ground on that point.

By then Unscom's focus had shifted to the list of companies which had assisted Iraq in pursuing its chemical and nuclear weapons programs. Fearing (rightly, as later events would show) that the list would end up with the CIA, Baghdad refused, insisting that Unscom must keep the list under wraps. Also, it wanted to barter the much-sought-after document for the lifting of the oil embargo. Ekeus refused, saying that the earliest he could recommend that would be in June 1994 after he had had the monitoring system working for at least six months. However, it was only after Unscom and the IAEA had signed a letter saying they would keep the list secret and use it only "for technical end" that Iraq submitted it. Baghdad also permitted Unscom to use its reconnaissance planes equipped with new surveillance gear such as sensors all over the Iraqi territory to record new construction as a means of monitoring Iraq's future weapons projects.

It was against this backdrop that, on October 15, Ekeus informed the Security Council that substantial progress had been made in getting Iraq to provide information about its programs for producing long-range missiles and chemical and biological weapons, and most of the demands on the nuclear weapons program had been met. However, he added, the data provided by Baghdad had to be verified before firm conclusions could be drawn. While the monitoring cameras at the missile test sites had been turned on, the larger issue of the long-term monitoring remained unsettled because of Iraq's continued rejection of Resolution 715.[3]

Playing on Unscom's keenness to see Resolution 715 accepted, Iraq tried to trade its acceptance for a guarantee that the petroleum embargo would be ended as soon as all the monitoring equipment had been installed and activated – as stated in Paragraphs 21 and 22 of Resolution 687, with the earlier paragraph referring to "easing" of the sanctions. But it failed. So, on November 26, 1993, it unconditionally accepted long-term monitoring as specified in Resolution 715, and set up its own National Monitoring Directorate (NMD) under Gen. Hossam Amin to liaise with Unscom's monitoring and verification department. Noting Ekeus's repeated assertions that he would test Iraq's compliance with the monitoring scheme for six months before concluding that Unscom's mission had been accomplished, thus paving the way for the lifting of the oil embargo by the Security Council, Iraq concluded that America would not allow relaxation of the sanctions under any circumstances.

Impact of sanctions

Already Washington had taken to insisting that Iraq must accept Security Council Resolution 833 on its boundary with Kuwait and the right to international access, adopted unanimously on May 27, 1993. The frontier had been delineated by a 5-member UN Iraq–Kuwait Boundary Demarcation Commission, as required by Resolution 687, and was based on "the Agreed Minutes" of a high-level meeting between the two neighbors in 1963. The Commission allocated the port of Umm al Qasr, and the waters of Khawr al Zubair on which it stands, to Iraq, and handed over part of Iraq's naval yard and some oil wells along the border to Kuwait. The net effect of this delineation was to reduce further the already insignificant length of the Gulf coastline that Iraq possessed, a fact likely to rankle in Iraqi minds of all political persuasions.

There was, of course, no question of Iraq being allowed to use Umm al Qasr, its only port, for commercial purposes. Since August 1990 the US navy had been in the forefront of an international naval force to maintain a maritime blockade of Iraq. During the first three years it had intercepted 18,000 ships in the Gulf, boarded 800 and turned away 430, of which only 20 were allegedly carrying prohibited cargo.[4] Overland the only legitimate outlet Iraq had was with Jordan. The UN 661 Sanctions Committee allowed Baghdad to supply 50,000 bpd of crude and 25,000 bpd of fuel oil to Jordan, half of it free and the rest at a discount. (Because of Jordan's refusal to join the anti-Iraq Coalition in 1991, the Gulf monarchies had stopped their financial or material aid to it, thus making it totally dependent on Iraq for its oil imports.) These exports earned Iraq $396 million in 1990, $267 million in 1991 and $428 million in 1992 – all of these sums being used to buy food and medicine.[5]

Three years of stringent economic sanctions brought about profound changes in Iraqi society, giving rise to new classes and their co-option into the political system. The main beneficiaries of the embargo were the smugglers, licensed importers and large landowners. By contrast, hyperinflation transformed the substantial middle class, earning salaries that had only doubled, into the new poor. A senior civil servant's average monthly salary of ID 300, worth $960 before the war, was now worth a mere $5. During that period flour prices had risen fiftyfold. Before the August 1990 economic sanctions, US$1 was worth ID 0.31; now it was worth ID 60, a nearly 200-fold depreciation. Though illegal, currency trading by individuals was tolerated by the government. At 1980 prices, the national Gross Domestic Product (GDP) fell from $54 billion in 1979 (when the population was 13 million) to $10 billion in 1993 for a population of 19 million, or one-thirteenth of the 1979 figure.[6]

The case of "Farida," a freelance journalist, epitomized the drastic fall in living standards. Before the Second Gulf War, as a ministry of information employee, she earned ID 100 ($310) a month. Her expenses were ID 80, with half the sum spent on rent. She had a car and a maid. After the War, she worked at a daily newspaper and a weekly magazine, and was also a television news producer. Her total monthly income was ID 35,000 a month, and her expenses: ID 100,000. The deficit of ID 65,000 ($33) was met by remittances from abroad. Her car and maid were gone. Like her, middle-class professionals survived by doing two or three jobs a day, with engineers deploying their cars as taxis after work, and hospital doctors seeing patients at home, and by using up their savings which had lost most of their value due to high inflation. Education suffered. As Nuha al Radi noted in her diary,

> Loma [a friend] was telling me about her university classes; she teaches computer studies. She has sixty students. They have no paper and no pencils. They write on the back of receipts, pharmacy bills, account books, anything that has a blank side to it. The university does not supply her with paper to photocopy the exams, so she has to write the exam on the blackboard; those at the back cannot see it, so when the ones in front have copied the questions, those at the back move to the front. There are only ten working computers, so they take turns on the machines.[7]

Unemployment soared in 1992 when the government officially demobbed 600,000 soldiers to reduce its soaring budget deficit, but there were no jobs for them in the economy – the only exception being reconstruction projects which required mostly unskilled workers. Small wonder that petty crime soared, with cars disappearing from parking lots for cannibalization for parts. Responding to the growing pauperization of the populace, and the dangerously wide gap between the few rich and the many poor, the authorities banned the sale of alcohol at private eateries owned by Muslims, thereby also highlighting its increasingly Islamic leanings and thus reflecting the growing piety among the suffering populace which sought refuge in religion.

Most smugglers were petty bourgeoisie with blood ties to influential village clans in central and southern Iraq, both Shia and Sunni. They were active along the borders with Iran, Turkey and Syria where controls were lax – exporting Iraqi oil and oil products and importing food and essential consumer goods. There was also a new category of middlemen, those who were licensed by the government to purchase UN-approved flour, rice, tea, cooking oil, baby food, etc. in Jordan, and then sell these to the authorities with high mark-ups. They and the smugglers became enthusiastic backers of the Baathist regime.

The official drive for self-sufficiency in food gave a financial and political boost to the fortunes of landlords with large holdings. Besides providing subsidized fertilizer and free diesel for farm machinery, the government paid high prices for foodgrains – up from ID 180 for a ton of wheat before the war to ID 5000. Additionally, it raised their social and official status by restoring the administrative and financial powers they enjoyed before the 1968 Baathist coup. Little wonder that within a couple of years annual wheat production rose by 50 percent to 1.5 million tons, allowing the authorities to raise the initial monthly per capita ration from 6 kg (13.2 lb) to 9 kg (19.8 lb).[8] Little wonder, too, that state-run Iraqi television took to showing tribal leaders singing and dancing the national *dabka* dance, and heaping praise on Saddam Hussein.

Emerging division at the Security Council

At the UN Security Council, also, the situation improved marginally for Baghdad. Following its acceptance, albeit grudgingly, of Resolution 715 concerning long-term monitoring in November 1993, a division developed among the Permanent Five (P5) members of the Council, all of them holding veto power – with the uncompromisingly hardline Anglo-Saxon US–UK axis on one side and the non-Anglo-Saxon China, France and Russia on the other. At the Council's closed door meeting on March 18, 1994, to conduct the sixty-day review of UN sanctions, the non-Anglo-Saxon bloc proposed that a paragraph be added to the customary presidential statement commending Iraq for moving towards meeting UN terms on disarmament. Speaking for the motion, the French ambassador pointed out that Resolution 687 had linked the lifting of the oil embargo to Iraq's compliance on arms-related matters. Opposing the motion, US ambassador Albright repeated her government's position that all Security Council resolutions on Iraq must be viewed in totality, including the ones on the border with Kuwait (833) and human rights (688). When the P5 failed to reach an agreement, it was decided not to issue any presidential statement at all, thus discontinuing a practice that had become established ever since sanctions were imposed on Iraq in August 1990.

China, regarding itself as the only (unofficial) representative of the Third World on the Security Council, had all along taken a moderate line towards Iraq. It had abstained on Resolution 678 (November 1990) which authorized UN member-states use to "all necessary means" to expel Iraq from Kuwait. Because of its threat to veto a Western-sponsored resolution regarding Baghdad's oppression of Kurds if it were put under Chapter VII of the UN Charter, the Western powers refrained from doing so. China then abstained on Resolution 688 as well.

Beijing had a pressing economic reason too: oil. With industrialization gaining unprecedented momentum in China, the country became a net importer of oil in 1993. Its modest imports of 25,000 bpd in 1993 would rise eighteenfold during the next three years.[9] This turned Beijing's attention increasingly to petroleum-bearing countries. Iraq with its proven reserves of 100 billion barrels, the second largest in the world, was high on the agenda of Chinese diplomacy. The China National Petroleum Corporation (CNPC) began courting the Iraqi oil ministry for development contracts in the future.

France's close economic and military links with Iraq dated back to the 1970s. During the Iran–Iraq War it openly backed Baghdad, arguing that its defeat would lead to the spread of Islamic fundamentalism in the region which would hurt Western interests. It was the French corporations that were building two nuclear reactors near Baghdad which were bombed by Israel in June 1981. By 1983 about 1,000 French companies were active in Iraq, and 6–7,000 French specialists were based there. As much as 40 percent of total French military exports were destined for Iraq. Military cooperation between the two states had developed to the extent that the French government decided to lease to Baghdad five Super-Etendard warplanes originally meant for use by the French air force. This raised the more immediate lucrative prospect of selling scores of expensive Exocet missiles to Iraq to be used by Super-Etendards to hit Iranian oil tankers in the Gulf. These missiles proved devastatingly effective. France also sold Iraq Mirage supersonic fighter aircraft.[10] Little wonder that from 1970 to 1989 France was the second largest supplier of military hardware (after the Soviet Union) to Baghdad, with contracts worth $6 billion. With civilian and military contracts worth FF 130–150 billion (i.e., $22–25 billion) between 1973 and 1989, France became Iraq's third largest trading partner. Now Baghdad owed Paris $4.5 billion in unpaid bills.[11] Elf Aquitaine and Total Société Anonyme (SA), the leading French oil companies, interested in developing richly-endowed Majnoon and Nahr Omar oilfields in southern Iraq, had signed contracts which would become operative once the UN sanctions ended.

Friendship between Moscow and Baghdad dated back to 1959 – soon after the republican military coup against the pro-Western monarchy in Iraq. The close links that developed covered military, diplomacy, industry and education. Over the years almost all of Iraq's military imports had come from the Soviet Union. In 1972 the two countries signed a twenty-year Friendship and Cooperation Treaty, agreeing to "develop cooperation in the strengthening of their defense capacity." [12] Except for the first two years in the 1980–88 Iran–Iraq War (in protest at Baghdad's aggression against Tehran), Moscow shipped weapons to the Saddam regime. Soviet petroleum experts enabled Iraq to develop its industry to the extent that Baghdad ended its reliance on Western oil companies. It became the first Arab country to nationalize a Western-owned oil corporation, Iraq Petroleum Company, in 1972. Cooperation in education translated into Iraq sending its students to Soviet universities for professional degrees. That is how Iraq built up a small corps of Soviet-trained doctors and engineers, all fluent in Russian.

Russia inherited the Soviet legacy of close and multifarious ties with Iraq, including an estimated $8 billion that Baghdad owed to Moscow. With the Russian economy going into a tailspin following the collapse of the Soviet Union, these billions of dollars acquired more importance than before. Moscow therefore had a vested interest to see that the oil embargo on Iraq was lifted so that it could start repaying its Russian debts. In October 1994 Iraq's oil minister was in Moscow to negotiate contracts with Russian petroleum companies to rebuild the Iraqi oil industry once the UN sanctions ended.

The Russian petroleum giant, Lukoil, was interested in exploiting Western Qurna and North Rumeila oilfields in the south. Diplomatically, Russia was eager to have an ally in the strategic Gulf region, which contains more than two-thirds of the world's proven petroleum reserves.

So the Chinese–French–Russian axis that had emerged at the Security Council was underpinned by economic interest as well as ideological and strategic considerations.

In the coming months, as the divide between the Anglo-Saxon duo and the non-Anglo-Saxon trio became sharper, the Anglo-Saxons would accuse their detractors of being guided solely by the prospect of picking up lucrative contracts in Iraq. In return their rivals would refer to the indecent haste with which American and British companies had signed massive contracts for weapons and infrastructure projects in Kuwait and Saudi Arabia after the Second Gulf War. They would argue that the staunch opposition by Washington and London to easing sanctions on Baghdad had more to do with the Kuwaiti and Saudi ability to pay for the huge arms and other deals they had contracted with US and British corporations than with the provisions of the Security Council Resolutions, since the re-entry of Iraqi petroleum into the world market would depress the price and reduce the oil revenues of Kuwait and Saudi Arabia.

In an article in the *New York Times* of April 29, 1994, the US secretary of state, Warren Christopher, said, "The US does not believe that Iraq's compliance with Paragraph 22 of Resolution 687 is enough to justify lifting the embargo." This flew in the face of the text, which reads,

> [The Security Council] Decides that upon the approval by the Council of the program called for in Paragraph 19 above and upon Council agreement that Iraq has completed all actions contemplated in

Paragraphs 8, 9, 10, 11, 12, and 13 above, the prohibitions against the import of commodities and products originating in Iraq and the prohibitions against financial transactions related thereto contained in Resolution 661 [1990] shall have no further force or effect.[13]

Christopher's statement set the scene for lasting animosity between Washington and Baghdad, which had expected at least some relaxation after it had accepted Resolution 715 on long-term monitoring in late 1993.

During the sixty-day Security Council review of the embargo in mid-May 1994, Tariq Aziz pleaded for relaxation, but to no avail. Instead, at Washington's behest, the Council urged Iraq to accept Resolution 833 on the Iraqi–Kuwaiti borders. And Unscom chief Ekeus said that there should be a period of six months or more to see how monitoring was working before he could give the final verdict. By now Unscom and the IAEA had moved their offices from the Ishtar (Sheraton) Hotel on Abu Nuwas Street to Canal Hotel[14] in the eastern district of 7th Nisan (old name Baladiyat), after leasing the property from the Iraqi government, installing a tall transmission tower and a vast satellite dish, and equipping it with the latest in counter-surveillance technology that American and British intelligence agencies could provide. It also became the home of the UN's Baghdad Monitoring and Verification Center (BMVC).

Bearing in mind Ekeus's timetable, Saddam concluded, realistically, that the status quo would prevail at least until early 1995. The news from the UN had a debilitating effect on the Iraqi Dinar whose value fell precipitately to ID 2,000 to $1. The calamitous fall in the value of Iraqi Dinar was illustrated by Nuha al Radi, in her diary thus: "Dinner at the Hatra Hotel; nouvelle cuisine – five bits of very charcoaled meat, three slices of tomato and three small triangles of bread for 4,000 Dinars. My Toyota Corona cost that much in 1981."[15]

Saddam, the supremo

In May 1994, Saddam sacked Prime Minister Ahmad Hussein Khodayir, who had been in the job for only about a year, on the grounds that he had failed to stabilize the Iraqi Dinar, and took over the post himself. Saddam's grip over power was now total. He was not only the republic's executive president and commander-in-chief, but also its prime minister, not to mention his two other positions: chairman of the Revolutionary Command Council, the highest state authority, and secretary-general of the ruling Baath Party.

It was also in 1994 that he unveiled the rebuilt television tower in the Mansur district of Baghdad, which had been demolished by the American missiles three years earlier, now renamed Saddam International (Challenge) Tower, making sure that, at 112 meters, the newer version was 12 meters higher than the original. It was topped by a two-level, rotating restaurants, called Babil (i.e., Babylon). The ground level enclosure of the Tower was dominated by a full-length statue of Saddam Hussein, in military uniform, carrying a revolver, his right arm outstretched. Around the bottom of the pedestal were scattered various parts of the US missiles, like the limbs of a carcass. The English text on the pedestal read:

> This high standing monument of President Saddam Hussein was made exclusively from the remains of the aggressive American missiles which aimed this situation on 17th January 1991 during the grand immortal Battle of Umm al Marik [Mother of All Battles] as the Iraqi challenge against American imperialism.[16]

An aerial view of Baghdad through the glass walls of Babil Restaurant especially at night brought home the dictatorial nature of the regime and its penchant for the personality cult of The Leader (*al Qaid*) and for monumental public buildings. To the east along the winding Tigris could be seen the twelve bridges – four of them constructed during the First Gulf War, and one after the Second Gulf War, popularly called the Double Decker Bridge (1995), an impressive achievement, which – built with deficit financing – played its part in fueling hyper-inflation. To the south-east at the bottom of the U-bend in the Tigris stood the eighteen-story Baghdad University building. In the near distance to the east were the Festival and Parade Ground, where huge parades were held on Army Day (January 5) and other state occasions, and the modernistic Monument of the Unknown Soldier, lit up in the three colors of the national flag – green, white and red. Beyond these public buildings, hugging the left bank of the Tigris, was the very private Republican Presidential Palace in Tashri which, along with several other presidential palace complexes, became the center of a deep crisis between Unscom and Iraq in early 1998. To the north was the Baghdad Clock Tower, sprouting out of the Museum of the Leader, displaying every detail of Saddam's life.

At the entrance to the Saddam International Tower, a sign (in English) informed the visitor that photography was strictly banned, and so the visitor was required to leave his or her camera behind with the sentry. Yet at night when Babil Restaurant was busy, in contrast to its deserted appearance during the day – and I had a meal there with an Asian ambassador– there was an official photographer who went around the tables, flashing his camera without even saying "Excuse me." Undoubtedly, his pictures were meant for the files of the General Security.[17]

A visit to the Saddam International Tower and Babil Restaurant and a view of the capital from there aptly summed up the megalomaniac and paranoid nature of The Leader-President and his ruthless regime.

On the ground, the signs of the personality cult were everywhere. To see five pre-eminent, yet different images of Saddam Hussein – statues, and stenciled and hand-painted portraits – within the first five minutes of a taxi ride in Baghdad on arrival from Amman was an experience likely to linger in the mind of even the most widely traveled journalist or commentator. On the eighth floor of the ministry of information, where officials dealt with foreign journalists, I counted seven larger-than-life color prints of The Leader-President – often dressed in traditional Arab dress, engrossed in a book against the background of a shelf of weighty volumes – decorating the external walls of various offices from top to bottom. During the journey from Baghdad to Karbala, Najaf and Babylon, no square in even the smallest village was complete without a portrait of Saddam Hussein, dressed variously. At each of the three holy sites in Karbala and Najaf – the tombs of Imams Ali, Hussein and Abbas – the image of Saddam at prayer had been built into the outside wall of the inner sanctum of the shrine, reconstructed after the post-Gulf War uprisings.[18]

One of Saddam's early decrees as prime minister, issued in June 1994, concerned punishment for thieving and robbery: the first-time offender for stealing will have his right hand amputated, and the second-time offender his feet, and the use of firearms during theft or robbery will result in capital punishment for the culprit. However, a few months later Saddam substituted cutting off ears for amputation of hands and feet after war veterans with missing limbs complained to him that they were being mistaken for common criminals.[19]

In this gloomy, depressive socio-economic environment, what brought some solace to the Baghdad government was that an internecine war had erupted among the Kurds in May 1994, and that at the UN Security Council differences between the Anglo-Saxon duo and the non-Anglo-Saxon trio on Iraq were sharpening.

On the eve of the sanctions review by the Security Council on July 20, President Clinton addressed letters to all Council members stressing that his administration gave "high priority" to maintaining the UN embargo against Iraq. The Council meeting ended without any consensus on the issue. So Russia and America issued separate statements.

Calling on the Council to note Ekeus's statement that notable progress had been made on identifying and eliminating weapons of mass destruction and installing a comprehensive monitoring system, and pointing out that Unscom would be ready to start its long-term monitoring system in September the Russian ambassador, Yuli Voronstov, proposed that the Council should now set a deadline after which it would consider lifting the oil embargo if satisfied with the progress on monitoring and verification. At the same time he urged Iraq to accept Resolution 833 on the border with Kuwait, and provide information about 623 missing Kuwaiti nationals.

In contrast to Voronstov's balanced stance, US Ambassador Albright dwelt exclusively on what Baghdad had not done or done insufficiently. Iraq, she said, had only minimally complied with Security Council requirements on weapons of mass destruction, and defied virtually all other requirements. She added that the monitoring program was not yet in place and that it would require rigorous testing. She demanded Iraqi compliance on the recognition of Kuwait's borders, cessation of terrorism at home and abroad, termination of the economic warfare against the Kurdish region, an end to repression in the southern marshes, and information on the fate of missing Kuwaiti nationals.

Among those who pointed out that the US had changed the rules unilaterally was the *New York Times*. It was on firm ground. The pertinent Paragraph 21 of Resolution 687 of 3 April 1991 states:

> [T]he Council shall review the provisions of Paragraph 20 above every sixty days in the light of the policies and practices of the Government of Iraq, including the implementation of all relevant resolutions of the Security Council, for the purposes of determining whether to reduce or lift the prohibitions referred to therein.

Clearly, the phrase "all relevant resolutions" applied to the ones that had been passed on or before April 3, 1991. But what Albright had done was to invoke also the Council resolutions passed *after* that date.

During the next sanctions review by the Security Council on September 18, Tariq Aziz attempted to get the Council's agreement to link Iraq's acceptance of Resolution 833 and the ending of the oil embargo. He failed. Once more Albright stressed Baghdad's failings, saying that there were gaps in its account of chemical precursors, problems with the missile count, and inconsistencies in the nuclear accounting. After the meeting the Council's president (Spain) said that since Ekeus had not yet submitted his final verdict there would be no change in the sanctions regime.

The focus now turned on Ekeus's report to be debated by the Security Council on October 10. An indication of which way his conclusions were leaning came from Unscom's field officer in Baghdad, Jaako Ylitalo. "Our Commission is convinced it [Iraqi disarmament] is all over," he said. "It is watertight."[20] However, it seems, Ekeus shied away from giving a clean bill of health to Iraq when he encountered an uncompromisingly anti-Baghdad stance by Washington and London. He reportedly said this to the Iraqis during his visit to Baghdad in early October.

It was then that Saddam probably decided to highlight his demand for easing of sanctions by creating a crisis. His government said that it would "reconsider" its attitude to Unscom if Ekeus went along with Washington's plan to block any easing of sanctions. More seriously, on the night of October 7–8, it dispatched two Republican Guard divisions to southern Iraq, with their advance units about 20 miles (32 km) from the buffer zone with Kuwait, and called on the Security Council to fix a date for lifting the embargo at its October 10 meeting.

Among other things Saddam's moves embarrassed Russia, which regarded them as counter-productive. And so they proved to be. At the Security Council, America proposed that the UN should demarcate a ground exclusion zone in southern Iraq, but encountered opposition from Russia, France and China. The non-Anglo-Saxon trio also opposed military action against Iraq. The Russian foreign minister, Andrei Kozyrev, intervened, and struck a deal with Saddam Hussein on October 13: if Iraq agreed to accept Resolution 833 regarding the border with Kuwait then Moscow would do its best to get the sanctions lifted within six months – that is, by April 1995.

Meanwhile, Washington raised the estimate of the Iraqi troops in the south to about 80,000 – two Republican Guard divisions and 50,000 regular soldiers – and claimed that the advance units of the Iraqi armed forces were only 12 miles (20 km) from the Kuwaiti border. However, the UN Iraq–Kuwait Observation Mission (Unikom) personnel, posted in the demilitarized zone – 3 miles (5 km) into Kuwait and 6 miles (10 km) into Iraq – saw no indication of a military build-up by Baghdad.[21] Equally exaggerated was the Pentagon's claim that it had bolstered the US military presence in Kuwait to 50,000, a step which French officials – questioning the accuracy of the Pentagon's intelligence on Iraqi troop movement – described as an over-reaction.[22]

At the Security Council, a stiff resolution drafted by America and Britain was being circulated among the members. Russia succeeded in getting it moderated. The resulting Resolution 949, passed unanimously by the Council on October 15 under Chapter VII of the UN Charter, coupled its demand for Iraq to return (and maintain) its troops at the pre-crisis positions with its approval for diplomatic efforts to normalize Baghdad's relations with the UN. On October 16, the US confirmed that the newly dispatched Iraqi forces were withdrawing from southern Iraq. The next day Kozyrev urged the Council that it should end the petroleum embargo within six months of Baghdad recognizing Kuwait within its UN-demarcated boundaries.

Kuwait insisted that Iraq's written recognition must be deposited with the UN and that it must put its signature to the UN map. Later Kuwait and America demanded that the acceptance of Resolution 833 – demanding the recognition of the State of Kuwait, its territorial integrity and political independence – be endorsed by the Iraqi National Assembly, then ratified by the RCC in a decree signed by Saddam Hussein, and published in the official gazette. Iraq met the last three conditions on November 10, 1994. And three days later Tariq Aziz personally handed over the documents to the president of the Security Council, who that month happened to be none other than Albright of the United States. None of this pacified her. Indeed, doggedly pursuing Washington's strategy of always showing Iraq in the wrong, during the Council debate on November 14 she said that Baghdad had not revealed full details of its biological weapons program.[23]

In the end, Iraq lost on both fronts. It did not get an all-clear certificate from Ekeus. And it failed to exchange its acceptance of Resolution 833 for an end to the petroleum embargo. Its resort to troop movement silenced the waverers among US policy-makers who had earlier expressed qualms about the administration constantly moving goal posts to deprive Baghdad of its entitlement under Paragraph 22 of Resolution 687, and strengthened the hands of the hawks who, insisting that Iraq must prove its "peaceful intentions" toward its neighbors, argued that this would be possible only when Saddam had been overthrown. On the other hand, for the first time Baghdad won Moscow's public commitment to push for the lifting of the oil embargo by the next spring.

Intra-Kurdish violence and Iraqi opposition

By late 1994 the intra-Kurdish violence, which had erupted in May and buoyed Baghdad, had come to a virtual end, but only after damaging the cause of Kurdish nationalism and Washington's plans to topple Saddam.

Fighting between the KDP and the PUK erupted on May 1, as a result of a dispute between a pro-KDP landlord and his pro-PUK peasants. Before a temporary ceasefire came into effect a week later, more than 1,000 people were dead, and the PUK had stormed the parliament building in Irbil and ransacked the government treasury. The event marked the end of the two-year-long coalition between the KDP and the PUK following parliamentary elections in May 1992.

Power-sharing between the two parties, carried to extremes, was applied even to policemen on the beat and teachers, with a KDP-appointee balancing a PUK-nominee. In the ministries two different command structures developed, and the administration became paralyzed. And the fact that both Masud Barzani (leader of the KDP) and Jalal Talabani (the PUK chief) agreed to stay out of the government meant that real power existed outside the ministries.

Also, power-sharing required each party to let the other operate in its traditional strongholds. So the PUK began functioning in the KDP-controlled north-western province of Zakho. And the KDP set up offices in the PUK bastion of the south-eastern Suleimaniya province. Each tried to build up its strength at the expense of the other. The resulting tension reached an intolerable point, leading to the resignation of the PUK premier, Fuad Masoum (balanced by the KDP speaker of parliament), in December 1993.

The differences between the KDP and the PUK were deep and rooted in history. The KDP was formed by Masud Barzani's father, Mustafa, a tribal chief, as a nationalist organization in 1945. The PUK was established thirty years later by Talabani as a Marxist–Leninist organization. Talabani, who had started out as a KDP activist, accused Mustafa Barzani of tribalism and cooperation with American imperialism. Over time, however, the PUK started drifting rightwards. After the Second Gulf War, while Barzani maintained clandestine contacts with Saddam, and with Iran and Turkey as well, Talabani did not do so. He continued to aid the leftist-secularist Kurdistan Democratic Party of Iran (KDPI), thus upsetting Tehran. As a predominantly urban party, the PUK was antipathetic toward the KDP's continuing tribal ways. The use of different dialects – Kermanji in the north and Sourani in the south – was another critical factor setting the parties apart.[24]

Besides the military and financial support of the West that fostered cooperation between the KDP and the PUK in 1992, the two camps shared an expectation that their arch-enemy, Saddam, would fall soon. But defying most predictions, he continued to wield supreme power in Baghdad. This frustrated many Kurds who had felt earlier that their successful experiment in democracy would encourage an anti-Saddam sentiment among ethnic Arabs and hasten his fall.

Now the internecine bloodletting in Kurdistan provided propaganda victory to Saddam. It also reinforced the case of those inside the Gulf region and outside that if, in the face of their mortal enemy in power in Baghdad, the nationalist Kurds could not close ranks, there was no chance of them doing so once he was gone, and that such a scenario would lead to a break-up of Iraq and create more problems than it solved.

The intra-Kurdish violence embarrassed America – all the more so since the CIA had been pursuing the strategy of turning Kurdistan into a staging-post to topple Saddam through its brain-child, the Iraqi National Congress. Based at Salahuddin, 20 miles (32 km) north of Irbil since October 1992, and funded by the CIA, the INC had been beaming propaganda radio broadcasts into the government-administered Iraq, gathering intelligence from Iraqi military deserters whose number had risen due to the drying-up of the southern marshes – a traditional safe haven – and building up its own army. In May 1994, following the outbreak of intra-Kurdish violence, it succeeded in brokering a truce and inserting its soldiers between the warring factions. However, it was not until September that the fighting stopped, and not until late November that the two sides signed a fourteen-point peace plan. They agreed to reconstitute the regional government on a 50:50 basis, and co-opt smaller groups. The result was a cabinet with five ministers each from the KDP and the PUK, and one each from Islamists, Socialists, Communists, the Turkoman Front and the Assyrian Democratic Party.

In December 1994 the plans of the CIA – now represented in Salahuddin by a team of five senior operatives – to overthrow Saddam received a boost when Wafiq Jassim al Samarrai, former head of the Iraqi Military Intelligence, defected to the opposition. He was by far the most important intelligence official to change sides, and he did so because he feared for his life. In the mid-1980s, during the Iran–Iraq War, when he was deputy head of Military Intelligence, Saddam had selected him as one of the three officials to liaise directly with the CIA to seek highly sensitive information on Iran. After the Second Gulf War, as head of Military Intelligence, it was his task to escort the Kurdish leaders when they negotiated with the central government in Baghdad in the spring of 1991. That is when he reportedly forged secret links with the Kurdish nationalists, who later claimed that they had put him on their payroll.[25] This sort of double-dealing was extremely risky as al Samarrai would have known that he was under surveillance by the Special Security. So when he was forced into semi-retirement in early 1992 and given a humdrum job at the presidential palace, he would have sensed that something had gone seriously wrong and that he would have to flee sooner rather than later to save his life. Now, in the safety of Iraqi Kurdistan, whether he knew it or not, he fitted the scenario perfectly for those US officials who advocated a military coup in Iraq.

However, at the policy-making level in Washington the debate between those who favored a war of liberation and those who recommended a military putsch remained unresolved. At the operational level, though, the CIA executive, Frank

Anderson, conciliated the competing strategies by subterfuge. While professing to be dealing with the INC as the sole representative of the Iraqi opposition, he maintained secret contacts with the INA (consisting chiefly of defectors from the Iraqi military or Baath Party), nominally one of the nineteen INC affiliates, which had its own base in Salahuddin.

Little wonder that by late 1993 a cat-and-mouse game had ensued in Salahuddin, with the INC and the INA spying on each other, fueled by INC leader Chalabi's pathological suspicion of anybody with a Baathist background; and both of them in turn being spied on by the KDP and the PUK. With the INC employing 5–6,000 Kurds and Iraqi Arabs as soldiers and civil servants by 1994, there was much to watch and hear on the various sides of this intricate CIA-funded conglomerate. Also active were the intelligence agents of not only the Baghdad government but Turkey, Iran and Syria as well.

Following al Samarrai's defection, pressure mounted from high up in Washington to move against the Iraqi dictator and replace him with a small committee of generals, including al Samarrai. Setting aside his suspicion of all former Baathist officers and civilians, Chalabi worked closely with al Samarrai. Together they came up with a plan which on paper combined the basic elements of a popular uprising and a military coup. It visualized suborning the commanders of the Iraqi military units in nearby Mosul and Kirkuk, and infiltrating these cities with INC partisans with the aim of triggering a popular insurrection as well as large-scale Iraqi troop desertions following attacks on Baghdad's forces by INC soldiers and Kurdish *peshmargas*. As Saddam Hussein focused on countering the INC threat in the north, he would be exposed to the machinations of the Baghdad-based army commanders in touch with al Samarrai. They would storm the barracks where Saddam had a residence. Thus a combination of a popular revolt and a military coup would end the bloody Saddam era, and usher in a peace-loving, democratic regime.

While this plan was being forged by Chalabi and al Samarrai in close collaboration with the five-man CIA team in Salahuddin, in January 1995 Anderson deputed a veteran operative with field experience in Afghanistan to Salahuddin, with a brief to aid a highly classified INA project, masterminded by General Adnan Nouri, a former Republican Guard officer, for a clean military putsch, the planning for which had started three months earlier.[26] But in the hothouse of Salahuddin there were very few real secrets. Chalabi was aware of the rival INA plan, and part of the reason why he, bereft of any military or intelligence training or experience, cooperated actively with al Samarrai was the latter's military rank and experience, which also impressed the CIA. So Chalabi and al Samarrai rushed their plan to beat the INA. Their D-day was March 4, 1995. Going by what they heard from the CIA team in Salahuddin, all participants believed that they had the backing of Washington in everything they did, including their planned offensive against the Iraqi army in which the armed forces of the INC, KDP and PUK were to participate.

As soon as General Adnan Nouri of the INA got wind of the final INC plan, he rushed to Washington. In meetings with his CIA handlers on March 1 and 2, he convinced them that a frontal attack by the INC and its Kurdish allies on the Iraqi troops in the north would result in a massive counter-offensive by Saddam Hussein, which would put the US in an awkward situation. If it did nothing, Saddam's troops would prevail, defeating the rebel forces. And if it decided to intervene, it would have to do so on a large scale, possibly committing its ground forces. Since the American policy-makers had no intention of getting embroiled in a unilateral war with Iraq, the US National Security Adviser, Tony Lake, after consulting the state and defense departments and the CIA, decided to withdraw Washington's support for the Chalabi–al Samarrai plan. The cable received by the seniormost CIA operative in Salahuddin on March 3, said in effect that the US would not support this operation militarily or in any other way.[27] What also turned Tony Lake and the US National Security Council against this project was the attempt of al Samarrai to incorporate his plot to assassinate Saddam (during the Iraqi leader's forthcoming visit to Samarra, the home base of al Samarrai) into the overall Chalabi– al Samarrai plan which would have violated a US presidential executive order dating back to the presidency of Gerald Ford (r. 1974–76), explicitly banning Washington's involvement in assassinating foreign leaders.[28] Immediately, the KDP pulled out of the project.

Despite this, on the D-day the INC and PUK forces attacked Iraqi troops. They had some success. But the predicted popular uprisings in Mosul and Kirkuk failed to materialize. Nor were there any mass desertions from the Iraqi ranks, or any moves by the military commanders supposedly in cahoots with al Samarrai in the Baghdad area. What is more, finding PUK fighters busy on the Iraqi front, the KDP's Barzani tried to recover the territory he had lost earlier to the PUK, especially Irbil, which had fallen to the PUK in December 1994. This exacerbated the already tense relations between the two sides. And the discredited al Samarrai soon left Kurdistan for Damascus.

But that did not stop Washington from putting out exaggerated reports of fighting between Baghdad's troops and the INC–PUK forces along the *de facto* border between Kurdistan and the government-controlled Iraq, purportedly based on its satellite pictures. This was a ploy to show that Saddam was on his way out. Also, much prominence was given in the Western media to al Samarrai's claim that Saddam was hiding 10 Scuds and 200 anthrax bombs in the Tikrit area.

Unscom and Iraq's biological weapons program

During his visit to Baghdad in early March, Ekeus pointed out to the Iraqis that they had not accounted for 17 out of the 39 tons of growth media – used for growing bacteria and viruses – for their biological warfare program, purchased in 1988–89. The latter explained that the material was bought for medical purposes, and that the records pertaining to the deficit of 17 tons had gone up in flames during the anti-regime insurgency that followed the 1991 Gulf War.

All this was part of a preamble to the March 13, 1995 Security Council review of the UN sanctions. With Unscom and IAEA inspections and the related destruction of the WMD materials and facilities virtually finished, and the six-month trial period of long-term monitoring nearing its end in April, opinion among the Council members was shifting towards lifting the oil embargo on Baghdad. Also, by now, the united anti-Iraq front that Riyadh had forged in the Arab Gulf, had broken down, with Qatar, Oman and the UAE calling for an easing of sanctions against Baghdad to alleviate the suffering of the Iraqi people. To consolidate its position at the Security Council, the Iraqi government sent Tariq Aziz to New York in early March to lobby its members. He had bilateral meetings with the ambassadors of all the member-states, except America and Britain.

On the other side, instructed by President Clinton, Albright had earlier under-taken a tour of six Council member-states – Britain, Italy, the Czech Republic, Oman, Argentina and Honduras – to muster the required nine votes (out of fif-teen) to maintain sanctions.

At the Security Council, opposing the French and Russian reasoning that, with the required arms' disarmament accomplished and monitoring in place, Paragraph 22 of Resolution 687 should be activated, Albright repeated the American line that any easing of sanctions must also be tied to human rights and the missing Kuwaiti nationals. She also pointed out that in the chemical weapons program Iraq had yet to come clean about its program on VX, a nerve gas ten times more lethal than sarin, the nerve agent that Iraq had used widely during the Iran–Iraq War: its statement that it had merely conducted laboratory experi-ments was not credible. Thus pressed, on March 25, 1995, Iraq gave a new account of its VX program, admitting production of 550 lb (250 kg) of VX at pilot plants, but denied weaponization of the agent.[29]

In the event, therefore, the Security Council decided to maintain the status quo.

The seventh Unscom report to be submitted by Ekeus, on April 10, was to be of extraordinary importance as it was to cover both the monitoring process and the dismantling of the WMD and the intermediate and long-range missiles and their manufacturing facilities. The verification and monitoring was now opera-tional, Ekeus concluded, signifying the end of the six-month trial period. By now the BMVC was linked directly to its headquarters at the UN in New York. (Later this system would be exposed as one riddled with eavesdropping devices installed by the American CIA and the National Security Agency (NSA) opera-tives working under Unscom cover.) Its director, Goran Wallen, an American, had eighty-one subordinates of whom twenty-nine were support staff. In Iraq they had the back-up of a 29-strong German helicopter unit, later to be replaced by Chileans. Monitoring focused on covering the "choke points" in the weapons production process. The five monitoring teams, each two to six strong, were: nuclear (with focus on isotope detectors in rivers to detect discharge of any radio-active material); chemical (using chemical monitors in chemical industries to detect key precursors and chemical agents); biological (which was hard to monitor, but the pharmaceutical industry was put under surveillance); intermediate- and long-range missiles; and aerial inspection.[30] Biological weapons and facilities were difficult to control as most laboratories engaged in medical research into disease control could produce them.

Having destroyed all known research, development and manufacturing facilities for nuclear weapons, the IAEA now focused most of its resources on the implantation and strengthening of its monitoring and verification regime.

Unscom's monitoring staff worked in association with Iraq's NMD. The monitoring system, installed in 1994 at more than 250 sites, was the most comprehensive ever designed. It covered not only the present facilities in building and plant and skilled manpower with previous experience in the research or production of banned weapons and long-range missiles, but also any future introduction of new building, equipment or senior scientists and engineers.[31] In the case of equipment, the focus was on dual-purpose machinery. For instance, a fermenter could be used for making beer or biological weapons; and a machine tool, car parts or missile components. The Unscom regime required the Iraqi government to submit every six months a fresh list of all dual-purpose equipment in the country. Later, following the Security Council's adoption of Resolution 1051 on March 27, 1996, Unscom introduced an import–export monitoring system which required Iraq and the government of the country where the supplier was based to inform it of a possible trade in any dual-purpose item covered by the Unscom's monitoring system.

As for monitoring tools, they were used on the ground and in the air. On the ground three different kinds of sensors were installed: visual, chemical and temperature. The visual sensors – cameras – installed at 150 sites were connected through a system of transmitters and repeaters across the country to the BMVC and to the UN in New York. And the video-cameras, installed at 150 locations to ensure that dual-purpose machines were not used for military purposes, were linked to a central panel in Baghdad. The chemical sensors, called sniffers, were used to detect the presence of certain compounds which might indicate banned activity. Finally, temperature sensors were installed at certain sites which could be used for biological weapons to detect if a factory was operating equipment in a certain heat range. Monitoring was also conducted by helicopters and weekly U–2 high altitude reconnaissance flights by aircraft owned and operated by the US, with communications links to the Pentagon in Washington. The function of helicopters and U–2 spy planes was to obtain aerial photographs to detect any signs of new construction, power lines or any other fresh activity.

The overall working of the system was well illustrated by the (former) laboratories of the General Establishment for Animal Development in Baghdad. In the past this plant produced one million vaccines annually for animals. But, since its laboratories could be used for producing biological agents, they were closed down by Unscom. Once a month Unscom's biological inspectors visited the facility to check the monitoring system which was installed to record all visitors to the site, to ensure that the two Unscom-tagged centrifuges (categorized as dual-purpose machines) had not been used, and to check that the hardening foam, pumped through the ventilation system and capped with concrete to seal the main chamber of the laboratories, had not been tampered with.

By now most of the daily visits by Unscom inspectors were for checking the monitoring system.

Though the chance of importing any machinery into Iraq before the oil-for-food plan went into operation in December 1996 was minuscule, Unscom was still on the look-out for equipment in the medical area, which had all along been exempt from UN sanctions, since it could be used for the biological weapons program.

With Unscom and the IAEA having almost wholly accomplished their missions in the fields of chemical and nuclear arms and missiles,[32] Ekeus's attention turned increasingly to biological warfare agents. On April 6–7, 1995, a seminar of international biological specialists in New York, convened by him, examined the evidence provided by Unscom, and concluded that Iraq had maintained a biological weapons production facility at Hakam, 38 miles (60 km) south-west of Baghdad.[33] "The importation of [growth] media by type, quantities and packaging is grossly out of proportion to Iraq's stated requirements for hospital use," Ekeus noted in his report to the Security Council on April 10. "With Iraq's failure to account for these items and materials for legitimate purposes, the only conclusion … is that there is a high risk that they have been purchased for a proscribed purpose – acquisition of biological warfare agents."[34]

In mid-May Tariq Aziz told the visiting Unscom delegation led by Charles Duelfer, its American deputy executive chairman since 1993, that Iraq would provide further information on its biological projects once Unscom had closed the files on Iraq's past missiles and chemical arms programs, and the IAEA the nuclear file; and the Security Council had promised to lift sanctions once Baghdad had provided full information on the biological warfare agents. If the next Unscom report due in mid-June made these statements and confirmed that the monitoring system was up and running, then in late June Iraq would address fully the sole remaining issue of the biological program, he added. Duelfer passed on the message to his boss, Ekeus.

In his next comprehensive report, Ekeus noted Iraq's refusal to cooperate unconditionally on its biological program and compared this unfavorably to its cooperation in other areas. In Tariq Aziz's view, the new document had both "negative and positive elements." At the Security Council, Russia and France agreed with him. Both countries, especially France – which had, much to the irritation of America, opened an interest section in the Rumanian embassy in Baghdad in January 1995 – urged Iraq that since the chances of lifting, or at least easing, of sanctions were high it should continue its cooperation with Unscom. So the Iraqi officials meeting Ekeus in Baghdad on July 1 told him that Iraq had a biological arms program, and that it had produced anthrax (bacillus anthracis) and botulinum (clostridium botulinum) in 1989–90.

From Iraq's viewpoint, once its officials had provided fuller details of its biological program in writing to Ekeus during his visit to Baghdad on August 4, including an explanation of how 17 tons of growth media were used to produce anthrax and botulinum, it had done all that was required of it according to Resolution 687. Ekeus said that if Iraq's claim to have destroyed unilaterally all its biological weapons before the Second Gulf War could be verified, then he would inform the Security Council that Unscom had fully accomplished its mission, thus paving the way for an end to the embargo. The next day Tariq Aziz repeated the statement made earlier by Iraqi foreign minister, Muhammad Said al Sahhaf, that Baghdad would withdraw its cooperation with Unscom if there was no progress on lifting sanctions by August 31, and asked Ekeus to pass on the message to the Council. He agreed to do so.

Since the Military Industrialization Commission had been deeply involved in the biological programme, Ekeus wondered if he could talk to Gen. Hussein Kamil Hassan, who ran the organization before the Second Gulf War, during his next visit. Aziz promised to help.

But, by the time Ekeus had returned to New York on August 7, Gen. Hussein Kamil Hassan, accompanied by a large entourage, was on the verge of defecting to Jordan, thus delivering Saddam's regime the severest domestic blow yet. For, besides having being minister of industry and mines, oil and defense and director of the Military Industrialization Commission and the MIE at different times, Hussein Kamil was married to Saddam Hussein's eldest daughter, Raghad.

3

A SHATTERING BETRAYAL, THEN LUCKY BREAKS FOR SADDAM

Leaving Iraq on the night of August 7–8, 1995, in an Amman-bound convoy of black Mercedes, ostensibly on his way to sign an important contract in Sofia, Bulgaria, was a clever move by 41-year-old Gen. Hussein Kamil Hassan, August 8 being an Iraqi national holiday to celebrate Baghdad's victory over Iran in the First Gulf War. Steeped in a celebratory mood on that day, the regime would be slow to react to his master-stroke – leading a large group of defectors, consisting of his family, and that of his younger brother, Col. Saddam Kamil Hassan, and their aides – he must have reckoned.

Though their flight from Iraq was sensational when it happened, in retrospect it emerged more as a natural progression than a dramatic event, with Hussein Kamil escaping with millions of dollars in cash, and crates of sensitive documents. In essence, his defection had to do with the rising star of Uday (b. 1964), the elder son of Saddam Hussein – variously described as arrogant, avaricious, brutal, overambitious, unpredictable, and a psychotic playboy – who, having brought down other leading figures of the regime in the spring and early summer of 1995, was planning to bring about Hussein Kamil's dismissal or demotion.

Uday, a child of average intelligence, had been pampered by his father. Soon after his graduation from Baghdad University's Engineering College, Saddam tried to groom him for public life. To indulge his love of sport, Saddam had him elected director of the Iraq Olympic Committee with its headquarters in an impressive eight-story building. But in November 1988, after he had murdered Kamal Hanna Jajo, a food-taster and bodyguard of his father, in a drunken bout, Uday fell from grace. Uday's reason for murdering Jajo at a party was that he had been the intermediary in his father's affair with Samira Shahbandar (the divorced wife of Nour al Din al Safi, the general manager of Iraq Airways), whom he later married and by whom he had a son, Ali. Uday was imprisoned and then banished to Geneva in disgrace. But not for long. He returned home and soon became re-elected as director of the Iraq Olympic Committee. By 1990, he was also into the food processing business. Saddam included him in the Iraqi delegation that met Kuwaiti Crown Prince Saad al Ahmad al Sabah in Jiddah two days before Iraq's invasion of Kuwait.

But it was only after he was licensed to publish a daily newspaper, *Babil* (i.e., Babylon), and run the Youth (*Shahab*) Television after the Second Gulf War, that he began to make political impact. The *Babil*, edited by Abbas al Janabi, a Shia, provided Uday Saddam Hussein with a powerful vehicle. Its attacks on Prime Minister Khodayir for his failure to arrest the rapid decline of the Iraqi Dinar paved the way for his dismissal in the spring of 1994. During Baghdad's crisis with Washington in October, following the Iraqi troop maneuvers in southern Iraq, Uday set up a volunteer force of young men, called *Firqat Fedayin Saddam* (*lit.*, Saddam's Self-sacrificers Division), which soon became 20,000 strong. Its task was to assist the regime in suppressing subversion. It assisted the forces of the SRG and General Security in quashing the riots that erupted in Ramadi, 70 miles (110 km) west of Baghdad, a stronghold of the (Sunni) Dulaimi tribe, in May 1995, following the execution of Gen. Muhammad Madhlum al Dulaimi for his alleged involvement in a plot to assassinate Saddam.

The *Babil* criticized the security lapses which had resulted in the Ramadi rioting, thus casting a shadow over the competence of the interior minister, Watban Ibrahim al Tikriti, and the head of General Security, Sabawi Ibrahim al Tikriti – Saddam's half-brothers by the second marriage of his mother, Subha Tulfah al Masallat. In mid-May Watban al Tikriti lost his job.

Taking note of the allegations against Gen. Ali Hassan al Majid of his involvement in smuggling in Kurdistan, Saddam Hussein demoted him as defense minister and put him in charge of the Baath Party's trade unions section. When he failed to name Ali Hassan's successor, rumors circulated that he was planning to appoint Uday as defense minister. In any case, Uday had evinced keen interest in military transport with a view to creaming off repairs and maintenance contracts from the defense ministry. He was also trying to carve out a place for himself in the burgeoning import-export business being conducted in Amman, in which Hussein Kamil Hassan and Watban and Sabawi al Tikriti were involved.

Uday pursued his multi-faceted ambition against the background of growing squabbling in the extended family, with Saddam Hussein receiving diverse advice on how to deal with Unscom and the IAEA, and how to bring about an end to the punishing sanctions regime – his sons, Uday and Qusay, opposing concessions to the UN; Watban and Sabawi advising compromise; with Hussein Kamil somewhere in between.

Hussein Kamil, a nephew of Gen. Ali Hassan al Majid – a cousin and senior confidant of Saddam Hussein for many years – trained to become an army officer. Eager to please, he cultivated Saddam's wife, Sajida. This won him promotion to colonel soon after Saddam became president. In March 1981 Sajida Hussein included him in her entourage when she visited New York on a shopping spree. Instructed by the president, during his stay in New York he established business contacts, including one with an American company which later acted as a front for Baghdad to purchase ammunition from Brazil and Chile.[1]

Three years later, at 30, he married 17-year-old Raghad, the eldest daughter of Sajida and Saddam Hussein. Promoted to brigadier-general in the latter half of 1985, he was put in charge of the elite Republican Guard. This force had existed before the 1968 Baathist coup, but it was only a brigade strong. In keeping with the expansion of the army, the Baathist regime bolstered the RG to two brigades, and added a special forces battalion, making sure that all new recruits came from the Tikrit area, the home base of both President Bakr and Saddam Hussein. When the Iran–Iraq War caused further bolstering of the Iraqi military, the strength of the RG rose to one division by early 1985 when it was headed by Major-General Talie Khalil al Duri (from Dur, just south of Tikrit). From 1983 onwards the RG, dispatched to the front at crucial moments, performed well. However, given the comparatively large casualties it suffered in combat and the limited manpower that the Tikrit area could provide, Saddam decided to open its ranks to the Sunni tribes outside the Tikrit region – especially the Dulaimi from west of Baghdad, the Jibouri from north-west of Tikrit, and the Ubaidi from north of Tikirit. Within a year of taking charge, Hussein Kamil Hassan enlarged the RG to seventeen mechanized brigades with a total strength of 25,000 troops. By the time the Iran–Iraq War ended in August 1988, the RG had thirty-seven brigades, and Hussein Kamil Hassan was major-general.

His next job, as a cabinet minister, was to supervise the merger of the ministry of industry and the Military Industrialization Directorate into the ministry of industry and military industrialization (MIMI). In that office he became familiar with Iraq's program of non-conventional weapons and intermediate- and long-range missiles. In December 1989 it was he who announced that his ministry had developed a surface-to-surface missile, Al Abid, with a range of 1,110 miles (1,850 km). Following the post-Second Gulf War uprisings, Saddam dispatched him to curb the insurrection in Karbala. He then did the mopping-up operations in Kurdistan after his uncle, Gen. Ali Hassan al Majid, had quashed the rebellion there in April 1991. He was then promoted to lieutenant-general, and appointed defense minister. In the following cabinet reshuffle in September he was made a presidential adviser. In 1992 he was appointed minister of industry and mines as well as director of the expanded Military Industrializaton Commission, renamed the Military Industrialization Establishment, which included not only the Industrial Engineering Company but also a construction section, called Fao Company. As the MIE boss, he had been negotiating a deal with Bulgaria, a task which took him to Amman periodically, and it was here that he now sought and secured asylum after his defection.

The career of his younger brother, Saddam Kamil, was less impressive although he followed his elder sibling by marrying Rana (b. 1968), a younger sister of Raghad Saddam Hussein. Trained as an army officer, his main asset was that he was a lookalike of Saddam Hussein. He made his mark on the First Family as well as the Iraqi public in 1982 when he played Saddam Hussein in *The Long Days*, a six-hour romanticized television documentary of the Iraqi leader's life. After his marriage to Rana, Saddam Kamil, now a lieutenant-colonel, was drafted into Special Security.

In 1992 he became commander of the presidential guard, and head of the Tribal Chiefs' Bureau. Yet security around Saddam Hussein tightened so much subsequently that by 1994 Kamil had lost his unhindered access to the president, and only Qusay, and Abid Hamid Mahmoud, the president's private secretary, supervisor of his office and close relative, knew the leader's whereabouts.

The defection of the Kamil Hassan (al Majid) brothers was a dramatic illustration of the squabbling that had become endemic in the extended ruling family centered on Saddam Hussein. Its members belonged to several extended families – al Majid, al Ibrahim, al Muhammad, al Sultan and al Khatib – of the Begat clan belonging to al Bu Nasir tribe based in the Tikrit area, the source of al Tikriti family name used by many of them. The al Majid and al Ibrahim extended families became closer when, following the death of her first husband (Hussein al Majid), Saddam's mother, Subha Talfa (al Masallat) (d. 1982), married Ibrahim Hassan, by whom she had three sons. Thus Saddam Hussein became the blood link between the al Majids (Ali Hassan, Hussein Kamil and Saddam Kamil) on the paternal side and the al Ibrahims (Barzan, Watban and Sabawi) on the maternal side. When Saddam's regime faced a series of crises during the long Iran–Iraq War, he resorted to tightening his grip over the military and the security and intelligence agencies by appointing his close and distant relatives in top positions. Nepotism thrived and merit suffered, resulting in the shrinkage of the support base of the regime, ostensibly run by the governing Baath Party and open to all those who accepted its ideology and discipline. While this enabled Saddam to have a tighter grip over power than before, it had its downside. A single defection from this narrow circle could do his regime much damage, as the actions of Hussein Kamil Hassan (al Majid) would amply show.

Having secured asylum in Jordan and moved into one of the royal guest houses in Amman, Hussein Kamil wasted little time in launching a frontal attack on a regime of which until a few days earlier he had been a leading light. At a press conference on August 12, he denounced the Baghdad government and appealed to army, RG and SRG officers to revolt. He contacted the Iraqi opposition groups in exile. While buoyed by his defection and predicting Saddam's fall within six months – thus making the US more uncompromising on Iraq at the Security Council – they kept their distance from him. So, in December, Hussein Kamil ended up forming his own Higher Iraqi Salvation Council – committed to democracy, pluralism and free elections in post-Saddam Iraq – where officials of the current regime would be spared witch-hunt or revenge.[2]

Hussein Kamil gave extensive briefings to US National Security Agency and CIA officials as well as the Unscom chief, Ekeus, whom he also supplied with thousands of documents. Among other things, he told them that Iraq had developed a biological weapons program. He furnished Unscom with highly sensitive information detailing *inter alia* Baghdad's retention of proscribed weapons in violation of the UN disarmament regime. This aided America's efforts to block the French and Russian moves for the easing of sanctions against Iraq. Furthermore, he and his aides provided the CIA and NSA with details of the highly classified military communications systems, which the two agencies went on to exploit to gather intelligence for Washington through the American inspectors working for Unscom.

Eager to discover the Iraqi government's tactics to hide proscribed materials and documents from the Unscom teams, Ekeus questioned Hussein Kamil on the subject, to which the latter's response (in Ekeus's words) was "quite forthcoming."

Having recovered from the shock of the defections, involving not only the Kamil brothers but also his two daughters, Saddam tried to turn the disastrous events to his advantage. He now blamed Hussein Kamil for all that had gone wrong in Iraq's dealings with Unscom. The day after the chief defector's press conference in Amman, Ekeus received a fax from Hussein Kamil's deputy, General Amr Rashid (al Ubaidi), a British-trained engineer, who had been liaising with Unscom. It said:

> The government has ascertained that General Hussein Kamil had been responsible for hiding important information on Iraq's prohibited programmes from the Commission and IAEA by ordering the Iraqi technical personnel not to disclose such information and also not to inform Mr Tariq Aziz or Gen. Amr Rashid of these instructions.[3]

The following day Aziz telephoned Ekeus to say that the August 31 deadline for cooperation with Unscom was off.

In Baghdad, on hearing of the defections on the morning of August 8, Saddam ordered the severing of telephone links with the outside world, and put on high alert the RG and the SRG. He deployed the RG units in the streets of the capital, and they resorted to searching people. The black-uniformed Firqat Fedayin Saddam, now 30,000 strong, were posted along the 340 mile (550 km) Iraqi–Jordanian highway ostensibly to prevent further defections. Saddam followed up the dismissal of Hussein Kamil from his official posts with the promotion of Gen. Ali Hassan al Majid as commander of the First Corps based in Kirkuk. In an extensive swoop, Special Security arrested some 600 people.

In a nationwide broadcast on August 11, Saddam Hussein condemned his senior son-in-law, Hussein Kamil, comparing him to Cain (who murdered his brother Abel), Judas (who betrayed Jesus Christ) and Abu Lahab (who opposed Prophet Muhammad, his nephew). Among other things he accused Hussein Kamil of spying for the CIA and defrauding the state treasury of many millions of dollars through front companies.[4]

The next day, speaking on behalf of the al Majid extended family, to which Hussein Kamil belonged, Gen. al Majid said,

> This small family [of al Majids] in Iraq denounces Hussein Kamil's cowardly act and strongly rejects the treason which he has committed and which can only be cleansed by inflicting punishment on him in

accordance with the Law of God … His family has unanimously decided to permit with impunity the spilling of [his] blood.[5]

In other words, were somebody to kill Hussein Kamil, his family would not demand retribution along the principle of "eye for an eye, tooth for a tooth", as was a tribal custom and a code of the Islamic law, Sharia.

As Saddam brooded over the enormous blow his government had suffered at home and abroad as a result of Hussein Kamil's defection, he realized that the root cause of the disaffection in the regime's innermost circle was the insatiable ambition and unpredictable violence of Uday. In the latest of his brutal out-bursts, Uday had gate-crashed a party given by his uncle, Watban al Tikriti, in mid-July after he had been informed by telephone by one of the guests that Watban – blaming him for the loss of his job as interior minister – had been speaking ill of him. Arriving with a sub machine-gun, he sprayed the guest-filled hall with bullets, killing three to six people, including the gypsy dancers and sing-ers, and wounding Watban in the leg. His unrestrained arrogance and ambition had led him to interfere through the columns of the *Babil* in several ministries, including the foreign ministry which for years had been headed by the veteran Tariq Aziz, a deputy prime minister and a member of the RCC. The unchecked behavior of Uday, who was not a member of the RCC, had begun seriously undermining the role and influence of Saddam Hussein's loyal, long-serving aides, as well as the Iraqi constitution which described the RCC as the country's supreme authority.

Now Saddam stripped Uday of all the official positions he had garnered for himself, including his command of the Firqat Fedayeen Saddam, leaving him only the chairmanship of the Iraq Football Association. He orchestrated criticism of Uday in the Iraqi media. His foreign minister, Muhammad Said al Sahhaf, found Uday "unfit to govern." Barzan al Tikriti, still Iraq's ambassador to the UN in Geneva, was more forthright in attacking both Hussein Kamal and Uday Hussein in a long interview with the London-based *Al Hayat* (The Life) on August 31, 1995. "There is a deep chasm between Hussein Kamil and the Iraqi Kurds," he said. "How could the Iraqi Shias cooperate with him when he was the one who attacked the tomb of Imam Hussein ibn Ali [in Karbala]?" He described Uday Hussein as "an impetuous, rough and aggressive boy who knows nothing of civility." Scorning Uday's over-ambition, he added,

> Iraq is not a monarchy with a son or brother succeeding the king. It is a republic ruled by a revolutionary party …. Problems arise from people who do not know their true calibre …. The notion of inheriting power is not acceptable in Iraq. People do not accept Uday or Hussien Kamil. Neither of them has the legitimacy to govern.[6]

What is more, Saddam later went on quietly to expropriate Uday when he thought his son's wealth might be used to finance a coup.[7] To emphasize that it was the Baath Party and the RCC that mattered, he went on to offer himself as the party's sole candidate for president in a referendum which the constitution does not specifiy.

Saddam's somber, reflective mood, combined with a resolve to turn a new page, percolated down fast. When Ekeus, accompanied by fifteen experts, arrived in Baghdad on August 17 he found Iraqi officials in a chastened state of mind, vowing cooperation and transparency in their future dealings with Unscom without any time limits, along with promises of pursuing good neighborly policies in the region and channeling future resources only into economic development.

They made a clean breast of Iraq's WMD programs, admitting among other things that the government had not only succeeded in producing biological weapons but had also loaded them into 166 bombs and 25 warheads of Al Hussein missiles, with a range of 360 miles (570 km), after the August 1990 invasion of Kuwait. The total of 193 munitions filled with biological warfare agents roughly tallied with the figure of 200 that Gen. Wafiq al Samarrai had mentioned earlier in 1995.[8]

Ekeus listened to his briefings carefully and wondered if any written evidence would follow. When none did, he complained about it at his press conference in Baghdad on August 20. Later that day, just as he was departing for the military airport used by Unscom at Habbaniya, 53 miles (85 km) west of Baghdad, an Iraqi official informed him that the authorities had discovered that Hussein Kamil had hidden a pile of documents on proscribed weapons and that these had just been located at his farmhouse near Haidar village en route to Habbaniya.

So Ekeus and his party stopped by at the farmhouse – a villa with a few outhouses. In a locked chicken shed, they were shown some forty wooden and metal boxes containing documents, photos, videofilm, microfilm and microfiche, which – by Unscom's estimation – amounted to 650,000 pages of text.[9] What struck the team was the cleanliness of the crates found in a dusty, disused shed. Later examination of the contents showed that the documents had been tampered with, and highly classified material removed.[10] Nonetheless, the haul was rich in detail about the prohibited arms, especially nuclear weapons where, interestingly enough, Ekeus had found Hussein Kamil deficient during his interrogations. Apparently, this was the archive that the Iraqi authorities had removed from the ministry of agriculture and irrigation nearly four years earlier.[11] In Amman when Ekeus mentioned the Haidar farmhouse and stored documents to Hussein Kamil, the latter denied any knowledge of the property or archives.

On September 4, Ekeus told a press conference that Iraq had admitted possessing germ- or toxin-filled artillery shells, aerial bombs and ballistic missile warheads for possible use in the 1991 Gulf War, and that it had produced larger quantities of anthrax (8,500 liters) and botulinum (19,000 liters) than previously declared. The Iraqis also revealed that they had initiated a crash program in August 1990 to produce one nuclear bomb within a year.[12] In practice, the Iraqis failed to obtain the crucial triggering device either by designing and manufacturing it or by procuring it clandestinely.

Hussein Kamil's defection to Jordan, about which King Hussein ibn Talal had foreknowledge, provided the Jordanian monarch with a chance to ingratiate himself with Washington, from which he had been alienated due to his pro-Baghdad neutrality in the 1991 Gulf War. Yet Jordan was so dependent for its fuel on Iraq that it could not afford to break the strong economic links it had built with its eastern neighbor over the past two decades. In September 1995, Jordan's energy minister renewed the annual oil contract in Baghdad and signed a $500 million deal for a 375 mile (600 km) pipeline from Iraq to the oil refinery in Zarqa to be implemented after the anti-Iraq sanctions were removed. King Hussein announced that his government would not play a significant role in trying to overthrow Saddam Hussein.[13]

The Jordanian monarch's statement came as the Baath Party in Iraq was getting into stride to promote its candidate, Saddam Hussein, in the presidential referendum on October 15. Its campaign went hand in hand with unending glorification of Saddam. "By God we have always found you [Saddam Hussein] in the most difficult conditions a roaring lion and a courageous horseman, one of the few true men," declared Gen. Ali Hassan al Majid, a luminary of the Baath.[14]

So confident was the government of popular participation in the referendum that it invited about 500 foreign journalists to witness the exercise. Though the official turnout of 99 percent was undoubtedly inflated, it was large enough, at least in Baghdad, to impress the visiting reporters. But the official result – 99.96 percent of the voters saying "Yes" to "Do you want Saddam Hussein to remain president for another seven years?" – was an example of over-kill. The most frequent statement that foreign correspondents heard from ordinary Iraqi voters was that Saddam had managed to keep their country together and provided strong leadership in fiendish times, implying that his overthrow would lead to civil war and chaos that was then rampant in Bosnia, and that had blighted Lebanon from 1975 to 1990.

As expected, things went badly for the Iraqi leader at the UN Security Council. In his six-monthly report of October 11, 1995, Ekeus noted that Iraq had developed more powerful weapons than had been thought before. Biological warfare agents had been loaded into bombs and missile warheads and posted at four locations (not two as Iraq had said before) after the Iraqi invasion of Kuwait. There had been a clandestine production of the Scud type missile engine before the 1991 Gulf War. And Baghdad had concealed its chemical missile warhead flight tests. Therefore, said Ekeus, he would need more time to reach a final conclusion.[15]

Another report, released on October 19 by the UN's Rome-based Food and Agriculture Organization (FAO), painted a grim picture of the suffering being endured by Iraqis. The FAO's study of Greater Baghdad, accounting for nearly a quarter of the national population, showed that 28 percent of the children under five were "severely malnourished" – a figure higher than that in Ghana,

Mali or North Sudan. Lucielo Ramirez, head of the World Food Program (WFP, run by the FAO) in Baghdad, revealed that a quarter of the people living in Iraq below the 36th Parallel were vulnerable to continued shortage of food, and that included pregnant women and the elderly of both sexes. "If nothing is done to help these people then we will be counting dead bodies by 1996."[16] Reporting from Baghdad, Mariam Shahin, a visiting Arab journalist, wrote, "Iraqis appear to care less about democracy and reform than food on their plates … Now people speak much more frankly about their plight, visible need having torn down the veneer of false pride."[17]

Reflecting the general unease in the region, UAE president Shaikh Zaid al Nahyan called on Iraq's Arab opponents to reconcile with it, and do something to relieve the misery of its people. His statement was endorsed by Qatar, Oman and Bahrain.

In Baghdad, the WFP's warning made Saddam re-examine his stance on the oil-for-food Resolution 986 that the Security Council had passed unanimously on April 14, 1995. It was an improvement on Resolution 706 (August 1991) on the same subject. Now the six-monthly oil revenue allowed was $2 billion versus $1.6 billion before. Whereas 706 was just a one-off, the new resolution could be renewed every six months. Under it UN officials were only to "observe" the Iraqi distribution system of food, unlike in 706 which entitled them to "monitor" the distribution in the country. Also the new document said that "nothing in this Resolution should be construed as infringing the sovereignty and territorial integrity of Iraq."

But Saddam was as yet unconvinced. Since Resolution 986 still required Baghdad to deposit its oil revenue into a UN account, this amounted to the UN acting as the owner of Iraqi petroleum, thus violating Iraq's sovereignty, argued the Iraqi diplomats at the UN. They also feared that the implementation of Resolution 986 would indefinitely postpone the lifting of sanctions as specified in Resolution 687 – which Washington wanted – and put Iraq's major natural resource and economy under a long-term UN mandate.

By late 1995, however, Saddam was reassured that though Hussein Kamil Hassan fitted Washington's prescription for a suitable military successor to him – a Sunni, a general and a Tikriti – he had been shunned by the bulk of the Iraqi opposition, including the Iraqi National Congress and the Iraqi National Accord, and this had cooled the initial ardor for him by the CIA with whom he had established contact through a Western journalist before his defection.[18] The INC pointed out that Hussein Kamil was number six on its list of "war criminals" to be prosecuted in Nuremburg-style trials. Its main charge against him was that he had played a leading part in quashing popular uprisings in the south and the north after the 1991 Gulf War. So the CIA ended up exploiting Hussein Kamil as a vital source of inside information about the Baghdad regime and its weapons programs which could be used to prolong the UN's economic embargo, and then ignoring him.

Having first applauded Hussein Kamil Hassan, Ayatollah Muhammad Baqir al Hakim of the Tehran-based SAIRI called him a "criminal" when he realized that the defector was part of a US-backed scheme.

The defector returns

Once the initial excitement of defection wore off, and the CIA decided against giving Hussein Kamil Hassan a role in its anti-Saddam strategy, the wives, Raghad and Rana – now shunned by the Jordanian royal family and feeling bored – appealed to their mother, Sajida, to let them return home. They were encouraged to do so after they were convinced that their father had curtailed the powers of Uday who had earlier threatened their husbands. In any case, isolated in a hilltop villa near Amman's airport, they and their children had become so homesick that they were liable to believe what they wanted to, emotionally.

Deprived of power and unlimited resources, and gradually sidelined by the Jordanian monarch, Hussein Kamil became morose and depressed to the point of having a nervous breakdown in January 1996. He decided to move to Damascus, where Wafiq al Samarrai was now based, only to be told by King Hussein that he was free to go but without his family. That was out of the question. He therefore responded positively when Iyad Said al Tikriti, a former mayor of Tikrit, visited him in Amman to discuss the terms of his return to Iraq. On February 18, he made a formal, written request to Saddam Hussein for his return home as "an ordinary citizen" after he had been pardoned by the state in writing. Saddam pardoned him with the proviso that he would receive a written confirmation of his pardon signed by the RCC only if he arrived at the Iraqi border town of Trebil along with Saddam Kamil, and Raghad and Rana and their children. So when Saddam Kamil had second thoughts about returning to Iraq, Hussein Kamil forced him to change his mind. However, some other members of his original entourage, including his brother-in-law Izz al Din Muhammad al Majid, refused and stayed behind.

On February 20, when the Kamil brothers' motorcade arrived at Trebil, it was received by Qusay Saddam Hussein. After separating his two sisters and their children from the Kamil brothers, he gave the promised RCC's pardoning document to Hussein Kamil, and then put the two brothers into a separate black Mercedes. On their arrival in Baghdad the Kamil Brothers were taken to the headquarters of the General Intelligence Department, and questioned vigorously on their contacts in Amman with the Iraqi opposition and the Western and UN representatives. When released, they went to the house of their father, Kamil Hassan al Majid, a walled villa in the Greater Baghdad district of Saidiya sandwiched between Tamim and Maarifa on the western side of the Tigris. The next day, at a presidential palace office, Saddam Hussein gave them twenty-four hours to consider his demand that they instantly divorce their wives. While they prevaricated, Raghad and Rana submitted divorce petitions, on February 22, in which they said that they had been "deceived and misled by two failed traitors" to defect, and that during their first private meeting with King Hussein they had asked him to facilitate their return to Iraq. Their petitions were granted instantly. And on the morning of February 23, Baghdad's Youth TV reported that Raghad and Rana Saddam Hussein "are refusing to stay married to men who betrayed the homeland, the trust and the lofty values of their noble family and kinsfolk."[19]

Later that day, as military and police vehicles cordoned off the Saidiya district, Gen. Ali Hassan al Majid, leading a party of armed men, surrounded the villa of his younger brother, Kamil Hassan al Majid, and demanded the surrender of his sons, Hussein Kamil and Saddam Kamil. They refused to come out. A firefight ensued, lasting five hours, with the attackers using assault weapons. The occupants of the villa fought back until their ammunition ran out, killing two of their attackers. The assault party entered the house and murdered more occupants. But, to the frustration of Gen. al Majid, Hussein Kamil was not one of them. It was only after bulldozers had started to raze the house that Hussein Kamil emerged, half-naked and bleeding, brandishing a machine-gun and a pistol. He was gunned down. Dragging his corpse, Gen. al Majid shouted, "Come and see the fate of a traitor."[20] As the extended family elder of the al Majids he delivered what he had promised after the defection of the two Kamil brothers six months earlier. "We have cut off the treacherous branch from our noble family tree," Gen. al Majid said in his letter to President Saddam Hussein. "Your amnesty does not obliterate the right of our family to impose the necessary punishment."[21]

Saddam Hussein could, and did, claim that he had kept his written word, and that it was their own al Majid kinsmen who had killed the Kamil brothers because they had dishonored the family by their treason. "Had they [al Majids] asked me, I would have prevented them, but it was good that they did not," he said later.[22]

There has been much speculation as to what drove Hussein Kamil Hassan, who had known Saddam Hussein's wily ways for many years, to return to Iraq. The best explanation was probably offered by Shakir Jawhari, a Jordanian author of a political history of Iraq, who was in touch with Hussein Kamil during his exile in Amman. He said,

> The main feature in Hussein Kamil's personality was this extraordinary mixture of emotion and intelligence. His emotions had a very bad effect on his cleverness; and he was in this way a symbol of Iraqi character …. He was trying to correct his relations with President Saddam. I told him … his defection had a very serious result …. He said, 'President Saddam was my uncle before he was my father-in-law. We are one family'.[23]

So within seven months of suffering the most severe setback to his regime since the Second Gulf War, Saddam, to the despair and chagrin of his adversaries, had once again emerged virtually unscathed.

A month earlier, for a change, the Iraqi people had had a cheerful piece of news. On Wednesday January 20, 1996, the RCC announced that Iraq would negotiate the terms for implementing the oil-for-food Resolution 986 with the UN secretary-general. There were three chief reasons for this about-turn by Saddam. One was the threat of a famine issued by the WFP. Another was the realization by the Iraqi leader that with the US entering a presidential year in 1996, there was no chance of Washington agreeing to an end to economic sanctions, no matter how fully he cooperated with Unscom. Neither the Democrat nor Republican candidate for the White House could afford to be seen to be soft on him. The final reason was practical. The money that had been deposited clandestinely into a secret Swiss bank account, named the Fund for Strategic Development, by a three-member Committee for Strategic Development, chaired by Saddam Hussein, since 1975 – consisting of 5 percent of Iraq's oil revenue before it was credited to the Iraqi treasury plus commissions on large contracts[24] – was running out. Withdrawals from this account had been been used by the Iraqi government to finance imports of food and medicine since 1990.

The next day, the weekly shopping day, Baghdad's food market, the Shorja Souq near the Martyrs' (Shuhada) Bridge, was so packed that vehicular traffic came to a halt. As musicians struck up, men danced and women distributed sweets to the spectators. (Nearly four years later, traders at this market remembered the day fondly, recalling it with vivid descriptions.[25]) By the end of January 1996, free market prices of rice, sugar and edible oil dropped by up to 50 percent. Iraqis, who had been storing American dollars, began selling them, driving up the value of the Iraqi Dinar from ID 2,600 to ID 2,000 to US$1 in the open market. Even though the official rate remained fixed at ID 800 to $1, there was such a rush to sell US dollars that local banks often ran out of Dinars. The prospect of Iraq's oil re-entering world markets reduced the price of a petroleum barrel from $18 to $16 in January.[26]

However, the actual exporting of oil was not to commence until December. But that did not stop Saddam Hussein from announcing that the much-postponed parliamentary poll would be held in March. And when it was conducted, the official voter turnout was put at an incredible 93 percent. The Baath Party improved its size in the National Assembly from 150 members to 169.

In the anti-Saddam camp, the defection of Hussein Kamil Hassan had raised hopes and started a process which remained unaffected by his subsequent murder. This was particularly true of Washington where policy-makers took heart from Hussein Kamil's dramatic move, and recommitted themselves to overthrowing the Iraqi dictator through a military putsch – an enterprise in which they went on to secure the active cooperation of the intelligence agencies of Britain, Saudi Arabia and Jordan.

4

THE MOTHER OF
ALL FAILED COUPS

The idea of an anti-Saddam coup which mushroomed into the most ambitious, multi-national enterprise, coordinated by the CIA – to be staged in June 1996 – originated with a retired Iraqi general running an import–export business in Amman. He was Muhammad Abdullah al Shahwani, an ethnic Turkoman from Kirkuk, a former brigadier-general in the Republican Guard's helicopter force. In the autumn of 1994 he contacted Dr Iyad Muhammad Alawi, an Iraqi National Accord leader who had homes in Amman and London, with a plan. His three sons – Major Anmar al Shahwani, Captain Ayead al Shahwani and Lt. Atheer al Shahwani – serving in the RG wanted to organize an anti-Saddam coup. Their commitment to Baathism and active membership of the Baath Party had enabled them to enroll into the RG. But, as they did not yet enjoy high rank, they could solicit support among fellow-officers for their scheme without arousing the suspicion of any of the intelligence or security agencies. Alawi showed keen interest and alerted British Secret Intelligence Services, MI6, which passed on the information to the CIA. In due course it became the CIA's pet project. Indeed, in March 1995 it was this scheme that made US National Security Adviser Tony Lake withdraw the White House backing for the alternative Ahmad Chalabi–Wafiq al Samarrai plan.[1] The subsequent unilateral move by Chalabi, which failed, damaged his standing with the CIA, whose ardor for the INA project intensified against the background of continued rivalry between the INC and the INA, which would take a bloody turn several months later.[2] To impress its paymasters about its reach, from 1994 onwards the INA master-minded bomb blasts in the Iraqi capital and elsewhere. A bomb went off in a Baghdad cinema, killing many civilians. In early 1996 its chief explosions expert, Abu Amneh al Khadami, operating from Suleimaniya, dispatched a videotape to other opposition groups in which he complained about non-payment for the jobs he had performed.[3]

By the time Gen. Hussein Kamil Hassan arrived in Amman in August, King Hussein was aware of the CIA–INA plan which also had the backing of the MI6 and the Saudi intelligence agency. During his visit to Washington in September, he was briefed by the CIA at its Langley, Virginia, headquarters. Here Steve Ritcher, former CIA station chief in Amman, had replaced Frank Anderson as head of the Near East Division in the Directorate for Operations in January 1995. At the top, John Deutch, former provost of the Massachusetts Institute of Technology and deputy secretary of defense, had succeeded James Woolsey as the CIA director in May. His deputy was John Tenet, who, as the NSC intelligence director, had been supportive of a CIA-sponsored military coup against Saddam. No wonder that the CIA's new management committee on Iraq resolved to concentrate more on the core issue of toppling the Iraqi dictator and less on the peripheral issues of who would follow him and on what program. With King Hussein promising full cooperation in response to Clinton's appeal during his Washington visit, the CIA's dream scenario of using Amman as its operational base, with most of the funds coming from Saudi Arabia, came to pass. What had given further impetus to the CIA as well as the NSA was the detailed information that Hussein Kamil Hassan and his entourage had given them of Iraq's top-secret military and security communications systems.

Furthermore, at Unscom an American national, Scott Ritter, had emerged as the Commission's coordinator to crack Iraq's concealment procedures for banned weapons. Ritter, a former US Marine Corps intelligence officer with the rank of a colonel, who joined Unscom as a chief inspector in May 1991, carried much clout at the organization. Pursuing his new assignment zealously, he visited Israel, and proposed that its civilian and military intelligence agencies, Mossad (*lit.*, Organization) and Aman (der. of Amn, Hebrew acronym of Agaf Modein, Intelligence Branch), supply Unscom off-the-shelf all-frequency scanners and digital tape-recorders to record coded radio communications of Iraq's innermost military and security forces. Israel agreed. At Ritter's behest, Unscom chief, Ekeus, approved the formation of Special Information Collection Missions (SICMs) initially under Nikita Smidovich, and approached the US for technology to tap Iraqi security networks on frequencies that could not be picked up by American spy planes and satellites.

By October 1995, the anti-Saddam coup plan had progressed sufficiently for Deutch to dispatch a new station chief to Amman with a specialist team for the Iraq operation to liaise with a special unit of the Jordanian intelligence. In mid-December, King Hussein addressed the exiled Iraqi opposition groups, including the INA, in Amman, and proposed a federal set-up in post-Saddam Iraq which, in his view, would satisfy the three main groups in the country: Kurds, Shias and Sunnis. This about-turn by the Jordanian monarch, who had so far kept any anti-Iraq moves by him secret while professing neutrality in public, alarmed Saddam Hussein. Just after Christmas 1995, his government announced that Iraq's direct international telephone links were being cut because it did not have enough foreign exchange to pay the bills. Iraq also reduced the duration of the exit visa for its nationals from twelve months to one, thus restricting further foreign travel by Iraqi citizens.[4]

In mid-January 1996, at a high-level gathering of intelligence officials from the US, Britain, Jordan, Saudi Arabia and Kuwait in Riyadh under Prince Turki ibn Faisal, the Americans committed $6 million, the Saudis $6 million and the

Kuwaitis $3 million.[5] At about the same time Deutch got the go-ahead for an anti-Saddam coup at a top-level meeting at the White House.

Another indication of the Clinton administration's wholehearted backing for the project could be inferred from the speed with which the CIA and the NSA designed and delivered the appropriate technology to Unscom, pursuing its aim of discovering Iraq's concealment tactics. Equipped with the latest technology, Unscom's SICMs went into action under Ritter in January 1996. His team mapped the frequencies, and intercepted the communications of Iraq's NMD which, besides liaising with Unscom, was in regular contact with Special Security, the SRG and the Office of the Presidential Secretary. Ritter sent the intercepts by satellite relay to Bahrain, the regional headquarters of Unscom, where a computer filtered conversations for key words – "chemical," "missile," "biological," etc. – and relayed them to the NSA at Fort Meade, Maryland, for decoding and translation into English.

With all the preparatory work done, the special CIA team in Amman was now ready to establish direct contact with the al Shahwani Brothers in Iraq. This was an extremely risky task. All international calls to and from Iraq went through telephone operators and were invariably taped. To overcome this barrier, the CIA furnished the INA with the most up-to-date satellite communications system made secure by the latest high-technology encryption techniques. It had earlier provided the INA with a list of code words and phrases to be used in communication. The next step of handing over this equipment to the al Shahwani Brothers inside Iraq was equally tricky. There were no air flights into Iraq from Jordan or anywhere else. And the land journey from Amman to Baghdad was 560 miles (900 km) long.

There emerged three versions of what happened next. According to one, the CIA engaged an Egyptian intermediary to deliver the communications equipment to the al Shahwani Brothers, and he divulged his mission to the Iraqis probably for money, handing over the equipment to them.[6] In another version, the Iraqi GID infiltrated a group of Kurdish nationalists who were privy to the CIA's plans. And, according to a third version, the CIA used one of the Iraqi truck-drivers plying between Amman and Baghdad to deliver the equipment, and he got caught by the Iraqi GID which maintained a close watch on all such truck and taxi drivers, whether Iraqi or Jordanian.[7]

However, the CIA had devised a supplementary channel of communication with the Iraqi conspirators. It assigned the task of contacting the plotting officers in the RG and the SRG to those CIA operatives who had taken up jobs with Unscom while maintaining close links with their headquarters. According to Ritter, Moe Dobbs (a pseudonym), a member of the CIA's Special Activities Staff (SAS), and his colleagues, adept at handling communications and organizing logistics, had been planted into Unscom as inspectors as early as spring 1992 even though they were not arms experts. In mid-March 1996 the Moe Dobbs group was part of Unscom 143, led by Ritter, with the inspectors equipped with the Israeli-supplied radio scanners. This was the first of a series of deliberately confrontational inspection exercises which were designed to elicit a radio tele-phone response from the Iraqi organization hiding proscribed weapons and doc-uments (believed to be named Concealment Operations Committee) that could be picked up by Unscom's radio scanners. As expected, the Iraqis resisted and delayed access to five sites that Unscom wanted to inspect, which led to a UN Security Council warning to Baghdad and a demand that the inspectors be accorded unrestricted access. However, to Ritter's disappointment, the inspec-tions that were conducted yielded no evidence of "Iraqi wrongdoing."[8]

Meanwhile, working in close collaboration with the CIA, the INA unveiled psychological warfare against the Baghdad regime. Alawi announced the open-ing of the INA office in Amman on February 18 (two days before Hussein Kamil Hassan's return to Baghdad), followed by the inauguration of the INA's radio station Al Mustaqabal (*lit.*, The Future) a fortnight later. "We regard Jordan as the door to Iraq, and it is important for us to talk to the people inside" he told a Cable News Network (CNN) interviewer.

By then Jordan had permitted the opening of a reception camp for Iraqi refu-gees near Qasr al Azraq, 50 miles (80 km) east of Amman, as a cover for the INA's military planning. This "refugee camp" became the operational base for mounting an anti-Saddam coup sponsored primarily by the CIA and the INA, which had set up a Military Council consisting of Alawi, Gen. Adnan Nouri, Gen. Muhammad al Shahwani, Gen. Bara Najib al Rubaie and Col. Muhammad Ali Ghani.[9] Since Kurdistan, convulsed by the putative coup attempt in March 1995, had lost its attraction to the would-be defectors from Iraq, they now tended to opt for Jordan. As invariably happens in the world of espionage and counter-espionage, some of the defectors from the Iraqi Baath Party and military officer corps were double agents.

About then reliable news reached the INC's Chalabi in Kurdistan that the Iraqi GID knew the names of the coup plotters and that the special CIA commu-nications equipment was now with it in Baghdad. Chalabi, who had been a *per-sona non grata* with the CIA for the past year, saw his chance to rehabilitate himself with the agency. He flew to Washington and, in his meeting with Deutch and Richter, passed on the intelligence he had received. However, Deutch and Rich-ter viewed Chalabi's action as motivated by his hostility to the INA,[10] which had been implicated in blowing up the INC's Salahuddin office in October. Ruling out the aborting of the well-advanced plan, they chose to accelerate it. They fixed June 26 as the D-Day, and decided to use CIA operatives working under Unscom cover to contact the crucial Iraqi conspirators in the RG and the SRG.

Little wonder that Unscom's next confrontation with Iraq came in early June. Unscom's BMVC team, headed by Baghdad-based Goran Wallen, an Ameri-can, and the Unscom 150 team led by Ritter, demanded access to two RG and SRG sites in and near Baghdad. As before, Ritter's team included Moe Dobbs and eight other CIA Special Activities Staff. Iraq refused on the grounds that such visits would threaten its national security. This led to a stand-off for five days as negotiations continued at the UN in New York, with the Iraqi ambassador, Nizar Hamdoun, describing these sites as "extremely sensitive" and access to them as a violation of Iraq's sovereignty.

Anything to do with the SRG was particularly sensitive. Saddam formed the SRG in the wake of two serious assassination attempts on him in 1991 after the Second Gulf War and an ambush of his motorcade in the following year. He did so by handpicking the best that the Republican Guard officer corps could offer. The SRG became a super-elite force with its officers and men receiving higher salaries than their RG counterparts, and better perks. Designed to amalgamate the best in the regime's security-intelligence system and armed forces, it was organized into two basic structures – combat and security, the latter being the larger. It had four brigades, an artillery command, an air defense command, and force-level units managed directly by its headquarters. According to the written orders posted at various SRG sites, it had four missions: safeguard the president; protect all presidential facilities; prepare for combat; and perform any other task that may be assigned to it.[11] Since the SRG worked in close collaboration with the Special Security and the COC – the organizations Unscom was desperately trying to monitor – the objections of Ambassador Hamdoun were genuine.

On June 12, 1996, the Security Council passed a resolution calling for "immediate, unconditional and unrestricted access to any and all places." Baghdad refused to budge. Whether the Iraqis blocked Unscom's access to these sites for the general reason of "national security" they expressed publicly, or whether they had inside information about the details of the US-sponsored coup – with the CIA operatives under Unscom cover contacting the plotting Iraqi officers at these RG and SRG bases – remains a matter of conjecture. What is known though is that among those executed later for conspiring to overthrow the regime were many officers of the RG (to which the al Shahwani Brothers belonged) and the SRG.[12]

The CIA proceeded as planned, and so did its partner, the INA. "The uprising should have at its center the armed forces," Alawi told the *Washington Post* on June 23, 1996. "We preach controlled, coordinated military uprising, supported by the people, that would not allow itself to go into acts of revenge or chaos." The interview was a signal for the coup three days later. It never happened.

As early as mid-June the Iraqi authorities had begun arresting the plotters. By the end of the month over 120 officers, from captains to generals, were in jail. They included officers from the RG, the SRG 3rd Battalion, General Security, Special Security (Gen. Muwafiq al Nasiri from Tikrit), GID (Col. Riyadh al Duri), army and air force – and even Unit B32 (its commander, Gen. Ata al Samawal), Saddam's special unit to communicate securely with military units but without using a telephone, an instrument he had shunned just before the Iraqi invasion of Kuwait in 1990 to evade detection by the US administration deploying highly sophisticated devices to locate him.[13] Most of them were tortured for information and then executed.

True to the dream scenarios of the Bush and Clinton administrations, all conspiring officers were Sunni from the Sunni heartland of Tikrit, Dur and Mosul in the north, and Ramadi, Falluja and Baghdad in central Iraq. In Baghdad, the successful recruitment by the CIA-sponsored plotters of many officers of the SRG and Special Security – the innermost core of the regime's security-intelligence apparatus – sent alarm bells ringing within the Saddam regime. It immediately disbanded the SRG's 3rd Battalion, and the Special Security director issued an order banning contact between SRG personnel and aliens.[14]

Once the Iraqi regime had got over its alarm and shock, it stiffened its stance on Unscom inspections. It now perceived these exercises as part of communications channels for coordinating a coup to be staged after its attention had been diverted by US military strikes, which would also provide a chance for the Jordan-based INA insurgents to enter Iraq to carry out subversive acts. Soon Tariq Aziz would spell out his government's hardening stance to Unscom in his meetings with Ekeus in Baghdad, thus starting a process which two-and-a-half years later would culminate in an American blitzkrieg against Iraq and the end of the UN inspection and monitoring regimes.

For now, as a result of Baghdad's denial of access to the RG and SRG sites to Unscom, the Security Council passed Resolution 1060 on June 12, 1996, demanding that Iraq give unconditional access to any and all sites Unscom wanted to inspect. Washington hoped that, with Baghdad refusing to do so, Ekeus would brief the Council accordingly, providing it with an opportunity to persuade the Council to declare that Iraq was in "material breach" of Resolution 687, thus arming it with a basis to punish Iraq militarily. Instead, having heard Ekeus, the Council decided to dispatch him to Baghdad to persuade Iraq to accept Resolution 1060.

His first meeting with Tariq Aziz was on June 19. "There are two governments, the US and the UK, which officially or formally say they would like to change the government of Iraq," Aziz told Ekeus.

> Iraq cannot take lightly the fact that Unscom receives information mainly from these two governments, and then you send teams to the Special Republican Guard sites and find nothing … You sent your team, Unscom 150, anticipating a crisis … *I am complaining about the timing of the inspections* … If your proposals do not accommodate the principle of national sovereignty and national security and the reasonably early [end to sanctions], then we will not agree to them, even if the Americans threatened force.[15]

When faced with these facts, Ekeus had the option of either saying "No compromise," thus paving the way for American military strikes and the concomitant evacuation of Unscom for good, or reaching a compromise with Aziz. He chose the latter option. "The US and UK might have intended for Ekeus to be a messenger," notes Scott Ritter in *Endgame,* "but Ekeus was his own man and knew that he had a choice: be tough and lose the inspection process altogether, or seek a compromise and keep the inspection regime in place and functioning, even if flawed."

Ekeus's three days of talks ended on June 21, when he and Aziz signed a new plan that tackled four issues of concern, including Iraqi concealment, in exchange for Baghdad's acceptance of Resolution 1060. It required Ekeus to provide a final conclusion of Unscom's investigations into Iraq's past weapons programs in his next six-monthly report. Ekeus knew he was compromising. He did so because he realized that if he returned to the Security Council without a solution, Washington and London would strike Iraqi targets, and that such an action would not make Baghdad change its mind but would only result in the termination of the inspection regime, which needed to be saved. He and Aziz signed a confidential Agreement for Modalities of Sensitive Site Inspections (AMOSSI). The sixty Sensitive Sites selected in the light of Iraq's national security, dignity and sovereignty were various ministries, the RG and SRG facilities, the GID, Military Intelligence and Special Security. This permitted the Iraqis to "freeze" a sensitive or sovereign site if Unscom inspectors arrived unannounced until a senior Iraqi official appeared to escort the inspectors whose number was to be limited to four. Conscious that AMOSSI would be criticized by America and Britain, Ekeus impressed on the Iraqi side to keep it secret. But Aziz lost no time in informing France and Russia. And the word leaked to the UN missions of Britain and America; they were furious. When faced with criticism from them at the Security Council, Ekeus retorted that the presence of an Iraqi official was necessary from an operational point of view and that it did not affect the efficiency of inspections which were the strictest in the arms' control history, pointing out that during such an inspection movement of all vehicular traffic was banned to ensure that no material was removed from the site.[16]

Back in Amman, on June 26, the date of the putative anti-Saddam coup, the CIA station at the US embassy received a message from the Iraqi GID: "We have arrested all your people, and so pack up and go home." And the special CIA team did just that.

As if this were not enough, a further setback awaited the American hawks who had been relentless in their hostility to Saddam, this time in the mountain fastness of Iraqi Kurdistan.

The Kurdish fiasco

Relations between the Kurdistan Democratic Party and the Patriotic Union of Kurdistan, soured by their contrary stands on the March 1995 coup plans, continued to deteriorate, with Kurdistan virtually divided into two sectors, and the KDP and the PUK raising revenue mainly through customs duties on goods moving either between intra-Kurdish borders or across the Kurdistani frontiers with Turkey or Iran.

Washington's attempts to reconcile the warring factions between July and September failed. By then the internecine Kurdish violence, dating back to May 1994, had claimed 3,000 lives, and the PUK had expelled the KDP from half of northern Kurdistan, and established its jurisdiction over two-thirds of the 3.2 million people living in Kurdistan.

But it did not have corresponding resources to administer the territory under its control. The lucrative export of Iraqi oil to Turkey was being conducted through the area controlled by the KDP's Masud Barzani, who, unlike the PUK's Jalal Talabani, continued to maintain surreptitious contacts with Saddam Hussein, and even received weapons from him.[17]

Besides the old rivalries, a new factor had emerged to poison the political environment. It dated back to the period just before the Second Gulf War when, tempted by the funds from Baghdad, many tribal leaders had pressed young Kurds into the Iraqi auxiliary force, called Fursan. After Iraq's defeat in the war, this force broke up into many quasi-independent armed units. Fickle in their loyalty to the KDP or PUK, the commanders of these units often changed sides, depending on the size of the offers of money and weapons from Barzani or Talabani.

Another important element was the customs revenue collected by the two factions. With the cross-border trade increasing between 1994 and 1996, the KDP-PUK competition sharpened. The most lucrative source was the export of Iraqi petroleum, and petroleum products, to Turkey via the Habour border town controlled by the KDP. With 600 trucks using the crossing daily in each direction, the KDP was collecting an estimated $500,000 a day. Disregarding the agreement it had signed with the PUK in 1994, it refused to share any of this revenue with its rival. In return the PUK refused to share the control of Irbil, the administrative capital of the region, with the KDP. So while the PUK enjoyed political and demographic superiority, it lacked financial resources to administer the area under its jurisdiction. And the reverse was the case with the KDP, whose leader, Barzani, could not reconcile himself to the loss of Irbil, the largest city in the region, with a population of 7–800,000.

Militarily, each faction, with 12–13,000 troops and *peshmargas*, was about even in manpower. But the parties were unequal when it came to weaponry and ammunition. Given his financial dependence on the Iraqi petroleum exports, Barzani had interest in maintaining contacts with Baghdad without whose cooperation he could not obtain Iraqi oil and oil products at discounted prices for sale to the Turks at market rates. Baghdad was also the KDP's clandestine source of arms and ammunition. By contrast, Talabani had distanced himself from Saddam, and used every opportunity to condemn him. He was equally at odds with Iran and provided sanctuary to the secular-leftist KDPI. Over time, though, he realized that he could not afford to be antagonistic towards both Tehran and Baghdad, and that he would have to mend his fences with one or the other.

As the struggle between the KDP and the PUK continued, Baghdad offered to conciliate them. The offer was rebuffed summarily. Tehran, whose contacts with both parties dated back to the Iran–Iraq War, also tried and failed. In the process, however, Talabani, administering an area with a long border with Iran, realized that his only source of arms and ammunition was Tehran. So he decided to bury the hatchet with it. This went down badly not only with Barzani but also with Saddam, who resented Iran's renewed involvement in Iraqi Kurds' affairs. This led to increased clandestine cooperation between Barzani and Saddam.

Little wonder that when the KDP assaulted PUK units in Hrian on July 5, 1996, Talabani warned that the PUK "will not remain silent about these assaults, the source for which we believe is the KDP's relationship with Saddam, the executioner."[18]

Three weeks later, with the PUK's tacit support, Tehran mounted an assault on the KDPI base at Koy Sanjak, 40 miles (65 km) from the Iranian border, and captured it after a three-day battle. The defeated KDPI promised Talabani in writing that it would no longer attack Iran. With this, relations between Talabani and the Islamic Republic warmed. And Tehran proved generous in its supply of arms and ammunition to the PUK.

Thus bolstered, Talabani planned an offensive to dislodge the KDP from its stronghold of Hajj Umran near the Iranian border. On August 17, when KDP leaders were busy celebrating the founding anniversary of their party, the PUK staged its offensive. For the next few days fighting went well for it. On August 21, Robert Pelletreau, US assistant secretary of state for Near Eastern Affairs, urged Barzani to confer with Talabani. In response, Barzani stressed a point likely to appeal to Washington's anti-Tehran bias. "We request the US to … send a clear message to Iran to end its meddling in northern Iraq," he said in his fax to Pelletreau. "Our options are limited, and since the US is not responding politically … the only option left is the Iraqis."[19]

Without waiting for Pelletreau's response, the next day Barzani addressed a letter to "His Excellency President Saddam Hussein" via Gen. Ali Hassan al Majid, commander of the First Corps based in Kirkuk, requesting military assistance to "ease the foreign threat" from Iran. Saddam jumped at the opportunity. Here was his chance to poison KDP–PUK relations to an irreparable degree. Also, he reckoned that since he was acting to block the expansion of Iran's influence in the region Washington would not retaliate against him instantly were he to side with Barzani against pro-Tehran Talabani.[20]

On August 23, the US-mediated ceasefire lasted just one day. As the situation on the ground worsened for the Salahuddin-based KDP – facing a military threat from the PUK-controlled Irbil – Barzani again warned Washington that he might approach Baghdad for help. Indeed, the Iraqi troops stationed about 10 miles (16 km) south of Irbil – along the *de facto* border between Kurdistan and the centrally-controlled Iraq – were getting ready to move north. This was noted by the CIA, which on August 26 declared itself "reasonably confident" that Iraq's soldiers were planning a march on Irbil, and whose Near East division in Langley, Virginia, evacuated its team from Salahuddin. Two days later Talabani publicly confirmed the CIA's secret conclusion regarding Baghdad's intentions. Yet, when Pelletreau proposed that the KDP and the PUK dispatch envoys to London for a meeting on August 30 at the US embassy, Barzani agreed instantly – if only to stymie any suspicion in Washington.

In consort with Barzani, early on the morning of August 31, Saddam dispatched three Republican Guard armored divisions (30,000 soldiers and 400 tanks) towards Irbil, situated 10 miles (16 km) north of the 36th Parallel, with heavy Iraqi artillery targeting the city's outskirts, while taking care not to deploy aircraft and thus challenge the Western air umbrella. The PUK commander in Irbil with only 3,000 fighters ordered hasty evacuation. Both Barzani and the Baghdad government maintained that the latest military move was designed to expel the Iranian forces who, according to them, had penetrated 40 miles (65 km) into Iraqi Kurdistan. (Apparently, this was a reference to the Iranian assault on the KDPI base in Koy Sanjak a month earlier.) To set the record straight, Tariq Aziz released Barzani's written invitation to Saddam Hussein, on August 22, for military assistance.[21]

The fighting was over in thirty-six hours, with direct casualties numbering less than 200. By then, the evening of September 1, the Iraqi forces had captured Irbil, sealed off its exits to avoid creating a refugee problem, and replaced the PUK's green emblem with the yellow flag of the KDP *and* the tricolor of Iraq at the parliament building, the administrative heart of the region. Baghdad warned Washington to keep out of Iraqi Kurdistan, vowing to turn it into another Vietnam if it intervened militarily on the ground.[22]

On September 2, in a BBC World Service Radio interview, Barzani said,

> Saddam Hussein is still the president of Iraq. We have not separated from Iraq. We love our Kurdish flag, but there is also [in Irbil] the central [Iraqi] flag. If the Iraqis can meet our demands we can make an agreement.[23]

(On September 9, as Barzani appeared to be on the verge of signing an agreement with Baghdad on autonomy for Kurds within Iraq, he declared that Saddam Hussein was not an enemy of the Kurdish people.)

Along with Iraq's soldiers came its General Intelligence Department agents. Working in association with its KDP counterpart, with whom the Iraqi GID had long-standing contacts, the Iraqis rounded up all anti-KDP activists – including those of the PUK and SAIRI – with especial interest in the INC contingent working closely with the recently-departed CIA team. Earlier in the day, on their way to Irbil the Iraqis had captured ninety-six soldiers of the INC's 3rd Brigade and executed them. Other losses by the INC's military and intelligence wings raised the total to over 200.

On September 2–3, Baghdad began withdrawing its forces, but not before planting its GID personnel in the KDP-administered territory. "It is likely there are Iraqi intelligence agents and Iraqi secret police [i.e., General Security] here, but publicly there is no [Iraqi] organization here," conceded Karim Sinjari, the KDP intelligence chief, six months later.[24] On the diplomatic front, by recapturing Irbil with Saddam's overt military support, Barzani severely undermined Washington's stance of excluding the Iraqi dictator from the Kurdish affairs.

He also, inadvertently, showed that the Clinton administration's policy was in limbo. It refused to aid the quasi-independent Kurdistan to graduate to an independent state, and at the same time ruled out the option of the region reverting to Baghdad's jurisdiction. All it wanted to do was to use the Kurds as a lever to keep Saddam down. On the opposite side, this episode enabled Saddam to show – particularly to his neighbors – that his military was in a position to implement his political decisions, and that it was in a good mettle.

In an attempt to show that he was doing something, on September 3, President Clinton announced an extension of the southern no-fly zone, from the 32nd Parallel to the 33rd Parallel. (France disagreed with this step, originally proposed by British Prime Minister John Major, and said that its planes participating in the air surveillance of the southern no-fly zone would not cross the 32nd Parallel.) That night and the night after, in its Operation "Desert Strike", the US fired forty-four cruise missiles from its warships in the Gulf and B–52 bombers inducted from the Far East, at Iraq's command and control posts and air defense centers near Nasiriyeh, 400 miles (640 km) south of Irbil, hitting fifteen targets. Washington did so to "make Saddam Hussein pay a price for his latest brutality" and at the same time demonstrate its ability and willingness to contain Iraq in the long run.[25] However, the Pentagon's action elicited ridicule from some commentators who joked, "The Americans got the Iraqi map wrong way up" by hitting targets in the south whereas the problem was in the north.

But the truth was that the US had faced resistance to its preferred option of striking the Iraqi forces in the north. Ankara refused to let the Pentagon use its air bases for the purpose. It was quietly pleased about the resurgence of intra-Kurdish bloodletting after a period of comparative peace and five years of autonomous Iraqi Kurdish existence, which inspired the separatist Turkish PKK, that had been waging an armed struggle against Ankara since 1984, and using the quasi-independent Iraqi Kurdistan as its rear base. Of the three Western allies maintaining air surveillance in the north, France – contributing six of the sixty planes involved in the air surveillance exercise (with the UK doing the same) – publicly disagreed with the US, arguing that their common aim was to impose a no-fly zone, not a no-drive zone, and that by responding to Barzani's request for military assistance, Iraq had not violated the air exclusion limitation imposed on it. Therefore there was no justification either for US missile strikes against Iraq, or for extending the southern no-fly zone.[26]

In the Middle East, all Arab states except Kuwait, either opposed America's strikes or maintained silence. Russia and China strongly condemned them. This emboldened Saddam. On September 3, he announced that "hostile aircraft" in the northern and southern air exclusion zones would be shot down. It was only when the Russian foreign minister, Yevgeny Primakov, his old, Arabic-speaking friend, appealed to him to reverse his order that he did so ten days later.

By then the KDP had expelled its rival from almost all of Kurdistan, including the PUK bastion of Suleimaniya, with PUK leaders and fighters taking refuge in Iran. But this did not last long. On October 10 the PUK, freshly armed by

Tehran, launched a multi-prong counteroffensive from the border zone and recovered within days what it had lost a month earlier. By October 21, the PUK regained all lost territory except Irbil.

The total human cost to the two sides was about 2,000. Now Saddam warned Talabani publicly not to try retaking Irbil; and both Tehran and Washington advised likewise. On October 23, there was a US–UK-mediated ceasefire between the PUK and the KDP, which was later made permanent. Barzani and Talabani promised not to seek intervention by foreign forces. And they agreed to discuss a Temporary Local Administration, sharing of the customs revenue, and fresh elections. But the US mediator, who was assigned the job of conciliating the two sides, found them as intransigent as before on control of revenues and the contested areas, especially Irbil.

Whatever the reasons that propelled Barzani to invite Saddam to fight on his side, he did incalculable damage to the overall American strategy in Iraq. The CIA pulled out 2,000 agents immediately, followed by another 3,500, and wound up its four-year operation, costing $100 million, to develop Kurdistan as a territory from which to subvert and overthrow the Iraqi dictator.[27] Once this happened, Saddam lifted the economic embargo he had imposed on the Kurdish region almost five years earlier.

The ease with which Iraq's military marched into Kurdistan highlighted two depressing facts to Washington: the Kurdish troops and weapons were no match for Baghdad's soldiers and equipment; and, though much reduced from its peak of a million men under arms on the eve of the Second Gulf War, Iraq was still a substantial military power. Baghdad now had 380,000 men in its armed forces, including seven RG divisions, equipped with 2,700 tanks, 1,980 artillery pieces and 330 combat aircraft.[28]

The extent of the US setback was summed up by the testimonies given by the CIA chief John Deutch to the Senate Intelligence Committee in May and September 1996. In his first appearance he had said, "Saddam's chances of surviving another year are declining." But in his second appearance on September 19, he stated, "Saddam Hussein is politically stronger now in the Middle East than he was before sending his troops into northern Iraq in recent weeks," and added that there was "little prospect" of him being removed from power in the near future.[29]

Overt signs of this appeared within months. Having actively participated in an anti-Saddam coup plan for almost a year, King Hussein of Jordan did an about-turn. In December he held a much-publicized meeting with Iraqi foreign minister Muhammad al Sahhaf in Amman, thus pleasing the local business community, which was eager to have a share of the increased Iraqi trade following the implementation of the oil-for-food scheme.[30]

In Turkey, after renewing the six-month mandate for the Western Operation "Provide Comfort" ten times, the parliament let it lapse on December 31, 1996. It then immediately endorsed a six-month mandate for the Reconnaissance Force (Keshif Gucu, in Turkish), which the US and the UK renamed Operation

"Northern Watch" – with France pulling out of the exercise, chiefly as a result of its disgust at the endemic internecine Kurdish violence.

In the minds of Turks and others, there was much difference between Operations "Provide Comfort" and "Northern Watch". The former had both aerial and ground components – with American, British and French ground forces and intelligence agents stationed at the Turkish border town of Zakho, and a publicly declared objective of toppling the Saddam regime. But Washington's evacuation of several thousand Iraqi Arabs and Kurds, who had collaborated with the US, Britain and France, from northern Iraq meant an end to all ground presence. The fresh Operation "Northern Watch" also circumscribed the way the US and UK air forces were to conduct their mission. The new rules of engagement required that the Reconnaissance Force be led jointly by US and Turksih commanders, and that the planes refrain from any offensive action and use arms only in self-defense and only after the identity of the threatening aircraft had been confirmed and the pilot warned to turn back.[31]

Oil-for-food scheme gets going

A side-effect of the intra-Kurdish clashes was that the UN secretary-general, Boutrous Boutrous-Ghali, postponed the stationing of UN monitors in Kurdistan – to check the petroleum flow through a pipeline to Turkey (as required by the oil-for-food Resolution 986) – to ensure their safety. With the prospect of poor crops in the spring of 1996 severely undermining Iraq's fast deteriorating rationing system, which saved the bulk of the population from starvation, Saddam had agreed in January 1996 to discuss the terms under which Resolution 986 could be implemented. By so doing he meant to impress on Iraqis that whatever arrangement followed would be a result of negotiations of independent Iraq with the UN, rather than a mere Iraqi acceptance of a Security Council resolution. In May, Baghdad signed an MOU with the UN secretary-general, detailing the operation of the oil-for-food scheme. And in August the Security Council's 661 Sanctions Committee endorsed the scheme. Of the $2 billion worth of petroleum to be sold every six months by Iraq's SOMO, 30 percent would be allocated to the UN Compensation Fund; 13 percent to the relief in the Kurdish region to be administered by UN personnel; and another 7 percent to the administration of this and other programs by the UN (with its representatives monitoring export of oil and observing distribution of imported food and medicine), leaving Baghdad with only half of the total oil revenue.

Most of the foreign exchange was to be spent on foodgrains and medicine, with only $17 million left for the purchase of badly-needed fertilizers, chemicals for sewage treatment, and spare parts for water pumps.[32] Before the Second Gulf War, water drawn from the Tigris or Euphrates was treated in modern facilities using aluminum sulfate and chlorine. And sewage was treated and made bacteria-free before being discharged into rivers. Both these processes were driven by imported water pumps which need periodic repairs and maintenance. Due to the unavailability of spare parts for pumps, and the ban on the import of aluminum sulfate and chlorine, most water and sewage treatment plants had fallen into disuse or were functioning below capacity. Power shortages, leading to long and frequent breakdowns, accentuated the problem since water pumps failed to maintain pressure. Untreated sewage got discharged into rivers which continued to be the only source of drinking water. Therefore water-borne diseases – cholera, typhoid, dysentery and leishmaniasis – rose sharply among Iraqis already suffering the consequences of malnutrition, hitting children hardest.

According to an FAO report, in 1995 the urban–rural population ratio in Iraq was 71:29. Except those 10–12 percent in urban areas engaged in trade and other lucrative commercial activities, and three-quarters of rural inhabitants engaged in agriculture – where the government had encouraged farmers to grow wheat by keeping up its real price at the equivalent of $100 a tonne – the rest, about 70 percent of the total, were doing badly. Given the massive unemployment in towns and cities, there was a drift back to villages where agriculture was encouraged by the authorities. As a result, roughly 40 percent of the nation's labor force was now engaged in some form of agriculture, twice the figure before the 1991 war.[33]

Little wonder that public opinion in the Gulf region began to favor the ending of the UN embargo to provide relief to suffering Iraqis. Reflecting this, on October 15, 1995, addressing the newly accredited foreign ambassadors, UAE President Zaid al Nahyan called on Iraq's Arab opponents to reconcile with it, and added, "Iraqi President Saddam Hussein is only a human being who has made mistakes. It is time to lift sanctions because it is the Iraqi people who are paying for his mistakes." His statement was endorsed in the capitals of Oman, Bahrain and Qatar, whose rulers had re-established full diplomatic relations with Baghdad a year earlier.[34] Earlier in the year Boutros-Ghali had pointed out that the "International community has failed to confront the ethical question of whether the suffering inflicted in the target country is a legitimate means of exerting pressure on political leaders whose behavior is unlikely to be affected by the plight of their subjects."

No doubt the people in the region were relieved to learn in early December 1996, when the new oil-for-food scheme finally went into effect, that the rations of wheat flour, rice, cooking oil, sugar and lentils in Iraq would be raised to provide a daily per capita intake of 2,000 calories, up from the current 1,300. The increase was greeted with joy by Iraqis, the first truly good news for them for several years. At the same time it provided an opportunity to the state-run media to trumpet that the "steadfastness" shown by an independent Iraq, despite all odds, was paying off – a viewpoint that would, backed by evidence, gather strength with time.

Overall, so far, 1996 had brought a series of successes for Saddam. The year began with him securing the return of Hussein Kamil Hassan, the most damaging defector yet in his seventeen years in power, and seeing him killed. Then, in June, he had the quiet satisfaction of aborting the most serious coup attempt against him yet – masterminded by the CIA in conjunction with the INA and intelligence agencies of Britain, Jordan and Saudi Arabia. Two months later, due to the process started by Barzani's invitation to Saddam, the CIA ended its long-maintained strategy of turning Kurdistan into a staging area for his overthrow. And in early December his government announced a substantial increase in the rations of basic necessities, thus improving its standing among the populace. Between the beginning and end of 1996, the exchange rate for the Iraqi Dinar improved from ID 3,000 to ID 1,000 to US$1.

But before the year ended it had shocking news for Saddam. On the evening of Thursday December 12, a three-car convoy of Uday Saddam Hussein, on its way to a party being given by his maternal cousin, Luai Khairallah Talfa, was attacked by four gunmen at the T-junction of Mansur Street and International Street (*Sharia al Dawlee*) in the affluent Mansur neighborhood of west Baghdad. Armed with machine-guns, they killed the driver of Uday's car and one of his bodyguards, and pumped eight bullets into Uday, including one into his spine and another into his left leg, before fleeing. The bleeding Uday was rushed to the prestigious Ibn Sina Hospital. The sensational news spread fast. To curb rumor-mongering, the state-run media soon announced that Uday Saddam Hussein had been "lightly hurt." Yet it was not until June 1997 that Uday was discharged from hospital – in a wheelchair. By then Saddam Hussein had restored to Uday the funds and official positions he had taken away from him in the wake of the Hussein Kamil Hassan's defection.

Among those who claimed responsibility for the attack were al Daawa al Islamiya, a militant Shia constituent of the Tehran-based SAIRI; a Kuwait-based member of the Dulaimi tribe which nursed a gripe against the regime for the execution of Gen. Muhammad Madhlum al Dulaimi; and a Dubai-based group calling itself al Nahda (*lit.*, Awakening). But the government blamed Iran and its agents for the assassination attempt.

In a wide sweep the authorities arrested hundreds of people, most of them in the Mansur neighborhood. But it was not until twenty months later that they charged a dozen suspects with the attack.

Meanwhile, in July 1997, in an interview with Patrick Cockburn of the London-based *Independent*, Ismail Othman (a pseudonym), in his late twenties and belonging to the al Nahda, claimed to be one of the members of the hit team. The group was formed in 1991 after the Second Gulf War by Hamdoun Ali, an electrical engineer, who was executed in 1996. For the Uday project, their inside informant was an Al Nahda member, Raad al Hazaa, an officer in the Republican Guard and a nephew of Gen. Omar al Hazaa, who was executed in 1990 for openly criticizing Saddam Hussein for his conduct of the Iran–Iraq War. After the attack the hitmen and Raad al Hazaa escaped overland to Iran and Afghanistan, and then to a European destination. The rest of the tiny group got eliminated in February 1997. A clandestine meeting of eleven al Nahda activists in Greater Baghdad got exposed because one of them had parked a stolen car in the street, and it was detected by the police. In the ensuing melee they were all killed when the security forces fired a rocket-propelled grenade at the house they were occupying.[35]

Even though the Al Nahda team failed to assassinate Uday, Ismail Othman felt that much was achieved in psychological terms. "We wanted to end the common sense of hopelessness," he said. "The Iraqi opposition had all gone out of the country, with nobody left inside."[36]

Actually, unknown to al Nahda members, their action encouraged the Damascus-based Wafiq al Samarrai to spring into action, with the Iraqi president as his target. He had all along been a proponent of Saddam's assassination. Now he and his fourteen cohorts – all serving officers in Iraq – surmised that, fearing an attempt on his life, Saddam would retreat to his presidential palace in his home village of Auja just south of Tikrit. So, on December 13, they conspired to ambush his convoy the next day. The plan was that seven of them would monitor Saddam's convoy outside Dujayal – about halfway between Baghdad and Tikrit – and inform their seven co-plotters waiting outside Auja by using the local telephone system (mobile phones had yet to arrive in Iraq). It was standard practice for Special Security to sever telephone links in every settlement that Saddam passed in his journeys, and restore them after he was gone. But because of the Uday episode, Special Security cut off the telephone lines all the way between Baghdad and Tikrit during his travel. So the group outside Dujayil could not contact its cohorts outside Auja.

The non-event would have gone unnoticed but for the fact that one of the conspirators, the Basra-based Lt-Col. Ali Ahmad al Samarrai, failed to join his group outside Auja. On his way north, his car got a flat tyre 7 miles (11 km) south of Tikrit. He had no spare – tyres being in short supply in Iraq due to UN sanctions, with a single tyre costing as much as three months' salary of a civil servant – and found himself stranded. This drew the attention of Special Security agents who were posted along the highway and who questioned anybody who stopped. On searching his car they discovered a diary with codes across certain names used by him in his communications with Wafiq al Samarrai. Soon the authorities picked up the remaining co-plotters.[37]

So 1996, which started with the end of a crisis in the First Family of Iraq, ended with another shock to it, with the intermediate period yielding positive news to Saddam and his authoritarian regime.

US intelligence agencies and Unscom

Yet there were clandestine developments at Unscom and the CIA and the NSA – not to mention the intelligence agencies of Britain and Israel – that would have angered the Iraqi strong-man had he been privy to them in all their Byzantine details.

According to the *Washington Post*, Unscom's "remote monitoring system," begun in May 1993, expanded over the years to include over 300 weapons installations and research facilities in Iraq. Until February 1996, the video images and the logs of the electrical power consumed were recorded onto a magnetic tape at the remote sites. The Baghdad-based Unscom inspectors periodically visited the sites to collect the tapes. In March 1996, with Iraq's agreement, Unscom began transmitting images from the cameras back to Baghdad using radio signals, which were boosted by relays. This system provided Unscom with an almost real-time view of distant facilities. But, unknown to Unscom, the American signals-and-sensors technicians, who built and maintained the system, were intelligence operatives led by an innovative military intelligence technician. They constructed boosting stations with covert capabilities. Concealed in their structures were antennae capable of intercepting microwave transmissions. The US agents placed some of them near important nodes of Iraq's military communications system. Between September 1995 and March 1996 this team carried out many "maintenance" missions in Iraq. Also at least two other technicians lent by the US to Unscom to run the remote camera system were employees of the CIA.[38]

This system, incorporated into the monitoring facilities, ran in tandem with the second eavesdropping channel – both of them part of an operation code-named "Shake the Tree." It used commercial scanners to intercept low-powered Very High Frequencies (VHF) radio transmissions used by Iraq to direct its concealment efforts against Unscom. The "Shake the Tree" operation involved staging confrontational Unscom inspections to force the Iraqis to activate their concealment procedures which would be picked up by a quick synthesis of multifarious intelligence sources, thus enabling Unscom to catch the culprits red-handed as they moved contraband. The US-based director of "Shake the Tree" shared his information with a fellow-American, Charles Duelfer, deputy executive chairman of Unscom since 1993, to ensure that there was no change in Unscom's latest procedures – but not with his boss, Rolf Ekeus, a Swede, or, later, Richard Butler, an Australian.[39] (It was not the first time America had abused the UN for its own ends. Following the March 1975 Algiers Accord between Iran and Iraq, the Shah withdrew his support to the Iraqi Kurds fighting Baghdad from the Iranian soil. Due to the resulting humanitarian crisis, the UN sent its aid personnel, drawn from a few contributing member-states, to Iran. They included US intelligence agents with a mandate to salvage what they could of the Kurdish military campaign against pro-Moscow Iraq.[40])

So, it was not surprising when, following three SICMs by Unscom's Concealment Investigation Unit, the CIA–NSA failed to provide Ekeus with any report or conclusion drawn from the field data. In September 1996 Ekeus complained about this to CIA director Deutch. Yet nothing happened. It was noteworthy that around this time several articles accusing Ekeus of employing a large percentage of CIA operatives and using an American U–2 spy plane to provide sensitive information to US intelligence agencies had appeared in Iraq's semi-official newspapers. Disappointed with Washington, Ekeus approached Britain, with its decoding and translation facilities at Cheltenham, and Israel, with its de-encryption facilities at its Unit 8200, to provide the services that the US was then doing.

Both agreed, and went on to furnish complete transcripts of the SICM intercepts to Unscom.

Keeping his promise to Baghdad, in his next six-monthly report, Ekeus for the first time gave a summary of all that had been accomplished so far, including in the biological field, where in May–June 1996 Unscom supervised the destruction of Iraq's biological weapons production facilities at Hakam. His report noted that since its formation in April 1991, Unscom had dispatched 373 inspection teams, involving 3,574 experts, to Iraq, and that it had spent $120 million, most of it obtained from Iraq's assets frozen abroad. It also noted that there was an organized Iraqi mechanism for concealment of materials and documents concerning proscribed weapons.[41]

5

SADDAM AND
RE-ELECTED CLINTON

One of the first acts of Bill Clinton on his re-election as US president in November 1996 was to promote Madeleine Karbol Albright, then American ambassador to the UN, to secretary of state. This was bad news for Iraq. At the UN she had pursued an uncompromisingly hawkish policy on Baghdad. Nothing captured her stony-hearted attitude towards Iraq better than the statement she made during her interview with Lesley Stahl on Columbia Broadcasting Service (CBS) Television's "60 Minutes" program on May 12, 1996. "More than 500,000 Iraqi children are already dead as a direct result of the UN sanctions," said Stahl. "Do you think the price is worth paying?" Albright replied, "It is a difficult question. But, yes, we think the price is worth it." [1]

So it came as no surprise when on March 26, 1997, Albright said, "We do not agree with the nations who argue that if Iraq complies with its obligations concerning weapons of mass destruction, sanctions should be lifted." UN sanctions, she insisted, would remain. [2] This was a reprise of what President Bush's Deputy National Security Adviser, Robert Gates, had said in the aftermath of the Second Gulf War: UN sanctions would remain so long as Saddam exercised power in Baghdad, and meanwhile, "Iraqis will pay the price." [3] So there was no incentive for Saddam to cooperate with Unscom. But unlike in spring 1991 his position was far from hopeless.

Indeed, in those six years, the balance of power had gradually shifted in his favor. Several attempts by the CIA and Iraqi opposition to topple him had failed. This in turn had discouraged Washington's regional allies from letting the Pentagon use their territory for military strikes against the Saddam government. After all, they shared the same region as Iraq, and they did not want to stoke up the hostility of Baghdad by participating in subversive or overtly damaging actions against its regime. The rulers in the Gulf monarchies were also aware of the increasing sympathy for the impoverished Iraqis shown by their subjects, who compared unfavorably Washington's unwavering harsh treatment of Iraq with its indulgent attitude towards Israel, which over the past decades had either ignored or flagrantly violated a series of Security Council resolutions with impunity.

At the UN Security Council, France, Russia and China openly and repeatedly disagreed with America and Britain on how to deal with Baghdad. As

1997 unfolded, Iraq's relations with Unscom became more fraught, especially after Ekeus had been replaced in July by Richard Butler – a 55-year-old Australian disarmament expert, who retained Charles Duelfer, a former US state department official, as his deputy – and unconfirmed reports of Washington using Unscom for its national intelligence became more persistent. With these differences, the Anglo-Saxon duo and non-Anglo-Saxon trio at the Security Council became entrenched. This encouraged Saddam to demand an end to the UN embargo.

The charge of using Unscom for its national intelligence was also leveled against Israel, an arch-enemy of Iraq. Its civilian and military intelligence agencies, Mossad and Aman, had been cooperating with Unscom since October 1994.[4] These contacts were maintained chiefly through Scott Ritter, whose idea of setting up a Concealment Investigation Unit within Unscom had been adopted by Ekeus. By the end of 1996 Ritter's liaison with the Israeli intelligence, which involved *inter alia* sharing U–2 photographs of Iraq with it, had increased to the extent that the American FBI started an investigation against Ritter on the possibility that he had compromised American national security – an exercise that, four years on, had yet to finish. Unsurprisingly, it would be Ritter who would introduce Butler to Aman's director, Maj-Gen. Ami Ayalon on September 1, 1997, at a New York hotel.[5]

In the case of America, covert cooperation between it and Unscom had increased to the point where Ritter gave regular briefings to the US National Security Council in Washington. During one such meeting in early April 1997 in the White House Situation Room, he informed his audience of the results of his Unscom 182 inspection, which had been coordinated with a U–2 photo reconnaissance flight in a failed attempt to pinpoint a clandestine Iraqi missile force. What is more, he told them that Unscom "will have to start inspecting residences and properties associated with the president of Iraq." To gain stronger US-UK backing for "a more aggressive Unscom posture regarding Iraqi concealment activities," he went on to author a paper entitled *The Iraqi Concealment Mechanism*.[6]

Ritter's strategy outlined at the NSC chimed with the general tone of the last six-monthly report Ekeus submitted to the Security Council on April 11, 1997. In it he referred to "the Iraqi policy of systematic concealment, denial and masking of the most important aspects of its proscribed weapons and related capabilities."[7] While conceding that "Not much is unknown about Iraq's retained proscribed weapons capabilities," he warned that "what is not accounted for cannot be neglected." In the WMD, the unknowns were 17 tons of growth media used for reproducing toxins and 900 lb (400 kg) of anthrax, and in the delivery system, two of the 819 Scuds with a range of 190 miles (300 km). "Even a limited inventory of long range missiles would be a source of deep concern if those missiles were filled with the most deadly of chemical nerve agents, VX …. If one single missile were filled with the biological agent anthrax, many millions of lethal doses could be spread in an attack on any city in the region." On the other hand, he described Unscom's monitoring system as "effective", and added,

"For the most part, Iraq has sustained a fairly good level of cooperation in the operation of the monitoring system."[8]

During the first half of June 1997, Ritter, leading Unscom 194, inspected such holy of holies as the Special Security's training academy, the Special Security Institute, and the country's highest military academy, the al Bakr Military Institute. This alarmed and puzzled Iraqi officials. In his meeting with Ritter, Gen. Amr Rashid (who continued to liaise with Unscom even though he was now the oil minister) expressed his concern about "exposing our security organization to experts outside Iraq," especially when "some of your [Unscom] experts are from foreign intelligence agencies," according to an account given by Ritter. In response, Ritter claims to have referred to his paper, *The Iraqi Concealment Mechanism*, which he was then carrying, and listed Iraq's concealed materials and capabilities. "The hidden capabilities are fully covered by your inspections and monitoring teams," replied Rashid. "On hidden materials, we agree there is a discrepancy of a few missiles. On chemicals we are converging. On biologicals, we are working hard as well."[9] Contrary to Ritter's premonition that further inspections would be disallowed, that night his team inspected the headquarters of the SRG, and the following day three SRG sites, all of them on a "no notice" basis. It was only on the day after that his team was denied access to two more SRG sites – including the 2nd Battalion garrison in Greater Baghdad – it wanted to inspect unannounced.[10]

This was enough for America and Britain to raise an objection at the Security Council. On June 21, 1997, the Council adopted Resolution 1115, condemning Iraq for denying access to Unscom, threatening further sanctions if Unscom did not report total cooperation in its October report, and suspending the sixty-day sanctions review until then. Saddam protested. "Iraq has complied with and implemented all relevant [Security Council] resolutions," he said in a television address. "There is absolutely nothing else. We demand with utmost clarity that the Security Council fulfill its commitments toward Iraq …. The practical expression of this is to respect Iraq's sovereignty and to fully and totally lift the blockade imposed on Iraq."[11] In his broadcast on the 29th anniversary of the Baathist coup on July 17, he reiterated his position, adding that if the Council did not fulfill its obligations, then "Relations between Iraq and Unscom could reach a deadlock." The matter was of great urgency to his government, which had been nurturing an expectation among Iraqis that sanctions would be lifted in the last quarter of the year.

To help the process along, Tariq Aziz went out of his way to cultivate cordial relations with Butler when the latter visited Baghdad in July along with a small Unscom delegation, which included his American deputy, Duelfer. Wary of Aziz's charm offensive, Duelfer advised Butler to remain "tough and unyielding" in his demands for accurate disclosures.[12]

Duelfer need not have worried. Since Butler had decided to focus Unscom inspections on laying bare Iraq's concealment mechanism, preferably catching the Iraqis transporting the contraband, and Baghdad had been compiling evidence of some American employees of Unscom conducting espionage in Iraq, it was only a matter of time before another Iraq–Unscom crisis built up.

In early September Iraq submitted an 800-page document on its biological weapons program to Butler who resolved several points concerning Iraq's missile program during his September 5–9 visit to Baghdad.

However, on September 13 and 15, there were two instances when an Unscom team encountered obstruction in the course of its work. At a military barracks in Tikrit, when the team members waiting at the entrance saw trucks leaving the site, an Iraqi co-pilot in the hovering Unscom helicopter physically stopped an inspector taking pictures on the basis that photographing a military site was prohibited. There was a similar incident at the Sarabandi RG garrison two days later. On the other hand, the Iraqis allowed the inspection of the headquarters of the SRG's 2nd Battalion, the access to which had been denied to Ritter three months earlier.

On September 27, Ritter, leading Unscom 207, arrived in Baghdad. His demand to inspect a barracks complex housing three companies of the SRG's 2nd Battalion, suspected of having transported biological weapons in 1994, was denied. Two days later his team was denied access to the Jabal Maqbul (*lit.*, Accepted Mountain) presidential complex, situated 44 miles (70 km) north of Tikrit, on the grounds that the site was "residential presidential." This was conveyed to Ritter by Gen. Rashid who, during their meeting in June, had told him, "I could say I have two or more documents [on you] … I know your links to intelligence and I could go through them, say I have a document that proves this, that you are an American spy."[13]

The sources of Iraq's intelligence remained a matter of conjecture. On the human intelligence side, it was safe to assume that the Iraqi minders who accompanied Unscom and IAEA teams spied for the government. Also the movements of all Unscom and IAEA personnel would have been monitored, a fairly straightforward exercise, no matter which hotel they stayed at. So the Iraqi opposition's claim that the 120-strong "Bureau 28" – most likely run by Special Security – was engaged in spying on Unscom and IAEA personnel was credible. But this method yielded very little hard information. The key element in intelligence gathering was the high-technology eavesdropping equipment, where the Anglo-American intelligence agencies were streets ahead of their counterparts in the Western world, not to mention Iraq. As it was, aided by the West and the Soviet bloc during the First Gulf War in the 1980s, Baghdad had developed considerably its signals and electronic Intelligence (SEINT), codenamed Operation 858. Based in Rashidiya, 12 miles (20 km) north of Baghdad, the 1,000-strong Iraqi SEINT had half a dozen listening stations throughout the country. However, its ability to eavesdrop on telephone conversations inside Iraq did not enable it to pick up the conversations of UN inspectors who used scramblers and other secure communications equipment. In any event, SEINT's equipment was designed for the analogue system – in vogue in the 1980s – which was still in use in Iraq in the 1990s, and not for the latest digital system.

Since no telecommunications equipment had been imported into Iraq after August 1990, the reports published in Israeli and American newspapers in November 1997 that Iraq had equipment at Rashidiya capable of eavesdropping on UN inspectors' conversations by satellite telephone lacked credibility.[14]

In any case, Gen. Rashid's cautionary hint did not cool Ritter's zeal to crack the Iraqi concealment procedures.

His break came with Dr Diane Seaman, an American microbiologist. On September 25, she had conducted an unannounced inspection of the Iraqi Food and Drug Examination Laboratory (IFDEL) in Baghdad. Skipping the normal courtesy of having tea first with the boss of the establishment, Dr Hilal al Tikriti, on the ground floor, she rushed straight to the administrative office on the second floor. There she found two men with briefcases hurrying to leave through a back exit. But, giving chase, she managed to corner them in a laboratory room, where, assisted by her three colleagues, she snatched the briefcases from them. Containing documents, biological test kits and unidentified biological samples, they turned out to be important catches. Literate in Arabic, she noticed that many documents carried the letterhead, "Office of the Presidency, Special Security Directorate." A follow-up investigation revealed IFDEL's involvement in a project about gas gangrene – *clostridium perfringens* – which had been weaponized in the late 1980s.

At Unscom's Canal Hotel headquarters, Ritter was thrilled. "The [UN] Commission had been trying assiduously to find a link between the SSO [Special Security Organization] and prohibited weapons that could be brought before the Security Council," he said in his book *Endgame*. "We now had such a link."[15] But first he and Seaman needed to seek clarification from the appropriate Iraqi officials.

At the meeting they held that evening with them, the head of the Iraqi side, Dr Hamza Bilal, explained that the IFDEL had a verbal understanding with the authorities to do "biological testing" for the president and other top officials. Finding the explanation unsatisfactory, Ritter immediately told Gen. Hossam Amin, head of the Iraqi NMD, that he would undertake an inspection of an unspecified site that night and that they would be ready to leave the Unscom office at 2300 hours. (As it happened, Ritter had a spare "no notice" inspection notification signed by Butler, which his boss now allowed him to use.)

As the Unscom convoy of fourteen vehicles, accompanied by forty Iraqi minders, left the Canal Hotel, Ritter informed Gen. Hossam Amin that he would name the site on arrival and then he could tell him whether it was "sensitive." To the obvious relief of Amin, Ritter's convoy went past the Republican Presidential Palace in the Tashri neighborhood along the western bank of the Tigris. His (as yet undisclosed) destination was the Special Security headquarters, about three-quarters of a mile (1 km) from the Palace. But on their way to the site, the first car of the Unscom convoy got detached from the rest at a traffic light. This unforeseen situation drew the attention of a Special Security sentry and officer near the traffic light. They stopped all vehicles as the first car was ordered to reverse to rejoin the Unscom convoy, and several uniformed Iraqis in the area cocked their guns. It was only when Gen. Rashid arrived on the scene that a semblance of calm returned. By now Ritter was on his satellite phone conferring with Butler at the Unscom headquarters in New York. He attempted to negotiate with Rashid a resumption of the journey to the now named site – arguing that Unscom had the legal right to inspect the Special Security headquarters. Rashid disagreed. The Unscom convoy returned to its base at the Canal Hotel.

During the telephone conversation between Butler and Tariq Aziz that followed (according to Butler's published account), Aziz told his interlocutor that there was a section in Special Security that performed the task of testing the food eaten by top leaders. When Butler explained that it was important to inspect the Special Security head office because of the documents found along with the biological testing materials inside the snatched briefcases at the IFDEL, Aziz assured him that that building was "an empty shell." This was not so in the aerial U–2 picture of the area that Butler had in his office, and he said so. "The building is dilapidated," replied Aziz. "Nevertheless, it is within a presidential site. For reasons of the national dignity and sovereignty of Iraq, Unscom can never be allowed to visit a presidential site." He explained that a "presidential site" included "environs around a presidential palace."[16] By then Iraq had denied Unscom access to about 100 sites, usually contained inside the perimeter of a presidential palace, on national security grounds. According to Unscom, these sites included buildings where the SRG were suspected of hiding incriminating documents, weapons parts and biological warfare agents. Viewed in a broad context, this was Baghdad's counter-response to Unscom's strategy which – in Ritter's words – was to "gradually squeeze retained Iraqi weapons into a few sanctuaries which would then be subjected to no notice inspections."[17]

In his October 6 report, Butler noted some progress in the missile and chemical fields, but described biological warfare agents as an area "unredeemed by progress or any approximation of the known facts of Iraq's program." He also noted that the Iraqis had introduced a new category of "presidential sites" which was declared out of bounds to Unscom.[18] On October 23, the Security Council adopted Resolution 1134 threatening to impose a travel ban on certain Iraqi officials if Baghdad refused to give full details of the banned weapons program and failed to cooperate fully with Unscom. For the first time there was an open split on Unscom at the Council – with Egypt and Kenya joining France, Russia and China in abstaining.

This encouraged Baghdad to assume a defiant posture. There were other factors at work too. Due to the intransigent stance of hardline Israeli Premier Binyamin Netanyahu (r. 1996–99), the US-sponsored Middle East peace process had come to a virtual halt, disappointing Washington's Arab allies. The kid-gloves with which Clinton treated Netanyahu, who refused to implement the agreements he had signed with the Palestinians, contrasted sharply with the rigid stringency with which he interpreted and applied Security Council Resolution 687 in the case of Iraq. Also, Baghdad had by now most probably collected enough evidence to conclude that most Americans seconded from US military and intelligence to Unscom were, in the final analysis, working for Washington, and would therefore keep on finding pretexts to show its lack of cooperation so long as the Clinton administration wanted them to – which would be until Saddam's downfall. Therefore Saddam set out to diminish the pro-US bias of Unscom in personnel and equipment, and ensure that the lifting of sanctions was decided within the context of Resolution 687, and that alone. To give a high profile to the economic embargo against Iraq, he tried to bring the issue out of the Security Council portals and into the streets and bazaars of the Middle East, an objective he would realize to the full if the Pentagon were to attack Iraq, he reckoned. Furthermore, he calculated rightly, Washington's military action would jeopardize what it was trying to save – an ongoing monitoring regime.

On October 28, after Iraq's National Assembly had declared that "no more inspection teams should be allowed into the country until a deadline was established for lifting the embargo," Saddam Hussein presided over an RCC meeting. It declared its willingness to cooperate with Unscom provided it respected "Iraq's sovereignty, national security and dignity."

The following day Aziz told the Security Council that Baghdad would no longer accept American personnel in Unscom teams, since they had shown more loyalty to the US than to the UN, and demanded the end of flights by US reconnaissance aircraft, U–2, to monitor its compliance with the elimination of the WMD. Iraq had the sovereign right to expel foreigners it did not want on its soil, he added, charging that under the UN aegis the Clinton administration was engaged in spying on Iraq with the aim of changing its regime.

On October 30, Baghdad asked ten American inspectors out of a total of forty to leave the country within a week. When, on November 3, the Iraqis blocked an inspection of the Al Samoud short-range missile site because the team contained Americans, all other teams stopped work and returned to the Unscom headquarters. On November 3, claiming that the forthcoming U–2 flights on November 5 and 7 were linked to the military strikes that Washington was planning against his country, the Iraqi ambassador to the UN, Nizar Hamdoun, called on Butler to cancel the flights, especially when Iraq's air defenses were being activated to meet "the possibility of aggression."[19] Little did Hamdoun know that for the past few years Unscom had been sharing the U–2 intelligence with Iraq's sworn enemy, Israel, as well.

At the UN, while China called on Iraq and the Security Council to settle the dispute peacefully, the Russian foreign minister, Yevgeny Primakov, expressed his opposition to military action against Baghdad. To defuse the crisis, on November 3, the UN secretary-general, Kofi Annan (1997–), sent a team of three senior diplomats – Lakhdar Brahimi, an Algerian; Jan Eliasson, a Swede; and Emilio Cardenas, an Argentinian – to Baghdad.

After a series of meetings they finished their task on November 7. At a press conference Brahimi said that Iraq wanted Annan's personal intervention to defuse the crisis. (This would happen three months later.) Describing Unscom as "a mere instrument of US policy against Iraq," Tariq Aziz pointed out that Americans held 44 percent of the sensitive positions in Unscom in 1996, and 37 percent at present.[20] He demanded a change in Unscom's composition. During his meetings with the UN envoys, Aziz had provided them with evidence to back up his espionage charges and the allegation that American U–2 reconnaissance planes, based in Saudi Arabia, had been staking out potential targets in Iraq for attacks.[21]

In his published account of the UN envoys' visit to Baghdad in early November, Butler referred to Iraq giving them extensive briefings, "including documentary films about the way Unscom conducted its work," amounting to "elaborately contrived propaganda." Later he complained that

> Iraqi propaganda began to argue that Unscom was run by a bunch of out-of-control cowboys … Annan's trio helped confirm this view. They returned with videotapes provided by Baghdad of Unscom staffers interviewing Iraqi officials, tapes edited to make our inspectors appear like latter-day inquisitors.[22]

In the same book he later described the behavior of one of his chief inspectors, Scott Ritter, thus:

> His colorful style used to land him on Iraqi TV – of course, in the unenviable propaganda role of the "Ugly American." Iraqi television viewers would see Ritter towering over one of our Iraqi minders, gritting his teeth and chopping the air with his hands and spitting out demands: "We have a right to inspect this building! Now will you let us go through!"[23]

This could not have come as news to Ritter. In an interview with Peter J. Boyer of the *New Yorker*, he described his operating style while briefing his team thus:

> When I go into a site I am going to be polite. I am going to shake their hand, but I am the alpha dog. I'm going in tail held high. If they growl at me, I'm gonna jump on 'em. I'm gonna let 'em know who the boss is here. I'm in charge. They report to me, they do what I say. You work for me, so every one of you are [is] alpha dogs. When you go to a site, they're gonna know we're there, we're gonna raise our tails and we're gonna spray urine all over their walls – that's equivalent of what we're doing. So when we leave a site they know they've been inspected.[24]

Sticking to its position that the American U–2 plane, scheduled to fly over Iraq on November 7, was staking out potential targets for the Pentagon, Baghdad threatened to shoot it down. This went down badly at the Security Council whose Resolution 707 (August 1991) authorized such flights. On November 12, it adopted Resolution 1137 imposing international travel restrictions on the Iraqi officials responsible for non-cooperation with Unscom.

That day Iraq gave six US inspectors twenty-four hours to leave, and then expelled them. Of the remaining eighty-three Unscom staff in Baghdad, Butler withdrew all except seven technicians to safeguard the Unscom headquarters, and contacted the media in New York without bothering to inform the Security Council first. The Russian and Chinese ambassadors to the UN were livid with anger at Butler's behavior. To make matters worse, in an interview with the *New York Times*, Butler said, "Truth in some cultures is kind of what you can get away with saying." This remark was taken by many Arab diplomats at the UN and others as racist. Written complaints streamed into the office of the UN secretary-general, Annan, a Ghanaian.

In Washington, on the other hand, President Clinton was livid with anger at Saddam's behavior. "By expelling UN inspectors Saddam has ensured that the sanctions will be there until the end of time or as long as he lasts," he declared on November 14. Later he went on to describe Saddam as "clever-crazy."[25] He ordered a US military build-up in the region. Soon there were two US aircraft carriers, each with eighty-five warplanes, and seven cruisers, destroyers and sub-marines – carrying cruise missiles – as well as three guided missile frigates.[26]

Meanwhile his secretary of state, Albright, visiting the Qatari capital of Doha for the US-sponsored Fourth Middle East and North Africa (MENA) Economic Conference – aiming to foster economic ties between Israel and the Arab world – found herself without many peers to meet as only six of the twenty-two Arab League members turned up. On the eve of her subsequent arrival in Kuwait, the emirate's foreign minister, Shaikh Sabah al Ahmad al Sabah, said that his country was opposed to any military action against Iraq as it would harm the Iraqi people. His view was shared publicly by Egypt, Syria and Bahrain. Earlier Saudi Arabia had let it be known that it did not want its bases to be used for bombing Iraq.[27]

Were Clinton to ignore the Security Council disunity and official advice from his Arab allies, and act unilaterally against Iraq, he would end up substantiating Saddam's assertion that the dispute was between Baghdad and Washington, and not between Baghdad and the UN. Little wonder that when the Russian president, Boris Yeltsin, offered to mediate in the dispute, Clinton gave him a green light. At the same time he ordered another aircraft carrier to the Gulf to make it appear that he was acting tough.

On November 18–19, Tariq Aziz had meetings in Moscow with Primakov, an Arabist who had spent many years in the Middle East as a correspondent of the (Soviet) Tass Newsagency, had known Saddam Hussein since the mid–1970s, and had toured the Middle East soon after becoming foreign minister. There was also communication between Yeltsin and Saddam Hussein. Early on November 20 they announced an agreement. In return for Iraq's unconditional acceptance of Unscom's return, Moscow promised to work for speeding up Unscom's progress and its expansion by recruitment of non-American inspectors, the Security Council's formal recognition of what Unscom had achieved so far, and a timetable for the lifting of sanctions.[28] Meeting at the UN's Geneva office later that day, the foreign ministers of the Security Council's P5 endorsed the Iraqi–Russian declaration. Before the day was over Iraq invited Unscom back.

Washington and London could claim, rightly, that they had secured Unscom's unconditional return. But, overall, it was a big plus for Moscow. It was the first major diplomatic initiative undertaken by Russia since the break-up of the Soviet Union six years ago that had culminated in success.

All told, Saddam stood to gain from the crisis he had created. It exposed deep differences between the five permanent members of the Security Council, with Russia openly siding with Baghdad. Unable to handle the situation calmly as his predecessor, Ekeus, had done, Butler acted undiplomatically and unprofessionally, and drew fire from several Security Council members. Over the next few months, in contrast to his quietly efficient predecessor, who was a seasoned diplomat, Butler emerged as a confrontational bruiser. In the region, the Iraq–US impasse forced the Arab states to take a stand. Without exception they opposed military action against Baghdad. They argued that, unlike the situation in 1990, Iraq was not occupying another country now, and had recognized Kuwait as an independent state within its newly demarcated boundaries.

Saddam refocused world attention on the plight of Iraqis due to the 75-month economic siege imposed by the UN sanctions. According to the estimates of the WHO, over 500,000 Iraqi children under five had died as a result of malnutrition and lack of medicine caused by the UN embargo. (The Iraqi health ministry's figures were twice as high.) This fact weighed heavily on the consciences of the Arab public and governments. The warmth with which Tariq Aziz was received in the capitals of Morocco, Egypt, Jordan and Syria, on his way back to Baghdad from Moscow showed that Arab opinion was shifting in favor of Baghdad, a worrisome prospect for Washington.

To his credit, Saddam had chosen his timing well, a fortnight before the Fourth MENA conference, which was being held a fortnight before the 54-member ICO summit in Tehran to which Saddam had been invited. US bombing of Iraq before the MENA Conference would have aborted that event, and strikes just before the ICO summit would have provided the Iraqi leader with an opportunity to inflame anti-American feelings throughout the Muslim world.

However, Unscom sources said that Saddam had run out of technical contrivances to hinder its efforts to unearth all the missing elements in Iraq's program of chemical and biological weapons, and so decided to use a political ploy to achieve his objective.

In retrospect, the November 1997 crisis proved to be the first in a series which culminated in a four-day US bombing of Iraq a year later and resulted *inter alia* in Unscom staff being withdrawn from Iraq – by Butler.

Saddam's chief motive in bringing the simmering tension on the question of Unscom's unhindered access to all sites was to highlight the economic embargo on Iraq, an issue which had been at the center of a bitter debate among his close advisers since when he had settled on spring 1994 as the deadline for lifting of the sanctions.

Domestic front: oil-for-food and intra-Kurdish violence

The first food shipment under Resolution 986 arrived only in March 1997, and by the time the Security Council decided to renew the scheme for another six months in early June, three-quarters of the 800,000 tonnes of food – wheat, rice, pulses, vegetable oil and sugar – received had been distributed.[29]

The first medical supplies arrived only in May 1997. By then public health and water supply services in Iraq were in a dire state. This was the conclusion drawn by the director-general of the WHO, Hiroshi Makajima, after a visit to the country. The government's warehouses for medicine had run out of such basics as bandages, he said; and there was an acute shortage of syringes. The breakdown in clean water supplies had made the populace vulnerable to an epidemic of typhoid. Fatalities of children under five due to hunger and disease continued to run at 7,000 a month, representing a threefold increase in the mortality rate of 9 percent in 1991. "The situation [for children] is disastrous," said Philippe Heffnick, Unicef representative in Iraq. "Many are living on the very margin of survival."[30] Those who survived faced a bleak future. "The currently malnourished children will be mentally and/or physically retarded as adults," said Abdul Amir al Anbari, the Iraqi ambassador to the United Nations Educational, Social and Cultural Organization.[31]

"A Unicef survey showed that in 1994 about 68 percent of children went to school without breakfast, and in 1997 some 32 percent were malnourished," said Francesca Noe, a Baghdad-based Italian social worker, who studied the Iraqi educational system. "There is direct correlation between lack of nourishment and learning ability." Before the 1991 Gulf War there were free school meals for children, which were stopped after the conflict when they were needed most. Also, after the War the authorities ended the free bus transport they provided to pupils before, which was especially helpful in rural areas, she said. Before the War, only 6 percent of the children were not in primary school, and five years later the figure was 16 percent. "School-age children were being made to work for family business or engage in street vending or begging by their parents," she explained. The facilities at the educational institutions had deteriorated sharply. "The local authorities have been unable to maintain the buildings properly because the budgets for maintenance and cleaning were cut by 90 percent after the War," she continued. "So you see broken windows, no lights, and toilets in bad repair. And desks and chairs are in a bad state." Furthermore, due to the 688 educational buildings damaged or destroyed by the Coalition bombing, and the increase in the national population, there was such a shortage of premises that some of them in cities were being used on a shift basis. Then there was the psychological damage done by the bombardments, which occurred in 1991, 1993 (twice) and 1996. "A Unicef study showed that 80 percent of primary school children had fear of losing family or friends due to bombing," said Noe. Because of low salaries, many teachers left the profession and took up manual or semi-skilled jobs which paid better. So the average pupil–teacher ratio jumped from 30:1 before the War to the current 50–60:1. On top of that there was a shortage of textbooks and stationery. "Old, battered textbooks are being used," she continued. "Exercise notebooks, pencils and pens are too expensive. Before the War the government covered the full cost of the textbooks and stationery. Now it pays only for a half; and many parents find it hard to cover the rest. The UN Sanctions Committee has withheld permissions for producing paper in Iraq. It has also banned imports of pencils on the ground that the graphite in the pencils could be used for nuclear reactors." Given the acute shortage of paper, much of the teaching was being done orally with the help of audio and video cassettes – and by using radio and television programs.[32]

In the ultimate analysis, the fate of children was dependent on the state of Iraqi agriculture, irrigation, drinking water supply, public sanitation, public health service and electric supplies. With irrigation, water supply, public sanitation and electric power systems receiving only 10 percent of the needed resources, they were in a poor condition. Broken-down pumps, which could not be repaired without imported parts, adversely affected irrigation, water supply and sewage. All import contracts had to be scrutinized by the UN 661 Sanctions Committee, where America and Britain kept a hawkish eye. Since spare parts for machinery were neither food nor medicine, their purchase was repeatedly blocked by the US and UK representatives on the Sanctions Committee.

By the end of 1997, while 95 percent of the contracted foodgrains had been received by Iraq and distributed, only 25 percent of the contracted medicine had arrived. "It is hard ... to understand the hesitations of the [Sanctions] Committee in New York," said Dennis Halliday, head of the UN Office of Humanitarian Coordinator in Iraq (UNOHCI). Several foreign non-governmental organizations based in Baghdad blamed America for "political obstructionism." [33]

At the UN 661 Sanctions Committee, America and Britain barred international mail over 12 oz (340 g) to Iraq. "They embargo all business mail," said a doctor in Baghdad. "We see no professional literature and we cannot keep abreast of developments in our fields." [34]

This was just one manifestation of the educational, professional and cultural embargo, imposed since 1990, that had severely damaged Iraq's university system and its intellectual life. "Iraqi university teachers and students are cut off from the outside world, even from the neighboring Arab countries," said Francesca Noe.

> They are unable to import textbooks, journals, or even newspapers as sources of latest research. And they have no access to international computer data banks or even Internet. So they have to depend on outdated research material. They are not able to attend foreign seminars

or conferences even if they are invited because it is very expensive for them to go abroad.

The quality of teaching at the higher educational institutions has suffered. "The only way they can keep the university educational system going is by photocopying textbooks in violation of the international copyrights convention. But many photocopiers are out of order due to lack of spare parts." The drop-out rate at the university level was 30 percent due to the economic pressure on the students' families struggling to make ends meet.[35]

In November 1997 Unicef published a study of 53,000 Iraqi households and the rationing system. It concluded that the oil-for-food program had had no positive impact on the humanitarian situation in Iraq as yet. Actually, because of this scheme many previous donor countries had stopped contributing to the FAO's World Food Program for Iraq which provided free rations to indigent families. "It is clear that children are bearing the brunt of the current economic hardship," said Philippe Heffnick, the Unicef representative in Baghdad. "One million children are chronically malnutritioned." The report noted that the monthly rationing provided enough food only for about three weeks, and because of the poor quality of foodgrains, the calorie content was low. So most families had to buy food in the open market where the average price of basic necessities was fifty times higher than in 1991, and where 2.2 lb (1 kg) of meat cost ID 3,000, the monthly salary of a school teacher. Also, rations were supplied to a household on the basis of numbers, with no special provision for pregnant women.[36]

To earn $2 billion every six months, Iraq needed to export 650–750,000 bpd. But the actual amount available to Baghdad for importing food and medicine was about half of the total, with approximately one-seventh of the total going to the administrative authorities in Iraqi Kurdistan, a territory prone to periodic bouts of internecine violence.

Even though the INC and the INA maintained a presence in Kurdistan, the region had ceased to be the bastion of the armed anti-Saddam movement, and had instead become a turf where the KDP and the PUK constantly tried to get the better of each other.

The KDP–PUK truce signed in November 1996 had proved shaky even though the KDP, having tired of reaching a satisfactory political agreement with Baghdad, had repaired its damaged links with Washington – in the process formally agreeing to aid Turkey in its campaign against the separatist PKK (Kurdistan Workers Party) which among other things maintained an office in Irbil and used Iraqi Kurdistan as a safe haven. The KDP actively assisted Ankara in May 1997 when it sent 50,000 troops into Iraqi Kurdistan to attack PKK hideouts.

Barzani's military alliance with Turkey came against the backdrop of long-established trade links. There was much demand in Turkey for Iraqi petroleum products – especially diesel oil – supplied cheap by Baghdad to the KDP which sold them at market prices to Turkish truckers who carried them overland to

Turkey through the KDP-controlled sector. So although, yielding to US pressure, Masud Barzani severed his military links with Saddam, he maintained his economic relations with him. The Clinton administration was well aware of this, but turned a blind eye since there was no chance of its persuading the US Congress to give financial aid to the Kurdish factions to administer Iraqi Kurdistan. The political price that Barzani paid Saddam for his economic favor was to give free rein to Iraqi GID agents in the KDP territory.[37]

The latest estimate was that the trade in Iraqi oil products earned the KDP $800,000 a day. And customs duties and service charges brought in another $250,000 daily. The cash was deposited in the regional bank in Irbil, and controlled by the Kurdistan parliament with a KDP majority. So the PUK was deprived of cash, and Jalal Talabani was increasingly bitter about it.[38] He demanded that a joint committee or a neutral body be set up to collect and distribute the customs revenue. This was rejected by Barzani, who offered to pay the civil servants employed in the PUK-administered zone. Talabani also demanded that a fresh poll be held for the parliament since the current body was elected in May 1992. The KDP, enjoying predominance in the legislature, opposed this, arguing that conditions were not right for free and fair elections. In this it had the backing of Turkey which reckoned, rightly, that another parliamentary poll would set the current Kurdistan Autonomous Region on its way to full independence, which would give moral and material boost to the PKK's campaign for independence for Turkish Kurds.

As relations between the KDP and the PUK deteriorated, the latter began assisting the PKK – actively opposed by the KDP – by providing it with shelter in the area under its control. The PKK began hitting KDP targets and then withdrawing into the PUK-administered territory.

Matters came to a head in mid-September 1997 when the Turkish military staged a major incursion into northern Iraq with 15,000 soldiers, with an air cover, to push back the PKK from the frontier area, and destroy its stored supplies of food and ammunition in the mountains to stop it launching raids in winter. KDP *peshmargas* helped the Turkish soldiers on the ground.

In mid-October as the Turkish army, operating in Iraqi Kurdistan since May, began withdrawing, the PUK, backed by the PKK, attacked the KDP on three fronts, one of them near the Iranian border, and the other near Shaqlawa on the strategic Hamilton Road. It made gains. America, Britain and Turkey moved fast to mediate a ceasefire. Later they pressured Talabani to revert to the positions the PUK held before its offensives. Talabani refused, arguing that the truce was signed *in situ*, and that if the PUK adopted the logic of its rival, then the KDP should return to the PUK the territory it seized, including Irbil, in August-September 1996 with the active backing of Baghdad's troops and heavy weaponry.[39]

Around November 10, while the world attention was focused on the rising tension between Unscom and Iraq, the Turkish army and air force joined the KDP's 10,000 *peshmargas* in a counter-offensive against the PUK, and regained the territory the KDP had lost a month earlier. The latest fighting left 1,000

Kurds dead, the PUK militarily weak and the KDP's coffers depleted. The PUK–KDP ceasefire that Washington and London arranged proved as tenuous as the compromise Iraq was to reach with Unscom on November 20, 1997.

Unscom–US intelligence links

Butler sent an inspection team of seventy-five inspectors which arrived in Baghdad on November 21–22. He had signed confidential orders for no-notice inspections of the former headquarters of the 3rd Battalion of the Special Republican Guard. "Following a standard procedure that neither Unscom nor Washington officially acknowledges, Mr Butler's senior staff briefed a liaison officer from the CIA on the target, sources said," reported Barton Gellman of the *Washington Post*. Following this, Albright telephoned Mr Butler, urging him to delay the operation.[40] She did so for tactical reasons as she was to explain later in private: the US administration wanted to control the pace of confrontation with Baghdad to foster the most favorable condition where Washington and London would be able to blame Saddam for denying full cooperation to Unscom, and avoid provocative confrontation which would enable the Iraqi dictator to blame Unscom. Butler agreed. So, around midnight on November 22–23, at Unscom's Canal Hotel headquarters in Baghdad, the team received Butler's orders to abort the mission. Soon after, he issued a directive to his staff, ruling out new inspections until further notice at Special Security, RG, SRG and any other Iraqi sites designated "sensitive" by the Baghdad government.[41]

When the Security Council met on November 23 to debate the Iraq issue, it endorsed Butler's report of the November 20–21 proceedings of the Emergency Session of Unscom's College of Commissioners to discuss improving Unscom's composition and operational efficiency. Besides Butler, the chairman, there were twenty-one Commissioners – twenty of them from as many countries, appointed on an individual basis by the UN secretary-general, and one representative from the UN disarmament department. As a result of this meeting, three new Chinese inspectors were added to the Unscom staff; and for the first time since his appointment, Butler began briefing France, Russia and China at the Security Council. He also made sure that he was accompanied by a few of the Commissioners on his future trips to Baghdad. But the Security Council failed to agree on how Unscom should proceed henceforth. So it decided to let America and Russia negotiate bilaterally and come up with a common position – an exercise which would prove futile.

On November 28 the Iraqi foreign minister, Muhammad Said al Sahhaf, said that Unscom would not be allowed to visit "presidential and sovereign sites." During his meetings with Butler on December 14–15, Aziz confirmed the Iraqi ban. A week later the Security Council stated that Iraq's decision was "a clear violation" of UN resolutions. Another crisis was in the making.

6

"DESERT THUNDER" THAT
DIDN'T THUNDER

In the Iraq–United Nations chronicle, 1998 started with Unscom 227. Consisting of forty-three inspectors and their support staff, all working under Scott Ritter, it was divided into two operational teams, one headed by Ritter and the other by Dr Gabrielle Kraatz-Wadsack, a German biologist. On January 12, by Ritter's own account, Unscom 227 carried out seven inspections, including one at the General Security headquarters and another at the Abu Ghraib prison 6 miles (10 km) west of Baghdad. Following the earlier, incomplete inspection by Dr Diane Seaman, these investigations were focused on finding documents showing that the Iraqi government had conducted biological and chemical weapons experiments on political prisoners, arrested by General Security and held at the Abu Ghraib jail, in 1994–95. According to Ritter, his teams found the records on the dates in question missing.

Apparently, the Iraqis did not like the thrust of Unscom 227's investigation. But they could not possibly say so publicly. So they came up with an objection they had raised before and which had not been addressed – namely, the imbalanced composition of Unscom teams – and issued the following statement:

> Iraq has decided to stop the work of the inspection team headed by Scott Ritter, and to withdraw permission for him to undertake any activities on its territory, starting from today, until the composition of the team is changed with the balanced participation of the permanent Security Council member states.

Unscom protested, saying that its team members came from seventeen countries. However, two-fifths of Unscom 227 inspectors were from America and Britain, with the remaining from fifteen other countries. Ritter's 16-member operational team consisted of 9 Americans, 5 Britons, 1 Australian and 1 Russian.[1] With nothing to do, Unscom 227 left Iraq on January 15. While Russia and China at the Security Council called for a more balanced composition of Unscom inspection teams, Washington rejected Moscow's offer to replace the US-made and operated U–2 reconnaissance aircraft used by Unscom with comparable Russian planes.

On January 17, the seventh anniversary of the Second Gulf War, in a nation-wide broadcast, Saddam repeated what he had said before – namely, Iraq had met all its obligations under Resolution 687. Trying to bolster the morale of Iraqis, he referred to the journey undertaken by Abraham, born in the southern Iraqi town of Ur, to southern Turkey, armed with nothing more than a stick, but possessed of vision: "Prophet Abraham was neither timid nor afraid of the disparity in material resources." In other words, he reassured the Iraqi people that their vision and self-righteousness would more than compensate for their inferiority in weaponry. Nonetheless, he ordered the training of one million volunteers to prepare for a jihad if the UN embargo was not lifted within six months as demanded earlier by the Iraqi parliament.[2]

By one of those quirks of history, which some might be tempted to attribute to a supernatural power, some hours later a story broke on US television channels that President Clinton allegedly had an affair with Monica Lewinsky, a young White House intern, at his official residence. If Saddam needed evidence to illustrate the moral turpitude of America, the enemy of Iraq, to his people, here it was. America, mighty in weapons but depraved in morality, he could crow with glee. This scandal would dog Clinton for a year and culminate in his impeachment by the House of Representatives (lacking a two-thirds majority, the Senate failed to remove him from office, however), and impinge directly on his decisions on Iraq.

To resolve the latest Unscom crisis, Butler went to Baghdad, and had meetings with Tariq Aziz between January 19 and 21. In his report to the Security Council, he described the manner of the Iraqis as "disturbing and disappointing," and stressed the need to inspect "the sensitive and sovereign sites." His predecessor, Rolf Ekeus, had been through this sort of exercise time and again during his six years in office. He had had more than his share of stand-offs and recriminations with Iraq; but as a seasoned diplomat, he showed skill and flexibility to de-escalate disagreement and conflict. "In leading Unscom," he told the *Arms Control* monthly, "it has been necessary some time for me to finesse certain crisis situations by developing political solutions to a problem."[3] In contrast, a bruiser by nature, Butler tended to be confrontational, oblivious to the viewpoint of his disagreeing interlocutor. Little wonder that what Ekeus had managed to avoid in mid–1996 at the expense of upsetting America now began appearing on the horizon with a solidity it lacked before: American strikes against Iraq.

On January 25, US sources declared that the countdown to a Washington-led military action against Iraq had begun. An American armada of two aircraft carrier groups, comprising 15 warships and carrying 350 warplanes, was to be boosted by another aircraft carrier group. And B–52 bombers based on the Indian Ocean island of Diego Garcia were to be deployed. A build-up of US and UK naval and air forces in the Gulf enabled the Pentagon to mount Operation "Desert Thunder" – named after "Rolling Thunder" under which the US bombed North Vietnam from the mid-1960s to the early 1970s. It would translate into four days of non-stop air campaign with some 400 Cruise missiles fired, and 300 daily raids being mounted by combat planes, targeting Iraqi air defenses, command and communications centers, conventional weapons factories, RG and SRG premises, intelligence and security agencies headquarters, and the sites with a potential for producing missiles and chemical arms. Then there would be a brief respite to give Saddam a chance to relent. If he did not, there would follow another round of bombardment for a couple of days with its focus on such prestigious sites as the Presidential Palace near Tikrit in order to demoralize Iraqi soldiers and officers and encourage them to defect.

To fan the flames, in an interview with the *New York Times*, published on January 27, 1998, Butler asserted that Iraq had enough biological weaponry and missiles "to blow away Tel Aviv." His comment startled the Security Council to which he had presented no hard evidence to that effect. "We were shocked by the outrageous statements by Mr Butler," said Iraqi foreign minister, al Sahhaf. "I sent a letter to the UN secretary-general." As a result of the furor, UN Secretary-General Annan reprimanded Butler, and asked him to submit a written apology to the Council. He did.[4]

The prospect of US military strikes upset the Muslim world on one side, and Russia and China on the other. "Military action against Iraq will bring a new catastrophe with incalculable consequences for the region," warned the Islamic Conference Organization, based in the Saudi port city of Jiddah. China's foreign minister, Qian Qichen, expressed his country's "extreme opposition" to Washington's use of force as did Russian President Yeltsin. To further a diplomatic solution, he twice sent personal messages to his Iraqi counterpart through his deputy foreign minister, Victor Posuvalyuk. In Baghdad, on February 3, Posuvalyuk met Saddam Hussein, a rare privilege for a visiting foreign official. At the Security Council, having said repeatedly that it would veto a Council resolution authorising use of force against Iraq, Russia backed a draft resolution circulated by France and Arab League members which provided for unconditional access to Iraq's sixty sensitive sites for two months, and inspection of the eight presidential sites by a special committee to be appointed by the UN secretary-general.

By contrast, on February 7, appearing alongside the visiting British Prime Minister Tony Blair (r. 1997–), Clinton said that the objective of the Pentagon's action against Iraq would be not to unseat Saddam which, according to his National Security Adviser, Samuel (Sandy) Berger, entailed "unjustifiable costs in blood, treasure and political isolation."[5] Instead, the purpose was to degrade Saddam's potential for launching missiles carrying warheads filled with chemical or biological weapons. He dispatched Albright and the secretary of defense, William Cohen, to a string of world capitals to explain the US policy, which was to secure Unscom's unconditional and unfettered access to all Iraqi sites suspected of harboring proscribed weapons.

However, during Albright's visit to the Gulf monarchies, only Kuwait openly supported military action against Baghdad. She drew a blank in Riyadh. "There are those in Saudi Arabia who would grant the US use of Saudi facilities; there are also those who would refuse; and still others who want to see all Americans leave the kingdom," Crown Prince Abdullah, the effective ruler of the kingdom (due to King Fahd's ill health), reportedly told Albright. "Since I represent all these people, I am obliged to say 'no' to the use of Saudi facilities for attacks on Iraq." He also asked why Washington was prepared to use force against Iraq for failing to implement a few Security Council resolutions while Israel violated with impunity not only many Council resolutions but also refused to honor its internationally guaranteed treaty commitments to the Palestinians. "Saudi Arabia will not allow any strikes against Iraq under any circumstances from its soil due to the sensitivity of the issue in the Arab and Muslim world," said the official communiqué after the meeting.[6] Later, on the eve of Cohen's arrival in Riyadh, the Saudi defense minister, Prince Sultan, told the *Arab News*, "We are against striking Iraq as a people and as a nation."[7] The position of the UAE had been reiterated earlier by its president, Shaikh al Nahyan, who had proposed that a decision on accepting Iraq's return to the Arab League as a normal member should be reached through a majority rather than customary consensus. "Let us tell this man [Saddam Hussein] that you have erred towards us," he said, "but we now tell you 'Welcome back as a faithful brother.'"[8]

Little wonder that of the twenty countries to support the US publicly against Iraq now, only two were Arab (Kuwait) or African (Senegal). By contrast, in the Second Gulf War, of the twenty-eight nations in the US-led anti-Iraq Coalition, thirteen were Arab, African (Senegal and Niger) or South Asian (Pakistan and Bangladesh).

But that did not stop US sources saying, on February 14, that Operation "Desert Thunder" would be launched four days later, or General Henry Shelton, US joint chief of staff, forecasting that the air strikes could kill 1,500 Iraqis.[9]

Since the latest crisis was about eight presidential sites, which the Iraqis described as "sovereign," certain facts about them had to be established beyond doubt. Three of the palaces were in Greater Baghdad: Sijood, Republican and Radawaniye; and the fourth by the Tharthar Lake, 47 miles (75 km) north-west of the capital. Of the rest, three were in Auja, Tikrit and Jabal Maqbul; and one in Mosul. The sizes of these premises became contentious, with Butler overstating them in order to show that the Iraqis were excluding Unscom from large built-up areas of their country. These sites jointly measured 27 sq miles/70 sq km/18,000 acres, and had 1,500 buildings, he claimed. Kofi Annan sent a team of UN surveyors and cartographers, provided by Austria, to Iraq to check out the facts. They put the total area of the eight sites at 12.2 sq miles/ 31.5 sq km/8,160 acres, with 1,058 buildings.[10]

By contrast, US officials, citing U–2 photographs, claimed that one of the presidential sites alone covered 40,000 acres, and another 2,600 acres. This was part of the educational campaign that the Clinton administration had mounted in America. As part of it, the NSC made an arrangement with CNN to televise worldwide a "town hall" meeting at the Ohio State University stadium in Dayton to be addressed by Albright, Cohen and Sandy Berger. Normally, assured of his impressive persuasive powers and charisma, Clinton would have appeared solo at such a gathering. But because of the fresh Lewinsky scandal, he knew that the audience would question him about it persistently, and thus shift the focus away from Iraq; and politically, he could not afford that.

Now his ill-prepared trio faced a vociferous and unruly audience of 6,000 – composed of local residents, Vietnam War veterans and university students and staff – who kept heckling the speakers. The top US officials failed to convince the audience that bombing Iraq was the way to rid the country of its weapons of mass destruction, which they claimed was the overall aim. (As it was, the Pentagon had said earlier that it would not target the WMD or Saddam Hussein because it did not know their whereabouts; and among those who publicly questioned the air strikes' strategy was the retired Gen. Norman Schwarzkopf, who commanded the US-led Coalition's campaign against Iraq in the 1991 Gulf War.) The "town hall" event, meant to show the strength of US public support for military action against Iraq via CNN – which Iraqi officials, from Saddam Hussein down, watched avidly – ended up as a fiasco for Clinton. Little wonder that Iraqi TV aired the event uncut.[11]

Later the US government itself would acknowledge that its approach had been flawed. "The serious threat Mr Saddam poses was overblown [by the Clinton administration] in the effort to sell the possible [American] attack, some senior US officials now say," Steven Erlanger reported in the *New York Times* on November 8, 1998.

> Defence secretary William Cohen appeared on television brandishing a bag of sugar in an effort to describe how small a dose of biological and chemical weapons it would take to threaten Americans, but his own chairman of the Joint Chiefs of Staff, Gen. Henry Shelton, expressed serious reservations about the ability of the Pentagon to destroy such easily hidden and reconstituted weapons from the air."[12]

On February 22, a poll published by the *Newsweek* showed backing for military action against Iraq down to 18 percent from 40. Between February 1 and 17, according to the Gallup poll, the percentage of Americans favouring military action dropped from 50 to 40, and that for diplomatic solution rose from 46 to 54.[13]

Repeating what they had said in November, the Iraqis proposed intervention by the UN secretary-general, Annan. His mention of "a personal initiative", on February 13, opened the way for intense consultations with the Security Council's Permanent Members, which went on until he had the backing of all of them. Initially reluctant, the US came on board partly because the momentum for a diplomatic solution had become irresistible and partly because, having said repeatedly that the dispute was between Iraq and the UN, it could not block a visit to Baghdad by the UN's highest official. On February 19, Annan flew to

Paris, where President Jacques Chirac (r. 1995–), the main sponsor of Annan's trip to Iraq, lent him his white Falcon jet.

On his arrival in Baghdad Annan held talks with Tariq Aziz. These focused on three Iraqi demands: (1) an unambiguous public statement that once UN inspectors had expressed their satisfaction, sanctions would be lifted; (2) for inspection of the presidential sites, senior diplomats must accompany UN inspectors; and (3) the composition of the UN teams must reflect a wider range of nationalities than had been the case so far.

During a three-hour meeting with Saddam Hussein on February 22, Annan finalized a deal. In the middle of the night he was woken up by phone calls from Blair and Albright, each of whom insisted on seeing the draft before it was signed. Annan replied that it was against protocol to show it to one member of the Security Council and not others.[14] The seven-point MOU, which specifically mentioned Security Council Resolutions 687 (concerning the 1991 Gulf War ceasefire) and 715 (concerning monitoring), was signed the next day by Annan and Aziz. Annan returned to New York via Paris where he briefed Chirac.

Paragraph 3 coupled Iraq's undertaking to accord Unscom and the IAEA "immediate, unconditional and unrestricted access", in conformity with Resolutions 687 and 715, with Unscom's undertaking to "respect the legitimate concerns of Iraq relating to national security, sovereignty and dignity." Paragraph 4 stated that "inspection of eight Presidential Sites would be conducted by a Special Group – comprising senior diplomats and Unscom and IAEA experts chosen by the UN secretary-general – and headed by a [Special] Commissioner appointed by the secretary-general," who would report to Richard Butler. Paragraph 6 required Iraq and Unscom to "implement the recommendations directed at them as contained in the report of the Emergency Session of Unscom College of Commissioners held on November 21–22, 1997" to enable Unscom to report expeditiously to the Security Council under Paragraph 22 of Resolution 687. The last Paragraph required the secretary-general to bring the matter of lifting of sanctions to the attention of the Security Council.

In Baghdad the Iraqi president's aides called the MOU a victory of diplomacy over saber-rattling, with the Baath Party daily, *Al Thawra*, describing it as "Iraq's historic political victory" which had shown how "arrogant American imperialism had been defeated." In Washington the White House called it a "win–win" document – but only after Clinton had asked Butler to evaluate the MOU before making up his own mind, thus underlining Butler's centrality to his strategy. The White House stressed that Saddam had, unprecedentedly, agreed in writing to "immediate, unconditional and unrestricted access" to Unscom, and dropped his earlier two-month time limit on inspections.

Baghdad explained that Saddam Hussein made concessions because of "the goodwill" Annan brought with him, and because of the backing his mission had from Paris and Moscow, which had earlier declared that it would veto a Security Council resolution authorizing use of force against Iraq. This was a *quid pro quo* for the statement of Bill Richardson, the US ambassador to the UN, that if the

Council decided to ease or lift sanctions against Iraq before it had implemented "all relevant" Council resolutions, it would veto the resolution. Others saw Annan as offering Saddam a dignified way out after he had painted himself into a corner. Annan's visit to Baghdad and his talks with the top Iraqi officials gave the Saddam regime the kind of international legitimacy it had lacked since its 1990 invasion of Kuwait. Also by signing a deal with Annan, the Iraqis engaged him directly, and irretrievably, into the process, a major diplomatic gain by them. On its part the US argued, rightly, that but for its military build-up in the Gulf, Saddam would not have climbed down. Annan himself summed up the situation aptly: "You can do a lot with diplomacy, but of course you can do a lot more with diplomacy backed up by firmness and force."[15]

On his arrival at the UN, Annan was greeted as a hero of peace by hundreds of the staff in the foyer of the building, an unprecedented sight. At a press conference he said that Unscom inspectors had to handle Iraq, and Iraqis, with "a certain respect and dignity." In a closed-door meeting with the Security Council he referred to some Unscom inspectors as "cowboys" who threw their weight around, offended Iraqi sensitivities and acted irresponsibly. He also cited the Iraqi charge that some Unscom inspectors were assigned the job of hunting down Saddam rather than inspecting.[16]

"Some diplomats in Baghdad describe Unscom's previous behavior as 'obnoxious and a disgrace,'" reported Jon Swain in the (London) *Sunday Times.* "The worst offenders were the helicopter pilots and drivers, mainly Chileans and Spanish. 'They behave like an occupation force, shouting in public, leering at women and drinking,' one source said." Unscom shared the Canal Hotel with the UN's humanitarian office, which oversaw distribution of food and medicine. "The humanitarian workers are described by Unscom as 'bunny burgers' who help the SPIs, 'Starving Iraqi People,'" continued Swain. "Dennis Halliday, the UNOHCI head, removed all black UN identification stickers from the sides of his vehicles to distinguish his staff from Unscom."[17]

At the Security Council, America and Britain wanted to codify the Annan–Aziz agreement into a new resolution which would provide for automatic authorization of force if Iraq breached the accord. France opposed such a provision, and Russia saw no need for such a resolution.[18] While the Russian, French and Chinese delegations were quietly impressed by Saddam's surviving capacity and crisis management skills, their American counterpart could not conceal its frustrated anger at the turn of events. In the end, on March 2 the Council adopted Resolution 1154 welcoming the Annan–Aziz Agreement under Chapter VII of the UN Charter. This validated the agreement's authority. Politically, it allowed each side to claim victory, with the US–UK alliance claiming that the statement in Paragraph 3 – that any violation by Baghdad of its obligation to accord "immediate, unconditional and unrestricted access" to UN teams would have "severest consequences for Iraq" – was tantamount to authorizing military action, an interpretation vigorously disputed by the three non-Anglo-Saxon Permanent Members. Summing up their position, the Chinese Ambassador Qin

Hua Sun said, "This resolution in no way means the Security Council automatically authorizes any state to use force against Iraq." This interpretation was endorsed by Annan.[19]

By speedily choosing Jayantha Dhanapala, a Sri Lankan diplomat, to lead the Special Group to inspect the Presidential Sites, Annan apparently took on board Baghdad's complaint against the disproportionate US-UK involvement in the disarming of Iraq. On March 5, he appointed Prakash Shah, a former Indian ambassador to the UN, his personal envoy in Baghdad with a brief to monitor the situation in the country first-hand and try to de-escalate any future tension between Iraq and Unscom.

On the surface the February crisis had been defused, in reality not. For each of the two contending sides – Saddam and Unscom's Butler still working in tandem with Washington – had its own hidden agenda, which it was determined to pursue irrespective of the price. The Pentagon, assisted by Britain, maintained its armada in the Gulf at high alert, ready to strike should Baghdad fail to provide "immediate, unconditional and unrestricted access" to all sites other than the Presidential ones. And working in collaboration with Butler, Clinton was itching to strike Iraq, well aware that he would have to do so before the annual Muslim hajj pilgrimage in Mecca, due on March 15, 1998. For the planned six-day operation to finish before then it had to start by March 9 at the latest, and that meant Unscom insisting on inspections which were bound to provoke the Iraqis. "The cozy relationship between Butler and the US in aligning the inspection timelines with those for [US] military action was disturbing," noted Scott Ritter in his *Endgame.*[20]

So much depended on the progress, or otherwise, of the latest 50-strong Unscom team, arriving in Baghdad on March 5, led once again – despite Annan's advice to Butler to the contrary – by the controversial Ritter. In December, as head of Unscom's CIU, Ritter had approached the American NSA for technical support to accelerate the processing of Unscom data and relay it back quickly enough to impact on the inspection in progress. The NSA agreed, and made swift progress. It posted a special support team at Unscom's field office located in the military section of the Manama airport in Bahrain. And the function of one of the American "inspectors" in Ritter's latest team was to install an automated monitor at Unscom's headquarters in Baghdad. With this, the intercepts of the Iraqi military and security communications in Arabic were sent by satellite relay to Unscom's Bahrain office where they were filtered for key words – "chemical," "missile," "agent," etc. – the text decoded and translated into English, and relayed back to Unscom's Baghdad office within a short time.[21]

On March 6 and 7, 1998, the Unscom team, which included computer analysts and scientists, inspected various Special Security and SRG premises without any hitch. This happened despite the fact that Baghdad was incensed at Unscom inspectors making public the information gathered in the course of their duties tendentiously in a CNN documentary, "High Noon in Baghdad: the Inspectors' Story," aired on March 1. This was a blatant violation of the legal agreements between the UN and Iraq, prohibiting publication of material collected during inspections or monitoring. Baghdad lodged a strong complaint about it with Annan. But nothing came of it.[22]

The sites that were inspected included the Special Security headquarters, the access to which had been denied to Ritter in September. To his delight, Unscom's newly installed ambitious, clandestine eavesdropping system worked. He discovered that Special Security was receiving orders from Saddam Hussein's personal secretary, Abid Hamid Mahmoud, and that the Iraqis removed documents from one site, and delayed the arrival of his team at another – under false pretense – until the incriminating documents had been destroyed. Now he had evidence of Mahmoud's direct involvement in Iraq's concealment mechanism.[23] Later, through defector sources, Unscom would learn that Special Security used a fleet of Mercedes trucks to move the contraband around, the vehicles distinguished by white cabins with red stripes, red diesel tanks and wheel rims, and ministry of trade license plates with numbers between 30,000 and 87,000. Of the seven truck depots pinpointed by a defector, five were later discovered by Unscom's US-operated U–2 plane. However, the concealment unit headquarters in Al Fao Building in Baghdad's Palestine Street had been evacuated in January on the eve of the February 1998 crisis.[24] Responsible for implementing the rationing system, the trade ministry had a very large fleet of vehicles, some of which could easily be spared for extraneous purposes. Also, being a civilian ministry, it was less likely to be suspected of being involved in military matters.

For his current trip, Ritter knew that the center-piece of his inspections was to be Iraq's defense ministry – whose inspection had once been described by Aziz as "an act of war." In its ongoing contacts with Butler, the US had insisted on this site being included, expecting that Baghdad would refuse, thus providing it with a rationale for military strikes. On the morning of Sunday March 8, Ritter's team inspected the old defense ministry, and discovered nothing. In the afternoon he arrived at the new defense ministry with twenty-eight inspectors. There was a stand-off as he and Gen. Amr Rashid haggled over the number of inspectors to be admitted. Rashid started with six and went up to twelve while Ritter, in telephone contact with Butler at the UN, insisted on twenty. "Mr Ritter, we know that right now your government is kissing our feet to make a crisis," Rashid said. "We have no intention to do so. We know there is a threat of war, and we are not afraid. But we do not want a crisis." Once Ritter realized that the Iraqi officials knew what the US was up to, he settled for the half-way figure of sixteen. After eleven hours of paper chase covering different floors of the building, the inspectors discovered nothing.[25] So – for now – the Iraqis deprived Clinton of a chance to launch a blitzkrieg against their country.

Nor did Unscom have much luck with the presidential palaces. The first palace to be searched on March 26 in the company of twenty senior diplomats, including one American and one British, was Radawaniye in Greater Baghdad. It contained no contraband or related documents.[26] It was the same with the remaining seven such sites covered over a week. Dhanapala said so in his report to the Security Council on April 15. All of these sites had been sanitized, claimed Unscom sources.

The next day, in his six-monthly Unscom report Butler pointed out that due to the four-month-long crisis created by Baghdad, there was virtually no progress in verifying disarmament. Responding to it, in his letter of April 22 to the Security Council, Tariq Aziz said, "This report blatantly fails to demonstrate objectivity and fairness, denies and misrepresents facts, and flouts the basic precepts of dealing with the issues of disarmament. The report tendentiously ignores everything that Iraq has done over the past seven years." He then dealt with specific disarmament issues. He requested the Council to put an end to "the false claims which are used [by Butler] to justify intrusive inspections … [that] are, in fact, for the purpose of collecting intelligence information for the United States of America, which is determined to launch a new military aggression against Iraq."[27] Few outside observers would have guessed then that the targets hit by the Pentagon's Operation "Desert Fox" in December, and the revelations in the US press that followed, would substantiate Aziz's assertions.

Since Iraq had cooperated unconditionally with Unscom during the period covered by Butler's report, the Council, in line with its Resolution 1137 (November 12, 1997), decided, on April 27, to lift travel restrictions on certain Iraqi officials and revert to a sixty-day review of sanctions. The Iraqi government presented this as a major diplomatic victory which showed the correctness of the line it had been pursuing on Unscom. To celebrate the occasion, in May it organized a parade on the Festival and Parade Ground in Baghdad by half a million volunteers, who had signed up in response to Saddam Hussein's call four months earlier for a jihad against the UN embargo. Watched by foreign diplomats, it was an impressive exercise. It happened to coincide with the Pentagon's withdrawal of the extra force it had assembled in the Gulf in late 1997 and early 1998, reducing its 400 warplanes to 170.[28]

But since Unscom now had in place a monitoring and eavesdropping system in Iraq which worked in tandem with its regional office in Bahrain – with the US National Security Agency's employees playing a central role – and it had discovered a link between Saddam Hussein's personal secretary and Special Security to move or destroy contraband and related documents, Ritter resolved to catch the culprits red-handed and pass the incontrovertible evidence to the Security Council. The Iraqis on their part had finessed their recondite mechanism to the extent that they shifted the contraband around every 30–90 days, and removed or destroyed evidence on 15 minutes' notice.[29] So it was only a matter of time before the two sides clashed in the open again.

Iraqi suffering worsens

Along with the headline-grabbing disarmament drama, another process – less dramatic although more profound – centered on Iraqis' humanitarian needs, was in train. Dennis Halliday, the UNOHCI chief since the introduction of the oil-for-food program, summarized the situation in January 1998 thus:

> Roughly 30 percent of adults and children are suffering from malnutrition. We have acute malnutrition that can lead to death. We have chronic malnutrition that leads to stunting of physical and other capabilities … 25 percent of the kids are not going to school any more because they are out making money to support the family …. They [Iraqis] would need $15 to $20 billion a year in revenue to begin to get things moving properly.[30]

At Kofi Annan's initiative, on February 19, 1998, the Security Council passed Resolution 1153 which raised the six-monthly ceiling for the oil-for-food scheme from $2 billion to $5.26 billion. That was welcome news for Iraqis. The only problem was that at $15 a barrel, Baghdad would have to increase its oil exports from the current 900,000 barrels bpd to 2.34 million bpd. This and the local consumption of 450,000 bpd meant a total output of 2.8 million bpd. But Iraq's oil industry was so run down that its total output could not exceed 2 million bpd. Yet, at the UN's 661 Sanctions Committee, the US tried to add conditions on passing the $300 million requested for the Iraqi oil industry repairs over the next six months.[31]

On May 6, nearly 100 American peace activists, led by Ramsey Clark, former US attorney-general, flew to Baghdad, carrying $4 million worth of medicine, including antibiotics and anti-malarial drugs. In his letter to the UN Security Council, Clark, chairman of the New York-based International Action Committee, charged the Council with contravening the 1949 Geneva Conventions on War, which outlaw starving civilians as a means of warfare since, in his view, deaths occurring in Iraq "every two or three minutes" were a result of the UN sanctions. The figures released in 1995 and 1996 by the UN's FAO, WHO and Unicef showed that due to the UN embargo the mortality rate for Iraqi children under 5 had increased sixfold, and that for adults over 50 threefold. These statistics translated into 675,000 infant and 320,000 adult deaths in seven years.[32]

This was very much in the minds of the participants in the government-sponsored international seminar on UN sanctions in Baghdad, which was opened by Tariq Aziz. Among those participating were the visiting US peace activists, including the Pastors for Peace. They demonstrated in Baghdad outside the US interest section at the Polish embassy, claiming that millions of Americans were against the "genocidal sanctions against Iraq." The local media reported the event at length. And it got much exposure in the electronic media of the region as well as with several Arabic language terrestrial television channels based in London.

As far as the Clinton administration was concerned, it would have liked to see the Arab and other electronic media highlighting the latest report by the UN Special Rapporteur on human rights in Iraq, Max van der Stoel, a former Dutch minister. In his 22-page document released in April, he focused on the almost

20,000 Iraqis who were believed to have vanished during the last decade as a result of the bloody persecution by the Saddam regime, and another half a million, chiefly Kurds and Turkomans in the north, who had been displaced as a result of the government's scorched earth policy towards nationalist Kurds.[33]

In June 1998 Dennis Halliday referred to a recent UN survey, which showed that 10 percent of the children under five were suffering acute malnutrition, 25 percent chronic malnutrition, and another 25 percent were underweight. This was symptomatic of the run-down state of Iraq's infrastructure – electricity, telephone, transport and refrigeration. "Electricity is 40 percent of what it used to be," Halliday told Patrick Cockburn of the (London) *Independent*. "We have estimated we need $10 billion, and we are putting in $300 million [to rectify the situation]." With electricity off for twenty hours a day in rural areas, water pumps could not maintain pressure, and water became contaminated by sewage. In the absence of piped water, people drank straight from the heavily polluted rivers, which resulted in gastro-enteritis and death among children.[34] It would be another year before the UN 661 Sanctions Committee would agree to let Iraq "rehabilitate" its telecommunications network, installed in the early to mid-1980s, only to discover that the foreign companies which had supplied the equipment no longer made spare parts for the old analogue system. Faced with this, the 661 Committee agreed to let Iraq "upgrade" its telecommunications network. By the time a delegation of UN's International Telecommunications Union arrived in Baghdad in July 2000, another year had gone by.[35] Refrigeration and airconditioning in Iraq, where summers are unbearably hot, were badly affected by the 661 Committee's decision to bar the reverse osmosis equipment to desalinate water for use in the air-conditioning systems. In desperation the Iraqis desalinated water by other means and introduced it into the air-conditioning plants in public buildings, including hospitals. This choked the plants and ended in disaster.[36] Having failed to convey the gravity of the situation to the UN headquarters with a view to instituting remedial policies, Halliday offered his resignation in August 1998.

Persistent reports of Iraqi suffering had some impact on US lawmakers. In October, 44 US Congressmen and women, led by John Conyers, a senior black Democrat, wrote a letter to Clinton in which they called on him "to delink the economic sanctions, which have been a complete failure, from the military sanctions, end the crippling embargo, redefine the military effort, and focus on regional disarmament instead of singling out Iraq." (It was three months before Clinton responded, only to insist on "maintaining economic sanctions on Iraq.")[37]

After his resignation went into effect on September 30, Halliday became more vocal.

> If you've got a leadership which you can't communicate or have a dialogue with and that doesn't seem to want to conform to the standards that the UN is trying to establish, does that empower the

Security Council to kill a refugee, or to sustain malnutrition? I don't think so. Killing 6,000 kids a month is like a declaration of war. I don't think the Security Council is empowered to do that just because they don't like Saddam.[38]

The Anglo-American response to this argument was summed up by Sir John Weston, the British ambassador to the UN, thus: "They [Iraqi authorities] have prolonged the suffering of the Iraqi people for their own political ends." In other words, by refusing to cooperate fully with Unscom, the Baghdad government had dragged out the process, and thus shown that it was insensitive to the suffering of its citizens. Halliday, familiar with the situation on the ground, disagreed. "Before and during Resolution 986 the Iraqi government was supplementing its [rationing] quite extensively, feeding orphans, widows and single parents," he said.

In addition to 986, they're running an extraordinarily effective program through some 50,000 different agents in a country of about 18 million. Our [UN] observers watch that process from the border to the warehouse. It has worked, and we have no evidence of any significant leakage of foodstuffs. To say that they [the authorities] don't care about their own people is just rubbish.[39]

Unscom–Iraq tension rises

On the diplomatic front, after years of reactive behavior, the Saddam government mounted an offensive in May 1998. To reduce the influence that Washington had over the ten non-permanent and four permanent members of the Security Council, Tariq Aziz and the foreign minister, Muhammad al Sahhaf, undertook a worldwide tour. In Paris Aziz delivered a personal letter from Saddam Hussein to French President Jacques Chirac with a view to preserving France's backing for Iraq at the Security Council. While there, he also met the visiting Annan, and appealed to him to get Unscom to expedite its inspections and prepare the ground for an early lifting of sanctions. The rest of his European itinerary included Madrid, Rome and Brussels, the headquarters of the 15-member European Union (EU). Muhammad al Sahhaf set off on a tour of Africa, with his focus on Kenya, Gambia and Gabon, the three non-permanent African members of the Council. These tours were to be followed by similar missions to East Asia and Latin America.

At the UN, instead of urging a complete and swift ending of sanctions, Iraq now adopted a graduated approach. It was helped by the IAEA's six-monthly report on April 13, which stated that Iraq had compiled a "full, final and complete account" of its previous nuclear arms projects, and that since October 1997 the IAEA's monitoring and verification regime had not revealed "indications of the existence in Iraq of prohibited equipment or materials or of the conduct of prohibited activity."[40] Baghdad encouraged Russia to propose that the IAEA should end its search-and-destroy stage of disarmament and focus exclusively on monitoring and surveillance. But Washington threatened to veto such a resolution. Moscow then agreed to draft a joint Russian–American policy statement for presentation to the Security Council. This in essence called on the IAEA to submit a further report in early July.[41] By taking an obdurate stand on the subject, the US induced a similar stance in Iraq, as subsequent events would show.

Responding to Baghdad's repeated calls that Unscom should spell out specifically what it expected of Iraq, on June 3 Butler presented to the Security Council a paper entitled "Necessary Conditions for Resolution of Priority Disarmament Issues." It demanded that Iraq should account for special missile warheads and VX. And, in the biological field, it must provide information to enable Unscom to establish "material balance" – that is, to ascertain that the amounts of the ingredients and the final products matched. Butler stressed that these were "necessary" – not "sufficient" – conditions for Baghdad to meet to have sanctions eased or ended. Little wonder that Russia, France and China refused to endorse his document.[42]

By contrast, Butler's meetings in Baghdad with a top-level Iraqi delegation, led by Tariq Aziz, on June 13–14 went well. These resulted in "a measure of agreement" (according to Butler's account in his book), except for the unaccounted-for 500 tons of missile rocket fuel and VX. He added that he and Aziz had agreed to a work schedule that could use the road map outlined in his "Necessary Conditions for Resolution of Priority Disarmament Issues" in as little as two months, and close Unscom files on Iraq by October.[43] Aziz was more upbeat, describing the agreement as "specific in its nature, very precise," and adding that "A more practical approach is agreed on the biological weapons file" – the area where Unscom lacked a coherent picture of Iraq's development efforts. Aziz said so despite the fact that, having tackled the WMD issue fully during the meetings, Butler then told him that, assuming satisfactory progress on all subjects, "we would still need to discuss the Iraqi policy of concealment" – a statement which reportedly infuriated Aziz.[44] Evidently Aziz saw Butler, working in close collaboration with the US, shifting goal posts in technical and procedural fields, something Washington had been doing in diplomatic and political arenas since 1994.[45]

Reporting to the Security Council on June 18, Butler noted that while Baghdad agreed to provide detailed information about missile warheads, mustard gas shells and other weapons along with the documents, it had refused to deal with VX. The tale of VX was typical of the Iraqi behavior in other fields of proscribed armament: absolute denial, followed by partial admission with qualifications that kept changing, followed by what it declared to be the "final, full account." Having first denied making VX, Iraq said it produced some for experimental purposes in a laboratory – only to destroy it after having failed to weaponize it or finding a stabilizer for storage. Later, under pressure, it admitted that it had produced as much as 1.7 tons of VX, but not of weapons grade.[46]

Towards the end of June, Butler told the Security Council that Unscom had discovered the minutes of a meeting at which it was decided to hide evidence related to mobile missile launchers, and that the files found at the farm of Gen. Hussein Kamil Hassan after his defection in August 1995 had been put there just before their discovery by Ekeus, rather than previously assembled and stored there by Hussein Kamil Hassan.[47]

When considered in conjunction with Butler's earlier reference to the Iraqi government furnishing Unscom with details of its concealment policy and mechanism concerning proscribed weapons, his latest statements showed clearly that he was intent on dragging out the process and denying the easing or lifting of the UN embargo on Iraq.

It was against this backdrop that on July 18 a sixteen-strong team led by Dr Gabrielle Kraatz-Wadsack inspected Iraqi air force headquarters (a sensitive site) to seek documents to verify the past use of chemical and biological weapons. Once inside the building, she insisted on inspecting the air force command's operations room (an extra-sensitive site). She was allowed in along with one more inspector and an interpreter. Among the documents kept inside a safe, she found a file which contained a list of four special munitions – mustard gas, tabun, sarin and gas gangrene, *clostridium perfringens* – used by the air force in the past. She asked for a copy of the document which her senior Iraqi minder refused, saying she could take notes or have a copy with certain sections blacked out. When she protested the Iraqi official stopped further examination of documents. Following several phone calls between different officials, Butler and Gen. Amr Rashid agreed to seal the document jointly and keep it in the custody of the Iraqi National Monitoring Directorate, pending Butler's visit to Baghdad a fortnight later. By then, however, assisted by her interpreter, Kraatz-Wadsack had learnt that the document listed numerically the Iraqi air force's use of chemical weapons during 1981–88 in the Iran–Iraq War to a degree not reported before.[48] The unsealing of the document did not happen during Butler's next visit because by then Iraq was in the process of withdrawing its cooperation with Unscom.

In its report on July 4, the IAEA, after reiterating its earlier conclusion that Iraq did not possess nuclear weapons, referred to "Iraq's unwillingness to give the inspectors unfettered access to the Iraqi nuclear experts." In Baghdad's view, the issue of Iraq's nuclear specialists was extraneous. So the Iraqi Revolutionary Command Council addressed a letter to Annan on July 30, demanding that in the nuclear field the IAEA should now limit itself to long-term monitoring.[49] It also referred to its earlier statement about the lifting of sanctions within six months, and hoped that, at the Unscom's forthcoming meeting with Iraqi officials in Baghdad, it would recognize that Iraq had met all the requirements mentioned in Section C of Resolution 687.

During his meeting with Aziz on August 3, Butler brought up the subject of VX traces on a missile warhead that had been discovered by a US laboratory in Aberdeen, Maryland. "If Iraq filled warheads with VX, why should Iraq not say so to Unscom?" Aziz asked. "We declared that we filled warheads with anthrax. Anthrax, according to experts, is more lethal than VX. So as we admitted that we filled warheads with anthrax, why should we not [also] admit that we filled them with VX, if that was the case?"[50] Complaining that Butler was "focusing on minor issues that make no sense from the angle of disarmament," Aziz told him, "Since this is the wish of the American administration to perpetuate the situation – as long as this is the American wish, you are serving American policy." Little wonder that at the second meeting later that day, when Butler reportedly offered Aziz "a new accelerated schedule of work" to resolve most of the outstanding issues, Aziz told him, "There is no further work to be done, nor is there any additional information for Iraq to provide concerning its past programs of weapons of mass destruction … Go, and report to the Security Council that you have finished the job." Butler replied, "You have refused to give us the evidence required to support your claim."[51]

The issue of Iraq filling munitions with VX arose in mid-June 1998 when, during Butler's visit to Baghdad, his inspectors told him that fragments from a destroyed Scud showed traces of VX loaded just before the 1991 Gulf War (according to the laboratory tests at the US facility in Aberdeen, Maryland). It was one of the seven samples taken in March at the Nibai weapons dump near Taji, north of Baghdad. The Iraqis rejected the finding on four grounds: the Unscom inspectors had not given them samples of what they took; they had not taken the soil samples; and these should have been tested in a neutral country, not America. Finally, if VX was loaded in one warhead, the stabilizer would have been found in all samples. (Later tests carried out in Switzerland showed no traces of VX. The ones conducted in France showed traces of a chemical linked to VX. Finally, after examining three sets of results, seventeen scientists from seven countries concluded that there were "possible traces" of VX. In sum, the evidence was inconclusive.[52])

Following a call on August 4 by the Iraqi RCC and parliament to end cooperation with Unscom, Saddam ordered that cooperation with Unscom and the IAEA be suspended, and that no-notice inspections by them be discontinued. However, he exempted Unscom's monitoring activities; and so the cameras and sensors installed at suspected weapons sites remained intact. He demanded that Unscom be led by a new Executive Bureau that represented equally the five Security Council Permanent Members with a chairman chosen on rotation basis; that Unscom's offices in New York, Bahrain and Baghdad be reconstituted on the same principle; and that Unscom headquarters be moved from New York to Geneva or Vienna to insulate it from direct US influence.[53]

The Security Council president (the Slovene ambassador to the UN) was quick to declare that Baghdad's decision violated the Council's resolutions and the (February 23) Iraqi–UN Memorandum of Agreement.

But, unlike in the past, the Clinton administration chose to play down the Iraqi move. It did so not because it had become less hostile towards Saddam, but because Clinton had got mired in the Lewinsky sex scandal, and did not wish to embark on a foreign military campaign, especially when the lightning tour of nine Arab countries in four days by his defense secretary, William Cohen, revealed scant support for air strikes against Iraq. The bombing of the US embassies in the Kenyan and Tanzanian capitals on August 7, killing 250 people, mostly African, further distracted Washington.

While Albright described the latest crisis as "a confrontation between Iraq and the UN," leaving it to Annan and the Security Council to ensure that Saddam reversed his course, other top officials rationalized Clinton's restraint by describing Unscom as "one tool among many for containing Iraq" and – more significantly – one that had "outlived much of its usefulness."[54] So the implication was that Unscom had achieved almost all that it had set out to do. Yet, for domestic reasons, US policy-makers refrained from saying so unambiguously, aware that being seen to be soft on the Iraqi dictator was still unpopular with the American public.

What surprised many was the revelation made by the *Washington Post* on August 14 that for months the US had intervened secretly with Butler to dissuade his inspectors from mounting "challenge inspections", because it did not want to give Saddam a pretext to claim that the UN was being provocative, and that, on August 4, Albright had phoned Butler and urged him to rescind the no-notice inspections he had planned in New York before leaving for Baghdad via Beijing at the end of July. "News of Albright's call to Butler also reinforced Iraqi accusations that Unscom operated under US not UN auspices," noted Ian Williams, the UN correspondent of the London-based *Middle East International*. "It tended to strengthen the belief that US domestic politics rather than international legality were the factors which motivated its actions."[55]

A clear-cut example of US home politics impacting on Washington's behavior towards Iraq was recorded by Scott Ritter in his book, *Endgame*. While he, Charles Duelfer and Butler were discussing the Annan–Aziz Agreement in Butler's office at the UN in February 1998, decrying it as a betrayal of Unscom, the phone rang. Butler picked up the receiver. Taking their cue from him, Duelfer and Ritter left the room. When they returned, Butler said, "Madeleine [Albright] is very nervous. The heat coming down from Trent Lott [the Republican Senate majority leader] is upsetting the administration. She wants me to hold a press conference and endorse the Kofi Annan agreement [with Aziz]." He did.[56] That undoubtedly blunted Lott's attack.

It was against this backdrop of direct US interference in Unscom's operations that Ritter, the most hawkish and longest-serving inspector at Unscom, resigned on August 26, 1998. He did so in protest at the cancellation of his Unscom 255 by Butler under pressure from America which considered it to be too confrontational. He claimed that in July his inspectors had received two of the best pieces of intelligence information Unscom had had in a long time. Based on that, his Unscom 255 in August had targeted Saddam's personal secretary, Abid Hamid Mahmoud, responsible for orchestrating Iraq's effort to conceal WMD information and materials, and Special Security, which implemented his orders. He claimed further that between November 1997 and early August 1998 the US had made at least seven attempts to stymie Unscom investigations. "The United

States has undermined Unscom's efforts through interference and manipulation, usually coming from the highest levels of the administration's national security team," he said.[57]

Ritter's revelations undermined US standing at the Security Council. What had been surmised and expressed in private before now emerged as a fact – the Clinton administration's interference in, and manipulation of, Unscom to suit its domestic agenda. This provided a chance for France, Russia and China to have their say on the matter. The resulting Resolution 1194 that the Council adopted on September 9, 1998 was therefore a balanced one. While calling on Baghdad to rescind its decision of August 5, and suspending the normal sixty-day review of sanctions, it expressed readiness to consider a "comprehensive review" of Iraq's compliance with all Council resolutions if it resumed cooperation, and to draw up "a road map," describing what exactly Baghdad had to do to meet the UN requirements.[58]

Shifting regional balance

On September 8, to its relief, the Clinton administration was able to announce a piece of good news on Iraqi Kurds. Thanks to the tireless efforts of US assistant secretary of state, David Welch, Albright presented the KDP's Barzani and the PUK's Talabani to the press when they shook hands for the first time since May 1994, and announced that they had reached an agreement. Though the details were not divulged, an official statement referred to the two sides agreeing to share power and financial resources. The US state department spokesman said that the two leaders would not work directly to topple Saddam, but peace between them was essential to achieve that objective.[59]

Welch had intervened after an outbreak of intra-Kurdish violence in late 1997 and persistent reports that both Barzani and Talabani, unsure of what support they might receive from Washington and London in an open conflict with Saddam, were drifting towards clinching a deal with him. Indeed, on May 10, 1998, Tariq Aziz declared that the previous week he had received a KDP delegation in his office, and there was a PUK delegation waiting.[60]

Turkey expressed its disapproval of the Barzani–Talabani deal, seeing it as a potential threat to Iraq's territorial integrity. "It has been understood that the final goal [of the KDP and PUK] is a federated Iraq through a *fait accompli*," said Bulent Ecevit, the Turkish deputy premier. He announced that Turkey was restoring full diplomatic relations with Iraq by sending its ambassador (who had been withdrawn on the eve of the 1991 Gulf War) back to Baghdad.[61]

Ankara acted this way even though Washington had overlooked its breaching of the UN sanctions by letting its merchants trade in Iraqi oil and oil products since 1993. At 60,000 bpd, these imports amounted to about 10 percent of Turkey's fuel market. US officials knew this, but rationalized it on the grounds that Turkey had suffered so heavily as a result of UN sanctions on Iraq (with Ankara claiming a loss of $32 billion worth of two-way trade with Baghdad) that they decided to let it benefit from the Iraqi oil smuggling.[62] Thus Washington inadvertently conceded its critics' charge that it was being selective in its application of the UN embargo against Baghdad.[63]

Elsewhere in the region, a Syrian trade delegation visited Baghdad in May 1998, following Tariq Aziz's visit to Damascus six months earlier, the first sign of a thaw between the two neighbors who had broken off diplomatic relations seventeen years earlier. In August Syria and Iraq signed agreements to reopen the Kirkuk–Banias pipeline with a 1.4 million bpd capacity, once the UN sanctions had been lifted, and build a new pipeline with an enhanced capacity. Because of the shorter distance it would cost Iraq half the money to use the Kirkuk–Banias line than the Kirkuk–Yumurtalik line. In early September Syria opened a trade center in Baghdad, with Iraq planning to do the same in Damascus.[64] Even companies from Saudi Arabia, still hostile to Saddam Hussein, signed up $100 million contracts with Iraq for supplying food and medicine.[65]

Steady repairing of relations with the neighboring countries gave Saddam greater confidence as he prepared to face Unscom and its hawkish chief, Butler, with the aim of getting sanctions lifted by the end of 1998.

7

OPERATION "DESERT FOX"

Given the popular hatred of Saddam in America, it was no surprise that the 435-strong US House of Representatives adopted the Iraq Liberation Bill by 360 votes to 38 on October 6, 1998, followed by a larger plurality in the Senate. It authorized the president to spend up to $97 million for military aid to train, equip and finance an Iraqi opposition army, and authorized the Pentagon to train insurgents. A fortnight later Clinton signed it – turning it into the Iraq Liberation Act (ILA) – after ignoring the objection of the Iraqi National Assembly that "Such behavior contradicts the UN Charter, international law and the right of people to choose their own political system without foreign influence."[1]

The military strategy to destabilize Iraq was conceived by (Retd) Gen. Wayne Downing, a retired Special Forces officer, and Dewey Clarridge, a retired CIA officer who had worked with the anti-leftist Contras in Nicaragua in the 1980s. The plan involved the CIA, working in league with the Special Forces, to train opposition military officers who would then train their men. Next, protected by US air cover, they would start capturing lightly defended areas in southern and western Iraq as an opening gambit to attract defectors from the regular Iraqi army. As their guerrilla actions escalated, inducing an increasing deployment of Baghdad's air force, US air power would intervene to protect the insurgents. "[US] Support for an insurgency will send a signal to Saddam that we're getting serious and may encourage someone inside [Iraq] to stage a coup or assassination," said Clarridge. To get the ball rolling, Washington had first to designate groups eligible for military aid by end-January. For that Clinton had to be satisfied that a group had "broad-based representation" and "a record of support for democracy."[2]

Commenting on the ILA in its editorial, entitled "Fantasies About Iraq," on October 20, the *New York Times* wrote, "The intended beneficiaries of US support include the Iraqi National Congress, which represents almost no one and has failed to produce results with aid it previously received from Washington." A warning came from none other than Gen. Anthony Zinni, chief of the US Central Command, covering the Gulf. "I know of no viable opposition to Saddam in Iraq," he said. "Under such conditions any attempt to remove the Iraqi leader by force could dangerously fragment Iraq and destabilize the entire region." He added, "A weakened, fragmented, chaotic Iraq, which could happen if this isn't done carefully, is more dangerous in the long run than a contained Saddam now."[3] At a Congressional hearing in March he offered further elaboration. "I don't feel it is wise at this point to speak of providing weapons, creating camps for groups that are not viable," he said.

> Even if we had Saddam gone, we would end up with 15, 20 or 90 groups competing for power …. History teaches us in this region that you can change regimes if that's your goal but you could end up with an Afghanistan, an Iran, a Somalia. In the long run that could be more destabilizing … [Ultimately] it is stability in the region that counts … And whatever you do to effect regime change – a noble goal – it should be done with that in mind.[4]

In the region, opposition to Washington's plans came from one of its leading long-time allies, Egyptian President Hosni Mubarak. Referring to the anti-Baghdad activities of the American and British intelligence agencies, he said, "These projects won't get anywhere. Anyone who knows Iraq knows no action will succeed if it isn't led from the inside, by people living in Iraq." And Hamid Bayati, the London representative of SAIRI, the single most important Iraqi opposition group with a two-division-strong army based in Iran, said, "It is the Iraqi people who should do the job of toppling Saddam and his regime. But they should be able to work independently in their own ways to achieve this objective." Whatever the intention of the ILA, he continued, "it is undermining the Iraqi opposition by portraying them as American agents."[5]

At the UN, France was openly scathing. In an undisguised reference to the Americans, the French foreign minister, Hubert Vedrine, told the London-based, Saudi-owned *Al Sharq al Awsat* (The Middle East), "We cannot have the same people telling us that not the slightest detail must be changed in the [Security Council] resolutions and also announcing or advocating a policy which has nothing to do with the same resolutions."[6]

In late September, during a meeting with editors of the *Washington Post*, UN Secretary-General Kofi Annan summarized the feeling gaining ground among Security Council members about Iraqi disarmament. "I personally believe – as I think a lot of the Security Council members believe with 100 percent certainty – that Iraq being fully disarmed is never going to be possible," he said. "At the end of the day, the Security Council must decide whether Iraq is disarmed to the extent that it is not a threat to its neighbors, that it has no weapons of mass destruction, and that it has no capacity to make weapons of mass destruction."[7] So it was not surprising that as a follow-up to the Council's Resolution 1194 of September 9, 1998, he provided a draft of the terms of reference for a comprehensive review of Baghdad's compliance with Council resolutions which specified a timetable for Iraq's release from sanctions.

In contrast, Richard Butler's report on October 6, said that Iraq had prevented the disarmament phase of Unscom's mandate from being accomplished, and that it was planning to impede Unscom's monitoring function as well. His tone was in tune with the feelings of the Council president of the month, Sir Jeremy Greenstock of Britain. In the Council's discussions on the comprehensive review, America, backed by Britain, insisted that it should cover all the nine sections of the 34-clause Resolution 687 – including Sections D and G, concerning respectively "the return of all Kuwaiti property seized by Iraq" and "repatriation or return of all Kuwaiti and third country nationals or their remains present in Iraq on or after August 2, 1990." Baghdad rejected this, arguing that the review should focus solely on Section C since the crucial Paragraph 22 referred only to that section for easing or lifting of the sanctions.[8] Taking a mid-way position, Russia, France and China said that the review should consider all sections of 687 but that it should pay most attention to the current state of Iraqi disarmament.

At the end of the debate, the Council asked the British president to draft a letter to Baghdad. He did so. In it he crucially omitted the timetable for lifting sanctions on the grounds that Council members could not prejudge the result of the review in advance of the experts' reports on which it was to be based. This upset Baghdad which had set its sights on getting the embargo lifted by the end of the year.

Iraq's chances dimmed in late October when its officials failed to provide full cooperation during an Unscom inspection. The Security Council threatened to ban foreign travel by the Iraqi officials interfering with Unscom operations. Baghdad decided to expel those ten of the forty Unscom inspectors who were US nationals. The next day it turned back two American inspectors as they arrived from Bahrain. On October 31, it coupled its decision to stop cooperating with Unscom and the IAEA in inspecting and monitoring with a call for a rapid, comprehensive review of Iraq's compliance in disarmament linked to a timetable to lift sanctions. Baghdad's timing had to do with the mid-term US Congressional elections on November 3 where – in Saddam's estimation – tarred by Clinton's sex scandal, Democrats would do badly. In the event, the president's party improved its standing in the House – for the first time since 1934.

This, the temporary lifting of the Monica Lewinsky cloud, and the success that Clinton had in brokering a deal between Yasser Arafat and Binyamin Netanyahu at the Wye River Plantation in Maryland on October 23, made him reverse the policy of downplaying Saddam's defiance that he had pursued over the past year on the grounds that he did not want to dance to the Iraqi dictator's tune. Now he raised the temperature and brought the crisis to a boil quickly by not repeating the exercise of educating the American public to win its approval for bombing Iraq as he had done in February. What further aided him was the fact that the Security Council was being presided over in November by the US ambassador to the UN, Peter Burleigh.

As in the past, as the crisis deepened Clinton ordered a military build-up in the Gulf. But this time he faced a factor which did not exist before. Since his resignation from Unscom in August, Scott Ritter had regaled the world media in numerous interviews with sensational revelations, including the one that he had visited Israel many times to meet officials of its intelligence agencies, Mossad and Aman. In an interview with the Israeli newspaper, *Ha'aretz* (The Land), he mentioned Unscom sharing information with Israel, an admission that deeply embarrassed Butler, who now asked Ritter, a *former* Unscom inspector, to shut up, reminding him of his obligation not to divulge information collected in the course of his work – something Butler had not done with the *serving* inspectors who did the same in a CNN documentary in March. Ritter disclosed that "the key methodological breakthrough" to target Special Security to disrupt Iraq's weapons concealment program came from Mossad. (So far, US officials had credited Ritter with this breakthrough.) As stated earlier, his links with Mossad and Aman had developed to the extent that the FBI opened an investigation on him in 1996 to determine whether he had passed on classified US information to Israel.[9]

No wonder that in an interview with CNN on November 13, Tariq Aziz reiterated what he had said before: Unscom inspectors were spying for America and Israel. Referring to Washington's threat to strike Iraq, he said that "since the Americans were starving us and denying us medicine it was better to die under US bombs than to surrender."[10]

That evening, after five hours of deliberations at the Security Council, Annan sent a letter to Saddam Hussein, setting out what was required of him if he wanted to avoid an attack by the US and the UK, and promising him that once Iraq had resumed its cooperation with Unscom, the Security Council would tackle the issue of a comprehensive review of Iraq's disarmament. At about the same time there was a video-link contact between Saddam Hussein and the Russian ambassador Nikolai Kartouzov in Baghdad after he had delivered letters from President Boris Yeltsin and Prime Minister Yevgeny Primakov to the presidential office. The prime mover was Primakov on whose advice Yeltsin – acting on behalf of Russia, France and China – had advised Saddam to opt for a diplomatic solution, and confirm the agreement he had made with Annan in February. Yeltsin acquired this role after the Russian, French and Chinese ambassadors to the UN had held a separate meeting with their Iraqi counterpart, Nizar Hamdoun, who had provided them with a nine-point memorandum on the subject of the promised comprehensive review. Later this document would appear as an annex to Aziz's letter to Annan, and become a point of contention.

Meanwhile, other diplomatic sources conveyed to Saddam that the Pentagon would mount its blitzkrieg against Iraq within the next twenty-four hours if he refused to back down. So his government evacuated many important sites, including several barracks of the RG and Special Security and the GID headquarters.

Saddam Hussein convened a joint meeting of the RCC and the Baath Party Regional (i.e., Iraqi) Command Council. Then he and Aziz composed a reply to Annan which walked a tight-rope between "surrender" (as the US–UK alliance would see it) and "defiance" (as Iraqis would view it), and attached the nine-point memorandum on the comprehensive review as an annex. Signed by Aziz, it was passed on to Prakash Shah, Annan's personal envoy in Baghdad, and then to Annan at home in New York, who said that it met his requirements. It then reached the White House on November 14 at breakfast. There its two-page annex caused "frustration, anger and resolve."

The objective of Iraq's decisions of August 5 and October 31, 1998 was "to end the suffering of its embargoed people and to see the implementation of Paragraph 22 of the Security Council Resolution 687 as a first step for lifting the other sanctions," said the letter addressed to Annan. Referring to Annan's initiative on a comprehensive review of the matter, it stated that the deliberations of the Council "did not result in a clear picture ... America objected to the presentation of any clarity in regard to the objective of the comprehensive review." But, in view of "your [Annan's] letter and also the letters from Russian President Yeltsin and Premier Primakov," and in order "to give further chance to achieve justice by lifting sanctions, commencing with the implementation of Paragraph 22 ... the leadership of Iraq decided to resume working with Unscom and IAEA." Referring to the nine-point annex, the Aziz letter said, "We believe that ... the adoption of the points conveyed to the ambassadors of Russia, France and China, a copy of which I enclose, will render the [comprehensive] review serious, fair and fruitful."

But before his letter reached the White House, Aziz had declared on CNN that Baghdad had decided to let UN inspectors back into Iraq. By then US B–52 bombers, which had taken off from the bases in the southern state of Louisiana, were within an hour of unleashing their Cruise missiles. Informed of Aziz's statement on CNN by Sandy Berger, Clinton immediately aborted the mission. His decision was criticized at home by hawkish politicians and commentators, who called him "chicken-hearted." But if he had not aborted the mission, he would have been accused of killing hundreds of Iraqis just as Baghdad had run up a white flag.

"Saddam blinked first," declared most American politicians and pundits. "Victory after victory until we overcome sanctions," hailed *Al Thawra*, the organ of the ruling Iraqi Baath Party. "Victory" in this case meant not being bombed by America. Baghdad was aware that, given the close links of the CIA and the NSA with Unscom, the US knew more about Iraqi civilian and military facilities than ever before. And, aided further by continuous monitoring of some 460 sites in the country by the UN, any future bombings were going to be more deadly than the ones before. Unabashed, the Pentagon said that "it was inevitable that information supplied by the [UN] monitors had played a part in the careful selection of targets."[11] Small wonder that when Clinton aborted the US bombing mission Iraqis danced in the streets of Baghdad.

But the crisis was not over yet. At the White House, Berger said on the morning of November 14 that Aziz's letter to Annan was "unacceptable," and objected strongly to its annex. This led first to Hamdoun saying in writing that the annex to Aziz's letter was not a set of conditions attached to Iraq's decision, and then in another written statement in the afternoon that Aziz's letter constituted "a decree of the Iraqi leadership regarding the resumption of cooperation with [Unscom and the IAEA]. The two bodies will be permitted to carry out their regular duties."[12] By then Clinton had listed five conditions – including "unfettered access" to inspectors; all relevant documents to be handed over; and a bar on Iraq interfering with Unscom's "independence and professionalism" – for accepting the document, and warned that if Baghdad did not abide by its latest agreement, US forces would strike Iraq without warning. On November 15, the Security Council accepted Iraq's various statements as constituting a formal cancellation of its August 5 and October 31 decisions to withdraw cooperation from Unscom and the IAEA.

That day Clinton vowed to implement the recently passed Iraq Liberation Act as best as he could. The pledge emanated from his frustration and anger at the Iraqi dictator's escape from punishment through calculated brinkmanship, which enhanced his standing among Iraqis and other Arabs. "Over the long run, the best way to address that threat [to regional peace by Saddam] is through a government in Baghdad – a new government that is committed to respect its people, not repress them," he said. "Over the past year we have deepened our engagement with the forces of change in Iraq, reconciling the two largest Kurdish opposition groups, beginning broadcasts of Radio Free Iraq …. We will intensify that effort." As expected, Aziz objected vehemently. "I have to condemn strongly the statement of Mr Clinton, the plans of his government to overthrow the government of Iraq," he said. "This is a flagrant violation of the Security Council resolutions as well as international law."[13]

Clearly the Clinton administration had now publicly adopted the policy of "containment plus regime change" for Iraq. Consequently there needed to be a further tightening of US links with Butler. And there was.

"Sandy Berger … immediately met with Butler to coordinate inspection schedules in the framework of all-but-inevitable military strike," noted Scott Ritter in his *Endgame*.

> Butler had the customary test ready to go, one that he knew would be confrontational. It was a reworking of the Unscom 255 inspection [under me] that had been canceled in August on the grounds that it was too confrontational. Now, however, Butler and Berger knew what they wanted, and the newly numbered Unscom 258 delivered in spades. Delays, blockages, evacuated buildings – the classic pattern of Iraqi obstruction – were all provoked and catalogued … Butler appeared to have forgotten that he was a servant of the Security Council, not the United States. The Butler–Berger hand-in-glove relationship during Unscom 258 was too cozy. Prior coordination, daily Butler-to-Berger situation updates during the inspection, and a mutual review of Butler's report before its submission to the [UN] secretary-general infringed on the Security Council's powers.[14]

Unscom resumed work in Iraq on November 18, 1998, with its Unscom 258 team now led by an Australian, Colonel Roger Hill. Over the next week it carried out twenty-five inspections. The following day the Iraqis refused to hand over unconditionally certain documents – including the one Gabrielle Kraatz-Wadsak had discovered four months earlier – demanded by Unscom. On November 20, Butler released a list of twelve demands for documents and the responses of Riyadh al Qaisi, an undersecretary of the Iraqi foreign minister. The list included:

1 the minutes of the meetings of the Iraqi High Level Committee on the Retention of Banned Weapons and Materials formed in June 1991;

2 a report on Iraq's investigation of Gen. Hussein Kamil Hassan and his concealment of proscribed weapons capabilities and documents; and

3 the document detailing the Iraqi air force's use of chemical weapons during the Iran–Iraq War that Kraatz-Wadsack had briefly seen at the air force headquarters on July 18, 1998.

On 1, al Qaisi replied that the IAEA had earlier made this request and had been told that "there was no such committee in the technical sense of the word." Regarding 2, he said that Iraq did not formally investigate Hussein Kamil Hassan's defection. On 3, he replied that Iraq was ready to disclose "relevant portions" of the document in the presence of Prakash Shah, the special envoy of Annan in Baghdad.[15]

Butler declared that this violated President Clinton's statement about Baghdad handing over all the documents Unscom demanded. Baghdad replied that it did not accept Clinton's unilateral list of conditions. The Security Council refrained from judging whether or not Iraq's refusal constituted a violation of its promise of cooperation.[16]

Between December 4 and 9, the Iraqis prevented Unscom 261, a biological team, from inspecting one site, and a chemical weapons team from photographing a bomb. Finally, they blocked the inspection of the (Iraqi) Baath Party head office, which was suspected of harboring missile parts.[17] "Iraq will continue its fight against its enemies," declared Saddam Hussein. "After years of fighting, Iraq has become a model of resistance." Butler decided to cancel the forthcoming inspections on December 12 and 13, and mention this in his forthcoming report to the Security Council.

At the Council there was a growing consensus among the Russian, French and Chinese delegates that Iraq's disarmament was almost over, and that the comprehensive review should be completed by Christmas with the aim of lifting the oil, but not the financial, embargo against Baghdad. This view was shared by Annan's senior advisers. "You can never have 100 percent proof of disarmament because it is too easy to develop, manufacture and hide biological weapons, so at some point technical exercise gives way to political judgment," an adviser to the

UN secretary-general told Barton Gellman of the *Washington Post*. "At some point it becomes impossible to prove the negative."[18]

Pressured by the three non-Anglo-Saxon Permanent Members of the Council, Butler began submitting weekly reports, starting December 4. The day he handed in his second report, he had a meeting with the US National Security Adviser, Berger, at the American mission to the UN near the UN headquarters. The purpose of the face-to-face encounter seemed to be to manipulate the fast-moving situation in a way that it would provide Washington with a credible basis for bombing Iraq against the backdrop of imminent impeachment proceedings against Clinton at the US Congress. Berger then joined Clinton and his entourage on their way to Israel and the Palestinian Territories.

Chronology, December 13–19 1998

A factual chronology to disentangle the Iraq-Impeachment web

SUNDAY, December 13: Richard Butler gives the first draft of his report on Iraq to senior US diplomats at the UN. They communicate it instantly to President Clinton, then in Israel. He finds it weak, has a midnight meeting with National Security Adviser Sandy Berger and revives US bombing plans for Iraq. (*Independent*, December 18)

MONDAY, December 14: Clinton administration officials play "a direct role in shaping Butler's text during multiple conversations with him at secure facilities at the US mission to the United Nations." (*Washington Post*, December 16) At the UN, secretary-general Kofi Annan says that once the Security Council has decided that Iraq has met the disarmament qualifications mentioned by Resolution 687, there should be no grounds for maintaining sanctions against Baghdad. Later he adds, "The Council resolution does not talk about getting rid of [Iraqi] leadership." (Inter Press Service, February 3, 1999)

TUESDAY, December 15: At 2 p.m. Eastern Standard Time/9 a.m. GMT, the White House chief of staff, John Podesta, informs Congressional leaders that US forces will attack Iraq the following day. (*Washington Post*, December 18)

Peter Burleigh, the US ambassador to the UN, "advises" Butler to recall all UN inspectors, monitors and support staff from Iraq immediately. (Richard Butler, *Saddam Defiant*, p. 224.) Butler does so without even informing the higher body under which Unscom functions, the Security Council.

Before leaving Israel, Clinton tells Premier Netanyahu that Butler's Report is negative and that he will order bombing of Iraq.

Aboard his Air Force One jet, Clinton, accompanied by Albright and Berger, holds a telephone conference with Vice-President Al Gore, Defense Secretary

---

William Cohen and CIA Chief George Tenet. He orders "the priming of US forces to attack Iraq," and telephones British Premier Tony Blair to tell him to "get ready to bomb." (*Independent*, December 18)

At 6 p.m. EST/4 p.m. GMT, Butler delivers to Annan his ten-page report, which concludes that Iraq is not cooperating with Unscom.

At 9 p.m. EST/1 p.m. GMT, news agencies relay a summary of Butler's report. UN Security Council members then receive a copy of the report.

WEDNESDAY, December 16: Clinton returns to the White House just after midnight. He stays up till 1:30 a.m. to inform Congressional leaders of his plans to bomb Iraq.

All US breakfast TV news bulletins break the astonishing news just when the national interest is focused on the impeachment debate in the House of Representatives due the next day.

All Unscom staff have left Iraq.

Astonished Security Council members discuss Butler's report desultorily. Clinton has already made up his mind.

Democrat leaders in the House urge their Republican counterparts to postpone the impeachment debate as long the US commander-in-chief, Clinton, is engaged in a war with Iraq. Aware that the bombing could be an open-ended operation, extending beyond Christmas and the official end of the tenure of the House, and eager to wind up the House business a week before Christmas, Republican leaders agree to a postponement of just one day.

At 3:12 p.m. EST/8:12 p.m. GMT, the first Cruise missile is fired by the US. It reaches its target in Baghdad 100 minutes later.

At 4:45 p.m. EST/9:45 p.m. GMT, in an effort to show that the military operation, codenamed "Desert Fox," is bilateral, Blair issues a statement that bombing of Iraq has started.

The British contribution to "Desert Fox" is a mere 5 percent. (*International Herald Tribune*, January 6, 1999)

France did not join. Indeed, it discontinued its participation in the Southern Watch air surveillance in southern Iraq (up to 32nd Parallel, not 33rd Parallel), but made it public later. (*International Herald Tribune*, December 30, 1998)

At 6 p.m. EST/11 p.m. GMT, Clinton delivers a nationwide television address on hitting Iraq.

THURSDAY, December 17: Bombing of Iraq continues.

FRIDAY, December 18: The two-day debate on impeachment starts in the House of Representatives. The Muslim holy month of Ramadan begins after sunset. Night-time bombing of Iraq continues.

SATURDAY, December 19: At 1:30 p.m. EST/6:30 p.m. GMT, Clinton is impeached on the first article – perjury before a Grand Jury – followed by another on the third article – obstruction of justice – half an hour later by the House. This paves the way for the case to go before the US Senate, which has the final authority to dismiss him.

At 4:30 p.m. EST/9:30 p.m. GMT, Clinton halts the bombing of Iraq. By then the Pentagon has fired 415 Cruise and Tomahawk missiles (90 more than in the Second Gulf War) and dropped 600 laser-guided bombs.

Among those who welcome the end of the air campaign is Kuwait.

Sadly for Bill Clinton, his foxy plan to manipulate the Butler Report to get the House Republicans to defer the impeachment debate failed. Once that happened and the vote in the House went against him, and the anti-American sentiment in the Middle East began rising sharply, he stopped the bombing within three hours of the ballot.

Of the 650 sorties mounted during Operation "Desert Fox," 300 were from US aircraft carriers, and the rest from the ground bases in Saudi Arabia and Kuwait, resulting in the dropping of 600 laser-guided bombs. US warships fired 325 precision-guided Tomahawks while 90 Cruise missiles were launched by the B–52s flying from Diego Garcia. The Pentagon claimed to have hit 75 of the 100 targeted sites, which included the headquarters of the Military Intelligence, the Special Security, the Special Republican Guard and the Baath Party National (i.e., Pan-Arab) Command. However, the Iraqi authorities evacuated all likely targets, including Baghdad University's science laboratories and the Special Security headquarters, in the hours preceding the raids, as soon as Saddam gave a signal to take immediate evasive action and devolved power to four trusted aides in as many regions in which the country was divided. British planes dropped propaganda leaflets in the south on RG sites to stir up an anti-Saddam rebellion – a wrong move, as dissident Shia as well as Kurdish leaders were only too aware that hitting the Iraqi army while it was being attacked by foreign powers would be politically suicidal.[19]

Assessment of "Desert Fox"

The prime merit of Operation "Desert Fox" was to lend credibility to Clinton's repeated threats of force, and demonstrate once again the superiority of the US military-intelligence apparatus which achieved its aim of hitting enemy targets without causing many civilian casualties. But in the process Clinton lost considerable political-diplomatic ground in the region. This was aptly summed up by the public approval accorded to the end of the bombing by Kuwait. As for Saddam, he failed to transform the depiction of Iraq as a victim of the US–UK aggression into a popular protest in the Arab world, and use it as a lever to win Arab governments' support for the lifting of sanctions against his country.

Overall, the US-led air strikes resulted in ending the Unscom regime, with China joining Russia on December 23 to demand Butler's dismissal; reinforcing divisions among the Security Council's P5, with the US–UK axis on one side and Russia–China on the other, and France somewhere in between; alienating the UN secretary-general from the US–UK axis; precipitating damaging revelations of the American intelligence agencies' infiltration of Unscom in the American press; highlighting the dwindling support in the region for military action against Baghdad; making it harder for Washington to claim in future that its unilateral actions are taken on behalf of the world community; and moving the issue of anti-Iraq sanctions to the top of the Security Council's agenda.

Saddam's success on the last point was so obvious that, on December 22, the White House declared publicly for the first time that it was "willing to use its veto in the Security Council to keep the economic sanctions in place." [20] This was in stark contrast to the position of France which said that the embargo could no longer be defended as "it hurts the people of Iraq and keeps them hostages of their authorities."[21]

While Berger explained that the US struck Iraq to assert the credibility of its threat of force – a task which the Clinton administration found itself obliged to perform without much enthusiasm – another senior official described "Desert Fox" as a concrete illustration of "continuing American pressure" against Baghdad. Both claimed that the air strikes weakened the Saddam regime's power base, and damaged its military-industrial complex without hurting civilians, with Gen. Henry Shelton putting the Iraqi fatalities at 600–1,600 RG troops and "several key individuals."[22]

These claims were disputed by experts. "The initial assertions of significant damage inflicted on Iraq appears to be an awkward combination of propaganda and complete rubbish," said Anthony H. Cordesman, an American military analyst. "No change in Iraqi politics or Saddam's behavior should be expected. He has shown the Iraqis, the Gulf and the world that he can survive another US attack." Making the crucial distinction between immoveable buildings and their moveable contents – humans and materials – many US specialists concluded that any damage inflicted on Iraq pertained to the buildings and not to their contents which had been removed before the air strikes.[23]

However, the Clinton administration's unexpressed agenda was different. It wanted to show the Iraqi dictator that it had determined the constituents of his power base and was capable of striking them. That is why it targeted the headquarters of Special Security, Military Intelligence, SRG and Baath Party National Command. By hitting the command and control centers of Iraqi intelligence it conveyed a message of a more punitive action if Saddam posed fresh threats to the neighboring states. Having obtained highly secret information about the inner workings of his regime – most of it by infiltrating Unscom – it was eager to use it to impress on him his vulnerability. That explained its manipulation – on the eve of Operation "Desert Fox" – of Butler and his report to the Security

Council in the aftermath of its frustration at being deprived of striking Iraqi targets in mid-November when Saddam suddenly climbed down.

Moreover, by October 1997 the White House had concluded that Unscom, as constituted seven years earlier, had reached the end of the line. It also realized that the only basis on which it could justify future military action – lack of unconditional, unfettered access to Unscom inspectors – would be lost once Unscom ceased to exist or was deprived of its investigative role, which was bound to happen following its air strikes. So better to use the highly perishable intelligence information now, and be done with it.

But, by acting without the agreement of the Security Council's non-Anglo-Saxon Permanent Members, Washington and London violated the consensual principle that Annan had followed before flying to Baghdad in February to defuse an acute crisis. The resulting alienation that Annan felt from the US–UK alliance, and the statements by Ritter that the most important sites bombed during Operation "Desert Fox" had been derived from the inspections conducted by his team, paved the way for the disclosures of Washington's long-running clandestine exploitation of Unscom for unilateral purposes. These came in early January.

Also, with each day of the US-led air strikes, popular protest in the Arab world rose sharply. Besides the demonstrations in Cairo, Rabat (100,000-strong), Tripoli, Amman, Beirut and Damascus, there was one in Muscat, the first such event in the history of Oman. This, and the condemnation of the American military action as "unjust aggression" by Jordan's parliament, followed by a similar resolution on December 27 by the 16-member Arab Parliamentarian Union – providing the first non-governmental, pan-Arabic forum on Iraq since the Gulf War – buoyed Baghdad.

Aftermath of "Desert Fox"

However, Saddam's plan to have an Arab League summit to debate the issue, condemn the US–UK action and call for the lifting of UN sanctions, failed when the League foreign ministers' conference, called at the initiative of Yemen and the UAE, was postponed from December 23 to January 24. This happened at the behest of Saudi Arabia, Egypt and Kuwait, determined as they were to decelerate the process of assessing Operation "Desert Fox" by Arab leaders, hoping the anger over US bombardment would subside soon. It did.

Egyptian President Mubarak made a distinction between the Iraqi people and their regime. "We opposed the air attacks because in the final analysis it is the people of Iraq who pay the price," he told *Al Jumhuriya* (The Republic) on December 28. "We sympathize with them because we know that our brothers and sons in this fraternal country can do nothing about it. The regime in power is the root of all problems, and Egypt does not support this regime." The next day the *Babil*, run by Uday Saddam Hussein, described Mubarak as "the most wretched of the successors to the most wretched of the predecessors" and urged Egyptians to topple their "shameless ruler."

When, on December 31, *Al Jumhuriya* described Iraq as a country run by "The Gang of Four" (Saddam, Vice-President Taha Yassin Ramadan, Tariq Aziz and Speaker Sadoun Hamadi) who plundered the country, the *Babil* responded by printing a cartoon depicting Mubarak as a belly dancer performing before the Americans. On January 2, the Cairo-based *Akhbar al Yom* (News of the Day) portrayed Saddam resting on a pile of human skulls. Two days later the *Babil* suggested a truce to prevent "exploitation by the American and Zionist enemies." When Egypt ignored the offer, and its media continued to attack the Iraqi regime, on January 7 the *Babil* ran a cartoon depicting Mubarak as Clinton's dog. In response, Mubarak claimed in an interview with the *Al Jumhuriya* that Saddam was "actually inciting air strikes against his own country." This vituperative spat between Egypt and Iraq ended the reconciliation process that had gone on for some years and had picked up after Aziz's visit to Cairo in November 1997.

In his television broadcast on January 5, the Iraqi Army Day, aired on the Doha-based Al Jazeera satellite television channel, Saddam widened his verbal attack by pointing out that the attacking US–UK aircraft had come from Arab countries and from ships stationed in Arab waters, and that there were Western troops in "the Land of the Holy Sites" – that is, Saudi Arabia. Four days later the Iraqi parliament described the Kuwait–Iraq border demarcated in 1993 (and accepted by Baghdad in November 1994) as "illegal and savage," and called for reparations from Kuwait and Saudi Arabia for providing bases to America and Britain for air strikes against Iraq.[24] In response, the official Saudi Press Agency accused Saddam of killing and torturing thousands, and added, "The Iraqi people need revolution to topple the Baghdad tyrant." In a front-page article in *Al Thawra* on January 14, Tariq Aziz questioned the legitimacy of Kuwait's frontiers which he described as "a land mine that might explode in the future," and claimed that part of Kuwait's coastline belonged to Iraq.[25] This was enough to alert the Security Council whose members unanimously deplored Aziz's article and reaffirmed the sovereignty and territorial integrity of Kuwait.

Two days before the Arab League foreign ministers' meeting on January 24, Iraq released a secret letter that the US had addressed to the League members "urging them not to call for the lifting of sanctions or reforming Unscom." Washington acknowledged the authenticity of the document but described it as a memorandum for "discussing certain points."

The League foreign ministers' meeting in Cairo was the first to which Iraq was invited since its invasion of Kuwait in 1990. Before it were two draft resolutions, one drawn by Iraqi foreign minister Muhammad al Sahhaf, and the other jointly by his Egyptian, Saudi and Kuwaiti counterparts. The Iraqi version proposed that the League should condemn the American and British air strikes, urge its members to end the UN sanctions unilaterally, and declare illegal the no-fly zones imposed by Washington and London in northern and southern Iraq. The alternative draft called on Baghdad to implement the relevant Security Council resolutions to bring about the lifting of economic sanctions, and work out a diplomatic solution to the problem of weapons' inspection with the Council. Syria attempted to find a middle ground, and succeeded. The final draft was something of a compromise.

On "Desert Fox," the League's communiqué expressed "profound disquiet and concern at the use of the military option," and appealed for a diplomatic means to be used in the future. It urged Baghdad to implement the appropriate Security Council resolutions, and appointed a Contact Group to cooperate with the Council to facilitate the lifting of sanctions. On no-fly zones, it called on the Council to be "objective" and respect Iraq's sovereignty over "its national soil." Finally, it condemned Iraq for making "provocative" statements against Kuwait.[26]

What particularly riled Muhammad al Sahhaf and his delegation was the fact that the League's Contact Group contained Saudi Arabia and Egypt, but not Iraq. But the Group was indeed balanced. Besides Bahrain – the Arab bloc's representative at the Security Council – and the pro-American Saudi Arabia and Egypt, it contained Syria and the UAE, which were sympathetic towards Baghdad.

Unsurprisingly, the subject of Iraq's invasion of Kuwait cropped up. Kuwait's foreign minister, Shaikh Sabah al Ahmad al Sabah, demanded an apology from Muhammad al Sahhaf. He refused, but recognized that Iraq had made a "mistake" on Kuwait in 1990. Aware of this issue arising at the League meeting, Tariq Aziz had earlier told the Beirut-based *Al Nahar* (The Day) that Iraq was willing to apologize for its "mistakes" if other Arab governments did the same. "If all Arabs said sorry to one another, then Iraq will be ready to apologize," he added. But this was unacceptable to Kuwait's foreign minister at the Cairo meeting. As a precondition, he wanted the issue of some 600 Kuwaitis missing since the Second Gulf War settled to his satisfaction. He also wanted Iraq to promise in writing that it would not threaten its neighbors in the future. On his part, what the Iraqi foreign minister wanted was a promise from Kuwait that it would deny the use of its military bases to America and Britain in the future, something it had failed to do during "Desert Fox."[27]

The Iraqis walked out of the meeting in protest at the final communiqué, which was warmly received by America and Britain.

It gave further impetus to the newly unveiled American policy on Baghdad ("containment plus regime change"), with the US embarking on transforming the divided Iraqi opposition into a united force to become a viable alternative to Saddam's regime in the belief that "Desert Fox" had weakened him. It was also encouraged by the news of an attempted coup following the air campaign. The prime plotters were two generals – Lt. Gen. Kamil Sajit, a Sunni from Falluja, and Gen. Yelechin Omar, an ethnic Turkoman from Kirkuk – who inducted five other senior officers. But the authorities discovered the plot in late January. All seven conspirators were arrested and two were executed in early March, and their bodies delivered to their families.[28] Not that all those inside Iraq who wanted to get rid of Saddam were waiting for a military move against him by America. According to the April 1998 report by Max van der Stoel, the UN special human rights rapporteur on Iraq, the Baghdad government executed fourteen military officers in October for planning to assassinate Saddam Hussein, and a further twenty-three Iraqis were executed for "maneuvering" against the authorities.[29]

In Washington, once the White House had certified seven Iraqi groups eligible for US military aid on January 19, 1999, Albright named Frank Ricciardone, deputy chief of the US mission in Ankara, as "Special Representative for the Transition in Iraq" to coordinate opposition effort. Besides the INC, INA, KDP and PUK, the list of the eligible factions included the Tehran-based SAIRI, the Halabja-based Islamic Movement for Iraqi Kurdistan, and the London-based Movement for Constitutional Monarchy (MCM, led by Sharif Ali ibn al Hussein, a cousin of King Faisal II of Iraq). The KDP, SAIRI and MCM promptly rejected Washington's offer of aid, and attacked the whole enterprise. Undeterred, US officials leaked details of how the scheme would work to American and British newspapers. One such story, published in the (London) *Sunday Times* on January 24, 1999, described a plan whereby a score of groups of twenty men each, trained by the US in sabotage and use of arms, would infiltrate Iraq in summer and target roads, communications and power plants – and attack army patrols – in the western desert and the Shia-dominated south. They would report to the headquarters maintained in Iraqi Kurdistan, protected by a US–UK air umbrella. This would set off a process which would ultimately lead to large-scale defections of Iraqi soldiers and the downfall of Saddam.

In late January, Albright took Ricciardone with her on her visits to Cairo and Riyadh to spell out to the Egyptian and Saudi leaders the details of the new, proactive US policy on Iraq. The response of her hosts was not publicized. But the London-based Arabic newspapers, *Al Sharq al Awsat* and *Al Hayat*, owned by senior Saudi princes, said that Riyadh opposed any foreign role in changing Iraq's government, and that any change "should take place from within Iraq and by the people themselves."[30]

The top officials of Qatar, Oman and the UAE were not so diplomatic after they were briefed on the subject by Martin Indyk, US assistant secretary of state for the Near East. They feared that any change imposed on Iraq from outside could lead to rifts and civil war. Any external interference would not be in the best interests of anybody, they told Indyk.[31] Following his meetings with Albright and Cohen, the UAE president, Zaid al Nahyan, made public his refusal to join Washington's campaign to topple Saddam. "The present US policy of containment is harming the Iraqi people without weakening Saddam Hussein," a source close to al Nahyan told the *Middle East International*. "There is even evidence that sanctions are strengthening the regime. Iraq is too central, too powerful and too important to be treated this way."[32]

These developments encouraged Saddam to change tack on his regional policy. On February 19, he addressed a letter to the Arab League secretary-general, Esmat Abdul Maguid, offering to bury the hatchet with his Second Gulf War adversaries. By hosting American warplanes that were deployed against Iraq in Operation "Desert Fox," they had behaved in a manner similar to the one they accused Baghdad of doing in 1990–91, he reasoned, and so the two sides were now even, and should open a fresh chapter in their relations. But Saudi Arabia, the most important Gulf monarchy, showed no sign of thawing its relations with Saddam. Nor did Kuwait.

This strengthened the hands of hawks within Saddam's coterie of advisers. Intent on keeping the status quo, if only to benefit from the smuggling rackets – exporting oil and importing consumer goods and food from Turkey, Syria and Iran – they argued that it was futile to persuade the major pro-Washington countries like Saudi Arabia, Egypt and Kuwait to alter their policies. But his dovish advisers reasoned that it was in the medium- and long-term interests of Iraq to pursue confidence-building policies to wean away the pro-US Arab regimes from Washington. Since the tussle between the two sides remained unresolved, Saddam continued to swing from one position to the other while his leading adversary, the Clinton administration, remained resolute in its hostility towards him.

No-fly zones

With UN inspectors now out of his country, Saddam focused on the remaining overt violation of Iraqi sovereignty: the air exclusion zones. On December 26, 1998 Baghdad declared that it regarded the no-fly zones – covering 60 percent of Iraq and extending to the southern suburbs of Baghdad – as illegal and would defend its national airspace against violators. Iraq had made similar declarations in the past but, lacking the right missiles to hit the high flying aircraft enforcing the air exclusion zones, had failed to enforce them. The difference this time was that, having ended its participation in Operation "Northern Watch" in December 1996, France pulled out of Operation "Southern Watch" as soon as the US–UK alliance launched its "Desert Fox" campaign; and that China condemned the no-fly zones as "violations of the UN Charter and international norms."[33]

Over the next week Baghdad's decision led to periodic firing of Iraqi anti-aircraft guns at the American and British warplanes in both zones, and at least one air duel. The last time the south had witnessed such a confrontation was seven years earlier. As it was, the two American air surveillance operations were conducted by different branches of the Pentagon. The northern exercise was conducted by the US European Command headquartered in Stuttgart, Germany, with its aircraft stationed at the Turkish airbase of Incirlik; and the southern one by the US Central Command (Centcom) based at MacDill Air Force Base near Tampa, Florida, which maintained the Fifth Fleet headquarters in Bahrain, and had 23,500 troops in the Gulf, with almost half of them stationed on Kuwaiti and Saudi soils.[34]

In mid-February, while much media prominence was given to Tariq Aziz's failure to persuade Turkish Premier Bulent Ecevit to deny US and British war-planes the use of Incirlik air base, two important points were overlooked. Holding talks with Aziz was a clever maneuver by Ecevit, a socialist and an anti-imperialist, to offset Washington's pressure on him to cooperate actively in oust-ing Saddam. "It is not our tradition to make judgments on how countries should be ruled, especially neighboring countries, and how they should be changed," said a Turkish foreign ministry spokesman after the Ecevit–Aziz meeting. The other point was made by Aziz who traveled to the Turkish border overland through the Iraqi Kurdish area under the US–UK air surveillance. "They claim they are protecting the Kurds from the Iraqi government. Then how can an Iraqi deputy prime minister travel so easily?"[35] Even on the US use of its Incirlik base, reality was different from popular perception. Mindful of public resentment at repeated air strikes against a neighboring state, and unhappy at the consolidation of quasi-independence by Iraqi Kurds, Turkey later limited the number of days American jets could conduct Operation "Northern Watch" and barred night flights.[36] Regarding the strategic significance of the northern zone, even the US European Command conceded that it was marginal.

In the region, public disapproval of the air exclusion zones in Iraq was aired by the members of the 6-member Gulf Cooperation Council. Appearing along with US secretary of defense, Cohen, during his visit to Doha in March 1999, Qatari foreign minister, Shaikh Hamad ibn Jassim al Thani, criticized US strikes in the Iraqi no-fly zones.[37] In Riyadh a Saudi official said, "Whatever has to do with going out and hitting targets in Iraq will not have the support of the kingdom." On March 17, the Arab League called for "an immediate halt to all military activ-ity against Iraq which is only worsening the situation."[38]

None of this had any impact on Washington. Indeed, in mid-August American and British aircraft hit Iraqi targets outside the air exclusion zones. This led France, still basking in the glory of its participation in the US-led Nato campaign in the Kosovo region of Serbia, to protest loudly. It worked, with the US–UK alli-ance quietly returning to the original parameters of its operation. To cover its embarrassment at the turn of events, the Pentagon announced that over the past eight months the Anglo-American air forces had fired over 1,100 missiles at 359 Iraqi targets – more than three times the number during Operation "Desert Fox."

America justified its action on the basis of Security Council Resolution 688 (April 1991). But this document did not mention air exclusion zones. And, since it was not passed under Chapter VII of the UN Charter, it did not authorize mili-tary action by a UN member-state to enforce the resolution. When challenged, Washington argued that its action was "derivative" of Paragraph 6 of Resolution 688, which appealed "to all Member States and to all humanitarian organizations to contribute to these humanitarian relief efforts." By any criterion, this amounted to stretching the letter and spirit of the text to an unacceptable limit.

However, even that sort of exercise could not explain Operation "Southern Watch" which was imposed in August 1992 – sixteen months after Resolution 688 was passed. Following consultations with the British and French leaders, US

President Bush decided to enforce an air exclusion zone in the south to safeguard the Shias there. This had more to do with Bush punishing Saddam for his long stand-off with Unscom on disarmament in the previous month than protecting southern Shias.

The Pentagon's statement that "The purpose of the no-fly zone [in southern Iraq] is to ensure the safety of Coalition aircraft monitoring compliance with United Nations Security Council Resolution 688" was a glaring example of circular argument. And the fact that enforcing an air exclusion zone in the south did not stop Baghdad's ground-based attacks on the southern marshes providing refuge to Iraqi fugitives underlined lack of American concern for civilians.

"International law as created and interpreted through the Security Council is an approximate process," noted Sarah Graham-Brown in *Sanctioning Saddam*.

> The fact that there was no challenge to the use of force, some argue, constitutes de facto international acceptance that the terms of the resolution allow for it. Essentially, as one informed source put it, by dint of political power the main Coalition states (the US, the UK and France) won the day and established a precedent.[39]

Of the two air exclusion zones, the southern one, which had nothing to with protecting civilians had proved strategically important. The Pentagon perceived it as a means of denying Baghdad the chance to train its pilots in the southern Iraqi airspace and as a source of intelligence input in its early warning system for the US. In maintaining this zone, it had the active support of Riyadh and Kuwait, which footed the bill for the aircraft fuel and accommodation for the pilots and the ground staff, and which earned them Saddam's continuing ire. In the Pentagon's view, the Baghdad–Washington confrontation that occurred in October 1994 confirmed the strategic value of the southern zone.

Yet most of the Iraqi sites that the US warplanes kept hitting were in the north, and almost all of them were near Mosul, the third largest Iraqi city. A glance at a map explained why this was so and underlined the illogicality of the Western decision to impose a no-fly zone above the 36th Parallel to protect the Kurds. While almost half of the area and the population of the predominantly Kurdish Kurdistan Autonomous Region were below this parallel, the area above it contained a vast swathe of the overwhelmingly Arab sector of Iraq, with Mosul as its principal city. This zone was administered by the Iraqi government, which maintained a large military garrison and many air defense facilities in and around Mosul.

That the true reason for maintaining air exclusion zones in the north and the south was political, rather than humanitarian, became apparent when Albright herself said, "I believe that through our … continued patrolling of northern and southern no-fly zones, we are able to keep Saddam Hussein in his box."[40] Enforcing air exclusion zones and continued beefing-up of the Iraqi opposition – with tireless Chalabi bouncing up against all odds with yet another scheme to overthrow

Saddam – was the ongoing policy of the US. Within a fortnight of his demotion from chairman to ordinary member of the executive committee of the INC, Chalabi arrived in Washington with a plan to topple Saddam. It required the Pentagon or CIA to train 300 former Iraqi military officers to use anti-tank weapons, encryption and communications gear. Then they would train a further 1,000 Iraqis. This force would then infiltrate Iraq by land, sea and air, and seize an air base, which would then be protected by US air cover. It would become the destination for deserting Iraqi troops. This in turn would lead to the forming of a provisional government on Iraqi soil to be financed by petroleum revenue. "We need support, direction and training from the US," said Chalabi. "There is no shame in admitting that." But the problem was that no neighboring country was prepared to let the INC use its soil for infiltrating Iraq. And, as one Kurdish source told the London-based *Al Zaman* (The Time), Chalabi was unwelcome in Iraqi Kurdistan.[41] So Chalabi's latest plan did not get off the ground.

The confusion within the Clinton administration on the subject was well captured by the differing signals given by the State Department and the NSC. Following a meeting of the leaders of seven Iraqi opposition groups, including the INC, with Albright in Washington on May 24, 1999, the State Department spokesman, James Rubin, said that the US would provide the INC and the newly launched Democratic Centrist Current (critical of Chalabi) with non-lethal assistance. A month later the Senate Foreign Relations Committee heard Elizabeth Jones, deputy assistant secretary of the state department, say, "It would be unwise to arm Iraqi opposition groups right now. That could lead to more Iraqis being killed unnecessarily."[42] On the other hand, Jim Hoagland, a senior columnist at the *Washington Post*, wrote that during a meeting with Samuel Berger on May 25, the representatives of the seven Iraqi opposition groups heard him declare "a determination to get rid of the Saddam Hussein regime by the end of Clinton's second term."[43]

But the realities in the region were such that no government would let the reconstituted INC hold its conference on its soil. So its 300 delegates conferred on October 31 and November 1, in a New York hotel at the cost of $2 million, borne by the Clinton administration. Thomas Pickering, the US under-secretary of state, addressed them. They elected a 7-member executive committee, including Chalabi, with a member each from the INA, KDP, PUK and MCM, and two independents. Significantly, they left military matters "for later," meaning that they quietly buried Chalabi's latest insurgency scheme.[44]

Iraqis, victims of internal repression, external sanctions

As for the Iraqi opposition's nemesis, Saddam Hussein, he remained as brutally hostile to any sign of internal opposition as ever, keeping an ever-vigilant eye on the predominantly Shia south, especially on religious leaders. In 1994 Ayatollah Muhammad Taqi al Khoei, a son of the highly respected Grand Ayatollah Abol Qasim al Khoei, died on the road between Karbala and Najaf when his car was hit by a truck waiting for it by the roadside. In April 1998, Ayatollah Murtadha Ali Borujerdi, a Najf-based cleric, was shot dead by an unknown gunman after leading prayers at the Imam Ali mosque in Najaf, after he had ignored warnings not to lead prayers there as his sermons had become too uncomfortably popular for the regime. On June 19, 1998, Ayatollah Mirza Ali Gharavi and his son and son-in-law were shot dead while being driven to their home in Najaf. On both occasions the government blamed "foreign agents."[45] Perhaps in retaliation for these assassinations, Shia militants hurled two hand grenades at Izzat Ibrahim, vice-chairman of the Revolutionary Command Council, on November 22 as he emerged from his car in Karbala near Imam Hussein's mausoleum, where he had gone to deliver Saddam Hussein's speech at a ceremony marking Imam Hussein's birthday.[46]

On February 19, 1999, sixty-year-old Grand Ayatollah Muhammad Sadiq al Sadr and his two sons were shot dead as they left a mosque in Najaf after the evening prayers. He had been an official appointee, and his sermons drew tens of thousands of worshippers. The first sign that something was awry came when his weekly sermon was not broadcast on state television as usual. Once al Sadr was seen as close to the government which appointed him Grand Ayatollah to replace the late Abol Qasim al Khoei in 1992, despite the widespread popularity of another cleric, Ayatollah Mirza Ali Sistani. In August 1998, he issued a fatwa calling on Shias to attend weekly Friday prayers in mosques. This was seen as an attempt to distance himself from the regime and establish himself as an independent leader. Tens of thousands began attending his Friday sermons. His sermons also drew large crowds when he visited Karbala and Kufa. The government had made clear its disapproval of big crowds, but al Sadr had paid no heed to its wishes. After his assassination it blamed "foreign countries," and appointed Ayatollah Mirza Ali Sistani as Grand Ayatollah.[47]

These political murders were part of the state's repressive policies that had been in place ever since Saddam Hussein became vice-president nearly a quarter of a century ago. Deplorable though they were, there was nothing new or surprising about them. As an Asian ambassador in Baghdad, smiling sardonically, put it: "When you oppose Saddam Hussein inside Iraq, you are given two choices, 'Either leave the country, or leave the world.'"[48] Little wonder that in April 1999 the Geneva-based UN Commission on Human Rights strongly condemned "the systematic, widespread and extremely grave violations of human rights and of international law by the Government of Iraq, resulting in all pervasive repression and oppression sustained by broad based discrimination and widespread terror … [and] the summary and arbitrary executions", and "the widespread, systematic torture and enactment and implementation of decrees prescribing cruel and inhuman punishment as penalty for offenses."[49]

There were some in the anti-Saddam camp who argued that the Iraqi dictator was not really interested in seeing the end of UN sanctions as his close family members and cronies were benefiting from the smuggling rackets that had sprung up in the wake of the economic embargo. This viewpoint ignored the consistency and resolve with which Saddam and the Iraqi media had been campaigning for the lifting of sanctions since 1994.

After Unscom's failure to find any contraband at the listed eight presidential sites in March and April 1998, Saddam set his mind on seeing the sanctions lifted by the end of the year. This did not happen. What did happen, though, was that Butler pulled out all UN staff from Iraq in December on the eve of Operation "Desert Fox." That widened Saddam's area of maneuver. He could now state – or at least bargain – upfront the terms on which he would allow future UN inspectors and monitors into Iraq. In sum, politically, Saddam became the one to act, and Clinton the one to react.

At the Security Council the replacement in January 1999 of pro-American Japan and Kenya by independent-minded Malaysia and Namibia meant a greater chance of at least two non-Permanent Members siding with the three non-Anglo-Saxon Permanent Members on Iraq. The Council appointed panels on Iraq's disarmament and humanitarian situation, and on missing Kuwaiti nationals and property.

In its report at the end of March, the panel on missing Kuwaiti personnel and property was equivocal on personnel, but concluded that Baghdad had failed to account for all the Kuwaiti military hardware and archive material it carted off from the emirate. The disarmament panel said that while Unscom had uncovered "the bulk of Iraq's weapons program" there were "still unanswered questions." It added that since Baghdad's knowledge of the techniques and expertise in the bio-chemical field could lead to a rapid reconstitution of the WMD program, it was essential to install an ongoing monitoring and verification body with powers to mount inspections which would be "more intrusive than the ones so far practiced." It recommended that the new body should have more of its own technical experts (and not borrow them from member-states as Unscom had done) and its personnel should be more broadbased by nationality than was the case with Unscom. Its College of Commissioners should include the fifteen Security Council members, UN disarmament officials and representatives of the IAEA and the Organization for the Prohibition of Chemical Weapons. The humanitarian panel suggested various ways of improving the situation without compromising UN control over Baghdad's petroleum revenue and monitoring of the dual-use potential for imports. It recommended ending Iraq's cultural isolation by allowing educational materials and foreign publications.[50]

However, the impact of the oil-for-food scheme on the humanitarian situation was still far from significant. For instance, a UN report in 1999 showed that the per capita medical expenditure in Iraq was $12 a year whereas the annual per capita expenditure on drugs alone in Britain was $1,500.[51] This was due to two major reasons: Baghdad's low oil income, and bureaucratic impediments created mainly by America and Britain at the UN 661 Sanctions Committee to block the contracts Iraq wanted to sign, including those involving parts for electric plants. For any item to arrive in Iraq from abroad, it had to go through fourteen steps, most of these at the UN Sanctions Committee in New York.[52] So there were many points where the process could be blocked, and the American and British representatives on the Sanctions Committee took full advantage of that. Due to Washington's barring of vaccines for foot-and-mouth disease for Iraqi livestock on the grounds that the vaccines could be used for producing biological warfare agents, almost half of Iraq's livestock was dead by 1999.[53]

Due to low petroleum prices, Iraq's revenue from oil exports in 1998 was more than $3 billion short of the annual ceiling of $10.52 billion.[54] With a rise in oil prices in 1999, the situation was expected to improve, allowing Baghdad to make up, partially, for the previous shortfall. But the problem was that due to the continued disrepair of its petroleum industry, Iraq was unable to export enough to reach its UN-sanctioned ceiling. In October 1999, backed by the UN secretary-general, France called for the doubling of the $300 million budget over the next six months for Iraqi oil repairs, but the US refused to endorse the proposal. This was partly to get even with Saddam Hussein who banned the sale of Iraqi oil to American corporations in retribution for Operation "Desert Fox." On the eve of the implementation of the oil-for-food scheme in December 1996, Washington had announced that American companies were free to purchase Iraqi petroleum. And they did. Following Baghdad's ban on oil sales to them, they bought the commodity from Russian, French and Chinese intermediaries.

Among those critical of the bureaucratic inefficiency of the UN 661 Sanctions Committee and its "uninspiring administrators in Baghdad and the provinces", was Hans von Sponeck, the German head of the Baghdad-based UNOHCI. "It is not only about food and medicine," he said, "but it is also about intellectual genocide – with professional journals, international newspapers, books, writing materials, computers, all considered non-essential by the Sanctions Committee, and vetoed."[55] As a result not a single computer had been bought by Iraqi universities or colleges since 1990, and schools often lacked such basics as books and pencils.

It was this state of affairs in Iraq that led French foreign minister, Hubert Vedrine, in his speech at the UN General Assembly in October 1999 to accuse the Americans of insensitivity to the humanitarian situation of Iraqis and to denounce the continued UN embargo. Others argued that sanctions enabled Saddam to shift the blame for Iraq's severe economic and social problems from himself to the US, and that sanctions-busting was enriching his extended family and senior military officers.

"The Iraqi people have become inextricably dependent on the regime which provides their lifeline through the state-administered ration system," said Abdullah Mutawi, a lawyer associated with the New York-based Center for Economic and Social Rights (CESR) and a member of the American fact-finding missions to Iraq in 1991 and 1996. "This renders the regime stronger because the risk of having rations withdrawn is too high a price for dissent [as most people cannot afford to buy food in the open market]."[56] It cost the government $5 per capita to provide the monthly ration for which the recipient paid a nominal sum of ID 250, or US 12.5 cents, which went to the distributor, and which was enough to buy three eggs in the open market. Given the average family size of five in Iraq, the free rations amounted to a monthly income of $25, which was four times the remuner-ation of a typical civil servant and twice the salary of a judge.[57]

Sanctions had drastically reduced the size of the professional middle class – the foremost potential source of opposition to Saddam's dictatorial regime – through emigration and impoverishment. An estimated one million Iraqis had left the country since the Second Gulf War for Jordan, Lebanon, the Gulf monarchies, Western Europe and North America. Nuha al Radi's entries on the subject in her diary were illustrative. November 15, 1994: "Thamina [her friend] talking about emigration … Twenty-one members of her family have left, only eight remain in Baghdad." This happened despite the steps taken by the government to discour-age emigration. January 18, 1995: "He [my dentist] cannot afford to travel any-where. Doctors and engineers have to pay a million-Dinar [$10,000] guarantee to ensure their return; some mortgage their houses to get permission to leave."[58]

Those who remained struggled to survive. Many of them had taken to using their cars as taxis in spare time to earn much-needed cash.[59] Others had resorted to underhand means to cope with their dire economic condition. "Many of these methods are illegal, and illegal businesses are on the rise," said Hans von Sponeck. "Relying on them is creating in Iraq a generation of fixers, manipula-tors of the system rather than thinkers or strategists."[60] One of the illegal activi-ties was to deal with Jordan-based couriers who brought in US dollars in cash remitted by the Iraqis living abroad to their relatives in Iraq.

A nine-year economic siege had led to or aggravated various social ills. These included an alarming rise in crime – especially theft and burglary, prostitution, increased domestic violence, decline in women's employment, and a continuing fall in school attendance, with children put to work or begging. Thieving had become so rampant that foreign journalists, using four- and five-star hotels, reported thefts of cameras, even shirts, from their rooms. An entry in Nuha al Radi's diary on February 12, 1995 summed up the scene aptly: "When he [an Italian] arrives at the Rashid [Hotel], he calls the staff responsible for his room, lays out everything on the bed and tells them, 'I have so many shirts, trousers, socks, etc., and would like to keep that many.' He then gives them all a tip and manages to survive his stay relatively intact."[61]

Prostitution was on the rise. "In Baghdad you see prostitutes in the street in the middle of the night, something unheard of in Arab countries," said von Sponeck. "Shame-faced Iraqis would tell you, 'They are Sudanese.' You see young girls as prostitutes. Behind the Vatican embassy is a hotel where prostitu-tion goes on day and night."[62]

According to a recent Unicef study, the literacy rate of Iraq had fallen from 90 percent in August 1990 to 66 percent. During the academic year 1997–98 almost one million children did not sign up for school, and another 250,000 dropped out, thus pushing the total drop-out rate to 53 percent – twice the figure for the previous year.[63] Part of the reason for the high drop-out rate was that parents could not afford to buy exercise books and pencils for their children.

The negative impact of international isolation on Iraq's recent university graduates and young politicians will manifest itself in the coming decades. "The present generation of Baathists studied abroad, speak several languages, etc.," noted Phyllis Bennis, an American researcher, after a visit to Iraq. "The new generation has no such experience. They studied in Iraqi universities under conditions of sanctions, isolated from new books in their fields and from international conferences. Most have no direct experience of other Arab countries, let alone the world beyond their region."[64]

For the population at large, a whole generation was growing up with subnormal intelligence due to lack of protein in their diet during infancy. According to the latest Unicef report released in August 1999, the mortality rate among Iraqi children under five rose from 56 per thousand in 1984–89 to 131 in l994–99 as a result of an increase in malnutrition and disease, and dearth of medicine after the embargo precipitated the collapse of the national economy. These dry statistics turned into something concrete during my interview with Yassin Abdul Hamid, 62, a retired petty shopkeeper, in the Fathwat Arab neighborhood of Baghdad. "In 1997 my six-month-old baby son, Hikmat, got dysentry," he said. "There was no medicine for him at the hospital or any pharmacy. So he died of dehydration. A victim of the sanctions."[65]

While welcoming the chance to earn foreign exchange, albeit under strict UN supervision, to provide relief to its citizens, the Iraqi government was wary of the successive six-monthly renewals of the oil-for-food scheme. In the view of the semi-official *Babil*, America and Britain would turn the oil program into a permanent measure that would substitute for any eventual lifting of economic embargo.[66]

Iraqis had a reason to harbor such fears. In his article in the *Washington Post* in late January 1999, Samuel Berger established a direct link between UN sanctions and the oil-for-food program. "Our proposal to increase the flow of humanitarian aid to Iraq … is in direct opposition to the proposals to lift sanctions," he explained.

> If sanctions were lifted, the international community no longer could determine how Iraq's oil revenues are spent …. Billions of dollars now reserved for the basic needs of the Iraqi people would become available to Saddam Hussein to use as he pleased. Under the current program we … force Saddam Hussein to spend the nation's valuable treasure on the people of Iraq. That makes the oil-for-food program part of the sanctions regime … We are willing to lift the $5.2 billion ceiling to allow Iraq (under strict supervision) to use as much oil revenue as is necessary to meet humanitarian needs."[67]

What deeply concerned Hans von Sponeck, as had his predecessor, Dennis Halliday, was the linking of humanitarian aid to Iraqi disarmament. At a press conference at the UN in New York in November, he said, "Don't play the battle on the backs of the civilian Iraqi population by letting them wait until the more complex issues [of the UN inspections] are resolved." Warning against "the danger of using the human shield in the hopes of coaxing Iraqi concessions on arms issues," he appealed: "Please remove the humanitarian discussions from the rest in order to really end a silent human tragedy."[68]

This went down badly with Washington and London. According to James Rubin, the US state department spokesman, Hans von Sponeck "exceeded his mandate" by speaking on areas "beyond the range of his competence or his authority."[69] America and Britain tried to block his re-appointment by Annan. Ignoring it, Annan extended his term by a year partly because he himself had expressed similar views, partly because failure to re-appoint him would have upset the remaining three Security Council Permanent Members, and partly because von Sponeck had a long, illustrious career at the UN where he was an assistant secretary-general before his UNOHCI job.

But Washington did not give up. Trying to place the blame for the Iraqis' suffering on Saddam, it claimed that the Iraqi government was deliberately keeping food and medicine in warehouses, and not distributing them. But an inquiry conducted by the UNOHCI in Baghdad found that 87 percent of the imported food and medicine had been distributed by Iraq. With 400 UN monitors posted in the country to ensure that the Iraqi government did not divert oil income to programs other than food and medicine, and did not put dual-purpose imports to military use, the international body was well equipped to check out the American allegation.[70]

With Butler's withdrawal of the UN personnel from Iraq, Washington lost its main source of human intelligence. But the technical component of its intelligence remained in place, with satellite reconnaissance most likely complemented by periodic U–2 flights which, being conducted at 60,000 feet (20,000 m), escaped detection by the Iraqis.

The purpose of U–2 flights was to detect any major new construction or power lines in Iraq, which could imply that the authorities were reconstituting their WMD program. After the departure of the UN staff from Iraq in December 1998, President Clinton had remarked that he had "no doubt" that Saddam Hussein would revive WMD projects. But seven months later one of his spokesman conceded, "So far we have seen no evidence of reconstruction of the WMD." This was confirmed in mid-September by Martin Indyk. "We do not at this point have evidence of any kind that Saddam Hussein is attempting to rebuild his arsenal," he said. "Should he ever bring those weapons out or reconstitute, and we get evidence of that, then we will use force to take care of the problem."[71]

This was the backdrop against which the Security Council's P5 and Holland, a non-permanent member, haggled long and hard over a new draft resolution on Iraq, which would emerge finally as Resolution 1284, almost as long and weighty as Resolution 687.

8

IRAQ, A RETURN TO NORMALCY

On December 11, 1999, a draft resolution on Iraq prepared by Britain and Holland was presented to the UN Security Council, even though the five Permanent Members had not reached a consensus on it. The reason for the rush was that the Anglo-Saxon duo on the Council wanted to take advantage of Britain's presidency of the month. During the debate the objections raised by Russia, France and China were so strong that President Jeremy Greenstock feared a veto by one of them. To avoid this, he thrice postponed the vote, thus also giving an opportunity to the resolution's sponsors to amend it and make it palatable to the objectors. In the end the non-Anglo-Saxon trio abstained, as did Malaysia, when the vote was finally taken on December 17.

Like its all-inclusive predecessor, the 34-clause Resolution 687, the 39-clause Resolution 1284 was passed under Chapter VII of the UN Charter. Its Section A, dealing with disarmament, set up a new UN Monitoring, Verification and Inspection Commission (Unmovic) to replace Unscom. Unmovic was required to establish and operate "a reinforced system of ongoing monitoring and verification ... and address unresolved disarmament issues" and "identify ... additional sites in Iraq to be covered by the reinforced system of ongoing monitoring and verification." Within thirty days of the resolution being adopted, the UN secretary-general was required to appoint an Executive Chairman of Unmovic, subject to the approval of the Security Council, and a new College of Commissioners for Unmovic. The new Executive Chairman of Unmovic was to be given forty-five days to submit plans for organization and staff. And, from the date they started working in Iraq, Unmovic and the IAEA were to be given sixty days within which to produce a work program for the discharge of their mandates, which would include "the key remaining disarmament tasks to be completed by Iraq" and ensure that "each task shall be clearly defined and precise." Paragraph 6 stated that Unmovic staff would be regarded as international civil servants "subject to Article 100 of the Charter of the United Nations, drawn from the broadest possible geographical base." This would distinguish it from its Unscom predecessor to which personnel were loaned by member-states and who did not become part of the UN bureaucracy.

Section B referred to the missing Kuwaiti nationals and property. Section C dealt with economic sanctions and the related oil-for-food scheme. It authorized member-states to "permit the import of any volume of petroleum and petroleum products originating in Iraq," thus removing the ceiling on Iraqi oil exports forthwith. It also eased procedures for Iraq to "import foodstuffs, pharmaceutical and medical supplies, as well as basic or standard medical and agricultural equipment and basic or standard educational items." Furthermore, it allowed the Iraqi oil income deposited in the UN escrow account to be used for the purchase of locally produced goods. Paragraph 18 requested the UN 661 Sanctions Committee to appoint a committee of experts to "approve speedily contracts for the parts and the equipments necessary to enable Iraq to increase its exports of petroleum and petroleum products."

The final Section D outlined conditions and modalities for suspending sanctions. Paragraph 33 – where the Security Council expressed "its intention" to suspend sanctions for 120 days – read:

> Upon receipt of reports from the Executive Chairman of Unmovic and from the Director General of the IAEA that Iraq has cooperated in all respects with Unmovic and the IAEA in particular in fulfilling the work programs in all the aspects referred to in Paragraph 7 above … [and] the reinforced system of ongoing monitoring and verification is fully operational.

And Paragraph 35 stated that if the Unmovic or IAEA chief reported that Iraq was "not cooperating in all respects with Unmovic or the IAEA" or if Iraq was "in the process of acquiring any prohibited items," the suspension of sanctions shall terminate on the fifth working day following the report. Paragraph 38 reaffirmed the Security Council's intention to "act in accordance with the relevant provisions of Resolution 687 (1991) on the termination of prohibitions," which *inter alia* included a satisfactory outcome regarding Kuwait's missing personnel and property.[1]

Certain provisions of 1284 favored Iraq, others did not. On disarmament, an open-ended search for proscribed weapons was now to be replaced by specific demands on Iraq. While petroleum exports were delinked from disarmament, the sales were still to be administered by the UN, which effectively exercised a mandate over Iraq's most prized resource. The Security Council wished to see the Iraqi oil industry recover fully from the ravages of the Second Gulf War and sanctions had to be seen against the backdrop of rising world demand for oil, especially in the US.

On the other hand, since Resolution 1284 was adopted under Section VII of the UN Charter, it gave the member-states the option of using force to implement it. Also Baghdad had to readmit Unmovic and IAEA inspectors, agree to "a reinforced system of ongoing monitoring and verification," address "unresolved disarmament issues" and "identify additional sites in Iraq to be covered by the reinforced system of ongoing monitoring and verification." Most importantly, the latest resolution mentioned only a temporary suspension of the embargo. And the basis for that (spelled out in Paragraph 33) – Iraq cooperating "in all respects" – was far too vague. From Baghdad's viewpoint, it compared adversely with Paragraph 22 of Resolution 687 which stated that once the Council had agreed that "Iraq had completed all actions contemplated in Paragraphs 8, 9, 10, 11, 12, and 13 above, the prohibitions … contained in Resolution 661 (1990) shall have no further force or effect."

Little wonder that Baghdad repeated in essence what the ruling Baath Party organ, *Al Thawra*, had said earlier: "We cannot tolerate the impact of the sanctions and the spies at the same time. But unjust sanctions are easier to tolerate than spies and their recurrent and concocted crises to prolong sanctions."[2]

The argument offered by the British and the Dutch that America had for the first time agreed to a graduated easing of sanctions as a trade-off for Iraqi cooperation with Unmovic and IAEA inspectors, instead of demanding cast-iron evidence of Iraq's total compliance on disarmament and/or Saddam's overthrow, failed to impress Baghdad, or even neutral observers. After all, as UN Secretary-General Kofi Annan had himself pointed out, there was no Security Council resolution calling for Saddam Hussein's ousting.

In any event, the Iraqi leader had no illusions about an end to economic sanctions.

"We have said that the embargo will not be lifted by Security Council resolution but will corrode by itself," he said in his address on the 79th anniversary of the country's military day on January 5, 2000. "The corrosion has already started."[3] As the year progressed, his statement would be taken seriously at home and abroad.

Among those who were unimpressed by Resolution 1284 was Hans von Sponeck, head of the UNOHCI. Considering it inadequate to address the humanitarian needs of Iraqis, he resigned his post in mid-February. "My commitment is for the Iraqi people as a group of deprived people whose tragedy should end," he told the Doha-based Al Jazeera Television. He repeated his earlier remark that deprivation in Iraq was also partly due to "a tightly controlled state with many limitations." A few days later his example was followed by Jutta Burghardt, the German head of the World Food Program, which fed nearly one million destitute Iraqis. She told CNN, "I do not see that Resolution 1284 can be implemented for its humanitarian part in the near future." UAE President Zaid al Nahyan repeated his call for an end to sanctions. And in Cairo an Arab League spokesman demanded that the UN Security Council should discuss the problem in the light of the resignations by von Sponeck and Burghardt.[4]

In Washington, seventy members of the US Congress addressed an open letter to Clinton, asking him to do "what is right: lift the economic sanctions." They cited the UN estimates that over 1 million civilians, mostly children, had died due to sanctions, and added, "Morally it is wrong to hold the Iraqi people responsible for the actions of a brutal and reckless government." They urged the president "to delink economic and military sanctions against Baghdad."[5]

The position of the Clinton administration became morally untenable as it emerged that US companies and their foreign subsidiaries were heavily engaged in buying Iraqi oil and selling petroleum-related equipment and spare parts to Iraq. Colum Lynch of the *Washington Post* reported that

> While the US and Britain carry out almost daily air strikes against military installations in northern and southern Iraq, executives and even some [former] architects of American policy toward Baghdad are doing business with Saddam's government and helping to rebuild its battered oil industry.

Citing diplomats, industry officials and UN documents, he said, "Placing bids through overseas subsidiaries and affiliates, more than a dozen [US] companies have signed millions of dollars in contracts with Baghdad for oil-related equipment since summer of 1998." According to the US state department, American citizens had received licenses to export only about $15 million worth of oil-related spare parts to Iraq, a tiny percentage of the total. But this statistic excluded the parts and equipment Iraq bought from the American subsidiaries abroad. Although this indirect trade was monitored by the UN 661 Sanctions Committee, it divulged scant information about it. "The UN helps both countries avoid embarrassment by treating the business arrangements as confidential," reported Lynch.[6]

On his part Saddam turned a blind eye to the fact that his ban on direct Iraqi oil sales to US companies was being subverted by the Russian, French and Chinese middlemen, who loaded their tankers at the Iraqi oil terminal in the Gulf destined for non-American ports, and then diverted them to American destinations. As a result, in 1999, according the Petroleum Industry Research Foundation, Iraq emerged as the fastest growing source of US petroleum imports, with the American companies buying more than a third of the 2 million bpd exported by Baghdad.[7] Part of the reason for US corporations seeking out Iraqi crude was Washington's 1995 ban on trade with Iran, OPEC's second largest producer, whose current output was slightly above Iraq's. They were paying extra for having to buy the Iraqi crude from the Russian, French and Chinese intermediaries, who pocketed the trading profits.

Small wonder that on March 24, at the Security Council, China, France and Russia delivered stinging attacks on America and Britain for subjecting Iraqi purchases to painstaking scrutiny at the UN 661 Sanctions Committee, and conducting frequent air strikes against Iraqi targets.[8]

They were also emboldened by Annan's 64-page report on Iraq's humanitarian situation. In it he said that "Iraq's oil industry is seriously hampered by lack of spare parts and equipment, and this threatens to undermine the [humanitarian] program's income in the long term," and added that "Many of the 'holds' on contract applications, imposed by the 661 (Sanctions) Committee, do have a direct negative impact on the humanitarian program, and on efforts to rehabilitate Iraq's infrastructure, most of which is in appalling disrepair. We need a mechanism to review these holds." He pointed out that

> The UN has always been on the side of the weak and vulnerable, and has always sought to relieve suffering, yet here we are accused of causing suffering to an entire population. We are in danger of losing the argument, or the propaganda war – if we haven't already lost it – about who is responsible for this situation in Iraq – President Saddam Hussein or the United Nations.

He referred in particular to "the situation of Iraqi children whose suffering, and, in all too many cases, untimely death has been documented in the report prepared by Unicef and the Iraqi health ministry last year."[9]

As a consequence, Washington relented. It immediately withdrew its objections to $100 million worth of contracts for humanitarian goods for Iraq. And on March 31, the Security Council unanimously approved doubling the money for spare parts and equipment for the Iraqi oil industry to $1,200 a year.[10] This happened against the background of rising oil prices which hit a ten-year record of $34 a barrel in early March and which drove President Clinton seriously to consider releasing oil from the US Strategic Petroleum Reserve, meant for use in war or emergency, to lower the price.

At the UN the Security Council had by then unanimously accepted Annan's recommendation that 71-year-old Hans Blix, the Swiss IAEA chief from 1981–97, be appointed as Executive Chairman of Unmovic.[11] This was a climbdown by Washington which had disapproved of his earlier statement that the IAEA and Unscom should close the files on all areas of Iraqi disarmament by accepting its word about it and forgetting Baghdad's past transgressions, and get on with monitoring and verification – a line that Paris had been pushing since the Pentagon's "Desert Fox" blitzkrieg on Iraq in late 1998.[12]

Once Blix had assumed his office, Annan dissolved Unscom and its committee of commissioners, and established a new College of nineteen Commissioners, to serve Blix as an advisory board. Besides the nominees of the Permanent Five of the Security Council, and a representative from the UN Disarmament Department, there was a representative each from Argentina, Brazil, Canada, Finland, Germany, India, Japan, Nigeria, Senegal, Sweden and the Ukraine. The list of commissioners, prepared by Jayantha Dhanapala, the UN under-secretary for disarmament, included political appointees chosen from the respective government's arms-control office. (The most prominent casualty of the new set-up was Charles Duelfer, the American deputy executive chairman of Unscom from 1993–2000, who had been privy to information from Washington that even his bosses – Rolf Ekeus and Richard Butler – had been denied, since the Clinton administration decided not to renominate him.[13])

After submitting his blueprint to the Security Council for a new, tightly structured Unmovic, Blix struck a hawkish note by stressing that Unmovic retained powers "to designate inspection sites, conduct interviews, take samples and photos, and use aerial surveillance." [14]

Meanwhile, Washington maintained the air exclusion zones in northern and southern Iraq. This was an elaborate exercise with a US fighter F–15, heavily armed with air-to-air missiles, followed by an RC–135 reconnaissance plane, a Boeing 707 with surveillance equipment, two Navy EA–6B planes with electronic jammers, and F–16s carrying missiles to hit Iraqi radar. During the eighteen months since mid-December 1998, when Baghdad decided to challenge the US–UK overflights, the Anglo-American warplanes had penetrated Iraqi airspace 21,600 times, and killed 300 Iraqis and wounded 800, according to Baghdad. This happened mainly because Washington and London had authorized their warplanes to attack any Iraqi defense target even when unconnected with a specific attack or well after any challenge in response to anti-aircraft fire, radar illumination or missile launching which – as was to be revealed later – were often provoked by the American warplanes. Flying at 20,000 feet (6,000 m), these planes were invisible from the ground, and despite repeated Iraqi attempts, none of them had been known to have been hit. [15]

Every week Iraqi foreign minister Muhammad al Sahhaf routinely addressed a letter each to the president of the UN Security Council and the UN secretary-general, providing details of the violations of Iraqi airspace by American and British aircraft. For instance, between June 1 and 8, total US–UK sorties were 82 from Saudi Arabia, 84 from Kuwait, and 112 from Turkey, giving an average of forty violations per day. [16]

Due to the increasingly equivocal attitude of Ankara to Operation "Northern Watch" (which it called "Reconnaissance Force"), and the embarrassing bombing and strafing of Iraqi livestock, the Pentagon had moderated its missions in the north. During 1999 US planes patrolled aggressively, often buzzing a heavily fortified area around Mosul – with the pilots of F–16s, armed with air-to-ground missiles – and lighting flares over the Saddam Dam, thus inviting anti-aircraft fire and creating a rationale for hitting Iraqi air defense facilities. From early 2000 onwards the Pentagon stopped this practice and also the practice of dropping bombs emptied of explosives – so-called cement bombs – on the anti-aircraft batteries situated near mosques. Its pilots now let such batteries well alone. [17]

From February onwards, due to an increasingly tight oil market which impacted positively on Baghdad's economic and diplomatic standing, Saddam grew more confident. As a result he held the National Assembly elections on time for the first time since 1984.

At stake were 220 of the 250 seats, with the rest from the Kurdistan Autonomous Region to be nominated by Saddam Hussein. The electorate was 8.5 million strong. As in the past, the 552 candidates were either Baath Party members or independents loyal to the Baathist revolution. The electoral law banned public rallies or political manifestos. It allowed contestants perfunctory use of newspapers, radio and television. And it permitted them the use of only 10 banners, 300 cards and 400 black-and-white A4-size posters each. (One such poster pasted on a shop frame in the main market of Najaf, carrying a picture of the Baathist candidate Abdul Manaf Issam, three months after the March 24 poll, looked inconspicuous amidst multicolor portraits of Saddam Hussein in various guises – from an administrator to a field marshal to a religious devotee – that every shopkeeper displayed.[18]) "A candidate cannot use his personal wealth to influence voters and is encouraged to cooperate rather compete with other politicians for the greater good," explained Hassan Abdul Hamid, an Iraqi writer.[19] As a result none of the major issues troubling the electorate – the two-year drought to the ruined economy to the international isolation of Iraq – was discussed. The contrast to the parliamentary election in the adjoining Iran in February could not have been more stark.

Of those elected, 142 were Baathists. But a more noteworthy outcome of the poll was the election of Uday Saddam Hussein to the chamber. By now he had recovered enough from the gunshot wounds sustained more than three years earlier to be able to stand up unaided by crutches, and had received a medal of valor from his father. He was already chairman of the Iraqi Journalists Union and the Iraqi Youth Federation which among other things imparted civics and military training to young people. Those who voted for him hoped he would revitalize the National Assembly as he had done with print media with his *Babil* newspaper, and television with his Youth TV channel. But the National Assembly was an advisory body which only made legislative recommendations to the RCC presided by Saddam Hussein. However, were Uday to be elected Speaker of the Assembly he would sit on the RCC as an *ex-officio* member, an important move up the political power ladder.

At the UN, Hans Blix announced in July with much fanfare that Unmovic's forty-four inspectors from nineteen countries were to undergo a month-long training at New York's Columbia University to familiarize themselves with the historical, legal, administrative and political aspects of inspections and monitoring, and become "sensitive" to Iraqi culture.

As the end of this course neared – and with it the scheduled date for the deployment of a small Unmovic team in Iraq – Tariq Aziz said, "Iraq will not receive any person who has a relationship with Resolution 1284 and its results; Iraq will not cooperate."[20] When Blix presented his draft report for the Security Council to his College of Commissioners for review, four of the five Permanent Members of the Security Council – including America – advised him to change his conclusion. They suggested that instead of saying that Unmovic was "now in a position to start activities in Iraq," he should say that "the arms experts could plan and commence preliminary tasks to prepare for future inspections." Elaborating on this, an American official, while agreeing that Unmovic had finished its first stage of preparation, emphasized that it was not yet ready to launch a full-scale program in Iraq. Indeed, in an astonishing reversal of roles on the disarmament issue, Washington lined up with Moscow. "The US and Russia agreed that it was not appropriate to give the impression that Mr Blix and the Commission were ready to go back into Iraq [as] this might create a climate of confrontation at an inappropriate time," explained a Security Council diplomat. Little wonder that half of the forty-four trained inspectors were sent back home.[21]

From the Clinton administration's viewpoint, the timing was "not appropriate" to confront Saddam for the following reason: a shortage of petroleum in the world market gave the Iraqi leader a leverage he did not have before, and any stand-off with him would highlight the fact that there had been no inspections for proscribed weapons in Iraq since December 1998, which would damage Democrat Al Gore's electoral chances on November 7.

Chiefly due to the thriving economies all around the globe, the world demand for petroleum exceeded supply, and any interruption in Iraq's oil output, running at 3.6 million bpd in August, the highest ever, would spike up the prices even further – so reckoned American policy-makers, and rightly so. Furthermore, given Iraq's exemption from the OPEC quota, Washington was now keen to see it raise output to the maximum to ease the market and help lower the prices. With Iraqi oil exports running at 3 million bpd, equaling the two recent OPEC increases, Baghdad was in a strong position. Equally, President Clinton was discomfortingly aware of American dependence on oil imports. The US was importing 60 percent of the 19 million oil barrels it consumed daily – a twofold increase since 1983 – and the trend was set to rise. In the 1990s oil output in America declined by 15 percent while consumption rose by 11 percent.[22]

After the OPEC decision on September 11 to raise output by 800,000 bpd failed to calm oil traders and prices remained firm, Iraqi oil minister, Gen. Amr Rashid, reflecting Saddam Hussein's thinking, threatened that Baghdad would shelve its plans to increase output if the US continued to put holds on its contracts for food, medicine and economic infrastructure before the UN Sanctions Committee.[23] With Iraq's oil export income at a hefty $7.1 billion from January to June 2000, Saddam had a reason to feel cocky. Ever eager to use whatever leverage he could muster to strike a bargain, he had this time found himself armed with a tool that could not fail.

Washington moderated its stance towards him considerably. On September 12, Albright repeated the US position that it would not use force if Iraq did not comply with Security Council Resolution 1284 which led to the forming of Unmovic. But that did not pacify the oil traders who noted nervously that inventories of home heating oil in the six north-eastern states of America (called New England) were 60 percent below last year's, and the crude oil inventories in the US were 10 percent lower than last year's. On Wednesday September 20, the West Texas crude future rose to $37 a barrel. This caused panic in the White House. On Friday Clinton announced that his administration would release one million bpd for thirty days, in November, from the US Strategic Petroleum Reserve. That calmed the market. On Monday the oil futures in London dropped by $3.[24]

The panic on the oil market provided Saddam with a lever he did not have before. His government claimed that by carrying out slant drilling near the Kuwaiti–Iraqi border, Kuwait was stealing 300,000 bpd of Iraqi petroleum. It addressed a letter to the UN Security Council holding Saudi Arabia responsible for the losses that Baghdad suffered when Riyadh closed the oil pipeline from southern Iraq to the Saudi Red Sea port of Yanbo in August 1990.[25] Saddam's purpose behind putting Kuwait and Saudi Arabia – major petroleum producers – on the defensive was to destabilize the oil market and spike up prices, the opposite of what Clinton was trying to achieve.

Tide turns for Saddam

In August an already ebullient Saddam had received a morale-boosting visit from President Hugo Chavez of Venezuela, the current chairman of OPEC. Chavez became the first foreign elected leader to visit Baghdad since 1990. He did so in the course of a tour of OPEC member-states, inviting each head of state personally to attend the organization's summit in Caracas in late September to mark OPEC's fortieth anniversary. "The time has come for OPEC to show its power," he said in Baghdad on August 10. "The only way to counter international pressure is for OPEC to strengthen its political will." With OPEC's eleven members, including Iraq, pumping 32.5 million bpd, or 42 percent of the global total, Chavez's words carried weight.[26] A leftist who had forged friendly relations with Cuba's Fidel Castro and China's Communist leaders, Chavez had an additional reason to meet Saddam Hussein. Since Iraq was extracting oil outside the OPEC quota he wanted to ensure that Saddam would cooperate with his overall policy of maintaining discipline within OPEC regarding sticking to the allocated production levels. Chavez was conscious that before he was elected president in December 1998 (and re-elected in July 2000 under a new constitution), Venezuela, a major source of oil imports for the US, frequently broke the OPEC quota, thus subverting its price objectives.

Chavez's two-day visit to Baghdad was hailed as historic in Iraq and most of the Arab world. "Who is the next hero?" asked the *Babil* rhetorically. "Chavez knows the true meaning of independence as other thrones tremble when the American administration waves its big stick at them."[27]

This set the scene for "air diplomacy" – or more appropriately, airflight-busting – a process that started with a Russian plane arriving on August 17 at the newly reopened Saddam International Airport near Baghdad from Moscow, the first such flight since Iraq's invasion of Kuwait. Within two months this trickle would turn into a flood, abetted by the Israeli-Palestinian violence that erupted in late September and caused the Arab countries to close ranks.

The Russian plane, belonging to Vnukovo Airline, the largest domestic carrier, brought an official delegation led by Ruslan Tsalikov, deputy minister for emergencies, along with medicine, baby food and medical equipment.[28] Breaking with the protocol dating back to Security Council Resolution 670 of September 25, 1990, Moscow did not seek permission for this flight from the UN 661 Sanctions Committee. It argued that since Resolution 670 banned only flights carrying cargo other than foodstuffs or medicine, there was no need to obtain the

Sanctions Committee's permission when the shipment of food or medicine was involved. America, Britain and the Sanctions Committee disagreed, and wanted the intending party to inform the Committee twenty-four hours in advance so that an objection could be raised by any of the Security Council members.

On the wider issue of civil flights to and from Iraq, they maintained that these would constitute economic resources whose reinstatement would violate the embargo. But Russia, France and China retorted that the prohibition on flights stemmed from Resolution 670 and applied only to the flights carrying commercial cargo.[29] The Iraqis went one step ahead and argued that sanctions did not prohibit civil aviation in and out of their country, and that the reason they had withdrawn their aircraft from abroad was to ensure that they did not get confiscated after Resolution 661, imposing sanctions, was passed on August 6, 1990.[30] Their position was endorsed by France whose ambassador to the UN, Jean-David Levitte, said, "For many years now, we have considered that there is no flight embargo against Iraq." So on September 22 France merely notified the Sanctions Committee of a flight from Paris to Baghdad that day, carrying medical support teams and athletes. Three days later the French representative at the Sanctions Committee proposed that instead of seeking the Committee's prior permission by informing it twenty-four hours in advance, the intending country should only notify it, providing it with a route map. It was also proposed that the aircraft should be inspected by independent inspection agents at departure, at any stopover and on arrival in Baghdad to ensure that no unauthorized cargo was on board. Peter van Walsum, the Dutch chairman of the Committee, agreed that the matter deserved to be discussed.[31]

Just then, France, actively backed by Russia, got the Security Council to lower the percentage of the Iraqi oil income to be paid into the UN Compensation Fund from 30 percent to 25, thus leaving more money for Baghdad to repair its shattered infrastructure. France and Russia had initially wanted the percentage to be lowered to 20, but compromised when America agreed to $15.9 billion as compensation to the Kuwait Petroleum Corporation instead of its original claim of $21 billion.[32]

However, the big political break for Iraq came on September 26, when a Jordanian plane carrying a large delegation of cabinet ministers, parliamentarians, trade unionists, politicians, businessmen and medical personnel – along with medical supplies – arrived in Baghdad after Amman had merely notified the Sanctions Committee about it. Jordan's lead was quickly followed by Yemen. When the aircraft from Sanaa, carrying Abdul Qadir Bajammal, Yemen's deputy prime minister, and many other officials – and medicine – arrived in Baghdad via Amman on September 29, it was received by Tariq Aziz, the counterpart of Bajammal.

During the next four weeks the Baghdad airport received one foreign aircraft daily. Leaving aside the small or geographically peripheral countries like Comoros Islands, Djibouti, Mauritania, Somalia and Sudan, almost all members of the 22-strong Arab League participated in flight-busting. The most notable exceptions were Kuwait and Saudi Arabia. Both allowed the use of their air bases to the Pentagon to enforce an air exclusion zone in southern Iraq. So it was doubtful whether Saddam would have permitted a plane from either country to land in Baghdad until and unless it had withdrawn its cooperation from the US on maintaining a no-fly zone in southern Iraq.

The most notable among the flight-busters was Syria. When a plane from Damascus arrived at the Baghdad airport on October 8, with a 34-member delegation of high level officials and public figures, led by Muhammad Mufdi Sifo, minister for cabinet affairs, along with food and medicine, it became the first such aircraft since 1980. "The flight shows the total support of the Syrian people for the Iraqi people to ease their suffering caused by the embargo," said Sifo.[33] This happened after the meetings of Tariq Aziz with Syrian President Bashar Assad and his foreign minister, Farouq al Shaara, in Damascus in late September. "Syria supports the call for the lifting of sanctions imposed on Iraq," said al Shaara. "We expressed this position during the recent meetings of the UN General Assembly and the Arab League." [34] Indeed, instead of waiting for the termination of the embargo, the two governments announced that they would reopen the Kirkuk–Banias oil pipeline in November.[35]

By early October the Arab world was shocked by the inordinate force that the Israeli military used against stone-throwing Palestinians, who rioted in the West Bank and Gaza in protest at the visit to Islam's third holiest shrine on the Haram al Sharif (i.e., Noble Sanctuary) in Jerusalem's Old City by Ariel Sharon, the hardline leader of right-wing Likud bloc, on September 28. With a death toll of Palestinians rising above eighty, on October 7 the UN Security Council condemned Israel for "the excessive use of force against Palestinians" by 14 votes to none, with the US abstaining.

The need for closing Arab ranks against this background was so urgent that the Egyptian President Hosni Mubarak – in consultation with Saudi Crown Prince Abdullah – decided to close the chapter on Arab divisions caused by Iraq's occupation of Kuwait, and invite Iraq to the emergency Arab League summit in Cairo to discuss the grave situation in the Palestinian Territories and its impact on the peace process. This signaled the formal end of ten years of Iraq's ostracism by the Arab League. Given the vehemence with which Baghdad had denounced Israel and the zeal with which it had offered to help the Palestinians in their struggle to liberate themselves from the Israeli occupation, it would have been inexcusable for the Egyptian host not to invite Iraq to the top-level conference.

Saddam did not attend the summit on October 21–22, partly because he could not be certain of the security that the Egyptian government could provide, and partly because he reckoned that his health would become a focus of attention, not least by the intelligence agents attached to the US and Israeli embassies in Cairo. A report published in early September in the London-based, Saudi-funded *Al Sharq al Awsat* had cited an Arab doctor "with an excellent reputation" saying that a team of five European doctors was treating Saddam Hussein for lymph cancer after he had suffered from inflamed joints, breathing difficulties, poor vision and temporary loss of memory.[36] Since he did not show any loss of hair – a consequence of chemotherapy treatment – the report lacked credibility.

Instead Izzat Ibrahim, vice-chairman of the Iraqi RCC, attended the summit. He repeated the essence of the communiqué issued by the Iraqi cabinet on the eve of the Arab conference: "Iraq is calling [for] and working to liberate Palestine through jihad because only jihad is capable of liberating Palestine and other Arab lands [from Israel]." He added that Iraq could provide a plan for a jihad if Arab leaders decided to follow that course.[37] It was noteworthy that in the Gulf region the only other country to advocate such a policy was Iran.

At the summit Ibrahim was pleased to hear what King Abdullah II of Jordan had to say about the UN sanctions. At the risk of upsetting Washington and losing badly needed US financial aid, the Jordanian monarch declared, "Our [Arab] nation can no longer stand the continuation of this suffering, and our people no longer accept what is committed against the Iraqi people from [UN] embargo."[38] A day earlier his government had announced that it would remove independent Lloyd's of London inspectors from their posts overseeing Iraq-bound shipments arriving at the Jordanian port of Aqaba, as part of the UN oil-for-food scheme. It did so under pressure by Baghdad.[39]

Just as the Arab summit met in Cairo, Saddam dispatched a convoy of forty trucks loaded with food and medicine to the Palestinian Territories via Amman. Some days later a Palestinian plane arrived in Baghdad with many wounded Palestinians on board for medical treatment. These were the sorts of gestures likely to boost Saddam's already high standing among young Palestinians, accelerate his rehabilitation among Arabs, and create a symbiosis between him and Arab public opinion, which, he hoped, would pressure the Arab rulers to break the UN sanctions on Iraq.

Encouraged by the flight-busting, which accelerated to the point of seven flights a day on the eve of the annual Baghdad International Trade Fair on November 1 – with a record 1,500 companies from forty-five countries participating since its resumption in 1995 – the Iraqi government announced that it would resume domestic flights on November 5, including the ones to Mosul (in the northern no-fly zone) and Basra (in the southern no-fly zone). First London and then Washington said that they would not challenge civilian flights as the air exclusion zones were imposed to prevent military activity[40] while insisting that they would go on monitoring air traffic to ensure that military craft did not enter the prohibited sectors.

As it was, on the appointed day, Iraqi Airways, lacking civilian aircraft like the US-made Boeing, deployed refurbished Russian-built military aircraft – Anton and Ilyushin – painted in civilian colors for the flights. Unquestionably, this was more of a diplomatic defiance of America and Britain by the Saddam regime than a commercial decision by Iraqi Airways. "These flights will continue despite the threats, as they aim to smash the American–British criminal act of imposing illegal no-fly zones," declared the Iraqi foreign minister, Muhammad al Sahhaf.[41] By then Baghdad airport had chalked up a total of forty incoming international flights, one of which brought Jordanian Prime Minister, Ali Abu Ragheb, accompanied by 100 journalists and politicians. As the highest ranking Arab official to visit Iraq since the 1990 Kuwait crisis, he was invited to meet Saddam Hussein.

Another regional leader that Saddam had seen recently was Kamal Kharrazi, Iran's foreign minister. He arrived in Baghdad on October 13 from Tehran by an Iran Air carrier, a participant in the flight-busting exercise, for a three-day trip, and became the highest ranking Iranian official to do so since the revolution. His state visit had been arranged by Khatami during his meeting with Iraqi Vice-President Ramadan on the fringes of the OPEC summit in Caracas in late September.

After his meeting with Saddam Hussein, Kharrazi announced that both sides had agreed to re-activate the joint commissions they had set up under the 1997 accord to resolve their differences. The subjects these bodies dealt with included border demarcation, economic cooperation, the pilgrimage to the Shia holy places in Iraq by Iranians (suspended since July 2000), and security cooperation. The issue of the exchange of prisoners of war was almost settled. Since 1988, Iran had released some 57,000 prisoners of war and Iraq about 40,000. In dispute were 3,000 Iranian POWs which Tehran said Baghdad was holding.[42] Also, Baghdad wanted Iran to reopen an air corridor for Russian planes to enter Iraq to facilitate the planned resumption of scheduled flights between Moscow and the Iraqi capital. In exchange Tehran wanted an air corridor through Iraq for flights to Syria and Lebanon. A mutually beneficial deal was in the offing.

Saddam expressed his "willingness and determination to normalize relations with Iran." Most significantly, Kharazi said, "We have decided to activate the 1975 [Algiers] agreement in order to set up balanced and good-neighborly relations."[43]

So twenty years after Saddam invaded Iran after tearing up the Algiers Accord during a television address, the two neighbors were – as it were – returning to square one, with the prospect of a future visitor to the Shatt al Arab near Khorramshahr finding its banks devoid of any signs of the wars of the recent past.

But not quite. The Iraq that Saddam led into war against Iran was utterly different from the one he ruled in 2000. In 1980, Iraqi living standards had been rising by 20 percent annually since the mid–1970s due to the quadrupling of oil prices. Baghdad's annual petroleum revenue was an impressive $30 billion, and its foreign reserves totaled $35 billion. The country and its people were then imbued with unprecedented confidence and optimism.[44]

Equally, the Iran that was invaded by Iraq in 1980 was quite distinctive from the one that existed twenty years hence.

After the 1980s War the two countries had progressed along diverse lines. Following Saddam's brutal invasion of Kuwait, as his country had become isolated and impoverished his control over the state and society had become even tighter than before. By contrast, the Iranian regime had loosened up, and the country had progressed substantially in its reconstruction drive, and liberalized both its economy and politics.

Above: President Saddam Hussein chairing a cabinet meeting in Baghdad, July 2000. On his immediate left is Tariq Aziz. The inset shows another cabinet meeting where, to Saddam Hussein's extreme left, sitting in a corner, is his personal secretary, Abid Hamid Mahmoud (al Khatib)

Left: Saddam Hussein decorating his elder son, Uday, in Baghdad, January 2000

Right: Taha Yassin Ramadan, vice-president of the Republic of Iraq

Left: Saddam Hussein with his younger son, Qusay, in Baghdad, December 1996

Right: Izzat Ibrahim, vice-president of the Revolutionary Command Council of Iraq

Left: A painting
the Liberation
Square, Baghd

Above: Saddam Hussein's family tree at
Imam Ali's shrine in Najaf, July 2000

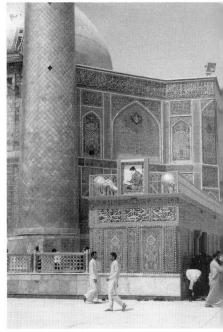

Above: A portrait of Saddam Hussein at pray
at Imam Ali's shrine in Najaf, July 2000

Right: Iraqi Dinar 250 bank note, the
highest Iraqi denomination, worth
US$800 before August 1990 and
US 12 cents in August 2000

Above: The United Nations headquarters in Baghdad, housing the offices of various UN agencies – from the humanitarian UNOHCI to the weapons monitoring BMVC

Below: Repairing sundry equipment, from hurricane lanterns to transistor radios, is a major activity at Shorja Souq, Baghdad, August 2000

Below: The dilapidated state of a water treatment plant in Baghdad, August 2000

Above: Open sewage is a common site in Baghdad, July 2000

Above: A wall mural in Baghdad shows an Iraqi prisoner of war being tortured, with his arms being torn apart by two Iranian jeeps during the 1980–88 Iran–Iraq War

Below: Iraqi prisoners of war at an Iranian military camp near Tehran, demonstrating against Saddam Hussein and for Ayatollah Ali Khamanei, the then President of Iran, September 1986

Above: An Iranian military outpost along the Shatt al Arab/Arvand Rud near Khorramshahr, January 1989

Below: A spokesman for the UN Iran–Iraq Military Observer Group briefing journalists near Khorramshahr, January 1989

Left and above: A senior cleric addressing a Friday prayer congregation in Tehran, January 2000

Below: The Iranian Majlis, Tehran

Above: (from left to right) Hojatalislam Muhammad Khatami, Hojatalislam Ali Akbar Hashemi Rafsanjani, Ayatollah Ali Khamanei, Ayatollah Muhammad Hashemi Shahroudi and Hojatalislam Mehdi Karrubi, Tehran, November 2000

Below: Office of the cleric attached to the Saadi Tile Factory at Islamshahr, with the picture of Ayatollah Ruhollah Khomeini on the wall, September 1986

Above: Shrine of Hadrat-e Maasuma, sister of Imam Ali Reza, Qom

Below: Mural of the Dome of the Rock, Jerusalem, near a mosque in Tehran. The inse shows a slogan reading 'Death to America 13 (Iranian calendar)/1999' outside the Friday prayer site in Tehran

Part II

IRAN

9

RAFSANJANI'S RECONSTRUCTION AND ECONOMIC LIBERALIZATION

For Iran, the overall result of the Second Gulf War was positive, economically and diplomatically. The conflict helped it to project a high profile internationally, and benefit from the soaring oil prices, which almost trebled between August 1990 and March 1991. This improved its economy even though it was lumbered with the deleterious legacy of the 1980s war, poor performance of the national-ized industry, scarcity of basic materials, and inadequate distribution, transport, and import and export systems. In 1990–91 the annual growth rate soared to 10.5 percent while inflation declined to 8 percent. This encouraged President Ali Akbar Hashemi Rafsanjani to accelerate the pace of privatization even though his radical plan to end the oil and gas monopoly by the state-owned National Ira-nian Oil Company (NIOC) was rejected by the Guardians Council.

The booming economy also encouraged him to implement long-overdue rationalization in government bureaucracy. Guided by him, the Majlis decided to combine the police, gendarmeric and revolutionary komitehs (i.e., commit-tees), that sprouted in the late 1970s, into the Organization of Security Guards – also known as Law Enforcement Forces (LEF). It became operational on March 21, 1991, the Iranian New Year. The amalgamation of the revolutionary komitehs into a larger national force went a long way to reassure the public about the sanctity of the rule of law. In February 1992 at Rafsanjani's behest, Ayatollah Ali Khamanei ordered that there should be one head of the military and the Islamic Revolutionary Guards Corps, to be called the chief of staff of the Armed Forces General Command. He named Hassan Firoozabadi, then deputy chief of staff of the military, as the first chief of staff of the amalgamated force.

In foreign affairs, Iraq's aggression against a fellow Arab state opened up unprecedented opportunities for Iran. While shunning Iraq whom they had actively backed during the First Gulf War, the Gulf monarchies now hastened to improve relations with Tehran. In March 1991 Saudi Arabia restored diplomatic relations with Iran that had been severed in July 1987 after the Saudi police shot dead over 400 mainly Iranian pilgrims during a demonstration in Mecca at the time of the annual hajj pilgrimage, when there was a strict ban on marches or demonstrations, even displays of pictures or placards, due to the Saudi ruling that the hajj was a purely religious ritual.[1] As a goodwill gesture, Riyadh doubled

Iran's quota for hajj pilgrims, from the standard 55,000 – on the basis of one pilgrim for 1,000 Muslims – to 110,000. However, as the next hajj season approached, differing views on the subject surfaced from Rafsanjani and Khamanei. While Rafsanjani had privately assured Riyadh that the Iranian pilgrims would not mount a demonstration in Mecca, Khamanei instructed the hajj leader, Hojatalislam Ahmad Khomeini, to ensure that the pilgrims denounced American and Israeli crimes at a time "when treacherous regimes in the region had invited sacrilege against Islam's most sacred soil."[2] This angered Riyadh. As a compromise, just before the start of the hajj in mid-June, Ahmad Khomeini resigned, and the Saudi authorities allowed the Iranians to perform their ritual of "disavowal of infidels [meaning, to them, Americans and Israelis]" only in their own allocated compound and out of sight of other pilgrims.

But on the vital issue of Gulf security, disappointment was in store for Tehran. Two months after agreeing to form a joint peacekeeping force with Egypt and Syria to maintain post-war security in the Gulf in early March 1991, the Gulf Cooperation Council – composed of Bahrain, Kuwait, Oman, Qatar, Saudi Arabia and the United Arab Emirates – changed its mind. That led to Egypt withdrawing its troops from Saudi Arabia on May 5. Three days later the US secretary of defense, Dick Cheney, arrived in the region to confirm a series of bilateral defense ties with each of the Gulf monarchies, including a formalized defense agreement with Riyadh.[3] This nipped in the bud Tehran's plan to become part of a regional security arrangement to be devised by the countries around the Gulf except Iraq, and facilitate the departure of American forces from the region. In September, when Kuwait signed a formal ten-year defense pact with Washington, Iran denounced it, arguing that it would encourage more US military intervention than before. Kuwait paid no heed.

As a counter-move to the Middle East Peace Conference in Madrid on October 30, 1991, under the joint sponsorship of America and the Soviet Union, Iran hosted the International Conference for the Support of the Muslim Palestinian People's Revolution, which was attended by all radical Palestinian groups, Islamic and secular. Encouraged by Khamanei, the conference decided to set up a permanent secretariat, to be funded by Iran, to coordinate pro-intifada (*lit.*, uprising) activities. Iran tightened its links with the radical Palestinian Hamas and Islamic Jihad. This angered Washington, the prime mover behind the Madrid Peace Conference.

While promoting hardline policies abroad, Khamanei continued to cooperate actively with Rafsanjani to contain radical leftist forces at home chiefly to smooth the way for much-needed economic reform. Guided by him, on the eve of the Experts Assembly election in October 1990, the Guardians Council rejected 60 such candidates out of a total of 169 ostensibly either for their "dubious behavior in the past," or for their lack of expertise in jurisprudence, or for their refusal to take the theological test proposed by Khamanei which many with the rank of hojatalislams (*lit.*, proof of Islam) and above found unacceptable. The rejected candidates included such clerics as Abdul Karim Musavi-Ardebili, a former chief justice, Mehdi Karrubi, Sadiq Khalkhali and Ali Akbar Mohtashami. In protest, Ayatollah Muhammad Musavi Khoeiniha, who had been cleared by the Council, withdrew his candidature. When Khalkhali warned Khamanei that "the very moderates and liberals now supporting you will not hesitate to stab you in the back when the time is ripe," Khamanei retorted, "Some ignorant religious people are more dangerous for Islam than the religion's known enemies."[4]

Khamanei's backing for economic liberalization was crucial for Rafsanjani, given the odds against him in the Majlis, where his pragmatic, modernist supporters were in a minority. His opponents remained firm in their resistance to economic reform. In an open letter in November 1990, two-thirds of the 270 MPs called on the government "to bring the nation closer to the Line of Imam Khomeini," arguing that "According to the Imam's policy, our Islamic revolution was not [engineered] to fill the people's bellies but to serve the will of God."[5] Outside of economic matters, however, these MPs were open to change in a liberal direction. This was reflected in the Majlis legalizing chess and amateur boxing. Such an environment fostered growth in the theater, and revived traditional Iranian and western classical music.

Given the irksome incompatibility that had emerged between the Majlis and President Rafsanjani, the next parliamentary poll due in April 1992 was set to be of extraordinary importance. It was.

Rafsanjani and Khamanei worked together to bring about the electoral fall of leftist radicals. In a Friday prayer sermon in March, Khamanei upheld the vetting system used by the Guardians Council for candidates for national public office, and gave his backing to Rafsanjani and his cabinet. He urged the electorate to vote for the candidates favoring economic reform.[6] The fact that they ran under the general banner of "Loyalty to the Imam's [i.e., Khomeini's] Line, Support for Rafsanjani" improved their chances of winning. In contrast, their opponents adopted the bland title of "Grand Coalition."

Using his influence, Rafsanjani ensured that such leftist stalwarts as Mohtashami, Karrubi and Khoeiniha were rejected by the Guardians Council through the rulings of its Competence and Qualification Committee, a tactic used earlier in the Experts Assembly poll. But, when the rejected candidates threatened public protest, the Council backed down and allowed them to contest. The election campaign was quite lively with many outdoor rallies and colorful posters. But most of the leftists lost when the results of the first round were announced on April 10. Their defeat was attributed to the changed mood of a public now more interested in bread-and-butter issues than slogans. In the first round 18.8 million electors, forming 70 percent of the total, voted; and in the second, held in May, 7.5 million. The number of clerical MPs fell sharply, from 122 to 71, about a quarter of the total. Winning 150 seats, economic reformers, who were social conservatives, emerged as the majority. And their leftist opponents' strength halved, from 180 to 90. With Karrubi's failure to win a seat, the speakership went to 49-year-old Hojatalislam Ali Akbar Nateq-Nouri, a social conservative, who was a leader of the Association of Combatant Clergy.

The overall result satisfied Rafsanjani who could now count on active cooperation by the Fourth Majlis, and implement his plan to weld his supporting constituencies of bazaar merchants, moderate clerics and technocrats into a strong alliance to underwrite his re-election in 1993 by a handsome majority.

However, within weeks of the Majlis poll, the Rafsanjani government was shaken by riots in Shiraz, Shushtar and Arak, culminating in three days of bloody rioting in Mashhad in which six people were killed. The violence in Mashhad was so severe that the authorities imposed a news black-out and martial law. Many of the defeated leftist Majlis candidates were not unhappy to see the Rafsanjani administration find itself in the embarrassing situation of having to shoot at rioting civilians in the holy city of Mashhad.[7]

The pattern of violence was the same everywhere. The LEF would tear down illegally built shanty towns near cities, the squatters would fight back, march to the city center and attack public offices, loot shops and burn cars and buses. The interior minister, Abdullah Nouri, denounced the protesters as "corrupters on earth," and the courts executed eight of them. (But such denunciations would not save Nouri from being made a scapegoat and dropped from the next cabinet by re-elected President Rafsanjani in 1993 for failing to forecast rioting.)

Underlying the apparently insignificant grievances that triggered the riots were deeper factors of impoverishment of the populace caused by high inflation and static earnings, which resulted from a drop in oil prices that followed the end of the Second Gulf War, from an average of $30 a barrel to about $20.

To reduce high inflation – one of the rioters' major grievances – by increasing the supply of goods, the government eased import restrictions, and allowed virtually unrestricted imports of goods. In the process it incurred high foreign debts, which in a year soared to $13 billion.[8]

The clerical establishment attributed the violence to a decline in revolutionary values which, in its view, needed to be refurbished. The newly elected social conservative MPs, vehemently opposed to "Westoxication" (their term for Western cultural imperialism), began attacking Muhammad Khatami, who had been minister of culture and Islamic guidance since 1982, for his failure to tackle seriously the threat posed by the encroaching Western culture, and being indulgent towards Westernized Iranian intellectuals and artists. Their views were given wide publicity by the largely conservative press. Around that time Khamanei delivered a series of speeches urging *inter alia* the IRGC and its auxiliary, Baseej, to implement the Quranic injunction of "Enjoin virtue and suppress vice" (*amr be al marouf va nahian al munkar*) – a signal to them to enforce strictly the Islamic dress code and behavior. The 1981 Islamic Dress Law specified *hijab* (*lit.*, screen) for women, and prescribed a maximum jail sentence of one year for violating it. It required a woman not to show her hair, arms or legs. The Bureau for Enjoining Virtue and Suppressing Vice was led by 66-year-old Ayatollah Ahmad Jannati, who was also the seniormost member of the Guardians Council and the head of the Islamic Propagation Organization. In that capacity he had set up a 5,000-strong enforcement brigade, with each member equipped with a motorcycle for a speedy deployment.[9] Yielding to this pressure, Khatami resigned in July. His job went to Ali Larijani, a social conservative, then deputy minister of the IRGC.

On the economic front, Rafsanjani's liberalization drive had so far focused on the domestic scene, where he had an almost unanimous backing of the social conservative majority in the Majlis. But as he extended the process to the external dimension of the economy – abolishing the Iranian Rial's three-tier exchange rate, devaluing it, securing foreign loans, setting up free trade zones, and encouraging foreign investment and return of exiled capital and expertise – his Majlis backers split among economic nationalists and internationalists, with the former securing the support of Khamanei.

The disgruntled leftist radicals had by now gravitated around Ayatollah Hussein Ali Montazeri, who attacked economic reform as the brain-child of the "satanic" International Monetary Fund (IMF), and denounced Rafsanjani's policy of seeking accommodation with the West as misguided and dangerous, which would, in his view, ultimately turn Iran into a secular state.

Undeterred, Rafsanjani embarked on the next stage of economic reform, rationalizing the Rial's three-tier exchange rate: R 70 to US$1 for essential imported goods; R 600 to US$1 for the industrial sector; and a floating rate for trade and services. There was widespread debate on the merits and demerits of a single floating rate and its impact on the economy. Despite much opposition in the press and the Majlis, in mid–1992 the Rafsanjani administration introduced a phased rationalization plan which culminated in a single exchange rate on March 21, 1993, when the Rial was devalued by 95.6 percent.[10] With the government's foreign revenue made up almost exclusively of earnings from petroleum shipments, the devaluation of the Rial left its income untouched. But the cost of imports skyrocketed and unleashed high inflation, hurting salaried employees, including 2 million civil servants and some 600,000 soldiers. Being the sole owner of foreign currencies, the government ended up enriching itself at home at the expense of the general public.

While ordinary Iranians were grappling with their worsening economic condition, Khamanei focused on recharging revolutionary fervor with the aid of Hizbollahis (*lit.,* Followers of the Party of God), a generic term for those dedicated to the Islamic revolution and its values. "Radical Hizbollahi elements must always be given priority over non-Hizbollahis," he told a clerical group.

> They must be present at all key levels in the administration and in the armed forces. All our commanders, officers, directors, writers, artists, teachers and ministers must be true Hizbollahis, since our main enemy, the main enemy of Islam and Muslims, remains the arrogance of the world, with America at its head.

At another meeting in mid-August 1992, he urged writers, journalists, intellectuals and researchers to strike back against the "West's bombardment of our Islamic position with its corrupt culture." Rafsanjani chimed in. He called on the

Hizbollahi elements to help the Islamic Republic overcome "its present difficult times," warning that "If we fail to come out positively from the present situation, both Islam and the Iranian clergy will suffer such a blow that it will be generations before they are able to recover."[11]

Following a long meeting with Khamanei in mid-August, Rafsanjani restated the aims of economic liberalization which implied that he was yielding to the economic nationalist faction within the social conservative MPs. He reiterated the assurance he had given earlier to a gathering of clerics. "No foreigner has so far offered to invest a penny in this country," he told them. "I can assure you that we will not accept foreign investments unconditionally."[12] The key word was "unconditionally." This pacified economic nationalists, but only up to a point. Their continued unease was expressed by Ayatollah Jannati, a confidant of Khamanei, in October:

> Iranian Muslims did not make the revolution for land, bread, water or a better life, but only for Islam. This is what we have to save and cherish … But the government is encouraging the corrupt, Westernized Iranians whom we booted out to come back and help create better life [for the people]. This is surely a crime.[13]

It was noteworthy that the statement about Iranians making the revolution for Islam was exactly the one that radical leftist MPs had made earlier to attack Rafsanjani's economic reform.[14] It seemed to be a handy stick to use to beat one's opponents with.

Foreign affairs

In regional affairs, Iran's interference in the post–1991 Gulf War uprisings in southern Iraq had soured relations with Baghdad. Since the Tehran-based SAIRI was pre-eminent in these rebellions, Saddam Hussein decided to get even with Iran by boosting his support to the Mujahedin-e Khalq Organization (MKO, People's Combatants' Organization). Established in Iran in 1965, and led by Masud Rajavi (b. 1947), the MKO moved its headquarters from Tehran to Paris after clashing with the Islamic regime in June 1981. Pressured by Iran, in 1986 the French government expelled the MKO which then moved to Baghdad. Saddam allowed the MKO to set up training camps near the Iranian border after the Second Gulf War. Within a year MKO activists resorted to staging pinprick raids into Iran. In April 1992 Tehran retaliated by staging air raids on the main MKO base in central Iraq. Baghdad then sent its warplanes to intercept the Iranian aircraft. Though by so doing Iraq did not violate the northern air exclusion zone being enforced by America, Britain and France, Washington was quick to note the Iraqi action and broadcast it as the first time Baghdad had flown its warplanes since the end of the Second Gulf War.

But Washington's continued hostility towards Baghdad had not resulted in any perceptible moderation towards Tehran. Having kept in touch with his Iranian counterpart through the American interest section in the Swiss embassy in Tehran during the Kuwait Crisis to ensure Iran's compliance with the Security Council resolutions, especially regarding the UN embargo against Iraq, US President George Bush made little effort after the Second Gulf War to thaw relations with the Islamic Republic. Popular opinion in America, still mindful of the humiliation Iran had inflicted on the US by holding Americans hostage for almost fifteen months, was hostile towards Iran.

Animosity towards both Iran and Iraq was given a legal basis in 1992 in the form of the Iran–Iraq Nonproliferation Act. Sponsored by Senators Al Gore (Democrat, Tennessee) and John McCain (Republican, Arizona), this bill was passed by the US Congress with an overwhelming majority, and signed into law by Bush. It specified penalties to be imposed by the president against countries that sold advanced weaponry to Iran or Iraq. Since Iraq was under the most comprehensive embargo ever imposed by the UN, the new American law was aimed primarily against Iran, and stemmed out of Washington's concerns about some of the sophisticated weapons that post-Communist Russia was selling to Tehran.[15]

In retrospect the 1992 Iran–Iraq Nonproliferation Act could be seen as a preamble to the dual containment policy unveiled by the newly installed Clinton administration. In his speech to the Washington Institute for Near East Policy on May 18, 1993, Martin Indyk, special assistant to the US president on Near East and South Asian Affairs, described Iran and Iraq as "pariah states." After having described the danger that Iraq still posed to the security of the region and America, Indyk turned to Iran.

> Containing the threat from Iran is a more difficult though no less necessary undertaking. When we assess Iranian intentions and capabilities we see a dangerous combination for Western interests …. It is the foremost state sponsor of terrorism and assassination across the globe …. We will pursue the effort of active containment unilaterally, maintaining the counter-terrorism sanctions and other measures enacted by previous administrations to encourage a change in Iranian behavior …. The necessity to act now derives from the fact that Iran's threatening intentions for the moment outstrip its capacity. But this moment will not last for long. If we fail in our efforts to modify Iranian behavior, five years from now Iran will be much more capable of posing a real threat to Israel, to the Arab world and to Western interests in the Middle East …. To the extent that the international community succeeds in containing Iraq but fails to contain Iran, it will have inadvertently allowed the balance of power in the Gulf to have tilted in favor of Iran, with very dangerous consequences.[16]

In reality, almost five years to the day, US Secretary of State Madeleine Albright would publicly offer Iran an olive branch!

"The exaggerated Iranian threat [aired by America] has been used to sell more defense equipment to the Arabian Peninsula," said Rosemary Hollis of the London-based Royal Institute of International Affairs. Between 1990 and 1993, a staggering $55 billion worth of arms were sold to Middle Eastern countries, with the US garnering $19 billion, the UK $14 billion and Russia $8 billion.[17]

Being put in the same column as Iraq by America was one of the reasons why the Tehran government protested against the Pentagon's missile strikes at targets in Baghdad in June 1993, describing them as "an act of pure barbarism and state terrorism." It expressed "compassion and confraternity with the innocent Iraqi people." And for the first time it did not hold Saddam Hussein jointly responsible for the hardships imposed on Iraqi Muslims. Its stance was widely backed by the Majlis and media.[18]

While Indyk was busily warning of Iran becoming "much more capable" of threatening "Western interests in the Middle East," Germany paid scant attention to this. In early October 1993, Iran's intelligence minister, Hojatalislam Ali Fallahian, arrived in Bonn at the invitation of Bernd Schmidbauer, the German minister who coordinated all intelligence and reported directly to Chancellor Helmut Kohl. Fallahian revealed that there had been close collaboration between his ministry and the German Bundes Nachrichten Dienst (Federal Intelligence Agency) and the Bundesamt Für Verfassungsschutz (Office for the Protection of the Constitution) for more than two years chiefly on the smuggling of drugs originating in Afghanistan. Actually, intelligence cooperation between Iran and Germany dated back to the latter half of 1991 when Tehran helped Bonn to secure the release of two German businessmen held hostage in Lebanon. As part of that deal, Germany freed Abbas Hamadi, an Iranian, after he had served half of his ten-year jail term for kidnapping two local businessman in 1988. Then, at Israel's behest, the Germans began negotiating the release of the Israeli airman, Ron Arad, who had been captured by the pro-Tehran (Lebanese) Hizbollah in south Lebanon in 1986. (This would come to fruition in 1996 and involve the exchange of the corpses of Israeli soldiers and Hizbollah fighters.) Given this, Germany claimed that its contacts with Iran were for humanitarian purposes – and for countering the drugs trade.[19] That failed to pacify an angry Washington. It alleged that Germany had agreed to supply Iran with spying computer equipment which would enable it to keep track of its dissidents at home and abroad.

British foreign secretary, Douglas Hurd, also protested, saying the German action was contrary to the Western policy of isolating Iran in the wake of the Salman Rushdie affair. Following the publication of the American edition of the novel *The Satanic Verses* by Salman Rushdie, an India-born author and a British national, in February 1989, Ayatollah Khomeini issued a fatwa (religious decree) after repeated protests by many Muslims in Britain, India and Pakistan against the book for insulting Islam and Prophet Muhammad. "I would like to inform all the fearless Muslims in the world that the author of the book entitled *The Satanic Verses* (which has been compiled, printed and published in opposition to Islam, the Prophet and the Quran), as well as the publishers, who are aware of the contents, have been sentenced to death. I call on all zealous Muslims to execute them quickly, wherever they find them, so that no one will dare to insult Islamic sanctity. Whoever is killed on this path will be regarded as a martyr."[20] Britain and other Western governments objected vehemently to this call for murder. After Khomeini's death in June, they pressured the Iranian government to rescind Khomeini's fatwa. When it argued that this could not be done as a dead man's verdict could not be countered by it, they insisted that it should publicly dissociate itself from the fatwa. Since this was not forthcoming from Tehran, diplomatic relations between it and the West remained fraught.

However, commercial links between Iran and Western Europe remained strong. In 1992 Germany sold $5 billion worth of goods to Iran, and was its number-one trading partner; and British and Italian exports to Iran amounted to $1 billion each.[21]

Also, whereas in the spring of 1993 Indyk was warning of Iran becoming "much more capable" of threatening the Arab world, the latter was cultivating better relations with Tehran. Ties with Qatar had improved to the extent that its Crown Prince, Hamad ibn Khalifa al Thani, had visited Tehran in November 1991 to sign several mutual cooperation agreements.

However, relations with the single most important monarchy in the Gulf, Saudi Arabia, seesawed. In late May 1993 Iran's foreign minister, Ali Akbar Velayati, started a tour of the Gulf monarchies with a cordial meeting with King Fahd of Saudi Arabia, which had raised Iran's quota for hajj pilgrims to 120,000. But hardly had he left Riyadh than trouble erupted between the Iranian hajj pilgrims and the Saudi authorities. Contrary to the prior agreement, the Iranians tried to mount an anti-American and anti-Israeli demonstration as part of the hajj ritual of "disavowal of infidels" in their Mecca camp. This was promptly suppressed by the Saudi security forces. Undeterred, the pilgrims staged a demonstration inside their compound in Mina near Mecca – an event for which the Saudis had been unprepared. The Iranians got the demonstration videotaped, and the broadcasting authorities in Tehran aired the tape, thus showing the world at large that the Iranian pilgrims had successfully defied the Saudi government, which had lost no time in expelling the pilgrims' leader, Hojatalislam Muhammad Muhammadi Reyshahri.[22] On May 31, Eid al Adha (*lit.*, Festival of Sacrifice), King Fahd attacked "Islamic militancy," and on the anniversary of Khomeini's death a few days later, Rafsanjani warned the Gulf rulers that by suppressing Islamic militancy they would fall just as the Shah of Iran had fourteen years earlier. Khamanei attacked "the American puppets," and was backed by 150 MPs.[23]

As for Iraq, the other target of Washington's dual containment policy, Iran declared its intention to build bridges with it. In October, Rafsanjani sent a personal message of reconciliation to Saddam Hussein through one of his deputy foreign ministers, Muhammad Javad Zarif. Commenting on it, the *Tehran Times*, close to Rafsanjani, said, "As the standard bearer of independence and anti-imperialism, Islamic Iran has a duty to take the first steps in reconciling with Iraq, regardless of its record of aggression and animosity."[24]

Rafsanjani's second term

This was after Rafsanjani had been re-elected president in a poll on June 11, 1993. The poll was held barely three months after the floating of a single open market rate for the Rial and its simultaneous devaluation by over 95 percent which caused severe economic pain to ordinary Iranians. This, and the absence of real choice, resulted in the lowest voter turnout yet, 56 percent. And, of those who voted, only 63 percent favored Rafsanjani (32 percent down on the 1989 result) with an unprecedented 24 percent voting for his nearest rival, Ahmad Tavakali, a former labor minister.[25]

Since Tavakali, a free market economist who was close to bazaar merchants, had no policy differences with Rafsanjani's economic liberalization, those who voted for him were protesting against the corruption and economic mismanagement that had plagued the regime – especially after the end of the Iran–Iraq War and Khomeini's death a year later. Tavakali's slogan, "Less Luxury and More Austerity for Leaders", hit home. It was aimed at the luxury cars and spacious villas of influential mullahs in the affluent north Tehran which are increasingly setting the religious leadership apart from their less fortunate compatriots. Many among the Islamic hierarchy, far from emulating the spartan life of the Republic's founder, Khomeini, had succumbed to the lures of high living and corruption. This happened at a time of growing impoverishment of the bulk of the populace due to rising unemployment, officially put at 14 percent, and high inflation running at over 30 percent. These stemmed from a combination of factors: removing or cutting subsidies on basic goods and services; a drastic devaluation of the Rial; high budget deficits; and low oil revenue due to falling petroleum prices.[26]

Unlike in 1989 when the electorate went to the polls in the aftermath of Khomeini's death, and voted almost unanimously for Rafsanjani seeking presidency for the first time, they now judged him on his record. On the credit side, using his considerable manipulative skills and sheer ruthlessness, he had avoided the quagmire of endemic internecine fighting among influential clerics, and undertaken much-needed, though unpopular, economic reform. On the debit side, he had failed to arrest a slide into economic and administrative corruption and mismanagement.

An eternal optimist, Rafsanjani put a positive spin on the electoral outcome. "While passing through the difficult period of economic adjustment, two-thirds of the voters have approved the difficult path of adjustment and given their approval to this [reformist] program," he declared. He assured Iranians that "the reconstruction path has nearly reached the uphill (*sic*) and is now approaching the era of a plateau." Next day the price of cooking oil shot up from R 7,000 to R 11,000 per kg.[27]

But Rafsanjani, the realist, knew that his lackluster electoral performance would encourage the social conservative majority in the Majlis to challenge his program of a fresh round of privatization and reduction in state subsidies, and a controversial package of investment incentives, including the establishment of free trade zones in Kish and Qeshm Islands, which had still to be cleared by the Guardians Council.[28]

The falling oil prices, fluctuating around the mid-teen US dollars, worsened the budget deficit and led to the rise of Iran's foreign loans to a staggering $30 billion by the end of 1993, due largely to the excess of imports over exports, which in 1991–92 was $10 billion on a two-way trade of $47 billion. The Rial's value fell from R 1,500 to US$1 to R 2,000. The government imposed import quotas and limited export of foreign currencies.[29] The falling living standards of Iranians were confirmed by the Central Bank's per capita income estimate of $540 in 1993, which was 22 percent lower than under the Shah in 1978.[30]

The first sign of a parliamentary challenge to Rafsanjani's fresh package of economic reform came in August 1993 in the voting for individual ministers of his new 23-member cabinet. The Majlis confirmed all of them except Muhsin Nourbaksh, a fervent advocate of economic liberalization and foreign investment, as minister of economy and finance. Of the 261 MPs voting, he secured 127 ballots, four less than the minimum (50 percent plus one) required. Undeterred, Rafsanjani made him vice-president for economic and financial affairs. (In September 1994 Rafsanjani would re-appoint him head of the Central Bank, a position Nourbaksh had held from 1982 to 1988.) The number of clerics in the new cabinet was down from four to two – with the justice ministry run by Hojatalislam Muhammad Shushtari, and the intelligence by Hojatalislam Ali Fallahian. Two other ministries – interior, and culture and Islamic guidance – which in the past often went to clerics, were now headed by laymen. With eight PhDs and nine engineers, the cabinet was dominated by technocrats. In October, Rafsanjani succeeded in having Muhammad Khan, a deputy of Nourbaksh, endorsed as minister of economy and finance by the Majlis.

Following the death, on December 9, of the Qom-based Grand Ayatollah Muhammad Reza Golpaygani, the centenarian Marja-e Taqlid al Alaa (*lit.*, Supreme Source of Emulation), a religious-constitutional controversy erupted in Iran when his family objected to the invitation given to Khamanei to lead Golpaygani's funeral services, due to Khamanei's comparatively junior status in the Shia hierarchy. (Had he been allowed this privilege his religious standing would have gone up.) Golpaygani's demise created a leadership vacuum in the Shia religious order which needed to be filled. It raised the possibility of Ayatollah Khamanei being elevated to a grand ayatollah and thus becoming a marja-e taqlid to his followers.

On this subject differences developed between the clerical establishment which wanted Khamanei to be both the Rahbar (Leader) and Marja-e Taqlid (just as Khomeini had been), and senior theologians in Qom who wanted to keep the two offices separate, and regarded Khamanei as too junior to merit the rank of

a marja-e taqlid. The latter backed the idea of naming 94-year-old Grand Ayatollah Muhammad Ali Araki (to whom Khomeini's followers had turned after
his death) as the successor to Golpaygani. Their ranks included Ayatollah
Ibrahim Amini, head of the Association of Teachers of Qom Seminaries. This
prestigious organization valued religious knowledge more than political experience. Formed in the early 1980s, it set up the Resalat Foundation in Qom,
which published the daily *Resalat* (Mission). It was opposed to government
intervention in the economy. "The office of the marja is [now] exclusively
established in Grand Ayatollah Araki," Amini declared. On the other side were
Ayatollah Muhammad Yazdi, the head of the judiciary, and Hojatalislam Ali
Akbar Nateq-Nouri, the Majlis Speaker. They argued that besides religion and
piety, a marja-e taqlid should also be well versed in political, military and social
issues so that he can lead the Muslim community in this age. "The esteemed
Leader of the revolution [Khamanei] is the most qualified of all his peers
regarding his awareness of the age, managerial ability, administrative skills and
the ability to understand the issues and affairs of the time," said Yazdi. "Therefore Khamanei should be regarded as both Leader [Rahbar] of the revolution
and the only marja [Marja al Aala]." The balance tilted in favor of Qom's
senior theologians when, on December 24, 80-year-old Ayatollah Ali
Meshkini, chairman of the Assembly of Experts, backed Araki as the marja-e
taqlid. He convened the Assembly to secure its backing, but its deliberations
were inconclusive as many members felt that the matter should be decided by
senior theologians on their own.[31] So, in the end Araki became the Marja-e
Taqlid al Alaa, not Khamanei.

This debate, conducted publicly, reflected the degree of freedom of speech
that existed in Iran. It also reflected the continued existence of different centers of
(political) power and influence, which had created a virtual impasse between a
pragmatic government, led by Rafsanjani, a socially and economically conservative Majlis, chaired by Nateq-Nouri, and leftist radicals inside and outside the
Majlis who opposed economic reform.

"In reality there is considerable freedom of expression in Iran, provided one
remains within the accepted ideological parameters and does not threaten the
established political order," noted Andrew Whitely of the New York-based
Middle East Watch. "Behind closed doors in the past few days [in September
1993] the Majlis has been debating the hottest issue of all – the future of vilayat-e
faqih [rule of religious jurisprudent]." At the same time Whitely expressed the
Middle East Watch's criticism of the regime's attitude towards "genuine dissent
or independent thinking of any kind, of the government's failure to curb the vigilante activities of the revolutionary zealots."[32]

The debate on the religious status of Khamanei revived after Araki's death in
Qom, following a month-long illness, on November 29, 1994, at 102 (or 105,
according to the lunar Islamic calendar). Hojatalislam Ahmad Khomeini, the
only son of the Islamic Republic's founder, said that the choice of the next
Marja-e Taqlid al Alaa should be left to the highest theologians of the realm.

Most of them regarded Khamanei as lacking the degree of piety and learning as well as teaching experience that the title required.

Calling on the government not to interfere in the selection of the supreme marja-e taqlid, the Association of Teachers of Qom produced a list of seven candidates, including Khamanei, Montazeri and Grand Ayatollah Muhammad Qomi Tabatabai (Khomeini's former teacher), and Ayatollah Muhammad Rouhani (a one-time opponent of Khomeini). After studying the list, the 150 social conservative MPs declared Khamanei "to be the most informed person concerning Islam and the Islamic world and the most qualified authority for the leadership of the Muslim society."[33]

They reached this conclusion on the basis that political experience was as important as theological learning. Ayatollah Jannati, a loyal supporter of Khamanei, attacked those who wanted the marja-e taqlid to be non-political. On December 9, the head of Iranian judiciary, Ayatollah Yazdi, declared Khamanei as Iran's marja-e taqlid, and warned the clergy not to challenge his decision. The senior theologians in Qom took offense, and let this be known to Ahmad Khomeini who, like his father, maintained a balance between the two competing sides, and acted as an intermediary. A compromise was devised in private. Five days later Khamanei declined the post of marja-e taqlid inside Iran due to already high volume of work, but added that he was willing to be the marja-e taqlid for Shias outside Iran.[34] However, most Shias outside Iran were the followers of 73-year-old Grand Ayatollah Mirza Ali Sistani, based in Najaf, Iraq.[35]

The year of 1994 began inauspiciously for Rafsanjani. On February 1, he was the target of an unsuccessful assassination attempt. Later that month, his younger brother, Muhammad Hashemi, lost his managing directorship of the state-owned radio and television, a job he had held since 1981, to Ali Larjani, then minister of culture and Islamic guidance. He then appointed his brother vice-president for executive affairs.

On Ashura – the day Shias mourn the death of Imam Hussein, a grandson of Prophet Muhammad – which fell on June 20, a bomb exploded in the women's section of the mausoleum of Imam Ali Reza (the 8th Imam of Twelver Shias) in Mashhad, shattering a wall and the prayer hall dome, and killing twenty-six people. The government blamed the MKO which immediately denied the charge. Its denial was plausible. Since the MKO's ideology was an amalgam of Shia Islam and Marxism, it was hard to see why it would try to blow up the shrine of a revered Shia Imam. The culprits were most likely anti-Shia Sunni militants of Iran and the neighboring Afghanistan and the drugs mafia operating along the Afghanistan-Pakistan border whose smuggling activities through Iran were hampered by Tehran's stringent anti-drugs policy. The fact that the authorities had allowed the demolition of a Sunni mosque in Mashhad to make way for a Shia mosque earlier in the year, thus upsetting the local Sunnis, apparently created the right environment for their terrorist action.

But a worse crisis was to face the government in early August when bloody rioting erupted in Qazvin, 80 miles (130 km) north-west of Tehran when the

Majlis refused to raise its status from a district to a province. It claimed thirty lives. When the LEF failed to restore law and order, the central government dispatched IRGC units to assist them. But still the rioting continued. What disturbed the Rafsanjani administration even more was the reported refusal of the commander of the local army units to accept the order from the interior ministry to assist the LEF and the IRGC. Ultimately the violence was curbed but only after many lives had been lost. On August 14, four senior officers of the army, air force, IRGC and LEF addressed a letter to the political leadership, warning it against the deployment of armed forces to crush civilian unrest or internal conflict, and adding that the armed forces could no longer remain silent while Iran was threatened by "aggression from outside and disintegration from within."[36]

The reference to a threat of "aggression from outside" was surprising. None of Iran's immediate neighbors had displayed aggressive intentions towards it. Indeed, after the collapse of the Soviet Union in December 1991, Iran had found itself surrounded by the friendly Central Asian and Caucasian states of Turkmenistan, Azerbaijan and Armenia. It had developed cordial relations with Russia – one of the five littoral states of the Caspian Sea – since mid-1989 when it and the Soviet Union signed agreements on commercial, economic, scientific and technical cooperation.

Within a year of the break-up of the Soviet Union, on August 25, 1992, Russia agreed to build a nuclear power plant at Halile near Bushahr and supply nuclear research units to run on 20 percent enriched fuel provided by Moscow, with Iran participating in the construction. (The work, begun originally in 1974 by the West German company Siemens, was suspended indefinitely after the revolution, and the site was bombed by the Iraqis during the First Gulf War.) In December 1994 the Atomic Energy Authority of Iran signed an $800 million contract with Moscow to rebuild two 1,000 mW light water, nuclear-fueled generators, as part of a nuclear power plant, to be finished by May 2003, with Iranian participation in the construction. But because progress on the joint venture was slow, Tehran switched to a turnkey arrangement in February 1998. Resisting pressure from Washington, Russia confirmed the contract.

In acute need of foreign exchange, it could not afford to cancel such a lucrative commercial deal. Nuclear technology was one of its most successful exports, and it had made inroads in several Asian countries, including China and India. It reassured the US that its reactors could not be used to produce weapons-grade plutonium, and reminded the Clinton administration that it, and South Korea, had agreed to supply similar reactors to North Korea. Washington reasoned that as an oil-rich state, Iran did not need nuclear-powered electrical plants, a point it never made when the Shah originally gave the contract for the Bushahr nuclear power plant to a West German company in the mid–1970s.[37] Despite Russia's repeated reassurances, both America and Israel were firm in their belief that Iran was bent on obtaining nuclear arms, and they intended to put as many hurdles in its way as they could to gain time to devise, jointly, appropriate response capabilities and doctrines.

In any event, Moscow's cooperation with Tehran went beyond the nuclear power project. Both were actively trying to end the civil war in Tajikistan between the secular government and the Islamist rebels, an enterprise that would be crowned with success in mid–1997. Both agreed that Washington had raised its armed presence in the Gulf to an unnecessarily high level. And both of them had adopted an identical policy on sharing the resources of the Caspian jointly among the five littoral states.

They were both offended by the way the US administration and oil corporations had tried to elbow them out of the lucrative contracts to exploit the offshore oilfields of Azerbaijan. However, Russia managed to muscle its way into the leading Western-led oil consortium by destabilizing Azerbaijan through its henchmen in the government. As a result, Lukoil of Russia obtained a 10 percent stake in the development of two offshore oilfields in a $7 billion deal signed in September 1994 by the State Oil Company of Azerbaijan (SOCAR). That was only one-seventh of the share that went to the Western-dominated consortium, Azerbaijan International Operating Company (AIOC), with the rest retained by SOCAR, which handed over a third of its equity to Lukoil. When Iran protested about its exclusion, Baku offered it half of SOCAR's remaining share, then reduced it to 5 percent of the total equity in exchange for help in raising capital. Tehran found the offer too low. Also, the four US oil companies in AIOC were so uneasy at the prospect of sharing the same negotiating table with the Iranians that they were determined to vote against Tehran's full participation. Therefore, in early April 1995, Baku withdrew its offer of equity to Iran altogether.

This happened almost a month after President Bill Clinton issued an executive order barring American individuals or companies from working in Iran's oil and gas industry in order to contain and isolate Iran while adding credibility to US efforts to rally international pressure against Tehran. He thus blocked a $650 million deal made in early March by Conoco, a unit of Du Pont, to develop Iran's Sirri A and E offshore oilfields, arguing that the arrangement undermined his efforts to crack down on Tehran.[38] Under the US law then in force, the oil contracts signed by American companies with Iran were not illegal provided the petroleum did not enter the US.

As for Iran, Article 43 (8) of its constitution specified "prevention of foreign economic domination of the country's economy." That precluded equity or production-sharing rights for foreigners. But the 1987 Complementary Law to the Establishment of Oil Ministry (1979) allowed contracts between the oil ministry, state companies and local and foreign persons and legal entities. Within this framework the oil ministry devised a buy-back formula which allowed it to pay the "guest company" in oil and gas to the point of enabling it a rate of return of 15–18 percent on its investment within four to five years.

In 1991, the Majlis opened Iran's offshore fields to foreigners on a buy-back basis. The reasons were technical and socio-political. Offshore fields required complex technology. Also, the foreigners stayed out at sea, which suited both sides. The foreign oil company (often already operating in one of the six Gulf monarchies) moved its equipment by ship from a nearby location, and its personnel were not subject to such restrictions as a ban on alcohol and the compulsory use of *hijab* (veil) for women.[39]

It took four years for the National Iranian Oil Company (NIOC) and Conoco to reach an accord on the Sirri A and E offshore fields. After Clinton's executive order, Iran gave this contract to Total SA of France, formerly Campaigne Petroles de France. As with Conoco, the NIOC did not give Total SA any rights on the reserves and the project had to be completed in five years, when Total was required to hand over operational control to the NIOC.

In the US, on April 30 (Remembrance Day in Israel), Clinton announced at the World Jewish Congress meeting in New York that he was banning trade with Iran forthwith. That put a stop to US oil corporations buying $4 billion worth of Iranian crude annually, and American companies exporting $326 million worth of goods – mainly corn, rice and oil industry equipment – to Iran.[40]

Domestic affairs

Clinton's move had an adverse impact on the Rial. Between January and May 1995, its value fell by 50 percent – to R 6,000 to US$1. Given that the Second Five Year Plan (March 1995–February 2000) was launched on March 21, the fall in the local currency was inauspicious for the authorities, especially when it had come on top of a 40 percent loss for the Rial in the latter half of 1994. Delinking itself from the floating market rate, the government announced a fixed rate of R 3,000 to US$1 on May 22. It also announced heavy punishments for those breaking the new regulations.[41]

The inauguration of the Second Five Year Plan, far more ambitious than the First, had been combined with the doubling of fuel prices and thus of bus fares. This went down badly with the Iranian public which had resented all along the bitter medicine of economic liberalization. Its disaffection came to the surface once more – in Islamshahr, a city of a quarter of a million, 12 miles (20 km) southwest of Tehran. A protest about water supplies turned into a riot against economic hardship. Workers from a nearby shanty town revolted, ostensibly against the inadequacy of water supplies, marched to Islamshahr, smashed shop windows, and set alight banks, petrol stations and public buildings. In the LEF firing that followed several people were killed. By nightfall order was restored. But the authorities did not release the figures of the dead, and banned their public mourning.[42]

The Islamshahr rioting was symptomatic of the continuing division within the political–religious establishment on such vital issues as managing the economy, the degree of freedom of expression, and the exact role of the Vali-e Faqih, the Guardian of Jurisprudence, in administering the state and his place in the theological hierarchy.

Whereas the Rafsanjani administration drew comfort from the World Bank report, published in December 1995, which stated that the previous six years had registered an impressive advance in the implementation of structural reform in the economy, and commended Tehran for being vigilant in repaying its foreign debts on time, its opponents denounced it as another sign of Iran surrendering its independence to foreigners.

While accepting much latitude in debates on theological-political subjects, the social conservative majority in the Majlis was resolved to carry on resisting "Westoxication." In January it passed a law banning the private use of satellite television equipment at a time when there were an estimated 250,000 satellite dishes in the country, and a state-owned factory was selling them at $400 a piece. But the Act permitted the state-run television to air satellite programs which were compatible with Islamic values. During the debate the fear of losing Iranian viewers to better-produced programs of Western television was widely expressed by the bill's proponents. "When a 15-year-old or 18-year-old sees attractive programs by satellite, when he or she listens to CNN or BBC News … will they be willing to listen to our news?" asked Nafiseh Fayazbaksh rhetorically.[43]

The debate on the role of the Vali-e Faqih, the Guardian of Jurisprudence, was also in progress. In an article published by the Center for Strategic Studies, attached to the President's Office, Hojatalislam Muhsin Kadivar, who was close to Rafsanjani, argued that a democratically elected *vali* (ruler or guardian) was part of Shia philosophy. He then defined the *vali*'s role and the manner in which he ought to be selected/elected. This implied that Kadivar was suggesting limiting his authority to religious affairs and/or amalgamating the offices of the *vali* and the executive president into one. "There are no conclusive theories [in Shia Islam]," he concluded. "All theories should be subjected to continuous debate."[44]

While these differences presented a fractious picture of the Islamic Republic abroad, they had their merit domestically. "Internal friction has created room for dissent," said a secular writer in Tehran to Lamis Adoni, a visiting Arab journalist. "This has enabled different trends, including the secular, to raise questions challenging the state's policies and practices." However, the chance of secularists leading the challenge to the status quo was minuscule. "The movement for change will only be effective if it is led by reformist and democratic Islamists," said Murad Saggafi, editor of the *Goft-e Gou* (Dialogue), a cultural magazine. "Secularists cannot lead such a movement." In other words, a reformist movement that offered progressive interpretations of Islamic thinking and laws was needed to end the monopoly that conservative clerical scholars currently exercised.[45]

Then there was 50-year-old Dr Abdul Karim Soroush, head of the Research Faculty for History and Philosophy of Science at Tehran University, and a leading Islamist thinker. After obtaining a Master's degree in pharmacy at Tehran University, he received a doctoral degree in chemistry at London University in the mid–1970s, where he also studied philosophy. After the Islamic revolution he was appointed to the Supreme Council of Cultural Revolution by Khomeini. He belonged to that school of Islamist intellectuals who wanted to reconstruct

Islamic civilization by "Islamization of modernity." This, they reasoned, was best done by presenting religious thinking in a way that incorporated modernity. They drew their inspiration from Indian-born Sir Muhammad Iqbal who published a seminal book, *The Reconstruction of Muslim Thought*, three years before his death in 1937. They differentiated between religion and science of religion – that is, thoughts of religion. Taking his cue from Iqbal, Soroush distinguished between religion and the understanding of religion the latter of which, in his view, was defined by time and place. Therefore, he reasoned, there could be no official guardianship of religious thought in Islam. Those who insisted on such guardianship needed to answer the crucial question, "Who guards the guardians?" In the ensuing multiple understandings of Islam, which must be tolerated and accepted, his own choice lay with incorporating modernity and pragmatism into religion. In his Persian-language book, *Contraction and Expansion of the Theory of Sharia* (Qabzo Bast-e Theorik Shariat), published in 1990, he tried to adapt the eternal nature of Islam to the modern conditions of popular revolts and globalization. His approach was perceived by many as paving the way for a pluralist Islamic society where different understandings of Islam were represented in various state organs.[46]

At this time a debate on the role of women in society was also taking place, in which the weekly *Zanan* (Women), edited by 31-year-old Faizeh Hashemi Rafsanjani, daughter of the president, and the quarterly *Farzaneh* (Wise), edited by Mahboubeh Qolizadeh, played a prominent role. They argued that the centuries-old interpretations of Islam were erroneous, and that a series of misinterpretations of Islam had been perpetrated by male scholars to rationalize male domination of Muslim society. President Rafsanjani was sensitive enough to enlightened female opinion to appoint 35-year-old Shahla Habibi (b. 1958) as an adviser on women's affairs with the status of a deputy minister. Faizeh Rafsanjani had emerged as the reform movement's foremost spokesperson on women. A former volley-ball coach, she organized the first Islamic Women's Olympics in Tehran in 1993 in her capacity as president of the Solidarity Council for Women's Sport Organizations. It was attended by 700 athletes from eleven Muslim countries. "In most of the Islamic world, women have cultural problems," she told a visiting *New York Times* reporter in January 1995. "They are regarded as a commodity, often forced into domesticity. [But] for Iranian women, the values have changed." They went skiing in hijab (veil). Prodded by her, the government gave strong support to women's sport. An example was the 5-acre Bahman cultural complex in the underprivileged south Tehran, with a sports center that had more facilities for women than men.[47]

Bare statistics about women showed that having to wear a veil in public had not stopped them from advancing socially and economically. In 1994 about a third of civil servants were women. Among university students 40 percent were female – versus 12 percent in 1978. The government had removed restrictions in higher education to let women train as engineers and assistants to judges – but not as judges (in accordance with the official interpretation of the

Sharia). Changes in personal law for Muslims authorized women for the first time to initiate divorce proceedings. Furthermore, faced with an unbearable population growth of 3.9 percent in the 1980s, the authorities encouraged family planning to the extent that the rate fell to 2.3 percent in the early 1990s, and then to 1.8 percent in the mid–1990s. This happened despite the fact that, between 1975 and 1996, life expectancy rose from 55 to 68, and infant mortality fell from 104 per 1,000 to 25.[48]

Iran and the West

Such facts were at odds with the negative impression that Western governments and people had of the way women were treated in Iran. They certainly had no impact on the policy-makers in Washington where Clinton pursued relentlessly his hard line on Iran which had the enthusiastic support of his secretary of state, Warren Christopher. As deputy secretary of state under President Jimmy Carter (r. 1977–80), Christopher had developed deep animosity towards Iran for holding American diplomats hostage for 444 days and humiliating the US by making it appear helpless domestically and abroad. Little wonder that in his speech to the UN General Assembly in late September 1995, Christopher singled out Iran for his frontal attack. Accusing Tehran of sponsoring international terrorism and of seeking to produce nuclear weapons, he urged the international community to isolate it. His Iranian counterpart, Ali Akbar Velayati, was so incensed that he rewrote this speech to rebut him. Calling the US an arrogant power, he declared that Iran would not be bullied. He called on Washington to stay out of the politics of the Gulf, and reiterated that Gulf security was the sole responsibility of the regional countries.[49]

Washington had scant regard for such views. In July 1995 President Clinton announced the formation of a new, permanent Fifth Fleet – consisting of 2 nuclear-powered submarines, 15 ships, 1 aircraft carrier with 70 warplanes, manned altogether by 10,000 sailors and marines – to patrol the Gulf, chiefly to police Iran and enforce the naval blockade of Iraq. It was to be headquartered in Bahrain. Such a military presence by the Pentagon in the Gulf was likely to exacerbate relations between Iran and the US.

Tehran could only draw some comfort from the fact that, despite its untiring lobbying, America had failed to convince the 15-member European Union and other Western allies to shun it just as they had Baghdad since 1990, despite the fact that (unlike in the case of Iraq) there was not a single UN Security Council resolution against Iran. In early May 1995, the EU, then chaired by France, came out against imposing trade sanctions on Tehran. Australia and Canada followed suit. They did so because they were aware of the large size of both the Iranian market and the country's oil and gas reserves. So they saw much merit in pursuing "constructive engagement" as a means to bring about changes in Iran's policies, with the EU advising each member-state to work out an individual solution with Iran on the Salman Rushdie affair.

In its tussle with America, the timing favored Tehran. In early April there was an agreement between Denmark and Iran whereby the latter promised not to undertake any measures to carry out Khomeini's death sentence. On the eve of a meeting between Iranian and EU officials in late May 95, Tehran's policy was that Khomeini's fatwa against Rushdie could not be revoked, but that the Iranian authorities would not take any steps to implement it. "Our government is not going to dispatch anybody, any commandos, to kill anybody in Europe," Velayati told the BBC World Service Radio. Yazdi, the head of Iran's judiciary, declared, "The fatwa is an independent legal position [taken by Khomeini], outside the legal system of Iran."[50] And, finally, Nateq-Nouri, the speaker of the Majlis, the legislative organ of the state, said, "The [Khomeini] fatwa is irrevocable, but we will not send commandos to kill Rushdie. That is up to Muslims [in general]."[51]

While this reassured the EU, it upset hardliners in Iran. In a letter to Khamanei, Colonel Muhammad Baqir Qatinaf, in charge of the IRGC's Operation "Sajil" to assassinate Rushdie, said:

As you know, Operation Sajil ordered by Imam Khomeini and confirmed by you, is being stopped after a government decision, and the agents of the information [i.e., intelligence] ministry stationed at the Iranian embassies abroad are ordered to stop mutual cooperation. Knowing that Imam Khomeini's fatwa is irrevocable, I seek your order to the government and the foreign ministry to continue their active collaboration [in pursuing the Operation Sajil] or face the wrath of angry Muslims.

There was no evidence to suggest that this appeal to Khamanei resulted in a change in the official policy. This was confirmed by Muhammad Javad Larijani, the conservative chairman of the Majlis's foreign policy committee in mid-August. "Iran has dissociated itself from the [Khomeini] fatwa," he told the London-based *Independent*. "There will be no Iranian hit squads trying to carry out the death sentence. These assurances ought to be sufficient for you, but Britain wants more. Britain wants that we sign a paper that amounts to an admission of guilt. That is unacceptable." On the other hand, the 15 Khordad Foundation – named after the date of a national uprising, June 5, 1963, in protest at Ayatollah Khomeini's first arrest by the Shah[52] – still offered a $2.5 million bounty to anyone who assassinated Rushdie. Iran countered that it could not interfere in the affairs of a private foundation.[53] So, if there was still an impasse, in a formal sense of the word, between Tehran and London, it was headed for a resolution sooner or later.

Overall, European diplomats were aware too that geography had endowed Iran with a most strategic location, and it was not in their medium- and long-term interests to alienate Tehran. Iran had land frontiers with the Indian sub-continent, Afghanistan, Turkmenistan, Azerbaijan, Armenia, Turkey and Iraq, and fluvial borders with Kazakhstan and Russia. Since its shoreline covered all of the Gulf which, at its narrowest, was only 35 miles (56 km) wide, it enjoyed proximity to all of the six Arab Gulf states. It was the only country in the oil-rich Gulf region which was also part of the Caspian basin endowed with large petroleum and gas reserves.

More importantly, populated by nearly 60 million people, and possessing 93 billion oil barrels (or 9.2 percent of the global total) and 20,700 billion m^3 of natural gas, the second largest reserves in the world, Iran was of much commercial interest to the EU. As it was, after Conoco's formal withdrawal from its deal on the Sirri oilfield with Iran in 1995, Total SA of France picked up the contract. This upset Washington. A top American official told Nicholas Bethel, a British politician, "We make sacrifices in an effort to tackle a problem that threatens the security of us all, only to see our allies making profits out of what we have voluntarily given up."[54] Also, the fact that the World Bank issued a favorable report on Iran in late 1995 displeased Washington.

Birth of a centrist force

While the World Bank document buoyed the Rafsanjani administration, its leftist detractors used it as evidence that Iran was surrendering its hard-won independence to foreigners, a subject that had engaged Iranian politicians and theologians since 1872 when Nasir al Din Shah of the Qajar dynasty gave Baron Paul Julius de Reuter, a British businessman, exclusive rights in Iran for railways, tramways, roads, telegraph lines, irrigation works, all minerals except gold and silver, a state bank and customs collection for an advance of $40,000 and 60 percent of the profits from the customs concession.[55] This view was also shared by economic nationalists in the social conservative camp. Indeed, their persistent opposition to the Rafsanjani government's economic liberalization plans, much whittled down, had led to the president's supporters drifting away from the traditional rightwing camp which drew its inspiration from the highly influential Association of Combatant Clergy.

The opening shot, signifying a formal split, came in January 1996 when sixteen top technocrats and politicians published an open letter, calling on the electorate to vote for those Majlis candidates who were dedicated to the prosperity and modernization of Iran as exemplified in "the line followed by President Rafsanjani." This led to the founding of the Servants of Construction (SOC, *Kargozaran-e Sazandegi*) to contest the forthcoming Majlis poll. The new group included Faizeh Rafsanjani, and Gholam Hussein Karbaschi, who was elected the secretary-general of the SOC. He was typical of other founder-members. Born in the household of a theology teacher in Qom, he enrolled at the seminaries in Qom, and then studied engineering in Tehran. After the revolution he joined Ayatollah Khomeini's secretariat, and then supervised a program on Iranian television. In 1982, at 25, he was appointed governor of the Isfahan province. Eight years later President Rafsanjani named him mayor of Tehran, a city of eight million. He instituted modern management methods at the City Hall, and became a popular figure.

In its national economic policies the SOC's differences with conservatives – now also described as the traditional right – were more on degree than substance. While it advocated curtailing state subsidies and lifting foreign currency restrictions, as recommended by the IMF, it wanted less privatization than the conservatives led by Speaker Nateq-Nouri, who was close to Khamanei. It proposed economic regeneration through industrial capital, not mercantile, which had been a consistent backer of the traditional right. A proponent of détente in foreign policy, the SOC wanted to expand contacts with the West to which conservatives were still antipathetic. Whereas the SOC was for political liberalization, the traditional right, with its belief in "society under a guardian (*majma-e vali*)," argued that the degree of political freedoms should be determined by senior religious leaders, not the popularly elected Majlis or president.

The remaining major faction, the leftists, were for political reform, and for retaining a strong public sector and state subsidies, the removal of which, it argued, would hurt the needy, who should be the prime beneficiaries of the Islamic revolution. It fought the general election under the banner of the *Salaam* (Peace) newspaper, edited by Ayatollah Khoeiniha.

In the election campaign conservatives resorted to populist revolutionary rhetoric to retain the loyalty of the older generations. Nateq Nouri warned that liberal Majlis and cabinet would lead to the destruction of revolutionary precepts, and accused his (disparate) opponents of establishing dialogue with America. In his New Year speech on March 21, 1996, in his native city of Mashhad, Khamanei warned the electorate not to be deceived by candidates who wanted to enfeeble the foundation of Islamic thought under the guise of "freedom and liberalism." Muhsin Rezaie, commander of the IRGC, called on the personnel of the Baseej, a large IRGC auxiliary force, to vote against "liberals," meaning centrists and leftists. The conservative faction tried to revive the alliance between bazaar merchants and the lower social strata which had been the driving force for the successful overthrow of the Shah. It succeeded. But in the process it lost the support of the modern middle class which switched its loyalty to the SOC, a centrist faction.

Because of the loss of its base in the modern middle class, the conservative faction's strength in the Fifth Majlis declined to 100–120. And due to the emergence of the centrist SOC, the number of its opponents rose from 30-odd to 80–90. The rest were independent. Reflecting the national results, the list of the thirty winners in Tehran was headed by Nateq Nouri followed by Faizeh Rafsanjani. The voter turnout of 25 million in the first round was 60 percent. The number of clerics fell in the new Majlis from 71 to 49, the lowest figure since the revolution, and that of women rose from 4 to 9. More remarkably, only twelve of the MPs of the First Majlis had survived, an indication of how competitive the position of a parliamentary deputy had become.

Iran and the world

While a vigorous election campaign for Iran's Majlis highlighted the participation of citizens in the running of their country, the events in Bahrain, the only Gulf monarchy with a Shia majority, demonstrated the alienation of its subjects from their political system. From December 1994 onward, an increasing number of Bahrainis had resorted to street protest for the restoration of the 1973 constitution, providing for an elected parliament, that the Emir had suspended in August 1975. This happened against the background of a sectarian disjunction between the subjects – 60 percent Shia – and the ruling family, which was Sunni. Instead of addressing the genuine desire of its citizens for a representative government, the authorities resorted to blaming Tehran for the continued unrest which by early 1996 had claimed sixteen lives and resulted in the arrest of 1,600.[56] On June 3, they arrested six suspects, alleging that they were trained by Tehran to carry out terrorist actions. They claimed that Iran's IRGC had set up the Hizbollah-e Bahrain in April 1993. In protest, the emirate recalled its ambassador from Tehran.[57]

But a far more serious allegation was leveled against Iran by Washington after the explosion on June 25, 1996, of a 4,500 lb (2,000 kg) bomb, planted in a fuel tanker, outside the perimeter of the guarded and fortified compound of a residential eight-story block in Khobar, part of a vast complex used by US servicemen stationed at the Dhahran airbase. Creating a 35 foot (11 m) crater, and sending sound waves that traveled 40 miles (65 km) to Bahrain, it tore into the front of the building, killing 19 servicemen and injuring 400. Two men were seen leaving the fuel truck and speeding off in a car, giving the security men a few minutes to begin an evacuation before the blast. Following the explosion, the Pentagon officially acknowledged that 6,000 US servicemen were based on Saudi soil. (Later, 4,000 of them were moved to a sprawling air base in Al Kharaj desert region 60 miles (100 km) south-east of Riyadh, and accommodated in a complex that stood in the middle of nowhere, and was therefore easy to secure.) Washington rushed seventy FBI agents to Saudi Arabia.[58] The timing of the blast indicated that there was probably a link between this terrorist act and the explosion, on November 13, 1995, of a 220 lb (100 kg) car bomb in the parking lot of the Saudi National Guard training center in Riyadh run by the US, killing 7, including 5 US military officers, and injuring 60, the majority of them American. For this too Washington had blamed Iran. But the four suspects arrested in April 1996 and executed in early June – Abdul Aziz al Mithan, Khalid al Said, Muslih al Shamrani and Riyad al Hajja – were all Saudi citizens and Wahhabi, a sub-sect within Sunni Islam, which held Shias in low esteem. Three of them had participated in the jihad against the Soviets in Afghanistan in the 1980s after receiving training in the Pakistani camps run by the US Central Intelligence Agency. Significantly, before the suspects' sentence was carried out, the Saudi authorities and US embassy in Riyadh had received threats of retribution if they were beheaded.[59]

Washington alleged that the perpetrators of the Khobar explosion were trained in Iran. The CIA went on to claim that it had identified eleven terrorist camps deep inside the Islamic Republic where, in its view, the Dhahran bombers were trained. (However, CIA-supplied maps, published in the [London] *Sunday Times* of August 11 and December 15, 1996 respectively, showed only two and four training camps – in Qazvin and Hamadan; and in Tehran, Qom, Abyek and Nahavand.) These sites were purportedly hiding about 5,000 men and women, many of them learning how to make suicide bombs – the chief culprit being the Imam Ali training camp (at an undisclosed location) which had allegedly been established by President Rafsanjani himself in 1994.

Rejecting the accusations, Tehran repeated "its unwavering commitment" to rejecting "both hegemony and hegemonization" perpetrated, in its view, by America. While the CIA's top managers released satellite and intelligence data to the *USA Today* which published it on August 3, other American officials close to the Saudi investigation said there was no evidence of Iran's involvement.[60] In an ominous move, on August 3, US warplanes violated Iran's airspace near Bushahr, where two nuclear reactors were being built by Russia – so said Tehran in its complaint to the UN Security Council.

In a concerted effort to demonize Iran, Washington also blamed Tehran for the TWA flight crash (following an explosion) on July 17, 1996, near Long Island on the eastern coast of the US, with a loss of 230 lives, and the July 27 bombing at the Olympics in Atlanta, Georgia. Four years on, American investigators had failed to establish whether the TWA blast was caused by sabotage, or a mechanical or electrical failure. And the allegation about the Atlanta explosion soon proved to be false.

On August 5, amidst fanfare, Clinton signed the Iran–Libya Sanctions Act (ILSA) – also called D'Amato Act, named after Senator Alfonso D'Amato, head of the US Senate Banking Committee – saying that "Iran and Libya are two of the most dangerous supporters of terrorism in the world." The Act was to remain in force for five years, after which the US Congress could extend it.

In the case of Iran, the terrorism charge pertained chiefly to the assassinations that Tehran's intelligence operatives had carried out abroad. It was estimated that in the seventeen years since the revolution, the Islamic regime had liquidated eighty militant opponents in Europe, Turkey and Iraq.[61] Its targets fell into two categories: former top officials under the Shah, a fast-dwindling number; and, more importantly, those groups which had taken up arms against the Iranian regime, the most prominent being the Baghdad-based Mujahedin-e Khalq Organization, and the secular, leftist Iranian Kurdish factions, operating from Iraqi Kurdistan. Following the Second Gulf War, the KDPI set up its headquarters in the Iraqi border town of Qala Diza and the Komala-e Jian-e Kurdistan (*lit.*, Association of Revival of Kurdistan) near Suleimaniya. These Iraq-based Iranian groups staged pinprick raids on Iran, which resulted in the deaths of IRGC personnel, and they were in return attacked by the Iranian forces. This was the background against which Kazem Darabi, an Iranian intelligence agent, and his four Lebanese cohorts assassinated four Kurdish leaders, including the KDPI chief, Sadiq Sharaf-Kandi, in September 1992 at the Mykonos Greek restaurant in Berlin, where the Kurds had come to attend a meeting of the Socialist International. Tension between Iran and its armed opponents rose sharply after the US adopted the dual containment policy in May 1993. Tehran feared that Washington would use the rebellious Iranians' Iraqi Kurdistan base to undermine the Islamic regime. Iran had made no secret of its policy of retaliating with force against violent rebellious groups, no matter where their activists were based. As it was, Israel had been pursuing such a policy since its inception in 1948. In more recent days, in October 1995 its intelligence operatives assassinated Dr Fathi Abdul Aziz Shikaki, head of the Islamic Jihad (of Palestine), in Malta.[62] But neither America nor any other Western country had considered putting Israel on the list of nations that supported international terrorism.

Tehran's fears were fueled when, following the passage of a secret directive by the US Congress on December 31, 1995, sanctioning $18 million for a covert action program against Iran, the White House announced that the sum would be spent *inter alia* to cultivate new enemies of the Islamic regime. In retaliation, on January 23, 1996, the Iranian Majlis authorized $20 million to "uncover and neutralize US government conspiracies and interference in Iranian affairs, to sue the US in international legal bodies, and to inform world opinion about American violation of the UN Charter."[63]

In June, the Voice of America (VOA) began beaming its non-jammable broadcasts into Iran from a powerful 600 kW transmitter in Kuwait. Four months later it inaugurated simultaneous radio and television broadcasts in Persian, beaming television transmission of an existing weekly one-hour radio phone-in program via the AsiaSat2 satellite. This magazine program included popular Iranian entertainers based in America, Iranian pop music, and legal advice on how to emigrate to the US. Despite a ban on satellite dishes since March 1995 as part of a campaign to counter the Western cultural invasion, with fines of up to $1,500, an estimated 250,000 out of 2 million households in Tehran had satellite dishes.[64] Depending on the diameter of its receptor, an Iranian family could watch up to thirty Western and Asian channels, including the pop music channel MTV, Star and the BBC World Service. When the new VOA television program in Persian proved popular, with pirated versions being rented out in Tehran and elsewhere, the government launched a crackdown. Although the VOA broadcasts were apolitical, it acted swiftly to stifle any political after-effect that might follow. At the same time the popularity of this VOA program in Persian made the Iranian broadcasting officials sit up and take notice. It made them realize that their audiences, especially the young, wanted more entertaining output. But they did not know how to achieve this without transgressing the fundamental values of the Islamic revolution. Nonetheless, as a tentative start, they decided to permit the IRGC to run its own national television channel with stress on light entertainment and music almost free of ideological content. To balance this, they considered establishing a nation-wide Islamic radio network with its headquarters in the holy city of Qom.[65]

But the diffuse cultural challenge from the West that Iran faced paled in contrast to the provisions of the freshly passed ILSA. It gave the US president discretionary power to impose two of the six sanctions against any individual or company anywhere in the world that invested $40 million or more in an Iranian or Libyan oil or gas project: a ban on imports of the goods or services of the offending entity; a federal government ban on the purchases from the sanctioned entity; a ban on all American financial institutions to lend it $10 million or more; prohibiting the sanctioned entity from acting as a primary dealer of US Treasury Bonds, or as an agent of the US government or as a repository for US government funds; a ban on US Export–Import Bank assistance; and a denial of licenses for the export of controlled technology to the sanctioned entity.[66]

Arguing that these sanctions violated international trading laws, the EU threatened retaliatory action were the US president to take action under ILSA. With its oil companies engaged heavily in Iran, France was vocal in its protest. Germany expressed its disapproval by renewing its export-credit guarantees to Iran. Japan said it would lodge a complaint with the World Trade Organization (WTO) as ILSA violated WTO rules. Aware that at the current rates of extraction of 192 million m^3 of natural gas and 3.62 million bpd of oil, the Iranian reserves would last 360 years and 70 years respectively, the European, Japanese and Chinese oil companies were in no mood to kowtow to US legislators, especially when they were convinced that the extra-territorial application of the American law was illegal.[67]

To Washington's dismay, during his visit to Tehran on August 12, 1996, Turkish Prime Minister Necmettin Erbakan signed a $20 billion natural gas deal with Iran, scheduled to run until 2020. A pipeline was to be laid to carry initially 3,000 million m^3 of Iranian gas, rising to 10,000 million m^3 in 2005. Trade between the two neighbors was to double to $2 billion in two years.

Against this backdrop Tehran's statement that President Clinton's decision "lacked international backing" sounded rather mild.

This stemmed partly from the confidence Iran had in its intrinsic strategic value which had been proven with the inauguration of a 90 mile (150 km) rail link between its border town of Sarakhs and Tejan in Turkmenistan in May 1996, the culmination of a five-year project costing $210 million. The opening event was attended by twelve leaders and presidents (five Central Asian republics, Iran, Turkey, Azerbaijan, Armenia, Georgia, Pakistan and Afghanistan). With this, the old Soviet rail system, covering all eight landlocked republics of the southern tier of former Soviet Union – Kazakhstan, Kyrgyzstan, Tajikistan, Turkmenistan and Uzbekistan of Central Asia and Azerbaijan, Armenia and Georgia of the Caucasus – became linked to the Iranian railway network. This provided the landlocked Central Asian states with access to the warm-water ports of Iran in the Gulf and the Arabian Sea, and thus released them from their dependence on Russia. Instead of selling their cotton exclusively to Russia, Uzbekistan and Turkmenistan could now explore world markets and deliver the commodity without the involvement of Moscow in any form. The new link was expected to move 2 million tonnes of cargo and half a million passengers annually between Tejan and Mashhad.[68]

The inauguration of the rail link coincided with Tehran's agreement with Kazakhstan whereby Iran would receive Kazakh oil by tanker at a Caspian port and would deliver the same amount to Kazakhstan's customers from one of its Gulf terminals.

None of this discouraged America from pursuing its policy of demonizing Iran. It now alleged that Tehran was carrying out a nuclear weapons program at its facilities at Neka, a town near the Caspian coastline, Moalem Kalayeh, and Karaj, a suburb of Tehran – despite repeated statements by the IAEA in 1995 and 1996 that its inspectors had found no evidence of "suspect, military-related activity" in Iran.[69]

The US strategy seemed to be preparing the ground for a military strike against Iran as punishment for its alleged involvement in the Khobar blast. Responding to this, Khamenei said that, though the American allegations were worthless, they were designed to create a psychological pretext for possible strikes. "An American strike against Iran would prove costly to the US and its regional allies," he warned.[70] In the event, the Pentagon did not hit Iranian targets.

In the spring of 1997, to Washington's delight, relations between Tehran and the EU soured. At the end of a three-year trial of the defendants (three Lebanese and an Iranian) – accused of murdering dissident Kurdish leaders in Berlin in September 1992 – Judge Frithjof Kubsch found them guilty. He added that "Senior clerics were also part of the plot." At the outset, he had said that the Iranian government was not in the dock. Nonetheless, it was critical for him to conclude who first conceived the assassinations and made them happen. The evidence suggested the decisions had been taken by the highest echelons of Iran's government, he concluded. He identified the Supreme National Security Council under President Rafsanjani as "the planning center for assassinations abroad [which] gives final approval to the missions initiated by the Intelligence Section of the President's Office."[71]

Citing a well-connected source in Beirut, Robert Fisk of the *Independent* wrote,

> These liquidations are not carried out on the specific orders of President Rafsanjani or the Spiritual Leader Khamanei. There are long standing orders [since the mid-1980s] to neutralize all armed opposition wherever it is, even in Europe. They come from the intelligence committee of the IRGC.

Every week five or six Iranian revolutionary guards get killed, with the Iranian Kurds coming in from Iraq, continued the source; and Tehran did not give out casualty figures for security reasons.

> The regime's security will always come first, and that means killing opponents who use violence … The CIA openly states that it has $20

million to destabilize Iran and Iraq – and it supports the armed Kurds who want to destroy the Tehran regime.[72]

Following the Berlin verdict, Holland, as the EU's chairman, proposed that all members recall their ambassadors from Tehran and suspend "critical dialogue" with it. They did so, except for Greece. Washington considered the moment propitious to pressure the EU to sever trade ties with Tehran. But an EU diplomatic source said, "Cutting off trade would have to be done within a UN context." And that was not in the offing. The commercial links between Iran and the EU, involving the vital oil trade, were too tight to be loosened or cut. Overall the EU imported 10 percent of its crude oil from Iran, with France, Italy and Germany being major buyers. On its part Tehran sold one-third of its $17 billion worth of petroleum exports to the EU, and imported goods worth $11.5 billion.[73]

While Iran's diplomatic relations with the EU entered a rocky phase, its ties with Saudi Arabia took a sudden turn for the better. At the ICO summit in the Pakistani capital of Islamabad in mid-March 1997, Rafsanjani had a much-publicized meeting with Saudi Crown Prince Abdullah, who had become the virtual ruler following King Fahd's severe illness in late 1995. This was the highest-level contact between the two states since the founding of an Islamic republic in Iran.

Both the Saudi and Iranian media reacted positively. Rafsanjani's efforts to strengthen links with Riyadh had been frustrated by the Iranian hardliners' resistance, Saudi Arabia's wariness towards Tehran, the continued heavy presence of the American forces in the Gulf, and Washington's pressure on the kingdom to distance itself from Iran. Rafsanjani had prepared the ground for a fruitful meeting with Abdullah by declaring that the hajj pilgrimage was strictly a spiritual ritual, thus disagreeing with radicals at home, who maintained that it was also a political congregation where anti-American and anti-Israeli sentiment must be expressed. Now Abdullah left it to Rafsanjani to prove Tehran's good intentions by ensuring that the Iranian pilgrims obeyed the Saudi rules strictly during the upcoming hajj.[74]

By now the main contours of Iran's foreign policy in the post-Khomeini era had become well defined. Tehran wanted to have close commercial ties with the EU, its largest trading partner in 1996, with annual two-way trade of nearly $17 billion. This suited the EU in general, and Germany, France and Italy (which imported a substantial part of their oil requirement from Iran) in particular. But in diplomatic and security spheres, Tehran had decided to forge strong links with Russia, China and India, as part of its overall strategy to frustrate the designs of the "hegemonist" America. In the aftermath of the EU ambassadors' withdrawal from the Iranian capital, Rafsanjani said that the recent developments strengthened Iran's inclination to give priority to its ties with Asian countries.[75]

Tehran gave especial importance to its relations with Moscow, which had emerged as its chief arms' supplier. The two had maintained a common position on the sharing of the Caspian Sea resources. They worked together to secure ceasefires between Azerbaijan and Armenia – at war over the enclave of Nagorno-Karabakh – in 1994, and in the Tajik civil war three years later. James Goodarzi, a London-based Iranian academic, noted in the *Middle East International:*

> [W]ith Nato's planned expansion into Russia's previous sphere of influence, the Kremlin sees its alliance with Iran as a linchpin in its overall strategy to preserve its influence in Transcaucasia, Central and Southwest Asia, and concomitantly, to prevent 'Western – particularly American – interference in its near abroad.'[76]

As its second most important supplier of weapons, China too loomed large on Tehran's diplomatic screen. Indeed, between 1986 and 1990, of the $2.9 billion that Tehran spent on foreign weapons, just under $1.5 billion went to China.[77] Iran's Chinese imports included speed patrol boats, gunboats, anti-ship missiles and Cruise missiles. With Beijing becoming a net importer of oil in 1993, it became more interested in strengthening ties with Tehran than before, with the latter supplying China with some 100,000 bpd in 1996. Finally, the Indian navy helped Iran modify its three Russian-made Kilo-class submarines to improve their operating efficiency in the Gulf's warm waters.

The last of these submarines became a center of controversy between Moscow and Washington and in American domestic politics. During the race between Democrat Vice-President, Al Gore, and Republican Governor, George W. Bush, for the US presidency in October 2000, the *New York Times* disclosed that on June 30, 1995, Gore, who had been given wide powers by President Clinton to deal with Russia, had signed a secret agreement with Russian Prime Minister Victor Chernomyrdin (r. 1993–98), which allowed Moscow to fulfill existing military contracts with Iran – including a Kilo-class diesel submarine, torpedoes, anti-ship mines and hundreds of tanks and armored personnel carriers – by December 1999, but barred any further weapons' sales to Tehran. The Kilo-class submarine was of particular concern to the Pentagon since it was difficult to detect and had long-range torpedoes, and could therefore be a threat to oil tankers or US warships in the Gulf. In the view of Senator John McCain, the co-sponsor of the 1992 Iran–Iraq Nonproliferation Act, a case could be made that the Russian delivery of weapons to Iran, especially the Kilo-class submarine, should have triggered sanctions against Russia under the 1992 law. "If the [US] administration has acquiesced in the sale then I believe they have violated both the intent and the letter of the law."[78]

What this episode underscored was a relentless effort by Washington to deprive Iran of access to advanced weaponry from all possible sources. Tehran was equally determined to frustrate America's designs, and continue to forge strong links with such major players on the international stage as Russia, China and India. In Iran foreign policy was decided by the SNSC, where its chairman, President Rafsanjani, was only the first among equals. So his imminent departure from the president's office was unlikely to alter the thrust or direction of the country's foreign policy.

Domestically, as Rafsanjani neared the end of his term in the spring of 1997, the economy was in a bad shape. The annual growth rate had plummeted from 8 percent in the early 1990s to 1 percent in 1996. The per capita GDP was below $1,000 a year. The economy was creating only two-fifths of the 700,000 jobs required annually to keep pace with the rising number of graduating students.[79] There were rising allegations of nepotism and corruption directed *inter alia* at Rafsanjani's inner circle. While he had followed the recommendation of the IMF and the World Bank regarding structural adjustments in the economy and reduction in state subsidies, his policies had proved inflationary. His efforts to trim the bloated civil service had failed, as also had his attempts to attract investment – domestic and foreign.

This was the backdrop against which conservatives adopted Speaker Nateq-Nouri as their candidate in December 1996 for the forthcoming presidential contest – an event signaling the start of the race for the presidency.

10

KHATAMI, A MODERATE
WITH A MISSION

Once the traditional right had adopted Ali Akbar Nateq-Nouri as its presidential candidate, with the conservative Association of Combatant Clergy lining up behind him, the centrist SOC had to decide whether to name a candidate from within its own ranks or ally with leftists or conservatives. When the left's first choice, Mir Hussein Musavi, a former prime minister, failed to win a nod from the Leader's office in early 1997, its chief spokesman, Ayatollah Muhammad Musavi Khoeiniha, managing editor of the influential *Salaam* newspaper, approached Hojatalislam Muhammad Khatami, then head of the National Library, to run for presidency as the emerging (political) reform movement's candidate. Khatami, a mild-mannered, academically-inclined man, reportedly became angry at the thought of entering the world of power politics. Later, how-ever, he calmed down and agreed to run.[1] His candidacy got a boost when Rafsanjani, working behind the scenes, decided to put his weight behind those preparing to challenge the traditional right, which had resisted his economic lib-eralization drive. So he advised the SOC to ally with the left in the presidential race. It did. Khatami also got the endorsement of the left-of-center Society of Combatant Clerics – popularly known as Majme – which in the earlier contests had backed Rafsanjani. His election campaign was masterminded by the SOC's Gholam Hussein Karbaschi, mayor of Tehran, and Khoeiniha, who turned his *Salaam* newspaper premises into the campaign headquarters.

The main plank of Khatami's platform was political reform, with its stress on the rule of law, respect for civil rights, greater openness in society, acceptance of political criticism, greater social justice, and reinforcement of the institutions of civil society. He also advocated administrative reform and fairer distribution of wealth. He called for greater participation in politics by young people. The driving force behind his program was the belief that a more open political environment – where the government took into account popular opinion – would reinforce the Islamic regime rather than enfeeble it. By contrast, his rival, Nateq-Nouri, stood for the status quo, seeing little need for political or cultural reform. He represented a socially conservative and internationally assertive trend in Iran.

The contest between Khatami and Nateq-Nouri was quite bitter. "Some alleged [during the campaign] that upon my assuming office, the country's security, Islam and the Islamic revolution would be undermined," Khatami recalled three years later. "Despite those allegations people voted for my program and elected me their president."[2]

On polling day, May 23 (2 Khordad in Iranian Calendar), an unprecedented 88 percent of the 33 million electors participated. Of these, 20 million, or 69 percent of the total, favored Khatami, and only 25 percent Nateq-Nouri. The rest of the ballots went to two minor candidates.

With this, 54-year-old Khatami emerged as the second most powerful man in Iran. Born in a religious family in Yazd, his father being a sayyid, a descendant of Prophet Muhammad, he pursued religious education in Qom where he obtained a degree in advanced theology. He then secured degrees in philosophy at Isfahan University and educational sciences at Tehran University. In Tehran he became an active member of the Association of Militant Clergy of Tehran. In 1978 he was sent to Hamburg, Germany, to head the Islamic Center that ran a Shia mosque. There he learnt English and German. After the revolution, he was elected an MP to the First Majlis. Ayatollah Khomeini appointed him head of the state-owned Kayhan Newspapers. In 1982 he became minister of culture and Islamic guidance in the cabinet of Prime Minister Mir Hussein Musavi, a position that was confirmed by the two subsequent parliaments. When the conservative-dominated 1992 Majlis objected to his liberal views, he resigned. President Rafsanjani then appointed him an adviser to the presidential office. He also became head of the National Library.[3]

Khatami won decisively for a variety of reasons. In general, electors wanted the government to tone down its ideological rhetoric and focus more on tackling such problems as inflation, joblessness, drug addiction, and pollution in cities. In Khatami they saw a potential for a more down-to-earth approach by the authorities. In particular, two large constituencies – women and youth – voted almost unanimously for him. The nation's youth perceived in him a mild, tolerant personality, ready to pay attention to their grievances, both social (such as strict segregation of sexes) and economic (such as the dearth of jobs). He advocated freedom and equality for women within an Islamic context, calling on them to be more active in the socio-economic sphere. Women also feared that the socially conservative traditional right would further restrict their social activities. Khatami's emphasis on the rule of law appealed especially to the modern middle class, the mainstay of the centrist SOC. Finally, by having the courage to discuss publicly the role of ethnic and religious minorities – Christian, Jews, Zoroastrians, Azeris and Baluchis – he won their vote.

Compared to this alliance of four major constituencies, the coalescing forces behind Nateq-Nouri were small. He had the backing of the traditional middle classes as represented by various merchant and guild associations under the umbrella of the Miscellaneous Islamic Committees and the socially conservative older generation.

Despite his overwhelming victory, Khatami reached an understanding with his conservative opponents inside the Majlis and outside, and urged greater cohesion and coordination within the center-left alliance that had propelled him to power. As a consequence, within a week of his defeat in the presidential race, Nateq-Nouri was unanimously re-elected Speaker for a year. And the Majlis endorsed entirely Khatami's 22-strong cabinet that he presented after taking office on August 3, 1997. Only five ministers of the Rafsanjani government survived. The intelligence ministry went to Hojatalislam Qorban Ali Najafabadi, a conservative cleric and an MP, who replaced Ali Fallahian. The new culture and Islamic guidance minister was Sayyid Ataollah Mohajerani, a liberal, often attacked by conservative mullahs. And the interior ministry went to Hojatalislam Abdullah Nouri (who had held that job from 1989 to 1993), a left-wing reformist. The veteran Velayati, foreign minister since 1980, was replaced by Kamal Kharrazi, who had been Iran's ambassador to the UN. Ayatollah Khamanei, the Leader, then appointed Velayati his adviser on foreign affairs. And he made Rafsanjani head of the Expediency Consultation Council System.

Disappointingly, Khatami's cabinet did not include a woman. But he made up this lacuna by appointing the first ever female vice-president. She was 37-year-old Dr Masoumeh Ebtekar, with a doctorate in immunology, a member of the editorial board of the *Kayhan International* newspaper, and the acting head of the national Non-Governmental Women's Organizations.

In the West, Khatami's surprise victory was widely welcomed. Even President Clinton paid a compliment to Iranian democracy. "There clearly was an interesting election in Iran – unexpected to the Iranians and unexpected to those who follow Iran carefully," said his secretary of state, Madeleine Albright, later. "Everyone has been intrigued by the election of Mr Khatami, but actions speak louder than words."[4] The chances of a US–Iran rapprochement improved when Warren Christopher, who had turned hostility to Tehran into a personal crusade, was replaced by Albright in January 1997 during the second Clinton administration. With this, Christopher's stance that America should respond positively to Iran only after the issues of state terrorism, acquiring of weapons of mass destruction, and its stand on the Middle East peace process had been resolved, gave way to the new policy of "parallel responses." That is, if Tehran made a gesture, Washington would reciprocate, even if the outstanding issues remained unaddressed – the start of a minuet between Iran and America.

Many Western reporters and commentators hastily and wrongly interpreted Khatami's win as signifying a rejection of the Islamic Republic's socio-political system by the voters. Interestingly, almost invariably they referred to him as a former minister of culture, omitting "Islamic guidance" from the ministry's title. This was all the more misleading since in Iran this ministry was popularly known as *ershad-e Islami* (Islamic guidance) – or just *ershad* – and its officials were to be found even in the countryside. This overarching Western view ignored the fact that Khatami was a cleric wearing a black turban, indicating that he was a sayyid, and ranked higher in the religious hierarchy than the white-turbaned clerics like Nateq-Nouri and Rafsanjani, who were not sayyids. As someone active with the Association of Combatant Clergy since its formation in 1974,

Khatami had been an integral part of the clerical establishment running Iran since the revolution.

Another misconception shared by most Western analysts was that, backed by an overwhelming popular mandate, Khatami would just forge ahead with the much-needed political reform. This view overlooked the fact that the Iranian constitution was more full of checks and balances than any of its Western counterparts, and major changes, whether social, political or economic, were difficult to implement as Khatami's predecessor, Rafsansjani, elected by an almost unanimous vote in 1989, had come to realize. There were five primary centers of power in Iran: the Leader who was both the spiritual and temporal ruler of Iran, the ultimate arbiter of power; the Assembly of Experts for Leadership that elected him, and which monitored his performance; the President, who was the chief executive; the Majlis, the legislative organ; and the judiciary. There were two secondary centers of power: the Council of Guardians (of the Constitution), which ensured that the legislation was not at odds with the Sharia, the Islamic law, or the Iranian constitution, and supervised elections to the Assembly of Experts for Leadership, President and Majlis; and the ECCS which resolved differences between the President, the Majlis and the Guardians Council. Both of these bodies were appointed by the Leader, as was the chief of the judiciary.

The 13-member ECCS consisted of the chairman, six (clerical) jurisprudents of the Guardians Council, the heads of the three organs of the government, the interior minister, the minister for the specific subject under discussion, and the chairman of the appropriate Majlis committee.

The Guardians Council, with a six-year tenure, consisted of six Just Jurisprudents (*adil fuqaha*), selected by the Leader, and six jurists, specializing in different areas of the law, elected by the Majlis from among the list provided by the head of the judiciary. On the compatibility of legislation with the Sharia, only the Just Jurisprudents were allowed to vote, and the decision was by majority. But the right to judge legislation's compatibility with the constitution lay with all members. The Council had a long record of vetoing reformist bills adopted by the Majlis. For instance, in 1981 it vetoed a land reform legislation, which imposed ceilings on land ownership, on Islamic grounds, arguing that an individual's right to own property was inviolable according to the Quran.[5] In the summer of 1993, it objected to the setting-up of Free Trade Zones in the offshore islands of Kish and Qeshm on constitutional grounds, and returned the bill to the Majlis for amendment.[6] All six jurisprudents on the Council were conservative. So too was Ayatollah Muhammad Yazdi, the head of the judiciary, a post with a five-year tenure, renewable once.

So, with conservatives entrenched in the judicial system, the Guardians Council, the Majlis and the Assembly of Experts, the chances of Khatami carrying out political reform speedily were remote.

Pragmatism in foreign policy

Nonetheless, in the region, Khatami's victory reassured the Gulf monarchies, especially Saudi Arabia whose Crown Prince, Abdullah, had, during his cordial meeting with Rafsanjani in March 1997 in Islamabad, invited him to undertake the hajj pilgrimage. More importantly, the peaceful way the Iranian pilgrims behaved during the hajj (in April) reassured Riyadh, and paved the way for Iran to host the triennial conference of the Jiddah-based ICO in December.

Such behavior by Riyadh, a close diplomatic, military and economic ally of the US, left Washington puzzled and dismayed. This had come after Saudi officials had refused point blank to let the American FBI agents get directly involved in the investigation of the 1996 Khobar explosion. They did so partly to show that Saudi Arabia was a sovereign state and partly to demonstrate that their intelligence apparatus was efficient enough to do its job unaided.

Iran also improved its relations with Iraq. On September 26, Iranian foreign minister Kamal Kharrazi met his Iraqi counterpart, Muhammad al Sahhaf, at the UN headquarters in New York, the first meeting of its kind. Given the international isolation of Baghdad, the Iraqi media gave the event much publicity despite the impasse on the 30,000 unaccounted-for Iraqi prisoners of war and the 135 Iraqi aircraft that had taken sanctuary in Iran during the Second Gulf War which, Baghdad claimed, had been absorbed into Iran's air force and civilian airline.[7]

Three days later Iran's air force hit two MKO military camps inside Iraq, thus highlighting the sponsorship that each side provided to the rebel groups from the other. In October when the US state department produced a list of thirty terrorist organizations worldwide, as required by the country's 1996 Anti-Terrorism and Effective Death Penalty Act, it included the MKO. That barred it from raising funds in America. "The MKO qualified for the designation under US law and the move was not made to curry favor with the Khatami government," said James Rubin of the US state department.[8] Nonetheless it pleased Tehran.

Tehran was also pleased when, on September 28, an oil consortium, led by Total SA (later TotalFinaElf) of France, and including Gazprom of Russia and Petronas of Malaysia, with 40:30:30 shares in the equity, signed a $2 billion contract with the NIOC to develop its vast offshore South Pars gasfield (phases 2 and 3), after an NIOC subsidiary, Iranian Offshore Engineering and Construction Company, had finished the first phase. The plan was to extract 20 billion m^3 of natural gas annually by 2001, enough to satisfy two-thirds of France's demand. Total SA was the favorite because it was already developing the adjacent part of Pars gasfield under the Qatari jurisdiction. The full exploitation of this vast field with total reserves of 300,000 billion m^3 of gas and condensates was to be carried out in eight phases.

Though Total's president, Thierry Desmarest, had told the Paris-based *Le Monde* (The World) that "The French law prohibits French companies submitting to US extra-territorial legislation," he took no chances. Before signing the contract with the NIOC, Total sold whatever minor holdings it had in the US.[9] Washington declared that Total, Gazprom and Petronas had violated its Iran–Libya Sanctions Act, and that it would penalize them. But it never did.

On the diplomatic front, Tehran got a boost – albeit inadvertently – from the hardline stance of Israeli Premier Netanyahu towards the Palestinians in the peace talks. The helplessness displayed by President Clinton in handling an intransigent Netanyahu damaged his standing in the Arab world, and made Tehran's view of America as a biased broker in the Middle East peace process more acceptable in the region.

An indication of this came on November 10, 1997, in Riyadh. Egyptian President Hosni Mubarak found himself preceded by Kamal Kharrazi, Iran's foreign minister, in his audience with King Fahd even though Mubarak was there to concur with the monarch on boycotting the US-sponsored MENA economic conference – held annually to encourage trade between Israel and the Arab world – in Doha, Qatar, on November 16, unless there was a breakthrough in the Israeli–Palestinian negotiations.

The MENA conference, boycotted by most of the invited Arab states, was a fiasco. Seen against this backdrop, the ICO summit in Tehran on December 9 would appear all the more successful.

With a full turnout of the leaders of the fifty-five nations of the ICO, addressed by the UN secretary-general, Kofi Annan, Iran achieved a major diplomatic coup. By delivering a moderate, erudite speech, President Khatami impressed the audience. "Islamic and Western civilizations are not necessarily in conflict and contradiction," he declared. Citing the Greek and Roman roots of the West, he said, "We should never be oblivious to the careful acquisition of the positive accomplishments of the Western civil society."[10]

The summit ended with the adoption of the Tehran Declaration. Denouncing Israel for its occupation of the Arab land, its expansionist policies and its state terrorism, it resolved to regain Al Quds (i.e., Jerusalem) and the Al Aqsa mosque and restore "the inalienable national rights" of the Palestinians. It urged member-states to respect Iraq's territorial integrity, and to sever military ties with Israel.[11] It rejected unilateralism and extra-territorial application of domestic laws and urged all states to consider the so-called D'Amato Law of the US as null and void. Finally, it condemned terrorism "while distinguishing terrorism from the struggle of peoples against colonial or alien domination or foreign occupation." It said that killing of innocents was forbidden in Islam, and urged the international community to "deny asylum to terrorists and assist in bringing them to justice."[12]

On the fringes, Khatami had a meeting with Iraqi vice-president, Taha Yassin Ramadan, who came instead of Saddam Hussein who had been invited. This was the first high-level contact between the two neighbors since their 1980–88 War. After the meeting Khatami said, "If we learn from the bitter experience of the past, we can have a fruitful future." Referring to historical ties between the two countries, he added, "The two brothers should use mild language with each other. Your pains and problems resulting from the aggressions of the great powers are regarded as our pains and problems." [13] He followed up this gesture with a congratulatory message to Saddam Hussein on the eve of the Muslim holy month of Ramadan, on December 31, 1997.[14]

Breaking with protocol, Khatami had two private meetings with Saudi Arabia's Crown Prince Abdullah, when the latter reportedly advised his host that Iran must convince Washington that it was no longer a threat to the Gulf monarchies. Since Abdullah also had a meeting with Ayatollah Khamanei, known for his hostility towards the US, which he routinely described as "the arrogant power," it was assumed that he conveyed a similar message to Khamanei as well.

American diplomats regarded the prestige that Iran gained from hosting the ICO summit as a setback to their policy of isolating Tehran. Much as they disliked the event they could not ignore it altogether. The US state department even found some nice words to say about the condemnation of terrorism in the Tehran Declaration. Responding to this, at his December 14 press conference Khatami referred to "the great American people," and added that he wanted a dialogue in "the not too distant future." The next day Clinton said that he would welcome that "as long as we have an honest discussion of all relevant issues" – meaning of course Iran's sponsorship of international terrorism and its efforts to acquire nuclear weapons.[15]

On January 7, 1998, Khatami gave a 45-minute interview to CNN in two parts – an unedited speech, followed by questions by Christiane Amanpour, an American journalist of Iranian origin. Khatami said, "First there must be a crack in this wall of distrust" between the two governments, and that "we must definitely consider the factors that led to severance of relations and try to eliminate them." He added, "If negotiations are not based on mutual respect, they will never lead to positive results." He then proposed an increase in the exchange of cultural, academic and sports delegations. In his answers to Amanpour, he said, "Iran feels no particular need for relations with America because it can obtain financial assistance through other sources, mainly European." Turning to domestic politics, he told her, "Differences of opinion are a natural consequence of a democratic system, and as long as the opposition [to him] operates within the constitutional framework I will tolerate its activities." Having expressed these views on CNN, Khatami declared on Iranian television that "The revolutionary tradition in foreign policy will continue."[16]

The next day, the US state department spokesman, James Rubin (who was later to marry Christiane Amanpour), confirmed that top US officials had watched the program. He said,

President Khatami's extensive comments with respect to US civilization and values were interesting. We appreciated the spirit in which those remarks were offered. We also noted the president's comments that the conduct of relations between nations must be based on mutual respect and dignity; we agree …. We noted with interest his regret concerning the hostage-taking [resulting from the November 1979 take-over of the US embassy in Tehran by Islamic revolutionaries that led to 444 days of captivity for the American hostages]. We welcome his statement that this period in Iranian history is over, and that the rule of law should be respected both domestically and internationally. On terrorism, President Khatami's rejection and condemnation of all forms of terrorism directed at innocents was noteworthy.

But, he added, "Characterizing our foreign policy since World War II as mistaken is also unfounded. Similarly, the characterization of the US–Israeli relationship was simplistic and wrong, and a continued reference to Israel as a racist, terrorist regime is not acceptable." Finally he said, "We will look closely at what President Khatami has said regarding people-to-people exchanges and people-to-people dialogue." But "The best way to address our bilateral differences would be to engage in a government-to-government dialogue." He then spelled out the three major subjects Washington wanted to discuss: Iran's support of international terrorism; its program to acquire nuclear weapons; and its opposition to the Middle East peace process.[17] Of course he made no mention of the subjects that Iran wanted to discuss, such as the US efforts to dominate the Gulf region and flood it with its weapons, and its strategic alliance with Israel, or the more specific Iranian demand of the unfreezing of its assets of some $10–12 billion in American banks.

It was noteworthy that a US official, explaining the Dual Containment policy, told Jane Hunter of the *Middle East International* that it was different in "motivation and application" in the two cases. "Iraq's government itself is problematic, incapable of being civilized and incapable of fulfilling its obligations." On the other hand, "Iran has a real government that has some political legitimacy." In electing Khatami last spring, "The [Iranian] people made a choice and said they wanted change." But Iran pursued policies that the US found problematic, and we seek to "change those policies through dialogue or pressure."[18]

As for Iran, it had its own agenda regarding Iraq, and pursued it irrespective of Washington's latest interpretation of its dual containment policy. Following Ramadan's successful visit to Tehran in December, the Iraqi foreign minister, Muhammad al Sahhaf, visited Tehran. The two countries set up five working committees on their outstanding disputes and to thrash out the details about the Iranian pilgrims to the Shia holy places in Iraq.

During the Iraq–UN crisis in February 1998, Iran showed its sympathy for Iraq. "The Americans are looking for a pretext for a military strike against Iraq," warned Ayatollah Hassan Rouhani, secretary-general of Iran's SNSC.[19] On the whole, though, Tehran kept a low profile, realizing that any overt interference by it would provide an excuse to Washington for even greater military presence in the Gulf. To Iran's relief, UN Secretary-General Annan defused the Iraqi crisis.

In early April the Iranian foreign minister announced that the two countries had agreed to exchange all remaining prisoners of war. The following month they launched their first joint search for the Iranian soldiers Missing in Action (MIAs). And finally, in August Iraq inaugurated a program to receive 3,000 Iranian visitors a week via the Iranian border town of Qasr-e Shirin to undertake a pilgrimage to the sites holy to Twelver Shias. The places were Najaf, Karbala, Kufa (containing the house of Imam Ali), Kadhimiya, a suburb of Baghdad (containing the shrines of two Shia Imams) and Samarra (where the last of the twelve Imams, Muhammad al Qasim, disappeared in 873A.D.). Two months later Iran and Iraq signed an accord to expand commerce, with Tehran agreeing to increase its food and medicine exports to Iraq under the UN oil-for-food scheme.[20]

Relations between Tehran and Washington too began to thaw. Iran gave visas to an American wrestling team in February 1998 to participate in the international Takhti tournament in Tehran. The wrestlers were allowed to display an American flag. They received such an enthusiastic welcome from the 12,000-strong audience that on the last day American wrestler Zeke Jones, holding up an Iranian flag and Khamanei's portrait, ran round the stadium to the chants of "Jones! Jones!" On that day the tournament's closing ceremony was attended by Speaker Nateq-Nouri, which implied Khamanei's approval of the Americans' presence in Tehran.

However, following the *New York Times'* story on March 26 that Washington had proposed posting a US Information Agency official at its Interest Section at the Swiss Embassy in Tehran, Iran acknowledged the report, but rejected the proposal.[21] Meanwhile, on the Iranian New Year – Spring Equinox, March 21 – Clinton sent a message of greetings to Khatami, hoping that "the day will soon come when the United States can once again enjoy good relations with Iran." Reciprocating the sentiment, Khatami had Clinton's message broadcast on the state-run radio.[22] Equally significantly, by now American spokesmen had stopped accusing Iran of complicity in the 1996 Khobar explosion in Saudi Arabia.

But in April, when a dozen Iranian wrestlers traveled to the US to participate in a tournament in Oklahoma, they were fingerprinted and photographed when they arrived at Chicago's airport. The 1991 instructions of the US Immigration and Naturalization Service (INS) required immigration officers to fingerprint and photograph first-time visitors from Iran, Iraq, Libya and Sudan, the countries listed by the state department as supporting international terrorism.[23]

The annual US state department report, published in May, described Iran as "the most active sponsor of state terrorism in 1997," with its agents held responsible for at least thirteen assassinations, mainly the anti-regime activists of the KDPI and the MKO, both based in Iraqi Kurdistan. Also, claimed the US document, Iran continued to provide money, training and weapons to various Middle East terrorist organizations like the (Palestinian) Islamic Jihad and Hamas, and that the leaders of various terrorist organizations had gathered the previous autumn in Tehran to discuss enhanced coordination and seek more funds."[24]

On the other hand, later that month, the Saudi kingdom publicly precluded Iran's involvement in the Khobar blast. Its interior minister, Prince Nayif, said,

"Saudi nationals alone were responsible for the bombing in June 1996 at the al Khobar complex near Dhahran airport." Iran was quick to respond. "The Saudi acknowledgment was a sign of courage on the part of the Saudi government," said its foreign minister Kharrazi.[25]

Riyadh's announcement disappointed Washington but did not cause it to alter its own course of action. Its Persian-language trial broadcasts by Radio Free Iran from the studios of Radio Free Europe/Radio Liberty (RFE/RL) in Prague went ahead in mid-May with a plan to launch a regular program in October. Tehran protested, saying that this was a violation of the 1981 Algiers Agreement, signed on the eve of the American hostages' release, whereby Washington agreed not to interfere in Iran's internal affairs; but to no avail.[26]

Just then America suffered a major diplomatic setback – at the hands of the European Union. Following a meeting in London of Clinton, British Premier Tony Blair, the current EU president, and Jacques Santer, president of the European Commission, on May 18, 1998, the US yielded to the EU on the issue of the ILSA and the earlier Burton-Helms Act, concerning trade with Cuba, with Santer repeating his condemnation of the American legislation as "illegal and counter-productive." Six months earlier the EU had lodged a formal complaint against Washington at the WTO in Geneva, challenging the American law, to be applied extra-territorially, on two grounds: it ran counter to the principle of free trade on which the WTO was built; and any punitive action taken under it against a non-American company or individual would violate the international law. After initial skirmishes the two sides decided on a truce, and told the WTO that they would try to settle the matter bilaterally. It soon became apparent that a solution could be found within the ILSA provision that permitted the US president to waive sanctions for a specific project on the grounds of "national interest" (Section 4c), or for those countries that had taken specific steps to counter state terrorism by Iran or Libya (Section 9c). At first Washington offered to grant a presidential waiver to Total SA on the basis of Section 4c. But the EU insisted on the Section 9c waiver. It succeeded at the London meeting.[27]

On his return to Washington, Clinton issued the waiver to the Total-led oil consortium with some reluctance, afraid that the Republican-majority Congress would deprive him of his right to waive sanctions. In the event, nothing of the sort happened. Indeed Senator Alfonso D'Amato, the Congressional sponsor of ILSA, and other Republicans encouraged the state department to press ahead with its review of the Iran policy, which resulted in Albright's speech on the subject a few weeks later.[28] (To show that he was not totally helpless in punishing those trading with Iran, in July – after Iran test-fired a medium-range missile, Shahab–3 – Clinton signed an executive order under the 1992 Iran–Iraq Nonproliferation Act, barring seven Russian organizations, including the Baltic State Technical University in St Petersburg, from receiving US financial assistance or trading their goods in America, for having assisted Tehran in its missile program.[29])

On June 17, addressing an Asia Society meeting in New York, Albright called for improved relations between America and Iran, and said that Washington was ready to have "a road map for normalization of relations." The following day Clinton said the US was seeking "a genuine reconciliation based on mutuality and reconciliation [with an Iran now] changing in a positive way under the reformist influence of President Muhammad Khatami." Significantly, a week later the Mobil Corporation took out a prominently displayed advertisement on one of the opinion-editorial pages of the *New York Times*, congratulating Albright for her initiative, and calling on "the US administration for some modest policy options that would engage Iran with the international community."[30]

In the World Cup football fixtures the match between Iran and America in Lyon, France, on June 21, ended with victory for the Iranian side. On its return to Tehran, the Iranian team was received ecstatically by hundreds of thousands of people, men and women alike, in the early hours of the morning, for having beaten the "Great Satan."

In mid-July US Attorney-General Janet Reno signed a regulation which allowed exemption to the 1991 immigration rule when such action was deemed to be "in the interest of foreign policy or national security." So later that month and in early August the INS made exceptions for the arriving Iranian wrestlers.

On the weightier, diplomatic issue, Khatami, in his conversation with twenty American journalists at the UN in September 1998, clarified the Iranian stance thus: "There seems to be a misinterpretation of what I have tried to say in this respect – and that is not to confuse a dialogue among people and cultures with political dialogue." He added that Tehran had no intention of opening a political dialogue with the US until it had taken "concrete steps to change its policies towards Iran."[31]

Much sharper statements came from Ayatollah Khamanei in his speech to thousands of Iranian students on the eve of the nineteenth anniversary of the US embassy seizure in early November. "Severing of relations between Iran and America has been to the 100 percent benefit of the Iranian people," he said. "The Americans only want to recover the position they had before the revolution … Our importance around the world and in the eyes of other peoples is based on our standing up to America." Referring to the economic problems facing Iran, he said, "Iran does not need America to overcome its economic crisis [due to low oil prices]. The rehabilitation and reform necessary to tackle Iran's economic problems requires the will and determination of the Iranian people and not relations with America."[32]

Conservatives strike back

By then public attention in Iran had been focused on the high-profile arrest and trial of Gholam Hussein Karbaschi, mayor of Tehran and secretary-general of the SOC, and the underlying issues it raised. He was charged with bribery, fraud and embezzlement of public funds, including a charge that he had sold five plots of land at 20 percent discount to the directors of the Tehran City Hall. But the Khatami government insisted that he was still the mayor and would conduct his affairs from prison. After his arrest in early April, he was refused bail and prison visits, and his access to his lawyer was restricted. A protégé of Rafsanjani, Karbaschi had transformed Tehran, a city of nine million (in the late 1990s), with cheap housing, new highways and provided more municipal services than ever before. He had the poor, seedy neighborhoods of southern Tehran cleaned up. On the negative side, he was ruthlessly ambitious, levied high taxes, and turned a blind eye to corruption. But then corruption was a national problem, not local. Faced with high inflation and low salaries, public service employees at all levels had taken to accepting bribes to survive. But the main reason for Karbaschi's arrest, said his supporters, was his successful launching of the *Hamshahri* (Fellow Citizens) which, with a circulation of 450,000, became the most popular daily, and its energetic backing for Khatami in the presidential race and later. The court's refusal to grant bail to Karbaschi created a crisis. After a meeting with Khatami, Rafsanjani, the head of the Expediency Consultation Council System, Yazdi, the judiciary chief, and Speaker Nateq-Nouri, Khamanei ordered that Karbaschi be released on bail, and defused the crisis.[33]

An open trial of Karbaschi began on June 7. The main charge against him pressed by Judge Gholam Hussein Muhsini Ejaei was that he had ordered a payment of $2.7 million to a private company without registering the transaction. Karbaschi denied the charge. He read out a letter from one of his top aides, Kamal Aziminia, whose statement had been used as evidence against Karbaschi. "When they [the investigators] brought me into court, I had been beaten so badly in prison with whips and clubs that I could hardly walk. They forced me to write and sign lies about myself and other prisoners and persons." In writing he had confessed to corruption and embezzlement at the municipality, and to providing illegal funds for Khatami's campaign.[34] Unprecedentedly, the authorities broadcast the trial twice daily on radio and television. It turned into a political opera and a vehicle for civic enlightenment for millions of viewers and listeners. In July Karbaschi was found guilty as charged and sentenced to five years in jail and 60 lashes, and ordered to pay a fine of R 1 billion ($330,000) to the government, and pay a further R 600 million ($200,000) to the municipality. He was also banned from any governmental job for twenty years. The next month Karbaschi appealed. But in December his appeal was rejected. Later Ayatollah Khamanei would intervene and reduce his sentence to two years in jail.

The Karbaschi episode highlighted two important aspects of the socio-political system in Iran. First, the three state organs – the executive, legislature and judiciary – were truly independent in practice, a feature that Iran's constitution had in common with Western democracies. Second, the Leader, elected by the Assembly of Experts electoral college, was the supreme authority in the country, and stood above the conventional organs of the state, a feature that set the Islamic Republic aside from Western republics.

Karbaschi's case and the way it was handled encouraged political debate that had started soon after Khatami's election a year earlier. Commenting on the current state of affairs in Iran, Foreign Minister Kharrazi said: "You have to see the trends in the whole system … Civil society is in the making." And referring to the lively press and increasing participation in political life by people as "very valuable in bringing about changes," he added, "But you should not expect the whole system to collapse, the constitution to change … President Khatami has his own ideas. He is pushing for them, but there are other trends in Iranian society. We have to see the outcome of these interactions."[35]

Earlier, on the first anniversary of his electoral victory, addressing a huge crowd in Tehran, Khatami, whose popularity rating held steady at 70 percent, had argued that a constitutional government, the rule of law and orderly social evolution were "intrinsic elements of a modern democracy," and that Islam was capable of providing a framework for political development along these lines. He warned that anarchy lay in store for a government which sought to ignore the vote of the majority.[36] The next day 20,000 students of conservative Qom seminaries held a rally protesting against Khatami's views. And a week later Nateq-Nouri was re-elected the Majlis speaker, with 165 (out of 258) MPs voting for him, a clear sign that the Majlis was out of step with the president.

In August, during a radio phone-in program as part of Government Week, Khatami stressed that any change had to be within the constitution.

> Our law, which is our constitution, has outlined the framework of that [legal] freedom, and has given the people the right to speak, think and express their views within that framework, and to place society in a position whereby its right to choose is enhanced.[37]

A practical result of this view of the president was that his government issued many licenses for new publications. Given Iranians' distrust of the state-run broadcasting system dating back to the era of the Shah, the print media was far more influential in Iran than in a Western country. The 890 publications in 1998 were nearly four times the figure during the unprecedented freedom that dawned after the Shah's fall. Whereas the 15 dailies accounted for most of the readership of 2 million in 1996, two years later the corresponding figures were 50 and 3.5 million. Ten of the new dailies were pro-Khatami – with *Hamshahri* topping the circulation table.[38] Whereas most of the conservative papers traced their origins to the Islamic revolution and the period soon after, the first properly reformist weekly, *Kiyan* (Existence), was founded only in 1992 after Khatami's resignation as minister of culture and Islamic guidance.

Some of the newly established publications began to push the boundaries within which the press had so far operated by printing articles that focused on the Leader, asking whether he derived his legitimacy from God – in which case he was infallible and above the law, which ran counter to the constitution's Article 107 that "The Leader is equal to the rest of the people of the country in the eyes of law" – or from the people, in which case he was fallible and could be removed from office by the popularly elected Assembly of Experts for Leadership which had appointed him in the first place. The warning in March 1998 by Rafsanjani that the current debate, though "necessary and constructive," was too sharp, was ignored by most reformist newspapers. One of their notable characteristics was that they did not give wide coverage to the activities of Ayatollah Khamanei, thus intentionally or unwittingly reducing his influence to shape public opinion, and another was that they did not shy away from attacking Rafsanjani, the second seniormost politician in the country.

Little wonder that the nature of the debate unleashed by the freshly established pro-reform press annoyed Khamanei and his close advisers, as did the criticism by the reformist press that the judiciary was dispensing political justice – that is, its verdicts were often politically motivated.

In mid-September 1998, within hours of Khamanei issuing an ultimatum against "the creeping excesses" of an increasingly free-wheeling press, and calling for a crackdown on "the enemies of the revolution in the press," the Press Court closed down the *Tous* (Peacock) edited by Mashaallah Shams al Wazien. The *Tous* had been launched after the *Jame* (Association), edited by Shams al Wazien, had been shut in June when its circulation had soared to 300,000 within five months of its launch, with the declared aim of defending civil society against the excesses of the state, and questioning the conventional wisdom of the social system. The longer-established *Salaam*, representing the Islamic left and edited by Khoeiniha, had been advocating a faster movement towards recognizing people's political rights within the constitution. Reflecting this phenomenon within society at large, there had been a parallel growth on university campuses of the reformist camp represented by the pro-Khatami University-Seminary Unity Consolidation Bureau (*Daftar-e Tahkim-e Vahdat-e Howze va Daneshgah*).

Acknowledging the change in popular opinion, the political establishment undertook horse-trading at the highest level behind the scenes. Ataollah Mohajerani, the reformist minister of culture and Islamic guidance, authorized to issue licenses for new publications, went along with the ban on the *Tous*. In exchange Khamanei went along with Khatami's moderate interpretation of Ayatollah Khomeini's fatwa on Salman Rushdie, thus paving the way for resumption of normal diplomatic ties with Britain, where the controversy had originated in 1989. There was a meeting between the Iranian and British foreign ministers at the UN in late September. "The British government and the EU do not support insults against religious sanctities," said Robin Cook, Britain's foreign minister. "Iran will not aid or reward anyone who kills Rushdie," said Kharrazi. He also disassociated his government from the 15 Khordad Foundation, which had offered $2.5 million for Rushdie's head. The two ministers then agreed to exchange ambassadors. The next day the 15 Khordad Foundation raised the bounty to $2.8 million, and 160 MPs issued a statement saying that Khomeini's fatwa was irrevocable, and that Muslims had a religious duty to implement it.[39]

As part of the above understanding, the leaders of the Ansar-e Hizbollah (*lit.*, Helpers of Hizbollah) were instructed (apparently by the Leader's office) to control their followers, some of whom had assaulted Mohajerani, and Abdullah Nouri, interior minister, after Friday prayers in Tehran in early September 1998. The Ansars behaved this way after they had legitimacy for their violent actions from some senior ultra-conservative theologians who condoned such behavior by individuals as a means of establishing a truly Islamic society if and when the state failed to do so. The most prominent among such clerics was Ayatollah Muhammad Taqi Mesbah-Yazdi, a religious teacher in Qom.[40] At the same time the investigation to find the assailants of Mohajerani and Nouri was intensified. It would lead to the arrest of three Ansars in January, and their sentencing to six to eighteen months in jail and 20 to 40 lashes.[41]

But on larger issues the reformist camp was in for disappointment. The Guardians Council disqualified 229 of the 396 candidates for the 86-member Assembly of Experts for Leadership to be elected on October 23, 1998. Some of them were rejected because they refused to take an obligatory examination to prove their theological expertise, others because they failed the test. However, the Council offered no official explanation because – in the words of its secretary-general, Ayatollah Jannati – "The Council does not want to confront anyone."[42] However, heeding the calls by such politicians as Faizeh Rafsanjani that the Assembly, hitherto monopolized by male clerics, should include women and pious laypersons, the Council ruled that non-clerics could be candidates if they met the high standards of religious expertise.

In practice, however, all 37 male and 9 female non-clerical candidates failed the theological test. And so did most of the pro-reform ones. The Islamic left refused to endorse any list after its candidates were rejected. The centrists, concentrated in the SOC, produced a skeleton list of theirs. This happened only after Rafsanjani intervened to reconcile the conservative and reformist camps, when the latter was persuaded not to issue a boycott call it had been considering seriously.[43]

Even then the voter turnout was only 50 percent, well below the 88 percent for the presidential poll. And the socio-political composition of the new Assembly – 54 conservatives, 16 reformists and 16 independent – came as no surprise.[44]

The debate on political reform continued against the background of a faltering economy mainly because of falling oil prices – at their lowest in four years – caused by a severe economic downturn in south-east Asia in the summer of 1997, and compounded by OPEC's decision in November, taken at Riyadh's behest, to raise output by 10 percent to 27.5 million bpd. Khatami's lack of personal experience of economic policy or public finance made matters worse. In any case, in his view, there was no realistic hope of fundamental economic revival until and unless some degree of political reform had been achieved.

At a growth rate of 1 percent and an inflation rate of 25, the economy was stagnant. It was creating only about the half the jobs needed to absorb the rising number of graduating students.[45] The government had been keen to curtail military expenditure, allocating it only 8 percent in its March 1998–February 1999 budget of some $50 billion, while maintaining the total cost of state subsidies at about 20 percent of the total.[46] With the falling price of oil – a commodity normally providing 30 percent of the annual budget revenue and three-quarters of foreign earnings – set to cut Iran's income in 1998 by about a third to $10.5 billion, the prospects for the economy looked bleak.

Little wonder that Rafsanjani had the Iranian oil minister, Bijan Zanganeh, in tow when he undertook a ten-day trip to Saudi Arabia in February 1998, which included an *umra*, a short hajj, by him. After his meeting with King Fahd the latter instructed his oil minister, Ali al Naimi, to increase cooperation with Iran to reach a "more just" price for oil, then fluctuating around $15 a barrel down from an average of $19.50 in 1997.[47] At this rate, Saudi petroleum exports income was expected to fall by a third in the current year from $45 billion in 1997.

The pressure of declining oil prices, combined with the US Iran–Libya Sanctions Act which – in the estimation of Ali Shams Ardekani, secretary-general of Iran's Chamber of Commerce, Industries and Mines – cut Tehran's normal annual oil income by 6 to 12 percent,[48] had made even the economic nationalists in the conservative camp realize that the only way to cope with the escalating demographic and economic pressures was to open up the oil industry to foreign investment. Indeed, in March 1997 the Majlis authorized the oil ministry to sign $5.4 billion worth of contracts with foreign companies during the financial year ending next February. The ministry's endeavor culminated in a seminar in London in September 1998 to interest foreign companies in its projects.

As it was, despite Washington's resolve to exclude Tehran from the oil and gas industry of former Soviet republics, Iran made steady progress there. In early June 1998 the NIOC invited tenders for a $400 million contract for a 250-mile (400-km) pipeline, between the Caspian port of Babol Sar and Tehran, to carry oil supplied by tanker by Kazakhstan and Turkmenistan, with the project to be finished by 2001. The pipeline was designed to handle 200,000 bpd, with Iran exporting the same amount from its Gulf ports to the customers of Kazakhstan and Turkmenistan.[49] Six months earlier Khatami and his Turkmen counterpart, President Saparmurad Niyazov, had inaugurated a 125-mile (200-km) pipeline to carry natural gas from Turkmenistan's Korpeje gasfield to Kord-Kui in northeast Iran. The initial 2 billion m^3 of gas to be pumped annually were to be raised first to 4 billion m^3 in 1999, and then to double that amount. Iran funded the $200 million project, with Turkmenistan, short of foreign exchange, repaying its share of the cost in gas deliveries. As neither Iran nor Turkmenistan approached the World Bank or the IMF – dominated by America – for loans to finance the project, the US never got a chance to veto it.[50]

Unlike in the West, there was little interest at the official or popular level in the Muslim-majority Central Asian republics, ruled by authoritarian leaders of the Soviet era, as to how the struggle for political reform was going in Iran.

11

POLITICAL REFORM
AND REACTION

At home the modern middle class was shocked by the assassinations of several writers and dissident politicians in late 1998. In November three authors, who were in the process of founding a secular Writers Association, were kidnapped and killed, and their corpses thrown in the streets of Tehran. The next month 70-year-old Dariush Foruhar, a leader of the secular National Front, and his wife, Parvane, were fatally stabbed at home by someone who had made an appointment to see him. Ayatollah Khamanei strongly condemned the murders and instructed the intelligence agencies to apprehend the culprits. Declaring that "Islam is a religion of compassion," he alleged that unrest was being promoted by "Islam's enemies" and "foreign elements."[1] Khatami appointed a three-member committee, consisting of the intelligence minister, Qorban Ali Najafabadi, the interior minister, Abdul Wahid Musavi-Lari, and a representative of Leader Khamanei.

On 12 January the committee announced the arrest of ten suspects, some of them intelligence ministry agents. Six of them were later released. The remaining four worked for the intelligence ministry, and included a deputy minister, Said Imami, who had held this job since 1990 despite the purported disapproval of Presidents Rafsanjani and Khatami. They were alleged to have a death list which included Abbas Abdi, a prominent reformist journalist.[2] Najafabadi said that "evil and deviant agents" within his ministry were responsible for "the monstrous crimes which have brought the Islamic system into disrepute." Conservative politicians joined the chorus of condemnation that followed. And reformists claimed that conservative Najafabadi had been "imposed" on Khatami and that it was high time the ministry was restructured. Khatami acted. In late February he replaced Najafabadi with Ali Yunusi, who won the endorsement of 197 MPs.

The pro-reform press was rife with rumors and revelations. And in mid-June the plot thickened when the chief judicial investigator revealed on television that Imami had hanged himself in his cell. "Iranians are not used to such transparency about matters of this kind and the revelations have left them perplexed and confused," reported Saeed Barzin in the *Middle East International*.

Until recently the intelligence ministry was spoken of only in hushed voices, in dark corners or in private places. Now newspapers – which are becoming more investigative and independent in their newly found and jealously guarded freedom – have pounced on the story like hungry beasts. They are cornering the ministry of intelligence and clawing for more information and explanations … A former intelligence minister, Ali Fallahian, is already being implicated in the press.[3]

This case and Imami's alleged actions would hang over Iranian politics like a cloud for almost a year.

Soon after the twentieth anniversary of the Islamic Revolution on February 11, Iran had its first local elections – thirteen years after the law on them had been passed – an exercise that Khatami described as "a giant step towards decentralization which is a goal of my government."[4] Equally importantly, this poll was expected to engender a new class of elected officials with a vested interest in local politics, and committed to Khatami's vision of a civil society.

There was another unique feature of the latest poll. Whereas vetting for the candidates for the president, parliament or Assembly of Experts was conducted by the Guardians Council, vetting for municipal candidates was done by the Election Supervisory Board, appointed by the Majlis, which worked in conjunction with the interior ministry. So the number of candidates shot up dramatically, especially in cities. In Tehran, for instance, there were 1,400 hopefuls for the 15-member local Islamic Council. Overall though there were only 330,000 candidates – including 5,000 women – for 200,000 Council seats to run local government in cities, towns and villages, which involved electing mayors and supervising local budgets.

So, almost overnight, the latest electoral exercise created a vast body of politicians with varied backgrounds and viewpoints. They ranged from mullahs and hardline Islamic ideologues to professionals with Western training and former aristocrats. The campaign in cities was lively – with candidates holding rallies, and plastering cars and city walls with fliers and posters. They published a variety of manifestos, and debated such issues as pollution, male–female relationships and various freedoms. The media gave extensive coverage to the campaign, thus raising popular interest.

Of the nearly 39 million Iranians above 15 and eligible to vote, more than 24 million did so. At 62 percent, the voter participation in Iran's local elections was higher than in the American presidential poll with an average voter turnout of around 50 percent. The high turnout and an impressive win by moderates indicated that Khatami's attempt to extend the framework of democracy had a popular backing.

In local elections, as in parliamentary ones, there was an absence of recognized political parties. But in big cities like-minded politicians put together a common list under an attractive slogan. For example, in Tehran, reformist Abdullah Nouri – managing editor of the *Khordad* (the Iranian month when Khatami was elected president), a popular daily – headed the list entitled "Islam of love." At the other end was a group of conservatives who tried to win popular support on the slogan of "Islam and clean air" – well aware of the heavy pollution that beset the national capital. But the "Islam of love" slate won all fifteen seats on the city's Islamic Council.

In most of the twenty-five major cities, the reformist coalition consisting of the recently formed Islamic Iranian Participation Front (IIPF, popularly known as Mosharekat, i.e., Participation) and the centrist SOC won. In Tehran they secured all the seats. In Isfahan and Shiraz they won handsome majorities. But in the holy cities of Qom and Mashhad they lost to conservatives. By contrast, in 700 towns and 33,000 villages, most winners were independent, more focused on local affairs than national politics. Interestingly, in Hamadan the majority of the seats went to women.

For Iranians it was their first-ever experience of grass-roots politics. This, and a feeling among ordinary citizens that the recent poll gave them a real voice in the running of local affairs was expected to liberalize the political system set up in the heat of a revolution and consolidated during the eight years of a bloody war with Iraq.

On the second anniversary of his electoral victory, May 23, Khatami addressed 100,000 newly elected local councilors, reassuring them that freedom was compatible with Islam, and that freedom of expression and association within the law would not lead to moral or social anarchy. In private he had been reassuring senior theologians that "political freedom will not undermine the authority of religion."[5]

As a sign of the times, and for the first time since the 1979 revolution, the regime fully approved Nawruz (*lit.*, New Day) – Iranian New Year – festivities. Hundreds of thousands of city dwellers began a fortnight-long holiday on the day of the spring equinox. Despite the Islamic revolution, the pre-Islamic Nawruz, celebrated *inter alia* by jumping over fire and having family reunions, never lost its importance at the popular level, and remained an official holiday. Indeed, on the first Nawruz after assuming the office of Leader in June 1989, Khamanei gave an official reception for the nation's dignitaries and MPs, and explained the significance of Nawruz and the traditions attached to it.

The slogan "Islamic government, Iranian identity" aptly summed up the ideology of the regime, which perceived the revolution as specifically Iranian and fostered Islam as the primary instrument to create and maintain national cohesion. More specifically, it was a particular interpretation of Islam, sanctified by the regime and enshrined in the constitution, that had to be safeguarded, and any criticism of it was to be suppressed. It was therefore not surprising that when Hojatalislam Muhsin Kadivar, argued that the concept of vilayat-e faqih (i.e., Rule of Jurisprudent) on which the Iranian constitution was founded was an innovation in Islam, which was not allowed, he angered the religious–political establishment. In April 1999 the Special Court for Clergy (SCC) tried him on charges of spreading lies and fomenting public unrest, found him guilty, and gave him an 18-month prison sentence. He was a popular teacher at seminaries, and his conviction led to student protest, which fizzled out. But, interestingly, his books propounding his unconventional ideas remained unbanned.

In foreign affairs, the Iran–America minuet, which had started with Khatami describing the 1979 American hostage-taking as "a tragedy" in a CNN interview in early 1998, continued. "I think it is important to recognize that Iran, because of its enormous geopolitical importance over time has been the subject of quite a lot of abuse from various Western nations," said Clinton on April 12, 1999.

> And I think sometimes it's quite important to tell people, look, you have a right to be angry at something my country or my culture or others that are generally allied with us today did to you 50 or 60 or 100 or 150 years ago. So we have to find some way to get dialogue [started] – and going into denial when you're in conversation with somebody who's been your adversary, in a country like Iran [which] has often worried about its independence and its integrity, is not exactly the way to begin.[6]

Later that month, Clinton signed an executive order permitting US exports of food and medicine to Iran, Libya and Sudan even though they continued to be on his administration's terrorist states list. The reasons given by the state department's undersecretary for business and economic affairs, Stuart Eizenstat, were that denying food and medicine hurts innocent people, damages the US image, strains relations with friendly (European) countries, and has little impact on the targeted governments or leaders.[7]

But Tehran considered this gesture inadequate. Its response came on July 2 on the eve of the eleventh anniversary of the downing of the Iran Air carrier by the US navy in the Gulf, killing 290 people. Addressing the Friday prayer congregation in Tehran, Rafsanjani said that two major crimes committed by America were shooting down an Iranian civilian aircraft and freezing Iran's assets, estimated to be worth more than $10 billion.[8]

Street riots in Tehran

A few days later Iranians became engrossed in the longest street protest in Tehran since the revolution. On July 7, the Majlis passed the first reading of a bill to amend the existing Press Law by 125 to 90 (with 55 MPs deliberately abstaining to deprive the house of its quorum, a plan which failed). The existing Press Law had been shepherded through the Majlis originally in 1985 by Khatami as minister of culture and Islamic guidance. The new bill required newspaper publishers to submit the list of their employees to the judiciary, and journalists to reveal their sources, and empowered the Press Court to overrule jury verdicts, conduct summary trials, and pass on extremely serious cases to revolutionary courts, charged with prosecuting those accused of such serious high crimes as treason and endangering national security.

This event coincided with the closure of the *Salaam*, edited by Ayatollah

Khoeiniha, after it had published a secret memorandum that detailed efforts by Said Imami of the intelligence ministry to rein in the pro-Khatami media. It was the same Imami who had been allegedly implicated in the assassinations of the intellectuals. The intelligence ministry complained to the court that by publishing a confidential document the *Salaam* had created doubts in the public mind. And the SCC summoned Khoeiniha to its chamber.

Late on July 8, about 500 Tehran University students held a peaceful protest meeting about the *Salaam*'s closure at the university dormitory complex in Amirabad, a Tehran suburb, several kilometers from the downtown campus. They were attacked by Ansar-e Hizbollah activists.

During the night of July 8–9 some LEF units attacked the university dormitories and killed one off-duty soldier who was staying as a guest, injured many, and arrested about 200 students. According to the LEF, some officers had entered the dormitories earlier without authorization and were taken hostage, and so other officers, also acting without orders, stormed the hostels to rescue their colleagues.

The next day the students first demanded punishment for those who had attacked their residence halls, and then added other, wider demands, including a thorough political reform, and an end to the conservatives' grip on certain important organs of state power. At the Tehran University campus, protesting students were joined by their colleagues from other universities and colleges. The single most important student body was the pro-reform University-Seminary Unity Consolidation Bureau, which had emerged from the earlier Islamic Associations among students. Some 10,000 protesters rallied and blocked the main thoroughfare. Others began a sit-in. When Khamanei's representative arrived to address the students, he was heckled and driven away. The protesters then marched to the interior ministry (in charge of the LEF), shouting, "Death to Despotism, Death to Dictators," and clashing with the LEF on the way. Some protesters shouted, "Freedom or Death" while others, more daring, "Khamanei must quit." The pro-reform press gave wide coverage to the events.

On July 10, the Supreme National Security Council, chaired by Khatami, condemned the LEF raid, and appointed a committee of inquiry. Khatami's statement, read on the state-run radio, stated that the SNSC had dismissed the LEF captain whose unit had stormed the student dormitories, reprimanded the LEF commander of the Tehran region, Brig. Gen. Farhad Nazari, ordered the release of all detained students, and promised compensation for those injured. The SNSC also promised to scrutinize radical rightwing vigilante groups like the Ansar-e Hizbollah.[9] Later the LEF commander-in-chief, Gen. Hedayat Loftian, would tell a closed session of the Majlis that 98 LEF personnel had been arrested for raiding the dormitories. And the number of Ansars arrested would reach 100.[10] The SNSC coupled its statement about the dismissals and arrests with a warning that no further demonstrations should be held without the prior permission of the interior ministry.

However, the following day the protest spread to universities in Isfahan,

Tabriz, Mashhad, Yazd and Hamadan despite the fact that Ayatollah Khamanei condemned the dormitory raids as "a bitter and unacceptable incident." The authorities imposed a blanket ban on meetings and demonstrations. Among the protesters a split developed, with the moderate majority arguing that they had achieved their aim of highlighting their backing for the *Salaam* and political reform. It was the radical minority among university students which disagreed and took to the streets, inadvertently providing a foil for disgruntled non-students to escalate the protest. The demonstration on July 13, when a section of the protesters shouted "People are hungry, but the clergy live like kings", turned bloody. Rioting erupted, and there were running battles between the demonstrators and the LEF now backed by the paramilitary Baseej. At the Grand Bazaar in south Tehran rioters set ablaze two banks. With the mild protest escalating into anti-regime riots, President Khatami had no choice but to condemn the unrest as harshly as did Khamanei. That evening in a television speech Khatami deplored the destruction of buildings in the city center and the Grand Bazaar, and pointed out that some of those arrested had no links with academic circles and were not even students. He added that a peaceful protest by students had degenerated into a riot led by "people with evil aims [who] intend to foster violence in society," and declared that "We shall stand in their way." Defense Minister Ali Shamskhani added his voice, saying that order would be restored "at any price." In practice, the security forces achieved this aim without having to resort to shooting. As Tehran's LEF commander, Brig. Gen. Farhad Ansari, said later, "The turmoil that followed the attack on the students' dormitories on July 9 was controlled by the LEF without the firing of a single bullet." [11] Such restraint by riot police in a Third World country was rare. Nonetheless the episode created tensions within the establishment. Privately, twenty-four IRGC commanders addressed a letter to Khatami warning him that their patience was running out and that he must curb violations against the Islamic system.[12]

On July 14, the political–clerical establishment banded together. The followers of both Khatami and Khamanei joined hands to organize a popular show of support for the regime. In Tehran between 500,000 and 1 million people participated in a peaceful march. Addressing the vast rally Ayatollah Hassan Rouhani, the SNSC's secretary-general, said, "We will resolutely and decisively quell any attempt to rebel." He coupled this with a promise that "security agencies will continue probing the tragic dormitory incident until all the roots which caused the incident are investigated and reported to the public." (The SNSC committee's report later cleared Gen. Loftian, and blamed a number of Tehran LEF captains, who acted "more out of anger than necessity." Also, it concluded, that far-right vigilantes – meaning Ansar-e Hizbollah – played a significant role in provoking the LEF to attack the students, and called on the intelligence ministry to investigate them.)

Both Rouhani and Khamanei went out of their way to say that students played an outstanding role in society and were its valued members. But there were certain sociological and historical facts that the leaders like them had to face and overcome. Between 1979 and 1996 whereas the population nearly doubled, the student body rose almost threefold, from 7 to 19 million, with 700,000 at universities and colleges of higher education. This section of the populace had no direct experience or memory of the pre-Islamic regime of the Shah, and therefore their commitment to the Islamic regime was less than total. "More than half of the 65 million Iranians are under 21," said Shirzad Bozorgmehr, a senior Iranian journalist.

> They have no direct experience or memory of how things were under the Shah, and the clergy have yet to find a way to get through to them. The post-revolutionary educational system has not socialized them in the way they would like.[13]

A recent study in Iran revealed that whereas 83 percent of university students watched television, only 5 percent watched religious programs. Of the 58 percent who read books other than textbooks, barely 6 percent showed interest in religious literature.[14]

The six-day-long student protest, which was reported at length and without censorship by foreign journalists based in Iran, aroused much interest and comment in the West, especially America. James Rubin of the US state department said, "We have made it clear that we are concerned by the use of violence to put down demonstrations by Iranian students in support of freedom of expression and democratic values and the rule of law."[15] This drew immediate official protest from Tehran, but that did not stop the US Senate passing a resolution in early August condemning "the repressive actions taken by the Iranian government against the democratic movement in Iran." On August 20, addressing the Friday prayers congregation in Tehran, Ayatollah Ahmad Jannati said,

> The American support for the [student] agitators is an attempt to overthrow the Islamic regime. The enemy wants to insinuate that it was the fault of the regime [which caused riots] whereas the attack [on the student dormitory] was the work of certain police officers, and there was no link between them and the government.[16]

Courts and pro-reform press

On July 25, the SCC's verdict went against the *Salaam*'s managing editor, Khoeiniha. The 9-member jury found him guilty under Articles 608 and 698 of the Criminal Law for publishing a classified document, slandering provincial officials and accusing MPs and the late Said Imami of complicity in an anti-press campaign, thus inciting public opinion and spreading lies. He was deprived of becoming an editor for three years, and his newspaper was banned for five years.[17]

In mid-August reformists saw a ray of hope when Khamanei appointed centrist Ayatollah Mahmoud Hashemi Shahroudi as head of the judiciary after the allowable second five-year tenure of the incumbent, Muhammad Yazdi, ran out. A diehard conservative, Yazdi had gained a fearsome reputation for giving too much power to the dreaded revolutionary courts, which dealt with high crimes, and favored political appointments of judges. Born in 1948 of Iranian parents in Najaf, Iraq, Sharoudi received his theological education in Qom. Before his appointment as the chief judicial official, he was a clerical member of the Guardians Council, which gave him a seat also on the ECCS. A quiet, scholarly man, he was acceptable to both conservatives and reformers.

Shahroudi declared that the judiciary would not align itself with any political faction and that it would continue its crusade against bribery and corruption. He sacked several key judiciary officials, and they included graduates of the hardline Haqqani Seminary in Qom and members of the conservative Miscellaneous Islamic Committees. He promised judicial reform, consulted independent lawyers on the subject, and appointed outsiders to see it through. But the reform was not going to be easy. "The judiciary has an extremely complicated structure," said an academic expert on constitutional law in Tehran. "It contains a massive load of laws, rules and regulations that have been in force and have become institutionalized. At the same time we have political elements that act like parasites. Because of this, reform will be very difficult."[18]

When, on September 5, the Press Court decided to suspend the six-month-old pro-reform *Neshat* (Vibrant), which had the third highest circulation, it did not even bother to inform Shahroudi. And the announcement by the Revolutionary Court that the four accused in the July student protest could face execution (for endangering national security) came as a surprise to him.[19]

The suspension of the *Neshat* – the successor to the previously shut *Jame* and *Tous* – came after it published an article questioning the legitimacy of capital punishment in Islam, thus challenging the "eye for an eye" principle enshrined in the Sharia – as well as an unsigned letter by "a veteran politician," believed to be an opposition figure with a secularist background, which, while questioning Leader Khamanei's authority (an illegal act), urged him to switch sides from conservatives to reformers. After trying Latif Safari, the newspaper's managing director, the Press Court found him guilty of insulting the basic tenets of the Quran and fanning student protest in July, and sentenced him to thirty months in jail and barred him from journalism for five years.[20]

While disagreeing with the Press Court, the culture and Islamic guidance minister Mohajerini called on reformist publications to exercise restraint so as not to give conservatives pretexts for action against them. This was seen as a conciliatory move which was soon reciprocated at the highest level. On October 1, 1999, delivering a sermon on the 100th birthday of Ayatollah Khomeini (according to the Islamic calendar), Khamanei said in the presence of Khatami, "The authorities today are pious. The President is a cleric, he is pious, he loves the household of the Prophet, and he is working for the rebirth of Islam." He then went on to attack those who were attempting to drag the government into the controversy surrounding the two-page satirical sketch, *Resurrection of the Messiah at the University Examination Time*, that had arisen recently. The short scene written by two students and published in a college journal with a circulation of fifty, depicted a student refusing to accompany the reappeared Twelfth Imam of Shias (who disappeared in 873 A.D.) to fight the forces of darkness because he had to sit for a university entrance examination the next day. Khamanei suggested that the insult to the Disappeared Imam might turn out to be an innocent mistake.[21] That meant ruling out the death sentence demanded by rightwing hardliners. (In the event, one of the two authors got a three-year jail sentence.) Later in the week in another sermon Khamanei lashed out at those who were trying to take the law into their own hands, a thinly disguised reference to such radical right vigilantes as the Ansar-e Hizbollah.

A far more serious case opened on October 12, when the SCC summoned Hojatalislam Abdullah Nouri, managing editor of the *Khordad*, to answer the charges of opposing the views of Ayatollah Khomeini and publishing sacrilegious articles. A native of Husseinabad in the Isfahan province, Nouri was 30 at the time of the revolution. He was elected an MP to the First Majlis, and was close to Khomeini who appointed him his representative to the IRGC. Under President Rafsanjani he became the interior minister, a post he occupied until 1993. He returned to this post under President Khatami in August 1997. In that capacity he sacked several hundred rightwing hardliners from the ministry. He appointed some sixty new provincial governors who became a driving force behind political reform. This displeased the conservative Majlis which passed a motion of no-confidence in him in June 1998. Khatami then appointed him vice-president, an office he left to launch the *Khordad*, which soon became the most popular daily. This made him the prime target of conservatives.

After the initial hearing, the SCC, in a 44-page indictment, formally accused Nouri of using his newspaper to insult Prophet Muhammad and his direct descendants, and Shia Imams; oppose the teachings of Khomeini; support banned political parties such as the Liberation Movement of Iran and the National Front; and propose friendly ties with America and Israel.[22]

At his trial, which opened on October 30, he refused to recognize the SCC. It had been set up by Khomeini by a personal decree in the mid-1980s as an *ad hoc* measure to deal specifically with clerical malfeasance, and it had a prosecutor, a judge and a 9-member jury, all appointed by Ayatollah Khomeini. Functioning outside the judicial system, it reported directly to him. Even the amended constitution of 1989 made no mention of it. Under Leader Khamanei it continued to function as before. Nouri reasoned that not even the Leader had the right to establish courts outside the constitution. The judge overruled his argument.[23]

During the two-week open trial, Nouri defended himself for three days. Replying to the charge of challenging the absolute authority of the Leader, he cited Article 107 which said that "The Leader is equal to all people of the country in the eyes of the law." Therefore, ran his argument, the Leader was in essence equal to the general population, and like any other individual had rights and duties, and had to obey the law, and possessed no powers above those granted to him under the constitution. Nouri reiterated his support for Ayatollah Hussein Ali Montazeri who had been put under house arrest after he had questioned the religious credentials of Khamanei.[24]

He stressed that Islam was not monolithic, and that he favored that version of it which recognized the right of the people to choose their own destiny, and which used state authority to serve the people rather than rule them. In foreign affairs he advocated full support for the Palestinian Authority rather than Hamas or the Islamic Jihad, and an acceptance of the current Middle East peace process. He also called for direct negotiations with Washington and the strengthening of the pro-Iranian lobby in the US, arguing that this would enhance Iran's international standing.[25]

Unlike in the case of Karbaschi, the state-run television refused to broadcast Nouri's trial. But his long written statement in his defense proved so popular that the pro-reform press published it as a series of articles, and the authorities refrained from interfering.

Again, unlike what happened in Karbaschi's trial concerning corruption and embezzlement, the charges against Nouri were in essence political, and his trial centered on the argument that lay at the heart of the debate in the Islamic Republic: should Islam be viewed as a monolithic ideology and value system (as conservative hardliners insisted) or as an ideology supple enough to adapt to the demands of modernity (as reformists wanted)? "The trial has opened a new way for us reformers to express our views," said Muhammad Reza Khatami, the leader of the leftist IIPF. "The political nature of the indictment against Nouri gave him a chance to express his views about social and political issues." And the pro-reform *Sobh-e Emruz* (Daily Morning) wrote, "Nouri's defense showed that one could offer a rational interpretation of the values and principles of the Islamic revolution, an interpretation that is different from the official readings broadcast by the propaganda speakers of the monopolist faction."[26]

According to many observers, underlying the specific charges against Nouri was a hidden agenda of conservatives – to bar him from contesting the forthcoming Majlis elections when, following his almost certain victory as the most popular MP of Tehran, he would emerge as the most eligible candidate for Speaker.

On November 11, the jury found Nouri guilty on fifteen counts. And a fortnight later the judge sentenced him to five years in jail. Addressing pro-reform MPs at the Majlis building on November 28, Khatami hoped Nouri would be able to return to politics. "It is to the detriment of the revolution, system and society if an impression is created that an individual's views are confronted in any other way than a satisfying analytical approach."[27]

Soon thereafter came up the case of Mashaallah Shams al Wazien, the former *Neshat* editor, who had set up the *Asr-e Azadegan* (Age of the Free) in October – his fourth newspaper in two years, all of them funded by members of a rising business class which backed political reform. The charges against him pertained to some objectionable pieces in the *Neshat*. When brought to the Press Court in early November, he tore up its documents, protesting at the "medieval inquisition" concerning the articles questioning the legitimacy of capital punishment in Islam. His case was not to be settled until next April when, like Latif Safari before him, he was given a 30-month jail sentence.

Iran, America and Iran's oil industry

In the ongoing battle between the pro-reform press and the conservative judiciary, the US refrained from public comment. And, despite the chill caused by the statements of the state department on the student protest in Iran, and the subsequent US Senate resolution on the subject, Clinton reportedly addressed a letter to Khatami in August, asking for Tehran's assistance to American officials investigating the Khobar bombing in Saudi Arabia, which was passed on to him by Sultan Qaboos of Oman. The request was based on US intelligence reports linking the bombing to three Saudi men who, it was believed, had taken refuge in Iran. They were said to be affiliated to the Saudi Hizbollah. The FBI was not satisfied with the information given to it by the Saudi authorities, and wanted to question these suspects. In return for his cooperation, Clinton promised better relations with Iran.[28]

In late August, John Limbert, an American state department official, speaking in Persian on the US-funded Radio Liberty, said that Washington was ready to enter into negotiations "without any preconditions." This was a departure from the previous position of the Clinton administration which had insisted on discussing only those issues that concerned it.

But Tehran was not satisfied. It wanted reduction in hostility as a precondition for direct negotiations. Its concerns were:

1 the 1996 Iran-Libya Sanctions Act,
2 the freezing of Iran's assets in America,
3 US interference in Iran's economic relations with the Central Asian republics,
4 pressuring Iran's neighbors to adopt anti-Iranian policies, and
5 beaming hostile broadcasts at Iran.

At the same time there was no softening in Leader Khamanei's stance. He declared that "the re-establishment of relations with America is a dream [of Americans] that will never come true," and that it was impossible to "show leniency" towards America because it was trying "to take control out of the hands of the Iranian government."[29] During his visit to France in late October, Khatami expressed a softer version of Khamanei's declaration. "It is necessary for one who has been an oppressor to try to put aside oppression and try to change policy," he told a group of journalists in Paris.[30]

In November, Washington proposed that as part of people-to-people exchanges, American consular officials should visit Iran periodically to promote such exchanges. James Rubin, the state department spokesman, said, "It is high time for Iran to allow such visits since we give routine permission to Iranian officials to visit the US to have contacts with private American citizens." Khamanei would have none of it. "The American interest in sending officials to Iran is to open an office for intelligence and political activities, and forge ties with their mercenaries," he said.[31]

Washington responded in kind. "The US has no intention of changing its policy of 'containing' Iran through economic sanctions while seeking a dialogue with the Iranian government – an overture Tehran has rejected so far – and promoting people-to-people exchanges among academics, athletes and the like," reported John Lancaster in the *Washington Post* on December 5, 1999. The previous day the immigration officers at the John F. Kennedy airport had photographed and fingerprinted Iranian clerics invited to attend a seminar on Islam and secularism at Georgetown University in Washington, DC, and caused the protesting mullahs to return home. Since visiting Americans were not photographed and fingerprinted in Iran, Tehran objected to Washington's practice.

Also the continued enforcement of the 1996 US Anti-Terrorism and Effective Death Penalty Act meant that the Clinton administration was required to lobby against any financial assistance to Iran – something Tehran could have done with, especially in 1998, when its oil income fell to $10.5 billion – by the IMF or the World Bank. With annual inflation officially at 20 percent, unemployment at 15 percent and economic growth at 2 percent (versus the predicted 5 percent), the economy was just limping along.[32]

In March 1999, at the behest of Iran, now the second largest producer in OPEC, the cartel cut 1.7 million bpd from its current output of 23 million bpd, with four cooperating non-OPEC countries – Mexico, Norway, Oman and Russia – reducing their production by 400,000 bpd.[33] The subsequent improvement in oil prices lifted Iran's oil revenue in 1999 to $13 billion at an average output of 3.52 million bpd.

The July rioting in Tehran increased the Iranian government's resolve to improve the economy, which had been ailing due to the depressed petroleum prices that prevailed from December 1997 to March 1999. Its prime tool to do so was raising its oil and gas production capacity.

Over the past quarter of a century the record of Iran's oil industry had been turbulent.

Following the trebling of petroleum prices in 1973–74, the Shah increased output sharply. It reached 6 million bpd in 1974, and was achieved by over-exploiting oil wells. During the revolutionary turmoil in 1978 the production was 5.3 million bpd.

After the 1979 revolution and the start of the First Gulf War in September 1980, output fell to 1.4 million bpd. It then rose but stagnated around 2.5 million bpd due to the war. After the war the output rose steadily to 3.6 million bpd.[34] But, overall, the industry had suffered due to the 1980s war which had raged in the oil-bearing region, chronic under-investment, a ban on oil and gas concessions to foreign companies, and the US sanctions.

The March 1995–February 2000 Five Year Plan called for an investment of $30 billion in oil and gas, with $9 billion to come from abroad. By mid–1998 Iran had signed up $4 billion in foreign investment. Also the NIOC set up new subsidiaries such as Naftgaran Engineering Service Company for exploration and development, and Iranian Offshore Engineering and Construction Company for offshore projects.[35]

In March 1998 the Majlis passed a law entitled, "Utmost Capacity of Local Technical and Engineering and Industry, and How to Materialize Projects and Facilities in order to Export." That is, it approved the Khatami government's plan to open much of the oil and gas sector, including onshore fields, to foreign companies.

Clinton's failure to apply sanctions under ILSA to the Total-led oil consortium in May 1998 was a breakthrough for Iran. It removed a major hurdle to large-scale foreign investment in its oil sector, and encouraged interest from European companies, especially British – BG (British Gas), Enterprise, Lasmo and Monument. In Iran it helped break down resistance to a more ambitious foreign investment program. In August the Iranian oil ministry unveiled 43 projects worth $8 billion before seventy foreign companies in London. Of the US companies, Mobil and Arco officially informed Iran that they were interested in the projects. Others expressing interest were Chevron, Conoco, Kerr-Mcgee and Unocal.

In March 1999 Elf, Agip of Italy and Bow Valley of Canada signed a four-year $540 million deal on Doroud offshore field with reserves of 7.5 billion barrels. This would increase oil output from 130,000 bpd to 220,000 bpd. And in April Elf and Bow Valley signed a contract for Balal offshore field. In late 1999 Royal Dutch-Shell signed an $840 million contract for Soroush and Nawruz offshore oilfields.

Explaining the procedure for selecting the winner of a bid, an NIOC official in Tehran said that the oil ministry made a short-list of four to six bidders after it had examined their overall track record, financial state and capacity to raise loans. Then it talked to each company separately. Next, its Technical Committee examined the track record of each company in a specific area – augmenting the present capacity, exploring, developing a virgin field, etc. – and how advanced its technology was in that field. Finally, it estimated what the chances were for NIOC employees of picking up the new technology during the project period which was often four to five years. Then its Economic Committee examined the price that the bidder was demanding for its services. Then the oil ministry reduced the list to two, and tried to play off one bidder against the other. "Just as in a football match, at the 89th minute nobody knows the winner, so also here," said the NIOC official. "The winner comes up at the last minute."[36] On the advice of the NIOC, the oil minister made his recommendation to the 10-member Supreme Economic Council (SEC), chaired by the President, since it was the SEC which handled contracts of international importance impinging on foreign policy.[37] The SEC's decision was then endorsed by Leader Khamanei. Because of the highly technical nature of the oil and gas industry, the SEC invariably endorsed the oil minister's recommendation.

Due to successive cutbacks in OPEC output in 1999, the petroleum price improved from $13 a barrel in the previous year to $18. This raised Iran's oil revenue by $2.5 billion to $13 billion in 1999, enabling it to reduce its long- and short-term foreign loans by about a quarter, to $11.6 billion. At home, though, the workforce was rising by 4 percent annually whereas the GDP growth was only half as much. The official privatization program was faltering due to lack of private capital.[38] And the government had failed to reduce the cost of subsidizing food and gasoline by targeting them at underprivileged groups. The $10 billion spent annually on state subsidies continued to drain the public exchequer and had a deleterious effect on the economy.

The Majlis poll

Curiously, economics did not figure in the debate that was in progress as the country prepared for the elections to the Sixth Majlis in mid-February 2000. Reformists feared that the conservative Guardians Council would veto candidates from their camp on a large scale. But this was not to be. Of the 6,800 aspiring candidates for the 290 Majlis seats (increased from the previous 270), only 11 percent were barred, including the 4 percent disqualified by the interior ministry. In the previous general election, the Guardians Council alone had rejected 35 percent.[39] The reasons for the rejection, as listed by the Council, were: breaking the law; taking drugs; past membership of the Rastakhiz (*lit.*, Resurgence), the sole ruling party under the Shah; disloyalty to the constitution or the Leader; and lack of full commitment to Islam.[40] That still left 600 candidates in the field for the thirty parliamentary seats in Tehran.

Twelve conservative factions, with only three with some weight – ranging from the Association of Combatant Clergy to the Miscellaneous Islamic Committees, an umbrella organization of various merchant and guild groups – formed an alliance called the Followers of the Imam's and Leader's Line. It emphasized improvement in economic conditions rather than political reform.

On the other side eighteen reformist factions, with only five of some substance – ranging from the Society of Combatant Clerics to the leftist IIPF to the centrist SOC – formed the 2nd Khordad/May 23 Front, named after the date on which Khatami scored his landslide victory in 1997. The IIPF's program included greater media freedom, including private radio and television channels and reform of government bureaucracy. Whereas it favored creating attractive conditions for private investment in industry, it opposed privatizing state-owned oil, power, telecommunications and tobacco industries as well as giving tax incentives to companies. With many of its activists being journalists, the IIPF had a substantial presence in the press.[41]

After a slow start, the election campaign picked up as Khatami undertook a nationwide tour of provincial capitals, culminating in a mammoth rally on February 11, Revolution Day, 2000 to urge people to participate in the poll, well aware that a large voter turnout would favor the reformist coalition, which offered an agreed slate of 200 candidates, including 9 in Tehran.

By contrast, the state-run radio and television, operating directly under Leader Khamanei, treated the elections in a determinedly low key. Given the legal prohibition of campaigning by electronic media, the public surmised that those given exposure on the broadcasting media were favorites of the conservative establishment.

In general, both camps put much stress on public rallies, which were well attended and widely reported in the print media, which played a crucial role. With pro-reform newspapers being more popular, reformists had a clear lead over their rivals. Actually, in the absence of conventional political party organization, newspapers became the central nervous system of the reform movement. They played a vital role in molding public opinion. The ambiance of most public rallies was well encapsulated by Howard Schneider of the *Washington Post*. "Establishment figures are booed," he reported.

> Catch phrases involving freedom, prosperity and "Iran for all Iranians" have replaced religious militancy in slogans from the right, center and left. Readings from the Quran still start the typical gathering, but they are followed by once-banned nationalist anthems and ancient Persian poetry.[42]

Summing up the electoral scene, a Tehran-based Western diplomat said, "A free and fair election. No holds barred. An open debate. This is supposed to be a clerical theocracy, and it is transformed, before our eyes, into a pretty lively democracy." [43]

On polling day, with 32 million electors participating, the turnout was 83 percent, a record for Majlis elections, and higher than the 71 percent in 1996. All but 66 seats were decided in the first run, but the results for Tehran, with 30 seats, were not declared. The May 23 Front, winning almost two-thirds of seats, emerged as the clear victor. The conservatives' score was 60, and the independents' 15. Only one-fifth of the previous MPs got re-elected. And there were fewer clerical winners than ever before.[44]

Though the results of Tehran polling stations were not validated by the Guardians Council, the unofficial score showed reformists to be firmly in the lead – with the IIPF leader, Muhammad Reza Khatami, the president's younger brother, topping the list; followed by Jamila Kadivar, wife of the reformist minister of culture and Islamic guidance, Mohajerani; Ali Reza Nouri, a younger brother of Abdullah, a jailed dissident; and Hadi Husseini Khamanei, a younger brother of the Leader.

While reformists were euphoric, conservatives were crestfallen. They knew they would lose but the extent of the defeat surprised and depressed them. Among those who lost was Muhammad Reza Bahonar, a prominent Tehran MP. "We will not change our principles and positions, but it is natural that we should reconsider our policies and methods," he declared. But those on the extreme right took the defeat badly. Masud Dehnamaki, a leader of the Ansar-e Hizbollah and editor of the *Jebhe* (Front), told a public rally in Tehran that Ansars should go on the offensive and "scare the bourgeois classes back into their homes."[45] A leading conservative MP, Muhammad Reza Taraqi, said, "We must not make a new religion of elections. If they help strengthen Islam they are good. If they weaken it they are evil." According to such radical right ideologues, divine commands authorizing violence in defense of faith overrode the laws of the state.[46]

Iran, America and the Gulf

In America, Clinton and Albright welcomed the reformists' success, and called for direct talks between the two countries. But the US Congress kept up its anti-Iran drive. On February 24, the Senate adopted by 98 votes to none the Iran Non-Proliferation Act, which had been passed five months earlier by the House of Representatives by 419–0. It required the President to report to Congress twice a year with a list of countries that could be subject to sanctions for providing Iran with materials to develop missiles or weapons, and impose sanctions at his discretion. Reversing its past policy to veto such a bill, the White House now said that the new law gave the president sufficient flexibility and that it would not veto it.[47] The new legislation was aimed primarily at Moscow whose tightening links with Tehran were a source of great unease both at the White House and Capitol Hill. They threatened to cut off US grants to Russia's International Space Station program. But defying continued American pressure, Russian Defense Minister Igor Sergeyev, during his visit to Tehran in January, confirmed that "Russia intends to maintain the dynamics of its bilateral ties with Iran in military, military-technical, scientific-technical and energy fields."[48] Among the scientific-technical deals being negotiated was a $3 billion contract for Moscow to license Iran to assemble Tupolev Tu–334 jet airliners, which came to fruition soon after. In the diplomatic field, after his meeting with Ivanov, Ayatollah Rouhani, secretary-general of the SNSC, reiterated that "Cooperation among Iran, Russia, India and China is very significant if one hopes to confront the hegemonic policies of America."[49]

As expected, the Iran Non-Proliferation Act elicited a sharp riposte from Tehran.

"On the one hand they [Americans] express willingness to have relations with Iran, and on the other they pass laws which seek to punish countries helping Iran with its weapons program," Rafsanjani told a Friday prayer congregation in Tehran on February 25. "America has to accept that it has made mistakes in the past regarding Iran and it must return to us what is rightfully ours, and prove its goodwill if it wants to have dialogue with Tehran."[50]

On March 13, Clinton renewed his executive order of 1995 barring trade with Tehran. "Iran's support for international terrorism, its efforts to undermine the

Middle East peace process, and its acquisition of weapons of mass destruction and the means to deliver them continue to threaten the national security, foreign policy and economy of the US," he said.[51]

Then, in the now-familiar pattern, came a step forward. Addressing the Princeton-based American-Iranian Council on March 17, Albright admitted that America had created a climate of mistrust with Tehran by playing "a significant role" in the 1953 coup against Iran's Prime Minister Muhammad Mussadiq and by providing long-standing support for the dictatorial Shah Muhammad Reza Pahlavi. She regretted the past "short-sightedness" in US policy, particularly during the Iran–Iraq War, when Washington backed Baghdad. She then held out an olive branch. She promised to "increase efforts" towards "a global settlement" of Iran's claims of its frozen assets in America – a departure from the case-by-case basis used by the Iran–US Claims Tribunal in the Hague since 1981. (After the hostage crisis in 1979, Washington froze $12 billion assets of Iran. Most of these were released in 1981 after the crisis was resolved, said the Americans; but the Iranians claimed that $10–12 billion, including the accumulated interest, still remained frozen.) Albright announced that the US was lifting its ban on imports of Iranian carpets, caviar, pistachios and dried fruit, thus reversing a decision taken in early 1987 by the Ronald Reagan administration. (However, at $85 million in 1985, these Iranian exports were only 8 percent of the total.) Furthermore, she declared that first-time Iranian arrivals in the US would not be photographed and fingerprinted by the immigration authorities. "I call upon Iran to join us in writing a new chapter in our shared history," she concluded.[52]

The Iranian response was mixed. "Iran thinks it [Albright speech] is positive and welcomes it," said Hamid Reza Asefi, the foreign ministry spokesman. He added that Iran would now allow imports of US food and medicine. But Ayatollah Rouhani called the Albright move a "new interference in Iran's domestic affairs." More importantly, addressing a religious gathering in Mashhad on March 24, Leader Khamanei said, "The Americans are presuming that such acknowledgments, which did not even include an apology, will cause us to forget America's acts of treason, hostilities and injustices. America can't do a damn thing."[53] Finally, a balanced response was provided by Foreign Minister Kharrazi, a moderate. He welcomed certain elements of Albright's speech, but added that her initiative was "polluted" by continued American interference in Iran's internal affairs.[54]

Albright's gesture deeply upset Baghdad, which had all along dreaded friendly relations between Iran and the US. On March 23, Tariq Aziz accused Albright of being "an expert liar" for saying Washington had made a mistake in supporting Baghdad in the Iran–Iraq War, and warned Tehran "not to be deceived by such lies." He referred to the Iran–Contra scandal – centered on a secret scheme by some American officials to fund anti-regime Contra rebels in leftist Nicaragua with the money earned by selling US-made weapons and spare parts clandestinely to Iran – and claimed that Washington "had plotted in secret to prolong the war to hurt both of our countries."[55]

As it happened, Aziz's spin to place Baghdad and Tehran in the same category in the chronicle of a past war chimed with the current policies that the two capitals had adopted on Gulf Security. They both wanted America to reduce its military presence in the region. By that token, they were opposed to Washington making further inroads, militarily, into the Gulf monarchies.

But this is precisely what US Defense Secretary Bill Cohen had in mind when he visited the region in early April. He aimed to persuade Qatar to let the Pentagon use its main armed forces base for a US air expeditionary unit, thus extending American military presence to the soil of four of the six Gulf monarchies, the others being Bahrain, Kuwait and Saudi Arabia. This was part of the Pentagon's plan to provide alternatives to US aircraft carriers to strengthen *inter alia* the air surveillance of the southern no-fly zone in Iraq. "Cohen wants to transform the Gulf into a US protectorate, and a warehouse for US weapons already paid for in order to guarantee the supplies and material needed by the US forces that are occupying large tracts of the Gulf," said *Al Thawra*, the mouthpiece of the Iraqi Baath Party, on April 9, 2000. Iran was equally hostile to Cohen. "America is trying to ensure that its illegitimate military presence in the Gulf will become permanent," remarked the state-owned Tehran Radio. "It is also trying to ensure that it will have a monopoly on military information and secrets in the Arab countries of the region. In this way, it is trying to prevent the formation of a regional security system in which all the littoral states participate."[56]

Such sentiments were shared by the two neighbors' business communities. During his visit to Tehran, Abdul Ghafour Yunus, chairman of the Iraqi Chambers of Commerce, said, "US efforts to tighten the embargo on Iraq will only be neutralized through a collaboration between Iranian and Iraqi officials, and especially their private sectors."[57] Already the public sectors of the two states were cooperating in helping Iraq smuggle its petroleum by using the territorial waters of Iran for hefty fees, thus enabling its government to earn foreign exchange outside the UN oil-for-food program. This trade started in 1997 with the oil-for-food scheme for Baghdad. After loading oil at Iraq's terminal, the tankers used the protected sealanes within the 12 mile (19 km) wide territorial waters of Iran to navigate the Gulf, and then sailed out to the high seas.

According to Vice Admiral Charles Moore of the US Navy, Iranian officials provided safe passage and false papers to Iraq for $7 a barrel. American sources put the value of this trade at $1 billion a year.[58]

Over time this scheme provided Tehran with a lever to punish Baghdad for unfriendly acts. The running sore between the two countries was their continued backing for each other's rebel groups. With reformists capturing the Iranian Majlis, the Mujahedin-e Khalq Organization leadership forecast an intensifying struggle between them and conservatives. It therefore decided to escalate its terrorist activity. On March 13, there were half a dozen mortar explosions in a residential area near the headquarters of the IRGC in Tehran, the apparent target of the MKO activists. The blasts injured four. The following day the MKO reported an air strike against one of its camps, and a hit-and-run attack by SAIRI militants, who later fired mortars at a Baghdad neighborhood, killing 4 and injuring 38. Then, reversing its earlier policy of collusion on oil smuggling, on April 1, Iran intercepted the Honduran-registered tanker, *Al Masru*, carrying 2,500 tons of Iraqi oil.[59] This was Tehran's clear warning to Iraq that it would pay an economic price for its failure to control the MKO.

But with internal tensions rising in Iran, MKO leaders were unlikely to cease their terrorist activities.

Khamanei's reaction

Buoyed by its stunning electoral success, the pro-reform press pushed the boundaries of the political debate even more. This trend got a further boost when there was an assassination attempt on 47-year-old Saeed Hajjarian, editor of the pro-reform *Sobh-e Emruz*, and a strategist behind the May 23 Front victory in the Majlis poll. As a former deputy minister at the intelligence ministry, he had good contacts there which he used to provide exclusive information in his newspaper and which helped to boost circulation. On March 12, as he stopped to take a letter from a man outside his office, he was shot in the face by another man who escaped on the back of a motorbike, the type used only by the security forces and the IRGC. He survived but was partly paralyzed. "The worst form of murder and violence is when bullets confront ideas," said Khatami after his meeting with him in hospital.[60] In Hajjarian the pro-reform press acquired a living martyr.

"Pro-reform newspapers went on the offensive, showing scant regard for the ideological principles that have guided the political establishment for the past 20 years," wrote Saeed Barzin in the *Middle East International*.

> Daily reports in the press about political violence and corruption attracted a huge readership and severely undermined the position of the conservatives. But this radicalization of the press also had the hallmarks of a classic Iranian rebellion, in which the absence of a supportive political institution soon leaves the initiative in the hands of even more radical elements and, ultimately, threatens chaos.[61]

It was incumbent upon Khamanei to see that Iran did not reach that brink.

The incident that reportedly exhausted the Leader's patience was the conference in Berlin on "Iran After the Parliamentary Elections," sponsored by the Heinrich Boll Foundation, on April 7–9. The twenty-one Iranian participants included Jamila Kadivar, the second most popular parliamentarian; Mehrangiz Kar, a feminist human rights activist; Akbar Ganji, an investigative journalist at the *Fath* (Victory); Abbas Abdi, a former columnist at the *Salaam*; Ali Reza Alavi-Tabar, acting editor of the *Sobh-e Emruz*; Hamid Reza Jalaipour, executive director of the *Asr-e Azadegan*; Izzatollah Sahabi, editor of the biweekly *Iran-e Farda* (Iran of Tomorrow), and a former leader of the Liberation Movement of Iran, the only opposition party in the country that had been allowed to function semi-clandestinely after the revolution; and Hojatalislam Hassan Yusufi-Eshkevari, who stood for separation of politics from religion. Most of the audience was from the Iranian diaspora in Germany, including large contingents from foreign-based anti-Tehran groups. The proceedings included discussion of such subjects as violation of human rights, the three-million-strong Iranian diaspora, the treatment of ethnic and religious minorities, the role of women, and political and social freedoms. Some reformist speakers questioned whether Iran should have a religious regime and whether women should be obliged by law to wear veils. During discussion the hardcore opposition elements took to barracking and heckling, and disrupted the conference. When asked by the chairman to contribute to the debate some of them danced and even stripped before the television cameras. This got reported widely and adversely in the rightwing media in Iran.

The state-run Iranian television inflamed the feelings at home by airing certain provocative parts of the proceedings.[62] This angered conservative politicians and clerics. Denouncing the Berlin conference as anti-Islamic, they demanded punishment for all the Iranian participants and the publications they represented. Rightwingers went on to present the event as part of a plan to build bridges between the pro-reform camp in Iran with the foreign-based leftist, secular opposition, despite the fact that the event was held with the full knowledge and acquiescence of the Iranian government, which had not barred anyone from attending it.[63] However, the conservatives' biased interpretation of the conference was apparently accepted by Leader Khamanei and his close aides.

Taking its cue from his office, on April 17, the about-to-be-dissolved Fifth Majlis passed the latest batch of clauses in the Press Law in an ongoing process that dated back to July 1999. These extended responsibility for press violations to journalists and commentators besides the publication's director, banned a publication from receiving financial support from foreign governments or organizations, and outlawed criticism of the constitution.[64]

On April 20, addressing 100,000 young people at the Grand Mosque of Tehran, Khamanei attacked reformist papers for subverting the Islamic revolution, but warned hardliners not to take the law into their own hands. "There are 10 to 15 newspapers which undermine Islamic principles, insult state bodies and create social discord," he said. "Unfortunately, some of the newspapers have become the bases of the enemy. They are performing the same tasks that the BBC Radio and the Voice of America, as well as the British, American and Zionist television broadcasts intend to perform."

Referring to the attack on Hajjarian, he said, "A shooting happens. Investigations have not produced any results, and these newspapers accuse the Islamic Revolutionary Guards Corps … of involvement. This trend is detrimental to the state, the revolution, the youth and the faith of the people." The audience chanted, "Death to mercenary writers" and "Shame on you hypocrites, leave the press." Concluding his speech, he warned, "I condemn any illegal action taken by any person due to emotion and support for this or that person. I will not allow it."[65]

Khamanei's speech and the Majlis's amendments to the Press Law were signals to the judiciary to move against the pro-reform press. It did. Between April 20 and 26, it closed down fourteen reformist publications, with a total circulation of 1 million, for insulting Islam and spreading corruption. It summoned all Iranian speakers at the Berlin conference and several student leaders. It imprisoned or summoned six prominent columnists (including Akbar Ganji) for engaging in unconstitutional or unIslamic activities, or pressed such charges against them. In a series of articles published before the Berlin conference, Ganji had chronicled the plots by the rogue elements in the intelligence ministry, some of whom were implicated in assassinating three writers and one dissident politician, and had then attacked Rafsanjani, accusing him of giving indirect approval to earlier, undisclosed political murders during his presidency.[66] To Rafsanjani's embarrassment, these articles were reprinted as books, which became best-sellers.

Significantly, the order to close the pro-reform newspapers was ostensibly based on a rarely used pre-revolution statute of 1957 that allowed the government to arrest people or suspend an activity to prevent a possible crime. "This time they closed the papers according to the law even though the law is questionable," said Hussein Ramazanzadeh, an aide to Khatami. "The reform movement has actually forced the opposition to play by the same rule."[67]

Endorsing the clampdown on the pro-reform press, Khamenei urged his followers to speak up. "A deviant media movement that is trying to shape public opinion and turn it against Islam, the revolution and the Islamic Republic, has been at work, creating new worries among the public," he said. Rafsanjani joined in. "What is being attacked is the Islamic content of the revoluton," he told the Friday prayer congregation in Tehran on April 27. Describing the critics of the regime as "agents of foreign powers hostile to Islam," he said, "Now they are putting freedom before Islam, freedom before faith." He referred to writers who, "perhaps unwittingly or perhaps intentionally, question all our accomplishments," and by so doing, "these people pave the way for those who want to take over the country."[68]

"The hardliners' fear of a moderate Majlis … coalesced with their simmering anger at the reform press which has stridently criticized conservative politicians," explained Susan Sachs of the *New York Times*.

> The result was intense pressure on Khamenei to represent the clerical establishment. The general shutdown of the moderate press, approved by Khamenei, was in the hope of calling a time-out in the increasingly vicious battle between the two sides being waged after the [first round of] Majlis elections through the newspapers.[69]

Along with the official crackdown went a barrage of reprobation at the reformist camp by the conservative press, well aware of the second round of the Majlis elections on May 5. It criticized Khatami for ignoring the clerical establishment when it came to canvassing support for his vision of a civil society, being less than transparent in the performance of his job, and failing to condemn blatant transgressions of the law by pro-reform newspapers. In its view, these publications had, willfully or inadvertently, affronted or revised Islamic principles and cardinal revolutionary precepts, caused social discord, and indulged in rumor-mongering which undermined citizens' belief in and loyalty to the socio-political system of the Islamic Republic.

The concerted conservative onslaught infuriated many in the reformist camp, especially the young, who wanted to demonstrate their anger in the streets. But older politicians urged them to exercise vigilant self-restraint since that was the best way to defeat the aims of – what they disparagingly called – "the Political Mafia." Khatami was particularly cautious. "We have to move through this sensitive period with calm, tranquillity and composure," he said.[70]

On the other hand, the rumors of an impending coup by the military had to be treated with skepticism in view of Khamanei's declared opposition to the armed forces' involvement in politics.

Indeed, having delivered a severe blow to the pro-reform press, Khamanei held out an olive branch to the reformist camp which, despite the shut-down of its press, went on to win a majority of seats in the second round of Majlis elections. Having maintained for years that there was no factionalism within the political–religious establishment, Khamanei now reversed his viewpoint. In a Friday sermon in mid-May he publicly acknowledged not only the existence of different factions within the establishment but also their right to co-exist. "The two factions, the progressive and the faithful, are as necessary as the two wings of a bird," he declared. He then pointed out where progressives had gone astray. Some of them had joined forces with the factions outside the Islamic establishment, even those who believed in secularism. This had to stop, and progressives must cut their ties with secularists and de-escalate their rhetoric, he demanded.[71]

Most conservatives and many centrists regarded Khamanei's speech as conciliatory, especially when it came amidst reports that the supreme judicial official, Shahroudi, was considering amalgamating a plethora of public courts – family, civil, criminal, press, civil service, revolutionary, specially for clergy – into one, operating under a single code. He was also considering reverting to jury trials in criminal cases which had been the practice during the Shah's regime and after – until 1994. In that year, at the behest of Ayatollah Yazdi, the chief judicial official, the Majlis had adopted a 16-article law entitled, "Public and Revolutionary Courts, and the elimination of the parquet system." It had replaced the old system whereby the Prosecutor General, after weighing the evidence, decided whether to prosecute or not, with the new practice of letting investigating judges decide. Having satisfied himself with the quality of the collected evidence, an investigating judge now worked alongside the presiding judge in court. Unlike the Prosecutor General, who could only prosecute, the investigative judge had the right to arrest the accused. In short, the new Act switched the proceedings in a criminal case from the English to the Continental European model, and dispensed with jury trials, which are part of the English legal system. In the public debate on the subject that preceded and followed the passage of this law, its proponents pointed out that the functions of the investigator, prosecutor and judge were performed by the same person in the early days of Islam: this was the custom among the tribes of pre-Islamic Arabia, and the early religious–legal scholars of Islam adopted it. But that had not stopped the Majlis in 1985 from specifying jury trials under the Press Law, or inhibited Ayatollah Khomeini from doing the same in his decree to establish the SCC.

Following Khamanei's speech, Mohajerani, the reformist minister of culture and Islamic guidance, addressed a letter to all publications urging them to stick to the Press Law strictly.

The draconian move against pro-reform press did not ostensibly damage the reformist camp in the second round of the Majlis poll. Nor did the voiding of thirteen first round results by the Guardians Council (with some seats going to conservatives) alter the overall picture. But the final tally was still not in sight.

This was due to the Guardians Council's prevarication about the thirty Tehran seats where, according to unofficial reports, Rafsanjani had just scraped through as the last winner, an outcome which led many to suspect an underhand manipulation. Finally, pressured by Khamanei, on May 20 (three months after the first polling day) the Council validated 26 victories for reformists, voided 2 results, and gave the remaining 2 to conservatives, including Rafsanjani, who had been formally put at the top of the list backed by the Followers of the Imam's and Leader's Line coalition. He now moved up ten places to become the twentieth winner. This happened when the Council invalidated 726,000 votes, a quarter of the total, due to ballot irregularities mostly in the pro-reform north Tehran. When some newspapers cried rat, the state-run radio warned that unsubstantiated allegations against the Council would lead to prosecution. But sensitive to popular unease, the reformist wing within the centrist SOC – which regarded Rafsanjani as its mentor – reportedly drafted his letter of resignation from the Majlis, and pressured him to sign it. He did. In it he attributed his withdrawal from the Majlis to "a heavy dose of adverse and poisonous propaganda by enemies [which] created an ambiguous and doubtful atmosphere."[72]

This finally destroyed the high ambition of Rafsanjani who wanted to succeed Khamanei, reportedly suffering from serious health problems, as the Leader. Within a decade of being elected president almost unanimously in 1989, Rafsanjani's popularity had declined precipitately. "What Rafsanjani created in the economy was a half-way house, with the negative features of both sectors, the public and the private," said a senior Iranian journalist during the run-up to the first round of the Majlis poll. "Also the entourage around him is corrupt, and they have made a lot of money." The corrupt ways of the men around Rafsanjani had become grist to the gossip mill – as was revealed to me in informal conversations in the Grand Bazaar of south Tehran, the heart of the Islamic regime.[73] Aware of this, the leftist IIPF had refused to include his name on the list of the May 23 Front. So Rafsanjani ended up as a joint candidate of the conservative Followers of the Imam's and Leader's Line and the centrist SOC in Tehran. He tried to present himself as someone above partisan politics.

He also lobbied hard behind the scenes to get Gholam Hussein Karbaschi freed from jail before the February poll and see that his project to launch a new newspaper, *Ham Mihan* (Our Country), got off the ground. Following a request by Sharoudi, on January 25, Khamanei ordered the release of Karbaschi after only eight months in prison instead of the original 24.[74] Despite this, and the enthusiastic backing of the *Ham Mihan*, Rafsanjani performed poorly, thus shattering the conservatives' hopes of installing him as the Majlis Speaker, and thus slow down the reformists' plans. His poor popular standing also hurt the SOC. In contrast to the 95 seats won by the IIPF, it scored only 30. These developments were perceived by many Iranians, especially the young, as just deserts for Rafsanjani. In a larger context, it signified the loss of popularity of the founders of the Islamic Republic among the populace, a majority of which was below the age of the 1979 revolution.

Contrary to the rumors of the Sixth Majlis becoming still-born, it met as scheduled on May 27, with all but 20 of the 268 new MPs, including 11 women, attending. It elected Hojatalislam Mehdi Karrubi, a leader of the leftish Society of Combatant Clerics, Speaker by 186 to none, with 62 abstentions. The fact that Karrubi had been Speaker from 1989 to 1992 helped to reassure the conservative establishment. His predecessor, Nateq-Nouri, who did not run for a parliamentary seat, was appointed to the Guardians Council by Leader Khamanei.

Those voting for Karrubi included almost all of the 95 MPs loyal to the leftist IIPF, 30 left-of-centre Society of Combatant Clerics; 10 from the longer-established leftist Mujahedin of Islamic Revolution (MIR); 30 right-of-centre Servants of Construction; and 15 independents.

Having conceded the Speakership to Karrubi, the IIPF, the largest faction, ensured that its leader, Muhammad Reza Khatami, became First Deputy Speaker when the election for the post was held on June 11. And the job of the Second Deputy Speaker went to Bahzad Nabavi, the leader of the MIR. The MIR came into being shortly after the Islamic revolution as a leftist group and provided an alternative for the young Iranians who belonged to secular Marxist groups. It was active in the take-over of the US embassy in late 1979. Three of its leaders, including Nabavi, became ministers in the government led by Mir Hussein Musavi.[75] It now favoured political liberalization.

Reformists thus consolidated their hold over the Sixth Majlis. This had implications beyond the proceedings or program of the chamber. The debate that had been in train in the pro-reform press before its recent closure was now likely to move to the corridors of the parliament.

12

REFORM RESTRAINED

The agenda of the reformers included reviving a vibrant press, encouraging the formation of conventional political parties, streamlining government ministries and enacting budget. But above all else, they had to work out a *modus operandi* with their conservative adversaries and foster a genuinely democratic culture, which had been missing so far. "The factions have to learn how to cooperate with each other – and they will learn," said Abbas Salimi Namin, the managing director of the *Tehran Times*.

> Iran's politicians are still new at competing as pragmatic political adver-
> saries and not as arch enemies bent on destroying one another. We don't
> have much experience in this. The role of the parties – how they should be
> controlled, how they should work with each other – it's not very clear to
> us.[1]

Iran's parliamentarians also had to realize that however sweeping their popular mandate, the Majlis was just one of several power centers, and that it was hemmed in by the Guardians Council, a bastion of conservatives. In the case of a dispute with the Council, the Majlis majority could take its case to the Expediency Consultation Council System, presided by Ali Akbar Hashemi Rafsanjani. But, given the ignominious battering he had received in the parliamentary poll at the hands of leftist reformers – constituting the bulk of the reformist camp – he was unlikely to take kindly to it.

As expected, the first test came with the Press Law. On June 18, a letter signed by 150 MPs, forming a clear majority, was read out in the chamber. Noting the closure of eighteen publications with a total circulation of over one million, it urged the judiciary chief, Ayatollah Shahroudi, to free the press and respect the rights of prisoners of conscience.

But this had no impact on the Press Court which persisted in curbing the remnants of the pro-reform print media. Five days later it shut down the *Bayan* (Narrative) daily edited by Hojatalislam Ali Akbar Mohtashami, chairman of the reformist May 23 Front. In mid-July it sentenced Imameddin Baqi, an Islamic thinker and an editor at the *Neshat* (before its closure), to five-and-a-half years in jail for questioning some aspects of the Sharia regarding the death penalty and accusing Ali Fallahian and Ali Akbar Hashemi Rafsanjani of complicity in the murders of five dissidents in late 1998.[2]

However, public opinion, especially in the capital, remained strongly pro-reform.

Mohtashami, contesting one of the two remaining parliamentary seats in Tehran, won handsomely. And the other seat too went to a reformist, Elias Hazrati, popular with student groups.[3]

But the undiminished hostility of the judiciary and Leader Khamanei toward the pro-reform print media made the IIPF leadership review its program. It dropped its plan to scrap the present, much-amended Press Law and replace it with new legislation. It decided instead to amend the present statute.

The absence of the pro-reform press did not mean that the debate about the future path of Iran had subsided. If anything, its closure compelled the top leadership of the reformist camp to join the fray.

In his speech to a national gathering of local councilors in Tehran on the eve of the third anniversary of his victory (on May 23, 1997), President Khatami dwelt on the conservative argument that religion was more important than democracy when setting the country's direction, and highlighted the republican aspect of the Islamic Republic.

"Imam Khomeini always emphasized that he was setting up an Islamic Republic rather than an Islamic State," he said. "This meant that Imam Khomeini himself believed in the combination of Islamic principles and the voice of the people."[4] Voting for the 1979 constitution meant that "Our people voted for freedom to speak, freedom to assemble, freedom to criticize – all these are inalienable rights of the people." As for Islam, he said,

> Our people voted for [an] Islam, which has a clear definition – not for those who wrongly see themselves as the embodiment of a pure Islam, those who excommunicate or kill their opponents … Iran needs to find and tear out by the roots the cancerous tumor within the state that had used fear and violence to support its narrow view of Islam.[5]

Along with "the cancerous tumor within the state" were such organizations as the Ansar-e Hizbollah, which had disrupted his election campaign speech in Mashhad on April 19, 1997, and which Khatami had described in early 1998 as illegal and fascist, and whose political violence he had promised to end. But the Ansars had continued to exist and carried on their violent activity, functioning as the intimidating arm of their powerful ultra-conservative political–religious masters. They were the ones to attack the peaceful student protesters in July 1999 as the LEF stood by idly, triggering five days of street rioting. Khatami used the first anniversary of the episode to express again his opposition to violent intimidation by the far-right vigilantes and the underlying thinking. "We must not expect the people to behave as we would like and [threaten] to suppress them if they do not. People must be allowed to speak freely and criticize their government. If people are left unsatisfied, this will one day lead to an explosion."[6]

But this did not avert the violence that erupted on July 8, 2000 in Tehran. On one side were the students, joined this time by thousands of disgruntled non-students, and on the other the LEF aided by the Ansars. A peaceful rally on that day to celebrate the first anniversary of the student protest turned violent when thousands of protesters from Tehran's poorer areas joined the pro-reform students at Revolution Square. A popular slogan of the past year – "People are hungry, but the clergy live like kings" – reappeared along with a new one, "Khatami, show your power or resign." While the LEF fired tear gas to disperse the rioters, the Ansars attacked them with knives, chains and bottles. There were street battles between the two sides. By the evening, having succeeded in dispersing the protesters, the LEF and Ansars sealed off Revolution Square. Many were injured, but no one was killed. The several dozen rioters arrested by the LEF turned out to be non-students. Remarking on the day's event, Leader Khamanei warned that Western powers were behind plans to bring down the Islamic system just as the Soviet system had been brought down.[7]

Khamanei's reference to the Soviet Union was pertinent although his placing of the blame on the West was flawed. Under reformist Mikhail Gorbachev (r. 1986–91), the Soviet Union entered a period of glasnost (*lit.*, transparency) and perestroika (*lit.*, restructuring). The disclosures and condemnations of the past injustices and cruelties that the Soviet people had suffered during several decades of a repressive, authoritarian rule under the Communist Party of the Soviet Union surfaced with such an unrestrained force that they severely undermined popular faith in the 70-year-old Marxist-Leninist system *per se*, and paved the way, inadvertently, for the collapse of the Soviet Union in late 1991. While willing to liberalize the Islamic system in Iran, both economically and politically, Leader Khamanei and his close aides apparently wanted to control the speed and direction of the process to avoid the recent fate of the Soviet Union as well as a severe backlash by conservatives.

Conscious of the success that reformists had in gaining control of the parliament and presidency over the past three years, Khamanei probably saw merit in maintaining the supremacy of conservatives in the judiciary. A fresh reminder of the conservative dominance of the judicial system came in mid-July with the verdicts by a military court on Brig. Gen. Farhad Nazari, former Tehran LEF commander, and nineteen LEF officers on charges of attacking university students in defiance of the interior ministry's orders a year earlier. The judge acquitted eighteen of them, including Nazari, on the grounds of insufficient evidence. The remaining two were found guilty of stealing an electric shaver and "improper conduct," and given three-month and two-year jail sentences respectively.[8] The interior ministry publicly criticized the verdict. The leftist IIPF, the largest group in the Majlis, expressed regret. And the leaders of the pro-reform University-Seminary Unity Consolidation Bureau staged a one-day hunger-strike in front of the Majlis, the first such gesture in Iran.[9]

Since the judicial system, including the Press Court, had attracted a lot of public attention recently, Leader Khamanei thought it appropriate to address the issue. The time was opportune also because it was almost a year since his appointment of Ayatollah Shahroudi as the judiciary head to succeed Ayatollah Yazdi, a diehard conservative. At a meeting with judges in late July he accused reformists of trying to hobble the courts and conservatives of attempting to exploit them for their own aims. He urged his audience to shun political bias and function strictly in accordance with the law. "May be Khamanei fears that abandoning the judiciary to reformists would rearrange the political configuration too far and too fast," remarked Saeed Barzin in the *Middle East International*.[10]

Taking an overall view, it could be seen that reformists had won the basic argument that all actions of the regime had to be within the law, and that it must punish the law breakers, no matter who they were – intelligence officials, policemen or Ansars. Their success in the matter could be gauged by the fact that conservative MPs had by now dropped their opposition to political reform, saying only that it should be institutionalized and moderated to ensure that it did not subvert Islam. They even called for the establishment of an official Reform Headquarters.[11] On the other side Khatami and his pro-reform followers had abandoned any plans for sweeping political reforms if only to avoid a perilous showdown with conservatives in the Majlis and outside.

"Short of a determined crackdown by ultra conservatives, the ultimate success of Khatami's drive to liberalize Iran may be less of an issue than its speed and sweep," reported Howard Schneider of the *Washington Post*.

> Despite a seemingly seesaw battle in which momentum swings between Khatami's supporters and their hardline rivals, key institutions are gradually being brought under more open and rational management. Abuses by hardline security agents and others are being more vigorously policed, and political victories [of reformists] such as the takeover of the Majlis appear to be taking place without crippling interference [by conservatives].

Schneider went on to point out that law enforcement officers, intelligence agents and others who had killed, beaten or abused citizens were being charged and tried with some consistency, and that such behavior seemed now to be more the exception than the rule.[12]

More specifically, the situation at the intelligence ministry, a major center of extra-legal activities in the past, had improved since the appointment of Ali Yunisi as its head in early 1998. He had actively encouraged the old, diehard employees to retire. He had also closed down the businesses run by the ministry as a source of independent funding, a device used to avoid scrutiny by the Majlis.

Little wonder that Hamid Reza Jalaipour, executive director of the *Asr-e Azadegan* – who was being prosecuted for participating in the Berlin conference on Iran, condemned as anti-Islamic by conservatives – was on the whole sanguine. "Such setbacks as the closure of my newspaper and my own arrest are not impeding the underlying trend toward more political and social freedom, more open and accountable institutions and stronger civil government," he said.[13]

Indeed, many in the reformist camp believed that Ayatollah Khamanei recognized the need for political liberalization and that behind the scenes he was helping it along in his own way, backing Khatami at crucial points. Between April 1998, when Gholam Hussein Karbaschi was arrested on corruption charges, and March 2000, when pro-reform editor Saeed Hajjarian became a target of assassination, Leader Khamanei had acted several times to placate the reformist camp. In Karbaschi's case the Leader ruled that he must be released on bail. He ensured that the assailants of Abdullah Nouri and Ataollah Mohajerani in September 1998 were apprehended and punished; and so too were those involved in trying to assassinate Hajjarian. (The five culprits received prison terms of 3 to 15 years, the longest one for Saeed Asghar, a university student, who pulled the trigger.[14]) Khamanei condemned the political killings in late 1998 in no uncertain terms. In July 1999 he was quick to describe the student dormitory raids as "a bitter and unacceptable incident." And it was during this crisis that his followers coalesced with those of Khatami to demonstrate their solidarity with the Islamic regime.

So it came as no surprise when Khatami announced in late July that he would seek re-election as president. "We are working according to the plan the people have voted for and confirmed," he told a gathering of university chancellors and research directors. "As long as the people have not withdrawn their votes, I will stand by my commitment ... The reform we propose is against dictatorship."[15]

Khatami's announcement delighted reformers, depressed conservatives and angered far-right vigilantes.

Reformist MPs pressed ahead with their plan to amend the restrictive Press Law to revive the lively print media which had played a vital role in their election. On August 6, the date for debating and voting on the amended law, Speaker Karrubi read out a letter from Leader Khamanei. "If the enemies infiltrate the press, it will be a big danger to the country's security and the people's religious beliefs," said Khamanei. "I do not deem it right to keep silent. The bill is not legitimate and not in the interest of the system and the revolution." His vetoing of the bill meant indefinite suspension of the matter. There were angry, shouted protests. Scuffles between reformists and conservatives broke out on the floor of the chamber. But Khamanei had acted within his powers: the constitution authorized him to intervene in the legislative process. "Our constitution has the elements of the Absolute Rule of the Supreme Clerical Leader, and you all know this and approve of this," said Speaker Karrubi. "We are all duty bound to abide by it."[16]

The next day thousands of raucous conservatives assembled outside the Majlis building to demonstrate their backing for Khamanei's edict. The situation was so surcharged that many onlookers felt that the chanting crowd might storm the building. It did not.

On August 13, a motion pledging to advance reform and accusing the conservative bloc of manipulating Khamanei's letter was signed by 161 MPs (out of 274). "We call on the highest authorities not to allow certain political currents who separated from the people to continue carrying out immoral acts under the name of defending sanctities and values," said the reformers' statement.[17] As the law banned direct criticism of the Leader, the reformist bloc directed its anger at its conservative rivals.

The following day, Ayatollah Jannati, a pre-eminent conservative, spoke. "You cannot save Islam with liberalism and tolerance," he declared. "I am announcing clearly and openly that the closure of the [pro-reform] newspapers was the best thing the judiciary has done since the revolution." And yet, the same day, Ayatollah Hadi Marvi, the deputy judiciary chief, said that there was no judicial consensus on the mass closure of reformist papers, and that it was possible that some could reopen in the future.[18]

For the present, though, the banning of the pro-reform press continued, the latest victim being the *Ava* (Voice). With this, the total of newspaper closures rose to twenty-five, all of them pro-reform except the *Jebhe*, the mouthpiece of the Ansar-e Hizbollah. Moreover, by banning journalistic activity by those found guilty, the Press Court had blocked their previous tactic of starting a new newspaper once the old one was shut down. By now ten journalists were serving prison sentences for their writings.[19]

Reformist leaders feared that continued pressure by conservatives on their followers would push the outer fringe of their camp into extra-legal activity – something that the far right had resorted to since the early days of the revolution. Their apprehension was realized on August 24. Holding its annual conference in the western city of Khorramabad, the pro-reform University-Seminary Unity Consolidation Bureau invited Hojatalislam Muhsin Kadivar, just released from jail, and Abdul Karim Soroush to address the delegates. When they arrived at the airport, it was besieged by dozens of noisy, frenzied Ansars. They were smuggled out and driven back to Tehran. Violent clashes erupted at the University, the venue of the gathering, and other parts of the city, when the authorities banned the conference and the Ansars attacked the delegates. The incensed students, joined by pro-reform locals, rioted, setting fire to banks and other public buildings, and pelting the LEF with stones. At its peak some 10,000 people were involved, and the three-day episode led to the death of one LEF sergeant, and injuries to many. Some observers perceived the event as a preamble to a violent, escalating struggle between reformists and conservatives. But to calm nerves two official teams arrived in Khorramabad from Tehran a few days later to investigate the rioting. In its report on November 13, the Majlis committee said,

> Some people have tried to say that ethical and geographical issues are responsible for the outbursts of violence. But the real reason was political violence-mongering and the unlawful use of levers of pressure

by one faction in order to attain its own goals and to stop the other faction from continuing its programs.

The report stated that the IRGC looked the other way as the Ansars blocked the passage of Kadivar and Soroush to the pro-reform student conference, and later when the student delegates were beaten by the Ansars and Baseej. However, the authors of the report failed to provide documentary evidence for their claims.[20] So the matter remained unresolved, with the tension between the two factions at about the same level as before the Khorramabad episode.

However, the latest bout of violence, and the production of a videotape offering confidential information about the workings of the Ansar-e Hizbollah, raised interest in Ansars. The existence of this videotape became public when, in mid-July, court officials charged two lawyers, Shirin Ibadi (specializing in human rights) and Hojatalislam Muhsin Rahami (who among others had defended Abdullah Nouri) with "disrupting the political situation in Iran" by conspiring with Ilah-e Sharifpour Hicks, a representative of the New York-based Human Rights Watch, during his visit to Tehran in May, to produce and distribute the videotape. The Iranian lawyers and Hicks were also charged with coercing Amir Farshad Ibrahimi, a former member of the Ansar-e Hizbollah, to make the confession he did on tape. According to Ibrahimi, the Ansars had been given a go-ahead on disrupting public meetings, assaulting reformist activists and assassinating Abdullah Nouri. He alleged that powerful conservatives, including senior ayatollahs and politicians, approved their plans. He also revealed that the Ansar-e Hizbollah was funded by traditional bazaar merchants, who supported the conservative clerical establishment.[21]

In the early days of the Islamic Republic, the Hizbollah, led by Hojatalislam Hadi Ghaffari, was found to have surreptitious links with the ruling Islamic Republic Party (IRP). One of the Hizbollah's virtues to its political masters was that it was loosely structured. It played an important role in the street at crucial moments in the history of the revolution in confronting and intimidating those the regime regarded as counter-revolutionaries. It started with harassing all "unIslamic groups" that had established offices on university campuses. After Ayatollah Khomeini had denounced in particular the Mujahedin-e Khalq Organization in March 1980, it targeted the MKO, which led to many bloody skirmishes. Once political challenges to the Islamic regime had subsided, Hizbollahis concentrated on social matters such as the observance of women's Islamic dress and the ban on alcohol. They were unhappy at the promulgation in December 1982 of Ayatollah Khomeini's eight-point decree on civil liberties and the transfer of moral offences from Revolutionary Courts to Public Courts. ("To spy and search is contrary to Islam," stated Khomeini's decree. "We should not engage in oppression. We should not investigate what is going on in people's homes.") In February 1983 they demonstrated in the predominantly working-class south Tehran to demand strict adherence to Islamic morals and warn those who might be tempted to transgress them due to the recent liberalization.[22]

Later their self-assigned functions were taken over by the members of the official Baseej militia, an auxiliary of the IRGC. This has continued. Now it was the Baseej which checked to see that any young women in the company of men were either married or related, and ensure that the headscarves of the women in the street covered their necks and hair. On college and university campuses the Baseej maintained its own offices to enforce the Islamic dress code and other social behavior, and collect information – especially about the extra-curricular books students were reading – for its files and for the intelligence ministry.[23]

In the late 1980s, the Hizbollah's ranks were swollen by many veterans of the First Gulf War. Following Khomeini's death in 1989, it vowed to defend what it regarded as his legacy, and opposed pragmatic changes, economic and cultural, that were introduced in the post war period. The members of its associate, the Ansar-e Hizbollah, led by Hussein Panah and Masud Dehnamki, tore down advertisements for luxury Western products, damaged fashionable boutiques and harassed young, unmarried couples in parks. When, following Khatami's victory in 1997, reformists assumed a high profile, Ansars began attacking secular intellectuals, reformist and leftist newspapers, and liberal-minded university students. With the LEF and judiciary turning a blind eye, they went on to assault two senior cabinet ministers, Abdullah Nouri and Ataollah Mohajerani, and several progressive clerics. Following their role in triggering the student protest in July 1999, the intelligence minister, Ali Yunusi, publicly referred to "pressure groups" – meaning primarily the Ansar-e Hizbollah, and secondarily the small Fedayin-e Islam (Self-sacrificers for Islam), which dated back to pre-revolution times. Describing their members as "war veterans with elevated religious principles," he said,

> Legal political factions do not support these groups officially. But that does not mean that no one in the military or information [i.e., intelligence] ministry supports them … Many files have been opened on these groups, but officials are either frightened of pursuing these cases or are doubtful about the guilt of the accused.[24]

Little wonder that, despite repeated assertions by President Khatami that violent acts by the Ansars would be curbed, they continued to resort to violence, often in league with the LEF, to harass pro-reform forces in the street. Their ideological inspiration came from the graduates of the ultra-conservative Haqqani Seminary in Qom. Their leading ideologue, the Qom-based Ayatollah Mesbah-Yazdi, a member of the Assembly of Experts, was pre-eminent in speaking and writing about the role and legitimacy of violence in political affairs. He was foremost in the calls for tough action – even outside the law – against dissident students in July 1999.

> When people are convinced that plots against the Islamic state are endangering it, they must act because this is a case where the use of

force is necessary even if thousands get killed … Not using force against those who commit offenses will lead to more violence and chaos. Islam says *moharebs* (those who wage war [against the Islamic system]) should be executed, or their hands or feet cut off, or be deported.[25]

His views were widely and vehemently challenged by clerics and non-clerics.

Though the debate on Islamic norms and principles was not as vigorous as it was before the clampdown on the pro-reform press, it was far from dead. After his release from prison in July 2000, Hojatalislam Muhsin Kadivar was welcomed by 1,000 students at a Tehran university meeting presided over by Professor Hashem Agha Jeri.

"Those who believe Islamic jurisprudence is a kind of divinity on earth, that it cannot be criticized or judged by the law, must enter debates with Islamic thinkers, and let voters decide," said Jeri. "Governments that suppress thinking under the name of religion are not only not religious governments but are not even humane governments. It is time for the institutions of religion to become separated from the institution of government."[26]

The role and status of women was constantly under discussion because of lack of gender equality. On the whole the situation was mixed. "Compared with other countries in the region, such as Saudi Arabia, where women cannot drive, or Afghanistan, where they cannot work, or receive medical care or education, Iranian women do enjoy greater freedom," reported Christina Toomey of the *Sunday Times Magazine*.

> But their lives are full of contradictions. They can work beside men, but not socialize with anyone to whom they are not related. They can be MPs, be vice-president, but cannot go abroad or out after dark without their husband's consent. Married couples can be arrested for holding hands in public. On buses, there is strict segregation. It is sexual apartheid: women sit at the back.[27]

On one hand, females had the same educational opportunities as males. Indeed, at Tehran University 52 percent of the intake in the 1999–2000 academic year was female, and this percentage was expected to prevail nationally the following year.[28] On the other hand, in terms of blood money, a woman's life was worth half that of a man. So too was her testimony in court. In the case of her husband's death, his father had the first right over the couple's assets. Women were barred from becoming judges. And women candidates for the presidency were routinely disqualified by the Guardians Council. In November 1999, though, the Qom-based Ayatollah Yusuf Sanaie issued a fatwa saying that it was acceptable for a woman to be president, or even the Leader. Also, he asserted, a woman should be allowed to divorce her husband if he married more than one wife without the first wife's consent.[29]

What was remarkable was that 68-year-old Ayatollah Sanaei was a senior theologian and teacher with a high ranking in the political–religious establishment whose core consisted of some 165,000 qualified clerics, active and retired.[30] A substitute Friday prayer leader of Qom, he had been a clerical member of the Guardians Council. Unlike the majority of his peers, he was in tune with the rising generation of mullahs, most of whom felt that Iran's Islamic system must adapt to changing times to survive. "The younger generation of students at our religious seminaries is quite advanced and progressive," said parliamentarian Hojatalislam Muhammad Taqi Fazel Meibodi, a friend of President Khatami. "But most of the older generation, like those on the Guardians Council, have traditional views. This is the problem the government is faced with."[31]

There were two core ideological problems facing the Islamic Republic. One was the nature of freedom. The other concerned the role and status of the Leader: was he empowered by a popular mandate or by God? Many traditional clerics argued that the divine right to govern – implicit in the concept of vilayat-e faqih – made public accountability unnecessary. This interpretation was not in line with the provisions of the amended 1989 constitution concerning the Leader, especially Article 107, which equated him with "the rest of the people of the country in the eyes of the law." Nor was it in line with the practice of the popularly elected Assembly of Experts for Leadership which had set up a committee to judge whether or not the Leader's performance was within the constitutional limits and whether or not it was satisfactory. During its six monthly sessions the Assembly discussed the committee's report, and formed an opinion, but did not make it public if it was positive. Only if it found the Leader's performance questionable was it expected to issue a statement to that effect. Such constitutional provisions and practices helped marry Islam with democracy, according to the reformist proponents of the system in Iran. "Clerical rule is not incompatible with democracy so long as voters have the power to select and remove the Leader invested with ruling powers," said Ayatollah Muhammad Musavi Khoeiniha. "The conservatives advocate a system which has no compatibility with democracy. God chooses a person – and people must obey that person – who does not have to be accountable to the people, any institution or anyone in general."[32]

According to Khoeiniha, who was close to Khatami, "There is a serious difference of opinion [on issues such as freedom] between them [Khamanei and Khatami]." This is unlikely to be dissipated in a clear win for one or the other protagonist in the near future – if only because the nature of freedom is a highly complex issue which must take into account the culture and history of a society under discussion as well as its stage of economic development.

In terms of practical politics, Khatami was determined to keep alive the flame of reform while cautioning his followers against expecting too much too soon or overplaying their hand, thus jeopardizing the gains they had made, or resorting to violence. "People have a certain understanding of their rights, which may be more than the government can deliver," Khatami said at the Unesco conference on "Dialogue between Civilizations" in New York in September 2000.

"Demands should not rise beyond what is feasible. Certain expectations are out of tune with the possibilities of the times." At the same time it was crucial to see that reform did not fail. "Any effort that would lead to failure of reform will lead to a disheartening of the people and pave the way for destruction of the will of the people – and for extremist groups to enter the scene," he said. "Extremism in any form, in any direction is unwanted, whether it is in the name of freedom or of suppressing the rights of the people." Earlier, addressing a gathering of expatriate Iranians at the UN, he had pointed out that for the first time the government in Iran was for the people's freedom instead of against it.[33]

Iran–US relations

Without doubt these developments in Iran were being monitored with interest by the policy-makers in Washington. Indeed, on September 6, when Khatami delivered his speech at the Millennium summit at the UN General Assembly, both Clinton and Albright stayed on to listen to him. (Earlier in the day, he had listened to Clinton's speech at the General Assembly.) In his address, Khatami said, "No particular form of democracy can be prescribed as the only and final version. Hence the unfolding endeavors [in Iran] to formulate democracy in the context of spirituality and morality may usher in yet another model of democratic life." This was in line with his statement two months earlier during his state visit to Germany: "Every people has the right to its own understanding of human rights on the basis of its own culture and its own history."[34]

At a New York press conference on September 7, Khatami elaborated on relations with Washington. America must acknowledge and apologize for past wrongs, including the 1953 coup and "the damage done to Iran by the US-backed regimes since then," he said. "The Americans will have to confess to this," he added. "This confession – if the Americans agree to do it – will be a big step forward toward removing our misunderstandings." He then referred to Washington's adversarial acts. "There are various sanctions. There are animosities, there are allegations against Iran. We need apology for those as well as some practical measures that in reality the [American] behavior has changed."[35] In short, the US must "earn" renewed political and economic ties with Tehran.

Among Iran's complaints against Washington was the latter's continuing lobbying of its allies as well as the World Bank and the IMF not to aid Tehran financially. In 1994 it had succeeded in convincing Japan to withdraw its offer of credits for a dam on the Karun River. Since then Iran had continued to draw on the $800 million the World Bank had sanctioned for various economic projects. When its fresh application for $232 million loans for health care and sewerage projects from the World Bank came up in May 2000 before the 24-member executive board, the US opposed it. But Britain and Germany joined the majority and backed it.[36] This once again underscored the division between America and the EU on Iran.

In a move that many in Iran and elsewhere considered interference in the country's domestic affairs, the Clinton administration incorporated the case of the thirteen Jews in Shiraz accused of espionage for Israel into its ongoing, behind-the-scenes dialogue with Tehran.

In April 1999, thirteen Jews and nine Muslims were arrested in Shiraz on charges of cooperation with Israel, membership in an illegal spy ring, and recruitment of new agents. Three Jews were released on bail. Of those detained one was a rabbi and three were Hebrew teachers. The penalty for espionage ranged from a six-month jail sentence to execution, depending on the severity of the crime that varied from the first degree to the fifth. In the absence of any evidence of radio communication, any passing on of information to Israel would have been done by telephone or fax. Though officially illegal, such communication with the Jewish relatives settled in Israel was often tolerated in Iran, and many Iranian Jews openly admitted doing so. Given the alliance that existed between Iran under the Shah and Israel, the 80,000-strong Jewish community experienced no problem under his rule. Following the 1979 revolution, about two-thirds of the Jews migrated to Israel or America. Twenty years later the community was 35,000 strong, consisting chiefly of doctors, engineers and merchants, and maintained fifty-six synagogues. In the Majlis it was represented by one deputy, Dr Manuchehr Eliassi of Tehran. The relations between the community and the government were cordial, with the latter donating tonnes of flour to the Jews to make unleavened bread for the Passover (on April 19, 2000).[37]

The trial of the Jews and Muslims by a Revolutionary Court started in camera on April 13 and ended on June 29. In a 72-page verdict, read out in open court, the judge acquitted three Jews and two Muslims. The remaining Jews got 4 to 13 year jail sentences for espionage dating back to the mid-1980s. They were found guilty of being members of a spy ring that was established by Ishaq Belanas, who emigrated in 1991 (most likely to America), and who had trained them to collect information about the local military installations to be conveyed to Mossad, the Israeli foreign intelligence agency. Danny Tefilin, the leading culprit, got the longest prison sentence.[38]

The ten Jews appealed. In September Judge Hussein Ali Amiri, the provincial judicial chief, upheld only one of the three original charges – cooperation with Israel – reduced the prison sentences by two to four years, and ruled that the time already served would be included in the sentences. "These are the lowest possible sentences, and we have used the ultimate of Islamic kindness and generosity," said Judge Amini. "According to the law, these charges could have brought executions."[39]

Washington, which had taken a high-profile stand on the case since April 1999, said that the final verdict fell short of "its hopes." This upset Tehran. "They do not accept the Iranian Jewish trial, which is very arrogant," said Iran's foreign minister, Kamal Kharrazi. "I do not understand why a government from the outside intervenes in the internal affairs of other countries." American officials had put it about that Kharrazi (apparently approached at the UN in early September) had said, "These [Jewish] guys were going to get off or [that] most of them would be off and the rest would have nominal sentences." The next day the US admitted that all Kharrazi had done was to express "his hope that within the framework of the laws in Iran, sentences would be mitigated on appeal," and that he had always emphasized separation of powers in Iran and that "the court was adjudicating the case in Shiraz with full independence and uninfluenced by political considerations."[40]

From Tehran's viewpoint, this episode illustrated once more the hegemonist behavior of the US and its disregard for the sovereignty of other states. It provided further fuel to those who were against normalizing relations with Washington. They had earlier received a boost by the failure, in late July, of the talks between the Israelis and the Palestinians on a final settlement – including the future of Jerusalem – mediated by President Clinton, at the presidential retreat of Camp David in Maryland.

"In the current state of affairs, anything said in favor of rapprochement or negotiations with America is an insult and betrayal of the Iranian people," said Leader Khamanei in his televised address on July 27. "The weakening of the United States in the world, the growing opposition of countries to [US] sanctions, and in particular the failure of the Camp David negotiations are proofs of the decline of the country and its loss of influence." Turning to his own country, he concluded, "As Iran is a model for Muslim peoples, the US will never give up its hostility towards us."[41]

Following the failure of the Camp David negotiations, Palestinian Authority President, Yasser Arafat, toured the Middle East and North Africa to brief the regional leaders, who were particularly interested in the future status of Jerusalem whose walled Old City contained the Haram al Sharif (Noble Sanctuary), the third holiest site in Islam, where stood the Dome of the Rock and Al Aqsa Mosque.

In mid-August Arafat had a meeting in Tehran with Kharrazi, the foreign minister of Iran and the current chairman of the Islamic Conference Organization. "No Muslim can allow Holy Jerusalem to remain under occupation, and the Islamic Conference Organization will never let any deal be made over Jerusalem," said Kharrazi after the meeting. "Any desecration of Holy Jerusalem will provoke the Muslim world. No doubt, the situation in Palestine and Jerusalem needs a unified stand to liberate all occupied Palestinian territories."[42]

Iran had all along backed the Palestinian Hamas and the Islamic Jihad, which were committed to liberating all of the West Bank, Gaza Strip and East Jerusalem – lost to Israel by Jordan and Egypt in the 1967 Arab–Israeli War – from the military occupation of Israel. They had used terrorist actions to achieve their aim. And this was one of the major bones of contention between Tehran and Washington even though there had been no such attacks against Israeli targets since 1998.

There was nothing new in what Kharrazi or Khamanei said about Jerusalem or the US-mediated peace process. So, as in the past, such statements did not arrest the steady movement towards increased contacts between Tehran and Washington.

On August 30, the American-Iranian Council and the Internews held a reception at the Metropolitan Museum of Art in New York. Among those who turned up were five Iranian MPs, led by Speaker Karrubi, and four US lawmakers, including Senator Arlen Specter (Republican, Pennsylvania). The Iranian team – which included Mouris Motamed, the newly elected Jewish MP, and Elaaheh Kolahi, the only woman MP who refused to wear a black chador in the chamber, opting instead for a coffee-colored calf-length coat (called *rupoosh*) and a shoulder-length head-covering (called *rousari*) – was in New York for a summit meeting of the Inter-Parliamentary Union. On the American side, Senator Specter was accompanied by Representatives Robert Ney (R, Ohio), Gary Ackerman (Democrat, New York) and Eliot Engel (D, NY). They extended an invitation to their Iranian counterparts to visit US lawmakers in Washington, DC. The Iranians on their part showed interest in inviting the Americans to Tehran. "Since there isn't government-to-government dialogue, this parliamentary contact will be the way to break the ice," said Specter. Though it was reported that the informal meeting had the tacit approval of Leader Khamanei, when Karrubi was asked about it later, he described it as "an accidental encounter."[43]

It was noteworthy that during his stay in New York Karrubi met the representatives of Conoco, ExxonMobil and Chevron. These US petroleum corporations had maintained close contacts with the NIOC which had a large office in London. "The role that US companies may play in Iran's oil and gas plans is once again a subject of intense interest not only to Iranian officials, but to the mainly European firms … which have so far enjoyed an effective monopoly in the country," reported Vahe Petrossian in the *Middle East Economist Digest* in September 2000. "Indeed, there is speculation in the US that the biggest new oilfield discovery – Azedgan – has been set aside for the US firm Conoco."[44] That would be possible only if the US Congress allowed the 1996 Iran–Libya Sanctions Act to lapse in August 2001, preceded by the non-renewal of the annual Presidential executive order five months earlier.

That in turn would depend very much on the progress in the Middle East peace process, or its absence.

As it was, lack of progress in the Israeli–Palestinian peace talks – despite the defeat in the 1999 prime ministerial contest of the hardline incumbent, Binyamin Netanyahu, by his rival, Ehud Barak – had stoked up discontent among the Palestinians. When at Camp David Arafat refused to buckle under pressure from Clinton, especially on Jerusalem, the Palestinians welcomed him back home as a hero. It was against this backdrop that, on September 28, Ariel Sharon, the most hawkish mainstream Israeli leader, visited the Haram al Sharif, surrounded by 1,000 Israeli soldiers. This triggered protest by the Palestinians and an excessive use of force by the Israeli military.

The situation worsened when Barak refused Arafat's proposal for a UN-led international inquiry into the violence. Among those who tried to quench the flames of fire were UN Secretary-General Kofi Annan and President Clinton – as well as Egyptian President Hosni Mubarak, who invited the two protagonists and the two principal mediators to the sea resort of Sharm al Shaikh. Cajoled principally by Clinton, Arafat and Barak agreed, on October 17, to take a series of immediate, concrete measures to end the bloody Israeli–Palestinian confrontation. Unable to get Barak's agreement on an international inquiry into the recent violence under UN auspices, Arafat settled for an American-led probe.[45]

Iran described the agreement as "an imposed peace [that] has given the Palestinian nation nothing." And the Iraqi cabinet declared that Palestine would be regained "only through liberation and the mobilization of the Arab nations' forces for jihad until liberation." [46] Baghdad's statement chimed in with what Iran and the Palestinian Hamas and Islamic Jihad had been advocating since the late 1980s.

In a sermon to 100,000 military volunteers, on October 20 in Tehran, Leader Khamanei said that the only solution to the Middle East crisis was to "destroy the Zionist regime." His audience responded by chanting, "Ready, Leader, we're ready."[47] Their chant was very much in tune with the sentiment prevalent in Saddam Hussein's Baghdad.

Little wonder that, following an official briefing, Elaine Sciolino, a Washington correspondent of the *New York Times*, wrote: "Ultimately, the greatest fear of leaders in the region and Washington policy-makers is that the two battle-tested powers of the Gulf [Iran and Iraq] might forge an alliance against Israel, however temporary."[48]

CONCLUSIONS AND
FUTURE PROSPECTS

Iraq and Iran are two of three important players in the Gulf, the third one being Saudi Arabia. Since this region has two-thirds of the proven world petroleum deposits it is of vital importance to the West. Over the next decade or so they will be among a handful of countries that will be able to export crude oil. It is worth noting that petroleum is the source not only of gasoline for cars, but also asphalt for road construction, fertilizers for agriculture, jet fuel for aircraft, paints for domestic and other purposes, heating oil and synthetic rubber.

Most of the Gulf oil and natural gas lie underground or under the territorial waters of Iran, Iraq, Saudi Arabia, Kuwait and the United Arab Emirates. Of these states – aside from Saudi Arabia – Iran and Iraq are more significant than the rest. Together, they own the second largest natural gas deposits on the planet and one-fifth of its petroleum reserves, almost equaling those of Saudi Arabia. Home to large populations, their geographical position has endowed them with extraordinary strategic importance.

Iran shares land frontiers with the Indian sub-continent, Afghanistan, Turkmenistan, Azerbaijan, Armenia, Turkey and Iraq, and fluvial boundaries with Russia, Kazakhstan and Oman. Its coastline runs not only all along the Persian/Arabian Gulf, which is only 30–210 miles (50–340 km) wide, but also along the Arabian Sea. Iraq, the easternmost part of the Arabic-speaking world that stretches westward to Mauritania along the Atlantic Coast, has common frontiers with six countries, three of which are major oil producers.

In the Gulf region, Iranians made history by overthrowing a pro-Western, secular monarch with a septuagenarian Shia cleric, Ayatollah Khomeini, who set out to purge his country of all Western, especially American, influence. His Islamic revolutionary rhetoric and actions threatened the secular Baathist regime in the Shia-majority Iraq, headed by Saddam Hussein, a Sunni, more seriously than any other in the region.

The subsequent 1980–88 armed conflict, often called the First Gulf War, which ended in a draw, left a deep imprint on both nations as well as the region. It helped Khomeini to consolidate the revolution in Iran. On the other hand, backed actively by the West and the regional monarchs, Saddam Hussein succeeded in containing the tide of Islamic revolution – to the relief of his backers as well as his people who danced in the streets for days, believing (wrongly) that they had won. Stability was maintained in the region, but at a heavy price as the world community was made to realize two years later.

In the course of the Iran–Iraq War, Saddam Hussein quadrupled his military to over one million men, and raised huge loans from the West, Japan, the Soviet Union and the Gulf monarchies, including $12–$14 billion from Kuwait. Both these facts came to play key roles in the brief interregnum between the end of the First Gulf War and the Iraqi invasion of Kuwait.

Due to the 1980s war there was much change in Iraqi society and state. The long conflict helped Saddam to sharpen his propaganda tools, and to make his security and intelligence agencies more pernicious than before, since war conditions provided them with a much wider latitude than they had in peace time. It also set Saddam Hussein on the path of acquiring and deploying non-conventional weapons, such as poison gases, and actively developing nuclear and biological weapons.

Commanding the largest military force in the region and possessing an impressive military–industrial complex fueled Saddam's ambition. Attacking and occupying Kuwait in eight hours in August 1990 demonstrated the fierce might of his armed forces. Equally impressive was the fact that he marshaled 545,000 Iraqi troops in Kuwait and southern Iraq to face the 850,000 troops that the US-led Coalition of twenty-nine nations had mustered.

But his men did not stand to fight when the Coalition launched its ground campaign in late February 1991. They fled en masse. Saddam, well practiced in the arts of denial and distortion, described this as "a victory."

Since that time, given the numerous stand-offs the Iraqi strong-man has had with UN inspectors, charged with disarming Iraq of its weapons of mass destruction, many politicians and commentators in the West and the Middle East have repeatedly asked why the Coalition forces did not advance to Baghdad and overthrow him.

Actually, this question was addressed in full as early as 1992 by General Sir Peter De La Billiere, who commanded the troops of Britain, which contributed the second largest force, after the US, to the Coalition ranks. "We did not *have* a [UN] mandate to invade Iraq or take the country over, and if we had tried to do that, our Arab allies would certainly not have taken a favorable view," he explained in his book, *Storm Command*.

> Even our limited incursion into Iraqi territory had made some of them uneasy. The Arabs themselves had no intention of invading another Arab country. The Islamic forces [i.e., forces of the thirteen Muslim members of the Coalition] were happy to enter Kuwait for the purpose of restoring the legal government, but that was the limit of their ambition. No Arab troops entered Iraqi territory.

Sir Peter had no doubt that the Western troops would have reached Baghdad in another day-and-a-half.

> But in pressing on to the Iraqi capital we would have moved outside the remit of the United Nations authority, within which we had worked so far. We would have split the Coalition physically, since the Islamic forces would not have come with us, and risked splitting it morally and psychologically as well, thus undoing all the goodwill which we had taken so much trouble to achieve. The American, British and French would have been presented as the foreign invaders of Iraq and we would have undermined the prestige which we had earned around the world for helping the Arabs resolve a major threat to the Middle East. The whole Desert Storm would have been seen purely as an operation to further Western interests in the Middle East.

Finally, what would have been achieved by such a move?

> Saddam Hussein … would have slipped away into the desert and organized a guerrilla movement, or flown to some friendly state such as Libya and set up a government-in-exile. We would then have found ourselves with the task of trying to run a country shattered by war, which at the best of times is deeply split into factions … Either we would have to set up a puppet government or withdraw ignominiously without a proper regime in power, leaving the way open for Saddam to return. In other words, to have gone on to Baghdad would have achieved nothing except to create even wider problems.[1]

The theme that Iraqis were strong nationalists was well backed by history. They actively resisted the British mandate imposed on Iraq by the League of Nations in 1921, and did not rest until Iraq achieved independence in 1932. Then they resented the influence that London exerted over their king. A nationalist, anti-royalist coup in 1958 ended British dominance of Iraq. After that Baghdad forged cordial relations with the Soviet Union, culminating in a Friendship Treaty in 1972. But once Saddam Hussein became the executive president seven years later, he made it a point to show that he was strictly his own man. When Moscow intervened militarily in Afghanistan in late 1979, he openly criticized its action. He was all set to become the chairman of the Non-Aligned Movement after its triennial conference in Baghdad in 1983. But because his country became embroiled in a war with Iran, a fellow-member of the NAM, and because of the unsafe conditions in the Iraqi capital, the conference venue was shifted to New Delhi, and Indian Prime Minister Indira Gandhi became the NAM's chairwoman.

One of the chief political weaknesses of the bodies like the Iraqi National Congress, an umbrella organization, is that the US funding makes it appear a tool of a foreign power, and that militates against any prospect of its being taken seriously by Iraqis. Its association with the CIA is so close and so public that even the Iraqi National Accord, originally funded by Riyadh, withdrew its affiliation with the INC in late 2000.

Iraq

Ten years of UN sanctions and international isolation of Iraq, which Saddam Hussein has survived by staying in "resistance" mode, seem to have strengthened his obstinacy, independent-mindedness, inordinate capacity for denial, and subterfuge.

All these elements of Saddam's character came to the fore when the UN tried to disarm Iraq of WMD and the means to deliver them according to the Security Council Resolution 687. Section C of that document required Iraq to submit to the UN within fifteen days "a declaration of the locations, amounts and types of all items specified above." Yet it was not until September 1997 that Iraq made the fifth submission of "the final, full and complete disclosure" of its past biological weapons' program.[2]

Apparently Saddam Hussein had expected to get away with providing the least possible information to Unscom. Given the manner in which the Iraqis had pulled the wool over the eyes of IAEA inspectors since the 1970s, he must have thought his officials had a good chance of giving a repeat performance. But this was not to be. So as months and years passed, the number of stand-offs and crises on UN inspections grew.

To outsiders it seemed to be a straightforward struggle between the good guy and the bad guy. But the reality was murky. Within a year Washington had resorted to using Unscom as cover for spying on Iraq for its own purposes. It kept even the Unscom bosses – Rolf Ekeus and Richard Butler – in the dark on certain aspects. The apparent linchpin of its strategy was an official from the US state department seconded to Unscom, Charles Duelfer, who served as the deputy to Ekeus and Butler from 1993 until the dissolution of Unscom in early 2000. To see that nothing untoward happened to the American staff of Unscom while they engaged in espionage, and no spanners were thrown in the works, deliberately or unwittingly, by anybody, he was kept fully informed by the US National Security Agency. When these facts were exposed in the American press in early 1999, they corroborated the repeated Iraqi allegations of the US exploiting Unscom for spying, and damaged the standing of the UN. They also diminished the chances of a return of UN inspectors to Iraq for inspection and monitoring.

Saddam Hussein was not the only one who did not play by the rules. As early as April 1994, the US secretary of state, Warren Christopher, stated that Iraq's compliance with Paragraph 22 of Security Council Resolution 687 was not enough to justify lifting UN sanctions. When, yielding under pressure, and as a consequence of the defection of Gen. Hussein Kamil Hassan in August 1995,

Saddam Hussein gave further information about the proscribed weapons and facilities, Washington did not change course: it kept shifting the goal posts. It never considered rewarding Iraq for the cooperation it had offered, however grudgingly. Throughout, its policy was "all stick, no carrot."

Once Richard Butler became the executive chairman of Unscom in July 1997, for all practical purposes he adopted the American policy as his own. As Scott Ritter, a trained US intelligence officer and a chief inspector of Unscom since 1991, showed in his book, *Endgame*, Butler seemed to work for the US, not the UN. Ritter also noted Butler's close coordination of inspections and their timing with the US National Security Adviser, Sandy Berger. Evidently Butler had no intention of ever giving Iraq a clean bill of health, no matter what the latter did. According to his own account in *Saddam Defiant*, during his meeting with Tariq Aziz in June 1998, he told the Iraqi deputy premier that, assuming satisfactory progress, "we would still need to discuss the Iraqi policy of concealment."[3] He did not stop there. In his statement of November 20, 1998, he mentioned his demand that Baghdad should hand over the minutes of the meetings of the Iraqi High Level Committee on the Retention of Banned Weapons and Materials that, according to Unscom, Iraq had admitted forming in June 1991.[4] He would have known that under no circumstances would Iraq publicly admit forming such a committee and that there was no possibility whatsoever of its handing over documentary proof of such a committee to a foreign organization. This was undoubtedly a delaying tactic by Butler, to hold back the prospect of issuing a clearance certificate to Iraq.

In September 1997, once Iraq had submitted its fifth final and complete report on its biological warfare agents program, the policy-makers in Washington concluded, rightly, that Unscom had more or less reached the end of its usefulness. So it became irrelevant whether its inspectors stayed in Iraq or not. Their activities were now important only in so far as they could provide a basis for the Pentagon to use the detailed intelligence that US operatives under Unscom cover had painstakingly collected over the years. Little wonder that the Clinton administration was all ready to strike Iraq in February 1998. But, unexpectedly, UN Secretary-General Kofi Annan intervened and defused the crisis. Then nine months later the B–52 bombers were already on their way to hit Iraqi targets when they were turned around by Clinton when, again unexpectedly, Saddam backed down on Unscom inspections at the last moment.

Finally, in Operation "Desert Fox" in December 1998, the Pentagon put to use all the intelligence that the US had gathered so far.

But later the Clinton administration found itself having to pay a heavy price for this action, diplomatically and otherwise. It meant the departure of Unscom and IAEA inspectors from Iraq due to their withdrawal by Butler on the eve of Operation "Desert Fox." The public opinion in the Arab world hardened against America. The rupture that this US operation caused among the Permanent Five members of the Security Council was so deep that it took one year to draft and debate a follow-up resolution to replace Unscom, among other things. Even then, France, Russia and China abstained when Resolution 1284 was put to the vote in December 1999.

It was not until August 2000 that Unmovic, which replaced Unscom, was in a state where it could do preliminary work for inspections and monitoring in Iraq. By then the international petroleum market had become so tight that it had come to rely heavily on Iraqi oil exports. The decision of Hugo Chavez (the leftist president of Venezuela, and then chair of OPEC) to meet his Iraqi counterpart in Baghdad inadvertently paved the way for busting the UN airflight ban on Iraq. On top of that came the flare-up in the Israeli–Palestinian violence following the failure of Camp David talks between the two parties mediated by President Clinton on the final status of the Palestinian Territories including East Jerusalem in July, and the provocative visit to the Muslim Noble Sanctuary in the Old City of Jerusalem by the hawkish Israeli leader, Ariel Sharon, two months later.

Suddenly fortune began smiling on the Iraqi dictator, who was invited to an Arab summit for the first time in ten years. However, a decade is a long time in volatile Arab politics. And the reasons that put Saddam on the upswing were beyond his control. He had nothing whatsoever to do with the upsurge in the economies all over the globe which boosted demand for oil. Nor did he have anything to do with the US-mediated peace talks between the Israelis and Palestinians.

What further aided Saddam was the US presidential poll which made Clinton wary of using force against Saddam for fear of him retaliating by reducing or cutting off Iraqi exports running at a hefty three million bpd. The subsequent stand-off on the election result kept American politicians and public transfixed on the subject, with little interest or inclination to tackle any problem abroad.

However, an objective examination of the situation showed that the gains made by Baghdad were symbolic and psychological rather than solid and material. All the forty international flights between mid-August and early November that arrived in the Iraqi capital did so under the label of humanitarian journeys by loading token food or medicine on board, to stay within the context of UN Security Council Resolution 670 (September 1990). The practical impact of these flights on the supply of foodstuffs and medicine in Iraq was perfunctory. With the country importing 200 tons of food and medicine daily, it would need forty flights *a day* to replace its current UN-administered oil-for-food scheme.

In any event, the damage done by the decade-long economic embargo to the Iraqi economy, infrastructure and social fabric was so deep and wide that it would take several years of uninterrupted, high oil income to repair it. Iraq's class composition has been altered beyond recognition, with the salaried middle class reduced from being about a third of the population to less than a sixth. Unable to make ends meet, some middle-class professionals had taken up semi-skilled jobs, such as car or refrigerator repairs, while others had emigrated. It was the émigrés' remittances home in US dollars, sent through Jordan-based couriers, that were sustaining much of the middle class in Iraq. Reversing the long-established trend, the country had experienced migration from urban areas to rural.

Also the phrase "lifting of UN sanctions" needed a close examination. There were two parts to it, civilian and military. Nobody at the UN Security Council was even thinking of removing military sanctions against Baghdad. In the civilian sphere again there were two distinct aspects: goods – oil and non-oil – and financial transactions.

Since January 2000 there had been no limit on how much oil Baghdad sold abroad. But all petroleum transactions had to go through the UN. In that sense the UN had a mandate over Iraq's most prized resource – almost similar to the political mandate on Iraq that the League of Nations conferred on Britain during the 1920s. That was the reason why Saddam initially refused to accept the oil-for-food Security Council Resolution 986 passed in April 1995. The implementation of that program from December 1996 onward did not invalidate that argument of Saddam. As for financial transactions with Iraq, these were still banned. That was why foreign visitors could not use their credit cards in the country. So there was still a long way to go before the full lifting of sanctions in the civilian sector, assuming the US refrained from exercising its veto on such a resolution at the Security Council.

Equally importantly, it was hard to visualize an end to the economic embargo without Iraq agreeing to some form of inspecting and monitoring by the UN to ensure that it did not reconstitute its WMD programs. Therefore much negotiating and bargaining lay ahead, a process in which Saddam was likely to introduce the issue of the no-fly zones imposed by the US and the UK. The unannounced de-escalation in the air surveillance in the north by the Pentagon had much to do with the unease felt by Turkey in whose territory the American and British warplanes were stationed. Ankara had normalized diplomatic relations with Baghdad, and spoken in favor of the lifting of sanctions against Iraq which hurt its own economic interests.

In the south, the US and the UK used jets stationed on land bases in Kuwait and Saudi Arabia and on their own aircraft carriers in the Gulf. So even if Kuwait and Riyadh were to withdraw their cooperation, they would still be able to conduct Operation "Southern Watch," but their action would be deeply offensive to the Gulf Arabs.

Regarding Iraq's relations with the Saudi and Kuwaiti monarchies, Kuwait had the specific issue of the 623 missing Kuwaitis to settle with Baghdad. In return Iraq had raised the subject of 1,150 missing Iraqis. Then there was the more weighty matter of Iraq's invasion of Kuwait, for which the latter had demanded an apology. But Baghdad was prepared to say that it had made a "mistake" in Kuwait if the emirate and the Saudi kingdom did the same for providing land bases to Washington and London for imposing a no-fly zone in southern Iraq.[5] The Iraqi condition implied that Kuwait and Saudi Arabia would do so *after* they had asked America and Britain to withdraw their warplanes from their territories. But there was no sign that they were contemplating such a move.

So, the negotiations between the UN Security Council's five permanent members and Iraq were likely to be protracted – all the more so in view of Saddam

Hussein's freshly acquired cockiness. He was only too aware of the role that Iraqi oil exports played in affecting the price of the commodity, on which the West depended heavily, and the unprecedentedly high petroleum revenue of $15–17 billion Iraq expected to earn in the second half of 2000.

The Iraqi leader had arrived at this position after several ups and downs in his career following the defeat of Iraq in the Second Gulf War. For the first few years it was downhill for him at home and abroad. He set his mind on seeing the UN sanctions ended by the spring of 1994. That was not to be. Warren Christopher's published interpretation of Resolution 687 in April 1994, that disarming Iraq of its WMD was not enough to lift the embargo, dampened his hopes. And the defection of his senior son-in-law, Hussein Kamil Hassan, the seventh most powerful man in the republic with an insider's knowledge of Iraq's WMD program, in August 1995 was the nadir of Saddam's downhill slide.

But he proved resilient, recovering fast from this shattering blow. By deciding to offer himself as the sole presidential candidate, for which there was no provision in the constitution, he infused life into the ruling Baath Party, an organization which had so far never performed such a task. It rose to the occasion, and mustered enough people to the polling booths to impress the several hundred foreign journalists who had been invited to witness the event.

A turning-point in Saddam's post–1991 career came in 1996. The year began with the return and murder of Hussein Kamil Hassan. In June he pre-empted the most ambitious US-led plan for a coup against him. And in late August came an internecine blood-letting among the Kurds. To be invited by one Kurdish leader, Masud Barzani, to fight another, Jalal Talabani, was something Saddam simply could not refuse. But even though he had to withdraw his forces quickly from Kurdistan, after they had achieved the intended result, what pleased him most was the unceremonial collapse of the American plan to build up the Kurdish region as a launching pad to overthrow him and his regime. Also he forged clandestine commercial and intelligence links with Barzani. To their credit, both the Bush and Clinton administrations studiously, and rightly, avoided getting involved in the quagmire of internal politics of Iraqis, be they Kurds or Shias.

The year ended with the start of the UN-supervised oil-for-food program. This enabled Saddam to raise the daily ration of some 1,300 calories a day to 2,000 calories, an enormous gain for his long-suffering citizens.

From then on, the Iraqi president began to inch forward. In his dealings with Unscom he became pro-active, and turned his nemesis, the re-elected President Clinton, into someone who reacted. As Clinton neared the end of his second term of office, his subordinates would assure the strong anti-Saddam lobby in the US that the Iraqi dictator would be overthrown before Clinton left the White House in January 2001. This was not to be.

In late February 1991, with dejected Iraqi soldiers on the run in their thousands before the advancing forces of the US-led Coalition, very few would have bet on Saddam surviving a year, much less a decade.

There are several reasons why this has happened. His regime remains viciously intolerant of opposition, however muted or well-meaning. An atmosphere of fear prevails in the country. But this has been the case for so long that most people do not even realize that they habitually keep looking over their shoulders and that they speak the name "Saddam Hussein" in hushed tones, often using the term *al Rais* (the President) or *al Qaid* (the Leader), or both. The security and intelligence agencies remain loyal to Saddam and are brutally efficient. In the final analysis they underwrite his regime. After all he acquired the ultimate power as the boss of these agencies.

He was also helped, unwittingly, by the repeated bombings of Iraq by the Pentagon after the Gulf War – starting with the strikes in January 1993, on the eve of President Bush's departure from the White House, and ending with the ones in December 1998.

Since these bombardments had nothing to do with expelling Iraq from Kuwait, most Iraqis failed to perceive the logic behind them. Indeed, in the case of Operation "Desert Fox," they saw President Clinton trying to divert attention away from the impeachment proceedings against him in the House of Representatives by authorizing air strikes against Iraq. So they increasingly put the blame for their misery on America, not Saddam.

Also, most Iraqis feared the unknown future they believed would befall them if Saddam Hussein were assassinated or toppled.

So, given the choice between a repressive, but stable, regime they had lived under since 1968, and an uncertain future that would follow Saddam's overthrow, they thought it prudent to stay with the status quo. Well aware of the deep differences between Arabs and Kurds, concentrated in the mountainous north, and between the privileged Sunni minority and the long-marginalized Shia majority, they reckoned that once the oppressive lid of Saddam's regime was removed, a civil war would ensue and the country would break up into statelets. This is what had happened in the Lebanese civil conflict, emanating primarily from religious differences, that lasted from 1975 to 1990.

Interestingly, the popular Iraqi fear of instability in the post-Saddam Iraq was shared by top US policy-makers. It was forcefully articulated by General Anthony Zinni, chief of the US Central Command, covering the Gulf.[6] Washington also had another strong reason to prefer political stability in Iraq to an unpredictable future. It wanted to keep oil prices stable – an objective which would be seriously undermined by an outbreak of civil conflict in a country whose proven oil reserves were second only to Saudi Arabia's. That was why, while painting a picture of a multi-party democracy in post-Saddam Iraq (essentially for domestic consumption), both the Bush and Clinton administrations were firm in their plans to replace the Iraqi dictator with another strong-man, a pro-Washington Sunni general deriving his power from the armed forces and intelligence and security agencies. They reckoned, rightly, that only such an authoritarian figure would be able to control the bloodletting that would erupt after Saddam's departure as the relatives of some 30,000 victims of his regime settled scores with the security and intelligence agents – a repeat on a much larger scale of what happened in southern Iraq immediately after the Second Gulf War.[7] That is why they worked closely in planning anti-Saddam coups with the soldier-dominated Iraqi National Accord while lavishing praise in public on the civilian-led Iraqi National Congress.

On the ground, politics of the exiled Iraqi opposition meant little, if anything, to the people living inside Iraq. If they had an opinion at all, it pertained to the West in general, and America in particular. By and large they detested the US and its presidents.

One would have thought – as did the American policy-makers – that the Iraqi people would almost unanimously blame Saddam Hussein for the misery that has visited them since his invasion of Kuwait in 1990, and that they would see the connection between the cause (Iraq's aggression) and the effect (UN sanctions and international isolation). "There are various reasons why this is not the case," explained "Hatem," a London-based Iraqi professional who did not belong to any opposition group and who visited Baghdad periodically.

> Iraqis don't take individual responsibility for the invasion of Kuwait. The sanctions, that flowed from that event, have created a popular feeling of "us" and "them," the West. When it comes to apportioning blame, most Iraqis think at the first level, and don't get into secondary and tertiary reasons. They say that Saddam put them in harm's way but did not cause harm. That was caused by the West, led by America. "Saddam did not drop bombs on us, did not cut off our electricity and phones and water supplies; others did that," they say.

And sanctions had provided Saddam with a perfect alibi for all the ills in the country.

> If roads are potholed, if phones don't work, if there aren't enough medicines in hospitals, Saddam blames the sanctions. On the other hand, he takes full credit for any improvement, however slight – like, say, flower-beds appearing in Saadoun Street in Baghdad [a thoroughfare].

Sanctions had aided the Iraqi leader to tighten further his hold over society in which rationing was at the core of his control mechanism. "Furthermore," continued "Hatem",

> due to communications and educational embargo middle class Iraqis have lost touch with reality. They do not read foreign papers or watch foreign television. All they are exposed to are the Iraqi state television and radio which provide a highly distorted view of the outside world.

Most people in Iraq don't know what a fax is, or a mobile phone. E-mail is a rarity even in Baghdad, and very expensive.[8]

Though, despite its best efforts, America had failed to dislodge Saddam, at some point he must go as a result of death due to natural causes or an accident. What happens after him depends to a large extent on how he departs – suddenly or as a consequence of a long, publicly acknowledged illness. He was known to be suffering from a lymph glandular disorder since the mid-1970s which was kept under control by medicine. The recent reports that he was undergoing chemotherapy treatment for lymph cancer administered by a team of European doctors lacked credibility. "Saddam would never trust non-Iraqi doctors," said "Ilam," a London-based Iraqi specialist on the Gulf. "He knows that they would be bribed by Western intelligence agencies to leak information about his ill-health. So he would trust only local doctors living in Iraq who would be kept under constant surveillance."[9]

It is possible that with advancing age a still healthy Saddam may decide to lessen his work load by shifting some of his authority to one or more close family members, who include his sons, Uday and Qusay, half-brothers – Barzan, Watban, and Sabawi – and a senior cousin, Ali Hassan. He may then elevate himself to an elder statesman and oversee the performance of his chosen successor. From his viewpoint that would be the best possible scenario as it would provide an orderly transitional period.

But what if he develops an incurable disease, and the fact becomes known? He may then decide to groom his successor in the way Syrian president Hafiz Assad did by actively promoting his eldest son, Bashar. Only in the case of Saddam, his younger son, Qusay, is the more likely candidate. Since 1992 he has been in charge of the National Security Bureau, which oversees all security and intelligence agencies. Unlike his elder brother, Uday – notorious for his violence, short temper and public tantrums – Qusay is intelligent and quietly ruthless. However, now that Uday has almost fully recovered from the injuries he suffered during the assassination attempt on him in late 1996,[10] he should be considered an active aspirant for the top job.

Then there is the possibility of Saddam dying accidentally or clinically – on the operating table. That would leave no time for him or his immediate family to seize the reins of power and keep them. This could lead to infighting between the different factions in the extended family of Saddam – the al Ibrahims and al Majids. That in turn would most probably induct the twenty-two generals of the elite Republican Guard and the Special Republican Guard, the only force whose units are garrisoned in and around Baghdad. So in the end it may come down to a struggle between competing RG generals.

At the end, whosoever emerges triumphant may find himself or his group being courted by the US – on certain terms, the bottom line being protecting America's vital interests in the Gulf.

Iran

Since World War II, Washington's strategic objectives in the Gulf have been consistent:

1 there should be assured access on reasonable terms, for the US and its allies, to the oil and natural gas reserves of the Gulf;
2 security of Israel must be guaranteed;
3 (until the Soviet Union's collapse), Soviet influence in the Gulf must be kept out or minimized; and
4 no single Gulf state should be allowed to become the dominant power in the region.

It was in pursuit of the last objective that the US began siding with Baghdad during the Iran–Iraq War when Tehran acquired the upper hand in the conflict, raising the possibility of becoming the unchallenged leader in the Gulf.

Between World War II and the 1979 Iranian revolution, the US had successfully co-opted Iran under the dictatorial Shah into the tripod of Israel, Saudi Arabia and Iran on which its regional strategy rested. The prime agenda of this alliance was to maintain political stability in the Gulf and the rest of the Middle East, and keep in check revolutionary forces, whether Marxist or Arab nationalist. The loss of the Iranian leg of the tripod created a major problem for American policy-makers – all the more so when a revolutionary movement rooted in Islam, and virulently opposed to the US hegemony in the region, emerged triumphant. There was no precedent for such a popular movement in modern times. If it was a question of co-existing or even allying with a regime that administered the state along Islamic lines, America had enjoyed excellent relations with the Saudi kingdom, which had been run strictly according to the Sharia since its inception in 1932. Both Washington and Riyadh shared a deep hatred of Marxism and were committed to maintaining the political status quo. With US oil corporations running the Saudi petroleum industry the economies of the two countries were interlinked.

But Saudi Arabia was, and remains, a royal autocracy whereas America is a secular, democratic republic. In strictly ideological terms, the US, committed to promoting democracy worldwide, should feel an affinity with the Islamic Republic since the latter has had a representative government based on universal franchise since the 1979 revolution. During the first two decades of its history, it held three referendums (on establishing an Islamic republic, and adopting a constitution framed by a popularly elected body in 1979, and then on endorsing an amended constitution a decade later) and sixteen elections (3 Experts Assembly, 7 presidential, 5 parliamentary and 1 local council). Even during the war with Iraq, the Iranian regime did not alter the electoral timetable. And in all elections voters had a choice of candidates. Oddly enough, like the US president, the Iranian Leader was elected by an electoral college in the form of the Assembly of

Experts (of Islam). But whereas the American presidential college comes into being only to elect the chief executive, the Iranian Assembly has a tenure of eight years and monitors the performance of the Leader.

Judged purely by the standard of a representative government, America and India, the world's largest democracy, should have been allies ever since the Indian Republic adopted a multi-party system based on universal franchise in 1950. But they were not because there was a clash of interests. India wanted to be the regional superpower which Washington opposed since New Delhi was friendly with the Soviet Union, the superpower rival of the US. In this it had the active support of Pakistan, a traditional rival of India, which was often ruled by military generals.

Likewise, Iran under the ayatollahs wanted to be the regional superpower, a position it thought it deserved since it was the most strategic country in the area, its shoreline covered not only the Gulf but also the Arabian Sea, its population was one-a-half times the total of the remaining seven Gulf states, and it shared the same religion – Islam – with its neighbors. This ambition of Tehran was opposed by Washington, which had the support of the Gulf monarchies whose Arab subjects had been historically antipathetic towards Persians/Iranians.

In the absence of being accepted as the region's leader, Tehran insisted that the security of the Gulf should be the exclusive responsibility of the regional states, and that non-regional countries should stay out. Washington disagreed strongly. It regarded the Gulf and the Straits of Hormuz as international water-ways. And it made no bones about its economic and strategic interest in the continued supply of Gulf oil and gas at comparatively cheap prices to it and the rest of the Western world and Japan – an objective in which it was actively aided by the ruler of Saudi Arabia, possessing a quarter of the globe's oil deposits, and acting as the swing producer in OPEC. Small wonder that, until recently, Iran and Saudi Arabia were on the opposite sides in OPEC.

Riyadh's animosity towards Tehran was rooted in the fact that, after overthrowing the Shah of Iran, Ayatollah Khomeini attacked monarchy *per se* in the Muslim world, citing the Quran to support his argument that hereditary power had no sanction in Islam.[11] However, following Khomeini's death, pragmatism became the watchword in Iran's foreign policy in the region. This trend was aided by Iraq's invasion of Kuwait, which struck a near-fatal blow to Saddam's pan-Arabist pretensions and his drive to inflame historic Arab–Persian rivalry. In the wake of the Iraqi aggression, Iran's relations with the small Gulf monarchies improved, with the exception of the UAE which disputed Tehran's jurisdiction over the islands of Abu Musa, Lesser Tunb and Greater Tunb. In the case of Riyadh, while ideological impediments towards normal relations ceased to exist, Saudi Arabia's intimate links with Washington still jarred in Iran. It was not until the election of moderate Khatami, in May 1997, that prospects improved for a genuine rapprochement between the two leading Islamic states, one republican and the other monarchical. The hosting of the Islamic Conference Organization (where only Azerbaijan, Bahrain, Iran and Iraq were the Shia-majority members) by Iran in December put a seal on normalizing ties between Tehran and Riyadh. Saudi Crown Prince Abdullah went on to play a crucial behind-the-scenes role to thaw relations between Iran and America, resulting in Khatami's interview on the CNN.

However, Iran's opposition to the US extended beyond the region. Describing America as a hegemonist (not imperialist – the term used by the secular left worldwide) power, Tehran has encouraged, within its limited resources, anti-American, Islamic forces in the Muslim world. Its most notable contribution has been in Lebanon (where the Hizbollah succeeded in securing Israel's unconditional evacuation of south Lebanon after twenty-two years of occupation) and in the Occupied Palestinian Territories where, to the chagrin of Washington, it has supported Hamas and the Islamic Jihad.

On its part, the US has been active in its opposition to the Islamic Republic – from imposing economic sanctions on it in late 1979, following the American hostage taking in Tehran, to the adoption of the dual containment policy in 1993 to the 1996 Iran–Libya Sanctions Act.

The thaw in relations that started in early 1998, with President Khatami expressing regret at the American hostage-taking, has yet to result in talks at a government-to-government level, a preamble to normal ties between the two countries.

Meanwhile, the subject of relations with the one-time "Great Satan" – the defining term routinely used by Ayatollah Khomeini for America – will continue to engage Iranian politicians and journalists.

Having unveiled a socio-political system which combined the salient features of Islamic jurisprudence with the basics of democracy – universal suffrage, representative government, freedom of speech and association albeit within the limits of Islam – the leaders of the Islamic Republic have seen it evolve, as the polity has grappled with changing circumstances, from revolution to war to reconstruction.

"After the revolution President Abol Hassan Bani-Sadr antagonized the mullahs, and the Mujahedin-e Khalq went on a warpath, and then came the war with Iraq," said Sadiq Zibakalam, professor of political science at Tehran University.

> So the issue of political freedoms got marginalized. After the war, during his two terms, President Rafsanjani focused on reconstruction. It is only after Khatami's election [in 1997] that the issue of political reform got back on the agenda. Actually, this is not surprising. After all this is what the Iranian revolution was about. During the late 1970s we discussed such subjects as Islam and freedom, and Islam and the role of women.[12]

But since the nature of freedom is complex and shifting, and since there are reportedly differences between Leader Khamanei and President Khatami on the subject, the issue is unlikely to be resolved soon and without further convulsions.

Seen in a positive light, this can be described as the dynamic of Iranian politics.

Since the early days of the Islamic Republic there have been two main currents within Islamic politics, right/conservative/hardline and left/reformist/moderate. And measured by the size of Majlis deputies their fortunes have varied. In the First Majlis (1980–84), conservatives were in a minority. That was why it rejected President Ali Khamanei's first choice of prime minister. Ali Akbar Velayati, a conservative, was rejected by 80 votes to 74, and Mir Hussein Musavi, a leftist, was accepted by 115 votes to 39 in October 1981.[13] Even though neither faction had a majority in the Second Majlis (1984–88), it again endorsed Musavi after President Khamanei had presented him as his choice after his re-election in 1985. In the Third Majlis (1988–92) the leftist camp, which now included moderates, claimed the loyalty of two-thirds of the house. But its strength declined to 90 in the Fourth Majlis (1992–96) while the conservative total rose to 150. With the formal split in the traditional right leading to the formation of the SOC in 1996, a centrist force, backed largely by the modern middle class, emerged in Iranian politics. In the Fifth Majlis (1996–2000), the rightwing strength was 120 while the leftwingers and centrists together were 70 strong. After Khatami's election as president in 1997, the term "reformist" came into vogue, to encompass everybody who was not a conservative or hardline fundamentalist. They achieved the same strength in the Sixth Majlis (2000–) as had the leftwingers and moderates collectively in the Third.

The changing fortunes of different factions, the emergence of a centrist trend, the shift in political debate from economic to political liberalization – all these were signs of a functioning democracy within an Islamic framework. With major battles on running the economy behind them, the different factions had converged on such vital issues as further privatization (to include such sectors as telecommunications, railways and petrochemicals) and maintenance of highly popular subsidies on essential items like foodstuffs, fuel and medicine.

It was in the arena of political reform that the factions were at loggerheads. Fundamentalists and rightwingers wanted to maintain the status quo while centrists and leftists advocated widening of the freedom of expression, association and assembly within the constitution. The former warned that if the regime allowed political liberalization to advance unchecked, it would end up losing power, and regress to the last days of the Shah, when he conceded too much too quickly to his secular opponents. Their opponents referred to Chapter Three of the 1989 constitution, entitled "People's Rights," Articles 19–42. "Publications and the press have freedom of expression except when it is detrimental to the basic principles of Islam or the rights of the public," stated Article 24. "The details of this exception will be specified by law." And according to Article 27, "Public gatherings and marches may be held freely provided arms are not carried and they are not detrimental to the basic principles of Islam."

The differences between the two camps were encapsulated in the statements made during the trial of Ayatollah Muhammad Khoeiniha, the managing director of the *Salaam*, by the SCC in July 1999. "Our Islamic Republic can remain only if it guarantees the maximum legitimate freedom within the framework of the constitution," said Khoeiniha. "The *Salaam* is trying to create turmoil and instability in the basic pillars of the system and the revolution," countered one of his accusers, Hamid Reza Taraqi, a rightwing MP.

In the absence of well-organized and properly structured political parties, newspapers became surrogate parties, their circulations indicating the size of their support. Their number multiplied after Khatami's victory in 1997. Actually it was he who, as minister of culture and Islamic guidance, had piloted the first press bill in 1983 in the midst of the First Gulf War. "During the war with Iraq conditions were not right for press freedom, and nobody paid much attention to the subject," said Muhammad Sultanifar, the managing director of the English-language *Iran News*, established in 1994.

> Before the 1997 presidential poll there were several restrictions on the press. After Khatami's victory journalists realized the importance of the Press Law; and so did the Fifth Majlis. Both felt that it was time to amend the legislation. But reformist deputies wanted to do so to open up the press, conservatives to control it.[14]

By coincidence, the ban on the *Salaam* came on the day the Majlis adopted in principle restrictive amendments to the Press Law by a majority of 35 votes.

Press freedom was part of a wider demand for political and social liberalization. As expected, this was being resisted by conservatives not only in the parliament but also in the judiciary where they were in a majority. Since the Iranian legislation was based on Islamic canons, it was the qualified clerics who dispensed justice. A side-effect of their anti-reform verdicts was that the proponents of the regime could, and did, claim, rightly, that the three organs of the state – executive, legislative and judicial – were indeed separate as was the case in Western democracies.

There were, of course, several major differences between secular democracies in the West and the emerging Islamic democracy whereby, in Khatami's words, Iran was unprecedentedly trying to "formulate democracy in the context of spirituality and morality." One of them was that, unlike in Britain and North America, in criminal cases the roles of the investigator and prosecutor were combined in the investigating judge – a practice somewhat similar to that prevalent in medieval times in tribal societies in Muslim countries.

But a far greater difference lay in the fact that there was an overlay of mullahs in all important aspects of Iranian state and society. The Leader, who had to be a senior cleric, appointed his personal representatives not only to all the important institutions of the state at the national and provincial levels but also to the major private and quasi-official foundations, which possessed enormous assets. Mullahs were attached to the regular military as well as the IRGC, Baseej and LEF. They, of course, ran the Islamic Propagation Organization. They were on the payrolls of the ministry of culture and Islamic guidance which had its representatives in many large villages, not to mention 700 towns and 25 cities. In addition they were on the staff of the private and official foundations, including the richly endowed Foundation for the Deprived and Martyrs. Finally, there were many seminaries where all teachers and many administrators were clerics.

In political terms, Islam provided the Iranian regime with an ideology and a social cement. The image of women clad in chadors in the street – however repugnant to the Western eye – was the most dramatic and ubiquitous manifestation of Islam in daily life. The absence of alcohol, gambling and night-clubs was another.

In an Islamic state, the Sharia governs the life of a Muslim completely. Having studied all human actions, the early jurisprudents categorized them as: obligatory; recommended; allowed; unspecified; undesirable; and prohibited. From this they graduated to prescribing exactly how the obligatory, recommended and allowed acts were to be performed. The simple edict of Prophet Muhammad, that a believer must undertake ritual ablution with water (or sand) before prayers, became enmeshed into a profound debate on the purity and pollution of the human body. Religious jurisprudents conducted minute examination of all bodily functions – eating, drinking, breathing, washing, urinating, defecating, farting, copulating, vomiting, bleeding and shaving – and prescribed how these were to be performed, the main stress being on keeping the body "pure." Along with this went a code of social behavior, including contact between opposite sexes, which too was all-encompassing. (The twin codes were so demanding that, even with the best will in the world, a believer could not abide by them all the time. On the other hand, it was the introduction of these codes into the lives of those who embraced Islam that led to common behavioral patterns among Muslims whether they lived in the Mauritanian desert or Indonesian archipelago.) What emerged within a century of the rise of Islam in 622 A.D. was Islamic jurisprudence *(fiqh)*, which included all aspects of religious, social and political life – covering not only ritual and religious observances, the law of inheritance, property and contracts, and criminal law, but also constitutional law, laws concerning state administration, and the conduct of war.[15]

When it comes to interpreting the Sharia – that is, practicing *ijtihad* (interpretative reasoning) – there was often no difference between jurisprudents on the obligatory and prohibited subjects. Differences usually arose in the grey area of "allowed, unspecified and undesirable." Whether a woman was entitled to become president of Iran fell into this category. As stated earlier, at least one senior theologian, Ayatollah Yusuf Sanaei, has said "Yes." In general, though, older jurisprudents were conservative, sticking to traditional interpretations, whereas younger ones were flexible and progressive.

Then there was the specific issue of the concept of vilayat-e faqih (rule of the religious jurisprudent) which formed the backbone of the Iranian constitution adopted in 1979. This doctrine, developed by Ayatollah Khomeini in 1971 in his book *Hukumat-e Islami: Vilayet-e Faqih* (Islamic Government: Rule of the Jurisprudent), specified that an Islamic regime required an Islamic ruler who was thoroughly conversant with the Sharia and was just in its application: a Just

Faqih. He should be assisted by jurisprudents at various levels of legislative, executive and judicial bodies. The function of the popularly elected parliament and presidency, open to both lay believers and clerics, was to resolve the conflicts likely to arise in the implementation of Islamic precepts. However, judicial functions were to be performed only by jurisprudents who were conversant with the Sharia. Such jurisprudents would also oversee the actions of the legislative and executive branches. The overall supervision and guidance of parliament and judiciary rested with the Just Faqih (later officially called Leader, *Rahbar*, of the Islamic Revolution), who must also ensure that the executive did not exceed its powers.[16]

An important amendment to the constitution's Article 107 – authorizing the Assembly of Experts to choose the Leader – incorporated after Khomeini's death in June 1989, included the sentence, "The Leader is equal with the rest of the people of the country in the eyes of [the] law." Given this, those clerics who argued that the Leader was divinely chosen and not accountable to the people could only be a minority. Equally small was the number of those who were advocating an end to the monopoly over *ijtihad* (interpretative reasoning) that jurisprudents had so far enjoyed.

In this debate Professor Abdul Karim Soroush of Tehran University stood out for the boldness, if not originality, of his thought. It drew a line between religion, which was eternal, and religious knowledge (*maarifat-e dini*), which resulted from applying "knowledge of the day" to the study of the core scriptures. Summarizing Soroush's thesis, Valla Vakili, an Iranian scholar at Oxford University, wrote,

> While religion itself does not change, human understanding and knowledge of it does. Religious knowledge is but one among many branches of human knowledge … [It] is the product of scholars engaged in the study of the unchanging core of Shia Islamic texts – the Quran, the *hadiths* and the teachings of the Shia Imams. These scholars interpret the text through the use of various methods, ranging from the rules of Arabic grammar to inferential logic, from Aristotelian philosophy to contemporary hermeneutics. Religious knowledge changes then as a function of these methods. But it is also influenced heavily by the worldview that informs each scholar [i.e, his understanding of other human sciences] … Religious knowledge changes and evolves over time, as more comprehensive understandings replace previous, more limited interpretations. Yet all interpretations are bound by the era in which a religious scholar lives, and by the degree of advancement of the human sciences and religious studies within this era.[17]

Soroush's commonsensical thesis offered a convincing explanation for the gap that often existed between the interpretations given by the older jurisprudents, educated in earlier times, and the younger ones, educated more recently.

He wanted that religious knowledge be pursued as vigorously as possible by clerics and lay believers alike in a free-flowing environment, and whatever impeded that objective ought to be removed. He argued, for instance, that since using religion as a political ideology limited religious knowledge of the believer it should be discontinued. He found religiously based methodology in governing a modern state inadequate, and concluded that there were no specifically religious methods of governance. The only institutional role for religion in government he was prepared to concede was that of establishing a legal code that incorporated the *fiqh*, and was in compliance with it.[18]

In essence, Soroush was arguing in his articles in the pro-reform press for separation of religion and politics, a taboo subject in Iran. Little wonder that the clerical establishment found his reasoning subversive, although it had not tried him for that yet. In any case, he had expressed such views before the amendment of the Press Law in 1999 that outlawed criticism of the constitution and the Leader.

The conservative MPs in the Fifth Majlis feared that a debate along the lines suggested by Soroush would raise the possibility of a divorce between religion and politics, and threaten the system dominated by clerics, and had to be nipped in the bud. They had the backing of the Leader's office. It was in this context that the harsh response of the Leader and the judiciary to the reform movement – which was being advanced principally by a lively press – needed to be viewed.

Faced with this reactionary onslaught, the freshly elected reformist centrist-leftist majority in the Sixth Majlis in spring 2000 concluded that it was best to focus on consolidating whatever gains reformers had made in politics and culture in the past three years rather than push for further reform.

However, unless a social order, whether secular or religious, evolves with time, it will inevitably atrophy. The Islamic system in Iran was no exception. Indeed, by amending 40 of the 175 articles of the 1979 constitution and adding two more articles within a decade of its promulgation, the regime had acknowledged the indisputable need for change.

Whether such wise counsels will prevail over the coming years, and whether the regime will prove supple enough to adapt to changing times and the fast-emerging post-revolution generation, is hard to tell.

What could be said with certainty, though, was that, in Khatami, Iran had found a president who had the ability to bridge the gap between generations, between those who remembered their days under the Shah's oppressive dictatorship, and those who lacked any experience of the *ancien régime*. This was an extremely valuable quality, very much needed once the revolution had passed its twentieth anniversary.

Above all else, Khatami was a healer. He had shown his conciliatory nature not only at home but also abroad. Among other things he extended a hand of friendship to Saddam Hussein, whose aggression against Iran set off the twentieth century's longest conventional war, on the eve of the ICO summit in December 1997. Aware of the popular sympathy that Iranians developed for the suffering Muslim people of Iraq, he ensured that Iran participated in the airflight-busting that started in late summer 2000. By having Foreign Minister Kamal Kharrazi lead the Iranian delegation, Khatami underscored the significance of the Iran Air flight. By coincidence this occurred at a time when both Baghdad and Tehran found themselves advocating a jihad to liberate the Occupied Palestinian Territories from Israel, leading to fears in Washington that the one-time enemies might forge a tactical alliance, in which Syria would inevitably be drawn, to fight Israel.

Yet Iran and Iraq had still to tackle the contentious issue of the sponsorship each provided to the armed rebel groups from the other, especially SAIRI and the MKO. Unless each of these was expelled from Tehran and Baghdad respectively, the prospects were slim for a peace – much less friendship – treaty between the two neighbors which went to war in 1980. A chronicle of that conflict was offered in my work, *The Longest War* – the first in a trilogy that ends with the present book.

EPILOG

The stalemated result of the US presidential poll on November 7, 2000, between Democrat Al Gore and Republican George W. Bush was not resolved until December 12 when the Supreme Court ruled in favor of Bush by five votes to four. He chose as his secretary of state (Retired) General Colin Powell, former chairman of the US chiefs of staff during the 1991 Gulf War. Powell declared that he would "re-energize" sanctions against Iraq, and dismissed Saddam as "sitting on a failed regime that is not going to be around in a few years' time." In his confirmation hearings before a US Senate committee on January 17, he stressed the need "to be vigilant, ready to respond to provocations, and utterly steadfast in our policy towards Saddam Hussein."[1]

Powell's statements ran counter to the mood prevailing in the Gulf region and the Muslim world, which were steadily re-integrating Iraq into their folds. At the triennial Islamic Conference Organization summit in Doha in mid-November, the final statement dropped its traditional reference to "Iraqi aggression" and called for efforts to "prepare the ground for resolving the differences" between Iraq and Kuwait.[2] Soon Iraqi oil began flowing through the newly re-opened Syrian–Iraqi pipeline. It transpired later that Iraq was selling petroleum at the discount price of $15 a barrel to Syria and receiving the revenue outside the UN escrow account, and that the Syrian government was consuming the oil domestically and exporting the equivalent amount – 150,000 bpd – at the higher market prices.[3] By late November Saudi Arabia had reopened its border with Iraq and allowed vehicular traffic, and Egypt had upgraded its consulate in Baghdad to the ambassadorial level. "Iraq will soon be integrated into the Arab fold," said President Hosni Mubarak. "It is only a matter of time."[4] The month ended with Jordan starting weekly scheduled flights to Baghdad. The UN Sanctions Committee approved this if passengers could prove their journeys were not of commercial nature, a condition which in practice meant little. Jordan's lead was followed by Egypt and then Syria.

Reflecting the prevalent sentiment in the Arab world, Egyptian foreign minister Amr Moussa told the world economic forum in Davos, Switzerland, in January 2001, "We can't expect the people of Iraq to live under sanctions for ever. Since the Gulf War, public opinion in the Arab world has moved 180 degrees."[5]

What accelerated Iraq's rehabilitation in the Arab ranks was Saddam's anti-Israeli militancy which struck a popular chord against the background of continuing Israeli–Palestinian violence. Arabs noted that while Washington vehemently opposed sending UN peacekeepers to protect the Palestinians from the excessive use of force by Israel, its warplanes provided 24-hour air cover to rebellious Kurdish and Shia citizens of Iraq against the central government.

On January 5, the 80th anniversary of the Iraqi army, Saddam sent special greetings to "the vanguard of the striving people of Palestine" in their struggle "to liberate Palestine from the river (Jordan) to the (Mediterranean) sea" – a phrase highlighting Iraq's non-recognition of Israel.[6]

Saddam backed up his pro-Palestinian rhetoric with a proposal to the UN secretary-general that $875 million of the petroleum revenue earned by Iraq during the current six monthly period under the oil-for-food program be transferred as aid to the Palestinians. But it failed to win the UN Security Council's approval due to the opposition of America and Britain. That, however, did not stop an Iraqi representative in the Palestinian territories from handing over a $10,000 check to the family of the latest Palestinian martyr (in a list of 340) – compared to the $2,000 that the Palestinian Authority gave – and a $1,000 check to the family of an injured Palestinian (one among some 3,000).[7] With the annual per capita income of a Palestinian before the intifada (*lit.*, uprising) being $1,600 – versus an Israeli's $17,500 – Baghdad's handouts were over-generous.

The fact that an Iraqi's per capita income was less than a Palestinian's, and that, a decade after the Gulf War, Iraq was still dependent on the UN Security Council to be able to maintain its vital rationing system, evidently did not enter Saddam's thinking.

After protesting that the Security Council had turned the temporary oil-for-food program into a permanent one, Baghdad accepted its next six-monthly phase on December 1. The latest scheme liberalized its provisions by including electrical goods and housing supplies into the list of "pre-approved imports," and permitted Iraq to spend $525 million locally on repairing and maintaining its oil industry but under UN supervision.[8]

As January 17 (the tenth anniversary of the 1991 Gulf War) approached, regional and international attention turned to Iraqi–Kuwaiti relations. As an MP, Uday Saddam Hussein submitted a working paper to the Speaker, suggesting that the National Assembly's logo should be redrawn to include Kuwait as part of Greater Iraq. Among the regional countries that protested were the UAE, Bahrain and Oman, all of whom had recently restored diplomatic relations with Baghdad. In response, Tariq Aziz said that Uday was free to propose what he pleased, and that Kuwait got "what it deserved" in 1990 because it was undermining oil prices and stealing Iraqi oil by drilling horizontally across the border. When Kuwait voiced its protest, the semi-official *Al Thawra* threatened, in its editorial on January 21, that Iraq would withdraw its recognition of the emirate. The next day the Iraqi newspapers attacked Saudi Arabia for providing facilities to the American and British warplanes on its soil.[9] The spat highlighted the continuing tension between the principal regional adversaries in the 1991 Gulf War.

However, this did not arrest the movement toward closer economic ties between Iraq and Egypt, which had emerged as the fourth largest source of imports for Baghdad – after Russia, China and France. Taha Yassin Ramadan flew to Cairo in mid-January to sign a free trade agreement with Egypt, which visualized abolishing all tariffs and trade barriers between the two countries. A few weeks later Syria followed suit.[10] The ultimate objective was to create a common market of Iraq, Jordan, Syria and Egypt – a scenario that displeased Washington.

By then, going by its satellite intelligence of the past few months, the Pentagon had concluded that Iraq was about to link parts of its air defense system with the freshly installed fiber-optic network and improve its chances of hitting the US and British aircraft patrolling the no-fly zones. To abort such a possibility, it needed to target sites that lay outside the southern air exclusion zone. So it approached President Bush.

On February 15, Bush authorized such an action (leaving the timing to General Henry Shelton, chairman of the US chiefs of staff) and prepared for his imminent visit to Mexico. The Pentagon struck the next day at 12:30 p.m. EST/8:30 p.m. Iraqi time. Two dozen US and UK warplanes fired on five Iraqi air defense targets above the 33rd Parallel, around Baghdad, containing seven command and control nodes and twenty radar installations. The two-hour air strikes killed three and injured thirty.[11]

In Mexico City, Bush tried to downplay the raids by describing them, wrongly, as "routine." He said, "Saddam Hussein has got to understand that we expect him to conform to the agreement that he signed after Desert Storm. We will enforce the no-fly zone, both south and north. Our intention is to make sure that the world is as peaceful as possible, and we are going to watch very carefully as to whether or not he develops weapons of mass destruction. If we catch him doing so, we will take the appropriate action."[12] Bush's ignorance of the basic facts was pointed out by Mike Allen in the *Washington Post*: "In the 1991 agreement that ended the Gulf War, Mr Saddam pledged not to develop weapons of mass destruction. The agreement said nothing about no-flight zones."[13] Apparently President Bush was unaware that the US derived its authority for imposing the no-fly zones in Iraq from the UN Security Council Resolution 688, and not Resolution 687 which formalized the ceasefire in the 1991 Gulf War.

In their briefings the defense ministries in Washington and London first accused Iraq of having upgraded its air defense system and then modified their assertion by stating that it was on the verge of doing so.

The mainstream American press described the raids as "timely reinvigoration" of the US policy on Iraq and a signal to Saddam that the Bush administration was not averse to using force to contain any new Iraqi threat. Outside America, though, the speculative nature of the American claim about Iraq's improved air defense system did not convince the media or their readers or viewers. The ideas of warplanes flying at 20–25,000 feet (6,500–8,000 m) in the air, and improved radar and ground-launched missile systems were too abstract to grip popular imagination – especially in comparison to the earlier, actual disputes between Iraqi officials and UN inspectors.

Russia described the raids as "a threat to international security and the entire international community." But severest criticism came from France, with its foreign minister, Hubert Vedrine, asserting that Washington had "no legal basis" for this kind of bombing. "All other countries have expressed their disapproval, criticism, doubt and disquiet, as we have, because we do not see the point of this action," he said. "The new [US] administration told us it is reflecting on a new Iraqi policy, more focused on security and gentler on the population. What it has just done is neither."[14]

"All other countries" included members of the 22-strong Arab League. Criticism came from all except Kuwait, with Saudi Arabia adopting an equivocal stance. Following his signing of a free trade agreement with Syria in Damascus, Saudi foreign minister Saud al Faisal joined his Syrian counterpart, Farouq al Shaara, in issuing a communiqué which expressed "condemnation and concern at the latest escalation targeting southern Baghdad at a time when broad consultations are taking place to address the situation in its entirety at the forthcoming Arab summit in Amman in a manner that preserves the region's security and Iraq's safety and sovereignty over its territory."[15] On the other hand, according to Jim Hoagland, a senior *Washington Post* columnist, "Saudi Arabia insisted that the Pentagon keep secret its assistance in last week's strikes though AWACS [Airborne Warning and Control Systems] and other aircraft would have flown from at least one Saudi base."[16]

The popular belief among Arabs was that President Bush had manufactured the pretext of the upgrading of Iraqi air defense to punish Saddam for the vocal and material support he was providing the Palestinian intifada. By conferring on Saddam the image of a victim, Bush unwittingly boosted his already high standing among Palestinians. "A youthful countenance of Mr Saddam smiles from posters pasted on walls, taped to store windows and waved aloft at funerals," reported Molly Moore from the West Bank town of Ramallah. "His name is shouted at demonstrations … and in public opinion polls, Mr Saddam … has consistently outpolled the Palestinian leader, Yasser Arafat."[17]

During his four-day tour of the Middle East in late February, Powell discovered the wide gap that existed between the Arab nations' policies toward Iraq, and America's stance. In Cairo, after he had stated that "it is Saddam Hussein who refuses to abandon his pursuit of weapons of mass destruction [and] threatens not the US but the region," Egyptian foreign minister Amr Moussa retorted: "For us, I don't see the threat." Nonetheless, at the end of his tour he conceded that the UN sanctions were in "a disarray," an understatement. He promised to devise "smart sanctions" that would focus on military trade that could assist Iraq in developing WMD.[18]

In late March, the US state department came up with a scheme whereby UN monitors would be posted just outside Iraq's frontiers and at key airports to prevent Baghdad from importing military materials. To end Iraq getting under-the-counter commissions from oil traders, the UN would prepare a list of oil companies authorized to buy Iraqi crude direct from its State Oil and Marketing Organization. To secure their cooperation, Syria, Jordan and Turkey will be permitted to purchase Iraq's petroleum at discount prices and deposit the funds in special accounts that Iraq could use only to import goods from these countries. The UN would prepare a new, shortened list of prohibited items described in great detail to assist the exporting countries. All import contracts would still be reviewed by the UN 661 Sanctions Committee but the pre-approved items could pass automatically. If a Committee member raised an objection, then the exporter would be given time to clarify or offer an alternative item. That would end the current practice of a member vetoing a contract without any explanation – a procedure that has resulted in 1,500 frozen contracts worth $3.3 billion, with the US being responsible for $3.1 billion.[19]

Powell's team rushed to finalize its proposals for revised sanctions on Iraq before the Arab summit on March 27–28. Arab leaders, however, were interested not in the nuances of the UN sanctions but in the wholesale scrapping of them as their final communiqué would show. A consensus on the lifting of the embargo against Iraq emerged at the three-day Arab foreign ministers' conference on the eve of the summit. This was less than satisfactory to Iraq's Muhammad al Sahhaf who called on fellow League members to breach the sanctions just as they had done in the case of air flights.

The efforts of the summit host, King Abdullah II, and the "goodwill committee" of the ministers failed to reconcile Iraq and Kuwait, reportedly due to the hard line adopted by Saudi Arabia at the behest of Washington. To Baghdad's satisfaction, instead of discussing "Iraq's invasion of Kuwait," as previous Arab League foreign ministers and heads of state had done, this time they debated "the situation between Iraq and Kuwait." Also, according to one report, the Jordanian monarch managed to devise a compromise between the demands of Kuwait that Iraq must apologize for its 1990 invasion, promise in writing that it would not re-invade Kuwait, and accept all post-Gulf War UN Security Council resolutions, and Iraq's insistence that Kuwait must stop the use of its bases by US and UK warplanes. But at the last moment Kuwait pulled out reportedly under pressure from Saudi Arabia, represented by Saudi defense minister Prince Sultan ibn Abdul Aziz, who had played a leading role in assembling the anti-Iraq Coalition in 1990.[20]

On the other hand it was significant that the summit was held in the capital of Jordan, which had maintained pro-Baghdad neutrality before and during the 1991 Gulf War. King Abdullah II sent a personal invitation to Saddam Hussein through a special envoy to attend the summit. But Saddam did not, and, as before, dispatched Izzat Ibrahim instead. At the summit's open session, Ibrahim read out the message from his boss. Addressing the fellow-leaders, Saddam said, "The [Palestinian] intifada and the sanctions [against Iraq] are the same issue, and if you ignore any of this you are ignoring the main issues of the Arabs. Ignoring the people's stand in any area is tantamount to taking the stand of foreign powers."[21] By foreign powers Saddam meant Israel (which had elected Ariel Sharon, an uncompromising hawk, as its prime minister on February 6) and the US, and his message was directed at Kuwait and Saudi Arabia, which provided their bases to US and UK warplanes to patrol southern Iraq and bomb Iraqi targets.

The future of the air exclusion zones was one of the three areas of policy on Iraq under review in Washington, the others being UN sanctions and the Iraqi opposition. While Powell was wary of the Iraqi National Congress and the hazards of even low-level military support to it that could become open-ended and expensive, defense secretary Donald Rumsfeld was all for a pro-active plan to overthrow Saddam Hussein by arming and training the INC. This difference needed to be resolved before Bush could finalize his policy on Iraq. And that was not expected before June 2001.

Meanwhile the Bush administration threw an early hint of thawing of relations with Tehran, no matter who prevailed in the ongoing tug-of-war between conservatives and reformers there. "We've made an effort not to personalize our policy," said a state department official in early April. "We try to be careful not to support any political faction. We don't have a sentimental view of the reform movement."[22] Criticizing the Clinton presidency's public approval of the reformists' success in the February 2000 Majlis elections, the official promised that the new administration would refrain from expressing a preference in the upcoming presidential poll.

As yet President Muhammad Khatami had not declared his hand. What he had done was to be honest with the public about the achievements and failures of his presidency and spell out the limitations of his authority.

In his address to a conference on the constitution on November 26, 2000, Khatami said, "I declare that after three and a half years as president, I don't have sufficient powers to implement the constitution, which is my biggest responsibility. In practice the president is unable to stop the trend of violations or force implementation of the constitution." So far he had refrained from elaborating on the anti-constitutional activities of his opponents in order to avoid creating tension, he explained. To illustrate the constitutional violations he alluded to closed-door courts without jury being used to prosecute journalists and politicians, and the leveling of such ambiguous charges as "disturbing public opinion" and "undermining the establishment." Two days later the judiciary chief Ayatollah Muhammad Hashemi Shahroudi accused him of attempting to exploit the constitution.[23] Khatami did not respond, evidently to avoid "creating tension."

As it was, breaking with tradition, the revolutionary court in Tehran had opened to public the trial of the seventeen defendants accused of participating in a conference on Iran in Berlin in April that was judged to be "unIslamic." As part of that trial, Akbar Ganji, a reformist investigative journalist well known for his piety, was brought before the court on November 30. During his appearance, with television cameras turning, Ganji named those he held responsible for the deaths of some eighty dissidents between 1989 and 1998. He named Ali Fallahian, the intelligence minister from 1989 to 1997, as the "master key" who ordered the killings. He accused Gholam Hussein Muhsini Ejaei (a hard-line judge who had tried and convicted Gholam Hussein Karbaschi) of ordering the assassination of writer Pirouz Davani in August 1998. Generally speaking, he continued, political murders were the handiwork of the adherents of the ultra-conservative Haqqani seminary in Qom whose spiritual mentor, Ayatollah Muhammad Taqi Mesbah-Yazdi, argued in public sermons that if the faithful found the Islamic system or its sanctities being profaned and the state failing to act, they had the right and duty to take appropriate action. Defending the charge of defaming the Islamic system, Ganji said that he accused only 1 percent of the violent wrongdoers within the 20 percent right-wing nationwide minority. "Those who are repressing civil society, assassinating people with different ideas, imprisoning their critics, disturbing reformist gatherings and banning the independent press are not acting in a revolutionary manner but in a dictatorial, fascist way," he concluded.[24]

Ganji's performance caused a sensation and won him many admirers especially among young Iranians. Conversely, it secured him the stiffest punishment among the eleven defendants who were found guilty and sentenced on January 13, with three of them receiving either suspended sentences or fines. He got a ten year jail sentence followed by five years internal exile in the southern town of Bashagard.[25]

What impact this had on the reform movement as a whole remained unclear. However, according to Mashallah Shams al Wazien, the cell-mate of Ganji, "The loss of momentum for the reform movement can only take place when the people turn their backs on their demands, which are gaining freedom and liberty and participation in the political power structure. And the people of Iran are not turning their backs on these demands."[26]

Ganji's indictment sheet had included not only his participation in the Berlin conference but also a series of articles on the murders of intellectuals and writers in late 1998. The case against the eighteen defendants, all of them employees of the intelligence ministry, for the assassinations of Dariush and Parvene Forouhar, and Muhammad Mukhtari and Muhammad Jaafar Pouyande opened on December 23 and proceeded speedily behind closed doors before a military court presided by Muhammad Reza Aqiqi. Convinced that full truth would not emerge, the relatives of the victims boycotted the trial. All but two of the accused admitted complicity in one or more assassinations.

Judge Aqiqi acquitted three of the accused. He sentenced to death the three defendants who carried out the killings (as required by the Sharia), and to life imprisonment Mustafa Kazemi and Mehrdad Alikhani – former intelligence ministry departmental heads – for ordering the murders and preparing a list of forty victims to be targeted for assassination.[27]

The leftist Islamic Iran Participation Front denounced the verdict on the basis that the case had left many questions unanswered. Criticism also came from the victims' families who described the trial as "a damage limitation" exercise by the judicial authorities who were more interested in hastily closing the gory chapter rather than exposing the full extent of an episode, which many believed was linked to the assassinations of scores of dissidents stretching back a decade and involved politicians in higher places.

On the other side there were others who saw the glass half full rather than half empty. Summarizing their view, Jim Muir, head of the BBC bureau in Tehran, wrote, "The fact that the trial happened at all and that convictions were secured is perhaps the biggest tangible achievement scored by President Khatami in his struggle to establish the rule of law and transparency in public affairs."[28]

Khatami continued his crusade for political reform within the constitution while explaining his role in Iran's political–religious life. "We must abide by the principles of popular rule and pluralism in our constitution," he said in a speech in mid-February. "We are forced and doomed to make progress and do not have much time. Democracy is a must in today's world. Those who negate pluralism do not understand the spirit of the times."[29] About a month later, in an unprecedented "state of the nation" address to the Majlis, he said, "I cannot give up my commitment to God and to the noble people. As long as the people want me, I will continue to serve, with the thought that I can move forward in the face of all problems." He concluded on a somber note: "We should be worried that, God forbid, one day our people will feel the authorities are not meeting their real demands. Under such circumstances, no military, security or judicial power will be able to save the country."[30]

Soon 200 of the 276 MPs signed an open letter calling on Khatami to stand, arguing that failure to do so would doom political reform.

In a welcome sign of compromise, the press court closed down a hard-line weekly for "insulting Khatami" and "ridiculing his social and political program" on March 8, a decision that had been preceded by the Guardians Council's approval of a bill allowing single women to study abroad. However, the thrust of these decisions was neutralized by the press court's orders, on March 18, to shut down four reformist publications.[31]

This was a reflection of the division in the conservative camp, with moderates intent on reducing the vote for Khatami in the presidential poll, and hard-liners resolved to see that he did not run. Either way, this camp's strategy centered around showing that Khatami was weak and ineffective. Khatami knew this, and was also aware of the criticism by young reformers that he had no stomach for political fighting. But he was conscious too of the fact that as a people Iranians favored the underdog. So he continued to portray himself, rightly, as someone sinned against rather than sinning – someone who was being sidelined, despite the massive popular mandate he had won in the 1997 election.

While conservatives, lacking any credible rival to Khatami, were focusing on reducing the vote for Khatami, reformists were planning to turn the presidential poll into a referendum on his ideas and policies. Khatami was deliberately holding back his hand, planning to leave it to the last minute (the registration date being May 3), thus depriving his opponents of fielding a serious candidate.

He was widely expected to run and win. The only unknowns were the size of the voter turnout and his plurality – the factors which will determine the direction and pace of political reform over the next four years. But what seemed fairly clear was that, irrespective of the outcome of the presidential poll, Tehran's relations with Washington were unlikely to warm substantially. This had to do with the rising violence between Israel and the Palestinians, which by late April had claimed the lives of over 400 Palestinians (including thirteen Israeli Arabs) and 75 Israelis.

Iran strongly condemned Israel's excessive and disproportionate use of force against the Palestinians. Its reformist-dominated Majlis sponsored an international conference in support of the Palestinian intifada in Tehran on April 24–25. It was attended by 35 Arab and Muslim countries, and the large Palestinian delegation included many MPs and representatives of the pro-Yasser Arafat mainstream and militant Islamic groups.

Addressing the gathering, Leader Khamanei said, "First of all the Israeli regime must be isolated in the Occupied Territories, its political and economic lifelines severed, and then the armed resistance against Israel must be continued." President Khatami called for worldwide sanctions against Israel and the trial of Israeli "war criminals" before an international tribunal.[32]

In Baghdad Saddam Hussein was equally vehement in his denunciation of Israel, offering to unleash hundreds of thousands of Iraqi volunteers to help Palestinians to liberate their country through a jihad.

So, on this important regional issue, the two neighbors continued to share a common stance.

APPENDIX I

The Algiers Accord, 6 March 1975

During the convocation of the OPEC summit conference in the Algerian capital and upon the initiative of President Houari Boumedienne, the Shah of Iran and Saddam Hussein (Vice-Chairman of the Revolution Command Council) met twice and conducted lengthy talks on the relations between Iraq and Iran. These talks, attended by President Houari Boumedienne, were characterized by complete frankness and a sincere will from both parties to reach a final and permanent solution of all problems existing between their two countries in accordance with the principles of territorial integrity, border inviolability and non-interference in internal affairs.

The two High Contracting Parties have decided to:

First   Carry out a final delineation of their land boundaries in accordance with the Constantinople Protocol of 1913 and the Proceedings of the Border Delimitation Commission of 1914.

Second   Demarcate their river boundaries according to the thalweg line.

Third   Accordingly, the two parties shall restore security and mutual confidence along their joint borders. They shall also commit themselves to carry out a strict and effective observation of their joint borders so as to put a final end to all infiltrations of a subversive nature wherever they may come from.

Fourth   The two parties have also agreed to consider the aforesaid arrangements as inseparable elements of a comprehensive solution. Consequently, any infringement of one of its components shall naturally contradict the spirit of the Algiers Accord. The two parties shall remain in constant contact with President Houari Boumedienne who shall provide, when necessary, Algeria's brotherly assistance whenever needed in order to apply these resolutions.

The two parties have decided to restore the traditional ties of good neighbourliness and friendship, in particular by eliminating all negative factors in their relations and through constant exchange of views on issues of mutual interest and promotion of mutual co-operation.

The two parties officially declare that the region ought to be secure from any foreign interference.

The Foreign Ministers of Iraq and Iran shall meet in the presence of Algeria's Foreign Minister on 15 March 1975 in Tehran in order to make working arrangements for the Iraqi-Iranian joint commission which was set up to apply the resolutions taken by mutual agreement as specified above. And in accordance with the desire of the two parties, Algeria shall be invited to the meetings of the Iraqi-Iranian joint commission. The commission shall determine its agenda and working procedures and hold meetings if necessary. The meetings shall be alternately held in Baghdad and Tehran.

His Majesty the Shah of Iran accepted with pleasure the invitation extended to him by His Excellency President Ahmad Hassan Bakr to pay a state visit to Iraq. The date of the visit shall be fixed by mutual agreement.

On the other hand, Saddam Hussein agreed to visit Iran officially at a date to be fixed by the two parties.

H.M. the Shah of Iran and Saddam Hussein expressed their deep gratitude to President Houari Boumedienne, who, motivated by brotherly sentiments and a spirit of disinterestedness, worked for the establishment of a direct contact between the leaders of the two countries and consequently contributed to reviving a new era in Iraqi-Iranian relations with a view to achieving the higher interest of the future of the region in question.

United Nations Security Council Resolution 598, 20 July 1987 (adopted unanimously)

The Security Council,

Reaffirming its resolution 582 (1986)

Deeply concerned that, despite its calls for a ceasefire, the conflict between Iran and Iraq continues unabated, with further heavy loss of human life and material destruction,

Deploring the initiation and continuation of the conflict,

Deploring also the bombing of purely civilian population centres, attacks on neutral shipping or civilian aircraft, the violation of international humanitarian law and other laws of armed conflict, and, in particular, the use of chemical weapons contrary to obligations under the 1925 Geneva Protocol,

Deeply concerned that further escalation and widening of the conflict may take place,

Determined to bring to an end all military actions between Iran and Iraq,

Convinced that a comprehensive, just, honourable and durable settlement should be achieved between Iran and Iraq,

Recalling the provisions of the Charter of the United Nations and in particular the obligation of all member states to settle their international disputes by peaceful means in such a manner that international peace and security and justice are not endangered,

Determining that there exists a breach of the peace as regards the conflict between Iran and Iraq,

Acting under Articles 39 and 40 of the Charter of the United Nations,

1   Demands that, as a first step toward a negotiated settlement, Iran and Iraq observe an immediate ceasefire, discontinue all military actions on land, at sea and in the air, and withdraw all forces to the internationally recognized boundaries without delay;

2   Requests the Secretary-General to despatch a team of United Nations observers to verify, confirm and supervise the ceasefire and withdrawal and further requests the Secretary-General to make the necessary arrangements in consultation with the parties and to submit a report thereon to the Security Council;

3   Urges that prisoners of war be released and repatriated without delay after the cessation of active hostilities in accordance with the Third Geneva Convention of 12 August 1949;

4   Calls upon Iran and Iraq to co-operate with the Secretary-General in implementing this resolution and in mediation efforts to achieve a comprehensive, just and honourable settlement, acceptable to both sides, of all outstanding issues in accordance with the principles contained in the Charter of the United Nations;

5   Calls upon all other states to exercise the utmost restraint and to refrain from any act which may lead to further escalation and widening of the conflict and thus to facilitate the implementation of the present resolution;

6   Requests the Secretary-General to explore, in consultation with Iran and Iraq, the question of entrusting an impartial body with inquiring into responsibility for the conflict and to report to the Security Council as soon as possible;

7   Recognizes the magnitude of the damage inflicted during the conflict and the need for reconstruction efforts with appropriate international assistance once the conflict is ended and in this regard requests the Secretary-General to assign a team of experts to study the question of reconstruction and to report to the Security Council;

8   Further requests the Secretary-General to examine in consultation with Iran and Iraq and with other states of the region measures to enhance the security and stability of the region;

9   Requests the Secretary-General to keep the Security Council informed on the implementation of this resolution;

10   Decides to meet again as necessary to consider further steps to ensure compliance with this resolution.

APPENDIX III

United Nations Security Council Resolution 687, 3 April 1991 (12–1, 2 abs)

The Security Council,

Recalling its resolutions 660 (1990), 661 (1990), 662 (1990), 664 (1990), 665 (1990), 666 (1990), 667 (1990), 669 (1990), 670 (1990), 674 (1990), 677 (1990), 678 (1990) and 686 (1990),

Welcoming the restoration to Kuwait of its sovereignty, independence and territorial integrity and the return of its legitimate government,

Affirming the commitment of all Member States to the sovereignty, territorial integrity and political independence of Kuwait and Iraq, and noting the intention expressed by the Member States co-operating with Kuwait under paragraph 2 of resolution 678 (1990) to bring their military presence in Iraq to an end as soon as possible consistent with paragraph 8 of resolution 686 (1991),

Reaffirming the need to be assured of Iraq's peaceful intentions in light of its unlawful invasion and occupation of Kuwait,

Taking note of the letter sent by the Foreign Minister of Iraq on 27 February 1991 (S/122275) and those sent pursuant to resolution 686 (1990) (S/22273, S/22276, S/22320, S/22321, and S/22330),

Noting that Iraq and Kuwait, as independent sovereign States, signed at Baghdad on 4 October 1963 'Agreed Minutes Regarding the Restoration of Friendly Relations, Recognition and Related Matters', thereby recognizing formally the boundary between Iraq and Kuwait and the allocation of islands, which were registered with the United Nations in accordance with Article 102 of the Charter and in which Iraq recognized the independence and complete sovereignty of the State of Kuwait within its borders as specified and accepted in the letter of the Prime Minister of Iraq dated 21 July 1932, and as accepted by the Ruler of Kuwait in his letter dated 10 August 1932,

Conscious of the need for demarcation of the said boundary,

Conscious also of the statements by Iraq threatening to use weapons in violation of its obligations under the Geneva Protocol for the prohibition of the Use in War of Asphyxiating, Poisonous or Other Gases, and of Bacteriological Methods of Warfare, signed at Geneva on 17 June 1925, and of its prior use of chemical weapons and affirming that grave consequences would follow any further use by Iraq of such weapons,

Recalling that Iraq has subscribed to the Declaration adopted by all States participating in the Conference of States Parties to the 1925 Geneva Protocol and other Interested States, held at Paris from 7 to 11 January 1989, establishing the objective of universal elimination of chemical and biological weapons,

Recalling further that Iraq has signed the Convention on the Prohibition of the Development, Production and Stockpiling of Bacteriological (Biological) and Toxin Weapons and on Their Destruction, of 10 April 1972,

Noting the importance of Iraq ratifying this Convention,

Noting moreover the importance of all States adhering to this Convention and encouraging its forthcoming Review Conference to reinforce the authority efficiency and universal scope of the convention,

Stressing the importance of an early conclusion by the Conference on Disarmament of its work on a Convention on the Universal Prohibition of Chemical Weapons and of universal adherence thereto,

Aware of the use by Iraq of ballistic missiles in unprovoked attacks and therefore of the need to take specific measures in regard to such missiles located in Iraq,

Concerned by the reports in the hands of Member States that Iraq has attempted to acquire materials for a nuclear-weapons programme contrary to its obligations under the treaty on the Non-Proliferation of Nuclear Weapons of 1 July 1968,

Recalling the objective of the establishment of a nuclear-weapons-free zone in the region of the Middle East,

Conscious of the threat which all weapons of mass destruction pose to peace and security in the area and of the need to work towards the establishment in the Middle East of a zone free of such weapons,

Conscious also of the objective of achieving balanced and comprehensive control of armaments in the region,

Conscious further of the importance of achieving the objectives noted above using all available means, including a dialogue among the states of the region,

Noting that resolution 686 (1991) marked the lifting of the measures imposed by resolution 661 (1990) in so far as they applied to Kuwait,

Noting that despite the progress being made in fulfilling the obligations of resolution 686 (1991), many Kuwaiti and third country nationals are still not accounted for and property remains unreturned,

Recalling the International Convention against the taking of hostages, opened for signature at New York on 18 December 1979, which categorizes all acts of taking hostages as manifestations of international terrorism,

Deploring threats made by Iraq during the recent conflict to make use of terrorism against targets outside Iraq and the taking of hostages by Iraq,

Taking note with grave concern of the reports of the Secretary-General of 20 March 1991 (S/22366) and 28 March 1991 (S/22409), and conscious of the necessity to meet urgently the humanitarian needs in Kuwait and Iraq,

Bearing in mind its objective of restoring international peace and security in the area as set out in recent Council resolutions,

Conscious of the need to take the following measures acting under Chapter VII of the Charter,

1 Affirms all thirteen resolutions noted above, except as expressly changed below to achieve the goals of this resolution, including a formal cease-fire;

A

2 Demands that Iraq and Kuwait respect the inviolability of the international boundary and the allocation of islands set out in the 'Agreed Minutes Between the State of Kuwait and the Republic of Iraq Regarding the Restoration of Friendly Relations, Recognition and Related Matters', signed by them in the exercise of their sovereignty at Baghdad on 4 October 1963 and registered with the United Nations and published by the United Nations in document 7063, United Nations Treaty Series, 1964;

3 Calls on the Secretary-General to lend his assistance to make arrangements with Iraq and Kuwait to demarcate the boundary between Iraq and Kuwait, drawing on appropriate material including the map transmitted by Security Council document S/22412 and to report back to the Security Council within one month;

4 Decides to guarantee the inviolability of the above-mentioned international boundary and to take as appropriate all necessary measures to that end in accordance with the Charter;

B

5 Requests the Secretary-General, after consulting with Iraq and Kuwait, to submit within three days to the Security Council for its approval a plan for the immediate deployment of a United Nations observer unit to monitor the Khor Abdullah and a demilitarized zone, 10 kilometres into Iraq and 5 kilometres into Kuwait from the boundary referred to in the 'Agreed Minutes Between the State of Kuwait and the Republic of Iraq Regarding the Restoration of Friendly Relations, Recognition and Related Matters' of 4 October 1963; to deter violations of the boundary through its presence in and surveillance of the demilitarized zone; to observe any hostile or potentially hostile action mounted from the territory of one State to the other; and for the Secretary-General to report regularly to the Council on the

operations of the unit, and immediately if there are any serious violations of the zone or potential threats to peace;

6   Notes that as soon as the Secretary-General notifies the Council of the completion of the deployment of the United Nations observer unit, the conditions will be established for the Member States co-operating with Kuwait in accordance with resolution 678 (1990) to bring their military presence in Iraq to an end consistent with resolution 686 (1991);

C

7   Invites Iraq to reaffirm unconditionally its obligations under the Geneva Protocol for the Prohibition of the Use in War of Asphyxiating, Poisonous or Other Gases, and of Bacteriological Methods of Warfare, signed at Geneva on 17 June 1925, and to ratify the Convention on the Prohibition of the Development, Production, and Stockpiling of Bacteriological (Biological) and Toxin Weapons and on Their Destruction, of 10 April 1972;

8   Decides that Iraq shall unconditionally accept the destruction, removal, or rendering harmless, under international supervision, of:

(a)   all chemical and biological weapons and all stocks of agents and all related subsystems and components and all research, development, support and manufacturing facilities;

(b)   all ballistic missiles with a range greater than 150 kilometres and related major parts, and repair and production facilities;

9   Decides for the implementation of paragraph 8 above, the following:

(a)   Iraq shall submit to the Secretary-General, within fifteen days of the adoption of this resolution, a declaration of the locations, amounts and types of all items specified in paragraph 8 and agree to urgent, on-site inspection as specified below;

(b)   the Secretary-General, in consultation with the appropriate Governments and, where appropriate, with the Director-General of the World Health Organization (WHO), within 45 days of the passage of this resolution, shall develop, and submit to the Council for approval, a plan calling for the completion of the following acts within 45 days of such approval:

(i)   the forming of a Special Commission, which shall carry out immediate on-site inspection of Iraq's biological, chemical and missile capabilities, based on Iraq's declarations and the designation of any additional locations by the Special Commission itself;

(ii)   the yielding by Iraq of possession to the Special Commission for destruction, removal or rendering harmless, taking into account the requirements of public safety of all items specified under paragraph 8 (a) above including items at the additional locations designated by the Special Commission under paragraph 9 (b) (i) above and the destruction by Iraq, under supervision of the Special Commission, of all its missile capabilities including launchers as specified under paragraph 8 (b) above;

(iii) the provision by the Special Commission of the assistance and co-operation to the Director-General of the International Atomic Energy Agency (IAEA) required in paragraphs 12 and 13 below;

10 Decides that Iraq shall unconditionally undertake not to use, develop, construct or acquire any of the items specified in paragraphs 8 and 9 above and requests the Secretary-General, in consultation with the Special Commission, to develop a plan for the future ongoing monitoring and verification of Iraq's compliance with this paragraph, to be submitted to the Council for approval within 120 days of the passage of this resolution;

11 Invites Iraq to reaffirm unconditionally its obligations under the treaty on the Non-Proliferation of Nuclear Weapons, of 1 July 1968;

12 Decides that Iraq shall unconditionally agree not to acquire or develop nuclear weapons or nuclear-weapons-usable material or any subsystems or components or any research, development, support or manufacturing facilities related to the above; to submit to the Secretary-General and the Director-General of the International Atomic Energy Agency (IAEA) within 15 days of the adoption of this resolution a declaration of the locations, amounts and types of all items specified above; to place all of its nuclear-weapons-usable material under the exclusive control, for custody and removal, of the IAEA, with the assistance and co-operation of the Special Commission as provided for in the plan of the Secretary-General discussed in paragraph 9 (b) above; to accept in accordance with the arrangements provided for in paragraph 13 below, urgent on-site inspection and the destruction, removal and rendering harmless as appropriate of all items specified above; and to accept the plan as discussed in paragraph 13 below for the future ongoing monitoring and verification of its compliance with these undertakings;

13 Requests the Director-General of the International Atomic Energy Agency (IAEA) through the Secretary-General, with the assistance and co-operation of the Special Commission as provided for in the plan of the Secretary-General in paragraph 9 (b) above, to carry out immediate on-site inspection of Iraq's nuclear capabilities based on Iraq's declarations and the designation of any additional locations by the Special Commission; to develop a plan for submission to the Security Council within 45 days calling for the

destruction, removal, or rendering harmless as appropriate of all items listed in paragraph 12 above; to carry out the plan within 45 days following approval by the Security Council; and to develop a plan, taking into account the rights and obligations of Iraq under the Treaty on the Non-Proliferation of Nuclear Weapons, of 1 July 1968, for the future ongoing monitoring and verification of Iraq's compliance with paragraph 12 above, including an inventory of all nuclear material in Iraq subject to the Agency's verification and inspections to confirm that IAEA safeguards cover all relevant nuclear activities in Iraq, to be submitted to the Council for approval within 120 days of the passage of this resolution;

14   Takes note that the actions to be taken by Iraq in paragraphs 8, 9, 10, 11, 12 and 13 of this resolution represent steps towards the goal of establishing in the Middle East a zone free from weapons of mass destruction and all missiles for their delivery and the objective of a global ban on chemical weapons;

D

15   Requests the Secretary-General to report to the Security Council on the steps taken to facilitate the return of all Kuwaiti property seized by Iraq, including a list of any property which Kuwait claims has not been returned or which has not been returned intact;

E

16   Reaffirms that Iraq, without prejudice to the debts and obligation of Iraq arising prior to 2 August 1990, which will be addressed through the normal mechanisms, is liable under international law for any direct loss, damage, including environmental damage and the depletion of natural resources, or injury to foreign Governments, nationals and corporations, as a result of Iraq's unlawful invasion and occupation of Kuwait;

17   Decides that all Iraqi statements made since 2 August 1990, repudiating its foreign debt are null and void, and demands that Iraq scrupulously adhere to all of its obligations concerning servicing and repayment of its foreign debt;

18   Decides to create a Fund to pay compensation for claims that fall within paragraph 16 above and to establish a Commission that will administer the Fund;

19   Directs the Secretary-General to develop and present to the Council for decision, no later than 30 days following the adoption of this resolution, recommendations for the Fund to meet the requirement for the payment of claims established in accordance with paragraph 18 above and for a programme to implement the decisions in paragraphs 16, 17, and 18

above, including: administration of the Fund; mechanisms for determining the appropriate level for Iraq's contribution to the Fund based on a percentage of the value of the exports of petroleum and petroleum products from Iraq not to exceed a figure to be suggested to the Council by the Secretary-General, taking into account the requirement of the people of Iraq, Iraq's payment capacity as assessed in conjunction with the international financial institutions taking into consideration external debt service, and the needs of the Iraqi economy; arrangements for ensuring that payments are made to the Fund; the process by which funds will be allocated and claims paid; appropriate procedures for evaluating losses, listing claims and verifying their validity and resolving disputed claims in respect of Iraq's liability as specified in paragraph 16 above; and the composition of the Commission designated above;

F

20   Decides, effective immediately, that the prohibitions against the sale or supply to Iraq of commodities or products, other than medicine and health supplies, and prohibitions against financial transactions related thereto, contained in resolution 661 (1990) shall not apply to foodstuffs notified to the Committee established by resolution 661 (1990) or, with the approval of that Committee, under the simplified and accelerated 'no-objection' procedure, to materials and supplies for essential civilian needs as identified in the report of the Secretary-General dated 20 March 1991 (S/22366), and in any further findings of humanitarian need by the Committee;

21   Decides that the Council shall review the provisions of paragraph 20 above every sixty days in light of the policies and practices of the Government of Iraq, including the implementation of all relevant resolutions of the Security Council, for the purposes of determining whether to reduce or lift the prohibitions referred to therein;

22   Decides that upon the approval by the Council of the programme called for in paragraph 19 above and upon Council agreement that Iraq has completed all actions contemplated in paragraphs 8, 9, 10, 11, 12, and 13 above, the prohibitions against the import of commodities and products originating in Iraq and the prohibitions against financial transactions related thereto contained in resolution 661 (1990) shall have no further force or effect;

23   Decides that, pending action by the Council under paragraph 22 above, the Committee established by resolution 661 (1990) shall be empowered to approve, when required to assure adequate financial resources on the part of Iraq to carry out the activities under paragraph 20 above, exceptions to the prohibition against the import of commodities and products originating in Iraq;

24   Decides that, in accordance with resolution 661 (1990) and subsequent related resolutions and until a further decision is taken by the Council, all States shall continue to prevent the sale or supply, or promotion or facilitation of such sale or supply, to Iraq by their nationals, or from their territories or using their flag vessels or aircraft, of:

(a)   arms and related material of all types, specifically including conventional military equipment, including for paramilitary forces, and spare parts and components and their means of production, for such equipment;

(b)   items specified and defined in paragraph 8 and paragraph 12 above not otherwise covered above;

(c)   technology under licensing or other transfer arrangements used in production, utilization or stockpiling of items specified in subparagraphs (a) and (b) above;

(d)   personnel or materials for training or technical support services relating to the design, development, manufacture, use, maintenance or support of items specified in subparagraphs (a) and (b) above;

25   Calls upon all States and international organizations to act strictly in accordance with paragraph 24 above, notwithstanding the existence of any contracts, agreements, licences, or any other arrangements;

26   Requests the Secretary-General, in consultation with appropriate Governments, to develop within sixty days, for approval of the Council, guidelines to facilitate full international implementation of paragraphs 24 and 25 above and paragraph 27 below, and to make them available to all States and to establish a procedure for updating these guidelines periodically;

27   Calls upon all States to maintain such national controls and procedures and to take such other actions consistent with the guidelines to be established by the Security Council under paragraph 26 above as may be necessary to ensure compliance with the terms of paragraph 24 above, and calls upon international organizations to take all appropriate steps to assist in ensuring such full compliance;

28   Agrees to review its decisions in paragraphs 22, 23, 24, and 25 above, except for the items specified and defined in paragraphs 8 and 12 above, on a regular basis and in any case 120 days following passage of this resolution, taking into account Iraq's compliance with this resolution and general progress towards the control of armaments in the region;

29   Decides that all States, including Iraq, shall take the necessary measures to ensure that no claim shall lie at the instance of the Government of Iraq, or of any person or body in Iraq, or of any person claiming through or for the benefit of any such person or body, in connection with any contract or

other transaction where its performance was affected by reason of the measures taken by the Security Council in resolution 661 (1990) and related resolutions;

G

30   Decides that, in furtherance of its commitment to facilitate the repatriation of all Kuwaiti and third country nationals, Iraq shall extend all necessary co-operation to the International Committee of the Red Cross, providing lists of such persons, facilitating the access of the International Committee of the Red Cross to all such persons wherever located or detained and facilitating the search by the International Committee of the Red Cross for those Kuwaiti and third country nationals still unaccounted for;

31   Invites the International Committee of the Red Cross to keep the Secretary-General apprised as appropriate of all activities undertaken in connection with facilitating the repatriation or return of all Kuwaiti and third country nationals or their remains present in Iraq on or after 2 August 1990;

H

32   Requires Iraq to inform the Council that it will not commit or support any act of international terrorism or allow any organization directed towards commission of such acts to operate within its territory and to condemn unequivocally and renounce all acts, methods, and practices of terrorism;

I

33   Declares that, upon official notification by Iraq to the Secretary-General and to the Security Council of its acceptance of the provisions above, a formal cease-fire is effective between Iraq and Kuwait and the Member States co-operating with Kuwait in accordance with resolution 678 (1990);

34   Decides to remain seized of the matter and to take such further steps as may be required for the implementation of this resolution and to secure peace and security in the area.

Adopted by 12 votes to one (Cuba), with two abstentions (Ecuador and Yemen)

APPENDIX IV

United Nations Security Council Resolution 688, 5 April 1991 (10–3, 2 abs)

The Security Council,

Mindful of its duties and responsibilities under the Charter of the United Nations for the maintenance of international peace and security,

Recalling Article 2, paragraph 7, of the Charter of the United Nations,

Gravely concerned by the repression of the Iraqi civilian population in many parts of Iraq, including most recently in Kurdish populated areas which led to a massive flow of refugees towards and across international frontiers and to cross border incursions, which threaten international peace and security in the region,

Deeply disturbed by the magnitude of the human suffering involved,

Taking note of the letters sent by the representatives of Turkey and France to the United Nations dated 2 April 1991 and 4 April 1991, respectively (S/22435 and S/22442),

Taking note also of the letters sent by the Permanent Representative of the Islamic Republic of Iran to the United Nations dated 3 and 4 April 1991, respectively (S/22436 and S/22447),

Reaffirming the commitment of all Member States to the sovereignty, territorial integrity and political independence of Iraq and of all States in the area,

Bearing in mind the Secretary-General's report of 20 March 1991 (S/22366),

1   Condemns the repression of the Iraqi civilian population in many parts of Iraq, including most recently in Kurdish populated areas, the consequences of which threaten international peace and security in the region;

2   Demands that Iraq, as a contribution to removing the threat to international peace and security in the region, immediately end this repression and expresses the hope in the same context that an open dialogue will take place to ensure that the human and political rights of all Iraqi citizens are respected;

3   Insists that Iraq allow immediate access by international humanitarian organizations to all those in need of assistance in all parts of Iraq and to make available all necessary facilities for their operations;

4   Requests the Secretary-General to pursue his humanitarian efforts in Iraq and to report forthwith, if appropriate on the basis of a further mission to the region, on the plight of the Iraqi civilian population, and in particular

the Kurdish population, suffering from the repression in all its forms inflicted by the Iraqi authorities;

5   Requests further the Secretary-General to use all the resources at his disposal, including those of the relevant United Nations agencies, to address urgently the critical needs of the refugees and displaced Iraqi population;

6   Appeals to all Member States and to all humanitarian organizations to contribute to these humanitarian relief efforts;

7   Demands that Iraq co-operate with the Secretary-General to these ends;

8   Decides to remain seized of the matter.

Adopted by 10 votes to three (Cuba, Yemen and Zimbabwe), with two abstentions (China and India)

APPENDIX V

United Nations Security Council Resolution 986,
14 April 1995 (adopted unanimously)

The Security Council,

Recalling its previous relevant resolutions,

Concerned by the serious nutritional and health situation of the Iraqi population, and by the risk of a further deterioration in this situation,

Convinced of the need as a temporary measure to provide for the humanitarian needs of the Iraqi people until the fulfilment by Iraq of the relevant Security Council resolutions, including notably resolution 687 (1991) of 3 April 1991, allows the Council to take further action with regard to the prohibitions referred to in resolution 661 (1990) of 6 August 1990, in accordance with the provisions of those resolutions,

Convinced also of the need for equitable distribution of humanitarian relief to all segments of the Iraqi population throughout the country,

Reaffirming the commitment of all Member States to the sovereignty and territorial integrity of Iraq,

Acting under Chapter VII of the Charter of the United Nations,

1   Authorizes States, notwithstanding the provisions of paragraphs 3 (a), 3 (b) and 4 of resolution 661 (1990) and subsequent relevant resolutions, to permit the imports of petroleum and petroleum products originating in Iraq, including financial and other essential transactions directly relating thereto, sufficient to produce a sum not exceeding a total of one billion United States dollars every 90 days for the purposes set out in this resolution and subject to the following conditions:

    (a)   Approval by the Committee established by resolution 661 (1990), in order to ensure the transparency of each transaction and its conformity with the other provisions of this resolution, after submission of an application by the State concerned endorsed by the Government of Iraq, for each proposed purchase of Iraqi petroleum and petroleum products, including details of the purchase price at fair market value, the export route, the opening of a letter of credit payable to the escrow account to be established by the Secretary-General for the purposes of this resolution, and of any other directly related financial or other essential transaction;

    (b)   Payment of the full amount of each purchase of Iraqi petroleum and petroleum products directly by the purchaser in the State concerned into the escrow account to be established by the Secretary-General for the purposes of this resolution;

2   Authorizes Turkey, notwithstanding the provisions of paragraphs 3 (a), 3 (b) and 4 of resolution 661 (1990) and the provisions of paragraph 1 above, to permit the import of petroleum and petroleum products originating in Iraq sufficient, after the deduction of the percentage referred to in paragraph 8 (c) below for the Compensation Fund, to meet the pipeline tariff charges, verified as reasonable by the independent inspection agents referred to in paragraph 6 below, for the transport of Iraqi petroleum and petroleum products through the Kirkuk-Yumurtalik pipeline in Turkey authorized by paragraph 1 above;

3   Decides that paragraphs 1 and 2 of this resolution shall come into force at 00.01 Eastern Standard Time on the day after the President of the Council has informed the members of the Council that he has received the report from the Secretary-General requested in paragraph 13 below, and shall remain in force for an initial period of 180 days unless the Council takes other relevant action with regard to the provisions of resolution 661 (1990);

4   Further decides to conduct a thorough review of all aspects of the implementation of this resolution 90 days after the entry into force of paragraph 1 above and again prior to the end of the initial 180 day period, on receipt of the reports referred to in paragraphs 11 and 12 below, and expresses its intention, prior to the end of the 180 day period, to consider favourably renewal of the provisions of this resolution, provided that the reports referred to in paragraphs 11 and 12 below indicate that those provisions are being satisfactorily implemented;

5   Further decides that the remaining paragraphs of this resolution shall come into force forthwith;

6   Directs the Committee established by resolution 661 (1990) to monitor the sale of petroleum and petroleum products to be exported by Iraq via the Kirkuk-Yumurtalik pipeline from Iraq to Turkey and from the Mina al-Bakr oil terminal, with the assistance of independent inspection agents appointed by the Secretary-General, who will keep the Committee informed of the amount of petroleum and petroleum products exported from Iraq after the date of entry into force of paragraph 1 of this resolution, and will verify that the purchase price of the petroleum and petroleum products is reasonable in the light of prevailing market conditions, and that, for the purposes of the arrangements set out in this resolution, the larger share of the petroleum and petroleum products is shipped via the Kirkuk-Yumurtalik pipeline and the remainder is exported from the Mina al-Bakr oil terminal;

7   Requests the Secretary-General to establish an escrow account for the purposes of this resolution, to appoint independent and certified public accountants to audit it, and to keep the Government of Iraq fully informed;

8   Decides that the funds in the escrow account shall be used to meet the humanitarian needs of the Iraqi population and for the following other purposes, and requests the Secretary-General to use the funds deposited in the escrow account:

(a)   To finance the export to Iraq, in accordance with the procedures of the Committee established by resolution 661 (1990), of medicine, health supplies, foodstuffs, and materials and supplies for essential civilian needs, as referred to in paragraph 20 of resolution 687 (1991) provided that:

(i)   Each export of goods is at the request of the Government of Iraq;

(ii)   Iraq effectively guarantees their equitable distribution, on the basis of a plan submitted to and approved by the Secretary-General, including a description of the goods to be purchased;

(iii)   The Secretary-General receives authenticated confirmation that the exported goods concerned have arrived in Iraq;

(b)   To complement, in view of the exceptional circumstances prevailing in the three Governorates mentioned below, the distribution by the Government of Iraq of goods imported under this resolution, in order to ensure an equitable distribution of humanitarian relief to all segments of the Iraqi population throughout the country, by providing between 130 million and 150 million United States dollars every 90 days to the United Nations Inter-Agency Humanitarian Programme operating within the sovereign territory of Iraq in the three northern Governorates of Dihouk, Arbil and Suleimaniyeh, except that if less than one billion United States dollars worth of petroleum or petroleum products is sold during any 90 day period, the Secretary-General may provide a proportionately smaller amount for this purpose;

(c)   To transfer to the Compensation Fund the same percentage of the funds deposited in the escrow account as that decided by the Council in paragraph 2 of resolution 705 (1991) of 15 August 1991;

(d)   To meet the costs to the United Nations of the independent inspection agents and the certified public accountants and the activities associated with implementation of this resolution;

(e)   To meet the current operating costs of the Special Commission, pending subsequent payment in full of the costs of carrying out the tasks authorized by section C of resolution 687 (1991);

(f) To meet any reasonable expenses, other than expenses payable in Iraq, which are determined by the Committee established by resolution 661 (1990) to be directly related to the export by Iraq of petroleum and petroleum products permitted under paragraph 1 above or to the export to Iraq, and activities directly necessary therefor, of the parts and equipment permitted under paragraph 9 below;

(g) To make available up to 10 million United States dollars every 90 days from the funds deposited in the escrow account for the payments envisaged under paragraph 6 of resolution 778 (1992) of 2 October 1992;

9 Authorizes States to permit, notwithstanding the provisions of paragraph 3 (c) of resolution 661 (1990):

(a) The export to Iraq of the parts and equipment which are essential for the safe operation of the Kirkuk-Yumurtalik pipeline system in Iraq, subject to the prior approval by the Committee established by resolution 661 (1990) of each export contract;

(b) Activities directly necessary for the exports authorized under subparagraph (a) above, including financial transactions related thereto;

10 Decides that, since the costs of the exports and activities authorized under paragraph 9 above are precluded by paragraph 4 of resolution 661 (1990) and by paragraph 11 of resolution 778 (1991) from being met from funds frozen in accordance with those provisions, the cost of such exports and activities may, until funds begin to be paid into the escrow account established for the purposes of this resolution, and following approval in each case by the Committee established by resolution 661 (1990), exceptionally be financed by letters of credit, drawn against future oil sales the proceeds of which are to be deposited in the escrow account;

11 Requests the Secretary-General to report to the Council 90 days after the date of entry into force of paragraph 1 above, and again prior to the end of the initial 180 day period, on the basis of observation by United Nations personnel in Iraq, and on the basis of consultations with the Government of Iraq, on whether Iraq has ensured the equitable distribution of medicine, health supplies, foodstuffs, and materials and supplies for essential civilian needs, financed in accordance with paragraph 8 (a) above, including in his reports any observations he may have on the adequacy of the revenues to meet Iraq's humanitarian needs, and on Iraq's capacity to export sufficient quantities of petroleum and petroleum products to produce the sum referred to in paragraph 1 above;

12 Requests the Committee established by resolution 661 (1990), in close coordination with the Secretary-General, to develop expedited procedures as necessary to implement the arrangements in paragraphs 1, 2, 6, 8, 9 and

10 of this resolution and to report to the Council 90 days after the date of entry into force of paragraph 1 above and again prior to the end of the initial 180 day period on the implementation of those arrangements;

13 Requests the Secretary-General to take the actions necessary to ensure the effective implementation of this resolution, authorizes him to enter into any necessary arrangements or agreements, and requests him to report to the Council when he has done so;

14 Decides that petroleum and petroleum products subject to this resolution shall while under Iraqi title be immune from legal proceedings and not be subject to any form of attachment, garnishment or execution, and that all States shall take any steps that may be necessary under their respective domestic legal systems to assure this protection, and to ensure that the proceeds of the sale are not diverted from the purposes laid down in this resolution;

15 Affirms that the escrow account established for the purposes of this resolution enjoys the privileges and immunities of the United Nations;

16 Affirms that all persons appointed by the Secretary-General for the purpose of implementing this resolution enjoy privileges and immunities as experts on mission for the United Nations in accordance with the Convention on the Privileges and Immunities of the United Nations, and requires the Government of Iraq to allow them full freedom of movement and all necessary facilities for the discharge of their duties in the implementation of this resolution;

17 Affirms that nothing in this resolution affects Iraq's duty scrupulously to adhere to all of its obligations concerning servicing and repayment of its foreign debt, in accordance with the appropriate international mechanisms;

18 Also affirms that nothing in this resolution should be construed as infringing the sovereignty or territorial integrity of Iraq;

19 Decides to remain seized of the matter.

APPENDIX VI

United Nations Security Council Resolution 1284, 17 December 1999 (11–0, 4 abs)

The Security Council,

Recalling its previous relevant resolutions, including its resolutions 661 (1990) of 6 August 1990, 687 (1991) of 3 April 1991, 699 (1991) of 17 June 1991, 707 (1991) of 15 August 1991, 715 (1991) of 11 October 1991, 986 (1995) of 14 April 1995, 1051 (1996) of 27 March 1996, 1153 (1998) of 20 February 1998, 1175 (1998) of 19 June 1998, 1242 (1999) of 21 May 1999 and 1266 (1999) of 4 October 1999,

Recalling the approval by the Council in its resolution 715 (1991) of the plans for future ongoing monitoring and verification submitted by the Secretary-General and the Director-General of the International Atomic Energy Agency (IAEA) in pursuance of paragraphs 10 and 13 of resolution 687 (1991),

Welcoming the reports of the three panels on Iraq (S/1999/356), and having held a comprehensive consideration of them and the recommendations contained in them,

Stressing the importance of a comprehensive approach to the full implementation of all relevant Security Council resolutions regarding Iraq and the need for Iraqi compliance with these resolutions,

Recalling the goal of establishing in the Middle East a zone free from weapons of mass destruction and all missiles for their delivery and the objective of a global ban on chemical weapons as referred to in paragraph 14 of resolution 687 (1991),

Concerned at the humanitarian situation in Iraq, and determined to improve that situation,

Recalling with concern that the repatriation and return of all Kuwaiti and third country nationals or their remains, present in Iraq on or after 2 August 1990, pursuant to paragraph 2 (c) of resolution 686 (1991) of 2 March 1991 and paragraph 30 of resolution 687 (1991), have not yet been fully carried out by Iraq,

Recalling that in its resolutions 686 (1991) and 687 (1991) the Council demanded that Iraq return in the shortest possible time all Kuwaiti property it had seized, and noting with regret that Iraq has still not complied fully with this demand,

Acknowledging the progress made by Iraq towards compliance with the provisions of resolution 687 (1991), but noting that, as a result of its failure to implement the relevant Council resolutions fully, the conditions do not exist which would enable the Council to take a decision pursuant to resolution 687 (1991) to lift the prohibitions referred to in that resolution,

Reiterating the commitment of all Member States to the sovereignty, territorial integrity and political independence of Kuwait, Iraq and the neighbouring States,

Acting under Chapter VII of the Charter of the United Nations, and taking into account that operative provisions of this resolution relate to previous resolutions adopted under Chapter VII of the Charter,

A

1   Decides to establish, as a subsidiary body of the Council, the United Nations Monitoring, Verification and Inspection Commission (UNMOVIC) which replaces the Special Commission established pursuant to paragraph 9 (b) of resolution 687 (1991);

2   Decides also that UNMOVIC will undertake the responsibilities mandated to the Special Commission by the Council with regard to the verification of compliance by Iraq with its obligations under paragraphs 8, 9 and 10 of resolution 687 (1991) and other related resolutions, that UNMOVIC will establish and operate, as was recommended by the panel on disarmament and current and future ongoing monitoring and verification issues, a reinforced system of ongoing monitoring and verification, which will implement the plan approved by the Council in resolution 715 (1991) and address unresolved disarmament issues, and that UNMOVIC will identify, as necessary in accordance with its mandate, additional sites in Iraq to be covered by the reinforced system of ongoing monitoring and verification;

3   Reaffirms the provisions of the relevant resolutions with regard to the role of the IAEA in addressing compliance by Iraq with paragraphs 12 and 13 of resolution 687 (1991) and other related resolutions, and requests the Director-General of the IAEA to maintain this role with the assistance and cooperation of UNMOVIC;

4   Reaffirms its resolutions 687 (1991), 699 (1991), 707 (1991), 715 (1991), 1051 (1996), 1154 (1998) and all other relevant resolutions and statements of its President, which establish the criteria for Iraqi compliance, affirms that the obligations of Iraq referred to in those resolutions and statements with regard to cooperation with the Special Commission, unrestricted access and provision of information will apply in respect of UNMOVIC, and decides in particular that Iraq shall allow UNMOVIC teams immediate, unconditional and unrestricted access to any and all areas, facilities, equipment, records and means of transport which they wish to inspect in accordance with the mandate of UNMOVIC, as well as to all officials and other persons under the authority of the Iraqi Government whom

UNMOVIC wishes to interview so that UNMOVIC may fully discharge its mandate;

5   Requests the Secretary-General, within 30 days of the adoption of this resolution, to appoint, after consultation with and subject to the approval of the Council, an Executive Chairman of UNMOVIC who will take up his mandated tasks as soon as possible, and, in consultation with the Executive Chairman and the Council members, to appoint suitably qualified experts as a College of Commissioners for UNMOVIC which will meet regularly to review the implementation of this and other relevant resolutions and provide professional advice and guidance to the Executive Chairman, including on significant policy decisions and on written reports to be submitted to the Council through the Secretary-General;

6   Requests the Executive Chairman of UNMOVIC, within 45 days of his appointment, to submit to the Council, in consultation with and through the Secretary-General, for its approval an organizational plan for UNMOVIC, including its structure, staffing requirements, management guidelines, recruitment and training procedures, incorporating as appropriate the recommendations of the panel on disarmament and current and future ongoing monitoring and verification issues, and recognizing in particular the need for an effective, cooperative management structure for the new organization, for staffing with suitably qualified and experienced personnel, who would be regarded as international civil servants subject to Article 100 of the Charter of the United Nations, drawn from the broadest possible geographical base, including as he deems necessary from international arms control organizations, and for the provision of high quality technical and cultural training;

7   Decides that UNMOVIC and the IAEA, not later than 60 days after they have both started work in Iraq, will each draw up, for approval by the Council, a work programme for the discharge of their mandates, which will include both the implementation of the reinforced system of ongoing monitoring and verification, and the key remaining disarmament tasks to be completed by Iraq pursuant to its obligations to comply with the disarmament requirements of resolution 687 (1991) and other related resolutions, which constitute the governing standard of Iraqi compliance, and further decides that what is required of Iraq for the implementation of each task shall be clearly defined and precise;

8   Requests the Executive Chairman of UNMOVIC and the Director General of the IAEA, drawing on the expertise of other international organizations as appropriate, to establish a unit which will have the responsibilities of the joint unit constituted by the Special Commission and the Director General of the IAEA under paragraph 16 of the export/import mechanism approved by resolution 1051 (1996), and also requests the Executive

Chairman of UNMOVIC, in consultation with the Director General of the IAEA, to resume the revision and updating of the lists of items and technology to which the mechanism applies;

9   Decides that the Government of Iraq shall be liable for the full costs of UNMOVIC and the IAEA in relation to their work under this and other related resolutions on Iraq;

10   Requests Member States to give full cooperation to UNMOVIC and the IAEA in the discharge of their mandates;

11   Decides that UNMOVIC shall take over all assets, liabilities and archives of the Special Commission, and that it shall assume the Special Commission's part in agreements existing between the Special Commission and Iraq and between the United Nations and Iraq, and affirms that the Executive Chairman, the Commissioners and the personnel serving with UNMOVIC shall have the rights, privileges, facilities and immunities of the Special Commission;

12   Requests the Executive Chairman of UNMOVIC to report, through the Secretary-General, to the Council, following consultation with the Commissioners, every three months on the work of UNMOVIC, pending submission of the first reports referred to in paragraph 33 below, and to report immediately when the reinforced system of ongoing monitoring and verification is fully operational in Iraq;

B

13   Reiterates the obligation of Iraq, in furtherance of its commitment to facilitate the repatriation of all Kuwaiti and third country nationals referred to in paragraph 30 of resolution 687 (1991), to extend all necessary cooperation to the International Committee of the Red Cross, and calls upon the Government of Iraq to resume cooperation with the Tripartite Commission and Technical Subcommittee established to facilitate work on this issue;

14   Requests the Secretary-General to report to the Council every four months on compliance by Iraq with its obligations regarding the repatriation or return of all Kuwaiti and third country nationals or their remains, to report every six months on the return of all Kuwaiti property, including archives, seized by Iraq, and to appoint a high-level coordinator for these issues;

C

15   Authorizes States, notwithstanding the provisions of paragraphs 3 (a), 3 (b) and 4 of resolution 661 (1990) and subsequent relevant resolutions, to permit the import of any volume of petroleum and petroleum products

originating in Iraq, including financial and other essential transactions directly relating thereto, as required for the purposes and on the conditions set out in paragraph 1 (a) and (b) and subsequent provisions of resolution 986 (1995) and related resolutions;

16 Underlines, in this context, its intention to take further action, including permitting the use of additional export routes for petroleum and petroleum products, under appropriate conditions otherwise consistent with the purpose and provisions of resolution 986 (1995) and related resolutions;

17 Directs the Committee established by resolution 661 (1990) to approve, on the basis of proposals from the Secretary-General, lists of humanitarian items, including foodstuffs, pharmaceutical and medical supplies, as well as basic or standard medical and agricultural equipment and basic or standard educational items, decides, notwithstanding paragraph 3 of resolution 661 (1990) and paragraph 20 of resolution 687 (1991), that supplies of these items will not be submitted for approval of that Committee, except for items subject to the provisions of resolution 1051 (1996), and will be notified to the Secretary-General and financed in accordance with the provisions of paragraph 8 (a) and 8 (b) of resolution 986 (1995), and requests the Secretary-General to inform the Committee in a timely manner of all such notifications received and actions taken;

18 Requests the Committee established by resolution 661 (1990) to appoint, in accordance with resolutions 1175 (1998) and 1210 (1998), a group of experts, including independent inspection agents appointed by the Secretary-General in accordance with paragraph 6 of resolution 986 (1995), decides that this group will be mandated to approve speedily contracts for the parts and the equipments necessary to enable Iraq to increase its exports of petroleum and petroleum products, according to lists of parts and equipments approved by that Committee for each individual project, and requests the Secretary-General to continue to provide for the monitoring of these parts and equipments inside Iraq;

19 Encourages Member States and international organizations to provide supplementary humanitarian assistance to Iraq and published material of an educational character to Iraq;

20 Decides to suspend, for an initial period of six months from the date of the adoption of this resolution and subject to review, the implementation of paragraph 8 (g) of resolution 986 (1995);

21 Requests the Secretary-General to take steps to maximize, drawing as necessary on the advice of specialists, including representatives of international humanitarian organizations, the effectiveness of the arrangements set out in resolution 986 (1995) and related resolutions including the humanitarian benefit to the Iraqi population in all areas of the country, and

further requests the Secretary-General to continue to enhance as necessary the United Nations observation process in Iraq, ensuring that all supplies under the humanitarian programme are utilized as authorized, to bring to the attention of the Council any circumstances preventing or impeding effective and equitable distribution and to keep the Council informed of the steps taken towards the implementation of this paragraph;

22   Requests also the Secretary-General to minimize the cost of the United Nations activities associated with the implementation of resolution 986 (1995) as well as the cost of the independent inspection agents and the certified public accountants appointed by him, in accordance with paragraphs 6 and 7 of resolution 986 (1995);

23   Requests further the Secretary-General to provide Iraq and the Committee established by resolution 661 (1990) with a daily statement of the status of the escrow account established by paragraph 7 of resolution 986 (1995);

24   Requests the Secretary-General to make the necessary arrangements, subject to Security Council approval, to allow funds deposited in the escrow account established by resolution 986 (1995) to be used for the purchase of locally produced goods and to meet the local cost for essential civilian needs which have been funded in accordance with the provisions of resolution 986 (1995) and related resolutions, including, where appropriate, the cost of installation and training services;

25   Directs the Committee established by resolution 661 (1990) to take a decision on all applications in respect of humanitarian and essential civilian needs within a target of two working days of receipt of these applications from the Secretary-General, and to ensure that all approval and notification letters issued by the Committee stipulate delivery within a specified time, according to the nature of the items to be supplied, and requests the Secretary-General to notify the Committee of all applications for humanitarian items which are included in the list to which the export/import mechanism approved by resolution 1051 (1996) applies;

26   Decides that Hajj pilgrimage flights which do not transport cargo into or out of Iraq are exempt from the provisions of paragraph 3 of resolution 661 (1990) and resolution 670 (1990), provided timely notification of each flight is made to the Committee established by resolution 661 (1990), and requests the Secretary-General to make the necessary arrangements, for approval by the Security Council, to provide for reasonable expenses related to the Hajj pilgrimage to be met by funds in the escrow account established by resolution 986 (1995);

27   Calls upon the Government of Iraq:
       (i)   to take all steps to ensure the timely and equitable distribution of all

humanitarian goods, in particular medical supplies, and to remove and avoid delays at its warehouses;

(ii) to address effectively the needs of vulnerable groups, including children, pregnant women, the disabled, the elderly and the mentally ill among others, and to allow freer access, without any discrimination, including on the basis of religion or nationality, by United Nations agencies and humanitarian organizations to all areas and sections of the population for evaluation of their nutritional and humanitarian condition;

(iii) to prioritize applications for humanitarian goods under the arrangements set out in resolution 986 (1995) and related resolutions;

(iv) to ensure that those involuntarily displaced receive humanitarian assistance without the need to demonstrate that they have resided for six months in their places of temporary residence;

(v) to extend full cooperation to the United Nations office for Project Services mine-clearance programme in the three northern Governorates of Iraq and to consider the initiation of the demining efforts in other Governorates;

28 Requests the Secretary-General to report on the progress made in meeting the humanitarian needs of the Iraqi people and on the revenues necessary to meet those needs, including recommendations on necessary additions to the current allocation for oil spare parts and equipment, on the basis of a comprehensive survey of the condition of the Iraqi oil production sector, not later than 60 days from the date of the adoption of this resolution and updated thereafter as necessary;

29 Expresses its readiness to authorize additions to the current allocation for oil spare parts and equipment, on the basis of the report and recommendations requested in paragraph 28 above, in order to meet the humanitarian purposes set out in resolution 986 (1995) and related resolutions;

30 Requests the Secretary-General to establish a group of experts, including oil industry experts, to report within 100 days of the date of adoption of this resolution on Iraq's existing petroleum production and export capacity and to make recommendations, to be updated as necessary, on alternatives for increasing Iraq's petroleum production and export capacity in a manner consistent with the purposes of relevant resolutions, and on the options for involving foreign oil companies in Iraq's oil sector, including investments, subject to appropriate monitoring and controls;

31 Notes that in the event of the Council acting as provided for in paragraph 33 of this resolution to suspend the prohibitions referred to in that paragraph, appropriate arrangements and procedures will need, subject to paragraph 35 below, to be agreed by the Council in good time beforehand,

including suspension of provisions of resolution 986 (1995) and related resolutions;

32 Requests the Secretary-General to report to the Council on the implementation of paragraphs 15 to 30 of this resolution within 30 days of the adoption of this resolution;

D

33 Expresses its intention, upon receipt of reports from the Executive Chairman of UNMOVIC and from the Director General of the IAEA that Iraq has co-operated in all respects with UNMOVIC and the IAEA in particular in fulfilling the work programmes in all the aspects referred to in paragraph 7 above, for a period of 120 days after the date on which the Council's in receipt of reports from both UNMOVIC and the IAEA that the reinforced system of ongoing monitoring and verification is fully operational, to suspend with the fundamental objective of improving the humanitarian situation in Iraq and securing the implementation of the Council's resolutions, for a period of 120 days renewable by the Council, and subject to the elaboration of effective financial and other operational measures to ensure that Iraq does not acquire prohibited items, prohibitions against the import of commodities and products originating in Iraq, and prohibitions against the sale, supply and delivery to Iraq of civilian commodities and products other than those referred to in paragraph 24 of resolution 687 (1991) or those to which the mechanism established by resolution 1051 (1996) applies;

34 Decides that in reporting to the Council for the purposes of paragraph 33 above, the Executive Chairman of UNMOVIC will include as a basis for his assessment the progress made in completing the tasks referred to in paragraph 7 above;

35 Decides that if at any time the Executive Chairman of UNMOVIC or the Director-General of the IAEA reports that Iraq is not co-operating in all respects with UNMOVIC or the IAEA or if Iraq is in the process of acquiring any prohibited items, the suspension of the prohibitions referred to in paragraph 33 above shall terminate on the fifth working day following the report, unless the Council decides to the contrary;

36 Expresses its intention to approve arrangements for effective financial and other operational measures, including on the delivery of and payment for authorized civilian commodities and products to be sold or supplied to Iraq, in order to ensure that Iraq does not acquire prohibited items in the event of suspension of the prohibitions referred to in paragraph 33 above, to begin the elaboration of such measures not later than the date of the receipt of the initial reports referred to in paragraph 33 above, and to

approve such arrangements before the Council decision in accordance with that paragraph;

37 Further expresses its intention to take steps, based on the report and recommendations requested in paragraph 30 above, and consistent with the purpose of resolution 986 (1995) and related resolutions, to enable Iraq to increase its petroleum production and export capacity, upon receipt of the reports relating to the co-operation in all respects with UNMOVIC and the IAEA referred to in paragraph 33 above;

38 Reaffirms its intention to act in accordance with the relevant provisions of resolution 687 (1991) on the termination of prohibitions referred to in that resolution;

39 Decides to remain actively seized of the matter and expresses its intention to consider action in accordance with paragraph 33 above no later than 12 months from the date of the adoption of this resolution provided the conditions set out in paragraph 33 above have been satisfied by Iraq. Adopted by 11 votes to none, with four abstentions (China, France, Malaysia and Russia).

NOTES

PREFACE

1 BP Amoco plc, *BP Amoco Statistical Review of World Energy 2000*, London, 2000 p. 4.
2 A Saddam joke doing the rounds in Baghdad in August 2000 summed up the situation aptly. At a cabinet meeting he turned to his neighbor and asked, "What time is it?" The minister replied, "Whatever time you want it to be, Mr Leader-President."

INTRODUCTION

1 Twelver Shias believe in twelve Imams, religious leaders: Ali, Hassan, Hussein, Zain al Abidin, Muhammad al Baqir, Jaafar al Sadiq, Musa al Kazem, Ali al Rida/Reza, Muhammad al Taqi Javad, Ali al Naqi, Hassan al Aksari and Muhammad al Qasim. See further, Dilip Hiro, *Dictionary of the Middle East*, Macmillan Press, Basingstoke; and St Martin's Press, New York, 1996, p. 327.
2 Jasim M. Abdulghani, *Iran and Iraq: The Years of Crisis*, Croom Helm, London, 1984, p. 3.
3 Cited in Shahram Chubin and Sepehr Zabih, *The Foreign Relations of Iran: A Developing State in a Zone of Great Power Conflict*, University of California Press, Berkeley, CA, 1974, p. 183.
4 Edmund Ghareeb, *The Kurdish Question in Iraq*, Syracuse University Press, Syracuse, NY, 1981, p. 133.
5 *New Middle East*, July 1970, p. 25.
6 Cited in Dilip Hiro, *Inside the Middle East*, Routledge & Kegan Paul, London, and McGraw Hill, New York, 1982, p. 281.
7 Martin Short and Anthony McDermott, *The Kurds*, Minority Rights Group, London, 1977, p. 19.
8 Tariq Y. Ismail, *Iraq and Iran: Roots of Conflict*, Syracuse University Press, Syracuse, NY, 1982, p. 66.
9 See further Dilip Hiro, *Dictionary of the Middle East*, p. 10.
10 Committee Against Repression and For Democratic Rights in Iraq, *Saddam's Iraq: Revolution or Reaction?*, Zed Press, London, 1986, p. 66.
11 Dilip Hiro, *The Longest War: The Iran–Iraq Military Conflict*, Grafton Books, London, 1989, and Routledge, New York, 1991, p. 24.
12 Robert Graham, *Iran: The Illusion of Power*, Croom Helm, London, 1978, p. 243, note 43.
13 *Guardian*, February 28, 1979.
14 Dilip Hiro, *The Longest War*, pp. 28–9.
15 *Ibid.*, pp. 34–5.
16 *Foreign Information Broadcast Service*, April 18, 1980; *Washington Post*, April 18, 1980.
17 Dilip Hiro, *Iran Under the Ayatollahs*, Routledge & Kegan Paul, London and New York, 1985; and toExcel Press, Lincoln, NE, 2000, pp. 154–6.
18 Sharam Chubin, "Reflections on the Gulf War," *Survival*, July–August 1986, p. 308.
19 *MERIP Reports*, July–September 1981, pp. 3–4. According to a well-informed source, on the eve of the war the Iraqi president sent a word to the Kuwaiti ruler that General

Oveissi could be in Tehran "within days." Patrick Seale, *Asad: The Struggle for the Middle East*, I. B. Tauris, London and New York, 1988, pp. 361–2.

20 Dilip Hiro, *Dictionary of the Middle East*, p. 100. Iraq did not release official figures of the war dead.

21 Interview in Baghdad, July 2000.

22 *Al Thawra*, April 17, 1983.

23 Since the last Shia Imam disappeared in 873 A.D., the thirty generations after him with an average age of 25 would cover 750 years, bringing the top of the trunk to about 1625 A.D., followed by five more generations spanning 125 years, ending around 1750 A.D. – and not 1937 when Saddam was born. But Dr Haidar Muhammad Hussein al Kalidar, the caretaker of Imam Ali's shrine in Najaf, insisted that President Saddam Hussein's family tree had been constructed by Islamic scholars specializing in tribal and clan origins. Interview in Najaf, July 2000.

24 *Middle East Economic Digest*, August 12, 1988, p. 11.

25 After the initial financial assistance of $1 billion a month that Saudi Arabia and Kuwait provided Iraq during the first two years of the conflict, this settled down to an average of $300 million a month for the rest of the war – consisting of such items as oil countersales, payments for weapons bought in the Soviet bloc or France, and deposits made to Western companies doing business with Iraq. To this sum of $45,300 million must be added the grants and loans of some $500–700 million each by Qatar and the United Arab Emirates (UAE). These figures exclude the donations, running into hundreds of millions of US dollars, that Saudi and Kuwaiti citizens made to Iraq. See Dilip Hiro, *The Longest War*, p. 77 and p. 213.

26 *Ibid.,* p. 297 and p. 299.

27 Anoushirvan Ehteshami, *After Khomeini: The Iranian Second Republic*, Routledge, London and New York, 1995, p. 48.

28 *Middle East International*, February 16, 1990, p. 12.

29 In Shia Islam, *ruhaniyun*, the plural of *ruhani*, meaning a spiritual being, means more than its approximate equivalent in Sunni Islam, *ulama*, religious–legal scholars. Dilip Hiro, *Iran Under the Ayatollahs*, p. 158.

30 Dilip Hiro, *Iran Under the Ayatollahs*, p. 158.

31 Dilip Hiro, *Desert Shield to Desert Storm: The Second Gulf War*, HarperCollins, London, 1992, and Routledge, New York, 1992, p. 62.

32 Said K. Aburish, *Saddam Hussein: The Politics of Revenge*, Bloomsbury, London, 2000, p. 261.

33 The English translation of this memorandum, discovered at the headquarters of Kuwait's State Security Department by the (occupying) Iraqis, was placed before the UN secretary-general by Iraq's ambassador to the UN on October 29, 1990.

34 Cited in Dilip Hiro, *Desert Shield to Desert Storm*, p. 84.

35 *Ibid.,* p. 89.

36 *Ibid.*, p. 93.

37 *Guardian*, August 24, 1990; *Independent*, August 24, 1990.

38 *Middle East International*, June 8, 1990, p. 11. The exchange of prisoners dragged on for ten years.

39 *New York Times*, September 20, 1990 and March 21, 1991.

40 Cited in Dilip Hiro, *Desert Shield to Desert Storm*, p. 182.

41 See also Dilip Hiro, *Desert Shield to Desert Storm*, pp. 338–9. Of these 115 were warplanes and the rest civilian carriers. *Middle East International*, October 27, 2000, p. 17.

42 Cited in *Middle East International*, February 8, 1991, pp. 9–10.

43 *Washington Post*, February 8, 1991.

44 Dilip Hiro, *Desert Shield to Desert Storm*, p. 354.

45 *Ibid.*, p. 371.

46 *Ibid.*, pp. 387–8.

47 Dilip Hiro, *Dictionary of the Middle East*, p. 100.
48 *Ibid.*, p. 100; *Middle East International*, July 21, 1995, p. 18.
49 *Independent*, March 22, 1991.
50 Bush added, "The ghost of Vietnam [where America was defeated in 1975] has been exorcised." *Sunday Telegraph*, March 3, 1991.
51 *International Herald Tribune*, March 1 and 2, 1991.
52 *Middle East International*, March 8, 1991, pp. 18–19.
53 *Sunday Times*, March 10, 1991; *Guardian*, March 11, 1991.
54 *New York Times*, March 8,1991; *Independent*, March 8, 1991.
55 Dilip Hiro, *Desert Shield to Desert Storm*, pp. 97, 150, 179, 197.
56 Anthony H. Cordesman, and Ahmed S. Hashim, *Iraq: Sanctions and Beyond*, Westview Press, Boulder, CO; and Oxford, UK, 1997, pp. 101–2.
57 ABC News, February 7, 1998, cited in David Wurmser, *Tyranny's Ally: America's Failure to Defeat Saddam Hussein*, The AEI Press, Washington DC, 1999, p. 142.
58 Cited in Andrew Cockburn and Patrick Cockburn, *Out of the Ashes: The Resurrection of Saddam Hussein*, HarperCollins, New York, 1999 and Verso, London, 2000, p. 37.
59 Cited in *Middle East International*, 13 February, 1998, pp. 3–4.
60 *Independent*, March 17 and April 16, 1991; Anthony H. Cordesman, and Ahmed S. Hashim, *Iraq*, p. 26.
61 Islamic Republic News Agency, March 13, 1991. To get even with Iran for its backing of SAIRI, Saddam let the dormant, Baghdad-based, anti-Tehran Mujahedin-e Khalq Organization restart its military activities.
62 Interview with Dr Haidar Muhammad Hussein al Kalidar, caretaker of the Imam Ali shrine, Najaf, July 2000.
63 *Gulf States Newsletter*, February 22, 1999, p. 3.
64 *Daily Telegraph*, March 25, 1991; *International Herald Tribune*, March 25, 1991.
65 *Guardian*, March 28, 1991. Earlier the White House had said that the US would shoot down Iraqi helicopters used against the rebels *only* if they posed a threat to the Coalition forces. *New York Times*, March 27, 1991.
66 David Wurmser, *Tyranny's Ally*, pp. 10–11.
67 *Independent*, April 7, 1991.
68 Nuha al Radi, *Baghdad Diaries*, Saqi Books, London, 1998, p. 56.

1 SADDAM CENTER-STAGE, EXIT BUSH

1 *Observer*, May 19, 1991; *Independent*, May 21, 1991. "If a man like General Abdullah with his [military] following could not pull off a take-over, we don't honestly believe anyone could," said a senior Kurdish leader.
2 *New York Times*, June 4, 1991.
3 *Independent*, June 7 and 13, 1991.
4 *Middle East International*, July 26, 1991, pp. 9–10, 35; Tim Trevan, *Saddam's Secrets: The Hunt for Iraq's Hidden Weapons*, HarperCollins, London, 1999, pp. 397–8.
5 Before the UN sanctions of August 1990, Ishtar Sheraton Hotel was part of the Sheraton chain; afterwards it was run by Iraq's ministry of tourism as Ishtar Hotel.
6 *Middle East International*, September 27, 1991, pp. 9–10; Tim Trevan, *Saddam's Secrets*, pp. 103–9.
7 See later, pp. 63–4; Scott Ritter, *Endgame: Solving the Iraq Problem – Once and for All*, Simon & Schuster, New York and London, 1999, p. 107.
8 Sarah Graham-Brown, *Sanctioning Saddam: The Politics of Intervention in Iraq*, J.B. Tauris (in association with MERIP), London and New York, p.73.
9 *Middle East International*, November 8, 1991, p. 14.

10 In 1999 Muhammad Zubaidi was appointed a deputy prime minister, one of three, the others being Tariq Aziz and Hikmat al Awazi, a Sunni, who was also the finance minister.
11 *Middle East International*, November 8, 1991. pp. 13–14.
12 Cited in James Fine, "The Iraq Sanctions Catastrophe," *Middle East Report*, January–February 1992, pp. 36, 39.
13 Sarah Graham-Brown, *Sanctioning Saddam*, p. 77.
14 *Los Angeles Times*, May 9, 1991.
15 Dilip Hiro, *Desert Shield to Desert Storm: The Second Gulf War*, HarperCollins, London, 1992; and Routledge, New York, 1992, p. 443.
16 Said K Aburish, *Saddam Hussein*, Bloomsbury, London, 2000, pp. 76, 337.
17 Interviews in Baghdad, July 2000.
18 See Dilip Hiro, *The Longest War: The Iran–Iraq Military Conflict*, Paladin Grafton Books, London, 1989; and Routledge, New York, 1991, pp. 65–6.
19 Scott Ritter, *Endgame*, pp. 56, 125.
20 *International Herald Tribune*, November 12, 1998.
21 Andrew Cockburn and Patrick Cockburn, *Out of the Ashes: The resurrection of Saddam Hussein*, HarperCollins, New York, 1999; and Verso, London, 2000, p. 245.
22 Dilip Hiro, *The Longest War*, p. 98.
23 Scott Ritter, *Endgame*, p. 75.
24 Anthony H. Cordesman, *Iraq and the War of Sanctions: Conventional Threats and Weapons of Mass Destruction*, Praeger, Westport, CT, and London, 1999, p. 156.
25 Said K. Aburish, *Saddam Hussein*, p. 233.
26 Andrew Cockburn and Patrick Cockburn, *Out of the Ashes*, pp. 50–1.
27 *Nation*, May 10, 1999, p. 20. The conference was held in Austria because none of Iraq's neighbors was keen to host it.
28 See Introduction.
29 *Middle East International*, April 3, 1992, p. 8.
30 *Ibid.,* December 3, 1992, pp. 9–10; Said K. Aburish, *Saddam Hussein,* p. 320.
31 *Middle East International*, March 19, 1993, pp. 7–8.
32 Richard Butler, *Saddam Defiant: The Threat of Weapons of Mass Destruction, and the Crisis of Global Security,* Public Affairs, Washington DC, 1999; and Weidenfeld and Nicholson, London, 2000, p. 95.
33 Scott Ritter, *Endgame*, p. 107.
34 *Ibid.*, pp. 108–11.
35 Nuha al Radi, *Baghdad Diaries*, Saqi Books, London, 1998, p. 53.
36 Sarah Graham-Brown, *Sanctioning Saddam*, p. 171.
37 Anthony H. Cordesman, *Iraq and the War of Sanctions*, p. 209.
38 Interview in Baghdad, July 2000.
39 *Middle East International*, May 15, 1992, pp. 8–9.
40 *Ibid.*, September 11, 1992, pp. 6–7.
41 *Ibid.,* January 22, 1993, pp. 5–6; Anthony H. Cordesman, *Iraq and the War of Sanctions*, p. 196.
42 Anthony H. Cordesman, *Iraq and the War of Sanctions,* p. 197.
43 *New York Times,* January 13, 1993.

2 ENTER CLINTON, SADDAM'S NEW NEMESIS

1 US National Security Council release, May 18, 1993, Washington, DC. Report No. 84 of Washington Institute for Near East Policy, Washington, DC, May 21, 1993.
2 *New Yorker*, November 1, 1993.
3 *Middle East International*, October 22, 1993, p. 11.

4 *Ibid.*, December 3, 1993, p. 10.
5 *Ibid.*, July 23, 1993, p. 10.
6 Sarah Graham-Brown, *Sanctioning Saddam: The Politics of Intervention in Iraq*, I.B.Tauris (in association with MERIP), London and New York, 1999, p. 161.
7 Interview in Baghdad, July 2000; Nuha al Radi, *Baghdad Diaries*, Saqi Books, London, 1998, p. 76.
8 *Middle East International*, October 22, 1993, pp. 20–1.
9 *BP Statistical Review of World Energy 1997*, British Petroleum Corporation, London, 1998, pp. 7, 10.
10 Dilip Hiro, *The Longest War: The Iran–Iraq Military Conflict*, Paladin Grafton Books, London, 1989, and Routledge, New York, 1991, pp. 123–4.
11 *Middle East International*, July 23, 1993, p. 10, and April 15, 1994, p. 13.
12 See Dilip Hiro, *Dictionary of the Middle East*, Macmillan Press, Basingstoke, 1996; and St Martin's Press, New York, 1996, p. 130.
13 For full text of Resolution 687, see Appendix III.
14 The name came from the dried-up Old Nahrawan Canal, later called Army Canal.
15 Nuha al Radi, *Baghdad Diaries*, p. 63.
16 Visit to the Saddam International Tower, July 2000.
17 Visit to the Babil Restaurant, July 2000.
18 Visits to Baghdad, Karbala, Najaf and Babylon, July 2000.
19 *Middle East International*, September 23, 1994, p. 9.
20 Cited in *Middle East International*, October 7, 1994, p. 12.
21 Anthony H. Cordesman, *Iraq and the War of Sanctions: Conventional Threats and Weapons of Mass Destruction*, Praeger, Westport, CT, and London, 1999, p. 203.
22 *Middle East International*, October 21, 1994, pp. 3–8.
23 *Ibid.*, November 18, 1994, pp. 8–9.
24 See Dilip Hiro, *Dictionary of the Middle East*, pp. 170–1, 252–3.
25 Andrew Cockburn and Patrick Cockburn, *Out of the Ashes: The Resurrection of Saddam Hussein*, HarperCollins, New York, 1999, and Verso, London, 2000, p. 35.
26 See later, Chapter 4, p. 102.
27 *Washington Post*, June 15, 1996, January 26, 1997; Andrew Cockburn and Patrick Cockburn, *Out of the Ashes*, pp. 188–9.
28 Writing in the *Journal Du Dimanche* of March 7, 1999, Gilles Delafon, a French Middle East specialist, said that on their return to the US in March 1995, the five CIA officials were arrested by the FBI and charged with an attempted murder of Saddam Hussein, which contravened the presidential ban on assassinations imposed by President Ford in 1974. But the next year the charges against them were dropped, and they were, indeed, decorated for their work. Cited in *Daily Telegraph*, March 8, 1999.
29 Tim Trevan, *Saddam's Secrets: The Hunt for Iraq's Hidden Weapons*, HarperCollins, London, 1999, p. 312. However, the matter remained unresolved. On October 27 Unscom chief Richard Butler sent Tariq Aziz a proposal to discuss the VX program, alleging that Iraq was hiding 200 tonnes of VX.
30 *Middle East International*, March 15, 1996, pp. 20–1.
31 Inter Press Service, March 3, 1998.
32 For long-range missiles Unscom visited thirty sites, and for chemical weapons about fifty. *Middle East International*, March 17, 1995, p. 19.
33 Tim Trevan, *Saddam's Secrets*, p. 319.
34 Inter Press Service, April 19, 1995.

3 A SHATTERING BETRAYAL, THEN LUCKY BREAKS FOR SADDAM

1 Said K. Aburish, *Saddam Hussein*, Bloomsbury, London, 2000, p. 209.
2 Anthony H. Cordesman and Ahmed S. Hashim, *Iraq: Sanctions and Beyond*, Westview Press, Boulder, CO, and Oxford, UK, 1997, p. 68.
3 Report of the Executive Chairman of the Special Commission to the UN Security Council, S/1995/864, October 11, 1995.
4 *BBC Summary of World Broadcasts*, August 14, 1995; *Wall Street Journal*, August 14, 1995.
5 *Foriegn Broadcast Information Service*, August 14, 1995.
6 *Al Hayat*, August 31, 1995.
7 *Middle East International*, December 20, 1996, p. 11.
8 See earlier, Chap. 2, p. 85.
9 *Guardian*, October 15, 1995.
10 Tim Trevan, *Saddam's Secrets: The Hunt for Iraq's Hidden Weapons*, HarperCollins, London, 1999, p. 331.
11 See earlier, Chap. 1, p. 62.
12 *Middle East International*, September 8, 1995, p. 6.
13 *Ibid.*, October 20, 1995, pp. 16–17.
14 *BBC Summary of World Broadcasts*, August 14, 1995.
15 *Middle East International*, October 20, 1995, p. 13.
16 Inter Press Service, October 21, 1995.
17 *Middle East International*, September 22, 1995, p. 10.
18 Said K. Aburish, *Saddam Hussein*, p. 337.
19 Iraqi News Agency, February 23, 1996; *Independent*, September 24, 1996; Associated Press, October 1, 1998, citing an interview with Abbas al Janabi, editor of the *Babil*, after his defection to the West.
20 *Independent*, February 24, 1996; *Sunday Times*, February 25 and September 8, 1996.
21 Andrew Cockburn and Patrick Cockburn, *Out of the Ashes: The Resurrection of Saddam Hussein*, HarperCollins, New York, 1999; and Verso, London, 2000, p. 210.
22 Reuters, May 8, 1996.
23 Cited in *Independent*, February 28, 1996.
24 Said K. Aburish, *Saddam Hussein*, pp. 134–5.
25 Interviews in July 2000.
26 Inter Press Service, February 3, 1996.

4 THE MOTHER OF ALL FAILED COUPS

1 See earlier, Chap. 2, p. 84, note 26.
2 On October 31, 1995 a bomb blast wrecked the INC headquarters in Salahuddin, killing twenty-eight. The KDP arrested three suspects, who reportedly confessed to be working for the INA. The CIA conducted its inquiry but did not release its findings, out of embarrassment: both the INA and the INC were on its payroll. Andrew Cockburn and Patrick Cockburn, *Out of the Ashes: The Resurrection of Saddam Hussein*, HarperCollins, New York, 1999; and Verso, London, 2000, pp. 213–14.
3 *Independent*, April 11, 1997.
4 Inter Press Service, December 30, 1995.
5 Andrew Cockburn and Patrick Cockburn, *Out of the Ashes*, p. 220.
6 *Sunday Times*, April 2, 2000.
7 Andrew Cockburn and Patrick Cockburn, *Out of the Ashes*, p. 224.
8 Scott Ritter, *Endgame: Solving the Iraq Problem – Once and For All*, Simon & Schuster, New York and London, 1999, pp. 135–6; *Daily Telegraph*, March 8, 1999.

9   David Wurmser, *Tyranny's Ally: America's Failure to Defeat Saddam Hussein*, The AEI Press, Washington DC, 1999, p. 24.

10 Andrew Cockburn and Patrick Cockburn, *Out of the Ashes*, p. 227.

11 Scott Ritter, *Endgame*, pp. 124–5; Said K. Aburish, *Saddam Hussein*, Bloomsbury, London, 2000, pp. 325–6.

12 *Middle East International*, June 21, 1996, p.14; *Daily Telegraph*, March 8, 1999.

13 Interview with an Iraqi exile in London, January 2000.

14 Scott Ritter, *Endgame*, p. 143.

15 *Ibid.*, pp. 140–1. My italics.

16 *Middle East International*, July 19, 1996, pp. 14–15; Tim Trevan, *Saddam's Secrets: The Hunt for Iraq's Hidden Weapons*, HarperCollins, London, 1999, p. 411; Scott Ritter, *Endgame*, p. 141; Richard Butler, *Saddam Defiant: The Threat of Weapons of Mass Destruction, and the Crisis of Global Security*, Public Affairs, Washington, DC, 1999; and Weidenfeld & Nicolson, London, 2000, p. 96.

17 *Middle East International*, September 6, 1996, pp. 3–6; November 8, 1996, pp. 16–17.

18 *BBC Summary of World Broadcasts*, July 8, 1996.

19 Cited in Andrew Cockburn and Patrick Cockburn, *Out of the Ashes*, pp. 237–8.

20 Inter Press Service, September 3, 1996.

21 *Le Monde*, September 3, 1996.

22 Inter Press Service, September 3 and 6, 1996.

23 Cited in Inter Press Service, September 6, 1996.

24 *Guardian*, April 28, 1997.

25 Inter Press Service, September 6, 1996.

26 Inter Press Service, September 14, 1996.

27 *Middle East International*, September 20, 1996, pp. 5–6. Later, in a court case concerning one of the CIA's Iraqi agents in America, it was officially revealed that the US had evacuated 5,500 Iraqis and Kurds who worked for the CIA, INC and INA from Iraqi Kurdistan in September 1996. By then the INC and the INA had received a total of $20 million from the CIA.

28 Anthony H. Cordesman and Ahmed S. Hashim, *Iraq: Sanctions and Beyond*, Westview Press, Boulder, CO, and Oxford, UK, 1997, p. 211.

29 *Washington Post*, September 20, 1996; Andrew Cockburn and Patrick Cockburn, *Out of the Ashes*, p. 244.

30 Inter Press Service, December 10, 1996.

31 *Middle East International*, January 10, 1997, pp. 11–12; January 24, 1997, pp. 19–20.

32 *Ibid.*, December 20, 1996, pp. 11–12.

33 Cited in Sarah Graham-Brown, *Sanctioning Saddam: The Politics of Intervention in Iraq*, I.B.Tauris (in association with MERIP), London and New York, 1999, p.184.

34 Inter Press Service, October 22, and December 10, 1995; and *Middle East International*, November 3, 1995, p. 9.

35 *Independent*, July 8, 1997.

36 Cited in Andrew Cockburn and Patrick Cockburn, *Out of the Ashes*, p. 259.

37 It was in late September 1997 that the plotters' corpses were dumped in front of their homes, and that was when Wafiq al Samarrai leaked the story to the Western press. *Sunday Times*, October 12, 1997.

38 The names of three key US intelligence agents, known to *Washington Post* reporter Barton Gellman, were withheld for security reasons when he published the story on March 2, 1999.

39 *Washington Post*, March 2, 1999.

40 *Middle East International*, February 12, 1999, pp. 22–3.

41 *Ibid.*, October 25, 1996, pp. 9–10 ; November 22, 1996, p. 10; December 6, 1996, p. 13.

1 CBS TV transcript, May 12, 1996.
2 Andrew Cockburn and Patrick Cockburn, *Out of the Ashes: The Resurrection of Saddam Hussein*, HarperCollins, New York, 1999; and Verso, London, 2000, p. 263.
3 See earlier, Chap. 1, p. 52.
4 Scott Ritter, *Endgame: Solving the Iraq Problem – Once and For All*, Simon & Schuster, New York and London, 1999, p. 154.
5 Richard Butler, *Saddam Defiant: The Threat of Weapons of Mass Destruction, and the Crisis of Global Security*, Public Affairs, Washington, DC, 1999; and Weidenfeld & Nicolson, London, 2000, p. 154.
6 Scott Ritter, *Endgame*, pp. 150, 157.
7 *Middle East International*, May 16, 1997, p. 6.
8 United Nations Special Commission, "Report to the Security Council – S/1997/301, dated April 11, 1997."
9 Scott Ritter, *Endgame*, pp. 152–3.
10 *Ibid.*, p.154.
11 Iraqi TV, June 22, 1997.
12 Richard Butler, *Saddam Defiant*, p. 98.
13 Scott Ritter, *Endgame*, p. 152.
14 *Jane's Intelligence Review*, July 1997, pp. 312–16, and August 1997, pp. 365–7; *New York Times*, November 25, 1997; *Jerusalem Post*, November 28, 1997. Interviews in Baghdad, July 2000.
15 Scott Ritter, *Endgame*, p. 164.
16 Richard Butler, *Saddam Defiant*, pp. 99–100.
17 Scott Ritter, *Endgame*, p. 190.
18 United Nations Special Commission, "Report to the Security Council – S/1997/774, dated October 6, 1997."
19 Richard Butler, *Saddam Defiant*, p. 107.
20 "Of the approximately 1,000 people Unscom used during my administration, perhaps 250 were American; another 150 were British." wrote Richard Butler in *ibid.*, p. 94.
21 *Middle East International*, November 21, 1997, p. 3.
22 Richard Butler, *Saddam Defiant*, pp. 109, 122.
23 *Ibid.*, p. 198.
24 "Ritter's Private War," *New Yorker*, November 9, 1998, pp. 56–73.
25 *Sunday Times*, November 16, 1997; *Independent*, December 18, 1997. Strictly speaking, Iraq expelled only the Unscom's American inspectors, not UN inspectors *per se*.
26 *Middle East International*, November 21, 1997, p. 5.
27 *Observer*, November 16, 1997; *The Times*, November 17, 1997.
28 Inter Press Service, November 26, 1997.
29 Inter Press Service, June 3, 1997.
30 Inter Press Service, March 1, 1997; BBC World Service Radio, November 12, 1997.
31 *Middle East International*, May 16, 1997, pp. 16–17.
32 Interview in Baghdad, August 2000.
33 Inter Press Service, December 10, 1997.
34 *Middle East International*, March 7, 1997, p. 18.
35 Interview in Baghdad, August 2000.
36 BBC World Service Radio, November 26, 1997; *Independent*, November 27, 1997.
37 *Middle East International*, January 10, 1997, pp. 17–18.
38 Inter Press Service, October 17, 1997.
39 Inter Press Service, November 11, 1997.

40 *Washington Post*, August 28, 1998. My italics.
41 *Ibid.*

6 "DESERT THUNDER" THAT DIDN'T THUNDER

1 *The Times*, January 13, 1998.
2 Inter Press Service, January 20, 1998; *Guardian*, February 4, 1998.
3 Cited in Inter Press Service, March 3, 1998.
4 Richard Butler said that he had been misquoted, and a correction appeared in the *New York Times*, January 30, 1998, p. 33; Geoff Simons, *Iraq – Primus Inter Pariahs: A Crisis Chronology*, Macmillan Press, Basingstoke, and St Martin's Press, New York, 1999, p. 156. See also Anthony H. Cordesman, *Iraq and the War of Sanctions: Conventional Threats and Weapons of Mass Destruction*, Praeger, Westport, CT, and London, 1999, pp. 245–6; *Sunday Times*, March 1, 1998.
5 CNN Transcript, February 18, 1998; *Washington Post*, March 1, 1998.
6 Cited in *Middle East International*, February 13, 1998, p. 4; Anthony H. Cordesman, *Iraq and the War of Sanctions*, p. 246.
7 Cited in Inter Press Service, February 10, 1998.
8 Cited in Anthony H. Cordesman, *Iraq and the War of Sanctions*, p. 237.
9 *Daily Telegraph*, February 16, 1998.
10 *Observer*, March 1, 1998; Richard Butler, *Saddam Defiant: The Threat of Weapons of Mass Destruction, and the Crisis of Global Security*, Public Affairs, Washington, DC, 1999; and Weidenfeld & Nicolson, London, 2000, pp. 145, 147.
11 On February 20, Bill Richardson, the US ambassador to the UN, was hooted down in the middle of his speech at University of Minnesota when he tried to justify air strikes against Iraq.
12 *New York Times*, November 8, 1998.
13 Inter Press Service, March 2, 1998.
14 *Observer*, March 1, 1998.
15 Cited in *Middle East International*, February 27, 1998, p. 4.
16 *Washington Post*, February 24 and 25, 1998.
17 *Sunday Times*, March 1, 1998.
18 Inter Press Service, February 27, 1998.
19 Anthony H. Cordesman, *Iraq and the War of Sanctions*, p. 263.
20 Scott Ritter, *Endgame: Solving the Iraq Problem – Once and For All*, Simon & Schuster, New York and London, 1999, p. 187.
21 *Middle East International*, January 29, 1999, p. 21.
22 Iraqi foreign minister Muhammad al Sahhaf's letter to Kofi Annan, S/1998/204 dated March 8, 1998.
23 *Middle East International*, January 29, 1999, p. 21.
24 *Washington Post*, September 30, 1998.
25 Scott Ritter, *Endgame*, pp. 188–9; *Washington Post,* March 20, 1998.
26 *The Times*, March 27, 1998.
27 Richard Butler, *Saddam Defiant*, pp. 166–7; Tariq Aziz's letter to the UN Security Council, S/1998/342 dated April 22, 1998.
28 The beefing up of the forces in the Gulf cost the US treasury $2 billion annually. *Middle East International*, March 13, 1998, p. 11.
29 *Washington Post*, August 28, 1998.
30 Cited in Anthony H. Cordesman, *op. cit.*, pp. 241–2.
31 *Financial Times*, June 17, 1998.
32 Inter Press Service, May 14, 1998.
33 *Middle East International*, April 24, 1998, p. 14.

34 *Independent*, August 1, 1998.
35 Interviews in Baghdad, July 2000.
36 Interviews in Baghdad, August 2000.
37 *Middle East International*, February 12, 1999, p. 10.
38 *Ibid.*, November 13, 1998, pp. 6–7.
39 *Ibid.*, November 13, 1998, p. 7.
40 Anthony H. Cordesman, *Iraq and the War of Sanctions*, p. 315.
41 *Ibid.*, p. 300; Inter Press Service, May 14, 1998.
42 Richard Butler, *Saddam Defiant*, pp. 171–2.
43 Anthony H. Cordesman, *Iraq and the War of Sanctions*, p. 304.
44 Richard Butler, *Saddam Defiant*, p. 175. However, in his interview with the *New York Times*, Butler was more forthright, demanding that Iraq submit documentation "involving area of official decision-making, especially on Iraq's concealment policy." *New York Times*, June 17, 1998.
45 Associated Press, June 15, 1998; *Washington Times*, June 16, 1998; *Financial Times*, June 17, 1998. Regarding the biological file, after the July 17–23 meetings in Baghdad on the subject, Aziz reportedly told Butler in a letter that "the meeting[s] did not succeed in closing the gaps between the two sides." Richard Butler, *Saddam Defiant*, pp. 174, 179.
46 Inter Press Service, May 14, 1998; *New York Times*, June 19 and 25, 1998; *Independent*, July 13, 1998; Anthony H. Cordesman, *Iraq and the War of Sanctions*, p. 300.
47 Richard Butler's allegation was said to be backed up by satellite images collected by the US showing delivery of the materials at the farm *after* Hussein Kamil Hassan's defection in early August 1995. *Middle East International*, July 3, 1898, pp. 10–11.
48 Richard Butler, *Saddam Defiant*, pp. 177–8. According to Butler, over 100,000 special munitions allegedly consumed during 1981–88 remained unaccounted for.
49 Anthony H. Cordesman, *Iraq and the War of Sanctions*, p. 318.
50 Richard Butler, *Saddam Defiant*, p. 184.
51 *Ibid.*, p. 184.
52 *New York Times*, September 18, and October 7, 1998; Reuters, October 26, 1998.
53 *International Herald Tribune*, August 6, 1998; Richard Butler, *Saddam Defiant*, pp. 187–8.
54 *Washington Post*, November 16, 1998.
55 *Middle East International*, August 21, 1998, p. 5.
56 Scott Ritter, *Endgame*, p. 182.
57 *New York Times*, August 27, and September 4, 1998.
58 *Middle East International*, September 18, 1998; Richard Butler, *Saddam Defiant*, p. 189.
59 *Washington Post*, September 18, 1998.
60 Anthony H. Cordesman, *Iraq and the War of Sanctions*, pp. 298–9.
61 Associated Press, September 17, 1998.
62 *New York Times*, June 19, 1998.
63 "American intelligence officials say they believe [Masud] Barzani was enmeshed in Iraqi oil smuggling even when he was on the CIA payroll in the covert program." *Ibid.*, June 19, 1998.
64 Associated Press, September 3, 1998; *Middle East International*, September 4, 1998, p. 15; Anthony H. Cordesman, *Iraq and the War of Sanctions*, p. 322.
65 *Washington Post*, October 22, 1998.

7 OPERATION "DESERT FOX"

1 Associated Press, October 6, 1998.
2 *Washington Post*, October 22, 1998; *Middle East International*, November 27, 1998; *Nation*, May 10, 1999, p. 22.

3   *Washington Post*, October 22, 1998; *Observer*, November 15, 1998; *New York Times*, November 16, 1998.

4   *Middle East International*, March 26, 1999, p. 14.

5   *Washington Post*, November 23, 1998; *International Herald Tribune*, November 30, 1998; *Gulf States Newsletter*, February 22, 1999.

6   Cited in *Middle East International*, January 29, 1999, p. 13.

7   *Washington Post*, September 30, 1998.

8   For the complete text of Security Council Resolution 687, see Appendix III.

9   *New York Times*, October 2, 1998; *International Herald Tribune*, November 12, 1998; *Sunday Times*, November 22, 1998. By mid-2000, the FBI has still not concluded its investigation.

10 *Guardian*, November 14, 1998.

11 *Observer*, November 15, 1998; *Sunday Times*, November 15, 1998.

12 Richard Butler, *Saddam Defiant: The Threat of Weapons of Mass Destruction, and the Crisis of Global Security*, Public Affairs, Washington, DC, 1999; and Weidenfeld & Nicolson, London, 2000, p. 206. In any case, Clause 4.4 of the annex should have appealed to President Clinton. "If the Council sees, through an objective study, that there are matters which need to be done, a short period be determined for their completion," it read. "Until that completion is reached, the Council implements measures for lifting or reducing sanctions in proportion of what has been fulfilled of the requirements of Paragraph 22. Thereafter the Council should commence the implementation of Paragraph 22 immediately upon the completion of the required work." This was uncannily like the formula Clinton used to broker a deal between the Israelis and the Palestinians on 23 October 1998 at the Wye River Plantation: a phased, interrelated agreement which required Israel to vacate a certain percentage of West Bank land in return for the Palestinians meeting certain specified commitments.

13 Reuters, November 15, 1998.

14 Scott Ritter, *Endgame: Solving the Iraq Problem – Once and For All*, Simon & Schuster, New York and London, 1999, pp. 195–6.

15 Anthony H. Cordesman, *Iraq and the War of Sanctions Sanctions: Conventional Threats and Weapons of Mass Destruction*, Praeger, Westport, CT, and London, 1999, pp. 374–5.

16 Agence France-Presse, November 26, 1998.

17 Richard Butler, *Saddam Defiant*, pp. 218–19.

18 *Washington Post*, November 22, 1998.

19 *International Herald Tribune*, December 21, 1998, and January 2–3, 1999; *Sunday Times*, December 27, 1998. Eighteen months later, the skeletal Baath Party National Command headquarters had been rebuilt. Author's visit to Baghdad, July 2000.

20 *International Herald Tribune*, December 23, 1998.

21 *New York Times*, January 13, 1999.

22 *Ibid.*, January 8, 1999; *International Herald Tribune*, December 22, 1998.

23 *New York Times*, January 3, 1999.

24 *Ibid.*, January 10, 1999; *The Times*, January 11, 1999.

25 *International Herald Tribune*, January 15, 1999.

26 Inter Press Service, January 26, 1999; *Middle East International*, January 29, 1999, pp. 11–12.

27 Inter Press Service, January 26, 1999.

28 *Sunday Times*, March 14, 1999.

29 *Guardian*, April 15, 1998.

30 *Washington Post*, January 29, 1999.

31 Reuters, February 3, 1999.

32 *Middle East International*, February 12, 1999, p. 10.

33 Associated Press, December 29, 1998.

34 *International Herald Tribune*, March 23, 1999.
35 *Nation*, March 15, 1999, p. 5.
36 *New York Times*, October 8, 1999.
37 *Ibid.*, March 23, 1999.
38 See http://leb.net/iac/nofly.html (accessed February 2001).
39 Sarah Graham-Brown, *Sanctioning Saddam: The Politics of Intervention in Iraq*, I.B.Tauris (in association with MERIP), London and New York, 1999, p. 106.
40 Associated Press, November 26, 1999.
41 Cited in *Nation*, May 10, 1999, p. 22.
42 Associated Press, June 23, 1999.
43 *Washington Post*, August 6, 1999.
44 Associated Press, November 1, 1999.
45 On March 14, 1999, *Al Jumhuriya*, the organ of the Iraqi government, reported that the authorities hanged eight Iraqis the day before for the assassinations of Ayatollahs Murtadha Borujerdi and Mirza Gharavi.
46 *Los Angeles Times*, November 24, 1998.
47 *Observer*, February 21, 1999; *Sunday Times*, February 21, 1999. The government announced that, on April 5, four Iraqis, including three clerics, were executed for murdering Grand Ayatollah Muhammad al Sadr and his two sons. Agence France-Presse, April 6, 1999.
48 Interview in Baghdad, July 2000.
49 Cited in *Dialogue*, January 2000, p. 7.
50 *Middle East International*, April 9, 1999, p. 12–13.
51 *Observer*, December 19, 1999; *Sunday Times*, July 16, 2000. Only 46 percent of the contracted medical materials had arrived in Iraq by the end of 1999. Associated Press, January 6, 2000.
52 Interview with Hans von Sponeck in London, October 2000.
53 Interview with a UN source in Baghdad, July 2000.
54 Associated Press, October 4, 1999.
55 *Middle East International*, September 3, 1999, p. 20; Reuters, November 2, 1999.
56 Cited in *Middle East International,* April 10, 1998, p. 17.
57 Interviews in Baghdad, July 2000.
58 Nuha al Radi, *Baghdad Diaries*, Saqi Books, London, 1998, pp. 64–5, p. 79. The exchange rate in early 1995 was around ID 1,000 to US$ 1.
59 During my visit to Baghdad in July 2000, I ventured into such taxis several times.
60 Interview with Hans von Sponeck in London, October 2000.
61 Nuha al Radi, *Baghdad Diaries*, pp. 86–7.
62 Interview with Hans von Sponeck in London, October 2000.
63 Agence France-Presse, July 24, 2000. Also see earlier, Chap. 6, p. 145.
64 *Middle East International*, October 29, 1999, p. 22.
65 Interview in Baghdad, July 2000. As someone with a chronic heart problem, Yassin Abdul Hamid carried a medical card that entitled him to certain drugs. "Often the most important drug was not available," he said.
66 Associated Press, May 25, 1999.
67 *Washington Post*, January 28, 1999.
68 Reuters, November 2, 1999.
69 *Guardian*, February 17, 2000.
70 BBC World Service Radio, November 6, 1999; *International Herald Tribune*, December 28, 1999.
71 *Washington Post*, July 15, 1999; Associated Press, September 14, 1999.

1 For the full text of Security Council Resolution 1284, see Appendix VI.
2 Associated Press, November 26, 1999. The sponsors of Resolution 1284 did not consult Iraq at all. Interview with Hans von Sponeck in London, October 2000.
3 Associated Press, January 5, 2000.
4 Reuters, February 15, 2000; Agence France-Presse, February 15 and 16, 2000.
5 *Daily Telegraph*, February 17, 2000.
6 *Washington Post*, February 20, 2000.
7 *Ibid.*, February 20, 2000.
8 *International Herald Tribune*, March 28, 2000.
9 United Nations Press Release, SC 6834 dated March 24, 2000.
10 Associated Press, March 25 and April 1, 2000.
11 This was after Russia, France and China had rejected Annan's first choice: Rolf Ekeus, a former Unscom chief.
12 *Middle East International*, February 11, 2000, p. 13.
13 See earlier, p. 177.
14 *New York Times*, April 7, 2000.
15 Since the imposition of the no-fly zones – in June 1991 in the north and August 1992 in the south – there had been 280,000 sorties by the US and the UK, initially joined by France. *Washington Post*, June 17, 2000. In the north only six of the sixty aircraft were British. In the south, before the French pull-out in December 1998, France and Britain each contributed five percent of the total.
16 *Baghdad Observer*, June 14, 2000.
17 In 1999 American aircraft bombed and strafed Iraqi sheep and other livestock because analysts studying satellite imagery mistook an animals' water trough for a missile launcher. *Washington Post*, October 26, 2000.
18 Visit to Najaf, July 2000.
19 Associated Press, March 26, 2000.
20 *International Herald Tribune*, August 24, 2000.
21 *Washington Post*, August 31, 2000.
22 *Observer*, September 24, 2000; *BP Amoco Statistical Review of World Energy 2000*, London, 2000, pp. 7, 10. With less than 5 percent of the world population, America consumed 25 percent of the global oil output.
23 *International Herald Tribune*, September 15, 2000; *Middle East International*, September 29, 2000, p. 5.
24 Reuters, September 12, 2000; *Middle East International*, September 29, 2000, p. 7.
25 *Observer*, September 24, 2000.
26 *International Herald Tribune,* August 11 and September 6, 2000.
27 Cited in *Middle East International*, August 18, 2000, p. 14.
28 Vnukovo Airline later said that it expected to start a regular twice-weekly service between Moscow and Baghdad by the end of the year. Earlier, Aeroflot, 51 percent state-owned, had signed an agreement with the state-owned Iraqi Airways which allowed them to open offices in Baghdad and Moscow respectively. *International Herald Tribune*, October 5 and 13, 2000.
29 Associated Press, September 14, 2000.
30 Interviews in Baghdad, July 2000.
31 *New York Times*, September 22, 2000; *International Herald Tribune*, September 27, 2000.
32 By then the Compensation Commission, having settled all small claims, had moved on to big ones. *New York Times*, September 27, 2000.
33 Agence France-Presse, October 8, 2000.
34 *International Herald Tribune*, September 27, 2000.

35 *New York Times*, November 5, 2000. In August Syria reopened its rail link with Iraq after nearly two decades.
36 *Al Sharq al Awsat*, September 2, 2000.
37 Associated Press, October 21, 2000.
38 *Ibid.*, October 21, 2000.
39 *Washington Post*, October 21, 2000.
40 This was certainly not the case in 1992 when Iraq had to cancel its plan to resume internal flights due to the no-fly zone restrictions. *International Herald Tribune*, November 6, 2000.
41 BBC News, November 5, 2000.
42 *Middle East International*, April 21, 2000, p. 13. By contrast, some 10,000 Iraqi POWs had sought asylum in Iran. *Kayhan International*, August 24, 1999.
43 *International Herald Tribune*, October 16, 2000.
44 Dilip Hiro, *The Longest War: The Iran–Iraq Military Conflict*, Paladin Grafton Books, London, 1989; and Routledge, New York, 1991, p. 57.

9 RAFSANJANI'S RECONSTRUCTION AND ECONOMIC LIBERALIZATION

1 See Dilip Hiro, *The Longest War: The Iran–Iraq Military Conflict*, Paladin Grafton Books, London, 1989; and Routledge, New York, 1991, pp. 224–5.
2 Cited in *Middle East International*, April 19, 1991, p. 18.
3 *Economist*, December 5, 1992, pp. 39–40.
4 Anoushiravan Ehteshami, *After Khomeini: The Second Iranian Republic*, Routledge, London and New York, 1995, p. 74; *Middle East International*, October 12, 1990, p. 14.
5 *Middle East International*, December 7, 1990.
6 Anoushiravan Ehteshami, *After Khomeini*, p. 61.
7 Inter Press Service, June 15, 1993.
8 By contrast, during the First Gulf War, Iran actually reduced its foreign debts of $15 billion it had inherited from the Shah's regime. Inter Press Service, June 15, 1993.
9 *Middle East International*, September 8, 1995, p. 13.
10 Anoushiravan Ehteshami, *After Khomeini*, p. 108.
11 *Middle East International*, August 7, 1992, p. 13, and August 21, 1992, p. 11.
12 Cited in *ibid.*, July 24, 1992, p. 13–14.
13 Cited in *ibid.*, October 23, 1992, p. 14.
14 See earlier, p. 197.
15 *New York Times*, October 13, 2000.
16 US National Security Council release, May 18, 1993, Washington, DC. Also Special Report No. 84 of Washington Institute for Near East Policy, Washington, DC, May 21, 1993. See earlier, Chap. 2, pp. 69–70.
17 *Guardian*, March 24, 1995. By contrast, in 1995 Iran spent only $250 million on arms imports. *Sunday Times*, August 11, 1996.
18 *Middle East International*, July 9, 1993, p. 5.
19 *Sunday Times*, November 14, 1993.
20 Tehran Radio, February 14, 1989.
21 *Middle East International*, October 22, 1993, p. 13.
22 Inter Press Service, June 6, 1993.
23 *Middle East International*, June 11, 1993, p. 17, and April 15, 1994, p. 18.
24 Cited in *ibid.*, October 22, 1993, p. 11.
25 Anoushiravan Ehteshami, *After Khomeini*, p. 68; Dilip Hiro, *Dictionary of the Middle East*, Macmillan Press, Basingstoke, 1996; and St Martin's Press, New York, 1996, p. 270.
26 Inter Press Service, June 15, 1993.
27 *Ibid.*; Anoushiravan Ehteshami, *After Khomeini*, p. 68.

28 It was not until September 1993 that the Guardians Council passed the Free Trade Zones law.
29 *Middle East International*, December 3, 1993, p. 10 and January 7, 1994, p. 13.
30 *Sunday Times*, December 4, 1994.
31 *Middle East International*, January 7, 1994, p. 13, and February 4, 1994, pp. 20–1.
32 Hooshang Amirahmadi and Eric Hooglund (eds), *US–Iran Relations: Areas of Tension and Mutual Interest*, The Middle East Institute, Washington, DC, 1994, p. 39.
33 *Sunday Times*, December 4, 1994.
34 *Guardian*, December 15, 1994. Ahmad Khomeini's natural death at 48 in March 1995 removed an important link between the feuding factions.
35 See earlier, Chap. 7, p. 173.
36 *Middle East International*, September 9, 1994, p. 14.
37 *Middle East International*, January 20, 1995, p. 14 and December 11, 1998, p. 17; *Guardian*, March 24, 1995.
38 America's unilateral sanctions derive from its national emergency legislation of 1897 passed during its war with Spain, giving the president wide powers. The excessive use of this law in the 1980s and 1990s resulted in the US imposing sanctions against 75 countries. *Los Angeles Times*, 21 January 2001.
39 Interviews in Tehran, August 1999.
40 *Middle East International*, May 12, 1995, p. 21, and May 2, 1997, p. 5.
41 Inter Press Service, May 22, 1995.
42 *Guardian*, April 5, 1995; *New York Times*, July 16, 1999.
43 *Guardian*, January 2, 1995.
44 Cited in *Middle East International*, May 12, 1995, pp. 20–1.
45 *Ibid.*
46 See further Farhang Rajaee, "A Thermidor of 'Islamic Yuppies' ? Conflict and Compromise in Iran's Politics," Middle East Journal, Spring 1999, pp. 222–3.
47 *New York Times*, January 2, 1995.
48 *Ibid.*; *Mainstream*, June 14, 1997, p. 14; Anoushiravan Ehteshami, *After Khomeini*, p. 115.
49 Inter Press Service, October 2, 1995.
50 *Independent*, June 7, 1995; *Middle East International*, June 9, 1995, p. 13.
51 Cited in *Independent*, June 7, 1995.
52 See further Dilip Hiro, *Iran Under the Ayatollahs*, Routledge & Kegan Paul, London and New York, 1985; and toExcel Press, New York, 2000, pp. 47–9.
53 *Independent*, August 20, 1996.
54 *Ibid.*
55 Dilip Hiro, *Iran Under the Ayatollahs*, p. 16.
56 See Dilip Hiro, *Dictionary of the Middle East*, pp. 45–6.
57 *Middle East International*, June 21, 1996, pp. 8–9.
58 *Ibid.*, July 5, 1996, pp. 7–8.
59 Inter Press Service, June 29, 1996.
60 *Observer*, August 4, 1996.
61 *Guardian*, February 3, 1997.
62 See further, Dilip Hiro, *Sharing the Promised Land: A Tale of Israelis and Palestinians*, Coronet Books, London, 1997, pp. 563–4.
63 *Middle East International,* February 2, 1996.
64 *Guardian*, January 2, 1995; *Middle East International*, November 8, 1996, pp. 12–13, and December 6, 1996, pp. 10–11.
65 *Middle East International*, December 6, 1996, pp. 10–11, and March 21, 1997, p. 14.
66 Unless Iran showed signs of changing its terrorist behavior, after the first year of ILSA the limit on investment in its oil and gas industry was to be halved to $20 million a year.

67 Inter Press Service, August 10, 1996.
68 *Ibid.,* May 12, 1996; *Middle East International,* May 24, 1996, p. 3.
69 *Independent,* January 11, 1995; *Sunday Times,* August 11, 1996. Only low enriched uranium unsuitable for weapons was being used to fuel the US-supplied research reactor at Tehran University, according to the IAEA. *Guardian,* March 24, 1995.
70 Cited in *Middle East International,* December 20, 1996, p. 10.
71 *Guardian,* April 11, 1997. The Iranian government denied any involvement in the Berlin murders and blamed them on the infighting among the opposition groups. When Iranian-German tensions rose, the head of Iran's judiciary threatened to make public documents about Bonn's involvement in the Iraqi chemical weapons' industry during the 1980s – a subject of great embarrassment in view of the UN action against Baghdad on chemical and other non-conventional arms after 1991.
72 *Independent,* April 12, 1997.
73 *Middle East International,* April 18, 1997, p. 12, and May 16, 1997, p. 17.
74 *Ibid.,* April 4, 1997, p. 12.
75 *Ibid.,* June 13, 1997, p. 16.
76 *Ibid.*
77 Anoushiravan Ehteshami, *After Khomeini,* p.179.
78 *New York Times,* October 14, 2000.
79 *Financial Times,* May 2, 1997; Anoushiravan Ehteshami, *After Khomeini,* p. 115.

10 KHATAMI, A MODERATE WITH A MISSION

1 Interviews in Tehran, January 2000.
2 Reuters, July 26, 2000.
3 F. Moini, *Who's Who in Iran,* Media & Books Co., Bonn, Germany, 2nd Edition, 1998, p. 106.
4 Cited in *Middle East International,* August 8, 1997, p. 10.
5 Dilip Hiro, *Iran Under the Ayatollahs,* Routledge & Kegan Paul, London and New York, 1985; and toExcel Press, New York, 2000, p. 216.
6 Anoushiravan Ehteshami, *After Khomeini: The Second Iranian Republic,* Routledge, London and New York, 1995, p. 111.
7 Inter Press Service, September 30, 1997.
8 Cited in *Middle East International,* October 24, 1997, p. 14. The 1996 Anti-Terrorism and Effective Death Penalty Act, which required the US government to publish annually a list of terrorist organizations and states supporting international terrorism, also stipulated that the American representatives on the international financial institutions should lobby against extending credit to the states sponsoring terrorism.
9 Interviews in Tehran, August 1999.
10 *Daily Telegraph,* December 10, 1997.
11 This so upset President Suleiman Demirel of Turkey, which had recently forged military links with Israel, that he left Tehran a day before the end of the summit.
12 Reuters, December 11, 1997.
13 *Ibid.*
14 Anthony H. Cordesman, *Iraq and the War of Sanctions: Conventional Threats and Weapons of Mass Destruction,* Praeger, Westport, CT, and London, 1999, p. 241.
15 *Middle East International,* December 19, 1997, p. 10, and May 22, 1998, p. 16. In mid-January 1998 the Palestinian leader Yasser Arafat, who had attended the ICO summit in Tehran, told the *Los Angeles Times* that he had brought President Clinton a message from President Khatami expressing a desire for a phased resumption of formal relations.

16 *Middle East International*, January 16, 1998, pp. 10–11.
17 *Independent*, January 8, 1998; *The Times*, January 9, 1998; *Observer*, January 11, 1998; *Sunday Times*, January 11, 1998.
18 *Middle East International*, May 22, 1998, pp. 16–17.
19 Cited in Anthony H. Cordesman, *Iraq and the War of Sanctions*, p. 255. In June, during his meeting with Muhammad al Sahhaf, President Khatami reiterated Iran's opposition to the Pentagon's military action against Baghdad. *Middle East International*, June 19, 1998, p. 18.
20 Anthony H. Cordesman, *Iraq and the War of Sanctions*, p. 340.
21 Reuters, March 29, 1998.
22 *Washington Post*, March 27, 1998.
23 There was no mention of Cuba and North Korea – also on the US list of states that sponsor international terrorism – because the possibility of a first-time arrival from these countries, possessing an American visa, was almost nil. Mysteriously, nothing was said about Syria, the remaining terrorist state on Washington's list.
24 *Washington Post*, May 1, 1998.
25 BBC News, May 23, 1998.
26 When the Prague-based RFE/RL started its Persian language broadcasts on October 30, Iran recalled its ambassador to the Czech Republic.
27 Inter Press Service, May 26, 1998.
28 *Washington Post*, August 14, 1998.
29 Radio Free Europe/Radio Liberty, July 29, 1998.
30 *New York Times*, June 18 and 25, 1998.
31 *Ibid.*, September 22, 1998.
32 Agence France-Presse, November 4, 1998.
33 A few months earlier a group of provincial mayors had been imprisoned on similar charges. *Middle East International*, April 24, 1998, p. 16.
34 Associated Press, July 5, 1998.
35 *Washington Post*, June 10, 1998.
36 Cited in *Middle East International*, June 5, 1998, p. 11.
37 BBC News, August 27, 1998.
38 Interviews in Tehran, August 1999.
39 *International Herald Tribune*, September 28 and 29, 1998.
40 Interviews in Tehran, August 1999.
41 Reuters, January 14, 1999.
42 *International Herald Tribune*, October 24–5, 1998.
43 *Middle East International*, October 30, 1998, p. 12.
44 Associated Press, October 26, 1998.
45 *Washington Post*, September 7, 1998.
46 *Middle East International*, January 30, 1998, p. 13–14.
47 Reuters, February 22, 1998.
48 *Middle East International*, May 16, 1997, p. 16.
49 *Ibid.*, July 17, 1998, p. 17.
50 Inter Press Service December 30, 1997.

11 POLITICAL REFORM AND REACTION

1 Cited in *Middle East International*, December 25, 1998, p. 16.
2 Agence France-Presse, January 12, 1999.
3 *Middle East International*, July 2, 1999, pp. 15–16.
4 Inter Press Service, March 1, 1999.
5 *Middle East International*, June 4, 1999, pp. 16–17.

6 Cited in *ibid.*, April 23, 1999, pp. 17–18.
7 *International Herald Tribune*, April 29, 1999.
8 *Iran News*, July 3, 1999.
9 *Washington Post*, July 11, 1999.
10 BBC News, August 15, 2000, and *Middle East International*, August 20, 1999, pp. 20–1. In February 2000, nineteen LEF personnel along with Brig. Gen. Farhad Nazari were put on trial.
11 *Tehran Times*, August 26, 1999.
12 The confidential letter was published by conservative papers within a fortnight, but none of them was taken to task by the Press Court. *Middle East International*, July 30, 1999, pp. 17–18.
13 Interview in Tehran, August 1999.
14 Cited in *Middle East International*, July 30, 1999, pp. 20–1.
15 *New York Times*, July 14, 1999.
16 *Nation*, November 15, 1999, p. 4.
17 Reuters, July 26, 1999.
18 *International Herald Tribune*, September 23, 1999.
19 *Ibid.*
20 Reuters, September 26, 1999.
21 Reuters, October 1, 1999.
22 For the Liberation Movement of Iran and the National Front, see Dilip Hiro, *Dictionary of the Middle East*, Macmillan Press, Basingstoke, 1996; and St Martin's Press, New York, 1996, p. 187 and pp. 218–19 respectively.
23 *Middle East International*, December 10, 1999, p. 15. Leader Khamanei stood by the SCC, describing it as legal and necessary.
24 *Observer*, November 7, 1999; *International Herald Tribune*, November 13–14, 1999.
25 *Middle East International*, November 26, 1999, pp. 18–19.
26 *Ibid.*; *International Herald Tribune*, November 29, 1999.
27 Reuters, November 29, 1999.
28 *Washington Post*, September 29, 1999.
29 Cited in *Middle East International*, September 3, 1999, p. 16.
30 *International Herald Tribune*, October 30–1, 1999.
31 Associated Press, November 23, 1999.
32 *Economist*, August 14, 1999, p. 49; *Washington Post*, September 16, 1999.
33 *Middle East International*, April 9, 1999, p. 17.
34 See further Dilip Hiro, *Dictionary of the Middle East*, "Oil and gas industry, Iran", pp. 229–30.
35 Interviews in Tehran, August 1999.
36 Interview in Tehran, August 1999.
37 Besides the president, the Supreme Economic Council contained seven cabinet ministers, the governor of the Central Bank of Iran, and the head of the planning and budget organization.
38 *International Herald Tribune*, March 21, 2000.
39 *Middle East International*, February 25, 2000, p. 21.
40 *Iran News*, January 11, 2000.
41 *Middle East International*, January 28, 2000, pp. 16–17, and February 25, 2000, pp. 4–6.
42 *Washington Post*, February 18, 2000.
43 Cited in *ibid.*
44 *International Herald Tribune*, February 23, 2000. Significantly, reformists won all five seats in the holy city of Mashhad, a traditional stronghold of conservatives.
45 Cited in *Middle East International*, March 10, 2000, p. 15.
46 *Observer*, May 14, 2000.

47 Associated Press, February 25, 2000.
48 *Iran News*, January 16, 2000.
49 *Ibid.*, January 15, 2000.
50 Associated Press, February 26, 2000.
51 *The Times*, March 15, 2000. Two months earlier, countering an Israeli report, the CIA had said that there was no evidence that Iran had succeeded in building its own atomic weapon, or that it had stolen or acquired enough fissile material to make one. *New York Times*, January 17, 2000.
52 *Washington Post*, March 18, 2000. Regarding the permitted Iranian imports into the US, there was stiff competition in caviar from Russia, and Iranian carpets were already getting into America through Canada. In any event, with the US financial services embargo against Iran still in place, the Iranian exporters could not get their money at home.
53 BBC News March 25, 2000. "America cannot do a damn thing," was a slogan that Ayatollah Khomeini coined on his triumphant return to Tehran after fifteen years' exile on February 1, 1979, following the Shah's departure a fortnight earlier. See further, Dilip Hiro, *Iran Under the Ayatollahs*, Routledge & Kegan Paul, London and New York, 1985; and toExcel Press, New York, 2000, pp. 90–1.
54 Reuters, April 5, 2000.
55 *Middle East International*, April 7, 2000, p. 16.
56 Cited in *ibid.*, April 21, 2000, p. 14.
57 *Iran News*, January 15, 2000.
58 In 1999 the US-coordinated multinational naval force, that enforced the blockade of Iraq, queried 2,400 ships and boarded 700. Yet it impounded only nineteen ships carrying Iraqi oil. *Washington Post*, February 7, 2000.
59 *Washington Post*, April 6, 2000.
60 Reuters, May 2, 2000.
61 *Middle East International*, March 24, 2000, p. 14.
62 *Iranfile*, April–May 2000, p. 2. On their return home, most of the Iranian participants in the Berlin conference, including Jamila Kadivar and Mehrangiz Kar, were charged with endangering national security. *Sunday Times Magazine*, October 1, 2000, p. 22; *International Herald Tribune*, November 10, 2000.
63 Indeed, the Berlin conference was seen as a means to improve relations between Iran and the EU on the eve of President Khatami's state visit to Germany in July.
64 Reuters, April 17, 2000.
65 Associated Press, April 20, 2000. Some pro-reform newspapers had alleged that the instructions to kill Saeed Hajjarian were given at a religious center in Islamshahr. *International Herald Tribune*, July 20, 2000.
66 *International Herald Tribune*, April 24, 2000.
67 *New York Times*, April 25, 2000.
68 Associated Press, April 26, 2000; *International Herald Tribune*, April 29–30, 2000.
69 *New York Times*, May 4, 2000.
70 *Middle East International*, May 5, 2000, p. 5.
71 *Ibid.*, May 19, 2000, p. 17.
72 Associated Press, May 23, 2000; *International Herald Tribune*, May 27–8, 2000.
73 Interviews in Tehran, January 2000.
74 BBC News, January 25, 2000. Earlier, in May 1999, Khamanei had rejected calls by the Majlis to pardon Karbaschi: "The authority to resolve such matters lies with the judiciary," he said. "And it is in the good of the country and the people if legal rulings are not undermined by different motives." Agence France-Presse, May 6, 1999.
75 See further Dilip Hiro, *Iran Under the Ayatollahs*, pp. 114–15, 137, 187.

12 REFORM RESTRAINED

1 Cited in *New York Times*, July 5, 2000.
2 Associated Press, July 17, 2000.
3 BBC News, July 1, 2000. After the credentials of three conservative MPs were rejected in late September, the number of the newly elected MPs fell to 274. The elections for the remaining sixteen seats were expected to coincide with the June 2001 presidential poll.
4 In contrast, after overthrowing the leftist President Muhammad Najibullah of Afghanistan in 1992, the victorious Islamic Alliance of Afghan Mujahedin renamed the country the Islamic State of Afghanistan.
5 *Los Angeles Times*, May 23, 2000.
6 *Economist*, July 15, 2000, p. 70.
7 *International Herald Tribune*, July 10, 2000; *Middle East International*, July 14, 2000, pp. 18–19; *Economist*, July 15, 2000, p. 70.
8 *International Herald Tribune*, July 11, 2000.
9 *Middle East International*, July 28, 2000, p. 15. On the other hand, by dismissing Gen. Hedayat Loftian as the LEF commander-in-chief in late June, Leader Khamanei had belatedly conceded one of the main demands of the student leaders after the 1999 riots. *Ibid.*, July 14, 2000, p. 19.
10 *Ibid.*, July 28, 2000, pp. 15–16.
11 Reuters, July 26, 2000.
12 *Washington Post*, May 18 and June 10, 2000.
13 *Ibid.*, May 18, 2000.
14 Reuters, May 17, 2000.
15 *Ibid.*, July 26, 2000.
16 *International Herald Tribune*, August 7, 2000.
17 Associated Press, August 13, 2000.
18 *International Herald Tribune*, August 15, 2000.
19 *Ibid.*, August 11, 2000.
20 Reuters, August 31, 2000; *Middle East International*, September 15, 2000, pp. 12–13; *International Herald Tribune*, November 14, 2000.
21 *Ibid.*, July 20, 2000.
22 See further Dilip Hiro, *Iran Under the Ayatollahs*, Routledge & Kegan Paul, London and New York, 1985; and toExcel Press, New York, 2000, pp. 115, 159, 160, 195, 243.
23 Interviews in Tehran, August 1999.
24 *Middle East International*, October 15, 1999, p. 23.
25 *Ibid.*
26 *International Herald Tribune*, August 5–6, 2000.
27 *Sunday Times Magazine*, October 1, 2000, p. 27.
28 *Observer*, November 28, 1999; *Sunday Times Magazine*, October 1, 2000, p. 24.
29 *International Herald Tribune*, November 26, 1999.
30 Besides about 80,000 Shia clergy running 60,000 mosques, there were clerics in the judicial system (3,500 judges and another 2,500 in the supporting staff); the military, IRGC, Baseej and the LEF (some 18,000); the civil service, including teachers (about 7,000); the numerous foundations, including the multifarious Foundation for the Deprived and Martyrs (5,000); the Islamic Propagation Organization (2,000); and the seminaries (4,000) – giving a total of 122,000. To this must be added another 25,000 clergy functioning outside the official network, raising the aggregate to 147,000. Assuming another 12 percent of this figure to be either retired or too ill to work, the grand total came to nearly 165,000.

31 *International Herald Tribune*, July 6, 2000.
32 *Time*, July 17, 2000, p. 26.
33 *Los Angeles Times*, September 5 and 8, 2000; *Middle East International*, September 15, 2000, p. 13.
34 *Washington Post*, July 13, 2000; *International Herald Tribune*, September 7, 2000.
35 Associated Press, September 8, 2000.
36 *Financial Times*, January 29–30, 2000; Associated Press, May 20, 2000.
37 *Economist,* April 15, 2000, p. 74. See further Dilip Hiro, *Dictionary of the Middle East*, Macmillan Press, Basingstoke, 1996; and St Martin's Press, New York, 1996, p. 149.
38 Some Jewish suspects confessed on television. "This happened at a time when the foreign media had launched a big propaganda for the Jews," explained the reformist culture and Islamic guidance minister, Ataollah Mohajerani. "So our judiciary had to use its instruments to show that the Jews might be guilty, so it used the state television." *Observer*, July 2, 2000. On July 10, Iran issued an arrest warrant against Ishaq Belanas.
39 Associated Press, September 21, 2000.
40 *Los Angeles Times*, September 22, 2000; *New York Times*, September 24, 2000.
41 Agence France-Presse, July 27, 2000.
42 *International Herald Tribune*, August 11, 2000.
43 *Ibid.*, September 1 and 11, 2000. The gesture of the four US parliamentarians contrasted sharply with the statement signed by 253 of their colleagues on October 11 which called for "a tougher policy" toward Iran as it continued to violate human rights and President Khatami had failed to bring about any improvement. Reuters, October 11, 2000.
44 *Middle East Economic Digest*, September 8, 2000, p. 5.
45 *Washington Post*, October 18, 2000. It was not until November 7 that President Clinton announced the composition of the five-member investigative committee. Led by George Mitchell, a former US senator, it was to consist of Warren Rudman, another former US senator; Javier Solana, the security and foreign policy chief of the European Union; Thorbjorn Jagland, the foreign minister of Norway; and Suleiman Demirel, a former president of Turkey. *International Herald Tribune*, November 8, 2000.
46 Reuters, October 17, 2000; Associated Press, October 21, 2000.
47 *New York Times*, November 5, 2000.
48 *Ibid.*

CONCLUSIONS AND FUTURE PROSPECTS

1 General Sir Peter de La Billiere, *Storm Command: A Personal Account of the Gulf War*, HarperCollins, 1992, London, pp. 304–5.
2 Tim Trevan, *Saddam's Secrets: The Hunt for Iraq's Hidden Weapons*, HarperCollins, London, 1999, p. 412.
3 See Chapter 6, p. 148.
4 Anthony H. Cordesman, *Iraq and the War of Sanctions: Conventional Threats and Weapons of Mass Destruction*, Praeger, Westport, CT, and London, 1999, p. 375.
5 See Chap 7, p. 167.
6 See Chap 7, pp. 154–5.
7 Interviews in Baghdad, July 2000.
8 Interview in London, August 2000.
9 Interview in London, November 2000.
10 At his 36th birthday party, he was seen dancing a waltz with a visiting European journalist.

11 See further Dilip Hiro, *Islamic Fundamentalism*, Paladin Books, London, 1988; and as *Holy Wars: The Rise of Islamic Fundamentalism*, Routledge, New York, 1989 pp. 131, 209.

12 Interview in Tehran, August 1999.

13 Dilip Hiro, *Iran Under the Ayatollahs*, Routledge & Kegan Paul, London and New York, 1985; and to Excel Press, New York, 2000, p. 198. The earlier prime minister, Muhammad Javad Bahonar, was assassinated in June 1981.

14 Interview in Tehran, August 1999.

15 See further Dilip Hiro, *Islamic Fundamentalism*, pp. 28–9, 36–8; and *Dictionary of the Middle East*, Macmillan Press, Basingstoke, 1996; and St Martin's Press, New York, 1996, p. 85.

16 See further Dilip Hiro, *Dictionary of the Middle East*, p. 336.

17 Valla Vakili, *Debating Religion and Politics in Iran: The Political Thought of Abdolkarim Soroush*, Council on Foreign Relations, New York, 1997, pp. 10–11.

18 *Ibid.*, pp. 13, 19, 24.

EPILOG

1 Cited in *Middle East International*, December 22, 2000, p. 13 and January 26, 2001, p. 4.

2 *International Herald Tribune*, November 23, 2001.

3 *Los Angeles Times*, January 23, 2001.

4 *Washington Post*, November 23, 2000.

5 Cited in *Observer*, February 18, 2001.

6 *Observer*, January 7, 2001.

7 *Washington Post*, January 31, 2001.

8 *New York Times*, December 6, 2000.

9 *Washington Post*, January 15, 2001; *Middle East International*, January 26, 2001, pp. 6–7; *New York Times*, February 6, 2001.

10 *Washington Post*, January 14, 2001; *Middle East International*, January 26, 2001, p. 6.

11 The Pentagon targeted 25 parts of the Iraqi radar stations – dishes, telecommunication bunkers and other components. It damaged only eight. Another eight escaped damage. For the rest, satellite imagery failed to produce usable pictures of the targets. *Washington Post*, February 22, 2001.

12 *Ibid.*, February 17–18, 2001.

13 *Ibid.*, February 19, 2001.

14 *International Herald Tribune*, February 20, 2001.

15 *Al Hayat*, February 22, 2001.

16 *Washington Post*, February 21, 2001.

17 *Ibid.*, January 31, 2001.

18 *Middle East International*, March 9, 2001, p. 6.

19 *Washington Post*, March 26, 2001.

20 *Middle East International*, April 6, 2001, p. 7. Kuwaiti and Saudi leaders had arrived in Amman backed by a GCC foreign ministers' resolution calling on Iraq to implement its obligations under UN resolutions, and reproving it for threatening Kuwait and Riyadh for granting air base facilities to the US and the UK. *Ibid.*, March 23, 2001, p. 7.

21 *Washington Post*, March 28, 2001.

22 *International Herald Tribune*, April 3, 2001.

23 Associated Press, November 26, 2000; *International Herald Tribune*, December 1, 2000.

24 *Middle East International*, December 8, 2000, pp. 15–16.

25 Of the remaining seven, Saeed Sadr, a translator at the German embassy in Tehran got a ten year jail term for distributing opposition pamphlets; Khalil Rostamkhani, an interpreter at the Berlin conference, nine years for having dissident leaflets at home; Ali Afshari, a student leader, five years; Izzatollah Sahabi, a journalist,

four-and-a-half years; and publisher Shahla Lahiji and human rights lawyer Mehrangiz Kar four years each. *Middle East International*, January 26, 2001, p. 17.

26 This statement was part of the written interviews he and Ganji gave clandestinely to the *International Herald Tribune* from their prison cell. *Ibid.*, January 23, 2001.

27 Of the remaining ten defendants, three were given life sentence and the rest prison terms of two-and-a-half to ten years. *Ibid.*, January 29, 2001; *Middle East International*, February 9, 2001, p. 13.

28 *Middle East International*, February 9, 2001, p. 13.

29 *International Herald Tribune*, February 16, 2001.

30 *Washington Post*, March 12, 2001.

31 *Middle East International*, March 23, 2001, p. 18.

32 BBC News, April 24, 2001.

SELECT BIBLIOGRAPHY

Abdulghani, Jasim M., *Iran and Iraq: The Years of Crisis*, Croom Helm, London, and The Johns Hopkins University Press, Baltimore, MD, 1984.

Aburish, Said K., *Saddam Hussein: The Politics of Revenge*, Bloomsbury, London, 2000.

Afrsiabi, K. L., *After Khomeini: New Directions in Iran's Foreign Policy*, Westview Press, Boulder, CO, 1994.

Amirahmadi, Hooshang, and Hooglund, Eric (eds), *US-Iran Relations: Areas of Tension and Mutual Interest*, The Middle East Institute, Washington, DC, 1994.

Axelgard, Frederick W., *A New Iraq? The Gulf War and Implications for US Policy*, Praeger, New York and London, 1988.

BP Amoco plc, *BP Amoco Statistical Review of World Energy 2000*, London, 2000.

Butler, Richard, *Saddam Defiant: The Threat of Weapons of Mass Destruction, and the Crisis of Global Security*, Public Affairs, Washington, DC, 1999; and Weidenfeld & Nicolson, London, 2000.

Chubin, Shahram, and Tripp, Charles, *Iran and Iraq at War*, I. B. Tauris, London and New York, 1988.

Cockburn, Andrew, and Cockburn, Patrick, *Out of the Ashes: The Resurrection of Saddam Hussein*, HarperCollins, New York, 1999; and Verso, London, 2000.

Committee Against Repression and for Democratic Rights in Iraq, *Saddam's Iraq: Revolution or Reaction?*, Zed Press, London, 1986.

Constitution of the Islamic Republic of Iran of 24 October 1989, Ministry of Culture and Islamic Guidance, Tehran, 1990.

Cordesman, Anthony H., *Iraq and the War of Sanctions: Conventional Threats and Weapons of Mass Destruction*, Praeger, Westport, CT, and London, 1999.

Cordesman, Anthony H., and Hashim, Ahmed S., *Iraq: Sanctions and Beyond*, Westview Press, Boulder, CO, and Oxford, UK, 1997.

de La Billiere, General Sir Peter, *Storm Command: A Personal Account of the Gulf War*, HarperCollins, London, 1992.

Ehteshami, Anoushiravan, *After Khomeini: The Second Iranian Republic*, Routledge, London and New York, 1995.

Ghareeb, Edmund, *The Kurdish Question in Iraq*, Syracuse University Press, Syracuse, NY, 1981.

Ghareeb, Edmund, and Khadduri, Majid, *War in the Gulf 1990–91: The Iraq–Kuwait Conflict and Its Implications*, Oxford University Press, New York and Oxford, 1997.

Graham, Robert, *Iran: The Illusion of Power*, Croom Helm, London, 1978.

Graham-Brown, Sarah, *Sanctioning Saddam: The Politics of Intervention in Iraq*, I.B.Tauris (in association with MERIP), London and New York, 1999.

Haseeb, Khair el-Din (ed.), *Arab-Iranian Relations*, Centre for Arab Unity Studies, Beirut, 1998.

Heikal, Mohamed, *Illusions of Triumph: An Arab View of the Gulf War*, HarperCollins, London, 1992.

Hiro, Dilip, *Inside the Middle East*, Routledge & Kegan Paul, London, and McGraw-Hill, New York, 1982.

Hiro, Dilip, *Iran Under the Ayatollahs*, Routledge & Kegan Paul, London and New York, 1985; and toExcel Press, New York, 2000.

Hiro, Dilip, *Islamic Fundamentalism*, Paladin Books, London, 1988; and as *Holy Wars: The Rise of Islamic Fundamentalism*, Routledge, New York, 1989.

Hiro, Dilip, *The Longest War: The Iran–Iraq Military Conflict*, Paladin Grafton Books, London, 1989; and Routledge, New York, 1991.

Hiro, Dilip, *Desert Shield to Desert Storm: The Second Gulf War*, HarperCollins, London, 1992; and Routledge, New York, 1992.

Hiro, Dilip, *Dictionary of the Middle East*, Macmillan Press, Basingstoke, 1996; and St Martin's Press, New York, 1996.

Ismael, Tareq Y., *Iraq and Iran: Roots of Conflict*, Syracuse University Press, Syracuse, NY, 1982.

Kemp, Geoffrey, *Forever Enemies: American Policy and The Islamic Republic of Iran*, The Carnegie Endowment for International Peace, Washington, DC, 1994.

McDowall, David, *The Kurds*, Minority Rights Group, London, 1985.

Milani, Mohsen, *The Making of Iran's Islamic Revolution: From Monarchy to Islamic Republic*, Second Edition, Westview Press, Boulder, CO, 1994.

Moini, F., *Who's Who in Iran*, Media and Books Co., Bonn, Germany, 1998.

al Radi, Nuha, *Baghdad Diaries*, Saqi Books, London, 1998.

Ritter, Scott, *Endgame: Solving the Iraq Problem – Once and For All*, Simon & Schuster, New York and London, 1999.

Short, Martin and McDermott, *The Kurds*, Minority Rights Group, London, 1977.

Simons, Geoff, *Iraq – Primus Inter Pariahs: A Crisis Chronology*, Macmillan Press, Basingstoke, and St Martin's Press, New York, 1999.

Al Suwaidi, Jamal S. (ed.), *Iran and the Gulf: A Search for Stability*, The Emirates Center for Strategic Studies and Research, Abu Dhabi, UAE, 1996.

Tamimi, Azzam (ed.), *Power-Sharing Islam?* Liberty for Muslim World Publications, London, 1993.

Trevan, Tim, *Saddam's Secrets: The Hunt for Iraq's Hidden Weapons*, HarperCollins, London, 1999.

US News and World Report, *Triumph Without Victory: The History of the Persian Gulf War*, Times Books, New York, 1992.

Vakili, Valla, *Debating Religion and Politics in Iran: The Political Thought of Abdolkarim Soroush*, Council on Foreign Relations, New York, 1997.

Wurmser, David, *Tyranny's Ally: America's Failure to Defeat Saddam Hussein*, The AEI Press, Washington, DC, 1999.

NEWS AGENCIES, NEWSPAPERS
AND PERIODICALS

Agence France-Presse
Associated Press
Baghdad Observer (Baghdad)
BBC News (London)
BBC Summary of World Broadcasts (Reading)
Daily Telegraph (London)
Dialogue (London)
Economist (London and New York)
Financial Times (London and New York)
Foreign Broadcast Information Service (Washington)
Guardian (London)
Gulf States Newsletter (Crawley)
Al Hayat (London)
Independent (London)
Inter Press Service (Rome)
International Herald Tribune (Paris)
Iranfile (London)
Iran News (Tehran)
Jane's Intelligence Review (Coulsdon*)*
Kayhan International (Tehran)
Los Angeles Times (Los Angeles)

Mainstream (New Delhi)
Middle East Economic Digest (London)
Middle East International (London and Washington)
Middle East Journal (Washington)
Le Monde (Paris)
Nation (New York)
New York Times (New York)
New Yorker (New York)
Newsweek (New York and London)
Observer (London)
Reuters
Al Sharq al Awsat (London)
Sunday Times (London)
Sunday Times Magazine (London)
Survival (London)
Tehran Times (Tehran)
Al Thawra (Baghdad)
Time (New York and London)
The Times (London)
Washington Post (Washington)

INDEX

For a name starting with Al, El, Le or The, see its second part. A person's religious or secular title has been omitted.

369